KU-636-796

Contents at a Glance

Social Media Marketing

ALL-IN-ONE

FOR

DUMMIES®

A Wiley Brand

3rd Edition

by Jan Zimmerman
and
Deborah Ng

FOR

DUMMIES®

A Wiley Brand

Social Media Marketing All-in-One For Dummies®, 3rd Edition

Published by: **John Wiley & Sons, Inc.,** 111 River Street, Hoboken, NJ 07030-5774, www.wiley.com

Copyright © 2015 by John Wiley & Sons, Inc., Hoboken, New Jersey

Published simultaneously in Canada

For general information on our other products and services, please contact our Customer Care Department within the U.S. at 877-762-2974, outside the U.S. at 317-572-3993, or fax 317-572-4002. For technical support, please visit www.wiley.com/techsupport.

Wiley publishes in a variety of print and electronic formats and by print-on-demand. Some material included with standard print versions of this book may not be included in e-books or in print-on-demand. If this book refers to media such as a CD or DVD that is not included in the version you purchased, you may download this material at http://booksupport.wiley.com. For more information about Wiley products, visit www.wiley.com.

Library of Congress Control Number: 2014955782

ISBN 978-1-118-95135-4 (pbk); ISBN 978-1-118-95137-8 (ebk); ISBN 978-1-118-95136-1 (ebk)

Manufactured in the United States of America

10 9 8 7 6 5 4

Table of Contents

Chapter 2: Exploring Content Marketing Platforms 237

Chapter 3: Developing a Content Marketing Strategy 259

Chapter 4: Getting Your Content to the Masses 271

Introduction

You sat back, sighing with relief that your website was running faultlessly, optimized for search engines, and producing traffic, leads, and sales. Maybe you ventured into e-mail marketing or pay-per-click advertising to generate new customers. Then you thought with satisfaction, "I'll just let the money roll in."

Instead, you were inundated with stories about Facebook and fan pages, Twitter and tweets, blogs and podcasts, Pinterest, Google+, and all other manner of social media buzz. By now you've probably tried more than one of these social media platforms. Perhaps you haven't seen much in the way of results, or you're ready to explore ways to expand your reach, increase customer loyalty, and grow your sales with social media.

Much as you might wish it were otherwise, you must now stay up to date with rapidly changing options in the social media universe. As a marketer, you have no choice when 80 percent of Internet users visit blogs and social media and when your position in search engine results may depend on the recency and frequency of social media updates. Since the second edition of this book, social media marketing has become an essential component of online marketing.

The statistics are astounding: Facebook has more than 864 million daily active users; more than 60 million blog posts appear on the Internet each month; more than 500 million tweets are sent per day on average; and 6 billion hours of video are viewed each month on YouTube. New company names and bewildering new vocabulary terms continue to flood the online world: Instagram, Snapchat, pinning, location tagging, and sentiment monitoring, for example.

Should your new business get involved in social media marketing? Is it all more trouble than it's worth? Will you be hopelessly left behind if you don't participate? If you jump in, or if you've already waded into the social media waters, how do you keep it all under control and who does the work? Which platforms are the best for your business? Should you take advantage of new channels or stick with the comfortable ones you've already mastered? This book helps you answer both sets of questions: Should your business undertake social media marketing? If so, how? (Quick answer: If your customers use a social media service, use it. If not, skip it.)

About This Book

The philosophy behind this book is simple: Social media marketing is a means, not an end in itself. Social media services are tools, not new worlds. In the best of all worlds, you see results that improve customer acquisition, retention, and buying behavior — in other words, your bottom line. If this sounds familiar, that's because everything you already know about marketing is correct.

Having the most Likes on Facebook or more retweets of your posts than your competitors doesn't mean much if these achievements don't have a positive impact on your business. Throughout this book, you'll find concrete suggestions for applying social media tactics to achieve those goals.

If you undertake a social media marketing campaign, we urge you to keep your plans simple, take things slowly, and always stay focused on your customers. Most of all, we urge you to follow the precepts of guerrilla marketing: Target one niche market at a time; grow that market; and then reinvest your profits in the next niche.

What You Don't Have to Read

You don't have to read anything that seems overwhelming or insanely complicated, deals with a particular social marketing service that you dislike or disdain, or doesn't apply to your business. Content following a Technical Stuff icon is intended for developers or particularly tech-savvy readers.

Reading the case studies in sidebars isn't critical, though you might enjoy reading about honest-to-goodness business owners who successfully use the social marketing techniques we discuss. Often, they share a helpful tip that will make your social media life easier.

If you have a limited budget, focus your explorations on the free or low-cost tools and resources that appear in various tables, instead of enterprise-level options, which are designed for large companies with large marketing budgets. Sometimes, however, a tool with a moderate price tag can save you lots of time or expensive labor.

You can skip any of the minibooks on individual social media services if you don't include them in your social media marketing plan. If you decide to add one or more of them later, simply return to that book for freestanding information. Of course, if you're looking for a thorough understanding of the social media whirl, read the book straight through, from cover to cover. You'll find out all about social media — at least until a totally new service launches tomorrow.

Foolish Assumptions

In our heads, we visualize our readers as savvy small-business owners, marketers in companies of any size, and people who work in any of the multiple services that support social media efforts, such as advertising agencies, web developers, graphic design firms, copywriting, or public relations. We assume that you

✦ Already have or will soon have a website or blog that can serve as the hub for your online marketing program

✦ Are curious about ubiquitous social media

✦ Are comfortable using search terms on search engines to find information online

✦ Know the realities of your industry, though you may not have a clue whether your competitors use social media

✦ Can describe your target markets, though you may not be sure whether your audience is using social media

✦ Are trying to decide whether using social media makes sense for your company (or your boss has asked you to find out)

✦ May already use social media personally and are interested in applying your knowledge and experience to business

✦ May already have tried using social media for your company but want to improve results or measure return on your investment

✦ Have a passion for your business, appreciate your customers, and enjoy finding new ways to improve your bottom line

If our assumptions are correct, this book will help you organize a social marketing presence without going crazy or spending all your waking hours online. It will help you figure out whether a particular technique makes sense, how to get the most out of it, and how to measure your results.

How This Book Is Organized

We've built this book like a sandwich: The first two and last two books are overviews of marketing or business issues, or of social media tools and techniques. The five books in the middle are how-to manuals for incorporating blogs, podcasts, or image-sharing services, Twitter, Facebook, LinkedIn, or Pinterest into your social media marketing campaign.

Like most *For Dummies* books, this one enables you to get as much (or as little) information as you need at any particular moment on a specific topic.

You can return to it as a reference guide at any time. However, unless you're certain that you're interested only in a specific social marketing service covered in Books III through VII, we recommend that you read Book I first to establish your goals, objectives, and schedule for social media marketing.

For information on a specific topic, check the headings in the table of contents or look at the index.

Book I: The Social Media Mix

Book I gets you off on the right foot. Chapter 1 explains what social media services are, individually and collectively, categorizes the overwhelming number of social media options by type, and explores how social media are the same and different from other forms of online and offline marketing. In the next two chapters, you define your own marketing goals, objectives, and methods for social media, with a particular emphasis on return on investment (ROI), and learn how to research where your target audiences "hang out." The final chapter in this book offers some practical tips on how to manage your social media effort in terms of precious resources: time, money, and people.

This minibook includes three key planning forms: the Social Media Marketing Goals form, to establish the purpose of your campaign; the Social Media Marketing Plan, to select and document your tactics; and the Social Media Activity Calendar, to assign and schedule tasks.

Book II: Cybersocial Tools

Implementing and tracking social media marketing campaigns across multiple services is a daunting task. In the first chapter of Book II, we offer a variety of productivity tools to help you post content in multiple locations, notify search engines, and monitor your growing social notoriety. The second chapter deals in depth with integrating social media into a coordinated search engine optimization strategy, and the third deals with social bookmarking, social news, and social sharing as new methods of viral marketing.

Book III: Content Marketing

Your content is your most important online asset. It's through your content that you catch the attention of the search engines, raise brand awareness, and establish your expertise. We delve into the importance of content and what goals you hope to achieve with your content marketing strategy, and explore the different types of content available to you online. We also touch on blogs, podcasts, and videos for those of you who hope to expand beyond print to reach your online communities. Finally, we discuss sharing images and the legalities involved.

Book IV: Twitter

Twitter is an essential marketing tool for brands wishing to grow their online presence. Brevity is key, and though some find it challenging to communicate in 140 characters, most agree that it's a great way to learn more about the people using a product or service, and grow a community of supporters. In Book IV, we cover the basics of Twitter marketing and even some not so basic areas like hosting a Twitter chat, uploading a Twitter background, and using Twitter to search for brands, jobs. and clients.

Book V: Facebook and Instagram

Facebook is where the people are, and you owe it to yourself and your brand to be a part of the action. In Book V, we take you through setting up Facebook and Instagram accounts, as well as marketing to your community through conversation, photos, and other content.

Book VI: LinkedIn

In Book VI, we explore using LinkedIn as a marketing tool. We take you through setting up a LinkedIn business page, networking through LinkedIn, and using LinkedIn as a content platform.

Book VII: Pinterest

Book VII covers Pinterest, a social networking force to be reckoned with. With Pinterest, a picture really is worth a thousand words, and we show you how to find the photos that best tell your brand's story. But don't worry; we won't just toss you into the water without teaching you how to swim first. We take you through creating an account, uploading photos, and creating boards, and even touch on some unique uses for your Pinterest account.

Book VIII: Other Social Media Marketing Sites

In addition to the "big guys" covered in the Books III through VII, there are hundreds of social media services with smaller audiences. Some of them are networks specific to a demographically segmented audience, and some focus on narrowly targeted vertical markets. Book VIII analyzes the value of working with smaller services and surveys many stratified niche options, including geomarketing and group deal sites. This minibook also includes chapters on using Google+, popular new social media fad sites, and social mobile sites; and multiplying your social media impact with advertising, public relations, and e-newsletters.

Book IX: Measuring Results; Building on Success

Book IX returns to business principles with a chapter on the importance of measuring your results. The first chapter offers details on Google Analytics for your website in general, and on Google Social Analytics to assess the performance of your social media campaigns. We do a deep dive into the metric sea with details on internal performance measurements for content-sharing services, plus detailed instructions for measuring Twitter, Facebook, minor social media platforms, and social mobile sites. Book IX concludes with chapters covering how to compare results from social media metrics with other forms of online marketing and suggestions for using data to guide your marketing decisions.

Icons Used in This Book

To make your experience easier, we use various icons in the margins to identify special categories of information.

These hints help you save time, energy, or aggravation. Sharing them is our way of sharing what we've figured out the hard way — so that you don't have to. Of course, if you prefer to get your education through the school of hard knocks, be our guest.

This book has more details in it than any normal person can remember. This icon reminds you of points made elsewhere in the book or perhaps helps you recall business best practices that you know from your own experience.

Heed these warnings to avoid potential pitfalls. Nothing we suggest will crash your computer beyond repair or send your marketing campaign into oblivion. But we tell you about business and legal pitfalls to avoid, plus a few traps that catch the unprepared during the process of configuring social media services. Not all those services create perfect user interfaces with clear directions!

The geeky-looking Dummies Man marks information to share with your developer or programmer — unless you are one. In that case, have at it. On the other hand, you can skip any of the technical-oriented information without damaging your marketing plans or harming a living being.

Where to Go from Here

You can find helpful information on the companion website for this book at www.dummies.com/extras/socialmediamarketingaio. From the site, you can download copies of the Social Media Goals and Social Media Marketing Plan forms, which you can use to develop your own marketing plans. You can also find an online Cheat Sheet to print and keep handy near your computer at www.dummies.com/cheatsheet/socialmediamarketingaio. If you find errors in this book, or have suggestions for future editions, please e-mail us at books@watermelonweb.com. We wish you a fun and profitable experience going social!

Book I
The Social Media Mix

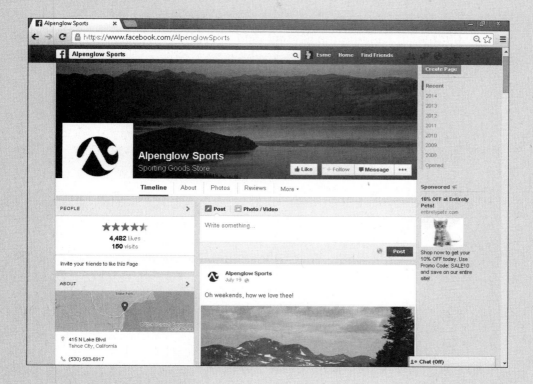

Contents at a Glance

Chapter 1: Making the Business Case for Social Media

In This Chapter

✔ Defining social media

✔ Accentuating the positives

✔ Eliminating the negatives

✔ Latching on to the affirmatives

✔ Integrating social media into your overall marketing plan

✔ Evaluating the worth of social media

*I*n the best of all worlds, *social media* — a suite of online services that facilitates two-way communication and content sharing — can become a productive component of your overall marketing strategy. These services can enhance your company's online visibility, strengthen relationships with your clients, and expand word-of-mouth advertising, which is the best type.

Given its rapid rise in popularity and its hundreds of millions of worldwide users, social media marketing sounds quite tempting. These tools require minimal upfront cash and, theoretically, you'll find customers flooding through your cyberdoors, ready to buy. It sounds like a no-brainer — but it isn't, especially as social media channels mature into a pay-to-play environment with paid advertising.

Has someone finally invented a perfect marketing method that puts you directly in touch with your customers and prospects, costs nothing, and generates profits faster than a perpetual motion machine produces energy? The hype says "yes"; the real answer, unfortunately, is "no." While marketing nirvana may not yet be at hand, the expanding importance of social media in the online environment may mean that your business needs to participate anyway.

This chapter provides an overview of the pros and cons of social media to help you decide whether to join the social whirl, and it gives a framework for approaching a strategic choice of which media to use.

Making Your Social Debut

Like any form of marketing, social media takes some thought. It can become an enormous siphon of your time, and short-term profits are rare. Social media marketing is a long-term commitment.

So, should you or shouldn't you invest time and effort in this marketing avenue? If you answer in the affirmative, you immediately confront another decision: What form should that investment take? The number of options is overwhelming; you can never use every technique and certainly can't do them all at once.

Figure 1-1, which compares the percentages of small businesses using various social media to attract new customers, shows that most businesses use LinkedIn and/or Facebook. Although some U.S. small businesses have taken a wait-and-see attitude, more and more are trying social media. According to an August 2013 survey from the National Small Business Association (`www.nsba.biz/wp-content/uploads/2013/09/Technology-Survey-2013.pdf`), 73 percent of small businesses used some form of social media, up from 47 percent in 2010. Those businesses on the sidelines give the best reason in the world for not participating — their customers aren't there.

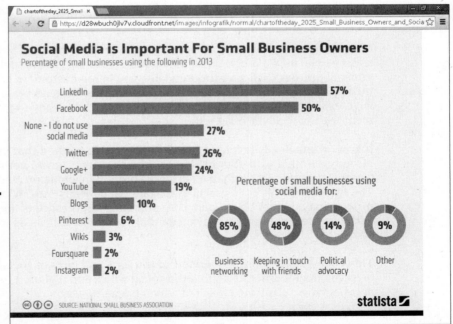

Figure 1-1: Most companies using social media focus on LinkedIn or Facebook.

Defining Social Media Marketing

The bewildering array of social media (which seem to breed new services faster than rabbits can reproduce) makes it hard to discern what they have in common: shared information, often on a peer-to-peer basis. Although many social media messages look like traditional broadcasts from one business to many consumers, their interactive component offers an enticing illusion of one-to-one communication that invites individual readers to respond.

The phrase *social media marketing* generally refers to using these online services for *relationship selling* — selling based on developing rapport with customers. Social media services make innovative use of new online technologies to accomplish the familiar communication and marketing goals of this form of selling.

The tried-and-true strategies of marketing (such as solving customers' problems and answering the question, "What's in it for me?") are still valid. Social media marketing is a new technique, not a new world.

This book covers a variety of social media services (sometimes called social media *channels*). We use the phrase *social media site* to refer to a specific, named online service or product.

You can categorize social media services, but they have fuzzy boundaries that can overlap. Some social media sites fall into multiple categories. For instance, some social networks and online communities allow participants to share photos and include a blog.

Here are the different types of social media services:

✦ **Social content-sharing services:** These services facilitate posting and commenting on text, videos, photos, and podcasts (audio).

- *Blogs:* Websites designed to let you easily update or change content and allow readers to post their own opinions or reactions.

  Examples of blog tools are WordPress, Typepad, Blogger, and Tumblr. Blogs may be hosted on third-party sites (apps) or integrated into your own website using software. Figure 1-2 shows an example of a blog at www.muybuenocookbook.com, which was built using a WordPress template.

- *Video:* Examples are YouTube, Vimeo, Vine.co, or Ustream. Figure 1-3 shows a how-to video from YouTube.

- *Images:* Flickr, Photobucket, Instagram, Snapchat, SlideShare, Pinterest, or Picasa.

- *Audio:* Podbean or BlogTalkRadio.

Figure 1-2:
The WordPress blog for Muy Bueno uses strong graphics to gain attention.

Reproduced by permission of Yvette Marquez-Sharpnack, MuyBuenoCookbook.com

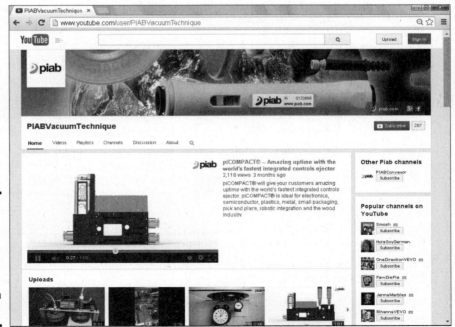

Figure 1-3:
A YouTube channel can be an integral part of a social media strategy.

Reproduced by permission of Piab AB

✦ **Social networking services:** Originally developed to facilitate the exchange of personal information (messages, photos, video, and audio) to groups of friends and family, these full-featured services offer multiple functions. From a business point of view, many social networking services support subgroups that offer the potential for more targeted marketing. Common types of social networking services include

- *Full networks,* such as Facebook, Google+, or MeetMe.com. Figure 1-4 shows how the Lodge at Mountain Springs Lake Resort uses its Facebook page to attract leads.

- *Short message networks,* such as Twitter or Plurk, which are often used for sharing announcements, events, sales notices, and promotions. Figure 1-5 shows how Blue Bottle Coffee uses its Twitter account at `https://twitter.com/bluebottleroast` to enable a dialog with its customers.

- *Professional networks,* such as LinkedIn and small profession-specific networks.

- *Specialty networks* (which target specific groups, rather than the general public) within a vertical industry, demographic, or activity segment, as opposed to by profession or job title.

Figure 1-4:
The Lodge at Mountain Springs Lake Resort uses its Facebook presence to attract leads for weddings.

Figure 1-5: Twitter can be used to make announcements (top) or facilitate dialogue with customers (bottom), as shown on the Twitter page for Blue Bottle Coffee.

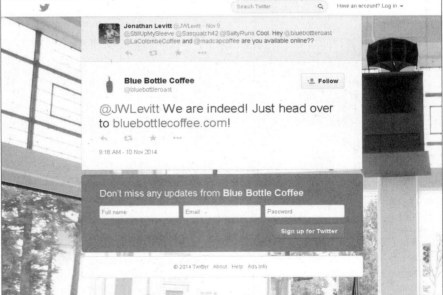

✦ **Social bookmarking services:** Similar to private bookmarks for your favorite sites on your computer, social bookmarks are publicly viewable lists of sites that others have recommended. Some are

- *Recommendation services,* such as StumbleUpon and Delicious

- *Social shopping services,* such as Kaboodle and ThisNext

- *Other bookmarking services organized by topic or application,* such as sites where readers recommend books to others using bookmarking techniques

✦ **Social news services:** On these peer-based lists of recommended articles from news sites, blogs, or web pages, users often vote on the value of the postings. Social news services include

- Digg

- Reddit

- Other news sites

✦ **Social geolocation and meeting services:** These services bring people together in real space rather than in cyberspace:

- Foursquare

- Meetup

- Other GPS (Global Positioning System) applications, many of which operate on mobile phones

- Other sites for organizing meet-ups and *tweet-ups* (gatherings organized by using Twitter)

✦ **Community-building services:** Many comment- and content-sharing sites have been around for a long time, such as forums, message boards, and Yahoo! and Google groups.

Other examples are

- *Community-building sites* with multiple sharing features, such as Ning

- *Wikis,* such as Wikipedia, for group-sourced content

- *Review sites,* such as TripAdvisor, Yelp, and Epinions, to solicit consumer views

As you surf the web, you can find dozens, if not hundreds, of social tools, *apps* (freestanding online applications), and *widgets* (small applications placed on other sites, services, or desktops). These features monitor, distribute, search, analyze, and rank content. Many are specific to a particular social network, especially Twitter. Others are designed to aggregate information across the social media landscape, including such monitoring tools as Google Alerts, Mention.net, or Social Mention, or such distribution tools as

RSS (Really Simple Syndication), which allows frequently updated data to be posted automatically to locations requested by subscribers

Book II offers a survey of many more of these tools; specific social media services are covered in their respective books.

Understanding the Benefits of Social Media

Social media marketing carries many benefits. One of the most important is that you don't have to front any cash for most social media services. Of course, there's a downside: Most services require a significant investment of time to initiate and maintain a social media marketing campaign.

As you read the following sections, think about whether each benefit applies to your needs. How important is it to your business? How much time are you willing to allocate to it? What kind of a payoff would you expect? Column 2 in Figure 1-6 shows how other small businesses rate the relative effectiveness of social media in meeting their goals.

Figure 1-6: The effectiveness of social media marketing compared to other marketing tactics.

Digital Marketing Tactics Used by US SMBs, March 2013 % of respondents	Currently in use	Most effective
Website	86.6%	33.9%
Social media	77.3%	24.9%
Email for marketing/promotion	65.8%	19.6%
Email for customer service	61.3%	14.0%
Videos and photos	54.6%	13.2%
SEO	53.8%	16.2%
Blogs and white papers	52.7%	13.4%
Email for prospecting	48.2%	9.5%
Online store or other ecommerce solution	26.3%	10.9%
Online events (webinars and shows)	26.3%	10.1%
Paid search words	23.2%	8.4%
Paid banner ads on search engines and/or other websites	22.7%	9.8%
Mobile/SMS communication	19.6%	3.4%
Mobile apps	18.2%	6.2%

Source: Vocus and Inc. Magazine, "The State of Digital Marketing for SMBs," June 12, 2013

159135   www.**eMarketer**.com

Reproduced by permission of eMarketer

Casting a wide net to catch your target market

The audience for social media is huge. In June 2014, Facebook claimed almost 1.32 billion monthly active users, of which 1.08 billion were mobile users. Slightly more than 81 percent of Facebook's traffic comes from outside the U.S. and Canada.

When compared to Google, this social media behemoth is in tight competition for the U.S. audience. In July 2014, Facebook tallied 167.35 million unique U.S. visitors, while Google surpassed it with 177.03 million. Keep in mind, of course, that visitors are conducting different activities on the two sites.

Twitter claims more than 271 million monthly active users and totes up about 500 million *tweets* (short messages) daily. A relatively small number of power users are responsible for the majority of tweets posted daily. In fact, about 44 percent of users create Twitter accounts without ever posting. More people read tweets than are accounted for, however, because tweets can be read on other websites.

Even narrowly focused networking sites claim hundreds of thousands of visitors. Surely, some of the people using these sites must be your customers or prospects. In fact, one popular use of social media is to cast a wide net to capture more potential visitors to your website. Figure 1-7 shows a classic conversion funnel, which demonstrates the value of bringing new traffic to the top of the funnel to produce more *conversions* (actions taken) at the bottom.

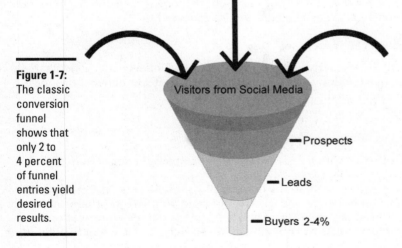

Figure 1-7: The classic conversion funnel shows that only 2 to 4 percent of funnel entries yield desired results.

The conversion funnel works like this: If more people arrive at the top of the funnel, theoretically more will progress through the steps of prospect and qualified lead to become a customer. Only 2 to 4 percent, on average, make it through a funnel regardless of what action the funnel conversion depicts.

In Book I, Chapter 3, we discuss how you can assess traffic on social media sites using Quantcast, Alexa, or other tools, and match their visitors to the profiles of your customers. Generally, these tools offer some information free, although several are freemium sites with additional data available only with a paid plan.

Branding

Basic marketing focuses on the need for branding, name recognition, visibility, presence, or top-of-mind awareness. Call it what you will — you want people to remember your company name when they're in need of your product or service. Social media services, of almost every type, are excellent ways to build your brand.

Social media works for branding as long as you get your name in front of the right people. Plan to segment the audience on the large social media services. You can look for more targeted groups within them or search for specialty services that may reach fewer people overall but more of the ones who are right for your business.

Building relationships

You will hear repeatedly that social media marketing takes time to produce sales results. If you're focused on short-term benefits, you'd better shake that thought loose and get your head into the long-term game. To build effective relationships in social media, you're expected to

+ Establish your expertise.

+ Participate regularly as a "good citizen" of whichever social media world you inhabit; follow site rules and abide by whatever conventions have been established.

+ Avoid overt self-promotion.

+ Avoid using hard-sell pressure techniques.

+ Provide value with links, resources, and unbiased information.

Watch for steady growth in the number of your followers on a particular service or the number of people who recommend your site to others; increased downloads of *white papers* (articles that provide detailed information on a topic); or repeat visits to your site. All these signs indicate you're building relationships that may later lead, if not to a direct sale, then to a word-of-web recommendation to someone who does buy.

In the world of social media, the term *engagement* refers to the length of time and quality of interaction between your company and your followers.

Social media is a long-term commitment. Other than little experiments or pilot projects, don't bother starting a social media commitment if you don't plan to keep it going. Any short-term benefits you see aren't worth the effort you have to make.

Improving business processes

Already, many clever businesses have found ways to use social media to improve business processes. Though individual applications depend on the nature of your business, consider leveraging social media to

✦ Promptly detect and correct customer problems or complaints.

✦ Obtain customer feedback and input on new product designs or changes.

✦ Provide tech support to many people at one time; if one person has a question, chances are good that others do, too.

✦ Improve service delivery, such as cafes that accept to-go orders on Twitter or Facebook, or food carts that notify customers where and when their carts will arrive.

✦ Locate qualified new vendors, service providers, and employees by using professional networks such as LinkedIn.

✦ Collect critical market intelligence on your industry and competitors by watching content on appropriate social media.

✦ Use geolocation, tweets, and mobile search services to drive neighborhood traffic to brick-and-mortar stores during slow times and to acquire new customers.

Marketing is only part of your company, but all of your company is marketing. Social media is a ripe environment for this hypothesis, where every part of a company, from human resources to tech support, and from engineering to sales, can be involved.

Improving search engine rankings

Just as you optimize your website, you should optimize your social media outlets for search engine ranking. Now that search engines are cataloging Twitter and Facebook and other appearances on social media, you can gain additional front-page real estate for your company on Google and

Yahoo!/Bing (who now share the same search algorithms and usually produce similar results).

Search engines recognize some, but not all, appearances on social media as inbound links, which also improve the page rank of your site.

Use a core set of search terms and keywords across as many sites as possible. Book II, Chapter 2 deals with search engine optimization, including tactics to avoid because they could get you in trouble for spamming.

Optimization pays off in other ways: in results on real-time searches, which are now available on primary search engines; on external search engines that focus on blogs or other social media services; and on internal, site-specific search engines.

Selling when opportunity arises

Conventional thinking says that social media is designed for long-term engagement, for marketing and branding rather than for sales. However, a few obvious selling opportunities exist, particularly for business-to-consumer (B2C) companies, that won't offend followers:

✦ **Sell music and event tickets.** SoundCloud and ReverbNation, which cater to music and entertainment, are appropriate social media sites for these products.

✦ **Include a link to your online store on social shopping services.** Recommend products — particularly apparel, jewelry, beauty, and decor — as Stylehive does.

✦ **Offer promotional codes or special deals to followers.** Offering codes or deals on particular networks encourages your followers to visit your site to make a purchase. You can also announce sales or events.

✦ **Place links to online or third-party stores like Etsy.com (see Book II, Chapter 1) on your profile pages on various services.** You can rarely sell directly from a social media service, but some permit you to place widgets that visually showcase your products and link to your online store, PayPal, or the equivalent to conclude a transaction.

✦ **Include a sign-up option for your e-newsletter.** It offers a bridge to sales.

The chart in Figure 1-8 shows a 2013 HubSpot survey of the percentage of companies that succeeded in acquiring a customer by way of a lead generated from a specific social media service. Survey respondents included both B2B (business-to-business) and B2C (business-to-consumer) companies.

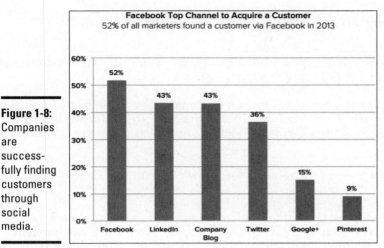

Figure 1-8:
Companies
are
success-
fully finding
customers
through
social
media.

Reproduced by permission of HubSpot, Inc.

Include sales offers within a stream of information and news to avoid turning your social media site into a series of never-ending advertisements.

Saving money on advertising

Although time is money, the magic word is *free*. If you're a start-up company, free social media is likely the only advertising you can afford. If you decide to approach social media for this purpose, construct your master campaign just as carefully as you would a paid one:

✦ Create a plan that outlines target markets, ad offers, publishing venues, and schedules for different ad campaigns.

✦ If necessary, conduct comparative testing of messages, graphics, and offers.

✦ Monitor results and focus on the outlets that work best at driving qualified visits that lead to conversions.

✦ Supplement your free advertising with search engine optimization, press releases, and other forms of free promotion.

Advertising is only one part of marketing!

As you see traffic and conversions building from your social media marketing campaigns, you may want to reduce existing paid advertising campaigns. Just don't stop your paid advertising until you're confident that you have an equally profitable stream of customers from social media. Of course, if your ad campaign isn't working, there's no point continuing it.

Understanding the Cons of Social Media

For all its upsides, social media has its downsides. As social media has gained in popularity, it has also become increasingly difficult to gain visibility among its hundreds of millions of users.

In fact, sometimes you have to craft a campaign just to build an audience on a particular social media site. It's quite similar to conducting optimization and inbound link campaigns so that your site is found in natural search results.

Don't participate in social media for its own sake or just because everyone else is.

By far, the biggest downside in social media is the amount of time you need to invest to see results. You need to make an ongoing commitment to review and respond to comments and to provide an ongoing stream of new material. An initial commitment to set up a profile is just the tip of the iceberg.

Keep in mind that you need to watch out for the addictiveness of social media. Individually and collectively, social media is the biggest-ever time sink. Don't believe us? Ask yourself whether you became addicted to news alerts during the 2012 presidential campaign or couldn't take your eyes off live coverage of the Mars landing. Or maybe you play Candy Crush or other video games with a passion, continuously run instant messaging, check email every ten seconds . . . you get the idea. Without self-discipline and a strong time schedule, you can easily become so socially overbooked that other tasks go undone.

As you consider each of the social media options in this book, also consider the level of human resources that are needed. Do you have the time and talents yourself? If not, do other people within your organization have the time and talent? Which other efforts will you need to give up while making room for social media? Will you have to hire new employees or contract out services, leading to hard costs for this supposedly "free" media?

Integrating Social Media into Your Overall Marketing Effort

Social media is only part of your online marketing. Online marketing is only part of your overall marketing. Don't mistake the part for the whole.

Consider each foray into social marketing as a strategic choice to supplement your other online marketing activities, which may include

✦ **Creating and managing a marketing-effective website:** Use content updates, search engine optimization (SEO), inbound link campaigns, and event calendar postings to your advantage.

✦ **Displaying your product or service's value:** Create online press releases and email newsletters. Share testimonials and reviews with your users and offer affiliate or loyalty programs, online events, or promotions.

✦ **Advertising:** Take advantage of pay-per-click ads, banners, and sponsorships.

Social media is neither necessary nor sufficient to meet all your online marketing needs.

Use social media strategically to

✦ Meet an otherwise unmet marketing need.

✦ Increase access to your target market.

✦ Open the door to a new niche market.

✦ Move prospects through the conversion funnel.

✦ Improve the experience for existing customers.

For example, the website for Fluid IT Services (www.fluiditservices.com) links to Facebook, Twitter, and LinkedIn profiles sites, as well as its blog (www.fluiditservices.com/blog), to attract its audience. For more information on overall online marketing, see Jan's book, *Web Marketing For Dummies,* 3rd Edition (Wiley Publishing, Inc.).

To get the maximum benefit from social media, you must have a *hubsite,* the site to which web traffic will be directed, as shown in Figure 1-9. With more than 1 billion websites online, you need social media as a source of traffic. Your hubsite can be a full website or a blog, as long as the site has its own domain name. It doesn't matter where the site is hosted — only that you own its name, which appears as www.yourcompany.com or http://blog.yourcompany.com. Though you can link to http://yourcompany.wordpress.com, you can't effectively optimize or advertise a WordPress address like this. Besides, it doesn't look professional to use a domain name from a third party.

Consider doing some sketching for your own campaign: Create a block diagram that shows the relationship between components, the flow of content between outlets, and perhaps even the criteria for success and how you'll measure those criteria.

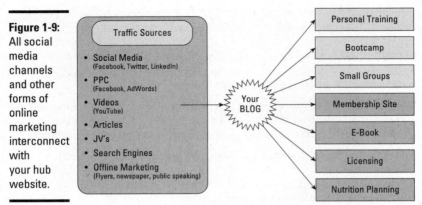

Figure 1-9:
All social media channels and other forms of online marketing interconnect with your hub website.

Reproduced by permission of Watermelon Mountain Web Marketing, watermelonweb.com

Developing a Strategic Social Media Marketing Plan

Surely you wrote an overall marketing plan when you last updated your business plan and an online marketing plan when you first created your website. If not, it's never too late! For business planning resources, see the Starting a Business page at www.sba.gov/category/navigation-structure/ starting-managing-business/starting-business.

You can further refine a marketing plan for social media marketing purposes. As with any other marketing plan, you start with strategy. A Social Media Marketing Goals statement (Figure 1-10 shows an example) would incorporate sections on strategic goals, objectives, target markets, methods, costs, and return on investment (ROI).

You can download the form on this book's website (www.dummies.com/ extras/socialmediamarketingaio) and read more about ROI in Book I, Chapter 2.

Here are some points to keep in mind when putting together your strategic marketing overview:

✦ The most important function of the form isn't for you to follow it slavishly, but rather to force you to consider the various facets of social media marketing before you invest too much effort or money.

✦ The form also helps you communicate decisions to your board of advisors or your boss, in case you need to make the business case for getting involved in social media.

✦ The form provides a coherent framework for explaining to everyone involved in your social media effort — employees, volunteers, or contractors — the task you're trying to accomplish and why.

Social Media Marketing Goals

Related to Hub Site (URL): _____

Prepared by: _____ **Date:** _____

Business Profile

Is the social media plan for a new or established company?
- ○ New company
- ○ Existing company, years in business:

Does the company have an existing brick-and-mortar operation?
- ○ Yes
- ○ No

Does the company have an existing website or web presence?
- ○ Yes
- ○ No

Does the company have an existing blog or social media presence?
- ○ Yes
- ○ No

If yes, list all current URLs for social media.

Will your site serve:
- ○ Business
- ○ Consumers

What type of business is the website for?
- ○ Manufacturer
- ○ Service provider
- ○ Retailer
- ○ Distributor
- ○ Professional

What does the company sell?
- ○ Goods
- ○ Services

Describe your goods or services:

What geographical range does the social media campaign address?
- ○ Local (specify)
- ○ Regional (specify)
- ○ National (specify if not US)
- ○ International (specify)

Social Media Campaign Goals

Rank the applicable goals of your social media campaign from 1-7 with 1 your top goal

- _____ Increasing traffic/visits to hub site
- _____ Branding
- _____ Building relationships
- _____ Improving business process (e.g. customer service, tech support)
- _____ Improving visibility in natural search
- _____ Increasing sales revenue
- _____ Saving money on paid advertising

Figure 1-10:
Establish your social marketing goals, objectives, and target market definition on this form.

Financial Profile

Social Media Campaign Budget for First Year

Outside development, contractors,
includes writing, design, technical $ _____

Special content production (e.g.
video, podcasts, photography): $ _____

Marketing/paid ads on social
media $ _____

Inhouse labor (burdened rate) $ _____

Other costs, e.g. tools, equipment $ _____

TOTAL: $ _____

Break-even point: $ _____   Within: _____ ◯ mo ◯ yr

Return on investment: _____ %   Within: _____ ◯ mo ◯ yr

Objectives

Repeat for appropriate objectives for each goal within timeframe specified
(for instance, 1 year).

Traffic objective (# visitors per month): _____   Within: _____

Conversion objective: _____ %   Within: _____

Sales objectives (# sales per month): $ _____   Within: _____

Average $ per sale: $ _____   Within: _____

$ revenue per month: $ _____   Within: _____

Other objectives specific to your site,
e.g. for branding, relationships, search
ranking   _____   Within: _____

_____   Within: _____

_____   Within: _____

Figure 1-10:
(continued)

Marketing Profile

Describe your target markets. Give specific demographic or other segmentation information. For B2B, segment by industry and/or job title.

What is your marketing tag?

Value proposition: Why should someone buy from your company rather than another?

Name at least six competitors and list their websites, blogs, and social media pages.

© 2012 Watermelon Mountain Web Marketing www.watermelonweb.com

Figure 1-10:
(continued)

Reproduced with permission of Watermelon Mountain Web Marketing, watermelonweb.com

Book I, Chapter 3 includes a Social Media Marketing Plan, which helps you develop a detailed tactical approach — including timelines — for specific social media services, sites, and tools.

In the following sections, we talk about the information you should include on this form.

Establishing goals

The Goals section prioritizes the overall reasons you're implementing a social media campaign. You can prioritize your goals from the seven benefits of social media, described in the earlier section "Understanding the Benefits of Social Media," or you can add your own goals. Most businesses have multiple goals, which you can specify on the form.

Consult Table 1-1 to see how various social media services rank in terms of helping you reach some of your goals.

Setting quantifiable objectives

For each goal, set at least one quantifiable, measurable objective. "More customers" isn't a quantifiable objective. A quantifiable objective is "Increase number of visits to website by 10 percent," "add 30 new customers within three months," or "obtain 100 new followers for Twitter account within one month of launch." Enter this information on the form.

Table 1-1	Matching Social Media Services to Goals			
Service	**Customer Communication**	**Brand Exposure**	**Traffic to Your Site**	**SEO**
Facebook	Good	Okay	Good	Good
Google+	Good	Good	Okay	Okay
Instagram	Poor	Good	Good	Poor
LinkedIn	Okay	Good	Good	Okay
Pinterest	Good	Good	Okay	Good
SlideShare	Okay	Good	Poor	Poor
Twitter	Good	Good	Good	Good
YouTube	Okay	Okay	Good	Okay

Adapted from data sources at www.cmo.com/articles/2014/3/13/_2014_social_intro.html

Identifying your target markets

Specify one or more target markets on the form, not by what they consume, but rather by who they are. "Everyone who eats dinner out" isn't a sub-market you can identify online. However, you can find "high-income couples within 20 miles of your destination who visit wine and classical music sites."

You may want to reach more than one target market by way of social media or other methods. Specify each of them. Then, as you read about different methods in this book, write down next to each one which social media services or sites appear best suited to reach that market. Prioritize the order in which you plan to reach them.

Book I, Chapter 3 suggests online market research techniques to help you define your markets, match them to social media services, and find them online.

Think niche! Carefully define your audiences for various forms of social media, and target your messages appropriately for each audience.

Estimating costs

Estimating costs from the bottom up is tricky, and this approach rarely includes a cap. Consequently, costs often wildly exceed your budget.

Instead, establish first how much money you're willing to invest in the over-all effort, including in-house labor, outside contractors, and miscellaneous hard costs such as purchasing software or equipment. Enter those amounts in the Cost section.

Then prioritize your social marketing efforts based on what you can afford, allocating or reallocating funds within your budget as needed. This approach not only keeps your total social marketing costs under control but also lets you assess the results against expenses.

To make cost-tracking easier, ask your bookkeeper or CPA to set up an activity or a job within your accounting system for social media marketing. Then you can easily track and report all related costs and labor.

Valuing social media ROI

Return on investment (ROI) is your single most important measure of suc-cess for social media marketing. In simple terms, *ROI* is the ratio of revenue divided by costs for your business or, in this case, for your social media marketing effort.

You also need to set a realistic term in which you will recover your invest-ment. Are you willing to wait ten weeks? Ten months? Ten years? Some forms of social media are unlikely to produce a fast fix for drooping sales, so consider what you're trying to accomplish.

Figure 1-11 presents a brief glimpse of how HubSpot clients assessed their average cost of *lead generation* (identifying prospective customers) in 2013, comparing social marketing to other forms of marketing. It's just a guide. Keep in mind that the only ROI or cost of acquisition that truly matters is your own.

Costs usually turn out to be simpler to track than revenues that are trace-able explicitly to social media. Chapter 2 of this minibook discusses tech-niques for figuring ROI and other financial metrics in detail.

Whatever you plan for online marketing, it will cost twice as much and take twice as long as anticipated.

A social media service is likely to produce results only when your customers or prospects are already using it or are willing to try. Pushing people toward a service they don't want is quite difficult. If in doubt, first expand other online and offline efforts to drive traffic toward your hubsite.

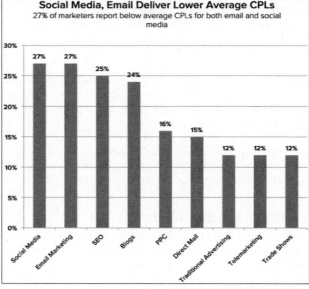

Figure 1-11: Social media and email show a lower cost per lead (CPL) generated compared to other forms of marketing.

Reproduced by permission of HubSpot, Inc.

Aglow with brand value from social media

Alpenglow Sports has been selling mountain gear on the north shore of Lake Tahoe, California, for more than 35 years, long before the existence of the Internet and web marketing. Now it uses social media to share its passion for mountain sports — skiing, trail running, hiking, backpacking, and rock climbing — and to convey its strong commitment to the community and to the environment.

According to owner and CEO Brendan Madigan, the company promotes itself regionally, with some social media posts targeted specifically to various locations in California. Alpenglow's market, he explains, is roughly 40 percent locals and 60 percent visitors, including many second-home owners who drive to Tahoe from elsewhere in the state.

Unlike many companies, Alpenglow has not used its eight-year-old website (`http://alpenglowsports.com`, seen in the following figure) for e-commerce, though that may change in the future. The site currently consists of a blog, a registration portal for its annual Alpenglow Mountain Festival, and a gallery of strong images that convey its brand message.

Madigan explains that in keeping with the company's spirit of adventure, Alpenglow began doing social media in 2009 without a master plan. "I've always felt that social media should portray the passion that we all have for the mountain sports we do. Accordingly, I just started a Facebook page [see the following figure] and began to learn as I went along." One summer, some of the shop employees ascended and then skied down Mt. McKinley (Denali) in Alaska, posting updates on Facebook of their adventure. When they returned, they discovered many people had been following their progress. "That was undoubtedly a light-bulb moment for me regarding the marketing power of a free resource!" Madigan exclaims.

With that triumph in hand, Alpenglow added Twitter and then Instagram. "When you are portraying a mountain lifestyle, there is rarely something as effective as simple images. One image can say a lot about your brand and what you love to do."

(continued)

(continued)

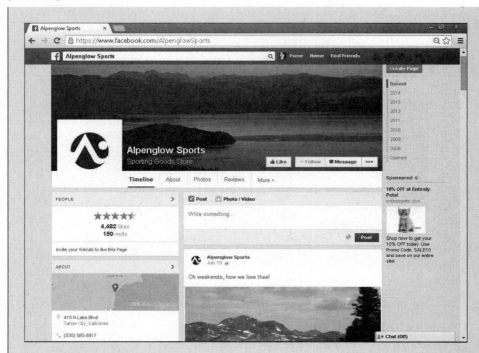

Alpenglow doesn't look for social media to provide a direct ROI through product sales. "I've always felt that if you are pitching sales your brand will lose, especially in the small brick and mortar arena." Madigan feels that if he conveys the fun and thrill of mountain sports, the ROI will come organically. It doesn't hurt that the company's employee-athletes are an amazing inspiration, as well as a great source of information and experience.

To keep things "authentic," Madigan manages the social media outlets himself, working with a creative partner only to develop content for larger events or offline advertising. "I try to abide by a 90/10 split for fun posts versus some type of product/sale post. I feel that anything more than that will turn off customers. Plus, while we have financial realities, promoting cheesy sales pitches just isn't as fun as posting a photo of the backcountry powder skiing you did that morning that had an epic sunrise!"

The effort is time-consuming, but to Madigan it's all part of an expression of life in the mountains. He tries to post to Facebook daily at either 9 a.m. or 4 p.m. Twitter and Instagram are more likely to be on the fly, when he catches a great photo of wildflowers, a sunrise, or glittering snow. On occasion, he will use Hootsuite for a more scheduled rollout of messages. Overall, social media is a six- to ten-hour-per-week commitment.

To monitor the results of all this activity, Alpenglow uses Talkwalker and Google Alerts. Madigan finds it essential to "keep an ear to the ground," so he can address both praise and criticism quickly, and respond promptly to any questions that arise. He uses Google Analytics to track web traffic primarily during mountain festivals.

Notwithstanding Facebook Insights, "I don't think there is a realistic way to actually measure a direct ROI for social marketing," Madigan says. "Because we aren't currently fixated on driving traffic to an e-commerce site, we have some degree of flexibility."

In addition to social media, Alpenglow includes e-newsletters, search engine optimization, press releases, and traditional print and radio ads in its marketing mix. For paid online advertising, Madigan uses Facebook advertising only to boost successful posts. (See Book V). "With the 8-percent Facebook algorithm, it is quite hard to reach our followers. Usually we only do this during our Mountain Festivals or other important events that warrant enhanced exposure. We generally target our audiences to sport-specific followers or geographic regions," he explains.

Madigan reemphasizes the importance of passion to other business owners. "You have only 8 seconds to make an impression — and as a business owner or marketer, it is your responsibility to capture [your customers' attention]. Be fun, educational, and daring in your social posts. I always ask myself 'Does this post portray what gets me out of bed in the morning?' Pretty simple when it comes down to it."

Here are addresses for Alpenglow Sports' web presence:

```
http://alpenglowsports.com
```

```
www.facebook.com/AlpenglowSports
```

```
http://instagram.com/alpenglowsports
```

```
http://twitter.com/AlpenglowSports
```

```
www.yelp.com/biz/alpenglow-sports-tahoe-city
```

```
http://alpenglowsports.wordpress.com
```

```
http://plus.google.com/100026260159126807522/posts
```

Chapter 2: Tallying the Bottom Line

*I*n this chapter, you deal with business metrics to determine whether you see a return on investment (ROI) in your social media marketing services. In other words, you get to the bottom line! For details on performance metrics for various types of social media as parameters for campaign success, see Book IX.

By definition, the business metric ROI involves revenues. Alas, becoming famous online isn't a traditional part of ROI; it might have a public relations value and affect business results, but fame doesn't necessarily make you rich. This chapter examines the cost of acquiring new customers, tracking sales, and managing leads. After you reach the break-even point on your investment, you can (in the best of all worlds) start totaling up the profits and then calculate your ROI.

To get the most from this chapter, review your business plan and financial projections. You may find that you need to adjust some of your data collection efforts to ensure that you have the information for these analyses.

If numbers make your head spin, ask your bookkeeper or accountant for assistance in tracking important business metrics from your financial statements. That person can ensure that you acquire the right data, set up spreadsheets to calculate key metrics, and provide regular reports — and then he or she can teach you how to interpret them.

You don't want to participate in social media marketing for its own sake or because everyone else is doing it. The following sections help you make the business case for yourself.

Preparing to Calculate Return on Investment

To calculate ROI, you have to recognize both costs and revenue related to your social media activities; neither is transparent, even without distinguishing marketing channels.

Surprisingly, the key determinant in tracking cost of sales, and therefore ROI, is most likely to be your sales process, which matters more than whether you sell to other businesses (business to business, or B2B) or consumers (business to consumer, or B2C) or whether you offer products or services.

The *sales cycle* (the length of time from prospect identification to customer sale) affects the timeline for calculating ROI. If a B2B sale for an expensive, long-term contract or product takes two years, expecting a return on your investment within a month is pointless.

For a *pure-play* (e-commerce only) enterprise selling products from an online store, the ROI calculation detailed in this chapter is fairly standard. However, ROI becomes more complicated if your website generates leads that you must follow up with offline, if you must pull customers from a web presence into a brick-and-mortar storefront (that method is sometimes called *bricks-and-clicks*), or if you sell different products or services in different channels. Table 2-1 provides resource sites that relate to these issues and other business metrics.

Table 2-1	Resources for Business Metrics	
Site Name	*URL*	*What You Can Do*
ClickZ	www.clickz.com/clickz/column/2140755/understanding-importance-social-media-roi	Measure social media success.
Frogloop.com	www.frogloop.com/social-network-calculator	Download or calculate online your social media ROI.
Harvard Business School Toolkit	http://hbswk.hbs.edu/archive/1262.html	Use the break-even analysis tool.
	http://hbswk.hbs.edu/archive/1436.html	Calculate lifetime customer value.

Site Name	URL	What You Can Do
Interactive Insights Group	`www.interactiveinsightsgroup.com/blog1/social-media-metrics-superlist-measurement-roi-key-statistics-resources`	Scan annotated super-list of dozens of articles on social media ROI and measurement; with a $5.95 cost.
National Retail Federation	`https://nrf.com/who-we-are/retail-communities/digital-retail-shoporg`	Research, news, and whitepapers from the NRF's digital retail community.
Olivier Blanchard Basics of Social Media ROI	`www.slideshare.net/thebrandbuilder/olivier-blanchard-basics-of-social-media-roi`	View an entertaining slide show introduction to ROI.
Panalysis	`www.panalysis.com/resources/sales-target-calculator.aspx`	Calculate online sales.
	`www.panalysis.com/resources/customer-acquisition-cost.aspx`	Calculate customer acquisition costs.
Search Engine Watch	`http://searchenginewatch.com/article/2079336/4-Steps-to-Measure-Social-Media-ROI-with-Google-Analytics`	Set up Google Analytics to measure social media ROI.
SearchCRM	`http://searchcrm.techtarget.com`	Find information about customer relationship management (CRM).
WhatIs.com	`http://whatis.techtarget.com`	Search a dictionary and an encyclopedia of business terms.

Include the business metrics you intend to monitor in the Business Goals section of your Social Media Marketing Plan, found in Book I, Chapter 3, and the frequency of review on your Social Media Activity Calendar discussed in Book I, Chapter 4.

Accounting for Customers Acquired Online

The *cost of customer acquisition* (CCA) refers to the marketing, advertising, support, and other types of expenses required to convert a prospect into a customer. CCA usually excludes the cost of a sales force (the salary and commissions) or payments to affiliates. Some companies carefully segregate promotional expenses, such as loyalty programs, that relate to branding or customer retention. As long as you apply your definition consistently, you're okay.

If your goal in social media marketing is branding or improving relationships with existing customers, CCA may be a bit misleading, but it's still worth tracking for comparison purposes.

The definition of your customers and the cost of acquiring them depend on the nature of your business. For instance, if you have a purely advertising-supported, web-only business, visitors to your site may not even purchase anything. They simply show up, or perhaps they register to download some information online. Your real customers are advertisers. However, a similar business that's not supported by advertising may need to treat those same registrants as leads who might later purchase services or pay for subscriptions.

The easiest way to define your customers is to figure out who pays you money.

Comparing the costs of customer acquisition

You may want to delineate CCA for several different revenue streams or marketing channels: consumers versus businesses; products versus services (for example, software and support contracts); online sales versus offline sales; consumers versus advertisers. Compare each one against the average CCA for your company overall. The formula is simple:

```
cost of customer acquisition = marketing cost ÷ number of leads
```

Be careful! This formula can be misleading if you calculate it over too short a time frame. The CCA may be too high during quarters that you undertake a new activity or special promotion (such as early Christmas sales or the introduction of a new product or service) and too low during quarters when actual spending is down but you reap benefits from an earlier investment in social media.

Calculate your CCA over six months to a year to smooth out unique events. Alternatively, compute *rolling averages* (taking an average over several months at a time, adjusting the start date each month — January through March, February through April, March through May, and so on) to create a better picture of what's going on.

In Figure 2-1, Rapport Online ranks the return on investment, defined as cost-effectiveness in generating leads, for a variety of online marketing tactics.

The lowest ROI appears at the bottom of the cube, and the highest appears at the top.

Figure 2-1: Social media would fit near the top of the ROI scale for Internet marketing tactics.

Reproduced with permission of Rapport Online Inc., ROI

Social media marketing runs the gamut of rapport-building options because it involves some or all of these techniques. On this scale, most social media services would probably fall between customer referral and SEO or between SEO and PR/link building, depending on the type and aggressiveness of your effort in a particular marketing channel. Traditional offline media, by contrast, would have a lower ROI than banner advertising.

As with performance metrics, business metrics such as CCA and ROI aren't perfect. If you track everything consistently, however, you can at least compare results by marketing channel, which can help you make informed business decisions.

If you garner leads online but close your sales and collect payments offline, you can frame CCA as the cost of lead acquisition, recognizing that you may need to add costs for staff, collateral, demos, travel, and other items to convert a lead.

For a rough idea of your cost of customer acquisition, fill out the spreadsheet (adapted from the spreadsheet at `www.forentrepreneurs.com`) shown in Figure 2-2 with your own data. For start-up costs, include the labor expense, contractors for content development, and any other hard costs related to your social media activities. Or try the CCA calculator at `www.panalysis.com/resources/customer-acquisition-cost.aspx`, substituting social media costs for web expenses.

To put things in perspective, remember that the traditional business school model for offline marketing teaches that the CCA is roughly equivalent to the profit on the amount a customer spends during the first year.

Cost of Customer Acquisition				Save As Excel | Exit Full Screen View
40R x 1C ■				
	A	B	C	D	E

	A	B	C
1	**Simple Cost of Customer Acquisition Calculation**		
2			
3	**Input Variables for 6 months**		
4	Total SMM Visiors	10,000	
5	Start-up SMM costs for content, programmer, contractors	$1,000.00	
6	CTR to site %	7%	
7	Conversion to customer %	4%	
8	No of Sales & Marketing Staff	1	
9	Ave 6 month labor cost for staff & contractors for SMM time app. 15 hr/mo @ $20	$1,800	
10			
11			
12	**Flow**	Qty	Conversion %
13	Total SMM Visits	10,000	
14	Site Visits	700	7%
15	Customers	28	4%
16			
17	SMM Marketing Spending (non-recurring)	$1,000	
18	Total Recurring Staff Costs	$1,800	
19			
20	**Cost of Customer Acquisition**		
21	Recurring staff costs only	$64.29	
22	Start-up costs only	$35.71	
23	Total costs	$100.00	

Sheet1

Figure 2-2:
Compare CCA for social media marketing (SMM) with the average CCA across your entire business.

Because you generally see most of your profits from future sales to that customer, you must also understand the *lifetime customer value* (how much and how often a customer will buy), not just the revenue from an initial sale. The better the customers, the more it's worth spending to acquire them. Harvard Business School offers an online calculator for determining lifetime customer value at `http://hbswk.hbs.edu/archive/1436.html`.

Be sure that the cost of customer acquisition (CCA) doesn't exceed the lifetime customer value.

In its *State of Retailing Online 2009* report for Shop.org, Forrester Research estimated that the cost of acquiring an online customer was about half the cost of acquiring an offline customer. In its 2014 update (`https://nrf.com/media/press-releases/shoporgforrester-search-marketing-tops-online-retail-customer-acquisition`), Forrester finds that retailers continue to invest in paid search and online display ads, including ads on social media to acquire new customers. As the cost of new customer acquisition through online advertising creeps up, marketing opportunities with free social media become increasingly attractive for small businesses.

Try to keep the total cost of marketing by any method at 6 to 11 percent of your revenues; you can spend less after you have an established business with word-of-mouth referrals and loyal, repeat customers. Remember, customer acquisition is only part of your total marketing budget; allow for customer retention and branding expenses as well.

Small businesses (fewer than 100 employees), new companies, and new products usually need to spend toward the high end of the scale on marketing initially — perhaps even more than 11 percent. By comparison, mature, well-branded product lines and companies with a large revenue stream can spend a lower percentage on marketing.

Obviously, anything that can reduce marketing costs offers a benefit. See whether your calculation bears out that cost level for your investment in social media.

One is silver and the other gold

You might remember the words to that old Girl Scout song: "Make new friends but keep the old; one is silver and the other gold." To retain customers, apply that philosophy to your policy of customer satisfaction. That may mean anything from sending holiday greetings to establishing a loyalty program with discounts for repeat buyers, from entering repeat customers into a special sweepstakes to offering a coupon on their next purchase when they sign up for a newsletter.

There's an old saw in marketing that it costs many times more to acquire a new customer than to retain an existing one. This assertion is hard to prove — and costs would vary with each business — but it's common sense to listen to customers' concerns, complaints, product ideas, and desires.

Thus, while you lavish time and attention on social marketing to fill the top of your funnel with new prospects, don't forget its value for improving relationships with current customers and nurturing their involvement with your brand. The same 2014 Forrester report on retailing online that we mentioned in the preceding section also noted the critical value of social media in building customer engagement.

Establishing Key Performance Indicators for Sales

If you track ROI, at some point, you must track revenue and profits as business metrics. Otherwise, there's no ROI to compute.

If you sell online, your storefront should provide ways for you to slice and dice sales to obtain crucial data. However, if your sales come from services, from a brick-and-mortar store, or from large contractual purchases, you probably need to obtain revenue statistics from financial or other external records to plug into your ROI calculation.

If you manage a bricks-and-clicks operation, you may want to integrate your online and offline operations by selecting e-commerce software from the vendor who provides the *point-of-sales* (POS) package for your cash registers. That software may already be integrated with your inventory control and accounting packages.

Just as with performance metrics, you should be able to acquire certain key performance indicators (KPI) for sales by using storefront statistics. Confirm that you can access this data before purchasing your e-commerce package:

✦ You should be able to determine how often customers buy (number of transactions per month), how many new customers you acquire (reach), and how much they spend per transaction (yield).

✦ Look for sales reports by average dollar amount as well as by number of sales. Plugging average numbers into an ROI calculation is easier, and the results are close enough as long as the inputs are consistent.

✦ You should be able to find order totals for any specified time frame so that you can track sales tied to promotions, marketing activities, and sale announcements.

✦ Look for the capability to sort sales by new and repeat customers; to allow for future, personalized offers; and to distinguish numbers for CCA.

✦ Your sales statistics should include a conversion funnel (as described in Chapter 1 of this minibook). Try to trace the path upstream so that you can identify sales initiated from social media.

✦ Check that data can be exported to a spreadsheet.

✦ Make sure that you can collect statistics on the use of promotion codes by number and dollar value so that you can decide which promotions are the most successful.

✦ Having store reports that break down sales by product is helpful. Sometimes called a *product tree,* this report shows which products are selling by SKU (stock keeping unit) and category.

Table 2-2 lists some storefront options that integrate with social media and offer sales analytics. Unfortunately, not all third-party storefront solutions offer ideal tracking. Many storefront solutions use Google Analytics, shown in Figure 2-3, to track transactions.

Table 2-2	**Social Media Store Solutions Offering Sales Statistics**	
Name	*URL*	*Type of Sales Stats Available*
Google Analytics ECommerce Tracking	`https://developers.google.com/analytics/devguides/collection/gajs/gaTrackingEcommerce`	Google Analytics for e-commerce
ProductCart	`www.productcart.com`	Google Analytics integration at the product level
Mercantec	`www.mercantec.com`	Google Analytics e-commerce tracking and statistics
Payvment	`www.ecwid.com/payvment`	Integrated storefront that works on social media, mobile, and blog sites

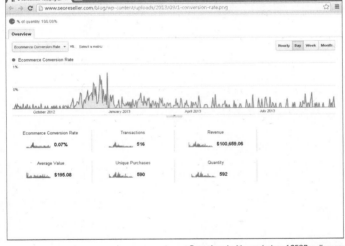

Figure 2-3:
Typical
e-commerce
statistics
available
on Google
Analytics.

Reproduced with permission of SEOReseller.com

If you created alternative SKUs for products sold by way of social media for tracking purposes, be sure to merge them into the same category of your product tree. Using multiple SKUs isn't recommended if your storefront solution includes inventory control.

You can input the numbers from your social media sales metrics into a sales calculator to forecast unit sales needed to meet your goals.

Figure 2-4 shows a calculator from Panalysis at `www.panalysis.com/`
`resources/sales-target-calculator.aspx`. Users enter values for the
variables in the fields at the top of the image and click Calculate; different
forecasts for monthly revenue appear below the fields.

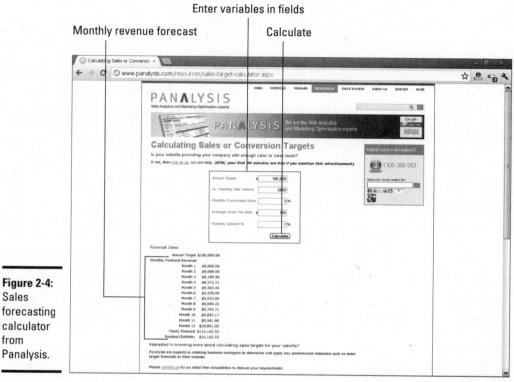

Enter variables in fields

Monthly revenue forecast   Calculate

Figure 2-4:
Sales
forecasting
calculator
from
Panalysis.

Tracking Leads

Often, your social media or web presence generates leads instead of, or in
addition to, sales. If your sales process dictates that some or all sales are
closed offline, you need a way to track leads from initiation to conversion.
MarketingSherpa, a marketing research firm, analyzed the conversion rate
of online leads, starting with the initial acquisition of customers' names or
email addresses, to offline sales. Percentages given are for each step compared to the original number of visitors. See Figure 2-5.

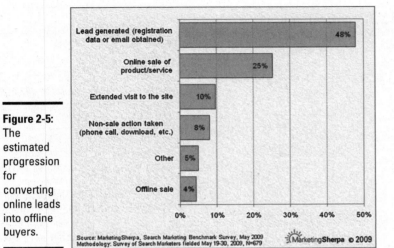

Figure 2-5:
The estimated progression for converting online leads into offline buyers.

Source: MarketingSherpa

Customer relationship management (CRM) software helps you track prospects, qualified leads, and customers in an organized way. A simple database might allow different managers, salespeople, and support personnel to share a client's concerns or track the client's steps within the selling cycle.

The process of CRM and lead management may also include qualifying and nurturing leads, managing marketing campaigns, building relationships, and providing service, all while helping to maximize profits. Table 2-3 lists some lead monitoring and CRM software options.

Table 2-3	Lead Monitoring and CRM Software		
Name	*URL*	*What You Can Do*	*Cost*
Batchbook	`www.batchblue.com`	Integrate social media with CRM.	Free 30-day trial with unlimited contacts; starts at $55 per month after free trial
HubSpot	`http://offers.hubspot.com/free-trial`	All-in-one software; manage inbound leads, lead generation, and more.	Free 30-day trial; starts at $200 per month after free trial

(continued)

Table 2-3 *(continued)*

Name	URL	What You Can Do	Cost
LEADSExplorer	www.leadsexplorer.com	See who's visiting your website.	Free 30-day trial; starts at $42 per month after free trial
SplendidCRM	www.splendidcrm.com/products/splendidcrmcommunity/tabid/71/default.aspx	Install open-source CRM software.	Free 30-day trial version; fee starts at $10 per user per month with two additional levels of features at a higher per user price
Zoho CRM	https://www.zoho.com/crm/zohocrm-pricing.html	Implement customer relationship management software.	Free for three users; starts at $12 per user per month for additional features, with increasing levels of features at a higher per user price

Though often thought of as the province of B2B companies offering high-ticket items with a long sales cycle, lead-tracking tools can help you segment existing and prospective customers, improve the percentage of leads that turn into clients, and build brand loyalty.

Figure 2-6 shows the distribution of leads and sales, respectively, with analytical tools provided by HubSpot. Note how the distribution of leads by marketing channels differs from the ultimate distribution of sales.

You can export your Google Analytics results to a spreadsheet and create a similar graphical display.

Figure 2-6:
HubSpot
offers lead
monitoring
software
that displays
web traffic
by source.

Reproduced with permission of HubSpot, Inc.

Understanding Other Common Business Metrics

Your bookkeeper or accountant can help you compute and track other business measurements to ensure that your business turns a profit. You may want to pay particular attention to estimating your break-even point and your profit margin.

Break-even point

Computing the *break-even point* (the number of sales needed for revenues received to equal total costs) helps determine when a product or product line will become profitable. After a product reaches break-even, sales start to contribute to profits.

To calculate the break-even point, first you need to figure out the *cost of goods* (for example, your wholesale price or cost of manufacturing) or *average variable costs* (costs such as materials, shipping, or commission that vary with the number of units sold) and your *fixed costs* (charges such as rent or insurance that are the same each month regardless of how much business you do). Then plug the amounts into these two formulas:

```
revenues - cost of goods (variable) = gross margin

fixed costs ÷ gross margin = break-even point (in unit sales)
```

Figure 2-7 shows this relationship. This graph of the break-even point shows fixed costs (the dashed horizontal line) to variable costs (the solid diagonal line) to plot total costs. After revenues surpass the break-even point, each sale contributes to profits (the shaded area on the right).

The break-even analysis tool from the Harvard Business School Toolkit (`http://hbswk.hbs.edu/archive/1262.html`) can also help you calculate your break-even point.

Profit margin

Net profit margin is defined as earnings (profits) divided by revenues. If you have $10,000 in revenues and $1,500 in profits, your profit margin is 15 percent (1500 ÷ 10000 = 0.15).

Revenue versus profit

One of the most common errors in marketing is to stop analyzing results when you count the cash in the drawer. You can easily be seduced by growing revenues, but it's profit that matters. Profit determines your return on investment, replenishes your resources for growth, and rewards you for taking risks.

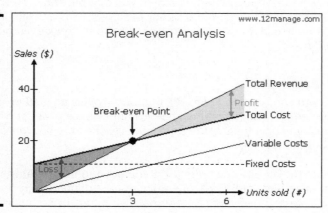

Figure 2-7: The break-even chart plots fixed plus variable costs; each sale after the break-even point contributes to profits.

Determining Return on Investment

Return on investment (ROI) is a commonly used business metric that evaluates the profitability of an investment or effort compared with its original cost. This versatile metric is usually presented as a ratio or percentage (multiply the following equation by 100). The formula itself is deceptively simple:

```
ROI = (Gain from Investment - Cost of Investment) ÷ Cost of
    Investment
```

The devil is, as usual, in the details. The cost of an investment means more than cold, hard cash. Depending on the type of effort for which you're computing ROI, you may need to include the cost of labor (including your own!), subcontractors, fees, and advertising for an accurate picture. When calculating ROI for your entire business, be sure to include overhead, cost of goods, and cost of sales.

You can affect ROI positively by either increasing the return (revenues) or reducing costs. That's business in a nutshell.

Because the formula is flexible, be sure that you know what other people mean when they talk about ROI.

You can calculate ROI for a particular marketing campaign or product, or an entire year's worth of marketing expenses. Or compare ROI among various forms of marketing, comparing the net revenue returned from an investment in social media to returns from SEO or paid advertising.

Run ROI calculations monthly, quarterly, or yearly, depending on the parameter you're trying to measure.

Try the interactive ROI calculator at `www.clickz.com/website-optimization-roi-calculator`, also shown in Figure 2-8. You can modify this model for social media by treating Monthly Site Visits as social media visits, Success Events as click-throughs to your main site, and Value of Success Events as the value of a sale. See what happens when you improve the *business metric* (the value of a sale) instead of, or in addition to, improving *performance* (site traffic or conversion rate).

ROI may be expressed as a *rate of return* (how long it takes to earn back an investment). An annual ROI of 25 percent means that it takes four years to recover what you put in. Obviously, if an investment takes too long to earn out, your product — or your business — is at risk of failing in the meantime.

Figure 2-8:
Play
around with
variables
like the
value of a
sale, as well
as perfor-
mance
criteria.

> **Calculating ROI: Website Optimization**   ⚡ ZAAZ
>
> *There is value in optimizing your website. How much value? Depending on your desired outcomes, the ZAAZ Calculator is designed to estimate the return on investment. Plug in the numbers and see how it changes the present and future value of your business.*
>
> **Current Site Behavior**
>
> Total Average Monthly Site Visits   `5,000` ⓘ
>
> Average Monthly Success Events   `250` ⓘ
> Identify specific targeted behavior (lead conversion, sales conversion, etc.)
>
> Success Event Conversion Rate   `5.00` % ⓘ
> Shows success event conversion from total site visits.
>
> Enter Average Value of a Success Event Visit $ `25` ⓘ
> Please refer to blogs.zaaz.com or here for more information on calculating this value.
>
> **Potential Improvement**   Enter the average value associated with a single Average Monthly Success Event Visit. Example: each visit is worth $25 on average.
>
> Increase Site Traffic by X%   `10` % ⓘ
> Enter a value (percentage) of the potential increase in site traffic (example 10%).
>
> Increase Conversion by X%   `10` % ⓘ
> Enter a value (percentage) of the potential increase in site conversion (example 10%).
>
> Estimated Cost to Improve Performance $ `3,000` ⓘ
> Enter estimated costs to optimize identified behaviors (e.g., agency fees, marketing and/or operational costs).
>
> **Estimated Impact of Site Optimization**
>
> ■ Monthly   ■ Annually
>
> Current Value $6,250
> $75,000
>
> Estimated Future $7,563
> Value $90,750

Reproduced with permission of ClickZ.com and Zaaz/Possible Worldwide

REMEMBER

If your analysis predicts a negative ROI, or even a very low rate of return over an extended period, stop and think! Unless you have a specific tactical plan (such as using a product as a loss leader to draw traffic), look for an alternative effort with a better likelihood of success.

Technically speaking, ROI is a business metric, involving the achievement of business goals, such as more clicks from social media that become sales, higher average value per sale, more repeat sales from existing customers, or reduced cost of customer acquisition.

Many people try to calculate ROI for social media based on performance metrics such as increases in

✦ The amount of traffic to website or social media pages

✦ The number of online conversations that include a positive mention of your company

✦ References to your company versus references to your competitors

✦ The number of people who join your social networks or bookmark your sites

✦ The number of people who post to your blog, comment on your Facebook, or retweet your comments

These measurements may be worth monitoring, but they're only intermediate steps in the ROI process, as shown in Figure 2-9.

Figure 2-9:
The relationship between performance metrics and business metrics for ROI.

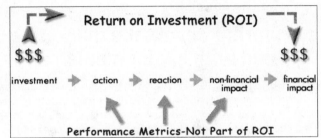

Source: BrandBuilder, "Olivier Blanchard Basics of Social Media ROI" www.slideshare.net/
thebrandbuilder/olivier-blanchard-basics-of-social-media-roi (#35)

Here's how to calculate your return on investment:

1. **Establish baselines for what you want to measure before and after your effort.**

   For example, you may want to measure year-over-year growth.

2. **Create activity timelines that appear when specific social media marketing events take place.**

   For example, mark an event on an activity timeline when you start a blog or Twitter campaign.

3. **Plot business metrics over time, particularly sales revenues, number of transactions, and net new customers.**

4. **Measure transactional precursors, such as positive versus negative mentions online, retail store traffic, or performance metrics.**

   For example, keep a tally of comments on a blog post or of site visits.

5. **Line up the timelines for the various relevant activities and transactional (business) results.**

6. **Look for patterns in the data that suggest a relationship between business metrics and transactional precursors.**

7. **Prove those relationships.**

   Try to predict future results on the basis of the patterns you see, and monitor your data to see whether your predictions are accurate.

Improvement in performance metrics doesn't necessarily produce better business results. The only two metrics that count toward ROI are whether your techniques reduce costs or improve revenue.

McKay Flooring covers the marketing ground with social media

McKay Flooring in Scotland (www.mckayflooring.co.uk, as shown in the nearby figure) is a second-generation family business that supplies and installs wood flooring throughout the United Kingdom. About 75 percent of its customers are commercial, with an emphasis on the sports flooring market. The company also does residential parquet installations and floor sanding. With 34 employees, McKay promotes itself primarily across the U.K. but sells its whisky-barrel flooring in the U.S. and Europe, as well.

Reproduced with permission of McKay Flooring Limited

McKay started social media marketing in 2008 using Twitter to promote its blog posts. "At the time, social media was relatively new, and we didn't really have a plan or strategy in place," explains Director Richard McKay. One by one, they added Facebook, Flickr, LinkedIn, Pinterest, YouTube,

Instagram, and Google+ (in roughly that order) to their list of multiple websites. McKay explains that he targets various social media platforms to very different market niches. For instance, he uses Pinterest (seen in the nearby figure), Instagram, and Facebook to focus on domestic customers and interior designers, while he builds awareness and trust for commercial clients via the McKay blog, LinkedIn, and Twitter.

"We recognized back in 2008 that having a social media presence was becoming increasingly important, but that we had to start creating content to put on these platforms," McKay says. The company started blogging about specific case studies and unique products to build brand awareness and improve its position in search engine rankings. Once the content was created, he distributed it to social media using the tool Buffer (`http://bufferapp.com`).

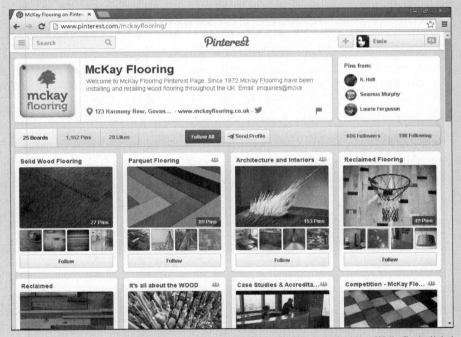

Reproduced with permission of McKay Flooring Limited

"One early win for us was the launch of our whisky-barrel flooring product made from reclaimed Scotch whisky barrels. We blogged about this and distributed our blog post to all our social media channels. It was picked up by some of the most viewed interior design blogs in the U.S. and in Europe, and sent huge traffic to our website. This year — nearly three years after launching our whisky flooring — we received an order from Google for their offices in Irvine, California. Not bad for a simple, free blog post!"

(continued)

(continued)

To cope with the challenge of constantly updating social media, McKay uses tools like Hootsuite, Buffer, DeliverThis.com, and IFTTT to update all its accounts. The operation is very organized! McKay has a content creation calendar and two staff people who spend two to three hours per day writing content, distributing it, and responding to social media enquiries.

Promoting its social media presence is simple with WordPress plugins on its sites. He also includes social media sharing icons on email signatures and print collateral. Early on in the process, McKay also posted on StumbleUpon, Technorati, and Digg. For analysis, McKay relies on Google Analytics to see which channels successfully generate leads. He uses Google Alerts for notification of brand mentions on social media, blogs, and websites.

To supplement its social media program, McKay Flooring makes active use of Google AdWords (supplemented by Unbounce for split-testing landing pages). AdWords produces the highest ROI results for the flooring company, but another of its companies, Love Salvage, does well with sponsored posts on Facebook. The company also produces a quarterly print and digital newsletter that targets commercial customers and prospects.

Given his success, it's worth listening to Richard McKay's advice. "I think the most important lesson we have learned . . . is to concentrate on creating compelling content. Social media can provide quick hits . . . but good blog content keeps paying for itself by providing inquiries years later."

McKay Flooring's web presence for its multiple product lines:

- **McKay Flooring:** www.mckayflooring.co.uk
- **Sports Flooring:** www.sportsflooring.co.uk
- **Classic Parquet:** www.classicparquet.co.uk
- **UK Floor Sanding:** www.ukfloorsanding.com
- **Whisky Flooring:** www.whiskybarrelflooring.com
- **Love Salvage** (reclaimed flooring and architectural salvage): www.lovesalvage.com

McKay Flooring's social media:

- **Facebook:** http://facebook.com/mckayflooring.ltd
- **Flickr:** www.flickr.com/photos/mckayflooring
- **LinkedIn:** www.linkedin.com/company/mckay-flooring-limited
- **Twitter:** http://twitter.com/mckayflooring
- **Pinterest:** www.pinterest.com/mckayflooring
- **Instagram:** http://instagram.com/mckayflooring
- **YouTube:** www.youtube.com/user/mckayflooring
- **Google+:** https://plus.google.com/+mckayflooringltd/posts
- **Blog:** www.mckayflooring.co.uk/blog
- **RSS:** www.mckayflooring.co.uk/feed

Chapter 3: Plotting Your Social Media Marketing Strategy

In This Chapter

✔ **Finding your audience online**

✔ **Segmenting B2C markets**

✔ **Conducting B2B research online**

✔ **Planning your strategy**

*I*n Book I, Chapter 1, we talk about making the business case for social media marketing, looking at the question of whether you should or shouldn't get involved. That chapter is about strategy, goals, and objectives — this one is about tactics. It helps you decide which social media services best fit your marketing objectives and your target market. Let your customers and prospects drive your selection of social media alternatives. To see the best return on your investment in social media, you need to try to use the same social media as they do. This principle is exactly the same one you apply to all your other marketing and advertising efforts. Social media is a new tactic, not a new world.

Fish where your fish are. If your potential customers aren't on a particular social media outlet, don't start a campaign on that outlet.

In this chapter, we show how to use online market research to assess the match between your target markets and various social media outlets. After you do that, you're ready to start filling out your own Social Media Marketing Plan, which appears at the end of this chapter.

Locating Your Target Market Online

Nothing is more important in marketing than identifying and understanding your target audience (or audiences). After you can describe your customers' and prospects' demographic characteristics, where they live, and what social media they use, you're in a position to focus your social marketing efforts on those people most likely to buy your products or services. (Be sure to include the description of your target market on your Social Media Marketing Goals statement, discussed in Book I, Chapter 1.)

Because social media techniques focus on inexpensive ways to reach niche markets with specific messages, they're tailor-made for a guerrilla marketing approach. As with all guerrilla marketing activities, target one market at a time.

Don't dilute your marketing budget or labor by trying to reach too many audiences at a time. People still need to see your message or brand name at least seven times to remember it. Trying to boost yourself to the forefront of everyone's mind all at once is expensive.

Focus your resources on one niche at a time. After you succeed, invest your profits in the next niche. It may seem counterintuitive, but it works.

Don't let setting priorities among niches paralyze you. Your choice of niches usually doesn't matter. If you aren't sure, go for what seems to be the biggest market first, or the easiest one to reach.

Segmenting Your B2C Market

If you have a business-to-consumer (B2C) company, you can adapt the standard tools of *market segmentation,* which is a technique to define various niche audiences by where they live and how they spend their time and money. The most common types of segmentation are

✦ Demographics

✦ Geographics

✦ Life stages

✦ Psychographics or lifestyle

✦ Affinity or interest groups

These categories affect not only your social media tactics but also your graphics, message, content, offers, and every other aspect of your marketing.

Your messages need to be specific enough to satisfy the needs and wants of the distinct subgroups you're trying to reach.

Suppose that you want to sell a line of organic, herbal hair care products using social media. If you described your target market as "everyone who uses shampoo" on your Social Media Marketing Goals statement (see Book I, Chapter 1), segment that market into different subgroups before you select appropriate social marketing techniques.

When you're creating subgroups, keep these concepts in mind:

✦ **Simple demographics affect your market definition.** The use of fragrances, descriptive terms, and even packaging may vary by gender. How many shampoo commercials for men talk about silky hair? For that matter, what's the ratio of shampoo commercials addressed to women versus men?

✦ **Consider geography.** Geography may not seem obvious, but people who live in dry climates may be more receptive to a message about moisturizers than people who live in humid climates. Or, perhaps your production capacity constrains your initial product launch to a local or regional area.

✦ **Think about life stages.** For instance, people who dye their hair look for different hair care products than those who don't, but the reason they color their hair affects your selling message. (Teenagers and young adults may dye their hair unusual colors in an effort to belong to a group of their peers; older men may hide the gray with Grecian Formula; women with kids may be interested in fashion, or color their hair as a pick-me-up.)

✦ **Even lifestyles (psychographics) affect decisions.** People with limited resources who are unlikely to try new products may respond to messages about value and satisfaction guarantees; people with more resources or a higher status may be affected by messages related to social grouping and self-esteem.

✦ **Affinity or interest groups are an obvious segmentation parameter.** People who participate in environmental organizations or who recycle goods may be more likely to be swayed by a "green shampoo" appeal or shop in specific online venues.

Different niche markets are drawn to different social media activities in general and to specific social media service providers in particular. In the following several sections, we look in detail at different online tools you can use to explore the parameters that seem the most appropriate for segmenting your audience and selecting specific social media sites.

For more information on market segmentation and research, see *Small Business Marketing Kit For Dummies,* 3rd Edition, by Barbara Findlay Schenck (Wiley Publishing, Inc.).

The most successful marketing campaigns are driven by your target markets, not by techniques.

Demographics

Demographic segmentation, the most common type of market differentiation, covers such standard categories as gender, age, ethnicity, marital status, family size, household income, occupation, social class, and education.

Sites such as Quantcast (www.quantcast.com) and Alexa (www.alexa.com) provide basic demographic information compared to the overall Internet population, as shown in Figure 3-1. Quantcast also displays the distribution by subcategory within the site. Alexa's free version now provides only limited information, although it does offer a seven-day free trial. As you can see, the sites don't always share the same subcategory breakdowns or completely agree on the data. However, either one is close enough for your social marketing purposes.

Use these tools to check out the demographic profile of users on various social media services, as well as your own users and those of your competitors. For instance, by comparing the demographics on Quantcast, you can see that LinkedIn appeals to an audience that is older, more male-dominated, and better educated than visitors to Facebook.

Look for a general match between your target audience and that of the social media service you're considering.

Always check for current demographic information before launching your social media campaign. For details by channel, try www.pewinternet.org/2013/12/30/demographics-of-key-social-networking-platforms.

Geographics

Marketing by country, region, state, city, zip code, or even neighborhood is the key for location-based social media outlets, such as Foursquare, or any other form of online marketing that involves local search.

Geographic segmentation also makes sense if your business draws its primary target audience from within a certain distance from your brick-and-mortar storefront. For example, geographic segmentation makes sense for grocery stores, barber shops, gas stations, restaurants, movie theaters, and many other service providers, whether or not your social media service itself is location-based.

Many social media services offer a location search function to assess the number of users within your geographical target area:

✦ **Twitter users near a specified location** (https://twitter.com/search-advanced)**:** Enter a zip code or place name in the Near This Place text box to find users within 15 miles of your designated location. On the search results page that appears, select both People and Near You in the left column. You may be able to alter the 15-mile default distance in the search box at the top of the results page.

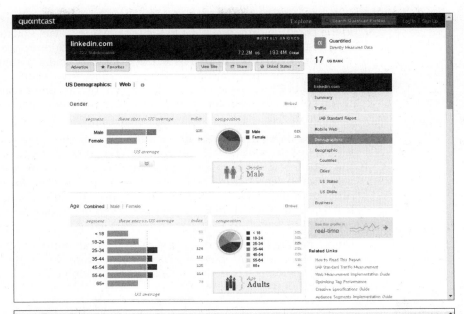

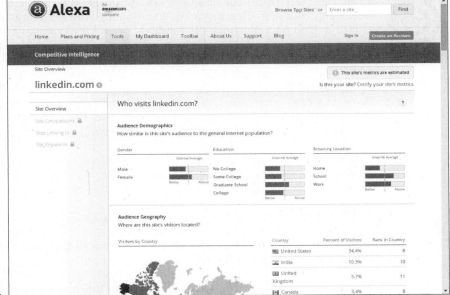

Figure 3-1: Quantcast (top) and Alexa (bottom) provide demographic profiles comparing users of a site (in this case, LinkedIn) with the general Internet population.

✦ **LinkedIn users within a certain radius** (www.linkedin.com/search): In the Location drop-down list in the left column, select Located In or Near in the Location drop-down list. Additional options appear, including a Country drop-down list, a Postal Code text box, and a Within drop-down list, with choices of radius from 10 to 100 miles. After clicking Search, the number of results appears at the top-left of the center column, above the list of names. You can filter further by the degree of connection, if you wish.

✦ **Facebook users near a certain location:** Click in the search box, and then select People I May Know from the drop-down list that appears. In the option box that appears in the right column, select the location where you want to search from the Current City drop-down list (for example, Albuquerque), and select Not My Friends from the Friendship drop-down list. Then click See More Filters at the bottom of the box. Select the filters you want to search by from the drop-down lists.

Unfortunately, Facebook doesn't give you a total number of the potential people you may want to reach. The most accurate way to size a potential target audience is to use the advertising option described in Book V, Chapter 2 of this book.

If you can't determine the number of potential users for a social media channel within your specific geographic location, use the Help function on the social media channel, check the blog, or contact the company.

Several companies combine geographical information with demographics and behavioral characteristics to segment the market more finely. For example, the Nielsen Claritas PRIZM system, available from Tetrad (www.tetrad.com/demographics/usa/nielsen/#tab-prizm), offers demo-geographic data organized into 66 distinct sub-segments, some of which are described in Table 3-1. (You can download the entire list at www.tetrad.com/pub/prices/PRIZMNE_Clusters.pdf.) These segments, shown in Figure 3-2, can be viewed at the zip-code level using the tool at www.claritas.com/MyBestSegments/Default.jsp?ID=20.

Life stages

Rather than look at a target market solely in terms of demographics, *life stage analysis* considers what people are doing with their lives, recognizing that it may affect media behavior and spending patterns.

For interesting details about the percentage of Internet users who access social media frequently sorted by age and gender, visit Pingdom's analysis of 24 social media sites (http://royal.pingdom.com/2012/08/21/report-social-network-demographics-in-2012). Usage may also differ by life stages, as shown in Table 3-2. Note that the set of life stages described in the table may not accurately reflect the wider range of today's lifestyles.

Table 3-1	Top-Level Demo-Geographic Social Groups from Nielsen PRIZM
Name	**Description**
Urban Uptown	Wealthiest urban (highest-density) consumers (five sub-segments)
Midtown Mix	Midscale, ethnically diverse, urban population (three sub-segments)
Urban Cores	Modest income, affordable housing, urban living (four sub-segments)
Elite Suburbs	Affluent, suburban elite (four sub-segments)
The Affluentials	Comfortable suburban lifestyle (six sub-segments)
Middleburbs	Middle-class suburbs (five sub-segments)
Inner Suburbs	Downscale inner suburbs of metropolitan areas (four sub-segments)
Second City Society	Wealthy families in smaller cities on fringes of metro areas (three sub-segments)
City Centers	Middle-class, satellite cities with mixed demographics (five sub-segments)
Micro-City Blues	Downscale residents in second cities (five sub-segments)
Landed Gentry	Wealthy Americans in small towns (five sub-segments)
Country Comfort	Upper-middle-class homeowners in bedroom communities (five sub-segments)
Middle America	Middle-class homeowners in small towns and exurbs (six sub-segments)
Rustic Living	Most isolated towns and rural areas (six sub-segments)

Reproduced with permission of The Nielsen Company; Source: Nielsen Claritas

You're looking for a fit between the profile of your target audience and that of the social media service.

With more flexible timing for going through life passages, demographic analysis isn't enough for many types of products and services. Women may have children later in life; many older, nontraditional students go back to college; some retirees reenter the workforce to supplement Social Security earnings. What your prospective customers do each day may influence what they buy and which media outlets they use more than their age or location.

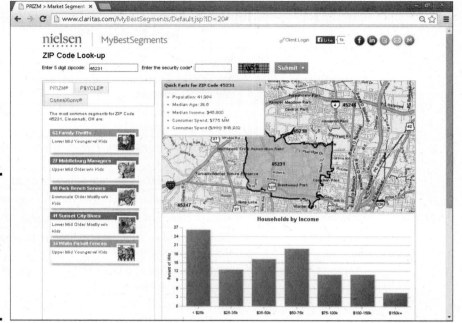

Figure 3-2:
Nielsen's Claritas tool allows you view market segmentation at the zip-code level.

Table 3-2	Life Stage Segmentation
Life Stage	*Products They Buy*
Single, no children	Fashion items, vacations, recreation
Married, no children	Vacations, cars, clothing, entertainment
New nesters, children under 6	Baby food and toys; furniture and new homes
Full nest, youngest over 6	Children's items, activities, and education
Full nest, children over 16	College, possibly travel and furniture
Empty nest, children gone	Travel, cruises, vacations
Retired couples	Moves to warmer climates, housing downsizing
Solitary working retiree	Travel, vacations, medical expenses
Retired solitary survivor	Medical expenses

Source: Adapted from http://academic.brooklyn.cuny.edu/economic/
friedman/mmmarketsegmentation.htm#C1.

For instance, the Pew Research Center's Internet and American Life Project found in January 2014 that 28 percent of cellphone users access a social networking site on a typical day, with the most likely users being higher educated, higher income, young, black, or Hispanic (www.pewinternet.org/fact-sheets/social-networking-fact-sheet).

Psychographics or lifestyle

Psychographic segmentation divides a market by social class, lifestyle, or the shared activities, interests, and opinions of prospective customers. It helps identify groups within a social networking service or other, smaller, social networks that attract users who meet your desired profile.

Behavioral segmentation, which is closely related, divides potential buyers based on their uses, responses, or attitudes toward a product or service. To obtain this information about your customers, consider including a quick poll as part of your e-newsletter, website, or blog. Although the results from those who reply may not be exactly representative of your total customer base — or that of prospective customers — a survey gives you some starter data.

Don't confuse the psychographic profile of a group with personality traits specific to an individual.

Psychographic segmentation helps you identify not only where to promote your company but also how to craft your message. For instance, understanding your specific target group, its mindset, and its lifestyle might help you appeal to customers such as the Innovators shown in Figure 3-3, who might be interested in your high-end line of fashion, home decor, or vacation destinations. Or you might target Experiencers for an amazing new cosmetics line, a wild new restaurant, or an energy drink.

To develop a better understanding of psychographic profiling, take the quick VALS (Values and Life Styles) survey yourself at www.strategicbusinessinsights.com/vals/presurvey.shtml.

Affinity groups

Segmenting by *affinity group* (a group of people who share similar interests or participate in similar activities) fills in the blank at the end of the "People who like this interest or activity also like . . . " statement. Because psychographic segmentation uses Activity as a subsection, that approach is somewhat similar.

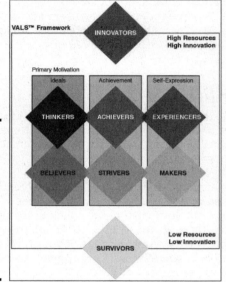

Figure 3-3:
Psycho-
graphic
segmen-
tation is
shown on
the VALS
(Values and
Life Styles)
chart.

*Reproduced with permission of Strategic Business Insights
(SBI); www.strategicbusinessinsights.com/vals*

For example, in Figure 3-4, Quantcast estimates other interests of visitors to Goodreads (www.goodreads.com) based on their browsing behavior under the Audience Interests option. (This data is available only for *Quantified sites* — for example, sites for which the site owners have verified the data.) An alpha symbol [α] in the upper-right of a Quantcast results page indicates a verified site, and a yellow caution symbol indicates an unverified one. On Alexa, scroll down to the Related Links section for a list of the top ten sites related to the target site in various ways, or click Categories with Related Sites to view sites that fit within the same classifications as the target site.

For information on clickstream analysis (where visitors come from and where they go), see Book IX, Chapter 6.

By using Quantcast and Alexa in this way, you can obtain public information about visits to specific social media services or to your competitors' or other related businesses' websites. You can also use these services to profile your own business, although your website might be too small to provide more than rough estimates. If your business is too small, estimate the

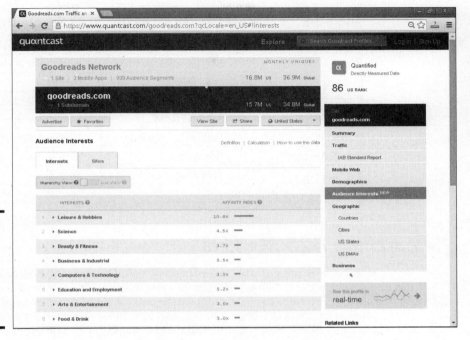

Figure 3-4:
Quantcast
estimates
topics that
interest
users of
Goodreads.

interest profile for your target market by running Quantcast for a verified, large corporation that offers a similar product or service.

Sign up for free, direct measurement of your apps and websites at `www.quantcast.com/user/signup`. Alexa charges for similar services, but it does allow you to claim your site for free at `www.alexa.com/site-owners/claim`. Otherwise, consider polling your customers to find out more about their specific interests.

You can also use Google Trends (`www.google.com/trends/explore#cmpt=q`) to search by the interest categories shown in Table 3-3. Click All Categories at the top of the page to open a drop-down list. Google Trends uses real-time search data to estimate customer interest in various topics over time. You can select specific keywords, time periods, or locations for additional detail.

Table 3-3	Main Categories Available on Google Trends	
Arts & Entertainment	Autos & Vehicles	Beauty & Fitness
Books & Literature	Business & Industrial	Computers & Electronics
Finance	Food & Drink	Games
Health	Hobbies & Leisure	Home & Garden
Internet & Telecom	Jobs & Education	Law & Government
News	Online Communities	People & Society
Pets & Animals	Real Estate	Reference
Science	Shopping	Sports
Travel		

Researching B2B Markets

Market research and social media choices for business-to-business (B2B) markets are somewhat different from business-to-consumer (B2C) markets because the sales cycle is different. Usually, B2B companies have a longer sales cycle, high-ticket purchases, and multiple people who play a role in closing a sale; consequently, B2B marketing requires a different social media presence.

In terms of social media, more B2B marketing efforts focus on branding, top-of-mind visibility, customer support, customer loyalty, and problem-solving compared to more sales-focused messages from B2C companies.

One key step in B2B marketing is to identify people who make the buying decision. Professional social networks such as LinkedIn, Networking for Professionals, or others on `www.sitepoint.com/social-networking-sites-for-business` may help you research people on your B2B customer or prospect lists.

According to research by the Content Marketing Institute, more than 90 percent of all B2B marketers use some form of social media (`http://contentmarketinginstitute.com/2014/01/planning-b2b-marketing-approach-social-media`). As shown in Figure 3-5, B2B firms may emphasize different forms of social media than B2C businesses. In many cases, the choice of social media varies by company size, industry type, experience with social media, and the availability of budgetary and human resources.

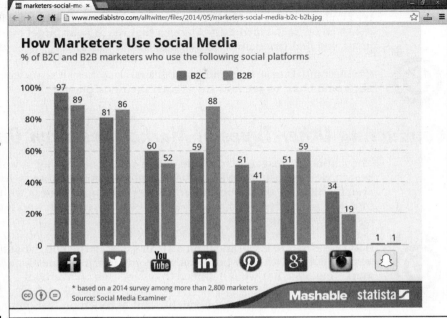

Figure 3-5:
B2C (left columns) and B2B (right columns) businesses often utilize different social media channels.

For more information on using social media for B2B marketing, visit one of these links:

```
https://smallbusiness.yahoo.com/advisor/83-exceptional-
    social-media-marketing-statistics-2014-160016146.html
www.socialmediaexaminer.com/
    SocialMediaMarketingIndustryReport2014.pdf
www.mediabistro.com/alltwitter/b2c-b2b-social-marketing_
    b57346
```

HubSpot (`www.hubspot.com/marketing-statistics`) also offers a range of B2B market research tools and webinars.

As always, the key is ensuring that your customers are using the type of social media you're considering. Use the search feature and group options on major social networking sites to test your list of existing customers. Chances are good that if a large number of your existing customers are using that service, it will be a good source for future customers as well.

In addition to participating in general market research, you might want to try SimilarSites (www.similarsites.com), which not only assists with research on social media alternatives that reach your target market, but also helps you find companies that compete with yours.

Check competing sites for inbound links from other sites, as well as their outbound links, to see how they reach their customers.

Conducting Other Types of Market Research Online

The amount of research available online can be paralyzing. A well-crafted search yields most, if not all, of the social marketing research you need. You aren't writing an academic paper; you're running a business with limited time and resources. Set aside a week or two for research, and then start laying out your approach.

Don't be afraid to experiment on a small scale. In the end, what matters is what happens with your business while you integrate social media into your marketing plan, not what happens to businesses on average.

Despite these statements, you might want to touch on two other research points:

✦ **The most influential sites, posters, or pages on your preferred social media:** You can learn from them.

✦ **Understanding what motivates people to use certain types of social media:** Make the content you provide meet their expectations and desires.

Identifying influencers

Whether you have a B2B or B2C company, you gain valuable insight by reviewing the comments of *influencers* (companies or individuals that drive the conversation within your industry sector). For example, to see the most popular posters on Twitter, use Twitaholic at http://twitaholic.com to view by number of updates or number of followers, as shown in Figure 3-6.

You may be surprised to find that the most frequent posters aren't necessarily the ones with the most followers, and vice versa.

For additional tools to identify influencers on various social media channels, check out the lists at Binkd (www.binkd.com/social-media/5-tools-to-identify-your-social-media-influencers) or Ragan (www.ragan.com/socialmedia/articles/9_tools_to_find_industry_influencers_47951.aspx).

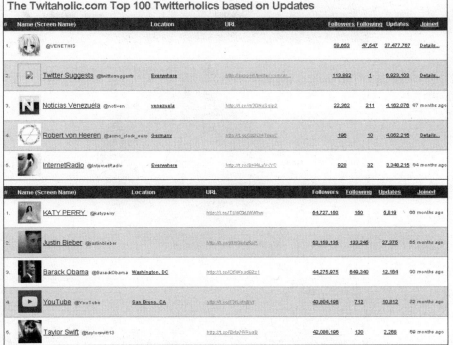

Figure 3-6:
Twitaholic
ranks
the most
influential
tweeters
by number
of updates
(top) or
number of
followers
(bottom).

Reproduced with permission of Twitaholic

These sites can help you identify people you might want to follow for research purposes. You can find more information about tools for identifying influencers for each of the major services in their respective minibooks.

Understanding why people use social media services

The expectation that people gravitate toward different types of social media to meet different needs seems reasonable. The challenge, of course, is to match what people seek with particular social sites. The advertising network Chitika surveyed its own clients, sorting downstream referrals from social networks to websites by vertical industry type, as shown in Figure 3-7 for Facebook and Twitter. Ask yourself whether these patterns match your expectations and whether they match what you see on these sites.

A review of successful social media models may spark creative ideas for your own campaign.

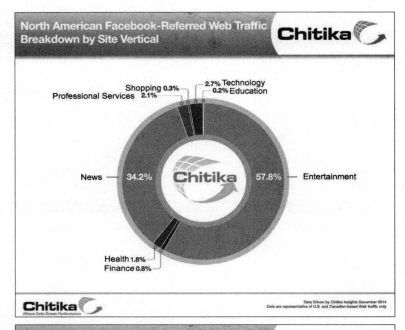

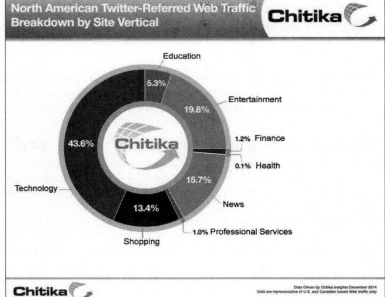

Figure 3-7:
Chitika analyzed referrals from Facebook (top) and Twitter (bottom) to various types of websites.

Setting Up Your Social Media Marketing Plan

You can dive into social media marketing headfirst and see what happens. Or you can take the time to research, plan, execute, and evaluate your approach. The Social Media Marketing Plan, shown in Figure 3-8, is for people taking the latter approach. (You can download the form at www.dummies.com/extras/socialmediamarketingaio.)

Plan your work; work your plan.

Depending on its complexity and availability of support, think in terms of a timeline of 3 to 12 months to allow time to complete the following steps. Estimate spending half your time in the planning phase, one-quarter in execution, and one-quarter in evaluation and modification. To set up your own custom social media marketing plan, follow these steps:

1. Do market research and online observation.

2. Draft marketing goals, objectives, and your marketing plan using the form in Figure 3-8.

3. Get your marketing ducks in a row with in-house preparation.

   • Hiring, outsourcing, or selecting in-house staff

   • Training

   • Team-building

   • Writing a social media policy document

4. Complete preparatory development tasks.

   • Designing advertising creatives

   • Content overview (an outline of which marketing messages you want to send out when)

   • Measurement plan and metric implementation

   • Social media tool selection and dashboard development

   • Social media activity calendar setup (see Book I, Chapter 4)

   • Programming and content modifications to existing website(s), as needed

5. Create accounts and a pilot social media program.

6. Evaluate the pilot program, debug it, and modify it, as needed.

7. Launch and promote your social media campaign one service at a time.

8. Measure and modify social media in a process of constant feedback and reiteration.

TIP

Don't be afraid to build a pilot program — or several — into your plan to see what works.

Social Media Marketing Plan

Company Name _____ Date _____

Hub Site (URL of website or blog with domain name traffic will be driven to)

_____

Standard Social Media Identification Name/Handle _____

Social Media Project Director _____

Social Media Team Members & Tasks _____ _____

_____ _____

Programming/Technical Team _____ _____

Social Media Policy URL _____

Check all applications used. Items noted by ☒ are strongly recommended.

SOCIAL MEDIA PLANNING

❑ **Dashboard (Select one: Enter URL & login info)**
- ○ Netvibes
- ○ Hootsuite
- ○ Other – Name:
- ○ Custom

❑ **Calendar (Select one: Enter URL & login info)**
- ○ Google Calendar
- ○ Yahoo! Calendar
- ○ Microsoft Office Calendar
- ○ Other – Name:

❑ **Social Sharing Service (Select one: Enter URL & login info)**
- ○ AddThis
- ○ ShareThis
- ○ AddtoAny
- ○ Other – Name:

❑ **Social Media Resources (Insert one resource site or blog to follow)**
- ○

SOCIAL MEDIA TOOL KIT

❑ **Monitoring (Select at least one: Enter name, URL, & login info for all used)**
- ○ Brand Reputation/Sentiment Tool with fee (e.g., BrandsEye)
- ○ Topic Monitoring Tool (e.g., Google Trends, Addict-o-matic)
- ○ HowSociable
- ○ IceRocket
- ○ Mention.com
- ○ Trackur
- ○ WhosTalkin
- ○ Blog Monitoring Tool
- ○ Twitter Monitoring Tool
- ○ Talkwalker Alerts
- ○ Google Alerts
- ○ Other – Name:

Figure 3-8:
Build a social media marketing plan for your company.

❑ **Distribution Tools** (Select at least one: Enter name, URL & login info for all used)
- ○ RSS/Atom Feeds
- ○ Buffer
- ○ Hootsuite
- ○ OnlyWire
- ○ TweetDeck
- ○ Other – Name:

❑ **Update Notification Tools** (Select at least one: Enter Name, URL & login Info for all used)
- ○ Pingdom
- ○ Feed Shark
- ○ GooglePing
- ○ King Ping
- ○ Other – Name:

❑ **URL Clipping Tool** (Select one: Enter URL & login info)
- ○ Bitly
- ○ Snipurl
- ○ TinyURL
- ○ Other – Name:

❑ **E-commerce Tool or Widget** (Select one: Enter URL & login info)
- ○ Ecwid
- ○ Storefront Social
- ○ Shopify
- ○ Etsy Widget
- ○ Amazon Widget
- ○ PayPal Widget
- ○ Other – Name:
- ○ Custom Widget

❑ **Search Engine Tools** (If needed, enter URL & login info; include submission dates)
- ○ Search Engine Ranking Tool (Select One)
- ○ Google Search Engine Submission
- ○ Bing/Yahoo! Search Engine Submission
- ○ Automated XML Feed
- ○ Specialty Search Submission Sites
- ○ Other – Name:

STANDARD SET PRIMARY KEYWORDS/TAGS
- ❑
- ❑
- ❑
- ❑
- ❑
- ❑
- ❑
- ❑

Figure 3-8:
(continued)

STANDARD PAGE DESCRIPTION TAG
(Enter 150-character description: Include at least four of the keywords above)

SOCIAL MEDIA SERVICES

☐ **Social Bookmarking Sites** (Select at least one: Enter name, URL, & login info for all used)
- ○ Delicious
- ○ StumbleUpon
- ○ Y! Bookmarks
- ○ Google Bookmarks
- ○ Other

☐ **Social News Sites** (Select at least one: Enter name, URL, & login info for all used)
- ○ Digg
- ○ Reddit
- ○ Newsvine
- ○ Slashdot
- ○ Other

☐ **Social Shopping & Specialty Bookmark Sites** (Enter name, URL, & login info for all used)
- ○ Kaboodle
- ○ This Next
- ○ StyleHive
- ○ Other

☐ **Blogging Site** (Enter name, URL, & login info for all used)
- ○ Primary blog
- ○ Blog directory submission site
- ○ Blog monitoring site
- ○ Blog measuring tool sites
- ○ Other

☐ **Primary Social Networking Services** (Select at least one: Enter name, URL, & login info for all used)

Facebook
- ○ Groups
- ○ Events
- ○ Metrics
- ○ Follow Us On/Like Us

Twitter
- ○ Hashtags/Lists
- ○ Tools
- ○ Metrics
- ○ Follow Us On

LinkedIn
- ○ Groups
- ○ Events/Answers
- ○ Metrics
- ○ Follow Us On

Google+
- ○ Circles
- ○ +1 (Ratings)
- ○ Metrics
- ○ Follow Us On

Figure 3-8:
(continued)

Pinterest
- ❍ Metrics
- ❍ Follow Us On

- ❍ Specialty Networks
- ❍ Other Professional Networks (e.g., Ryze)
- ❍ Other Vertical Industry Networks (e.g., DeviantArt)
- ❍ Other Demographic Networks (e.g., Grandparents.com)

❑ **Social Media Sharing Sites (Enter name, URL, & login info for all used)**
- ❍ YouTube
- ❍ UStream
- ❍ Vimeo
- ❍ Vine
- ❍ Instagram
- ❍ Snapchat
- ❍ Pinterest
- ❍ SlideShare
- ❍ Podcasts
- ❍ Other

❑ **Social Community Sites (Enter name, URL, & login info for all used)**
- ❍ Ning
- ❍ Forums
- ❍ Message Boards
- ❍ Other

❑ **Other Social Media Services (Enter name, URL, & login info for all used)**
- ❍ Geolocation (e.g., Foursquare, Google Latitude, Facebook Location)
- ❍ Collective Shopping (e.g., Groupon, Living Social)
- ❍ Social Gaming
- ❍ Social Mobile
- ❍ Other

SOCIAL MEDIA METRICS

Key Performance Indicators (Enter eight; e.g., Traffic, CPM, CPC, Conversion Rate, ROI)

❑	❑
❑	❑
❑	❑
❑	❑

❑ **Analytical/Statistical Tool (Select at least one: Enter name, URL, & login info for all used)**
- ❍ Google Analytics
- ❍ Yahoo! Analytics
- ❍ AWstats
- ❍ StatCounter
- ❍ SiteTrail.com
- ❍ Other

SOCIAL MEDIA ADVERTISING
- ❍ Facebook
- ❍ LinkedIn
- ❍ Twitter
- ❍ Other

❑ **Advertising Metrics (for reports on impressions, clicks, CTR, CPC, CPM, etc.)**

(Enter the following information for each social media advertising service, e.g. Facebook Ads, used.)
- ❍ Name/Account Log-in URL/User Name/Password
- ❍ Name/Account Log-in URL/User Name/Password

Figure 3-8: *(continued)*

Reproduced with permission of Watermelon Mountain Web Marketing; www.watermelonweb.com

It's no contest: Social media wins!

Originally founded in 1979, Whitehall Lane Winery in Napa Valley, California, was purchased by the Leonardini family in 1993. The winery now owns seven vineyards and has increased case production from 5,000 cases to almost 50,000. Whitehall Lane's first informational website, created in the late 1990s, was supplanted in 1999 with a site linked to Winetasting.com to allow online wine sales, one of the first wineries in the Napa Valley to do so.

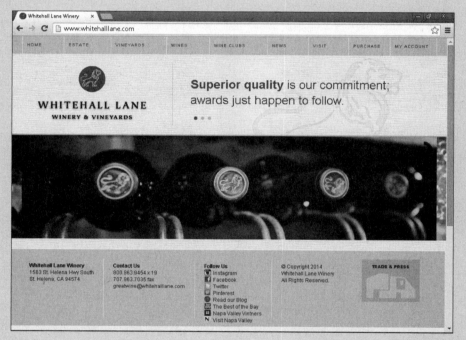

Reproduced by permission of Whitehall Lane Winery

In spite of the company's growth, the Tasting Room (direct sales) at Whitehall Lane took a tough hit during the recession starting in 2007. But by 2014, it had surpassed its pre-recession sales records. How? Katie Leonardini, co-owner and Vice President of Direct Sales (which includes overseeing the Tasting Room, e-commerce, Wine Club, and direct marketing), attributes some of the increase in the last two years to the winery's loyalty base. "Our fans don't just follow us on social media — they buy our wines, they visit our winery when they come to Napa Valley, and they join our wine club. Furthermore, they remain members of our wine club and don't cancel after 2 to 3 shipments as many members used to do in the past."

Leonardini turned to social media in 2008. "I was using it on a personal basis and knew that it would be a great way to engage those in their 20s and 30s to talk about Napa Valley and the wine industry. We had strong brand loyalty in the 50+ age group, but wanted to introduce our brand to younger segments." Her instincts obviously proved right.

She didn't have a master plan, but she knew she wanted to grow their list of friends and followers, especially those who lived outside Napa Valley so they would feel connected. "Our philosophy has always been to grow organically and not purchase followers," she explains. "We work hard to ensure that users who Like or Follow us do so because they are genuine fans of our brand and are interested in our content. We also like to reward those fans for following us faithfully.

Leonardini quickly found social media contests to be an effective way to grow the audience and build brand loyalty. The contests have strategic and tactical goals. "We use contests as tools to target specific areas on our social media, or to highlight events happening with the winery. For instance, in an effort to grow our Pinterest following and highlight different items for sale in the winery, we held a Pin and Win contest in March 2014," as shown in the nearby figure. She tries to run roughly one contest every other month. "Engagement on social channels depends on what type of contest we're running, but Facebook is generally highest based on our fan demographic there."

Reproduced by permission of Whitehall Lane Winery

(continued)

(continued)

Whitehall Lane also works hard to create consistencies between social media contests and what is going on in the winery, whether the goal of a contest is to build dinner attendance, increase sales from repeat customers, or increase wine club membership.

"Our contests are meant to engage our customers. We love to engage these followers, have some fun, and reward those that have been loyal to us. Finally, meeting these fans/followers in person really reinforces our philosophy." From Leonardini's point of view, social media efforts strengthen the quality of the guests, as well as the number of people, who visit the winery. "For example, if we gave away complimentary tastings on social media, our number of visitors would be larger in our tasting room, but those guests would be visiting for the free tasting, and not to explore the quality wines that we have to offer. The visitors that we gain due to our social media efforts are interested in learning more about our family business, the history of the winery, and what the advantages are in becoming a wine club member."

The company generally does not limit contests to specific market niches or segments. Because one of their goals is increased engagement, they take a more inclusive approach to getting people involved. Rather than targeting the audience narrowly by demographics, Leonardini tries to make contests that are more specific, like photo contests that every demographic can get involved in.

Wineries like Whitehall face constraints that many other businesses don't. Legally, Whitehall Lane must ensure that people submitting to its contests are above the legal drinking age. For the same reason, the company doesn't use wine as a prize for any contests. Whitehall Lane also enforces specific rules when collecting content from users (for example, in photo/video contests), so users who submit photos consent to allow use of these photos in marketing efforts.

For more than two years, Whitehall Lane has worked with Abbi Agency in Nevada. The agency manages the company's social media directly, but they work together to create the content. Abbi will generally put together the overall campaign ideas and contests and manage day-to-day operations, but the marketing team keeps the agency in the loop about specific happenings at the winery or things to be posted.

Success takes time! "The Abbi Agency follows a general schedule when posting to help keep content organized, consistent, and on-strategy," Leonardini says. "Each week, they schedule out content ahead of time, and then we check the content to ensure that it fits with our brand messaging before it goes live. All in all, between content creation and monitoring our social outlets, Abbi Agency spends 4 to 6 hours per week on our social media outlets, with more time spent during contests. Between launching and monitoring contests, they probably take a total of 8 to 12 hours, depending on how intensive they are. I correspond with my colleagues at Abbi Agency at least once a day. This ensures that we are all on the same page in terms of direction."

Whitehall Lane runs their contests and tracks analytics through Offerpop (`www.offerpop.com`), a well-known platform for social media contests and campaigns. With Offerpop, Leonardini can easily set up Facebook tabs for different types of social media contests with different goals, such as email collection, photo collection, increased engagement, customer referral, fan growth, and many more.

To determine a contest's success, Leonardini uses Offerpop analytics to see how much of the audience was engaged. Offerpop gives analytics to measure fan growth, shared contest links, entries and entry channel, page views, and many others." If we are working to establish a hashtag through a contest, we will use tools like Iconosquare and Topsy to measure the hashtag's growth during the contest's duration."

She actively cross-promotes their social contests throughout all of Whitehall Lane's social channels to reach their entire fan base. Depending on the contest, Leonardini will also blog about it and send out the information to the e-newsletter database. Whitehall Lane does include social icons on its website (see the figure above), but those drive users to Whitehall Lane's general social pages, where she posts frequently about contests to increase their visibility.

Leonardini has some very useful advice to share. "One huge lesson we have learned about social media contests is that it's important to put yourself in the user's shoes when considering whether a contest will be successful. Just because a contest is a creative, fun idea, it doesn't mean that it will be something that users will want to — or remember to — participate in. We've seen lower engagements with certain contests and have realized that these are too limiting . . . for users to participate in."

"Another great lesson we've learned is to be open to cross-promoting and working with others in our industry on social media. One of our most successful campaigns has been #MerlotMe, which was created by a dozen wineries in Napa Valley in 2013. With so many wineries working together to promote appreciation for Merlot in the month of October, it has allowed us to capitalize on the use of the hashtag and find ways to make the conversation unique for our brand."

Whitehall Lane Winery's web presence:

www.whitehalllane.com

http://instagram.com/whitehalllane

www.facebook.com/whitehalllanewinery

https://twitter.com/whitehalllane

www.pinterest.com/whitehalllane

http://blog.whitehalllane.com/

http://bestofthebaytv.com/view/887

www.visitnapavalley.com/wineries-whitehall_lane_winery_348.htm

www.napavintners.com/winery/whitehall-lane

Chapter 4: Managing Your Cybersocial Campaign

In This Chapter

✔ Scheduling social media activities

✔ Building a team

✔ Writing a social media policy

✔ Keeping it legal

✔ Protecting your brand reputation

After you create a Social Media Marketing Plan, one major task you face is managing the effort. If you're the only one doing the work, the simplest — and likely the hardest — task is making time for it. Though social media need not carry a lot of upfront development costs, it carries a significant cost in labor.

In this chapter, we discuss how to set up a schedule to keep your social media activity from draining all your available time. If you have employees, both you and your company may benefit if you delegate some of the social media tasking to them. You can also supplement your in-house staff with limited assistance from outside professionals.

For small businesses, it's your money or your life. If you can't afford to hire help to work on social media, you carve it out of the time you've allocated to other marketing activities — unless, of course, you want to add another two hours to your workday.

Finally, this chapter carries a word of caution. Make sure that everyone posting to a social media outlet knows your policy about what is and isn't acceptable, as well as how to protect the company's reputation and confidential material. As you launch your marketing boat onto the churning waters of social media, you should ensure that everyone is wearing a legal life preserver.

Managing Your Social Media Schedule

As you know from the rest of your business experience, if something isn't important enough to schedule, it never gets done. Social media, like the rest of your marketing efforts, can easily be swallowed up by day-to-day demands. You must set aside time for it and assign tasks to specific people.

Allocate a minimum of two hours per week if you're going to participate in social media, rather than set up pages and abandon them. Otherwise, you simply don't see a return from your initial investment in setup. If you don't have much time, stick with the marketing you're already doing.

Controlling the time commitment

Social media can become addictive. If you truly like what you're doing, the time problem might reverse. Rather than spend too little time, you spend too much. You might find it difficult to avoid the temptation of continually reading what others have to say about your business or spending all your time tweeting, streaming, and posting.

Just as you stick to your initial dollar budget, keep to your initial time budget, at least for the first month until you see what works. After you determine which techniques have the greatest promise, you can rearrange your own efforts as well as your team's.

Social media marketing is only part of your online marketing effort, and online marketing is only part of your overall marketing.

Selecting activity days

One way to control the time you spend on social media is to select specific days and times for it. Many business people set aside regularly recurring blocks of time, such as on a quiet Friday afternoon, for marketing-related tasks, whether they're conducting competitor research, writing press releases or newsletters for the following week, obtaining inbound links, or handling their social media marketing tasks.

Other people prefer to allocate their time early in the morning, at lunchtime, or just before leaving work each evening. The time slot you choose usually doesn't matter, unless you're offering a time-dependent service, such as accepting to-go orders for breakfast burritos via Twitter.

Whatever the case, allot time for every task on your Social Media Activity Calendar, followed by the initials of the person responsible for executing the task.

Allowing for ramp-up time

Even if you're the only person involved, allow time for learning before your official social media launch date. Everyone needs time to observe, master new tools, practice posting and responding, experiment, and decide what works before you can roll out your plan.

Bring your new social media venues online one at a time. This strategy not only helps you evaluate which social media venue works, but also reduces stress on you and your staff.

Developing your social date book

There are as many ways to schedule social media activities as there are companies. Whatever you decide, don't leave your schedule to chance.

Larger companies may use sophisticated project management software. Some offer a free trial such as Basecamp (`https://basecamp.com`) and Smartsheet (`www.smartsheet.com`), while others are available as freemium proprietary solutions, such as MOOVIA (`https://site.moovia.com`), or as open source programs such as GanttProject (`www.ganttproject.biz`) or ProjectLibre (`www.projectlibre.org`). For more options, see `http://alternativeto.net/software/smartsheet` or `www.techshout.com/alternatives/2013/17/smartsheet-alternatives`. Alternatively, you can schedule tasks using spreadsheet software.

However, the simplest solution may be the best: Calendar software, much of which is free, may be all you need. Paid options may merge schedules for more people and allow customized report formats. Several options are listed in Table 4-1. Look for a solution that lets you

+ Choose a display by day, week, or month or longer.

+ List events or tasks in chronological format.

+ Select different time frames easily.

+ Easily schedule repeat activities without requiring duplicate data entry.

If several people are involved in a substantial social media effort, select calendar software that lets you synchronize individual calendars, such as Google, Yahoo!, Mozilla Lightning, and others. Figure 4-1 shows a sample of a simple social marketing calendar using Yahoo! The calendar shows the initials of the person responsible. Clicking an event or a task reveals item details, including the time allotted to the task, the sharing level, and whether a reminder is sent and to whom. Figure 4-2 offers an example of an event detail listing in a Google calendar.

Table 4-1	Calendaring Software	
Name	*URL*	*Free or Paid*
Calendar & Time Management Software for Windows Reviews	`http://download.cnet.com/windows/calendar-and-time-management-software`	Free, shareware, and paid
Connect Daily	`www.mhsoftware.com/connectdaily.htm`	Paid, free trial
EventsLink Network Website Calendar	`www.eventslink.net`	Paid, free trial
Google Calendar	`www.google.com/calendar`	Free
Mozilla Lightning Calendar	`www.mozilla.org/en-us/projects/calendar`	Free, open source
Trumba	`www.trumba.com/connect/default.aspx`	Paid, free trial
Yahoo! Calendar	`http://calendar.yahoo.com`	Free

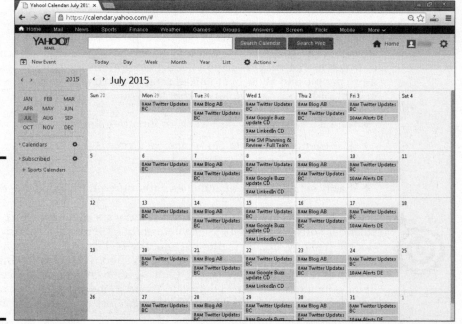

Figure 4-1: Using Yahoo! Calendar, you can easily schedule your social media activities.

Reproduced with permission of Watermelon Mountain WebMarketing, www.watermelonweb.com

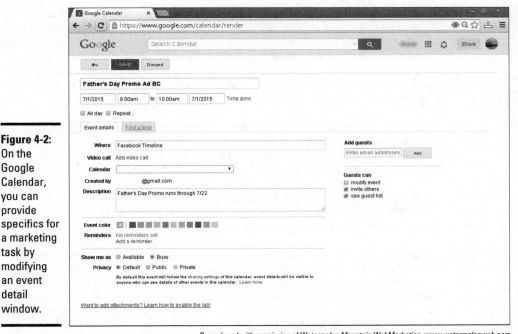

Figure 4-2:
On the
Google
Calendar,
you can
provide
specifics for
a marketing
task by
modifying
an event
detail
window.

Note: Google and Yahoo! require you to set up an account before you can use their calendars.

Throughout this book, we refer to this calendar as your *Social Media Activity Calendar,* and we add frequent recommendations of tasks to include on your schedule.

Set your calendar to private but give access to everyone who needs to be aware of your social media schedule. Depending on the design of your social media program, some outside subcontractors may need access to your calendar to schedule their own production deadlines.

Creating a social media dashboard

Your social media marketing efforts may ultimately involve many tasks: Post to multiple venues; use tools to distribute content to multiple locations; monitor visibility for your company on social media outlets; and measure results by using several analytical tools. Rather than jump back and forth among all these resources, you can save time by using a graphical dashboard or control panel.

Like the dashboard of a car, a social media dashboard puts the various required functions at your fingertips in (you hope) an easy-to-understand and easy-to-use visual layout. When you use this approach, the customized dashboard provides easy access in one location to all your social media accounts, tools, and metrics. Figures 4-3 and 4-4 show several tabs of a customized Netvibes dashboard — one for social media postings and another for tools.

The items on your primary dashboard may link to other, application-specific dashboards, especially for analytical tools and high-end enterprise solutions; those application dashboards are designed primarily to compare the results of multiple social media campaigns.

Table 4-2 provides a list of dashboard resources, some of which are generic (such as My Yahoo!) and others, such as Netvibes and Hootsuite (see Figure 4-5), which are specific to social media.

Before you try to build a dashboard, list all the social media sources, services, and reports you want to display, along with their associated URLs, usernames, and passwords. It will help if you indicate whether services are interconnected (for example, note whether you're using a syndication service to update multiple social media at the same time) and how often statistical reports should be updated for each service (hourly, daily, weekly, or monthly).

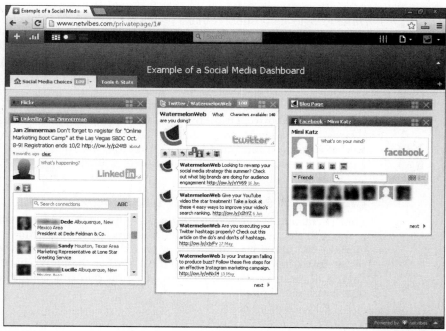

Figure 4-3:
This mock-up of a social media dashboard from Netvibes gathers the user's various social media services on the Social Media Choices tab.

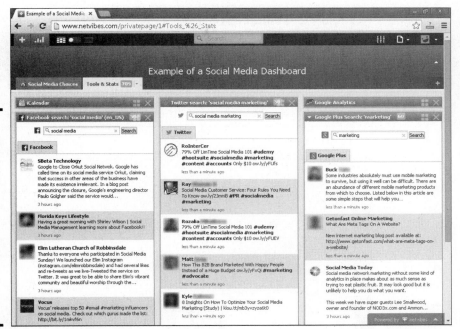

Figure 4-4:
The Tools &
Stats tab of
this mock-
up Netvibes
dashboard
displays
tools for
distributing,
monitoring,
searching,
and
analyzing
data.

Table 4-2		Social Media Dashboard Resources
Name	*URL*	*Description*
Hootsuite	www.Hootsuite.com	Free, customizable dashboard for social media; paid option available
MarketingProfs	www.marketingprofs.com/articles/2010/3454/how-to-create-your-marketing-dashboard-in-five-easy-steps	Instructions for customizing a dashboard (you can close the pop-up window asking you to sign up)
My Yahoo!	http://my.yahoo.com	Free, customizable Yahoo! home page
Netvibes	http://netvibes.com	Free, customizable dashboard for social media

(continued)

Table 4-2 (continued)

Name	URL	Description
Search Engine Land	`http://searchengineland.com/b2b-social-media-dashboard-a-powerful-tool-to-uncover-key-customer-insights-17839`	Tips on how to use a social media dashboard for B2B
uberVU	`www.ubervu.com`	Paid social media dashboard client

Figure 4-5:
The social media dashboard from Hootsuite allows you to monitor and update multiple social network services.

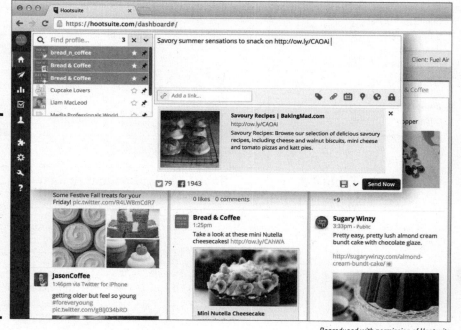

Reproduced with permission of Hootsuite

The more complex your social media campaign, the more functionality your dashboard needs.

Dashboards sound simple to use, but they can be a bit of a challenge to set up. In some cases, your programmer needs to create or customize *widgets* (mini applications). Plan to create and test several versions of the dashboard until everyone is satisfied with the results.

Consider implementing password access for approved users to various functions within the dashboard. Some users might be constrained to viewing reports, whereas others might be allowed to change the dashboard configuration.

Building Your Social Media Marketing Dream Team

Just for the moment, assume that you have employees who can — and are willing to — share the burden of social media. If you live a rich fantasy life, assume that you might even hire someone to take the lead.

In a larger company, the nexus for control of social media varies: In some cases, it's the marketing department; in others, corporate communications, public relations, sales, or customer support takes the lead.

Some companies disperse responsibilities throughout the company and have tens to dozens of people blogging and tweeting.

If your plan requires multiple employees to leverage LinkedIn profiles for B2B reasons, as well as post on multiple blogs in their individual areas of expertise and tweet current events in their departments, your need for coordination will increase.

Be cautious about asking employees to coordinate links and comments with their personal social media accounts. This task should be voluntary. Alternatively, on company time and on an account that "belongs" to your company (using a business email address), ask employees to develop a hybrid personal-and-business account where their personalities can shine. Now, individual privacy and First Amendment rights are respected on their separate personal accounts, and you have no liability for the content they post there.

 No matter who does the bulk of the work — your staff members, contractors, or a combination of the two — always monitor your program randomly but regularly. In addition to getting routine reports on the results, log in to your accounts for a few minutes at various times of the day and week to see what's going on.

Seeking a skilled social media director

A good social media director should have an extroverted personality, at least in writing. This person should truly enjoy interacting with others and take intrinsic pleasure in conversation and communication. You might want to look, based on your chosen tactics, for someone who can

✦ Write quickly and well, with the right tone for your market.

✦ Listen well, with an ear for your target audiences and their concerns.

✦ Post without using defamatory language or making libelous statements about competitors.

✦ Communicate knowledgeably about your company and your products or services.

✦ Recognize opportunities and develop creative responses or campaigns.

✦ Work tactfully with others, alerting them when problems or complaints surface.

✦ Articulate the goals of social media well enough to take a leadership role in encouraging others to explore its potential.

✦ Analyze situations to draw conclusions from data.

✦ Adapt to new social media and mobile technologies when they arise.

✦ Learn quickly (because this field is extremely fluid).

This combination of skills, experience, and personality may be hard to find. Add to it the need to reach different submarkets for different reasons. Now you have several reasons to build a team with a leader, rather than rely on a single individual to handle all your social media needs.

You usually can't just add social media to someone's task list; be prepared to reassign some tasks to other people.

Depending on the size and nature of your social media effort, your dream team may also need someone with production skills for podcasting or videocasting, or at least for producing and directing the development of those components. Though this person may not need extensive graphical, photographic, presentation, or data-crunching skills, having some skills in each of those areas is helpful.

Hiring 20-somethings (or younger) because they're familiar with social media may sound like a good idea, but people in this age group aren't as likely to be familiar with business protocol or sensitive to business relationships, as someone older and more experienced might be. You might need to allow extra time for training, review, and revision.

Looking inside

Before implementing a social media plan, speak with your employees to invite their input, assess their level of interest in this effort, evaluate existing skill sets, and ascertain social media experience. Consider all these factors before you move forward; by rearranging task assignments or priorities, you may be able to select in-house personnel to handle this new project.

Leave time for communication, education, and training both at the beginning and on an ongoing basis.

Hiring experts

Think about using professionals for the tech-heavy tasks, such as podcasts, videocasts, or design, unless you're going for the just-us-folks tone. Professionals can get you started by establishing a model for your staff to follow, or you may want to hire them for long-term tasks such as writing or editing your blogs for consistency.

Many advertising agencies, PR firms, search engine optimizers, marketing companies, and copywriters now take on social media contracts. If you've already worked with someone you like, you can start there. If not, select social media professionals the same way you would select any other professional service provider:

✦ Ask your local business colleagues for referrals.

✦ Check sources such as LinkedIn and Plaxo. If appropriate, post your search criteria on your site, blog, social media outlets, and topic-related sites.

✦ Request several price quotes. If your job is large enough, write and distribute a formal Request for Proposal (RFP).

✦ Review previous work completed by the contractors.

✦ Check references.

Creating a Social Media Marketing Policy

Even if you're the only person involved in social media marketing at the beginning, write up a few general guidelines for yourself that you can expand later. Figure 4-6 shows a sample social media policy; you can download other examples from `www.itbusinessedge.com/search/?q=social+media+policy&filter=ITDownload`. From the drop-down list for the first field at this link, select Policies. From the drop-down list in the second field, select Social Networking. Click Go and then download any of the sample policies from the list that appears.

ITBUSINESSEDGE
YOUR TECHNOLOGY INTELLIGENCE AGENT

NarrowCast Group, LLC ••• 10400 Linn Station Road, Suite 100 ••• Louisville, KY 40223

Sample Social Networking Policy

The following is the company's social media and social networking policy. The absence of, or lack of explicit reference to a specific site does not limit the extent of the application of this policy. Where no policy or guideline exists, employees should use their professional judgment and take the most prudent action possible. Consult with your manager or supervisor if you are uncertain.

1. Personal blogs should have clear disclaimers that the views expressed by the author in the blog is the author's alone and do not represent the views of the company. Be clear and write in first person. Make your writing clear that you are speaking for yourself and not on behalf of the company.
2. Information published on your blog(s) should comply with the company's confidentiality and disclosure of proprietary data policies. This also applies to comments posted on other blogs, forums, and social networking sites.
3. Be respectful to the company, other employees, customers, partners, and competitors.
4. Social media activities should not interfere with work commitments. Refer to IT resource usage policies.
5. Your online presence reflects the company. Be aware that your actions captured via images, posts, or comments can reflect that of our company.
6. Do not reference or site company clients, partners, or customers without their

Figure 4-6:
A basic social media policy may be enough to get you started.

Reproduced with permission of QuinStreet, Inc.

Most policies address the social media issue both in terms of what employees are allowed to do on behalf of the company and what they aren't allowed to do. For example:

✦ Employees may not be allowed to use personal social accounts on company time.

✦ Some trained employees may be allowed to post customer support replies on behalf of the company, whereas others are responsible for new product information.

For additional information and examples, see the resources listed in Table 4-3.

To increase compliance, keep your policy short and easy to read. Try to focus on what people *can do* rather than on what they can't do.

A typical policy addresses risk management, intellectual property protection, individual privacy protection, and the respect of your audience, company, and fellow employees. Given the rapidly changing world of social media, you'll have to keep your policy flexible and update it often.

Table 4-3	Social Media Policy Resource Sites	
Name	*URL*	*Description*
American Express	`www.americanexpress.com/us/small-business/openforum/articles/employee-social-media-policy`	Article titled "Employees Gone Wild: 8 Reasons You Need A Social Media Policy TODAY"
ITBusinessEdge	`www.itbusinessedge.com/search/?q=social+media+policy&filter=ITDownload`	Social media guidelines, templates, and examples; select Policies in the Type drop-down list, and Social Networking in the Topic drop-down list.
LikeableMedia Blog	`www.likeable.com/blog/2013/04/5-things-brands-should-consider-for-their-social-media-policy`	Article titled "5 Must-Haves For Your Brand's Social Media Policy"
LinkedIn	`www.linkedin.com/today/post/article/20140320152546-13721119-how-to-create-a-social-media-strategy-that-actually-gets-read`	Article titled "How to create a social media strategy that actually gets read"
Mashable	`http://mashable.com/2012/10/06/social-media-policy-update`	Article titled "Tips for Updating Your Company's Social Media Policy"
Netsphere Strategies	`www.netspherestrategies.com/blog/10-items-to-include-in-your-companys-social-media-policy`	Free checklist
PolicyTool for Social Media	`http://socialmedia.policytool.net`	Free social media policy generator
Rocket Lawyer	`www.rocketlawyer.com/document/social-media-policy.rl`	Free social media policy generator
Social Media Examiner	`www.socialmediaexaminer.com/write-a-social-media-policy`	Article titled "How to Write a Social Media Policy to Empower Employees"

(continued)

Table 4-3 *(continued)*

Name	URL	Description
Social Media Governance	`http://socialmedia governance.com/policies.php`	Free database of policies for review
TechRepublic	`www.techrepublic.com/ article/how-to-craft-a- social-media-policy`	Article titled "How to craft a social media policy"
Toolkit Cafe	`http://toolkitcafe.com/ social_media_policies.php`	Policies toolkit ($119)

Try to incorporate the following suggested concepts, adapted from Mashable (`http://mashable.com/2012/10/06/social-media-policy-update`):

✦ Hold individuals responsible for what they write.

✦ Be transparent. Disclose who you are, including your company name and title.

✦ Recognize that clients, prospects, competitors, and potential future employees are part of your audience.

✦ Be respectful of everyone.

✦ Understand the tenor of each social media community and follow its precepts.

✦ Respect copyright, trademarks, and privacy rights.

✦ Protect your company's confidential trade-secret and proprietary information in addition to client data, especially trade-secret information under nondisclosure agreements.

✦ Do *not* allow personal social media activity to interfere with work.

The complexity of your social media policy depends on the extent of your social media marketing effort and the number of people and departments involved. Generally, the larger the company, the longer the policy.

Staying on the Right Side of the Law

Just about everything in social media pushes the limits of existing intellectual property law. So much information is now repeated online that ownership lines are becoming blurred, much to some people's dismay and damage.

When in doubt, don't copy. Instead, use citations, quote marks, and links to the original source. Always go back to the original to ensure that the information is accurate.

Watch blogs such as Mashable and TechCrunch for information about legal wrangling. New case law, regulations, and conflicts bubble up continually.

Obtaining permission to avoid infringement

You can't (legally) use extended content from someone else's website, blog, or social media page on your own site, even if you can save it or download it. Nope, not even if you include a credit line saying where it came from. Not even if you use only a portion of the content and link to the rest. Not text, not graphics, not compiled data, not photos. Nothing. Nada. Nil. Zilch.

Though small text extracts with attribution are permitted under the fair use doctrine, the copyright concept is intended for individuals and educational institutions, not for profit-making companies. If you don't obtain permission, you and your company can be sued for copyright infringement. In the best-case scenario, you can be asked to cease and desist. In the worst case, your site can be shut down, and you might face other damages.

The way around this situation is simple: Send a permission request, such as the one in the nearby sidebar, "Sample copyright permission."

Be especially careful with photographs, which are usually copyrighted. Here are a few places to find free or low-cost images legally:

✦ Select from the wealth of material offered under a Creative Commons license (`http://creativecommons.org`). Search for items that can be used for commercial purposes or are in the public domain.

✦ Search for copyright-free images from the federal government.

✦ The Commons on Flickr (`www.flickr.com/commons`) has thousands of free photographs.

✦ Search `http://images.google.com`: Click the Settings link in the bottom-right corner of the window, and then select Advanced Search from the pop-up menu that appears. In the Advanced Search screen that appears, scroll down to the Usage Rights drop-down list and select Free to Use or Share, Even Commercially. Note that these images may still require attribution or have other limits on use; you should still contact the copyright holder for permission.

✦ Look for stock images from sources such as iStockphoto (`www.istockphoto.com`), Shutterstock (`www.shutterstock.com`), or Freerange Stock (`http://freerangestock.com`).

Sample copyright permission

Dear _____:

Watermelon Mountain Web Marketing wants permission to use your *(information, article, screen shot, art, data, photograph)* on our *(website/blog/social media page)* at *[this URL: WatermelonWeb. com]* and in other media not yet specified. We have attached a copy of the information we want to use. If it meets with your approval, please sign the following release and indicate the credit line you want. You can return the signed form as an email message, a PDF file, a digitally signed document, a fax, or a first-class mail message. Thank you for your prompt response.

The undersigned authorizes Watermelon Mountain Web Marketing to use the attached material without limit for no charge.

Signature:

Printed name:

Title:

Company name:

Company address:

Telephone/fax/email:

Company domain name:

Credit line:

Trademarks and logos also usually require permission to use, though the logos (icons) that social media companies provide for Share This or Follow Us On functionality are fine to use without permission. If you find an image in the Press or Media section of a company's website, you can assume that you have permission to reproduce it without further permission. Generally, a disclaimer that "all other logos and trademarks are the property of their respective owners" will suffice.

If it's illegal offline, it's illegal online.

Respecting privacy

Providing a disclaimer about keeping user information private is even more critical now that people sign up willy-nilly online. Individual privacy, already under threat, has become quite slippery with the Facebook Connect sign-in available on all sorts of third-party sites. Facebook Connect may make sign-ins simpler for a user, but it gives Facebook access to user behavior on the web while giving third parties access to users' Facebook profiles for demographic analysis.

Photographs of identifiable individuals, not taken in a public space, historically have required a waiver to use for commercial purposes. When individuals post their images on Facebook, LinkedIn, MySpace, or elsewhere, they may not intend to give permission for that image to appear elsewhere.

Respect a person's space; do not post publicly viewable images of people's faces on any of your social media pages unless you have permission. For a simple photo waiver, see www.nyip.edu/photo-articles/archive/basic-model-release.

Revealing product endorsement relationships

Taking aim at companies that were arranging paid recommendations from bloggers, the Federal Trade Commission (FTC) updated its regulations for digital advertising, including blogs, in 2013. The rule (found at http://www.ftc.gov/sites/default/files/attachments/press-releases/ftc-staff-revises-online-advertising-disclosure-guidelines/130312dotcomdisclosures.pdf) requires bloggers to disclose whether they've received any type of payment or free products in exchange for a positive review. For more information, see http://bloggylaw.com/ftc-guidelines-blogger-disclosures.

The rule doesn't appear to apply to individuals who post a review on public review sites (such as Epinions.com, TripAdvisor, or Yelp), but it applies if you review other companies' products on your blog or send products to other bloggers to request a review.

You can find out more about this requirement from the disclosure resources listed in Table 4-4. Some bloggers, offended by the rules, have found humorous or sarcastic ways to comply; others, such as Katy Widrick, whose blog appears in Figure 4-7 (http://katywidrick.com/about/disclosure-policy), are simply matter-of-fact about it.

Regardless of what you think of the policy, reveal any payments or free promotional products you've received. You can, of course, be as clever, funny, cynical, or straightforward as you want. Feeling lazy? Auto-generate a policy at DisclosurePolicy.org.

Table 4-4	Legal Resource Sites	
Name	*URL*	*Description*
American Bar Association	`www.americanbar.org/groups/ intellectual_property_law/ resources.html`	Intellectual property resource lists
BloggyEsq	`http://bloggylaw.com/ ftc-guidelines-blogger- disclosures`	Article titled "FTC Guidelines: Are You Making The Right Blogger Disclosures?"
DisclosurePolicy. org	`http://disclosurepolicy.org`	Generate free disclosure policies
Electronic Frontier Foundation	`www.eff.org`	Not-for-profit focused on free speech, privacy, and consumer rights
Federal Trade Commission	`www.ftc.gov/sites/default/ files/attachments/press- releases/ftc-staff-revises- online-advertising- disclosure-guidelines/ 130312dotcomdisclosures.pdf`	Federal guidelines for digital media disclosure
FindLaw	`http://smallbusiness. findlaw.com/intellectual- property.html`	Intellectual property resources
International Technology Law Association	`www.itechlaw.org`	Online legal issues
PublicLegal from the Internet Legal Research Group	`www.ilrg.com`	Index of legal sites, free forms, and documents
Nolo	`www.nolo.com/legal- encyclopedia/ecommerce- website-development`	Online legal issues
Social Media Examiner	`www.socialmediaexaminer. com/ftc-2013-disclosures`	Article titled "What Marketers Need to Know About the New FTC Disclosures"
Social Media Explorer	`www.socialmediaexplorer. com/social-media-marketing/ disclosures-for-bloggers- and-brands`	Blog and brand disclosure summary

Name	URL	Description
SocialMedia.org	`http://socialmedia.org/disclosure`	Social Media Disclosure Toolkit
U.S. Copyright Office	`www.copyright.gov`	Copyright information and submission
United States Patent and Trademark Office	`www.uspto.gov`	Patent and trademark information, databases, and submission
Word of Mouth Marketing Association	`www.womma.org/ethics`	WOMMA Code of Ethics resources

Figure 4-7:
This blogger sets out a clear acknowledgment policy on product endorsement.

Reproduced with permission of KPWidrick

Protecting Your Brand Reputation

It's important to start protecting your brand now by registering your company name for social media accounts. To avoid *brandjacking* (others using your company or product brand name on social media for their own purposes or to write misleading or negative things about your company), try to choose the most popular, available handle that will work across multiple sites. Use your company or product name and keep it short.

Even if you don't plan to do anything else in social media for a year or more, register your name now on Facebook, Twitter, LinkedIn, and Google+ and on any other sites you might want in the future, such as Pinterest or YouTube. You can register your name on every site while you read this book or reserve them all at once.

A number of companies now offer tools that claim to assess the quality of what people are saying about your company, products, or staff. In addition to counting how many times your name appears, they try to assess the *sentiment* of postings — whether statements are negative or positive. Some also offer an assessment of the degree of *engagement* — how enthusiastic or hostile a statement might be.

Some people then take this information, along with frequency of posting, and use their own proprietary formulas to assign a quantitative value to your online reputation, as shown in the example from Trackur (www.trackur.com) in Figure 4-8.

Figure 4-8: Trackur offers an inexpensive reputation-management tool that scales up for large companies.

Be cautious about assigning too much weight to these brand reputation tools, some of which are described in Table 4-5. They may produce widely varying results, and most rely on software that can't understand complex sentences or shortened phrases with words omitted. If you think your dense sibling doesn't understand irony, don't try sarcasm with a computer!

Table 4-5		Brand Sentiment Resources
Name	*URL*	*Description*
Attentio	`http://attentio.com`	Social media dashboard to track sentiment and more; paid
BrandsEye	`www.brandseye.com`	Online reputation tool; paid
Digital Sherpa	`www.digitalsherpa.com/blog/protect-online-business-reputation`	Article titled "How to Protect Your Online Business Reputation"
Mediabistro	`http://www.mediabistro.com/12-tips-on-fixing-your-brands-bad-reputation-a12012.html`	Article titled "12 Tips on Fixing Your Brand's Bad Reputation"
Naymz	`www.naymz.com`	Personal reputation on social media
Oracle Social Cloud	`www.oracle.com/us/solutions/social/overview/index.html`	Social relationship management tool
Reputation.com	`www.reputation.com/for-business`	Reputation monitoring tool; starts at $49/month
SDL SM2	`www.sdl.com/products/SM2`	Social media sentiment tool; paid
Sentiment 140	`www.sentiment140.com`	Twitter sentiment tool; free app
Social Fresh	`http://socialfresh.com/monitoring-your-brand-online-reputation/`	List of social monitoring tools
Trackur	`www.trackur.com/free-brand-monitoring-tools`	Reputation protection tool; freemium model

Notwithstanding the warnings, experiment with one of the free or freemium sentiment-measuring tools in Table 4-5 to see what, if anything, people are saying. (*Freemium* tools offer a free version with limited features; more extensive feature sets carry a charge.) Those results, such as they are, will become one of many baselines for your social media effort. Unless you already have a significant web presence, you may not find much.

Of course, many of these tools are designed for use by multinational corporations worried about their reputations after negative events, such as a General Motors auto recall or the British Petroleum oil spill in the Gulf of Mexico.

For you, the sentiment results might be good for a laugh or make excellent party chatter at your next *tweet-up* (your real-world meeting arranged through tweets).

Book II
Cypersocial Tools

Reproduced with permission of Mountain Springs Lake Corp.

Find out more about keyword metatags in the article "How to Keep Up with Keyword Metatags" at www.dummies.com/extras/socialmediamarketingaio.

Contents at a Glance

Chapter 1: Discovering Helpful Tech Tools

In This Chapter

✓ **Keeping current with social media**

✓ **Distributing content efficiently**

✓ **Keeping search engines in the loop**

✓ **Giving long URLs a haircut**

✓ **Selecting shopping tools that work with social media**

✓ **Monitoring the buzz**

*I*n Book I, you discover that the key to social media success is planning. This minibook reviews useful tools and resources to make your plan easier to execute. Before you start, you may also want to check out Book IX, which focuses on measurement tools for traffic, costs, and campaign performance.

As you select tools and schedule tasks from suggestions in this chapter, remember to enter them on your Social Media Marketing Plan (Book I, Chapter 3) and Social Media Activity Calendar (Book I, Chapter 4). You can also download blank copies of these forms at

www.dummies.com/extras/socialmediamarketingaio

Try to select at least one tool from each category:

✦ Resource, news, and blog sites that cover online marketing and social media

✦ Content-distribution tools

✦ Tools for notifying search engines and directories of updates

✦ URL-clipping tools

✦ Shopping widgets for social media, if appropriate

✦ Buzz-tracking tools to monitor mentions of your business

You can always jump right into the social media scene and figure out these things later, but your efforts will be more productive if you build the right framework first.

Keeping Track of the Social Media Scene

Unless you take advantage of online resources, you'll never be able to stay current with the changes in social media. Here's a quick look at how much the landscape changed in the course of just a few years:

✦ Use of social media continued its explosive growth. According to the Pew Center for the Internet and American Life, 72 percent of all Internet users also use social media. And one-fifth of Internet users access three or more social media channels.

✦ Facebook purchased WhatsApp, an instant messaging application, for $19 billion.

✦ The month-long FIFA World Cup tournament (for soccer) generated more than 3 billion interactions on Facebook and 672 million tweets in summer 2014.

✦ Social media fueled the remarkable fundraising phenomenon of the Ice Bucket Challenge for the ALS Society, raising more than $100 million for research into Lou Gehrig's disease.

✦ New social media platforms continued to pop-up, proving that the power of innovation is still strong. Watch for action on Spotify (music listing), Sobrr (short-lived social messaging), and Sulia (content sharing by experts), among others.

✦ Multiple social media services went belly-up. Casualties of the social media wars included Google's social network Orkut and Eons, a social media site targeted at baby boomers.

To keep current on the changing tides, subscribe to feeds about social marketing from social marketing blogs or news services; check at least one source weekly. Also, review traffic trends on social media services weekly; they're amazingly volatile. Table 1-1 lists some helpful resource sites.

Table 1-1	Social Media Marketing Resources	
Name	*URL*	*Description*
BIG Marketing for Small Business	`www.big marketingsmall business.com`	Social media, online, and offline marketing tips
HubSpot	`http://blog.hubspot.com`	Inbound marketing blog about attracting the right prospects to your site and converting them into customers

Name	URL	Description
Marketing Land	`http://marketingland.com`	Internet marketing news
MarketingProfs	`www.marketingprofs.com/marketing/library/100/social-media`	Social media marketing tips, including business-to-business (B2B)
MarketingSherpa	`www.marketingsherpa.com/library.html`	Social networking research
Mashable	`http://mashable.com/social-media`	Premier social media guide
TopRank Online Marketing Blog	`www.toprankblog.com`	Blog about online and social marketing
SiteProNews	`www.sitepronews.com`	Social media and search engine news
Social Media Examiner	`www.socialmediaexaminer.com`	Online social media magazine advising businesses on use of social media to achieve marketing goals
Social Media Marketing Group on LinkedIn	`www.linkedin.com/groups?gid=66325`	Professional, non-promotional discussion group
Social Media Today	`www.socialmediatoday.com`	Online community for marketing and PR professionals dealing with social media
TechHive	`www.techhive.com`	Technology news site
TechCrunch	`http://techcrunch.com`	Technology industry blog
Techmeme	`http://techmeme.com`	Top technology news site
Twitter Marketing Kickstart Tool Kit	`https://biz.twitter.com/download-our-marketing-kickstart-tool-kit`	Tool to improve Twitter performance by modifying your presence, profiles, and tweets

Saving Time with Content-Distribution Tools

Social media marketing obviously can quickly consume all your waking hours — and then some. Just the thought of needing to post information quickly to Facebook, Twitter, Google+, social bookmarks, blogs, Pinterest, or social news services might make any social marketer cringe.

Time to work smarter, not harder, with content-distribution tools to post your content to many places at once for tasks like the following:

✦ **Routine maintenance:** Use a content-distribution tool whenever you make updates according to your Social Media Activity Calendar. What a timesaver!

✦ **Quick event postings:** Share information from a conference, trade show, meeting, or training session from your phone by sending short text updates to Twitter and LinkedIn. Or take a picture with your smartphone and send it to Instagram, Twitter, and Facebook. To send something longer, use a distribution tool to post to your blog and Facebook.

✦ **Daily updates:** Group all social media services that you might want to update with rapidly changing information, such as a daily sale or the location of your traveling cupcake cart by the hour.

If you have more than three social media outlets or frequently update your content, choosing at least one distribution tool is a must-have way to save time.

Some businesses prefer to craft custom postings for Facebook, Twitter, and other services based on the specific audience and content needs of each channel, while others find this too time-consuming. Do what seems right for your business: Automate *cross-postings* (set up a service so that postings on one social media service automatically appear on others to save time), customize by channel, or mix and match.

In addition to, Hootsuite, OnlyWire, and other tools described in the next few sections, you can use really simple syndication (RSS) to feed content to users and to your various social media profiles. Keep in mind, however, that RSS works best with highly technical audiences.

Alternative content distribution services

You can select from several content-distribution services to *syndicate* (copy) your content from one social media service to another. All the services work roughly the same way, but each has its own peculiarities. Choose the one that's the best fit for you.

Reconfigure your settings on content-distribution tools whenever you decide to add or drop a social media service or create a new, special-purpose group for marketing purposes.

Buffer

An easy-to-use app, Buffer (`https://bufferapp.com`) allows you to pre-schedule content distribution to multiple social media platforms. It uses its own built-in link shortener to gather and compare data about the performance of posts on various channels.

Hootsuite

Self-described as "the leading social media dashboard," Hootsuite (`http://hootsuite.com`) has expanded from its origins as a way to manage only the Twitter experience. From scheduling to stats, Hootsuite now integrates more than 35 social media channels, allowing multiservice postings from one location to Twitter, Facebook, LinkedIn, Foursquare, Google +, Instagram, YouTube, and your blog, among others.

**Book II
Chapter 1**

Discovering Helpful
Tech Tools

OnlyWire

OnlyWire (`http://onlywire.com`) updates up to 50 social networks simultaneously. It also passes updates between WordPress sites, RSS feeds, and social media channels.

OnlyWire also offers several handy mini-apps at `http://onlywire.com/tools` to facilitate sharing items quickly:

✦ A developer API to custom-program content exchanges among your social media channels.

✦ A Chrome toolbar add-in that lets you quickly share web pages you like with your Facebook and Twitter accounts.

✦ A WordPress plug-in that automatically submits your WordPress posts to the social media services you've selected.

✦ An app to deliver material from RSS feeds to your selected social media channels

Postling

Like Hootsuite, Postling (`https://postling.com`) lets you cross-post to all major social networking services and blogging platforms: Facebook, Twitter, LinkedIn, WordPress, Tumblr, Flickr, CitySearch, and more. You can post immediately or schedule posts to go out at a later time. When people respond to your posts, Postling organizes those responses in one place and allows you to answer them from the Postling site. Postling emails a daily recap of the most recent activity on your social network sites, Yelp and Citysearch reviews, and relevant metrics, such as click through rates. You can also add other users for specific social media channels to help you respond to posts.

SocialFlow

SocialFlow (`www.socialflow.com`) is a high-end distributor of content and paid advertising across multiple social media networks. The company uses specific data to schedule posts and activities for times when your target audience is active on specific channels.

TweetDeck

Owned by Twitter, this tweet management tool at `https://about.twitter.com/products/tweetdeck` lets you schedule tweets, track engagement, and organize multiple accounts in one convenient location.

UberSocial

If you're on your smartphone all the time, UberSocial (`www.ubersocial.com`) may be perfect for you. This Twitter smartphone app, available for Android, BlackBerry, and iPhone, allows users to post and read tweets. Features vary slightly between the three devices, but all integrate LivePreview, which enables users to view embedded links next to tweets without closing the app and opening a new browser, making it an efficient way to use Twitter on your smartphone. Other features include cross-posting to Facebook, managing multiple accounts, and sending tweets of more than 140 characters.

Putting RSS to work

It almost sounds quaint, but RSS technology, which has been around for a decade, is still a viable way to distribute *(syndicate)* information for publication in multiple locations. The familiar orange-and-white icon shown in Figure 1-1 gained prominence years ago as a way to notify others automatically about often-updated content such as headlines, blogs, news, or music: an RSS feed.

Figure 1-1: The RSS icon.

The published content — *feed* — is provided for free in a standardized format that can be viewed in many different programs. RSS feeds are read on the receiving end in an RSS reader, a feed reader, or an aggregator. Readers come in three species:

✦ **Standalone:** Such as FeedDemon

✦ **Add-ons:** Compatible with specific applications, such as an RSS plug-in for a WordPress blog

✦ **Web-based:** Like Mozilla Firefox's Live Bookmarks, which adds RSS feeds to a user's Favorites folder

Feeds may be delivered to an individual subscriber's desktop, email program, or browser Favorites folder, or they can be reproduced on another website, blog page, or social media page.

You can offer an RSS feed from your site, blog, or social media pages — or display your own or others' RSS feeds on your pages. This feature requires some technical skills; if you're not technically inclined, ask your programmer to handle the implementation.

Subscribing is easy: Users simply click the RSS icon and follow directions. After that, the RSS reader regularly checks the list of subscribed feeds and downloads any updates. Users can receive automatic alerts or view their updates on demand. The provided material is usually a linkable abstract or headline, along with the publisher's name and date of publication. The link opens the full article or media clip.

Subscribers not only receive timely updates from their favorite sites, but they also can use RSS to collect feeds from many sites in one convenient place. Rather than check multiple websites every day, for instance, political junkies can have RSS feeds about Congress delivered automatically from *The Huffington Post, The Nation, The Washington Post,* and *The New York Times.*

Unless you're targeting a market that's highly proficient technically, be cautious about using RSS as your only option for sharing content except in technology fields. The general public sees RSS as too technical or complicated and many feed readers have been shut down recently.

Be sure to enter your choices for content distribution on your Social Media Marketing Plan and create a schedule for distributing updates (daily? weekly? monthly?) on your Social Media Activity Calendar.

If you're interested in RSS, you'll find the resources in Table 1-2 helpful.

Table 1-2	RSS Resources for Technical Audiences	
Name	*URL*	*Function*
Atom	`www.xml.com/lpt/a/1619`	Atom feed details
Feedage.com	`www.feedage.com`	Directory of RSS feeds
FeedDemon	`www.feeddemon.com`	Free-standing RSS reader for Windows
FeedForAll	`www.feedforall.com`	RSS feed creation tool
FeedBurner	`http://feedburner.google.com`	Create, manage, and monitor RSS feeds
Netvibes	`www.netvibes.com`	Combination personal aggregator and social network
NewsFire	`www.newsfirerss.com`	RSS reader for Macs
RSS Toolset	`http://oedb.org/ilibrarian/the_ultimate_rss_toolset`	Annotated list of 96 RSS tools

RSS offers a distinct advantage for sharing site content with readers: one-time-and-forget-about-it installation. After RSS is installed on your site or blog, you don't have to do anything except update your master site. You don't even have to type an entry like you do with the other content distribution tools. Everyone who subscribes gets your feed automatically, and you know that they're prequalified prospects because they've opted in.

From a user's point of view, RSS means that after requesting a feed, the user doesn't have to go anywhere or do anything to receive updates because updates arrive at her fingertips.

Unfortunately, RSS coordinates with social media distribution services only if you (or your programmer) enable your other social media pages to accept and display your RSS feed. Alternatively, your programmer might be able to use a tool like the OnlyWire API (`www.onlywire.com/socialapi`) to configure your RSS feed to accept updates for distribution to social media.

A newer format for syndication, an Atom feed operates similarly to RSS but uses different technical parameters. Although many blogs use Atom feeds, the older RSS format remains more popular overall. Some sites offer or accept only one or the other, so your choice of source and destination services partly drives your selection of syndication format. For more information about Atom and RSS, see `www.atomenabled.org` or `http://nullprogram.com/blog/2013/09/23`.

Notifying Search Engines about Updates

Some people think that search engines, especially Google, know everything about everybody's websites all the time. Not so. Even the Google grand-master needs a tip now and again. Even though all search engines routinely *crawl* or *spider* (visit and scan) websites to keep their own results current and relevant, your cycle for updates won't necessarily match their cycles for crawling.

Keeping search engines updated is valuable: Your site is not only more likely to appear in relevant search results, but its ranking will also improve from frequent updates.

The solution — pinging — is a simple way to get the attention of search engines and directories whenever you update your blog or website. Pinging has several other uses online: confirmation that a site or server is operating, as a diagnostic tool for connectivity problems, or confirming that a particular IP address exists.

Pinging can be done on demand by using a third-party service, or you can configure your blog, RSS feed, and some other sites to do it automatically. Generally, you simply enter the name of your blog or post, enter your URL, select your destination(s), and click the Submit button. The service then broadcasts a message that your site contains a new post or other content.

Select only one pinging service at a time. Search engines don't take kindly to double pinging.

WordPress, TypePad, Blogger, and most other blog services offer built-in, automatic pinging every time you post. On some smaller blog hosts, you may have to set up pinging (or submit to search engines) in a control panel. Table 1-3 summarizes some of the most popular pinging options.

Table 1-3	Pinging Resources	
Name	*URL*	*Description*
Feed Shark	`http://feedshark.brainbliss.com`	Free ping service for blogs, RSS feeds, and podcasts
GooglePing	`http://googleping.com`	Ping search engines without registering
King Ping	`www.kping.com`	Paid, automated pinging for blogs, tweets, and online publishers

(continued)

Table 1-3 *(continued)*

Name	URL	Description
Pingdom	www.pingdom.com	Paid service that monitors whether your site is up and running
PingFarm	www.pingfarm.com	Free ping service that notifies search engines when you update your site or blog
Pingler	http://pingler.com	Free and paid services for pinging multiple sites on a regular schedule; useful for developers and hosts
Ping-O-Matic!	http://pingomatic.com	Ping service for blogs to search engines
WordPress Pinging	http://htwp2.com/to-ping-or-not-to-ping	Article on the WordPress pinging service (owns Ping-O-Matic!)
Pinging and SEO	www.seostrategies.pro/seo/369/pinging-for-seo-explained	Article explaining Pinging and SEO benefits

Be sure to enter your choices for a pinging service on your Social Media Marketing Plan. If pinging isn't automatic, enter a task item for pinging below each update on your Social Media Activity Calendar.

Snipping Ugly URLs

The last thing you need when microblogging (on sites like Twitter) is a URL that takes up half your 140-character limit! Long, descriptive URLs that are useful for search engines are also messy in email, text messages, text versions of e-newsletters, and blogs, not to mention making it difficult to retweet within the limit. The solution is to snip, clip, nip, trim, shave, or otherwise shorten ungainly URLs with a truncating service. Take your choice of those in Table 1-4 or search for others.

Table 1-4	URL Snipping Services	
Service Name	*URL*	*Notes*
2 Create a Website	`http://blog.2createa website.com/2012/01/09/ popular-url-shorteners- for-redirecting-tracking- affiliate-links`	Comparison review article
Bitly	`https://bitly.com`	Free and paid versions, with history, stats, and preferences
Ow.ly	`http://ow.ly/url/ shorten-url`	Hootsuite's URL shortener, free
Snipurl	`http://snipurl.com`	Stores, manages, and tracks traffic on short URLs, free
TinyURL	`http://tinyurl.com`	One of the oldest and best-known truncators, free
Twitter	`http://t.co`	Link-shortening service; used only on Twitter, which automatically shortens links in tweets to a t.co link; can still use third-party link shorteners

The downside is that the true owner of shortened URLs may be a mystery, so it doesn't do much for your branding. Figure 1-2 shows a typical URL truncating service and the result.

As always, enter the name of your URL-snipping service on your Social Media Marketing Plan. To make it easier to track URLs and their snipped versions, select just one service.

Figure 1-2:
Enter a long
URL at Bitly
and receive
a short URL
in return.

Using E-Commerce Tools for Social Sites

If money makes the world go 'round, e-commerce takes the cybersocial world for a dizzying spin. There have been many different options for promoting or linking to your online store from blogs and social networks, but several applications now let you sell directly (or indirectly) from social media pages.

Always check the terms of service on social media sites to be sure you aren't violating their rules. Some services may prohibit selling directly from their site.

Selling through links

The easiest way to sell from social networks and blogs is simply to post a banner or a text link to your own website or to other sites (Etsy, for example) that sell your products. Additionally, you can post images on a site like Facebook with links to your website or other sites.

The electronic rock bank STS9 does this in a sophisticated manner, as shown in Figure 1-3. Clicking an item on its Facebook storefront (www.facebook.com/sts9/app_369666098814) takes shoppers to STS9's shopping website at http://sts9store.com/Store/ChooseMerch.aspx to fill their carts and check out.

Link to website store

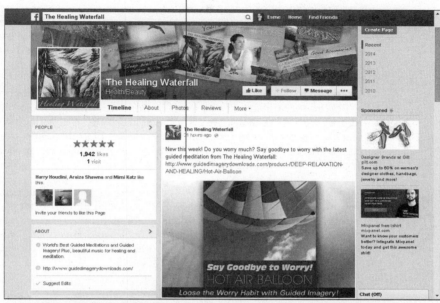

**Book II
Chapter 1**

**Discovering Helpful
Tech Tools**

Figure 1-3:
Product
offerings
can
begin on
Facebook
(top) and
then link to
a separate
shopping
website
(bottom).

Displaying products on social media services

If you're looking for a more seamless experience, consider e-commerce tools that display items from your existing online store on your blog or social media pages, and then either link automatically back to your web store to complete the transaction or permit users to purchase directly from the social media page.

E-commerce widgets are mini-displays of products; these changeable badges (which appear onscreen as a large button with multiple links) link to an existing web store. If you already have an online store, check your shopping cart or *check stand provider* (the section of your online store that totals orders and takes payments) to see whether it offers a widget for social media, like the one shown in Figure 1-4.

Many vendors of online stores offer widgets or apps with shopping or promotional functionality for use on specific social media services. For instance, SouthernTots.com uses the Soldsie app to conduct sales on Instagram (http://instagram.com/southerntots) and Facebook (www.facebook.com/southerntots) by using the comment function on those sites.

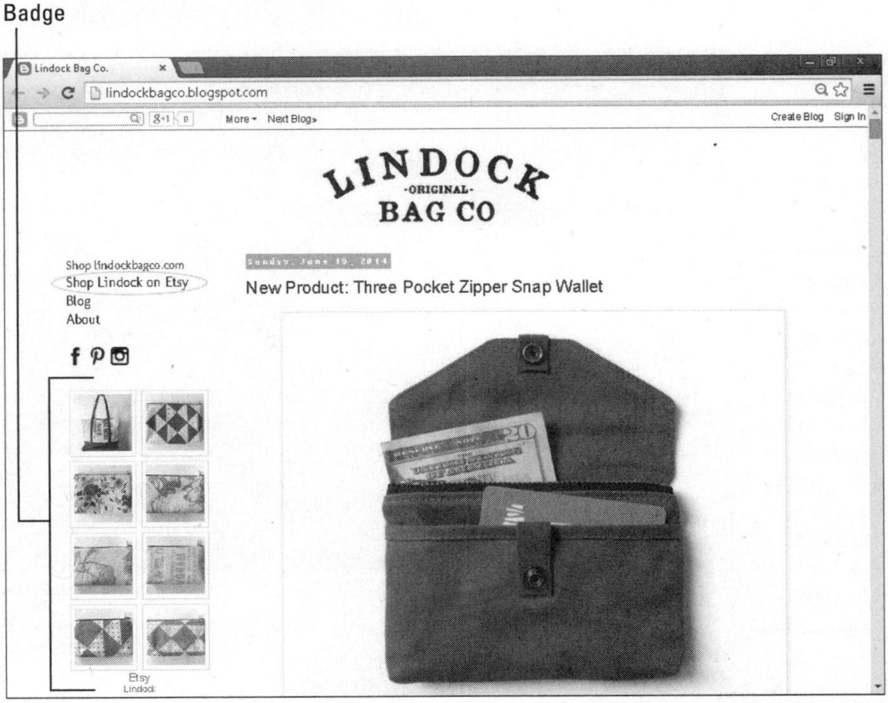

Badge

Figure 1-4:
The Etsy mini-badge on the left side of this blog drives traffic to the Etsy shop for the Lindock Bag Company.

Reproduced with permission of Julie Brzezinski

Combining a virtual storefront with a payment service

By comparison, a *virtual storefront* on a social media service either imports products from an online store already in place on your website or allows products to be uploaded directly from a freestanding, online store like Etsy. At the check stand stage, these storefronts link to your regular web store or to a third-party site to process the transactions. Although virtual storefront strategies may be a useful way to cast a wider net for customers, they may complicate your recordkeeping when used in addition to a web store.

E-commerce tools described in this chapter, which let you promote and sell only your own products, are quite different from social shopping services, which aggregate products from multiple sources, often suggested by consumers themselves and linking viewers back to your website. We discuss social shopping services — essentially, social bookmarks for products — in Book II, Chapter 3.

Third-party e-commerce tools that link to PayPal or other payment services generally don't integrate with inventory and accounting packages in the way that a full-featured shopping cart on your website might. If your business inventory system doesn't link to the shopping cart on your website, you may need to adjust those records manually.

If you use a virtual storefront in addition to an existing store on your own website but don't track inventory automatically, there's another way to track the source of sales: For tracking purposes, create separate SKUs for products that will be listed on different online store locations or set a different price — for example, discounting items specifically for your Twitter audience. However, this approach doesn't work with automated inventory controls.

Reviewing sample products for selling on social media

The following sections discuss some of the many specific tools and products available for selling products through social media. Consider these items examples in the range of products available. You should research and evaluate products to meet your own needs.

Ecwid

Ecwid (www.ecwid.com) is a complete e-commerce solution for websites, blogs, Facebook, Tumblr, and more. Facebook shoppers complete the entire process, including checkout, on Facebook. Additional social media integration to share purchases and recommend products is also available for Facebook, Twitter, Pinterest, Google+, and Tumblr.

Earthegy gains energy from Facebook sales

Chrisy Bossie founded Earthegy, a retailer of crystals and healing jewelry, in August 2010 with a shop on Etsy and products spread out on her dining room table. She soon added a blog, a Facebook page, and Facebook advertising to her marketing mix.

"Facebook advertising brought me a ton of qualified customers," explains Bossie, who tightly targets her Facebook ads to women, ages 35 to 60, who are interested in crystal healing and energy jewelry.

"Customers grew my business to the point [that] I outgrew other selling venues and needed my own e-commerce site." In 2012 she launched her site at www.earthegy.com (see the nearby figure) and quickly gained subscribers to a new weekly newsletter. At the same time, she continues her blog to capture Google rankings and drive traffic to her online store.

She added shopping to her Facebook presence, using an app provided by 3dcart (www.3dcart.com), which powers her online web store, as well. As seen in the following figure, Shop Earthegy appears as a tab in the top navigation (below the header graphic). It also appears to the left of the timeline on her main page. While Bossie has more than 1,000 products on her main website, the app previews only about 40 of them on Facebook. Because the app pulls products from one specified category in her store, Bossie cleverly created a New at Earthegy category in the top-left

Reproduced with permission of Earthegy

navigation column on her main site. Since products in the New category change constantly, this approach keeps the Facebook display fresh.

In the last year, Bossie says 35 percent of her sales appear to have come directly from Facebook, but she thinks those numbers are understated. "Customers who now go directly to my website often first found me on Facebook, but the Facebook referral doesn't show up now because they know how to find me directly."

Although she finds Google Analytics useful for keeping an eye on her website, Bossie prefers a real-time view. "I can see what people are searching for; if it's a product I don't carry, I'll start hunting for it." She even watches orders as they near the end of the checkout process. "A lot of the time, I'll be pulling those products from inventory and packing them while a customer is still checking out. It makes for faster shipping times, and a huge reason my customers become repeat customers is because I ship as fast as I possibly can."

While she plays around with Pinterest a bit, and cross-posts from Facebook to Twitter, Bossie keeps her marketing efforts focused. "Because of Facebook's effectiveness, I spend all of my time and effort there to generate sales and interest in my products."

She earned that effectiveness the hard way. Bossie offers some of her lessons learned for maximizing the potential of Facebook:

- Photos, photos, photos! Links and videos don't get nearly the reach as good photos do.

- Make sure your website information is easy to find. Fill out your About page on Facebook. There's no sense promoting your products on Facebook if people can't find where to purchase them. (For every product photo that Bossie posts, she includes a direct link to the store detail page in the caption.)

- Since people prefer information to ads, include stories and interesting tidbits about your products.

- Don't be afraid to use the Delete and the Block and Ban options if people post negative comments.

- Don't demand action from those who Like your Facebook page via your timeline. They are gracing you with an audience. If you start asking them to do things, they'll leave.

Passionate about her business, Bossie continues to run Earthegy as a one-woman band, working from dawn to dusk, like most entrepreneurs. Even when she's away from home, she constantly monitors her Facebook page on a smartphone. And, yes, she still has crystals spread out on her dining room table.

Earthegy's web presence:

- www.earthegy.com

- www.facebook.com/Earthegy

- www.facebook.com/Earthegy/app_30729455954 (store)

(continued)

(continued)

✔ www.blog.earthegy.com

✔ https://plus.google.com/114937442286552466800/posts?hl=en

✔ https://twitter.com/earthegy

Reproduced with permission of Earthegy

Since the contents of your web store are mirrored on several sites, it's easy to update your product catalog simultaneously at all sites and manage all the online locations from one dashboard. Prices range from free for up to ten products to $99 per month for unlimited products. All packages include a free Facebook store.

Shopify

Shopify (www.shopify.com) is a full-featured store builder that lets Facebook users browse your catalog and purchase products directly from Facebook. A free Facebook store is included with monthly web-based plans, which range from a $14 starter package to $179 for unlimited storage. If you don't already have or want a web-based store, you can select a Facebook-only plan (www.shopify.com/facebook) with unlimited products starting at $9 per month. Per-transaction credit card fees are charged in addition. All plans have a 14-day free trial.

When selecting a storefront solution for your website, investigate which ones offer either the ability to use the same solution on social media platforms or provide widgets for social media compatibility. Many companies have added this feature in response to demand.

Storefront Social

Made specifically for Facebook, Storefront Social (www.storefrontsocial.com) allows you to sell directly from Facebook using PayPal, Google Checkout, or Authorize.net for credit cards. You can forward shoppers to your web-based store to conclude the purchase or to see additional products. Offering a free seven-day trial and flat monthly fees from $9.95 for 100 products to $29.95 for 1,000 products, Storefront Social is an affordable selling solution for small-to medium-size stores.

StoreYa

StoreYa (www.storeya.com) is a cost-effective solution for selling on Facebook, blogs, websites, and/or in a mobile environment, with links to your primary store to complete a sale (see Figure 1-5). StoreYa allows you to import your products from other e-commerce programs. It includes multiple social media marketing tools to increase sales, as well as store statistics. Pricing varies by the number of products (SKUs) in your catalog, starting with a free version for 20 products and rising to enterprise level, with several affordable levels in between. It offers a free 14-day trial period.

Other resources for selling on social media

Table 1-5 lists other e-commerce widgets, storefronts, and resources you may want to check out.

Watch for news from Twitter about buying online directly from a tweet. Twitter began testing a Buy button with some test partners in Fall 2014 to make it fun and simple to shop from mobile devices.

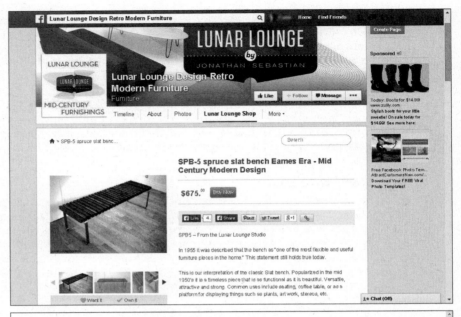

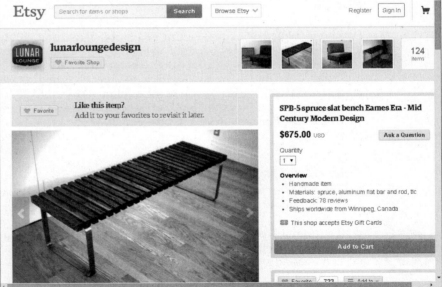

Figure 1-5: Lunar Lounge uses the e-commerce solution from StoreYa on its Facebook page (top); clicking the Buy Now button opens Lunar Lounge's Etsy shop (bottom).

Table 1-5   **Social E-Commerce Widgets, Storefronts, and Resources**

Name	URL	Notes
Amazon	`https://widgets.amazon.com`	E-commerce widgets for the Amazon store that can be placed on multiple social network, blog, or web pages
Big Cartel	`http://bigcartel.com`	Hosted e-commerce website geared toward artists, clothing designers, and bands; capability to set up free-standing e-commerce sites and add to a Facebook site
Bigcommerce	`www.bigcommerce.com`	E-commerce platform that allows you to design a web store and add a widget to Facebook
eBay	`http://developer.ebay.com/businessbenefits/money`	E-commerce widget for your eBay store
E-junkie	`www.e-junkie.com`	Cart or Buy Now buttons for social media or blog; fee based on size and volume; handles charges for downloaded items (for example, music or whitepapers)
Etsy	`www.etsy.com/storque/etsy-news/tech-updates-etsy-mini-679`	Directions for using e-commerce widget for your Etsy store
Highwire	`www.highwire.com`	Multichannel storefront for use on your own website and/or eBay, Facebook, Google, or mobile site
Mercantec	`www.mercantec.com/google`	Snippet generator that adds shopping cart to sites, blogs, or social networks; has analytics

(continued)

Table 1-5 *(continued)*

Name	URL	Notes
PayPal	`https://developer.paypal.com/docs/classic/products`	E-commerce Adaptive Payment API that lets programmers build small applications on social networks
Practical eCommerce	`http://search.practicalcommerce.com/search?q=social+media+e-commerce+widgets`	Articles about using e-commerce widgets with social media
Soldsie	`http://new.soldsie.com`	An app for Facebook and Instagram that allows you to sell on those sites through uploaded photos and user comments
Storefront Social	`http://storefrontsocial.com`	Allows you to create a Facebook shop in minutes
Wishpond	`http://corp.wishpond.com/social-promotions`	Apps to run promotions, such as coupons, contests, or group sales, on Twitter and Facebook

Keeping Your Ear to the Social Ground

The onslaught of data from social media sites can be overwhelming. To garner some value from all the noise, you can take advantage of certain tools to monitor what's being said about your company.

When should you start to worry? Some experts suggest that a negative comment appearing within the first 20 results on a Google search on your name, brand, or product could be a sign of trouble. Don't worry about a one-off negative comment on a minor site.

Social media *monitoring* is about who's saying what. It's about your brand, your products, and your reputation. It's not the same as social media *measurement,* which deals with traffic statistics, conversion rates, and return on investment (ROI). Measurement is covered in Book IX, including chapters about measurement tools specific to particular social networks.

Bring user feedback directly to you. Place a free feedback widget on your site from `http://shoutbox.widget.me`, `http://getbarometer.com`, or `www.makeuseof.com/dir/snapabug-visual-feedback`. This feature takes some programming knowledge; if you're not up to the task, ask your programmer. You can find some monitoring tools for specific types of services in the sections that follow.

Deciding what to monitor and why

If you didn't have anything else to do, you could monitor everything. That situation isn't realistic, so you need to set some constraints. Start with your goal and ask yourself what you want to accomplish. For example, you may want to

+ Track what's being said about your company and products, both positive and negative.

+ Conduct competitor or market research.

+ Stay up-to-date on what's happening in your industry.

+ Watch trends in terms of mentions, topics of interest, or volume of comments.

+ Gain a competitive advantage.

+ Monitor the success of a specific press release, media campaign, or product promotion.

+ Monitor infringement of trademark or other intellectual property.

+ Obtain customer feedback so you can improve your products and services.

After you decide your goal, it should be obvious what search terms or keywords to monitor. Your list might include

+ Your company name

+ Your domain name

+ Names of executives and staff who speak with the public

+ Product names and URLs

+ Competitors' names

+ Keywords

+ Topic tags

Deciding which tools to use

The number of monitoring tools is almost as great as the amount of data they sift through. Research your options and choose at least one tool that monitors across multiple types of social media. Depending on the social media services you're using, you might want to select one from each appropriate service category, as well.

The frequency with which you check results from these tools will depend on the overall visibility of your company, the schedule for your submissions to different services, and the overall intensity of your social media presence. For some companies, it might be a daily task. For others, once weekly or even once per month will be enough.

If you're not sure where to start, begin with weekly Google Alerts to monitor the web and daily Mention.com alerts to monitor social media. Add one tool each for blogs and Twitter, if you use them actively or think people may be talking about your business on their own. Adjust as needed.

Using free or inexpensive social monitoring tools

Pick one or more of the tools in the following sections to monitor across multiple types of social media.

Mark your choices on your Social Media Marketing Plan. If the tool doesn't offer automated reporting, you'll need to enter the submission task, as well as the review task, on your Social Media Activity Calendar.

Addictomatic: Inhale the Web

Addictomatic (`http://addictomatic.com/about`) lets you "instantly create a custom page with the current buzz on any topic." It searches hundreds of live sites, including news, blog posts, videos, and images, and it offers a bookmarkable, personalized dashboard for keeping track of your updates.

Brand24

An affordable brand-monitoring tool, Brand 24 (`http://brand24.net`) starts at $19 per month with a 14-day free trial. It includes both sentiment and data analysis to provide a good sense of the buzz around your product, brand, business, or search term. It covers multiple social media outlets, including Facebook, Twitter, and Blip TV, with alerts daily or more often. Additional features available with more expensive plans allow you to review customer behavior, actions, and posts.

Google Alerts

One of the easiest and most popular of free monitoring services, Google Alerts (www.google.com/alerts) are notifications of new results on up to 1,000 search terms. Alerts can be delivered via email or RSS feed.

You can receive results for news articles, websites, blogs, video, and Google books and forums.

You set the frequency with which Google checks for results and other features from your My Alerts dashboard page. Think of Alerts as an online version of a clipping service. Yahoo! (http://alerts.yahoo.com) offers something similar.

Google Trends

Google Trends (www.google.com/trends) is a useful market research tool. It not only provides data on the hottest current searches, but also compares the number of searches on the terms you enter to the total number of searches on Google overall during the same time frame. Click the word Trends in the top left of the navigation bar and select the Explore option in the drop-down list. Click Add Term to insert the search phrase that interests you.

From the top horizontal navigation you can choose to refine your research by selecting options from the dropdowns under Worldwide (location), 2004-Present (time frame), All categories (topic area), or Web Search (content type.) Select the Subscriptions option in the drop-down list to receive email notification of trending searches and stories.

HowSociable

Type any brand name at www.howsociable.com, as shown in Figure 1-6, to see how visible it is in social media. The free version checks "one brand with 12 different metrics and limited features." The paid upgrade checks 24 more channels. Click any element for additional detail, as shown on the report for the Department of Homeland Security in Figure 1-6.

IceRocket

Meltwater's IceRocket (www.icerocket.com) is a free monitoring tool that covers millions of blogs, as well as Twitter and Facebook, in 20 languages. By the way, this is one of the places left where you can post the URL for your blog to make sure it gets found in search engines.

**Book II
Chapter 1**

Discovering Helpful
Tech Tools

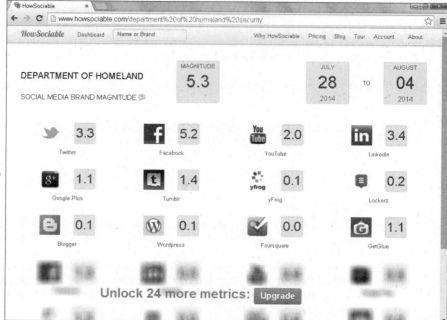

Figure 1-6:
HowSociable
displays
social media
visibility
for the
Department
of Homeland
Security.

IFTTT (If This Then That)

If This Then That (www.ifttt.com) is an automation tool that lets you write a script (called a *Recipe*) to receive notifications and accomplish other tasks online. You can easily use IFTTT to manage your online reputation. It's easiest to browse existing, public Recipes to find one that monitors your desired social media platforms; then tweak the Recipe to include the search terms you want to monitor.

Mention

Mention (https://en.mention.com) monitors multiple social networks, news sites, forums, blogs, or any web page in 42 languages. It offers several helpful features: first, the ability to export data, filtered by time and source, which allows you to compare your results to competitors' results; and second, real-time alerts plus a daily or weekly digest by email. Its free basic plan allows one user, one alert, and up to 250 mentions per month, but doesn't include analytics. Paid versions — which have higher limits on the number of alerts, mentions, and users — start at $29 per month, but all include a free 14-day trial.

social mention

social mention (`http://socialmention.com`) tracks and measures what's being said about a specific topic in real-time across more than 100 social media services. It provides a social ranking score based on its own definition of *popularity* — which includes self-defined criteria of strength, sentiment, passion, and reach — for every search. Figure 1-7 shows the results for the term Ice Bucket Challenge (which had received more than 1 billion views on YouTube by September 2014.) For more information on measuring sentiment, see Book I, Chapter 4.

Book II Chapter 1

Discovering Helpful Tech Tools

Figure 1-7: social mention provides a social-ranking score based on its definition of popularity.

You can select to monitor only specific services and choose among service categories of bookmarks, blogs, microblogs, comments, news, networks, video, audio, images, Q&A, or all. Although you can input only one term at a time, the results may go back 30 months or more.

If you select the CSV/Excel File option on the search results page, you can download all pages of the resulting display with details. This makes it easy to create graphs showing changes in various criteria over time. For instance, you might be able to pinpoint how an active social media campaign changes the Sentiment results for your company.

In addition, social mention aggregates trends (www.socialmention.com/trends) in near–real-time about social media discourse — which is also handy for doing market research.

Social Mention also offers real-time widgets (http://socialmention.com/tools) to place on your site or in your browser bar. The browser is a simple plug-in, but your programmer will need to copy and paste the widget code onto your site.

Sprout Social

A high-end package of social media tools, Sprout Social (www.sproutsocial.com) includes a comprehensive monitoring feature that combines all alerts, messages, and actions into a single stream that can be analyzed to discover trends. You can watch for social media comments about your business, brand, products, competitors, or industry topics in near real-time. Prices start at $59 per user per month but include a 30-day free trial.

Talkwalker Alerts

A comparable alternative to Google Alerts, Talkwalker (www.talkwalker.com/alerts) monitors the web for mentions of your brand, competitors, name, events, or other keywords. It provides email updates to your email inbox or RSS reader on a daily or weekly basis. Free for up to 100 alerts, Talkwalker Alerts does not cover social media. However, the paid Pro versions of Talkwalker (www.talkwalker.com/en/social-media-intelligence) include multiple social media sources, higher limits on the number of alerts, and other features. Prices start at approximately $650 per month, with a 14-day free trial.

Topsy

Topsy (www.topsy.com) is a free, real-time search engine for social media, including links, tweets, influencers, photos, and/or images. Ranking results based on daily conversations about terms entered, Topsy also offers social trends and social analytics.

Trackur

Trackur (www.trackur.com) tracks all forms of social media, including Facebook, Google+, Reddit, blogs, news, networks, RSS feeds, tweets, images, and video (some sources are available only with paid plans). In addition to displaying conversational content, Trackur presents trends and analyzes any website that mentions a term being monitored. You can get a free account that includes one saved search and 100 results. Monthly plans start with 50 search terms at $97 per month. All paid plans come with a free 10-day trial.

WhosTalkin.com

WhosTalkin.com (`www.whostalkin.com`) is another free, real-time search tool. It surveys 60 social media services for current conversations in the categories of blogs, news, networks, videos, images, forums, and tags. It lacks the reporting capabilities of social mention, but it does include actual comments. WhosTalkin.com provides results for only one term at a time but offers a browser search plug-in API.

Measuring the Buzz by Type of Service

The number of monitoring tools competing for market share is astonishing. The following tables are not intended to be comprehensive lists, but simply to provide some idea of what's out there.

Table 1-6 lists tools for monitoring blogs and forums; Table 1-7 tools for news, RSS, and geolocation sites; Table 1-8 tools for Twitter; and Table 1-9, some high-end tools at the enterprise level. You can always search for free tools in each category to get more options.

REMEMBER

To ensure that your blog appears in a timely fashion in blog-monitoring tools, submit your blog to each one and set up pinging (which you can read about in the section "Notifying Search Engines about Updates," earlier in this chapter).

Table 1-6	Blog- and Forum-Monitoring Tools	
Name	*URL*	*Description*
Attentio	`http://attentio.com`	Multilingual social media monitoring; fee.
Bloglines	`www.bloglines.com`	Delivers blog search content in an RSS feed.
BlogSearchEngine	`www.blogsearchengine.org/`	Search for blogs by topic area or search term
Meltwater IceRocket	`www.icerocket.com`	Trend and buzz monitor for blogs, Twitter, and Facebook.

(continued)

Table 1-6 *(continued)*

Name	URL	Description
sovrn	www.sovrn.com	Free tool to help publishers monetize their websites and social media, reach their target audiences, and build relationships. Includes reports on user behavior, demographics, and actions.

Table 1-7   **Social News and RSS Tools**

Name	URL	Description
Google News	http://news.google.com	Keyword search of Google News
Yahoo! News	http://news.yahoo.com	Keyword search of Yahoo! News

Table 1-8   **Twitter Monitoring Tools**

Name	URL	Description
Hashtagify.me	http://hashtagify.me	Manage your own hashtags and receive alerts when hashtags are used.
SocialOomph	www.socialoomph.com	Formerly TweetLater.com, one-stop shop to monitor and manage Twitter; paid version includes blogs, Facebook, LinkedIn, RSS feeds, and more.
Twitter's TweetDeck	https://about.twitter.com/products/tweetdeck	Twitter tool to create searches and track hashtags, events, or topics.
Twitter Search	https://twitter.com/search-home	Twitter's own search filter with advanced queries.

Table 1-9   Fee-Based, Enterprise-Level Monitoring Tools

Name	*URL*	*What It Does*
BrandsEye	`www.brandseye.com`	Paid service tracks online conversations with monitoring and insight tools.
eCairn Conversation	`www.ecairn.com`	Integrates and analyzes multiple social media sources for marketing and PR pros.
Lithium	`www.lithium.com/ products-solutions/ social-media- analytics`	Monitors community engagement as part of an integrated social media management package.
NielsenOnline	`www.nielsen.com/us/ en/solutions/ measurement/online. html`	Deep web analysis of consumer-generated content in online communities, message boards, groups, blogs, opinion sites, and social networks.
Salesforce. com	`www.salesforce marketingcloud.com/ products/social- media-listening`	Detailed monitoring of social media buzz about industry, competitors, and/or brand. Analyze customer desires, evaluate content engagement, and assess campaign reaction.
Spiral16	`www.spiral16.com/ technology`	Advanced software tool for brand monitoring and sentiment; includes sophisticated reporting.
Sysomos' Heartbeat	`www.sysomos.com/ products/ overview/ heartbeat`	Real-time monitoring and measurement tool for buzz and sentiment.

Figure 1-8 shows the results of a typical Twitter search.

Figure 1-8:
Results
page from
Twitter
Search for
Portland
Restaurants.

Chapter 2: Leveraging Search Engine Optimization (SEO) for Social Media

In This Chapter

✔ Understanding why SEO still matters

✔ Looking into the top search engines

✔ Focusing on the SEO basics of keywords and metatags

✔ Optimizing your web presence for search engines

✔ Conducting inbound link campaigns

✔ Gaining visibility in real-time search

*N*o matter how popular social media may be, search engine optimization (SEO) must still be a part of your toolkit for a successful, broad-spectrum web presence. The goal of SEO is to get various components of your web presence to appear near the top of search results — preferably in the top ten — on general search engines or in search results for specific social media services.

You accomplish this by selecting appropriate search terms or keywords and then optimizing content, navigation, and structure to create a web page or profile that's search-friendly for your selected terms. At the same time, you maximize cross-links from social media to increase the number of inbound links to your primary website.

Fortunately, you can optimize social media, from blogs to Facebook, very much the same way that you optimize a website. Some people call this social media optimization (SMO), referring to the application of SEO techniques to social media. SMO has become even more critical with search engines such as Google moving toward personalization and semantic analysis, which skews users' results on the basis of location and past searches.

If you do a good job optimizing multiple components of your web presence — your website, blog, Facebook page, Twitter profile, and more — they may all appear near the top of Search Engine Result Pages (SERPs) on selected terms, increasing your company's share of that premium screen real estate. As mentioned in Book I, Chapter 1, improving search engine ranking is one strategic justification for implementing a social media campaign in the first place.

Making the Statistical Case for SEO

News of the publicity about social media usage sometimes overshadows the actual numbers. For instance, comScore's Unique Visitor Table for June 2014 showed that Facebook (141.4 million unique visitors) has fallen behind Microsoft Sites (164.2 million), Yahoo Sites (171.3 million), and Google Sites (189.7 million). The numbers fluctuate, but keep in mind that press accounts and reality aren't always the same.

And just because more than 864 million people worldwide (82 percent outside North America) are called daily active Facebook users in September 2014 doesn't mean they're all using it to search for information that might lead them to your company.

In fact, a study in June 2013 by Forrester Research (How Consumers Found Websites In 2012, July 2013, Forrester Research, Inc.) showed that the majority of adult Internet users in the United States still opt for search engines more than social media networks or other sources to find websites, as shown in Figure 2-1. To reach that majority, SEO remains the technique of choice.

Sobering reminder: Older American audiences (over age 64) still gravitate toward print and television.

Figure 2-1:
In 2013, adult U.S. Internet users still favored search engines over social media to find websites.

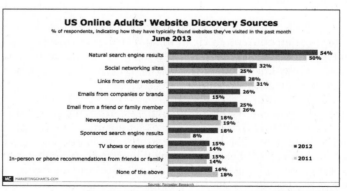

US Online Adults' Website Discovery Sources
% of respondents, indicating how they have typically found websites they've visited in the past month
June 2013

Natural search engine results	54% / 50%
Social networking sites	32% / 25%
Links from other websites	28% / 31%
Emails from companies or brands	26% / 15%
Email from a friend or family member	25% / 26%
Newspapers/magazine articles	18% / 19%
Sponsored search engine results	18% / 8%
TV shows or news stories	15% / 14%
In-person or phone recommendations from friends or family	15% / 14%
None of the above	16% / 18%

■ 2012
■ 2011

MARKETINGCHARTS.COM
Source: Forrester Research

Reproduced with permission. Source: "How Consumers Found Websites In 2012, July 2013, Forrester Research, Inc."

At the moment, no social media alternative covers as wide a base of web pages or as commanding an algorithm for assessing relevance as search engines.

What will happen in the future? Get out your crystal ball or watch eMarketer and other sites for more data. One thing about the web is for sure — like the world, it always turns.

Given these statistics, do you still need to bother with search engine optimization techniques for your hub website, as we discuss in Book I, Chapter 1? Absolutely. Here's why:

✦ Although the younger subset of Internet users is attracted to searching for trending topics on social media or relying on friends' recommendations of products, not all members of your target audience are active users of social media — especially if you have a business-to-business (B2B) company or target an older consumer audience.

✦ After you optimize your hub website or blog, registered under your own domain name, you can quickly transfer the techniques, tools, and results to social media, especially to blogs and tweets.

✦ Inbound links to a hub website remain a key to high ranking in search results, especially on Google. Your social media pages are a rich source of these links. Google treats social media channels, which are written in HTML, just like any other sites on the web for purposes of ranking and search.

Google can't review social media pages that have been set to private, no matter how much traffic or engagement those pages may have.

✦ Most social media services still aren't as flexible as a full-fledged website when it comes to handling e-commerce, database applications, forms, or other myriad features involving real-time data entry. Most third-party apps on social media that offer some of this functionality can't give you the same degree of control as you have on your website.

✦ Your website or blog benefits from links to your site from social media pages. In particular, make sure your profile is public and contains links to your site.

✦ SEO remains an essential, though not sufficient, method of ensuring site visibility based on a method other than the number of friends, fans, or followers you have. You're chasing profits, not popularity.

SEO isn't an end in itself. The goal is to draw qualified visitors to your website so that you can turn them into customers and clients. A strong SEO foundation helps direct traffic to your full-featured hub from your social media presence.

For more information about search engine optimization, see *Search Engine Optimization All-in-One For Dummies,* 2nd Edition, by Bruce Clay and Susan Esparza (Wiley Publishing, Inc.).

**Book II
Chapter 2**

Leveraging Search Engine Optimization (SEO) for Social Media

Thinking Tactically and Practically

The best results for SEO sprout from the best content — and so does the largest stream of qualified prospects. Though we talk about many SEO techniques in this chapter, none of them will work unless you offer appealing content that draws and holds the attention of your audience.

Two schools of thought drive SEO tactics for social media:

✦ Optimize your website and all your social media for the same search terms, occupying the first page of results with one or more pages of your web presence.

✦ Use your social media pages to grab a good position for some relatively rare search terms that your website doesn't use.

Get greedy. Go for the best of both worlds. Use your standard search terms on social media profiles and the more rarely used terms on individual posts, photo captions, or updates.

Use a free trial at sites such as `http://seosuite.com`, `www.webseoanalytics.com/free/seo-tools/keyword-competition-checker.php`, or `http://moz.com/tools` to see how your site ranks on different search terms. Your tactical decisions about keyword selection may depend on those results, as well as on the goals and objectives of your social media campaign.

Search engine jargon

Help yourself by mastering the terminology you see on search engine resource sites or in articles:

✔ **Natural or organic search** refers to the type of search results produced by a search engine's *algorithm* (set of rules) when indexing unpaid submissions.

✔ **Paid search results** are those for which a submission fee or bid has been paid to appear as sponsorships at the top of a search results page, in pay-per-click (PPC) ads in the right margin, or in some cases at the top of the list of search results.

✔ **Search engine marketing (SEM)** combines both natural and paid search activities.

✔ **Search engine optimization (SEO)** is the process of adjusting websites, web pages, and social media pages to gain higher placement in search engine results.

✔ **Social media optimization (SMO)** is the process of adjusting social media profiles and postings to gain higher placement in search engine results.

✔ **Spiders, crawlers, or robots (bots)** are automated programs used by search engines to visit websites and index their content.

In the later section "Choosing the right search terms," you discover how to select terms that people are likely to use and ones that give you a chance of breaking through to the first page of search results.

Focusing on the Top Search Engines

Ignore all those emails about submitting your site to 3,000 search engines. You need to submit only to the top two: Google, and Yahoo!/Bing (which share the same algorithm). When you submit to Bing, you're also listed on Yahoo! However, the results pages may not always be identical, particularly on local searches.

**Book II
Chapter 2**

Leveraging Search
Engine Optimization
(SEO) for Social
Media

Table 2-1 tells where to submit your sites to those search engines.

Table 2-1	Submission URLs for Key Search Engines		
Name	*URL*	*Search % in July 2014*	*Feeds*
Google	`www.google.com/ webmasters/tools`	67.4	AOL, Ask.com
Yahoo!	`www.bing.com/ toolbox/submit- site-url`	10.0	Lycos
Bing	`www.bing.com/ toolbox/submit- site-url`	19.3	Same submission site as Yahoo!

Source: comScore July 2014 U.S. Search Engine Rankings report (www.comscore.com/Insights/ Market-Rankings/comScore-Releases-July-2014-US-Search-Engine-Rankings)

According to comScore, these three search engines accounted for 96.7 percent of all searches in July 2014, with Google executing more than three times as many searches as Bing, its closest search competitor. All remaining search engines together accounted for the remaining 3.3 percent of searches. These primary search engines now send out spiders to crawl the web incessantly. You don't need to resubmit your site routinely. But you should resubmit your site to trigger a visit from the arachnids if you add new content or products, expand to a new location, or update your search terms.

Fortunately, you can ping search engines to notify them of changes automatically, as discussed in Chapter 1 of this minibook. After receiving a ping, search engines crawl your site again. Different search engines use different *algorithms* (sets of rules) to display search results, which may vary rapidly over time. To complicate matters further, different search engines tend to attract different audiences. Optimize your site for the search engine that best attracts your audience. Here are some facts about the top search engines and their audiences:

✦ About 72 percent of B2B buyers planning to purchase a product start with Google search.

✦ Alexa data show that users are somewhat more likely to use Yahoo! or Bing at school and Google at home.

✦ More than 70 percent of 18- to 29-year-olds preferred search results branded as Google; this number dropped to 64 percent of 30- to 44-year-olds. Those over 45 generally favored Bing results.

✦ People who search with Google tend to live in states with above-average median household incomes, above average college graduation rates, higher job growth rates, and older populations.

✦ States that favor Bing for search appear to lean towards the right of the political spectrum.

✦ Yahoo! users show a high correlation with very religious states but are found less often in areas with more Starbucks coffee shops or more college graduates. Because college graduation correlates to income, Yahoo! users also show a lower overall personal income.

✦ Market share is not even across the country. Google dominates both the West Coast (with a market share over 80 percent) and the East Coast (with a market share around 85 percent in Massachusetts, New York, and the District of Columbia). Of states in the U.S., only Delaware has a Google market share below 70 percent.

Knowing the Importance of Search Phrases

Users enter search terms into the query box on a search engine, website, or social media service to locate the information they seek. The trick to success is to identify the search terms that your prospective customers are likely to use.

For good visibility on a search term, your site or social media profile needs to appear within the top ten positions on the first page of search results for that term. Only academic researchers and obsessive-compulsives are likely to search beyond the first page.

Fortunately or unfortunately, everyone's brain is wired a little differently, leading to different choices of words and different ways of organizing information. Some differences are simple matters of dialect: Someone in the southern United States may look for *bucket,* whereas someone in the north looks for a *pail.* Someone in the United Kingdom may enter *cheap petrol,* whereas someone in the United States types *cheap gas.*

Other differences have to do with industry-specific jargon. *Rag* has one meaning to someone looking for a job in the garment industry and another meaning to someone wanting to buy a chamois to polish a car.

Other variations have to do with spelling simplicity. Users will invariably spell *hotels* rather than *accommodations,* or *army clothes* instead of *camouflage* or *khaki.* And users rarely type a phrase that's longer than five words.

The average length of a search query has been increasing. As of January 2012, it was between four and five words per search, but this number varies by search engine. Now that people are using voice to query their smartphones, search queries have become even longer and are often phrased as a question, rather than as a phrase. Now you need to think of search phrases in terms not only of what your content includes, but what your user might intend (take out your mind-reader hat), as well as how various concepts in your content relate to one another.

Longer search queries, which are sometimes called *long-tail keywords,* are more likely to land people on a specific page or post. Therefore, these long queries may be more likely to lead to conversions.

Choosing the right search terms

We recommend trying to come up with a list of at least 30 search terms that can be distributed among different pages of your website (more if you have a large site). You must juggle the terms people are likely to use to find your product or service with the likelihood that you can show up on the first page of search results. Here are some tips for building a list of potential keywords:

✦ Brainstorm all possible terms that you think your target audience might use. Ask your customers, friends, and employees for ideas.

✦ Be sure your list includes the names of all your products and service packages and your company name. Someone who has heard of you must absolutely be able to find you online.

✦ Incorporate all the industry-specific search terms and jargon you can think of.

✦ If you sell to a local or regional territory, incorporate location into your terms: for example, *Lancaster bakery* or *Columbus OH chiropractor.* It's very difficult to appear on the first page of results for a single word, such as *bakery* or *chiropractor.*

Book II
Chapter 2

Leveraging Search
Engine Optimization
(SEO) for Social
Media

✦ For additional ideas, go to Google, enter a search term, and click the Search button. Then click the Related Searches option in the left margin. You may be surprised by the other search phrases that users try.

✦ If you already have a website, look at your analytics results to see which search phrases people are already using to find your site.

✦ Use one or more of the free search tools listed in Table 2-2 to get ideas for other keywords, how often they're used, and how many competing sites use the same term.

Table 2-2	Keyword Selection Resources	
Name	*URL*	*Description*
Google Insights	`www.google.com/trends`	Research trending search terms
Google AdWords Keyword Planner	`https://adwords. google.com/ keywordplanner`	Free keyword generator and statistics available to AdWords users

KGen	`https://addons. mozilla.org/firefox/ addon/kgen`
	
	`https://chrome. google.com/webstore/ detail/kgen/ jkpcelefglapia hikhocfdcigfpaagcl`
		Shareware add-on for the Firefox and Chrome toolbar showing which keywords are strong on visited web pages

SEMrush	`www.semrush.com`	Research keywords used by competitors for Google and Bing organic search
Ubersuggest	`http://ubersuggest. org`	Free keyword suggestion tool
WordStream	`www.wordstream.com/ keywords`	Basic keyword tools; 30 free searches
Wordtracker	`www.wordtracker.com`	Keyword suggestion tool; free 7-day trial

✦ Figure 2-2 displays results and synonyms from the Google AdWords Keyword Planner (`https://adwords.google.com/keywordplanner`) for the phrase *dog grooming*. (Intended to help buyers of Google AdWords, this tool is also useful when you're brainstorming search terms.) To access this tool, you need to sign into an existing AdWords account or create a new one by clicking the links on the Keyword Planner page.

✦ Alternatively, you can reach this page by signing into your Google AdWords account at `https://adwords.google.com` or at. `http://google.com/mybusiness`. (See Book VIII, Chapter 2 for more on using Google My Business.) After you log in, navigate to the Tools tab and click Keyword Planner, which you can access without actually creating a campaign.

✦ Check your competitors' search terms for ideas. Visit your competitors' sites and right-click to view page source, or look in the browser toolbar for something like View⇨Source. The keywords are usually listed near the top of the source code for a page. If you don't see them, try using the Find command (Ctrl+F) to search for *keyword*.

Book II
Chapter 2

Leveraging Search
Engine Optimization
(SEO) for Social
Media

Figure 2-2:
The Google AdWords Keyword Planner displays the frequency of requests for related search terms and estimates the advertising competition for a term.

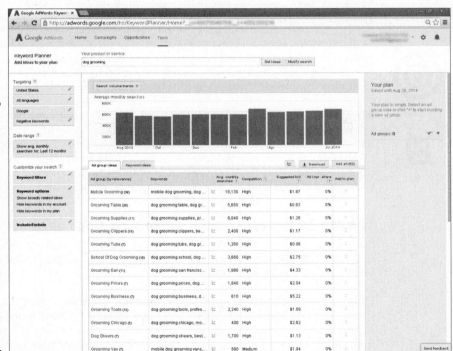

✦ Not sure who your competitors are? Enter one of your search terms to identify similar companies appearing on the first page of search results. Then you can go look at their other keywords, too.

✦ Look at the tag clouds for topics on social news services or blog search engines such as www.icerocket.com or www.blogsearchengine.org to assess the relative popularity of different search terms. *Tag clouds* visualize how often keywords appear in specific content or how often they're used by searchers, with the most popular terms usually appearing in larger type. (You can find more on tag clouds in the section "Understanding tags and tag clouds," later in this chapter.)

✦ Avoid using single words except in technical fields where the word is a term specific to a particular industry, such as *seismometer* or *angiogram,* with only hundreds of thousands, instead of millions, of competing pages. Not only will you have too much competition on generalized single words, but results for single words also produce too wide a range of options. People simply give up.

Crafting a page, blog post, or social media profile for more than four or five search terms is difficult. Break up your list of terms into sets that you think you can work into a single paragraph of text while still making sense.

Optimizing for search terms that real people rarely use doesn't make sense. Sure, you can be number one because you have no competition, but why bother? You will show up on these words anyway. The exceptions are your company and product names and terms highly specific to your business.

Always test your selected search terms to be sure that sites like yours show up in the results for that term. For instance, entering *artificial trees* as a search term yields inexpensive artificial Christmas trees, especially at the holiday season, and perhaps some silk palm trees. However, that term doesn't produce appropriate results if your company offers $30,000 tree sculptures designed for shopping malls, zoos, or museums.

Where to place search terms on your site

Sprinkle your keywords throughout the content that visitors will see. Although Google searches the entire page, it's a good idea to include search terms in the first paragraph of a page.

Opinions vary, but some experts recommend generally constraining your use to three to five search terms per page, aiming for a keyword density of 2 to 6 percent. The longer your content, the more search terms you can include on a page. Just be careful that the language remains readable!

Naturally, your home page should include your most important search terms and your brand names; you may want to include as many as eight terms. As you drill down in the navigation, the nature of the search terms may change. For instance, give your *category pages* (additional pages in the top navigation), which have general overview information, two to four general, short phrases.

Detailed pages that describe your products or services generally appear at secondary or tertiary levels in your navigation. Keep the search terms on these pages focused on one topic per page, and optimize for one to three brand names or longer search terms related to your topic.

You generally don't get much mileage from search terms on boilerplate pages such as your Privacy Policy, Terms of Service, or Contact Us unless you modify the content to include relevant information.

Book II
Chapter 2

Leveraging Search
Engine Optimization
(SEO) for Social
Media

Understanding tags and tag clouds

We want to dispense with one major source of confusion. *Tags* are the social media equivalent of search terms (several keywords together, such as *New Mexico artists*). Tags are commonly used on blogs, social media, and content-heavy sites other than search engines to categorize content and help users find material.

Tag clouds are simply a way to visualize either how often keywords appear in specific content or how often they are used by searchers.

Keywords in a tag cloud are often arranged alphabetically or with common terms grouped and displayed as a paragraph. The more frequently used terms (minus common elements such as articles and prepositions) appear in the largest font, as shown in Figure 2-3.

Tag clouds can help you quickly grasp the popularity of particular topics, the terms that people most often use to find a topic, or the relative size or frequency of something, such as city population or usage of different browser versions.

When you submit your site to social bookmarking or social news services (as we describe in Chapter 3 of this minibook), you're often asked to enter a list of helpful tags so that other people can search for your content. The first rule is to use tags that match your primary search terms and ensure that those terms appear within your text.

You can quickly generate a tag cloud for content by using a tool such as TagCrowd (`http://tagcrowd.com`) or Wordle (`www.wordle.net`). Simply paste in text from your website or enter the URL for your site and click to create a tag cloud. You can then enter the most frequently appearing words as the tags when you submit content to a social media service.

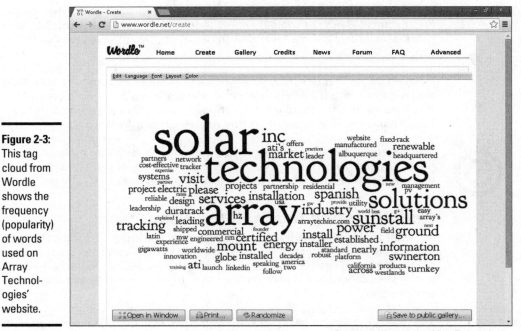

Figure 2-3:
This tag cloud from Wordle shows the frequency (popularity) of words used on Array Technologies' website.

Some social media services display tag clouds created on a running basis to identify trending topics. Use these tag clouds on social media to help determine the popularity of various topics while you decide which content to post. You can also modify the tags you use to categorize your postings. Include or default to commonly used tags when you make your submission to increase the likelihood that your posting shows up in search results.

Maximizing Metatag Muscle

Search engines use the title and description metatags to help rank the relevance of a website, blog, or social media page to a search query. Historically, engines needed many types of *metadata* (data that describes a web page overall) to categorize a website, but now search engines need only the title and description metatags for that purpose. Search engines can automatically detect the rest of the information they need, and too many metatags just slow them down.

The keywords metatag, while used more by human beings than by search engines, may be penalized by Yahoo!/Bing if the search terms don't also appear in the body copy for the page.

Title and page description tags have become even more important with the advent of social media. Facebook and some other platforms will pull content from these tags when a URL is shared.

Don't confuse the term *metatags,* which refers to specific entries that appear in page source code, with the term *tags,* the label used to refer to assigned keywords in social media.

To view metatags for any website, choose View➪Source in Internet Explorer; look for a similar command in other browsers. (You can also right-click a web page and choose View Source from the pop-up menu that appears.) A display appears, like the one shown in Figure 2-4, which shows the primary metatags for Array Technologies (`www.arraytechinc.com`).

Note that the detail boxes shown in Figure 2-4 (bottom) are optimized with the same search terms that appear in the keyword tag. Note also the page title above the browser toolbar, which also includes three of the search terms. We talk more about this metatag in the section "Tipping the scales with the page title metatag," later in this chapter.

If you see no metatags in the page source for your own site, you may be in trouble. That could partially account for poor results in search engines.

You can usually insert metatags and `<alt>` tags for photos quite easily if you use a content management system (CMS) to maintain your website or if you use blog software. If you don't, you may need to ask your programmer or web developer for assistance.

Tipping the scales with the page title metatag

Perhaps the most important metatag, the page title appears above the browser toolbar when users are on a website. (Refer to Figure 2-4, bottom, to see where the title tag's output appears on the screen.) A good page title metatag includes one or more keywords followed by your company name. Select one or more search terms from the set of keywords you've assigned to that particular page.

Because browsers may truncate the title display, place the search term first. Although you can use a longer title tag, we suggest an average length for the title tag of seven to ten words and fewer than 70 characters. Some search engines may truncate title tags that are more than 55 characters long anyway. A long, long time ago, way back in the dinosaur age of the Internet, page names were used to index a website. That method is now unnecessary; it's an absolute waste of time to use a phrase such as *home page* rather than a search term in a page title. It's almost as big a waste of time as having

Book II
Chapter 2

Leveraging Search
Engine Optimization
(SEO) for Social
Media

```
1  <!DOCTYPE html>
2  <html lang="en">
3  <head>
4  <meta http-equiv="X-UA-Compatible" content="IE=edge" />
5  <meta content="text/html; charset=utf-8" />
6
7
8
9  <title>Commercial Solar Systems | Lowest Levelized Cost of Electricity | PV Trackers: Array Technologies. Inc.
   </title>
10 <!--begin wp_head-->
11
12 <!-- BEGIN Metadata added by Add-Meta-Tags WordPress plugin -->
13 <meta name="description" content="Enjoy the lowest levelized cost of electricity through our flexible solar mounting systems. Our easy-
   to-install PV trackers are ideal for commercial solar system projects of any size. Become part of the clean energy movement. Contact us
   today!" />
14 <meta name="keywords" content="commercial solar systems, solar mounting system, pv trackers, levelized cost of electricity" />
15 <!-- END Metadata added by Add-Meta-Tags WordPress plugin -->
16
17 <link rel='stylesheet' id='colorbox-theme2-css'  href='http://arraytechinc.com/wp-content/plugins/jquery-lightbox-for-native-
   galleries/colorbox/theme2/colorbox.css?ver=1.3.14' type='text/css' media='screen' />
18 <link rel='stylesheet' id='wp-pagenavi-css'  href='http://arraytechinc.com/wp-content/plugins/wp-pagenavi/pagenavi-css.css?ver=2.70'
   type='text/css' media='all' />
19 <script type='text/javascript' src='http://ajax.googleapis.com/ajax/libs/jquery/1.8.3/jquery.min.js?ver=3.9.2'></script>
20 <script type='text/javascript' src='http://arraytechinc.com/wp-content/plugins/jquery-lightbox-for-native-
   galleries/colorbox/jquery.colorbox-min.js?ver=1.3.14'></script>
21 <link rel='prev' title='Product Related Services' href='http://arraytechinc.com/utility/utility-services/' />
22 <link rel='next' title='Utility/Commercial Project Map' href='http://arraytechinc.com/about-array-technologies/utility-commercial-map/'
   />
23 <link rel='canonical' href='http://arraytechinc.com/commercial/' />
24 <link rel='shortlink' href='http://arraytechinc.com/?p=679' />
25 <link rel="Shortcut Icon" type="image/x-icon" href="http://arraytechinc.com/favicon.ico" />
26 <!-- jQuery Lightbox For Native Galleries v3.2.2 | http://www.viper007bond.com/wordpress-plugins/jquery-lightbox-for-native-galleries/ --
27 <script type="text/javascript">
28 // <![CDATA[
29      jQuery(document).ready(function($){
30          $(".gallery").each(function(index, obj){
31              var galleryid = Math.floor(Math.random()*10000);
32              $(obj).find("a").colorbox({rel:galleryid, maxWidth:"95%", maxHeight:"95%"});
33          });
34          $("a.lightbox").colorbox({maxWidth:"95%", maxHeight:"95%"});
35          $(".videobox").colorbox({iframe:true, innerWidth:690, innerHeight:388});
36      });
37 // ]]>
38 </script>
```

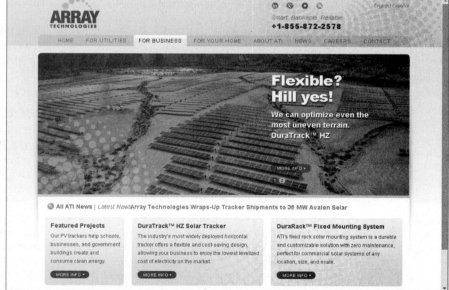

Figure 2-4:
The page source for the home page of Array Technologies (top). Their home page is at the bottom.

no `<title>` tag. The `<title>` tag (*Commercial Solar Systems | Lowest Levelized Cost of Electricity | PV Trackers: Array Technologies. Inc.*) that appears in Figure 2-4 (top) is a good example.

Because longer, more descriptive title tags may work better for social sharing, don't obsess about length. It's always better to write a title tag that gets clicks!

Google and other search engines dislike multiple pages with identical metatags. Changing the `<title>` tag on each page is one of the easiest ways to handle this preference. Simply pull another relevant search term from your list of keywords and insert it in front of the company name in the `<title>` tag.

Pumping up page description metatags

The page description metatag appears as several sentences below the link to each site in natural search results. It's important to write an appealing page description because you may want to repeat this tag in all your social media profiles.

Some search engines truncate description metatags after as few as 115 characters. Historically, description metatags used to be 150 to 160 characters. Just in case, front-load the description with all the search terms from the set you've assigned to that page. Search engines display the first line of text when a page description metatag isn't available.

Why pass up a marketing opportunity? Just because your site appears near the top of search results, you have no guarantee that someone will click through to your site. Write your page description metatag as though it were ad copy, including a benefits statement and a call to action.

Figure 2-5 displays natural search results on Google with the page description for a category page of Array Technologies, Inc. Note the inclusion of search terms (for example, *PV trackers, commercial solar system*) from the keywords metatag in Figure 2-4 (top), the benefits statement *(easy-to-install)*, and the calls to action *(Become part of the energy movement. Contact us today)*.

Book II
Chapter 2

Leveraging Search
Engine Optimization
(SEO) for Social
Media

Page description

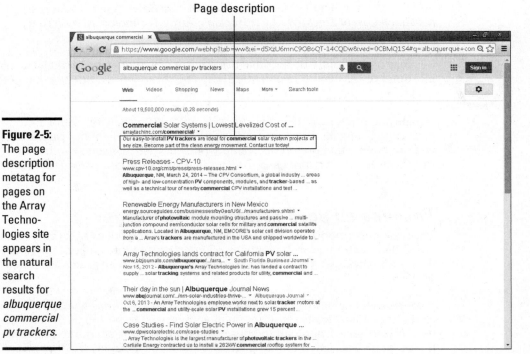

Figure 2-5:
The page description metatag for pages on the Array Technologies site appears in the natural search results for *albuquerque commercial pv trackers.*

Optimizing Your Site and Content for Search Engines

Optimization is the process of adjusting your site, blog, or social media profiles to play well with search algorithms. You optimize primarily by having plenty of relevant content, updating it often, and making sure that your web presence is easy for general and on-site search engines to discover with their spiders. I cover a few of the most important tricks of the trade in the following sections. For additional information on search engines and site optimization, check out some of the resources listed in Table 2-3.

Google has such a habit of modifying its search algorithms that the changes have been called *dances*. The 2014 version, which is called the Pigeon, is supposed to enhance the relevance and accuracy of local search results on both web search and Google Maps.

Because the changes will include improvements to Google's distance and location ranking variables, they are expected to affect local search engine rankings for some businesses. Google is rolling out Pigeon first for U.S. English results.

Table 2-3	Search Engine and Optimization Resources	
Name	*URL*	*Description*

Google Webmaster	`https://support.google.com/webmasters/bin/answer.py`
	
	`https://support.google.com/webmasters/answer/35291`
		Guidelines and suggestions for site optimization and SEO information for webmasters

Search Engine Guide	`http://www.searchengineguide.com/marketing.html`	Search engine articles, blog, marketing
Search Engine Journal	`www.searchenginejournal.com/seo-101-resources-learn-with-guides-tutorials-and-more/35740`	Best practices for URLs and SEO
Search Engine Land	`http://searchengineland.com`	Search engine news
Search Engine Watch (a publication of ClickZ)	`www.searchenginewatch.com`	Articles, tutorials, forums, blogs, SEO articles, and tips
Moz	`http://moz.com`	SEO learning resource with tools and community support.
UrlTrends	`www.urltrends.com`	Suite of SEO tools and reports

**Book II
Chapter 2**

Leveraging Search
Engine Optimization
(SEO) for Social
Media

Because these changes will unfold over time, your best option is to watch your search engine results weekly and take action as needed. To stay up to date on Google's jitterbugs, waltzes, cha-chas, quick-step, and other dances, you might want to bookmark `http://searchengineland.com/library/google/google-algorithm-updates`. You can also monitor any of the sources in Table 2-3 for news.

Writing an optimized first paragraph

First and foremost, use the search terms you've assigned to each page in the first paragraph of text or the first paragraph of a blog posting. (See Figure 2-6.) Although most search engines now check the full pages of entire websites or blogs eventually, it's better to have search terms visible near the beginning of page text for faster indexing.

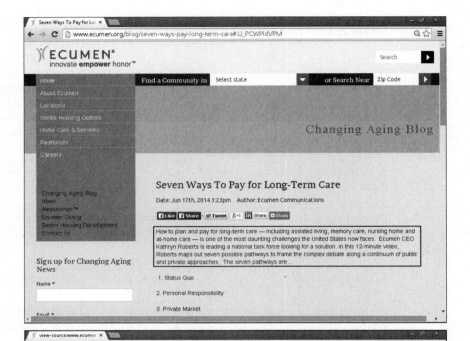

Figure 2-6:
Compare
the blog
post (top),
which uses
the keyword
phrase
*long-term
care* in its
title, page
URL, and
text to the
source code
(bottom).

There's nothing like on-site social media, such as a blog or forum, to generate keyword-rich content for search engines to munch on. Best of all, other folks are helping you feed the beast! Generally speaking, keep your copy per page to 150 to 300 words for SEO purposes.

Figure 2-6 (top) shows a well-optimized posting and its source code (bottom) from the Changing Aging blog. Ecumen, a nonprofit organization specializing in senior housing and services, owns the blog. This entry (at www.ecumen.org/blog/seven-ways-pay-long-term-care) includes the phrase *long-term care* in its URL, post title, and text. Note all the social media chiclets above the post. The source code uses the same term in the title and page description metatags, and it indicates that the Ecumen Changing Aging blog has both an XML site map and an RSS feed.

Try to arrange your navigation so every page on your site is accessible with no more than three to four clicks from any other page.

Don't try to force more than a few terms into the first paragraph. If another phrase or two fits naturally, that's fine. Trying to cram more words into your text may render it unintelligible or jargon-loaded to human readers.

No matter where the first paragraph of text appears on the page, place the text near the top of the source code. The text should appear above any tags for images, video, or Flash.

Updating often

Search engines, especially Google, love to see updated content. Regular updates are a sign that a website is loved and cared for, and easily updated content is one of many reasons for having a blog or content management system on your site. If changing content is simple and free, you're more likely to do it.

At least once a month, change a paragraph of content on your site. Include this task on your Social Media Activity Calendar. (See Book I, Chapter 4.) If you can't commit to this task, at least ask your programmer to incorporate some kind of automatically updated material, whether it's a date-and-time stamp, a quote, or an RSS feed, for example.

If you follow no other search optimization tips in this chapter, make sure that you follow at least these two: Update often and optimize the first paragraph of text on every page.

Guess what? You score extra jelly beans in the relevance jar if your search terms appear in particular places on your website, in addition to your title and page description metatags. Follow these tips to optimize your web page

Book II
Chapter 2

Leveraging Search
Engine Optimization
(SEO) for Social
Media

or blog for your selected set of search terms (however, if they don't work naturally, don't force them):

✦ **Links:** Use the words from your set of search terms as *text links* or *anchor text* (words that form an active link to another internal page or external site). Link liberally within text, but don't waste valuable real estate on meaningless phrases such as *Learn more* or *Click here.* They don't do a darn thing for your search ranking. Make sure that internal links open in the same window, while external links open in a new window so users don't lose track of your site.

If a clickable image opens another page, such as a product detail page, add a clickable caption that includes a search term or the product name. Score some points!

✦ **Headings:** Headlines and subheads help organize text and assist readers who are skimming your copy for the information they want. Headings that include your search terms can also improve your search engine ranking.

Onscreen, these words usually appear in bold and in a larger font size or different color (or both) from the body copy.

Headings must carry the `<h1>` to `<h6>` tags that define HTML headings, rather than appear as graphics. Search engines can't "read" words embedded in a picture.

✦ **Navigation:** Search terms that appear as navigational items, whether for main or secondary pages, also earn extra relevance jelly beans. Like with headings, navigation must be in text form, not in graphic form.

✦ **URLs:** Include search terms in understandable URLs for your pages. URLs not only help with search engines, but also are often used as link text elsewhere on the web — for example, when shared on social media.

✦ **Body text:** Use search terms intelligently in your content. Above all, make sure that the content makes sense to a human reader and is rich in information.

Avoid *keyword stuffing:* Don't overload a page with repetitive search terms or a long list of different terms in an effort to juice your standing on search engine results pages. Not only do words out of context ring an alarm bell for Google, they make readers very unhappy. If you stick with well-written, natural English and useful content, you'll do just fine in both human and search engine results.

✦ **Images and** `<alt>` **tags:** Not only may your images appear in image search results, they can also help with search engine results. The title, filename, caption, nearby text, and `<alt>` *tag* (the text that appears when hovering over an image on a PC) can contribute to a better ranking when they include a search term.

Sometimes you have to weigh the design considerations or limitations of your CMS or blog against search engine optimization needs. Some designers prefer the greater control and flexibility of font styles available in a graphic. Unfortunately, text in graphics is not readable by search engines. Ultimately, only you can decide what matters more to you.

Under no circumstances should you implement *black hat* techniques, which are scams promoted as the search engine equivalent of a get-rich-quick scheme. For instance, don't even think about hiding search terms in the same color as the background, installing magic pixels, or any other shifty tricks. These techniques might get you blacklisted from search engines.

Making your site search engine friendly

In addition to trying the techniques in the preceding section, which apply at the page level, you can take specific actions to make your site, as a whole, friendly to search engines.

Avoiding elements that search engines hate

If you expect a search engine to rank your site or blog favorably, you have to give it something to work with. Computers may be getting smarter all the time, but they can't yet "read" pictures, videos, or soundtracks, let alone minds. They need to be fed a rich diet of words. The list of search engine "detestable content" is short, but they can all be avoided without harming your message:

✦ **Graphics without descriptions:** As much as artists and photographers love pages without words, search engines hate them. Simple solutions can make your pictures search engine friendly: Provide an `<alt>` tag and/or caption; have text appear below the fold (as long as the text appears near the top of the code); or include a descriptive paragraph near the image. For an extra boost, include keywords in the filenames for photos.

✦ **Flash animations:** Whether developers provide Flash animation because it's lucrative or because their clients demand it, not all search engines can index Flash content. (Not to mention that Macs and mobile phones detest it.) Although Google can "read" Flash files, your best bet is to incorporate Flash much as you would incorporate a video — as an element on a page, not as an entire page.

✦ **Frames:** This old-fashioned (anything ten years old on the Internet is practically an antique) way of controlling the appearance of pages lets you modify content within a box. Unfortunately, search engines can't always see everything inside a frame or iFrame. Even Google can't guarantee that it will be able to associate content properly with the

Book II
Chapter 2

Leveraging Search
Engine Optimization
(SEO) for Social
Media

correct page URL. Many alternatives now exist, from tables to Cascading Style Sheets (CSS). If your developer insists on using frames, find a new developer.

✦ **Substantially duplicate content at different URLs:** The content may not be malicious; maybe it's just printer-only versions of your website. Be sure to delete old versions of pages that have been replaced. Even if they sit in archives, search engines may try to index these pages and reduce your page rank for duplicate information. Send your programmer to `https://support.google.com/webmasters/answer/66359` for direction about how to handle this situation. On the other hand, if Google thinks the duplication is deliberate, your site may be penalized or removed from the index.

✦ **Splash pages:** This misguided attempt to design a website as though it were a book with a cover may do real harm to site traffic. Generally, a site loses half its audience every time a click is required. Why cut your prospect list in half before you even have a chance to explain your benefits? Splash pages often consist of beautiful images or animations that make a statement about a company but carry no content or navigation. If you use rich media on a splash page, make sure to include a regular HTML link to a text-based page for search purposes.

   Often found on sites of companies specializing in entertainment, web development, architecture, arts and crafts, or graphic design, splash pages usually offer viewers an option to skip the introduction and an arrow cuing them to click to enter the "real" site. The simpler solution is to not include a splash page on your site.

If you insist on having a splash or entry page, at least don't annoy your visitors. Direct the navigational link for Home to the main page of real content, not to the splash page. With a bit of clever naming, you may be able to get search engine spiders to crawl over the first page of content and ignore the splash page.

Configuring URLs

The best URLs are readable and might include one of your search terms or a descriptive title: `www.yourdomain.com/social-media-small-businesses`. Using a search term from your set of keywords for your web or blog page earns you another point for relevance and lets users know what to expect. At least try to keep the URLs as readable text, as in `www.yourdomain.com/pages/socialmedia/article1234.htm`.

If the content in this entire section makes your eyes glaze over, just hand this chapter to your developer!

Problems with page URLs tend to occur when they're automatically assigned by a content management system (CMS) or when the pages are created dynamically. Those URLs tend to look like gobbledygook: www.*yourdomain*.com/shop/AS-djfa-16734-QETR. Although search engines can review these URLs, these addresses do nothing for your search engine ranking and aren't helpful to users.

You can improve your URL configuration several other ways:

✦ Use hyphens to separate words instead of using underscores, spaces, or plus signs.

✦ Keep your URLs as short as possible. Make your URL easier to copy and paste by minimizing the number of words and trailing slashes.

✦ Don't use database-generated URLs or pages created on the fly (called dynamic URLs) that include multiple non-alphanumeric characters: www.*yourdomain*.com/cgi-bin/shop.pl?shop=view_category=ASDFJ%20&subcategory=XYZ%6734. Search engines are less fussy than they used to be, but many still have problems indexing URLs that have more than four non-alphanumeric characters. Some still have problems with only three such characters.

Be careful when redesigning a blog or website, especially if you're changing developers or platforms. If the existing site is already doing well in search engines, try to preserve its URLs. Not all transitions to a new platform accommodate this strategy. Ask your programmer before you begin.

A badly configured URL may simply not be indexed. This problem can become significant with product databases on e-commerce sites, especially when you want every individual product detail page to appear in search engines. Note that this doesn't apply to tracking ID numbers appended following a ? to identify the source of a link. (For more on tracking URLs see Book IX, Chapter 1.)

Fortunately, a technical fix exists. You (or your programmer) can implement the Apache Mod_Rewrite module or ISAPI Rewrite for Microsoft, which convert URLs on the fly to a format that's search engine friendly. Have your programmer review www.digitalocean.com/community/tutorials/how-to-set-up-mod_rewrite or www.helicontech.com/isapi_rewrite, respectively, for more information.

**Book II
Chapter 2**

Leveraging Search
Engine Optimization
(SEO) for Social
Media

Indexing a site

You can easily create a virtual path to ensure that search engines crawl your entire site. A virtual path of links is especially important in two cases:

✦ When the top and left navigational elements are graphics, making it impossible for search engines to know which pages are really on the site

✦ When you have a large, deep, database-driven site without links to all pages easily available in the navigation

For a small site that has graphical navigation, you have a couple of simple fixes. You can create a parallel series of linkable main pages in the footer of your site or create a navigational bread-crumb trail at the top of the page, as shown in Figure 2-7. Either way can help both search engines and human beings know where they are within your site structure.

Bread crumb trail

Figure 2-7: Bread-crumb trails help both search-engine robots and real people navigate your site.

Reproduced with permission of Amritt Ventures, Inc.

A *bread-crumb trail* (think Hansel and Gretel) helps users track where they are on a complex website. It typically consists of a series of page links that extend horizontally across each page, just above the content. Bread-crumb trails, which may either display the site structure or the actual navigation path a user has followed, usually look something like this:

```
Home page > Main section page > Internal page > Detail page
```

Put these links in a Server Side Include (SSI) within the footer to ensure that links are displayed consistently on all pages. You then make future changes in only one place (other than in the site itself, of course).

For a site that has a significant number of pages, especially on several tiers, the best solution is to include a linkable site map or site index, shown in Figure 2-8. It looks a lot like a junior high school outline, which is a perfectly fine solution for both search engine friendliness and site usability.

Book II
Chapter 2

Leveraging Search
Engine Optimization
(SEO) for Social
Media

Figure 2-8:
Page links on a site index provide easy access to all pages on the site.

Reproduced with permission of The Fat Finch

Another solution exists for very large database-driven sites and large stores. Sitemap (XML) feeds that connect directly to Google or Yahoo!/Bing provide current content to all your pages. Direct your programmer to www. xml-sitemaps.com, https://help.yahoo.com/kb/yahoo-merchant-solutions/enable-sitemap-sln19495.html, www.bing.com/webmaster/help/bing-xml-sitemap-plugin-f50bebf5, or www.google.com/support/webmasters/bin/topic.py?topic=8476 for more information. If content on your site doesn't change very often, you can update these feeds manually every month. If you have continually changing inventory and other content, have your programmer upload these feeds automatically, at least once a day, using RSS.

If you want to index your site to see what pages you have, try one of these free tools:

✦ **Bing Webmaster Tools:** Use the Index Explore tool within the Reports & Data section to view how Bing sees your site (accessible in the top navigation after you log in).

✦ **Google Index Status page:** This tool provides stats about which URLs Google has indexed for your site over the past year. To get to this tool, sign in to Google Webmaster Tools at `www.google.com/webmasters/tools`.

✦ **Xenu's Link Sleuth:** Download and run this link-verification program (at `http://home.snafu.de/tilman/xenulink.html`). In the results, click the link labeled Site Map of Valid HTML Pages with a Title.

Minimizing download time

Google now includes download time in its methods for ranking websites in search results. Companies continue to post pages that take too long to download, testing viewers' patience and occasionally overwhelming mobile networks. Try to keep sites to less than 300KB to 500KB per page, especially now that 20 percent of website visits are from smartphones.

High-resolution photos are usually the main culprits when a page is too large. It isn't the number of photos, but rather the total size of files on a page that counts. A couple of tips can help reduce the size of your page:

✦ When saving photos to use online, choose the Save for Web option, found in most graphics programs. Stick to JPEG or GIF files, which work well online, and avoid larger, slower-to-load TIFF and BMP files, which are intended for print.

✦ Post a thumbnail with a click-to-view action for the larger version in a pop-up window. Be sure to save the larger image for the web. (Refer to the first bullet.)

Check the download size and time for your home page for free at sites such as `www.websiteoptimization.com/services/analyze`, or check out `www.compuware.com/en_us/application-performance-management/performance-test-center.html`, which tests both mobile and web download times. Call your developer if changes are needed.

Optimizing for local search campaigns

Local search has obvious value for brick-and-mortar retail businesses using the web and social media to drive traffic to their stores. However, it's just as valuable for local service businesses such as plumbers, or even for non-local businesses seeking online customers from a particular region.

Local optimization is needed for your site to appear near the top of results in spite of geolocation devices on smartphones (not always turned on), geographic tagging of images on Flickr and other photo-sharing sites, or the localization settings on Google results.

Chances are good that your business is not the only one of a particular type in your city or neighborhood. Localization is absolutely critical for restaurants, tourism, hospitality, and entertainment businesses.

**Book II
Chapter 2**

Leveraging Search
Engine Optimization
(SEO) for Social
Media

The concepts used for local optimization on websites apply equally well to social media:

✦ **Optimize search terms by city, region, neighborhood, or even zip code.** Rather than use a locality as a separate keyword, use it in a search term phrase with your product or service.

✦ **Include location in any pay-per-click ads.** This is equally true whether your ads appear on a search engine, Facebook, or other social media.

✦ **Post your business on search maps such as Yahoo! Local, Google My Business, Bing Places for Business Portal, and MapQuest on Yext.com (which is a paid site).** Consider using one or more of your social media pages as site link extensions (additional links that appear following your page description in search engine results). Appearing on search maps is absolutely critical for mobile search, as discussed in the following section.

✦ **Take advantage of local business directories, events calendars, and review sites to spread the word about your company and its social media pages.** In some cases, you might want to use one of your social media pages instead of your primary website as the destination link. Most directories are also excellent sources of high-value inbound links.

✦ **Use specialized local social media with a geographic component.** These options include social channels such as Foursquare, Meetup, or Everplaces. You can find more on these social media services in Book VIII, Chapter 3.

Optimizing for mobile search

The rapid adoption of smartphones and tablets is stunning: Nielsen estimates that 70 percent of all U.S. adults owned smartphones as of August 2014. Other usage statistics provide all the more reason to optimize for mobile search. Here are some percentages for how smartphone users actually use their phones:

+ Ninety-four percent search for local information via their phone.

+ Seventy-seven percent research products via their phone.

+ Forty-six percent made a purchase via their phone.

Combined with rapid technological advancements in location-based and integrated real-time search, this trend in smartphone adoption pushes business owners to ensure that their sites appear just as high in mobile search results and on mobile social media as they do on desktop computers. But not so fast. Alas, the process of optimizing for mobile search is not quite the same as for desktop search.

Users see even fewer results on mobile search than they do on a larger screen. With all that competition, you need to take every possible step to improve your rankings in results, including the local optimization techniques mentioned in the preceding section.

Here are a few techniques to incorporate:

+ **Mobile site ranking is much more susceptible to technical performance characteristics than desktop site ranking.** According to Search Engine Academy (`http://blog.searchengineacademy.com/blog/seo/ 7-mobile-seo-tips-for-2014-and-beyond`), your mobile site needs to be friendly for mobile search browsers based on such characteristics as usability, download speed, and screen rendering. Broken links or poor navigation will reduce your rank in results. If you render a large site in responsive design, it might look fine but take so long to download that no one will wait.

Your goal is to have a mobile site that downloads in less than one second!

+ **Your mobile site must work on all brands of smartphones.** It should use standard HTML coding. Better yet, incorporate next-generation languages such as HTML5 to enhance the performance of your mobile site, leading to higher rankings.

+ **Apply SEO optimization and localization techniques from earlier in this chapter to your mobile site.** Use appropriate keywords in headlines and text. It's critical to use geographically-targeted terms such as state, zip code, town, or neighborhood. That may be the only content scanned to produce mobile search results. Location and timeliness matter much more than search terms for mobile users.

+ **Aim at the top of the funnel with your mobile home page.** Try to reach many new prospects with keyword-focused content that explains who you are and the benefits of what you offer. On secondary pages, include content that adds value to the sale process, such as product specs, ratings, schedules, business hours, and prices. Also, include frequently updated offers, entertainments, and competitions that help build the business relationship.

✦ **Take advantage of the unique features of mobile devices.** Provide your visitors with click-to-call, mobile coupons, store locators, barcode scanners or QR codes, easy ways to share and recommend your business, and new mobile payment tools.

✦ **Incorporate outbound links to relevant sources and other elements of your social media presence.** Mobile users consume social media constantly, especially Facebook, Instagram, and Twitter. If your prospects are using mobile media, you might want to pay particular attention to incorporating and optimizing these channels in your social media strategic plan.

✦ **Include links to your mobile site in e-newsletters and social media.** More than 20 percent of email marketing is read from smartphones, and mobile users can share links quickly with their friends.

Search behavior on mobile sites is somewhat different from search behavior on a desktop in the home or office. Mobile searchers are highly focused on the task at hand and want results — often local ones — quickly. They may not have the time or patience to search beyond the first two or three results.

Well-optimized mobile sites can increase traffic, enhance brand loyalty, and improve revenue. It's worth the investment of your time. For more on mobile social media, see Book VIII, Chapter 5.

Book II
Chapter 2

Leveraging Search
Engine Optimization
(SEO) for Social
Media

Building Effective Inbound Links

An *inbound link* from another site to your website, blog, or social media page acts as a recommendation. Its presence implicitly suggests that visitors to the original site might find useful content on yours. Testimonial links are particularly important for social media, where they are measured in rating stars, number of views, retweets, Likes, and favorites. These recommendations enhance credibility and build traffic because they encourage other viewers to visit your original post.

Conversely, an *external link* goes from your page to someone else's, providing the same referral function. All these links form a web of connections in cyberspace. A site may require a *reciprocal link* back to its site before it will post one to yours.

It sounds simple. However, identifying places that will link to yours and getting them to post the link can be quite time-consuming.

Why bother? Although all search engines track the number of sites that link to yours, Google (and only Google) uses the number and quality of these inbound links to determine your position on search engine results pages. In essence, Google runs the world's largest popularity contest, putting to shame every high school's search for a prom king and queen.

Sometimes companies link to `http://yourdomain.com` and sometimes to `http://www.yourdomain.com`. Search engines consider them separate pages and may not give full credit for your inbound links. Do a permanent 301 redirect from one to the other. (Google likes www domains better.) Alternatively, you can accomplish this task from Google Webmaster Central, but it applies to only Google. Similarly, use Webmaster Central to make your site more secure with HTTPS secure protocols instead of standard HTTP or SSL conventions. Google is so committed to user security that it has started using HTTPS as a signal worth a few extra points in search engine ranking.

Google PageRank

A popularity contest is truly an apt metaphor for PageRank because not all inbound links are equal in the eyes of Google. Links from `.edu` and `.org` domains carry extra credit, as do links you receive from other sites that Google ranks as having good content and good traffic. Think of them as votes from the in crowd.

Google factors hundreds of variables including link quantity, link quality, keyword use, content, social metrics, site traffic, and brand visibility into its proprietary PageRank algorithm. For a graph showing how some of these variables are weighted, visit `http://dc8hdnsmzapvm.cloudfront.net/rand/wp-content/uploads/2013/08/rank-factors-pie-2013.gif`.

The algorithm ranks pages on an earthquake-style scale from 0 to 10. (Google search and *The New York Times* both have a page rank of 9.) Empirically speaking, a Google PageRank (PR) of 5 is usually enough to place your site on the first page of search results — with no guarantees, of course. Because PageRank adjustments are made only a few times each year, the visible PR may be slightly out of date. TechRanger suggests these interpretations of PageRank:

✦ **PR0 or ?:** Pages that haven't been ranked or have been penalized.

✦ **PR1:** Pages that Google has indexed and checked for correctness.

✦ **PR2:** A site is interesting and has potential.

✦ **PR3:** A page is a good informational resource, such as many news or business pages.

✦ **PR4:** Pages that are starting to break out from the pack as a noted authority.

✦ **PR5:** Pages more likely to appear near the top of search results once they reach this score.

✦ **PR6, 7, or 8:** Pages of clear and proven authority

✦ **PR9 or 10:** Only the *crème de la crème* (Google, YouTube, Twitter, and so on).

If you're serious about SEO, install the Google PageRank tool on your browser so that you can quickly check the PageRank of your site or blog, and that of your competitors. The PageRank display is built into Google's Chrome browser, or you can download it for Internet Explorer at `www.google.com/toolbar/ie/index.html`. (The Google toolbar may not work with all versions of all browsers; it is not supported on Firefox.)

Book II
Chapter 2

Leveraging Search
Engine Optimization
(SEO) for Social
Media

To install PageRank on your Google toolbar, follow these steps:

1. **On most browsers, choose View⇨Toolbars⇨Google Toolbar, and if that option is not already checked, do so.**

   The Google toolbar should now be visible.

2. **If the PageRank tool isn't visible on the Google toolbar, you must enable it. From the Tools tab on most browsers, select the Page Rank check box and click Save.**

3. **If you're using Chrome, click the three-bar icon at the far right instead of following Step 2.**

4. **From the drop-down list that appears, choose Settings. On the next page, select Extensions from the left navigation.**

5. **If PageRank appears in the list, click the check box to enable it.**

   If PageRank doesn't appear, click the Get More Extensions link, which appears below the list, and search for PageRank Status. Alternatively, you can navigate directly to `https://chrome.google.com/webstore/category/extensions` to search. Select an extension to enable from the list.

   You now see the PageRank tool on the Google toolbar. (See Figure 2-9 to see the Google PageRank tool in action).

6. **To see the page rank for a website, enter its domain name into the address box on your browser and wait for the page to load.**

7. **Hover your mouse pointer on the PageRank tool until the pop-up box that displays page rank results appears in the toolbar.**

   For more information, see `https://support.google.com/toolbar/answer/79837`.

To check page rank for multiple competitors' sites or potential inbound links at the same time, try the free tool at `http://multipagerank.com`.

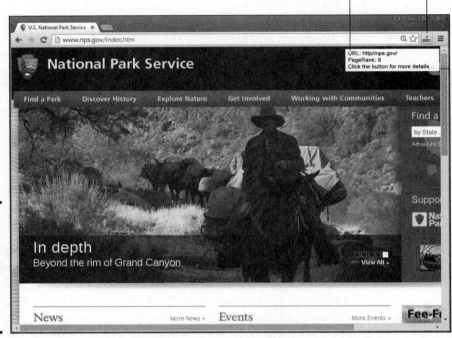

Page Rank icon

Additional Page Rank information

Figure 2-9:
The
National
Park
Service has
a Google
page rank
of 8.

Knowing what makes a good inbound link

In a nutshell, good inbound links (sometimes called *backlinks*) come from sites that have these characteristics:

✦ **Relevance:** The quickest way to determine relevance is to see whether the other site shares a search term or tag with your site. Use Google's search function to check, or view the source code on their pages.

✦ **A decent amount of traffic:** Check www.alexa.com or www.quantcast.com to estimate traffic on other sites.

✦ **Your target market:** Whether or not a link helps with PageRank, links from other appropriate sites help with branding and deliver qualified traffic to your site.

✦ **A good Google PageRank:** Look for a score of PR5 or higher in the PageRank tool. Higher-ranking sites, which often have high traffic volume and good content value, are considered more credible references; they pass along *link juice* (share page ranking) from their site to yours.

Lists of inbound links differ on different search engines. Because Google counts only sites with a high PageRank, the list on Google is always the shortest.

TIP

To see your own or others' inbound links on a particular engine, enter `link:http://yourdomainname.com` (where `yourdomainname.com` is replaced by your own domain name) in the search box for Google. For Yahoo!/Bing, you can check inbound links from their Webmaster tools at `www.bing.com/webmaster/help/using-the-inbound-links-tool-a75f3640`.

Hunting for inbound links

No matter how hard you try, it's difficult to find good sites from which you can request an inbound link to your own website or blog. Try link-checking tools such as the Link Popularity Checker (`webmaster-toolkit.com/link-popularity-checker.shtml`) or Majestic (`https://majestic.com`, shown in Figure 2-10), as well as the tools listed in Table 2-4.

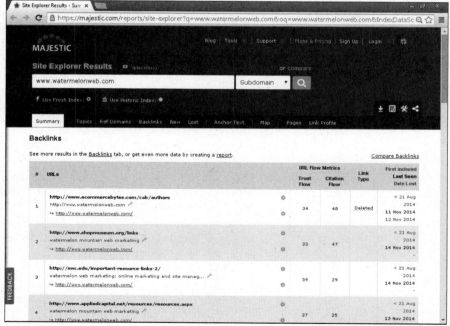

Figure 2-10: For each site it indexes, Majestic displays a list of backlinks.

Reproduced with permission of Majestic 12 LTD

Table 2-4   **Free Inbound Link Resources**

Name	URL	Description
Alexa	www.alexa.com	Link checker, related links, clickstream, and more; free version includes a site overview with global and U.S. ranks, demographics, audience, location, search traffic, top key-words, inbound links, and related links.
ClickZ	www.clickz.com/search?per_page=20&date=this_year&query=linking	Articles on link campaigns.
LinkPopularity	http://link popularity.com	Link checker for Google, Bing, and Yahoo!
Majestic	https://majestic.com	Check backlinks and history on other sites in bulk.
MultiPageRank Checker	http://multipage rank.com	Check Google PageRank and Alexa for multiple websites simultaneously.
Quantcast	www.quantcast.com	Audience Also Likes function.
Search Engine Colossus	www.searchengine colossus.com	Directory of international search engines.
Search Engine Guide	www.search engineguide.com/searchengines.html	Meta-index of topical search engines.
Search Engine Journal	www.search enginejournal.com/use-social-media-link-buiding-tool/80331	Article on how to receive backlinks from social media.
WhoLinks2Me	www.wholinks2me.com/	Backlink analysis.
Yext	www.yext.com	Check which directories link to your website.

You can hunt for potential links with a few tried-and-true techniques. Try looking at

✦ Inbound links to other sites that rank highly in Google on your search terms.

Be sure that your company truly has something in common with the other site. Shared terms may not be enough — there's a big difference between companies that run a fish restaurant and those that sell lead-free weights for catching fish.

✦ Inbound links to your competitors' sites.

✦ If data are available, the Alexa sections What Sites Are Related To and/or Upstream Sites for your competitors' websites.

✦ The resource lists of outbound links found on competitors' sites or other highly-ranked sites.

✦ Industry-based business directories.

✦ Yellow Pages and map sites.

✦ Local business directories.

✦ Blog-specific directories.

✦ Trade associations and other organizations you belong to or sponsor.

✦ Inbound links to suppliers' websites, including your web development and hosting company.

✦ Inbound links to sites owned by distributors, clients, customers, or affiliates.

✦ The implementation of cross-links with all your social media sites (even though some of these don't help with PageRank).

✦ Blogs you recommend in your blogroll from which you could request a link back.

✦ Inbound links to related, but not directly competing, businesses that your target audience might also visit.

Book II
Chapter 2

Leveraging Search Engine Optimization (SEO) for Social Media

Prequalify every potential link. Visit every link site to ensure that it accepts links, is truly relevant, has a Google PageRank of 5 or higher, and represents the quality and audience you want.

Stay away from *link farms* (sites that exist only to sell links), *web rings* (a closed loop of companies that agree to link to each other), and *gray-market link sites* (sites that sell links at exorbitant prices and guarantee a certain result). Your site can be exiled from search engines for using them. Besides, they don't raise your PageRank!

Implementing your link campaign

You need to email requests for a link to each of the potential sites you identify. Try for at least 50 links and hope that 30 of them come through. There's no upper limit — the more, the better.

✦ You might want to create a spreadsheet to track your link requests. Create columns for these elements:

✦ Domain name

✦ Appearance URL

✦ Submission URL or email address

✦ Submission date

✦ URL of the landing page you asked others to link to

✦ Reciprocal link requirement

✦ Date you checked to see whether a link was posted

Don't be afraid to group spreadsheet rows by target market. For instance, if you sell products for toddlers, you might have a group of links for sites used by single parents and another group for sites used by day-care centers.

Break this task into bite-size pieces so that it doesn't become overwhelming. On your Social Media Activity Calendar (found in Book I, Chapter 4), limit the search-and-submission task to only five to ten links per week.

After you qualify prospective links and add them to your spreadsheet, follow the directions on each site to submit your URL or email your request to the site owner.

Getting inbound links from social sharing, social bookmarks, and social news services

Leverage your social marketing activities to increase the number of inbound links to your site. If it's permissible, post your site to some of the social sharing, bookmarking, shopping, and news services described in Book II, Chapter 1 and Chapter 3. (Not all social bookmarks allow you to submit your own site, so you may need to ask a friend to help.) You're generally required to include either your domain name or a specific page URL with your submission.

These links encourage both inbound links and traffic. Some of these sites pass link juice, especially if you have multiple links from social news sites back to different news stories or content on your main site. For more information, see Chapter 3 of this minibook.

Not all link shorteners are equal. Choose ones that will pass link juice with a 301 redirect. The Bitly, Ow.ly, goo.gl, and cli.gs shorteners are safe bets. Of course, surround your links with relevant keywords. Just like with inbound-link campaigns for search engines, don't link everything from social bookmarking, news, or shopping services to your home page. For example, multiple product recommendations on social shopping sites should link to the appropriate product detail pages in your store.

Cross-link by submitting especially good blog entries to several social news services or by linking from one product recommendation to another on social shopping sites or from one review site to another.

Reaping other links from social media

Another easy way to build inbound links is by distributing *(syndicating)* content, as described in Chapter 1 of this minibook. By repurposing content on multiple social media sites, you not only increase your audience, but also increase the number of inbound links.

Taking advantage of the many places to post links on social media pages not only drives traffic to multiple elements of your web presence, but also improves your search engine rankings in the process.

Somewhere on your website or blog — at least on the About Us or Contact page — display a list of links to all your profiles on social media services, along with buttons for ShareThis and Google's +1. This form of passive link-building can pay off big-time with improved ranking in search results.

The more places these links appear, the better. You can also repeat text links to your social media pages in your linkable footer.

Don't be shy! Include calls to action to share your web page in the body copy of ads or e-newsletters. These links don't always have to hide their charms in the header or footer.

Here are a few other ideas for laying down a link:

✦ Every profile on a social network has a place to enter at least your web address and blog address, if you have one. If possible, link to both. The links in profiles usually provide link juice, although the ones in status updates usually don't.

✦ Include your web address when you make comments on other people's blogs, post reviews on recommendation sites, or submit someone else's news story. You may have to work it into the content. Use at least *your companyemailaddress@yourdomain*.com for branding reasons!

**Book II
Chapter 2**

Leveraging Search
Engine Optimization
(SEO) for Social
Media

✦ Include your company name for branding and your web address for linking when you post to groups on any social networking site, as long as it's appropriate, relevant, and not too self-promotional.

Read the Terms of Service on each site to be sure that you comply with requirements for use of email addresses, submissions, and links.

✦ Post events on LinkedIn, Myspace, Facebook, and elsewhere with a link to your site for more information.

✦ Include a share button, described in Chapter 3 of this minibook, to encourage additional distribution. People who receive content they like often pass it along or link to it from their own pages or blogs.

✦ Be sure to post cross-links on newsletters and on all your social media profiles to all your other web pages, including to your primary site and your blog.

Now that social media are included in ordinary search results, using search terms consistently can help you occupy more than one slot in search engine results pages. You can see an example in Figure 2-11.

Creating a resource page for outbound links

One item to include when optimizing your site for search engines is a Link Resources page — by that name or any other — for external or outbound links.

You need this page in order to post reciprocal links to other sites, but also to help viewers find useful, neutral information on .edu, .gov, and .org domains. Nestling reciprocal links within an annotated list of informational sites makes reciprocal links less noticeable and less self-serving. Good ideas about places for neutral links to appear are described in this list:

✦ Sites with information about materials used in your products or how to care for them

✦ Educational sites discussing the services you provide, such as *feng shui* for offices, the benefits of massage, or tips on tax deductions

✦ Sites for trade associations and other business organizations to which you belong

✦ Local, state, and federal government sites whose regulations or procedures may affect your business or customers

✦ Nonprofit sites that share your values; for example, sites talking about recycling electronics or supporting entrepreneurs in developing countries

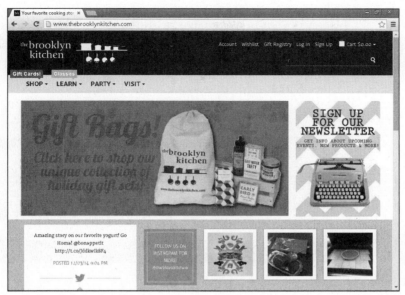

Book II
Chapter 2

Leveraging Search
Engine Optimization
(SEO) for Social
Media

Twitter listing   Yelp listing

Google+ listing

Figure 2-11:
The
Brooklyn
Kitchen
(top)
earns high
placement
in Bing
search
results
(bottom)
with
postings
from Yelp
reviews,
its Twitter
feed, and
its Google+
page.

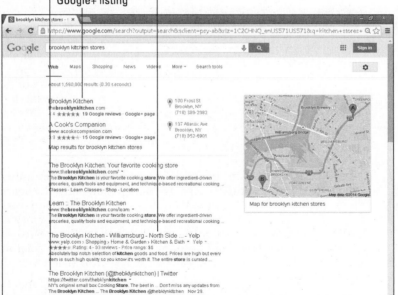

✦ Sites that talk about the history of your business or industry, or the local history of your brick-and-mortar storefront

✦ Other sites that may interest visitors to your site; for example, a hotel site that links to a local dining guide or events calendar

✦ HomeinSantaFeNM, for example, links to helpful sites at `http://homesinsantafenm.com/resources` (see Figure 2-12).

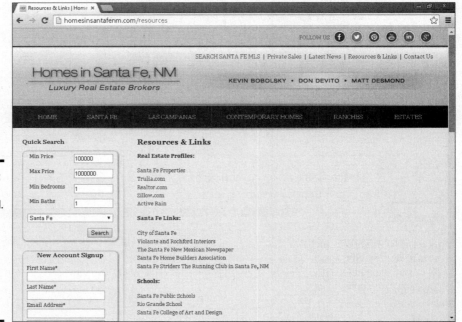

Figure 2-12: Homesin SantaFeNM. com offers visitors helpful external links to related sites.

A good starting place for neutral outbound links is to see inbound links for a high-ranked competitor. Enter its domain name into the search field on Alexa; then scroll down to the What Sites Link To" section to see the total number of inbound links to that domain, and the top identity of the top five inbound links. Scroll down farther to the section "What Sites Are Related To" to see ten related links, and perhaps more importantly, a list of Categories with Related Sites, which you can use as a search string to find other potential links.

Risking the personalized search

From a marketer's perspective, all bets are off with personalized search on Google. Google now defaults to a customized list of search results based on an individual's past searches, location, and the results she clicked. In theory, these search results, derived either from a cookie or web search history, are continuously refined to become more relevant to users' needs.

Google claims that with searches determined by location, visitors may be more likely to find new businesses in their area to support. Supposedly, the user's search history will remind her of links she has clicked previously, and those links will continually rank higher and higher in search results (because they aren't competing with the full pool of all relevant companies). In Google's mind, this process allows for repeat messaging, better branding, and increased customer loyalty for local business owners.

In practice, that relevance is debatable; users tend to see results that are more of the same, distorting the reality of what's out there and reducing the likelihood of receiving new information.

You must take a distinct action to turn off personalized search by clicking the gear icon in the upper-right corner of any Google search results page and selecting History. On the next screen, click the No Thanks button next to the Turn Web History On option. To turn it off, which is even more complicated, click the Pause button on your Account History page at `www.google.com/settings/accounthistory/search`.

Most users don't even know that personalized search exists, let alone how to turn it off or how to delete repeatedly occurring, undesirable sites from results to make room for new ones. (The latter option requires logging into your Google account to personalize settings for your Web History.) For more information, see `https://support.google.com/websearch/answer/54068`.

Unfortunately, the algorithm for personalized search tends to produce results reflecting a philosophy of "Them that has, gets." Your website may have more difficulty breaking through to new prospects or achieving a presence on the first page of some individuals' search results. Sadly, you can do nothing about it. Whether users who see your site are more qualified as prospects and more likely to buy remains to be seen.

Book II
Chapter 2

Leveraging Search
Engine Optimization
(SEO) for Social
Media

Optimizing Social Media for Search Engines

Here's the good news: Everything we cover earlier in this chapter about using SEO for your website or blog applies to other social media, too. Whew! You still have to implement the techniques, but you can save time by reusing search terms, metatags, inbound links, and optimized text.

Every search engine has its own rules. You may need to tweak your terms for not only general search engines, but also internal search engines on specific social media services.

Placing your search terms on social media

Start by reviewing your research for keywords and phrases. Decide on a primary set of four to six terms that best describe your company. Because your search terms must still relate to your content, you may want to reuse other sets for individual posts from your SEO research, mix them up, or include additional terms not optimized on your primary site.

You can place these terms in many locations:

✦ **Tags:** *Tags,* which are the social media equivalents of keywords, are assigned to specific content. Because many social media services place a limit on the number of tags that can be assigned to a given piece of content, pick a few from your primary set of search terms and select others (for example, brands, products, market, or competition) from your secondary list or elsewhere that are specific to your content.

If you're pulling tags out of thin air, remember to confirm which synonyms are most popular with the users of that service. For example, do people search for *Barack* or *Obama* or *president*? Use a keyword-selection tool for websites listed earlier in this chapter (refer to Table 2-2) or check a tag cloud (discussed in the section "Understanding tags and tag clouds," earlier in this chapter), if it exists, on the service you're using for the latest trends in tag usage.

✦ **Profiles:** Just about every form of social media asks you to establish an account. Most profiles ask for a brief description of your company and location, as well as the URLs for your website and blog. Work your primary set of keywords and brands into your profile and any other place you can comfortably integrate them, including featured products, department names, the marketing tagline, and staff bios.

Occasionally, a service requests only your email address. Of course, you use the one with your domain name in it.

If you haven't already set up email to forward from *you@yourdomain.com* to whatever email address you have from your ISP, do so now. Most hosting packages include at least five free email addresses. Email from *@yourdomain.com* not only makes you look more professional, but also adds to brand value.

✦ **Page content, status updates, and comments:** Obviously, you should include search terms in the first paragraph of text for each blog post. They don't need to be part of your primary set of terms, so you have some creative flexibility. Incorporate search terms in updates and comments, too, to increase the likelihood of being found in on-site search results.

✦ **Metatags, titles, and headlines:** Use search terms from your list in the title of your blog or page name; in the title of your post; in `<alt>` tags, captions, or descriptions for images; and within metatags. Each service handles these elements a little differently, as we discuss in the later sections on individual services.

If you use an automated service such as Hootsuite to update everything at one time, you may pay a bit of a penalty because Google considers automated, scheduled posts to be anonymous and doesn't index them. In addition, long, duplicate posts might set off warning bells. (There's no other evidence that search engines are penalizing third-party interfaces.) You should be okay if you combine scheduled posts through a service with personalized, spontaneous posts at other times. Facebook, and perhaps other social media platforms, may also see automated posts as spam; one study by HubSpot showed that Hootsuite posts got fewer Likes and clicks than manually posted ones, but that might have to do with the quality of the posts, not just the source. Only you can weigh the pros and cons based on your available time, staffing levels, and campaign objectives.

**Book II
Chapter 2**

Leveraging Search
Engine Optimization
(SEO) for Social
Media

Optimizing blogs

Because blogs (discussed in Book III, Chapter 2) are basically websites in a different format, the same principles of site optimization and configuration apply, including the need for inbound links and cross-promotion on social media services. Hard-learned lessons and best practices truly pay off because search engines crawl frequently updated blogs at least daily.

Integrate your domain name with your blog URL (*http://yourblog. yourdomain.com*) or buy a separate, related domain name (*http:// yourcompanyblog.com*), even if a third-party server hosts your blogs. For SEO purposes, you must own your own blog domain name. A blog at *www. mycompanyblog.blogspot.com* or *www.typepad.com/mycompanyblog* isn't acceptable.

Blogs are primo link bait. The casual sharing of relevant, text-based links within posts, the use of *blogrolls* (bloggers' linkable recommendations of other blogs), and related thematic material attract inbound links like black jackets attract white cat fur. With all that link juice, plus rapidly updated content, many blogs quickly zoom to Page One in search engine results.

Review all requests for inclusion on your blogroll or reciprocal link offers. Make sure that the requesting site is relevant, has a decent page rank, and is one that you feel good about recommending.

Different blog platforms operate somewhat differently, leading to some confusion on the part of bloggers trying to optimize sites for search engines.

Whatever your platform, the same methods you follow for websites still apply, with a multitude of additions:

✦ Include keywords from your primary list in your blog name, such as `http://yourcompany.com/social_media_blog`. The blog name should appear with an HTML `<h1>` tag on only the front page. On other pages of your blog, the heading level can be as low as `<h3>`.

✦ Include keywords in individual titles for each post. Use these keywords in the `<title>` tag in the source code for that entry, as well as in the page URL. Put those titles at the HTML `<h1>` level.

✦ Include primary keywords in the first sentence of content, which becomes the page description metatag by default, unless you write one manually. Use your secondary keywords in the body of your post.

✦ Fill out the tag box with your keywords, but do so judiciously. You don't need to bloat your blog tags with synonyms or terms you don't need to rank on.

✦ Incorporate search terms in anchor text for links on your blog.

✦ Use `<alt>` tags, captions, and descriptions with search terms for any images or media you upload to your blog.

✦ Post rich, appealing content with search terms regularly and often.

✦ Make sure the search engine spiders can crawl your blog easily by including a side navigation column on all pages and by offering access to archives and previous posts from all pages of your blog.

✦ Include a linkable bread-crumb trail that includes keywords without reaching the point of overstuffing.

✦ Provide internal text links to your own related posts, especially to relevant ones that are already ranking well.

✦ Submit your blog to blog directories and RSS submission sites. Two excellent lists are at `http://web-marketing.masternewmedia.org/rsstop55-best-blog-directory-and-rss-submission-sites` and `www.toprankblog.com/rss-blog-directories`.

✦ Use your blogroll as a resource — just having a blogroll isn't enough. Contact other bloggers to request a backlink or offer a reciprocal appearance on your blogroll in exchange for a backlink. Just be careful that you don't inadvertently create a link farm. For more on blogroll links, see `www.britmums.com/2014/07/blogs-sidebar-blogroll-yet`.

✦ Get backlinks to your blog with *trackbacks* (an automated way of notifying other bloggers that you've referenced their blog) or by posting comments on other blogs. Not all blogging hosts support trackbacks.

- ✦ Create an XML site map and submit it to search engines, just as you would for your website.

- ✦ Use *permalinks* (permanent links) to maintain blog URLs permanently.

- ✦ Use analytics tools to monitor traffic and user behavior.

If you need quick suggestions for good blog keywords, install the Wordtracker Keywords Tool (it offers a free seven-day trial) at `www.wordtracker.com/find-the-best-keywords`. It sits next to your blog editor on the screen so that you can consider tag suggestions while you write. Alternately, return to Google's free AdWords Keyword Planner, as described in the section "Choosing the right search terms," earlier in this chapter.

If you're an experienced blog writer, your posts are probably already written with one designated search term in mind. Review your top 10 to 15 most-viewed posts, make a list of the keywords you used for them, and use that list as input into the AdWords Keyword Planner.

Long blog pages with a lot of responses, including those from spammers, may end up with too many outbound links. Ask your programmer to place an HTML `nofollow` attribute in the code just before links from comments to discourage people from leaving fake comments that include links to their own sites in hopes of increasing their own search rankings.

**Book II
Chapter 2**

Leveraging Search
Engine Optimization
(SEO) for Social
Media

Optimizing WordPress

Although plug-ins for WordPress templates can be set to automatically generate title and page description metatags, you may want to tweak the automated SEO results for important posts. Auto-generation is fine for mundane posts or when you're short on time. For more information on selecting plug-ins, see Book III, Chapter 2.

For more flexibility and additional optimization features, try the Yoast plug-in at `http://wordpress.org/plugins/wordpress-seo` or the All in One SEO Pack at `http://wordpress.org/extend/plugins/all-in-one-seo-pack`.

Make your WordPress life easier by searching the list of WordPress plug-ins for items you need at `http://wordpress.org/plugins`. Compare plug-ins carefully — they're not all alike.

Here are a few things you can do to optimize your WordPress blog posts:

- ✦ **Swap elements of the blog post title.** Reverse the WordPress plug-in default arrangement by putting the post title first, which contains keywords, followed by the name of your blog.

✦ **Use a consistent format for keyword-rich page titles on all pages.** You can set up the format once in your template and apply it everywhere by using the Yoast or All in One SEO Pack plug-ins.

✦ **Insert a longer title description, with more search terms, into the image title field.** WordPress automatically uses the title you give an image as its `<alt>` tag. Unless you insert a longer title description with more search terms into the Image Title field, WordPress uses the filename as the image title.

When you write a post and add tags, WordPress automatically adds your tags to its global tag system. The global system determines the WordPress list of hot topics in real time. Users can click any word in the real-time tag cloud to view the most recent posts for that tag.

WordPress, like other blogs, often duplicates content by showing the same posts on archive, author, category, index, and tag pages. To remove duplicate content, which can have a negative effect on SEO, create a `robots.txt` file. See `www.problogger.net/archives/2013/08/14/how-to-stop-your-wordpress-blog-getting-penalized-for-duplicate-content`.

Optimizing Blogger

Contrary to myth, Google doesn't necessarily give preference to blogs hosted on its own service, Blogger. However, Blogger poses some unique advantages and challenges:

✦ Blogger templates place `<h1>` through `<h6>` tags into the source code through the What You See Is What You Get (WYSIWYG) interface, thereby helping with SEO. You can easily adjust page titles and blog names for the correct heading level in page templates.

✦ Blogger lacks theme-related categories, which makes it a little more difficult for you and for theme-based SEO. To overcome that problem, create permalinks that include your categories or directory names. We discuss permalinks in the following section.

✦ Because Blogger doesn't provide a related-links feature, create that list of related text links within or at the bottom of each post. These links should lead to your other postings on the same topic. Or take advantage of unlimited sidebar space to create a separate section for related links above your blogroll.

✦ Use labels on Blogger to categorize your posts. On the page where you're writing a post, click the Settings tab in the right column. Select Labels from the drop-down menu. In the box that appears, enter the terms you want to use, separated by commas, and click Done. For future posts, just click Labels in the drop-down menu. All the terms in the box appear below your post when it's published.

✦ Blogger defaults to weekly archiving, but the time-frames for archiving are malleable. Adjust the time-frame based on your volume of posts and comments to maintain good keyword density. If you post only weekly, it might make more sense to archive monthly. For an extremely active blog, you might want to archive daily.

✦ Creating text links is easy, so use your keywords in links whenever possible.

Assigning permalinks

Because most blogs are created on dynamic, database-driven platforms, their posts don't have fixed web addresses. Links to individual posts disappear after the posting is archived and no longer available on a page. Obviously, that's bad news for inbound links and SEO.

Permalinks (short for *permanent links*) solve that problem by assigning a specific web address to each post. Then individual posts can be bookmarked or linked to from elsewhere, forever.

Most blog software programs, such as WordPress and Blogger, already offer this as an option; you just have to use it. If your blog doesn't offer it, you can generate permalinks at www.generateit.net/mod-rewrite, although you may need help from your programmer to install them. Try to avoid links that look like this: www.*yourblog*.com/?p=123. Instead, choose an option to use one or more keywords, such as www.*yourblog*.com/contests/summer-travel-sweepstakes.

If you prefer to customize your permalinks, use the Permalink option in the Post Settings box. On the page where you're writing a post, click the Settings tab in the right column. Select Permalink from the drop-down menu that appears. Then you can create a URL that's different from your title, which you might want for search term reasons.

To generate WordPress permalinks, open the Settings option in the Admin panel, which appears in the left navigation. From there, select Permalinks from the second tier navigation and choose either the Common Structure option or the Custom Permalinks option to enter your own structure. (For example, you might want to insert a category.) For new blogs, that's it; for existing blogs, you may need to use the Redirection plug-in, as well. For more information, see http://codex.wordpress.org/Using_Permalinks. For directions about creating permalinks on Blogger, visit https://support.google.com/blogger/answer/2523525.

**Book II
Chapter 2**

Leveraging Search Engine Optimization (SEO) for Social Media

Optimizing images, video, and podcasts

Because search engines can't directly parse the contents of multimedia, you must take advantage of all opportunities to use your relevant search terms in every metatag, descriptive field, or `<alt>` tag. You can find more about podcasts and video in Book III, Chapter 3.

Make these fields as keyword- and content-rich as you can. In these elements, you can often use existing keyword research, metatags from your website or blog, or optimized text that you've already created:

✦ **Title and `<title>` metatag for your content:** This catchy name should include a search term.

✦ **Filenames:** Using names such as `image1234.jpg` or `podcast1.mp3` doesn't help with SEO; names such as `PlushBrownTeddyBear.jpg` or `tabbycats-sing-jingle-bells.mp3` are much more helpful. Use terms also in category or directory names.

✦ **Tags:** Use relevant keywords, just as you would with other social media.

✦ **`<alt>` tags:** Use these tags for a short description with a search term; for example, *Used cat tree for sale.*

✦ **Long description metatags:** Follow this example: `longdesc=for sale-gently used, gray, carpeted 6 foot cat tree with 4 platforms.`

✦ **Content:** Surround multimedia elements with keyword-rich, descriptive content.

✦ **Transcriptions:** Transcribe and post a short excerpt from a keyword-loaded portion of your video or podcast.

✦ **Anchor text:** Use keywords in the text link that opens your multimedia file.

✦ **Large images:** Upload large versions, as well as the thumbnails that are visible on your blog or website.

✦ **RSS and XML:** Expand your reach with media RSS and site maps.

For more information on indexing multimedia, see `https://support.google.com/webmasters/answer/114016`.

Even though search engines can't read watermarks, you may want to mark both videos and large images with your domain name and logo to encourage visits and for branding purposes, and to discourage unauthorized copying.

Optimizing Twitter

In addition to adhering to the standard admonishments about providing good content and using well-researched keywords, you can follow a few extra guidelines to improve your ranking in search results on both internal Twitter searches and on external searches:

✦ **Your name on Twitter acts like a `<title>` tag.** If you want to benefit from branding and to rank on your own or your company name, you have to use it! If you haven't already done this, log in to your Twitter account and click the Settings link. Then change your name.

✦ **Your username, or Twitter *handle*, should relate to your brand, company name, or campaign and be easy to remember.** It can include a keyword or topic area. Change it in the Settings area.

✦ **Pack your one-line bio with keywords.** Your Twitter bio serves as the page description metatag and is limited to 160 characters. Use résumé-style language and include some of your primary search terms. Talk about yourself or your company in the third person.

From the drop-down list at the top-right of the page (under your profile icon), select View Profile. After you click on the Edit Profile button, you can edit your profile photo, header graphic, name, business description, location, website URL, and theme color. Remember to click the Save Changes button when you finish.

✦ **On your Profile page, use your business address as your location.** Doing so helps with local searches. Remember to save your changes.

✦ **Brand your Twitter cover (header) image.** Use your standard business logo, logotype, or a photo showing one of your products or services, resized to the current cover dimensions of 1500-x-500 pixels.

✦ **Include keywords and hashtags in your tweets and retweets whenever possible so you have more to offer search engines than a time stamp.** With the 140-character limit, Twitter might be a good place to use those single-word terms. Use keywords in your Twitter #hashtags, too.

✦ **Remember the importance of the initial 42 characters of a tweet.** They serve as the `<title>` tag for that post. Your account name will be part of that count. Search engines will index the full tweet, however, and Twitter will include the entire post in the title tag if users click on an individual post.

✦ **Format your retweets.** Keep them under 120 characters so there's room for someone to add his or her retweet information at the front. When you retweet, avoid sending duplicate content by changing the message a bit. Use the Retweet button to paste the content into a new Tweet box. Add the letters RT and the @*username* of the original author. You can insert your comment at the beginning of the message if you want. Finally, click Tweet to post the retweet.

**Book II
Chapter 2**

Leveraging Search
Engine Optimization
(SEO) for Social
Media

✦ **Maximize retweets as a measure of popularity.** Write interesting content or share good articles, especially when the direct link to detailed content goes to your own site.

✦ **Increase your visibility.** When linking to your Twitter profile from other sites, use your name or company name rather than your Twitter handle as the anchor text for the link. (The @ in a Twitter handle, for example, @watermelonweb, isn't handled well by search engines.) If you happen to have a tweet with great keywords and hashtags, you can pin your tweet to the top of your timeline.

Because Twitter adds a nofollow attribute to links placed by users, linking to your site doesn't help with PageRank. Truncated URLs (such as the TinyURLs described in Chapter 1 of this minibook) behave just like their longer-version cousins because they're permanent redirects.

However, links from Twitter still boost branding and drive traffic to your site. More traffic to your site improves your ranking at Alexa (www.alexa.com), which in turn improves one of the quality factors Google uses for setting PageRank. It's all one giant loop. For more information on Twitter, see Book IV.

Optimizing Facebook

Take advantage of myriad opportunities to gain traffic from your Facebook pages by applying optimization techniques. Next to blogs, Facebook pages offer the highest number of opportunities to use SEO on social media to reach people who don't already know you. Fortunately, Facebook search engines can index all shared content on Facebook.

Every social network has different rules for its account names and profiles. Though consistency is preferable for branding purposes, follow the rules carefully. When you first create a Facebook Page for your business, as described in Book V, try these techniques:

✦ Use an easy-to-remember version of your business name alone or combined with a search term as your business's Facebook Page name. If possible, use the same username on both Twitter and Facebook for branding reasons. Facebook doesn't like generic names.

✦ Under Websites on the About page, list all your relevant domain names, including your website, your blog, and other social media pages. Later, you can also place links to your website or blog or another type of social media within your posts. Generally, it's easier to use the actual URL than to implement anchor text.

✦ Place keyword-loaded content in the first paragraph of each of the remaining boxes, which may vary depending on the type of page you elected to create. Include your contact information in the Company Overview box; address information also helps with local searches. Your page description metatag may work well in the Short Description box because it's already optimized for search terms. Be sure to include all your brand names and all the products or services that you offer in the Products box.

✦ More search-term opportunities abound if you use iFrame-based solutions (customizable sections for your Facebook pages) to create HTML boxes or Facebook Page apps from third-party developers. These additional iFrame boxes or apps can display text, images, and more links. Be sure to use a good search term in your box app's tab name (which is limited to ten characters) and include text links in your content. It's a bit of a pain, but you can do this on your own.

If you're a page administrator, you can use the apps at `www.hyperarts.com/social-media/tabpress-facebook-app.html` or `https://apps.facebook.com/static_html_plus`, or find a list at `www.facebook.com/search/results.php?q=static html&init=quick&tas=0.6347709277179092`. For more information about one of the most popular iFrame apps, see `www.wildfireapp.com`.

For more information on creating a Facebook account and business Pages, see Book V.

Optimizing Google+

Not surprisingly, the rules for optimizing Google+ track well with the principles for optimizing websites for Google. To maximize your search engine visibility on Google+, SEO Hacker recommends the following:

✦ Include one of your essential keywords and company name in the title of your Google+ page, just as you would for a `<title>` tag.

✦ Claim your custom, branded URL. You need more than ten followers, a profile photo, and a page that's at least 30 days old. Go to `https://support.google.com/business/answer/6068603` for directions.

✦ Copy the page description metatag for your website into the Meta Description field on your Google+ page. You already optimized that tag for several of your important keywords.

✦ Because the Introduction section is the body of your Google+ page, you can use the same keyword-optimized content that appears as the first paragraph on your home page or on other essential pages of your site.

✦ Use search terms in the descriptive filenames for the five main photos that appear on your Google+ page.

✦ In the Recommended Links section, first link your website home page to your Google+ page; that link allows your Google+ page to appear in the right section of search results (the Knowledge Panel). Then add links to and from your blog, all your other social media pages, as well as any other web pages to which you want to drive traffic (for example, to your online store).

✦ Like with your main website, update your Google+ page every two to seven days to indicate activity. When appropriate for marketing reasons, linking to your Google+ page can help boost your search rankings. It's just another example of Google's self-love!

  • As we discuss in Book VIII, Chapter 2, publish to your Google+ page what you're already publishing to other social channels.

  • Get Your Story straight. You might want to re-use the About section from your website. Your Story should include your marketing tagline, an introduction to your business, what sets you apart, and of course, some search terms.

  • Optimize the first 45 to 50 characters of your posts — they become the post's page title in Google search results; in other words, include one of your prized search terms.

✦ Even on social media, pictures are worth 1,000 words, maybe more. Include a lot of photos, videos, graphics, or GIF animations.

✦ Be sure that you and any other blog authors sign up for Google+ Authorship so that everyone's posts will be indexed. It helps your authors build their own personal credibility and following, as well. For more details about optimizing Google+, see www.slideshare.net/ HubSpot/8-tips-for-optimizing-your-google-page-posts-to-boost-seo. For more general information on creating a Google+ page, see Book VIII, Chapter 2.

Optimizing Pinterest

✦ With its visual content, Pinterest is perhaps the most challenging social media to optimize for search engines. Start by creating a business account or converting your personal one at www.pinterest.com/ business/create, as described in Book VII. Then take advantage of several tried-and-true techniques to give your Pinterest site some search oomph:

✦ Verify your website by clicking the Verify Website button next to the Website Text field. Follow the directions in the pop-up window so that your site will show up on profile and search results. For more details, see www.pinterest.com/settings.

Book II
Chapter 2

Leveraging Search
Engine Optimization
(SEO) for Social
Media

✦ Optimize your user and/or Business Profile name to include your company name and a search term describing what you sell or what business category you're in (unless you're a well-known brand). For instance, instead of listing only *Pretty Puppy*, use *Pretty Puppy Play Clothes for Puppies*.

✦ Use your four most important search terms and your page description metatag in the About You section of your company profile (under Settings).

✦ Optimize for local search by including your city, state, and zip code in the Location field of the profile. Of course, include the URL for your website and or blog in the Website field.

✦ Choose Settings⇨Business Account Basics and set the Visibility option to Off in your Profile; you *don't* want to hide your Pinterest profile from search engines. Choose Settings⇨Social Networks and be sure to select the cross-link options to Twitter, Facebook, and Google+. Also, upload your logo graphic under Settings⇨Profile.

✦ Use a descriptive filename that includes a keyword for each of the images you pin from your website or blog. The source link for each image will go back to your website or blog to increase your inbound links and drive traffic to specific pages. If you have optimized images on Flickr or other photo-sharing sites, you can use your Flickr URL as the image source for a pin.

At the moment, Pinterest passes link juice only for an image description. Unfortunately, Pinterest has added the `nofollow` attribute to the originating URL for pinned images themselves, thus diminishing the value of those links as repins.

✦ Include keywords in the title *and* description for each board and pin, whether the boards are employee headshots, photos of your company at tradeshows, or images also used on your blog. For local optimization, include your city. You might want to structure boards by customer type, product, service, or brand name to maximize the search terms you use.

✦ If you create data charts or infographics, be sure to include keywords in the title for your charts or graphics. (Try the infographics tool at `http://piktochart.com`, which offers a limited free account).

✦ Remember to add the linkable Pinterest icon and link to your suite of social media buttons on your website, blogs, and other social media pages.

For more ideas, visit `http://blog.piqora.com/5-ways-to-increase-your-traffic-with-pinterest-seo-that-you-can-implement-immediately`.

Use only images you own or have permission to use on Pinterest. You're liable for any copyright infringement. Respect the use of any credit lines required by Creative Commons or the owner of the image.

Like with other social media, Pinterest is a back-scratching site — you like me, and I'll like you. To increase traffic to your Pinterest posts (and eventually to your website), follow other Pinterest users and boards related to your company, repin relevant images, and click their Like buttons.

For more information on creating and using Pinterest for marketing purposes, see Book VII.

Optimizing LinkedIn

LinkedIn (discussed in Book VI) doesn't offer quite as many options for SEO as other forms of social media do. Start by including search terms within your profile text, in the descriptions of any LinkedIn groups you start, and within postings to a group. Just keep it gentle and unobtrusive. Follow these steps to optimize your profile and to pass along some SEO credibility:

✦ Use your name or company name in your LinkedIn URL (for example, www. linkedin.com/in/*yourcompanyname*). Because search engines look at keywords in URLs, this technique makes your company easier to find.

✦ Use content similar to your page description metatag within the first paragraph of your LinkedIn profile. It should already contain some of your primary search terms.

✦ Like links from Twitter, links from LinkedIn to other sites don't carry link juice. You can have as many as three links on your profile. Set one to your website and another to your blog. Use keyword-based link text on a third link to drive traffic to another page on your site or to another of your social media pages. Nothing says that all links have to lead to different domains.

For more optimization ideas, see www.linkedin.com/today/post/ article/20140320151331-142790335-11-seo-tips-for-your-personal-linkedin-profile or www.socialmediaexaminer.com/make-linkedin-company-page-useful.

Gaining Visibility in Real-Time Search

Needless to say, all the emphasis on social media has forced search algorithms to adjust accordingly. Search engines vary in how they handle social media services within natural search results. Google and Yahoo! note your social media presence but don't include individual tweets or posts in results because they're private. You may find that you need to resort to specialized search sites like www.socialsearch.com (shown in Figure 2-13) to see near real-time search results for Twitter, Instagram, and YouTube.

Bing offers two ways to see social content. First, it displays the results of topical posts from influencers and public figures in regular search results without users needing to connect to their social media accounts. However, if users connect Bing Social to Facebook on www.bing.com/explore/social, they'll see posts from their friends related to the search topic they've entered, such as their opinions on a movie or a recommendation for a Mexican restaurant.

Dedicated real-time search engines are available for different services, such as Facebook, Twitter, RSS feeds, and blogs. These engines, some of which are listed in Table 2-5, may also index comments and other elements found only on a particular social media service.

You can't benefit from real-time search unless you're active on Facebook, Twitter, and other services. Looking for something to say? Add your twist on the latest trends in your market sector. For ideas on current topics, use Google Trends (http://google.com/trends) or the hot-topic searches on most social media services.

Book II
Chapter 2

Leveraging Search
Engine Optimization
(SEO) for Social
Media

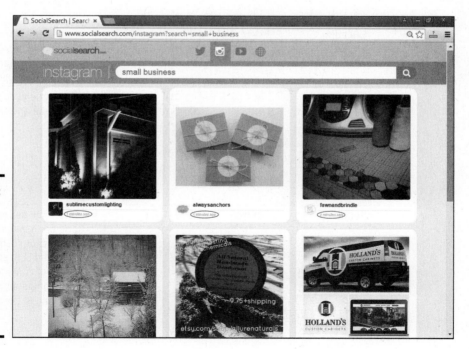

Figure 2-13:
Use tools like Social-Search.com to find real-time posts on Instagram, Twitter, or YouTube.

Table 2-5	Real-Time and Specialty Search Engines for Social Media	
Name	*URL*	*Description*
48ers	www.48ers.com	Real-time search of news and social media across the web; includes Twitter and Facebook.
Bing Social Search	www.bing.com/ explore/social	Near–real-time search includes Facebook and Twitter posts.
Facebook	www.facebook.com/ search.php	Search Facebook People, Pages, Places, Groups, Apps, Events, and Web Results.
Google Plus	https://plus. google.com	Search for people, pages, or posts on Google+.
IceRocket	www.icerocket.com	Real-time search of Twitter, Facebook, or blogs, or a combination of all three.
LinkedIn	www.linkedin.com/ search	Real-time search built-in for people, jobs, answers, groups, companies, universities, and posts.
Search Engine Land	http://search-engineland.com/ the-social-search-revolution-8-social-seo-strat-egies-to-start-using-right-now-113911	Resource article on real-time and social search.
Sency	http://sency.com	Real-time search engine that searches micro-blogs; can search selected U.S. and international cities for places and companies that are trending at the moment.

(continued)

Table 2-5 *(continued)*

Name	URL	Description
Stinky Teddy	http://stinkyteddy.com	Real-time search that allows you to choose what type of results you get (web, news, video, real-time, and images).
Topsy	http://topsy.com	Real-time search for the social web (primarily Twitter, blogs, images, video).
Twitter Search	http://search.twitter.com	Real-time Twitter search.
Yahoo!	http://search.yahoo.com	Real-time search from Yahoo! (includes Twitter, Yahoo! News, Yahoo! Shopping, several video channels, and more).

Gaining Traction on Google with Social Media

Sigh. Nothing ever stands still in the social whirl — or maybe social tornado is a better description.

Regular Google search results for the past hour may include near real-time results from Twitter, Facebook, Google+, or social media channels such as blogs and press release sites. (See Figure 2-14.) To view these, enter your search term on Google as usual. On the search results page, click the Search Tools tab⇨Any Time⇨Past Hour. If you're more concerned about time than content, switch from the default to Sorted by Date on Sorted by Relevance sub-tab that appears.

Although Google doesn't evaluate engagement on any social media platforms except Google+, it is aware of inbound links and search terms that appear in posts and profiles. Take action based on this information:

✦ **Enhance your Google+ listing with frequent posts, shares, and participation in Google+ circles.** Google+ results show up in both social search and standard, natural search. For more information on Google+, see Book VIII, Chapter 2.

✦ **Post early, post often.** Real-time search creates pressure to update frequently on social media so that you can stay near the top of the results stream. Like voting in Chicago, multiple recent posts can tip the scale. Schedule times on your Social Media Activity Calendar (found in Book I, Chapter 4) to post to your blog, add to your Facebook Timeline, or send tweets at least twice a day. Use management tools like those in Book I, Chapter 4 to make this process easier.

✦ **Share and share alike.** Post a lot of appealing, keyword-rich content on social media, and explicitly invite others to link to it. Good content on social media may draw a lot of Likes, but it's the number of links to that content that pushes up search results.

✦ **+1 +1 = 3, or maybe 30.** Put Google +1 buttons, as we describe in Book VIII, Chapter 2, anywhere and everywhere — on your social media, your website, your newsletters, your forehead. . . . Google incorporates +1 buttons but doesn't evaluate engagement (such as Likes, follows, and comments) on other social media.

✦ **Pin your hopes to Pinterest.** The Google spider now crawls pins and boards, looking for relevant keywords in descriptions. Use hashtag keywords for each pin for extra SEO-om-pa-pa.

✦ **Add Pin It and StumbleUpon buttons to your content.** For referral traffic, these two sites offer special value.

Figure 2-14:
Posts on Facebook, Twitter, and other social media are included in Google search results when you search by time.

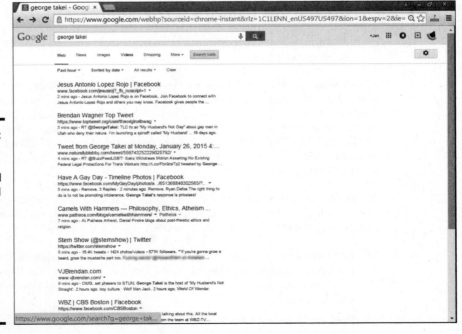

To view real-time results in Google+, enter your search term in the Search text box. When you see results, click the option for Most Recent at the top of the results list. From then on, relevant posts will appear in real-time.

Think about which messages are truly time-critical and save your real-time efforts for them. On your Social Media Activity Calendar, enter the times that you expect your target market might be searching, such as first thing in the morning or right before lunch. Make sure to ping all search engines with your updates.

Get some sleep! There's no point tweeting in the middle of the night when your customers are in bed (unless you're selling to insomniacs or international customers halfway around the world). Your tweets may be long buried by tweets from dozens — if not hundreds — of others by the time the sun rises. Better yet, schedule your tweets ahead of time with Hootsuite, Buffer, Netvibes, or other dashboard tools for specific social media channels.

**Book II
Chapter 2**

Leveraging Search
Engine Optimization
(SEO) for Social
Media

Monitoring Your Search Engine Ranking

If you're serious about SEO, you'll want to monitor how well you're doing. Table 2-6 lists some search engine ranking software that shows where your site appears on search engines by keyword or page. Most ranking software carries a charge, but some either offer a free trial or will rank a limited number of pages, keywords, or engines for free.

Table 2-6	Search Engine Ranking Services	
Name	*URL*	*Starting Price*
Rank Tracker	`www.link-assistant.com/rank-tracker`	Free download; licenses $125–$300
Search Engine Rankings	`www.mikes-marketing-tools.com/ranking-reports`	Free
SERank	`www.ragesw.com/products/search-engine-rank.html`	$49.95-$149.95; (other tools also available)
WebPosition	`http://webposition.com`	Free 30-day trial; then starts at $29/month
ZoomRank	`www.zoomrank.com`	Fee; contact representative for pricing

Kern the gnome scales the heights of social media

Described as crazy, goofy, unutterably weird, off-the-wall, and just-this-side-of-alien, the advertising campaign for the Gnome Experiment has become a famous example of how to use social media to turn the seemingly dull science of weights and measures into a participatory adventure enjoyed by millions.

In 2012, Kern & Sohn, a sixth-generation German company that manufactures extremely precise weighing scales, wanted to bring its products out of the laboratory and into consciousness of the wider world.

James Nester and Graham Jenks, a Creative Director team at OgilvyOne, London, put their noggins together and decided to send a garden gnome (seen in the nearby figure) on a round-the-world trip with a Kern & Sohn scale to see how much he weighed. Because the world is not, in fact, a perfect sphere, there are tiny variations in the pull of gravity around the earth. But it takes an extremely sensitive measuring device to detect the difference. The Gnome Experiment would enable Kern to precisely map these global fluctuations.

Reproduced with permission of J. Nester, Kern & Sohn

In the process, news reached 350 million people in 152 countries, while Kern the Gnome became a folk hero to students, teachers, scientists, geeks, and garden gnome lovers the world over. Within just two weeks of the experiment hitting the headlines, the Gnome Experiment escalated its client's Google search ranking for *precision scales* from page 12 to page 1, increased site visitors by 256 percent, lifted sales by 21 percent with a 1,042-percent ROI, and attracted more than 16,000 inbound links. (One fan even knitted the figurine a scarf for his visit to the South Pole (seen on location in the nearby figure.)

Reproduced with permission of J. Nester, Kern & Sohn

Book II
Chapter 2

Leveraging Search
Engine Optimization
(SEO) for Social
Media

The team packaged the gnome with a set of branded scales and asked a carefully selected group of scientists to weigh him as he traveled to different locations, including the Large Hadron Collider in Switzerland and SNOLAB in Ontario, Canada (the deepest laboratory in the world at almost one and a half miles below the surface).

Through websites, blogs, social and traditional media, millions learned about gravity, thousands joined the experiments, and Kern & Sohn became the world's most talked about precision scale company. The experiment was one of the only advertising campaigns to be turned into a dedicated TED talk. It was even adopted as part of the national curriculum in several countries, placing the Kern brand in front of the next generation of scientists.

Inevitably the advertising industry recognized such success — the Gnome Experiment was the most-awarded Direct Marketing campaign in the world in 2012 and the planet's most-awarded PR campaign in 2013.

So how did these guys pull it all off?" The Gnome Experiment is an inherently social idea," reflects co-creator James Nester. "It was something people wanted to talk about. So it didn't

(continued)

(continued)

rely on Twitter, Facebook . . . or any channel, actually. It was a conversation piece that tapped into genuine interests of real communities."

"In social media, *what* you say is vital," he points out. "But it's equally as important *who* says it. Tapping into the credibility and huge audiences of influencers was essential." After the gnome reached the South Pole, Ogilvy told the press, starting with a London commuter paper. After *The Metro* featured Kern the Gnome's story on its cover, publicity rolled in from the *New Scientist* magazine, *National Geographic,* the Discovery Channel, several European TV networks, and many more. "All these influencers helped spread the news much, much further than if we'd relied on our own social channels," Nester explains.

Naturally, the gnome had his very own Twitter account (see the gnome's Twitter page below), written by advertising creative director Nick Hearne. This was another big element in their success because journalists, influencers, and opinion leaders favor this platform, and it's easy for people to link from Twitter to a website.

Reproduced with permission of J. Nester, Kern & Sohn

"Search was actually an ingenious part of this idea — if we do say so ourselves," laughs Nester. "The Gnome Experiment was a highly effective link-baiting campaign that worked wonders on search performance." The Gnome Experiment website (`http://gnomeexperiment.com`) cross-linked with the Kern & Sohn website (`www.kern-sohn.com`), so the more people linked to the Gnome Experiment site, the higher up in search rankings Kern & Sohn's website shot. Because the gnome visited many Kern & Sohn resellers around the world, who were all added to the map with links to their websites, their sites rose in search results, too.

Although the Ogilvy team made sure to include relevant keywords on the Gnome Experiment site, the heavy lifting was done by the thousands of keyword-heavy articles published online by impartial, relevant, and credible sources.

Experiment co-founder Graham Jenks calls attention to the fact that they named the gnome Kern. "This was more than a nice touch; it was key. While journalists in traditional press will often cite the name of the company, you have no control in social media. As the story spreads, it's likely all references to the brand will be lost. Naming our gnome Kern helped make sure the most important keyword of all — the company name — showed up as much as possible."

With a project like this, Ogilvy had to keep track. For analytics, they used Radian6, Factiva, and Hootsuite to track the impact of the content they created and the volume of visitors. They also tracked social media results to evaluate fan engagement and how fans created their own content across every known social platform. The team actually engaged, however, only on channels for which they had developed profiles: Facebook, Twitter, Tumblr, and Flickr.

The project may not have been expensive, but it did chew up time, as social media often does. The team at Ogilvy handled the social media engagement, as well as influencer and media relations. Before news was launched to the press, Nester estimates it took about 20 hours per week to establish social channels and engage with influencers offline and online. After launch, they ramped up activities to around 35 to 40 hours per week. Some of these hours were in the middle of the night, holding live interviews with far-flung radio stations and overseas journalists.

The agency also created an online media kit for local and international media that included all travel photos of the gnome's adventures, a press release about his journey, and all the scientific information.

Nester sees no reason in theory why other small-to-medium size businesses couldn't be just as clever. The Gnome Experiment was a cost-effective project with a modest budget. "But great ideas that spread through social media while making press and TV headlines aren't easy to come by. So businesses would need to be able to spot the idea that will catch their audience's imagination – and then be set up and ready for the explosion of attention that follows," he cautions.

"The Gnome Experiment proves the power of getting it right," Nester observes. "And while social campaigns are nothing new — the best advertising has always been inherently social — we now have channels and techniques that help the best ideas travel the world. Just like Kern the Gnome did."

Web presence for Kern & Sohn and the Gnome Experiment:

(continued)

(continued)

- http://www.jenksandnester.co.uk/the-gnome-experiment
- www.ogilvypr.com/en/case-study/kern-sohn-gnome-experiment
- http://gnomeexperiment.com
- http://kernthegnome.tumblr.com
- https://twitter.com/hashtag/gnomeexperiment
- http://vimeo.com/34579945
- www.youtube.com/watch?v=_-R6k7UNcHY
- www.youtube.com/user/kernscales
- www.kern-sohn.com

SEO is a long-term strategy to deliver solid traffic over time to your hub website or blog. It takes time for your investment in SEO to pay off, and results can vary unpredictably from one week or month to the next. Generally, after you have everything set up and running smoothly, monitoring once per quarter should be enough, except for exceptionally large and constantly growing sites.

Enter your preferred SEO tools in your Social Media Marketing Plan and insert the tasks into your Social Media Activity Calendar.

Chapter 3: Using Social Bookmarks, News, and Share Buttons

In This Chapter

✔ **Differentiating between social bookmarks and social news**

✔ **Gaining marketing benefits from bookmarks**

✔ **Submitting to social bookmarking sites**

✔ **Submitting to social news sites**

✔ **Motivating people to bookmark and rate your site or content**

✔ **Using social share buttons**

Social bookmarks and social news services are essentially peer-to-peer referral networks. Each one is an expansion of the former tell-a-friend call to action. Rather than email a link to a site or some content to one or two people, users can notify many people at a time. Advocates of these recommendation services often argue that they filter the avalanche of websites that appear in standard search engines. Because social bookmarks and social news services rely on popular input from real people, rather than from algorithms, some Internet users place a greater value on these search results.

Hundreds of these services exist, which you can see on the All Services tab at www.addthis.com/services. In this chapter, we discuss the benefits of using these services, including higher search engine ranking, more traffic, and free visibility for minimal effort. We also emphasize using share buttons to encourage viral sharing of social media and website content.

Search engines recognize inbound links from many (but not all) of these services, so appearing on them can improve your search engine ranking. See Book II, Chapter 2 for more information on search engine optimization.

Bookmarking Your Way to Traffic

You most likely already know how to bookmark sites in a browser. Social bookmarking services work in much the same way, but you save bookmarks to a *public* website rather than to an individual computer. Then, users of bookmarking services can easily share links to their favorite sites, or content with friends or colleagues (or with the world) while enjoying convenient access to their own bookmarks from any browser, anywhere.

Social bookmarks act as testimonials from one amorphous group of web users to many others. Bookmarking services, such as StumbleUpon and Delicious (shown in Figure 3-1), recommend websites, blogs, videos, products, or content. At StumbleUpon, among other things, users can view bookmarks from their own list of favorites, friends' favorites, or everyone in the StumbleUpon database of submitters. Several subsets of bookmarking services are specific to certain applications (blogs only, for example) or activities (shopping only, for example).

Participating in social bookmarking is a no-brainer. Even if you do no other social media marketing, you should submit your site to several social bookmarking services, if they permit it, as part of your search engine optimization (SEO) efforts. Note that some services may not permit direct submission but will allow you to include a badge on your site to encourage your viewers to submit the site.

Users generally search for listings by *tag* (keyword), category, most recent, most popular, or individual submitter. Bookmarking services rank items by the number of people who have cited them.

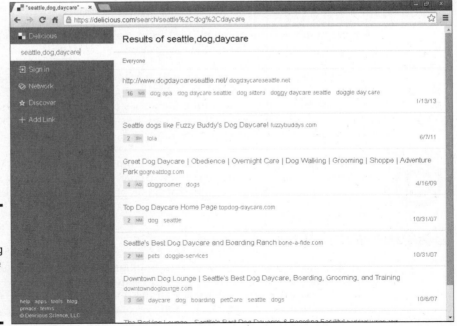

Figure 3-1:
Use bookmarking services like Delicious to recommend websites.

Table 3-1 lists some of the dozens of popular social bookmarking services and shows whether you're allowed to submit your own site. The Passes Link Juice column indicates whether search engines recognize a link from that service, as discussed in Book II, Chapter 2.

Table 3-1	Popular Social Bookmarking Services		
Name	*URL*	*Allows Self-Submission*	*Passes Link Juice*
Bing Toolbar	www.bingtoolbar.com	Yes	No
BlinkList	www.blinklist.com	No	No
Delicious	http://delicious.com	No	No
Google Bookmarks	www.google.com/bookmarks	Yes	Yes
Linkroll	www.linkroll.com	Yes	No
Mister Wong	www.mister-wong.com	No	No
Pinterest	www.pinterest.com	Yes	No for images; yes for description
StumbleUpon	www.stumbleupon.com	No	Yes
Yahoo! Toolbar	https://toolbar.yahoo.com	No	Yes

Book II
Chapter 3

Using Social Bookmarks, News, and Share Buttons

The visibility of your website on search engines improves when you have inbound links from a site that already has a high ranking in search results, but only if it passes link juice. Search the source code for a site to see whether it contains a `<nofollow>` tag. Sites with a `<nofollow>` tag do not pass link juice. Without that tag, links follow by default.

You can find more specialty bookmarks on the eBusiness Knowledgebase list of the top 15 social bookmarking sites:

www.ebizmba.com/articles/social-bookmarking-websites

The two largest search engines (Google and Yahoo!/Bing) also have bookmarking services. However, bookmarking on Yahoo!/Bing is available only through toolbars.

Later in this chapter, we discuss how to research bookmarking services, decide which ones to use, and then submit a site.

One type of bookmarking site deserves particular attention, especially if you have significant visual content. Pinterest, the online scrapbooking site, is attracting huge audiences and driving traffic to commercial websites, especially in the areas of weddings, home décor, women's apparel, and shopping. Green Wedding Shoes, an online wedding shop, is an example of a company using Pinterest (see Figure 3-2).

By July 2014, Pinterest surpassed 53 million unique visitors per month, with pinners spending an average of almost seven minutes a day on the site. According to RJmetrics.com, the demographics are a retailer's dream: About 80 percent of users are women. And, according to PewInternet.org, those women with higher household incomes and higher educational levels are more likely to use the site.

For more on Pinterest, see Book VII.

Traffic has skyrocketed for vendors specializing in home, lifestyle, apparel, food, and weddings, as users follow pins back to their source. If these are your target markets, start pinning!

Figure 3-2: At Pinterest, companies can use different boards (categories) of images (pins) based on product lines and users' interests.

Sharing the News

In comparison with social bookmarking services, social news services such as reddit and Digg (shown in Figure 3-3) point to time-sensitive individual postings and articles. Whereas bookmarking services look at sites without reference to timeliness, social *news* services focus on what's news now.

**Book II
Chapter 3**

Using Social Bookmarks, News, and Share Buttons

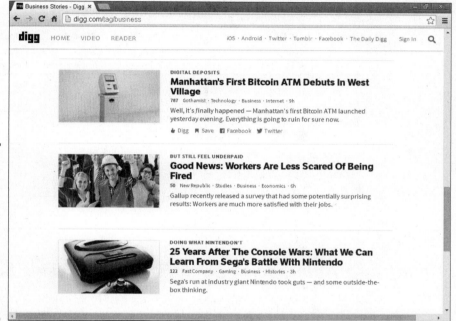

Figure 3-3: Digg shows links to individual articles submitted by hundreds of thousands of Internet readers.

Users can recommend dozens of different content pages on a particular website to a social news service, quickly driving significant amounts of traffic to the originating site. Many social news services rely on users to vote on submissions, with more popular results appearing on the service's front page. Unlike bookmarks, social news services aren't designed to share a list of recommendations with friends.

Figure 3-3 shows recently posted popular articles in response to a search for Business News on Digg. Although most entries link to standard news sources, business press releases and even special offers may appear.

Peer-based recommendations aren't always golden. Because they reflect whoever randomly happens to have posted, these posts may be volatile, biased, and nonrepresentative. They certainly don't reflect scientific results. In fact, you may find some recommended articles shocking or disgusting.

Watch the articles that appear for a few days to be sure you feel comfortable with the quality of what people recommend.

Table 3-2 lists some popular social news sites and whether you can submit your own site or press releases. The Passes Link Juice column indicates whether search engines recognize a link from that service.

Table 3-2	Popular Social News Services				
Name	*URL*	*Uses Popularity Voting*	*Allows Self-Submission*	*Allows Press Releases*	*Passes Link Juice*
Digg	http://digg.com	Yes	Yes	Yes	Yes
Fark	www.fark.com	No	Yes	Yes	No
MetaFilter	www.metafilter.com	Yes	Yes	Yes	Yes
Newsvine	www.newsvine.com	Yes	No	No	Yes
reddit	www.reddit.com	Yes	Yes, but not often	Yes	No
Slashdot	http://slashdot.org	No	Yes	Yes	Yes

Benefiting from Social Bookmarks and News Services

Social bookmarks and news services offer multiple benefits. To start with, they're free — always a positive factor for online guerrilla marketers. In addition, you may benefit in many other ways by using these services:

✦ **Improved search engine ranking:** By using your primary search terms in tags and other elements of your submissions, you may improve your overall web presence in general search engines. The appearance of your content on these services supplements your own site in general search results.

✦ **Inbound links:** Inbound links from social bookmarking and news services may dramatically improve your position in search engine results and your Google PageRank, as well as deliver visitors directly to your site.

✦ **Increased brand visibility and traffic:** The more people who see your website or content listed on one of these services, the more people will remember your name and visit your site. Like many other social marketing techniques, bookmarks and news services help fill the conversion funnel.

✦ **Increased readership and membership:** If you're a writer, pundit, professional speaker, or consultant, these services can be extraordinarily valuable. After you establish a reputation on a service, you may find that you have loyal followers, as well as many new readers, subscribers, clients, and speaking gigs.

✦ **Increased earnings:** You can consider people who visit your URL from social bookmarking and news services as prequalified prospects, pushing them farther down the funnel toward likely-buyer status. Be sure that your site validates the ratings it has earned, though.

✦ **Triggering the influentials:** Many online influentials watch social bookmarking and news services to spot trends and decide whether to mention a site or an article in their own blogs or tweets. Of course, submissions by these influential people carry additional value in the eyes of their followers.

Monitor comments about your site to confirm that recommended pages, content, or products continue to appear and that links still work. Visitors shouldn't see 404 File Not Found messages.

Your task is to ensure that your business is listed in the appropriate services and shows up near the top of results. Always review a potential social news service to make sure it's not just a spam aggregator, that postings are recent, what's permitted in its Terms of Use, and how it ranks on Google. Sounds a lot like the process of finding inbound links in Book II, Chapter 2, doesn't it?

In the following sections, we talk about researching social news services, selecting the right ones for your business, and submitting to them.

For more social news sites, check out

```
www.thehostingpool.com/50-social-news-websites/396
http://addthis.com/services/all?c=social_news
http://newinternetorder.com/get-backlinks-social-
    news-sites
```

Researching a Social Bookmark and Social News Campaign

Listing your website, blog, or content initially is easy. You, or others, can post your site on as many services as you want. Being listed high in the rankings is a more difficult task, though.

Check the Terms of Use on these services; in some cases, you can't submit your own site or content. Many news services have more constraints on the voting process than on submissions.

Here's how to post your site to the right services:

1. **Research appropriate social bookmarking and news services.**

   For an overview, try Quantcast or Alexa to review the user base, demographics, and traffic statistics for each prospective service. You can check sites like popurls, whose Popular Today section displays the most popular daily headlines on the Internet. Generally, you're looking for services that

   • Receive a lot of traffic.

   • Specialize in your market niche.

   • Attract your target market.

2. **Visit each site to confirm that it fits your needs and attracts your audience.**

   To understand more about the kinds of people who use a particular service, look at other top sites bookmarked in your category or at the content rated most favorably. Are the businesses and articles complementary to yours? To your competitors? Are the users of each service likely to try the products or services you offer?

   You can sometimes tell whether an audience might be receptive to your offerings by looking at who's paying for ads on particular pages.

3. **Sort by the names who submitted postings to see which individuals or companies are responsible for most of the public listings.**

   Don't be surprised if the results follow the 80/20 rule: 80 percent of posts will come from 20 percent of users. The top ten submitters are likely to be the influentials on that service.

Executing your plan

Because a distinct effort is involved in recruiting other people to submit your site to social bookmarking and news services, select just a few services from your research to begin. Start with the popular ones listed in Table 3-1 or 3-2 to see whether readers will vote for your content or repost your links on smaller services, saving you the effort.

Some groupthink takes place on these services. If you have a popular post on Digg, for instance, someone may copy it to reddit or StumbleUpon for you. Some services display a list of icons above every story for readers to share elsewhere.

Most users select only one social bookmarking service because they want only one place for their own favorites. That behavior complicates your task because you may need to submit to multiple services to obtain broad coverage. Strive for a realistic balance between coverage and the level of effort you can commit. If you're short of time, don't worry. Start small — you can always do another campaign later.

After you select your list of appropriate services, write them into your Social Media Marketing Plan (found in Book I, Chapter 2) with a schedule for regular postings and review. Then create an account and a profile, if appropriate, for each selected service. Finally, submit the URLs for your site (or sites) or content, as appropriate. Your schedule will probably reflect

✦ An initial mix of multiple one-time submissions to social bookmarking services

✦ Regular, repeat submissions to one or two social news services, within the constraints of their Terms of Use

✦ Occasional additions to your social bookmarks

✦ Regular monitoring of links to your site and mentions in the cybersocial whirl

Watch for scam services offering hundreds of automated social bookmark submissions. You don't need hundreds, any more than you need hundreds of search engines. Besides, you could end up blacklisted for using them.

Many services offer a toolbar add-in to help users easily submit sites or content whenever they find something they like. You might find it handy to install toolbar add-ins for the specific services you expect to use regularly. Better yet, install a share button (see the section "Using Social Media Buttons," later in this chapter) on your site and use the button to access your suite of accounts.

Monitoring results

As we discuss in Book IX, you always need to monitor the results of all your marketing techniques. Watch traffic statistics to identify which services produce the most referrals and when you see spikes in traffic. Stick with the services that become good referrers, of course — especially if they eventually lead to qualified prospects and sales. Replace the ones that don't work.

Consider trying a tool specifically designed for monitoring appearances on social bookmarking and social news sites, including when others have recommended or rated you. You can use these monitoring tools to assess these elements:

✦ The success of your social bookmarking and social news campaign

✦ The efficacy of one posting compared with another

✦ The unauthorized use of trademarks

✦ The effectiveness of a specific press release or sales promotion

✦ The appearances of your competitors on social bookmarks and news services

Book II, Chapter 1 discusses multiple tools for monitoring mentions of your business or website on social networks and blogs. Many of those tools also monitor bookmarking and news services. You might also want to try

✦ **Alltop** (`www.alltop.com`): Collects current headlines and lead paragraphs from websites and blogs and sorts by topic

✦ **BuzzFeed** (`www.buzzfeed.com`): Monitors hot stuff online to share

✦ **popurls** (`http://popurls.com`): Aggregates current headlines from the most popular sites on the Internet

✦ **Social Media for Firefox** (`http://addons.mozilla.org/en-US/firefox/addon/social-media-for-firefox-7888`): Status bar add-on that displays how many votes content has at Digg, StumbleUpon, Twitter, Delicious, and reddit

✦ **WhosTalkin.com:** A free topic search for multiple social media sites

Submitting to Bookmarking Services

Consider submitting URLs to bookmarking services from a personal, rather than business, address or have friends or employees use their personal email addresses as the submission source. Use neutral, non-promotional language in any comment or review. Figure 3-4 shows how to submit a site to Delicious, a popular social bookmarking service. Submitting to social bookmarking services is usually very simple: Create an account and submit a URL with a brief description.

Try to use appropriate search terms in category names, tags, text, or titles when you submit your site. Select terms that searchers are particularly likely to use. Generally, you can find those terms in traffic statistics for your website or in *tag clouds* (a graphic display of search terms that appear in an article, with the most frequently used terms appearing in a large font) from the target service. (Read about tag clouds in Book II, Chapter 2.) Enter your site in as many categories as possible.

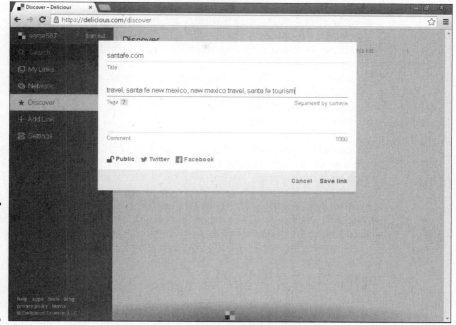

Figure 3-4:
A submission to Delicious, the social bookmarking service.

If you have separate domain names or subdomains for your blog or community site, submit a few of them as bookmarks, along with your primary website, as long as the number is reasonable (say, less than six). You can also post social bookmarks to where links are permitted on Facebook, LinkedIn, or other social networking pages to further enhance your visibility. Just don't personally submit too many of your own pages to one bookmarking site lest you become marked as a spammer.

Be discreet. Don't spam social bookmarking or news services with multiple frequent submissions. Although you can organize a few submissions from others to get the ball rolling, don't set up multiple accounts per user on a social news service to vote for yourself or use automated submitters, which not only might have malware but also might be prohibited. Like regular search engines, these social services act aggressively to detect and blacklist spammers. Read the Terms of Use on every site if you have questions.

Submitting to Social News Services

Think of social news services as peer-reviewed indexes to short-term, contemporary articles, whereas social bookmarks are more useful for longer-term content. Submitting frequently to social news services is not only acceptable but also practically obligatory, particularly if your site generates news within a particular industry or geographical region or if your livelihood is content dependent. Generally, with most social news services, you must create an account first and then submit content.

Because users are in and out of these services often, you always need new content to catch their attention. These users prefer peer-recommended stories versus ones selected by staff editors or that appear in an unfiltered RSS feed from other sources.

People who view your content are asked to vote stories up or down and are often given an opportunity to comment, as well. You generally need to create an account to post, vote, or comment on stories, but anyone can read the listings.

 Always select appropriate categories for your material, such as Technology, World News, Politics, Business, Entertainment, Lifestyle, or Environment. Avoid vague categories such as General, Other, or Miscellaneous — they're deep, dark pits from which your content may never escape!

Selecting content for social news services

Content choice is critical. Not every item on your blog or website will entice readers to submit or rate an article. Generally, the ones that drive the most traffic to your site will have timely content, such as breaking news, or entertainment, humor, or quality resource information not found elsewhere.

Keep the following in mind when deciding what to post on social news services:

✦ **Social news services are culturally dependent.** If you're trying to reach an international market, you may need to submit your content in languages other than English. Note that other countries and languages might have their own localized social bookmarking and news services. Visit www.searchenginejournal.com/50-social-bookmarking-sites-importance-of-user-generated-tags-votes-and-links or international search engines to identify the appropriate services.

✦ **Avoid out-of-date material:** If you must submit older stories, look for such items as features, interviews, how-to's, and essays that have longer-lasting interest. Those items are good for social bookmarking sites, too.

✦ **Match your content submissions to sites where readers like the types of stories you want to recommend:** Look at the tag cloud for frequency of use on tags similar to yours over the past 6 to 12 months.

✦ **Select the services with features that best match the content you have to offer and the audience you're trying to reach:** Some social news services allow links to images, video, and audio; others accept only links to text.

✦ **Think tactically:** Initiate posts for specific pages, posts, or articles that have the potential to lead to traffic, prospects, or sales, not for your everyday internal company news update.

If you get a reputation for posting meaningless items or using the comment space for hard-sell language, you might find it hard to gain traction on these sites; you might even be banned for posting junk.

Preparing social news stories for success

Although you might be tempted to splatter social news services with your stories, just give them a little thought. Set up tags, titles, and lead lines carefully. Follow these online journalistic tips for improved results:

✦ **Write a catchy headline, not an academic title.** Keep headlines short and memorable. Try to use vivid verbs (not just nouns) and active voice. Instead of "New social media app created by local company" for your star-gazing app, try "AstroWare's New App Rockets to the Stars."

✦ **Write a good lede.** The headline and first line of a story (the *lede*) are often the only elements that viewers see. Set a hook to catch readers and make them want to link back to your original content. Tell people what's in it for them or how they'll benefit by reading the story.

✦ **Write a good description, comment, or summary.** Keep it short (20 to 25 words!) and focus on benefits.

✦ **Check your facts, spelling, and links.** If you make errors, someone is likely to post a negative comment. If your links don't work, you lose potential traffic — a primary reason you're using social bookmarking and news services in the first place.

✦ **Prepare your site for success.** Just in case, be sure to structure your site to take advantage of new traffic. Links to related articles on your site or blog give interested readers more than one story to explore, thus increasing the number of page views per visit. To increase conversion rates, use calls to action and visual reminders to sign up for RSS feeds and newsletters, subscribe to a paid publication, or make a purchase.

✦ **Serving up your site.** Be sure that your hosting package allows for increased traffic. Traffic from social bookmarks tends to build slowly, but an appearance on the front page of a social news site can flood your server with more traffic than it's set up to handle. A quick call to your host or IT department should confirm your preparations.

These writing tactics not only help attract the kind of viewers who are more likely to click-through, but also help increase the time users spend on your blog or website.

Using Application-Specific Bookmarks

Some bookmarking and social news services are constrained to specific types of content, such as blogs or video, and others are specific to topic, or activity, such as shopping or product reviews. Table 3-3 provides some examples.

Table 3-3	Bookmarks for Specific Applications
Name	*URL*
Blogs	
BlogCatalog	www.blogcatalog.com
Bloglines	www.bloglines.com
Feedly	www.feedly.com
Reviews	
Epinions	www.epinions.com
SnapFiles	www.snapfiles.com/userreviews/latest.html
TripAdvisor	http://tripadvisor.com
Shopping	
Kaboodle	www.kaboodle.com
Stylehive	www.stylehive.com
ThisNext	www.thisnext.com
Sports	
FanNation	https://fannation.si.com
Video	
MyVidster	www.myvidster.com
Simfany	www.simfany.com

You can find more shopping bookmark sites at

www.pcmag.com/slideshow/story/293956/the-rapid-ascension-of-pinterest-and-social-shopping-sites/1

and more sports sites at

www.fangadar.com

Search for *topic area + bookmarking site* on any search engine to find more specialty bookmarking services.

Timing Your Submissions

Like with search engines, getting yourself on the first page of bookmarking and social news services can be difficult. You generally have only a 24-hour window on social news services to attract enough attention for either lasting value or timeliness. Remember that you may need to coordinate submissions by others to get things started.

There's no point in posting in the middle of the night, when many people are asleep on one side of the country or both. Generally, posting between 10 a.m. and 4 p.m. U.S. central daylight time works well, with an anecdotal peak of best results around 3 p.m. Workdays are generally better for generating traffic, although weekends see less competition. Of course, you need to adjust submission times if getting a scoop is critical or if you seek visibility on an international site.

On the other hand, if you're posting to specific bookmarking services (such as a social shopping or sports bookmarking site) that isn't time-dependent, weekends may find more of your audience available. It's a lot like scheduling an e-newsletter delivery or press release, both of which are audience dependent.

For lists of additional social bookmarking sites with a high page rank, visit `www.brightlivingstone.com/link-building/top-100-social-bookmarking-sites-list-page-rank` or `www.stuffskeleton.com/2014/04/top-200-high-page-rank-social-bookmarking-websites-in-2014.html`.

Your best bet is to experiment for yourself. Note that timing for news sites is not the same as timing posts for major social media channels. Based on AddThis (`www.addthis.com`) data, the best times to post on social media to ensure maximum engagement are

- ✦ **LinkedIn:** Tuesdays from 10 a.m. to 11 a.m.
- ✦ **Pinterest:** Wednesdays from 1 p.m. to 2 p.m.
- ✦ **Facebook:** Thursdays from 9 a.m. to 12 p.m.
- ✦ **Twitter:** Fridays from 2 p.m. to 3 p.m.

Try submitting the same post to different services at different times of the day, or try submitting different posts to the same service at different times. Monitor traffic to your site by the hour and day, and adjust your plans accordingly.

**Book II
Chapter 3**

Using Social Bookmarks, News, and Share Buttons

Adorning social media for marketing success

An online-only shop based in Vancouver, British Columbia, the Art of Adornment features hand-made and imported, vintage-inspired jewelry and accessories with a dark twist. Owner Elaine Barrick officially founded it in 2005 with an eBay store and main online shop, and added an Etsy shop in 2006.

Reproduced with permission of Elaine Barrick

Since Barrick was already familiar — as an artist and personal user — with the power of niche sites like LiveJournal and DeviantART to expose her work to the world, it made sense to add her business as well. Truly an experimenter and early adopter, Barrick soon opened accounts on other sites popular at the time (Myspace, Tribe, Friendster, and Flickr) and a few bookmarking sites like Stylehive, StumbleUpon, and Wists. When Facebook first started allowing business profiles, she expanded there and then started using Twitter, Tumblr, and Kaboodle. She hasn't stopped experimenting, though her business has outlived some of the sites she once listed on.

A few users had bookmarked her sites on Stylehive, StumbleUpon, and Wists, so she started receiving referrals from those sites in 2007. "However, it was Kaboodle," Barrick says, "that made the biggest impact in 2008, with referrals quickly outnumbering other bookmarking sites."

She created a Kaboodle "brand" page for Art of Adornment later in 2008 and began adding more product bookmarks to it. She still adds them manually since there is no automated process for that.

Reproduced with permission of Elaine Barrick

Barrick openly invites people to "Kaboodle" her products via the AddThis.com sharing toolbar, which appears on every product page in her web store. She also incorporates links to Kaboodle in newsletter email footers and profile pages on Facebook, Google+, and any other site that allows her to post links. "If site policy allows it, I won't waste an opportunity!"

She finds that bookmarking sites like Kaboodle and Pinterest that are geared towards shopping or collecting images are best for promoting specific products directly, but most have a very high bounce rate. "I get lots of traffic, but the traffic doesn't stay to look around. Social networking sites like Facebook, Google+, Twitter, and even Tumblr are less effective for individual products. I think," she observes," that's because the audience expects blog-like content and often views frequent product posts as spam. [Those sites] are better for engaging people directly, announcing special events, getting feedback, providing customer service, and sharing model shots of products in use."

"Social bookmarking sites have improved my market exposure and conversion rates from the very beginning," notes Barrick. "I wouldn't have survived this long without them. Revenue generated

(continued)

(continued)

from bookmarking sites in general has been waning over the past [few] years, in pace with a weakening economy. . . . But I keep in mind that people bookmark things because they can't buy right away, and Kaboodle users definitely like to bookmark my stuff. I'll see those conversions eventually, I'm sure."

Barrick's sole proprietorship is very small with almost no budget for advertising. Like many small business owners, she does almost all the marketing herself, and much of it manually. The practical aspect of marketing with limited time and limited resources makes Barrick very efficient. She spends anywhere from 15 minutes to about 2 hours a week, depending on what she's posting and whether she needs to respond to comments.

Given her location on the west coast, Barrick tries to post between 10 a.m and 11 a.m. Pacific daylight time, so her posts will reach the largest number of people around the world while they're awake. She has set up a "new product" feed via BufferApp.com, which picks up data from her shop's new product RSS feed and cross-posts it to LiveJournal, Twitter, Facebook, and Google+.

To see which sites and product posts provide the best quality traffic, Barrick relies primarily on Google Analytics and analytics from AddThis. Because there is so much duplication by activity type within her social media platform (for example, Pinterest and DeviantArt are both image-sharing sites), she mostly watches performance based on source URLs. "For instance, Pinterest refers enormous traffic, but has the highest bounce rate and generates few sales. DeviantArt refers very little traffic, but has a very low bounce rate percentage by comparison, and generates far more revenue than Pinterest."

Barrick says she learned very early on — and quite by accident — that she couldn't rely on her own product bookmarks, shares, or posts alone. "I'm a big online shopper myself and personally found Kaboodle fun to use," she says. She began bookmarking other businesses' products to her personal Kaboodle profile, along with some of her own products. (Her personal profile also links to her Kaboodle brand page and her store URL.)

"They were all products I was genuinely interested in, but were also closely related to those of my own. . . . It wasn't long before I noticed that my Kaboodle brand page feed was showing a sudden but steady increase in bookmark additions for my shop's products. Clearly more Kaboodle users were discovering my shop because they found one or more of my personal Kaboodle profile bookmarks." In short, she advises that for businesses wanting to get the most out of Kaboodle, setting up a brand page is essential. "But be aware that using just the brand page alone will limit your exposure."

Art of Adornment's web presence:

www.artofadornment.ca

www.behance.net/ArtOfAdornment

http://artofadornment.carbonmade.com

```
https://delicious.com/artofadornment
http://artofadornment.deviantart.com
http://stores.ebay.ca/Art-of-Adornment (shop)
https://ello.co/artofadornment
http://artofadornment.etsy.com (shop)
www.facebook.com/artofadornment
www.fotolog.com/artofadornment
https://plus.google.com/+ArtofadornmentCa/posts
www.kaboodle.com/store/artofadornment.ca
http://www.linkedin.com/company/art-of-adornment
http://artofadornment.livejournal.com
www.modelmayhem.com/artofadornment
https://myspace.com/artofadornment
www.pinterest.com/artofadornment
http://artofadornment.tumblr.com
https://twitter.com/artofadornment
www.youtube.com/user/artofadornment
```

Generally, social bookmarks drive traffic to your site slowly as people find your URL, but you can generate a spike in traffic by pushing your site on social news services (if they permit it). You can ask several people to submit your site, but leave it to others to vote it up or down.

Try to get 15 to 25 people to submit your posting within the first few hours of its publication. That's usually enough to get attention from others and build momentum for votes. Receiving 25 recommendations within a few hours means a lot more than receiving 25 recommendations within a week!

While your visibility on the service rises, so, too, does traffic to your site.

For all the value these services may have as recommendation search engines, the traffic on them is nothing compared with traffic on major search engines, such as Google and Yahoo!/Bing. Optimization for general search engines is still absolutely necessary, as discussed in Book II, Chapter 2, and forms the basis for your success.

Encouraging Others to Bookmark or Rate Your Site

Like most political campaigns, the popularity contest on services that rely on votes or frequency of submission can be managed to your advantage. It just takes a little preplanning. Although illegal vote-rigging and outright manipulation are forms of cyberfraud, the following techniques are valid ways to encourage others to submit or rate your site:

✦ **We all get by with a little help from our friends.** Always have other people submit your material; on some services, submission by others is required. One easy way is to email a circle of employees, colleagues, and friends to help when you post a new page or content, or help them set up RSS feeds from your selected services. Ask them to submit or comment on your posting within a few hours after being notified.

✦ **Scratch backs.** In addition to posting your own stories, recommending material on other sites that complement yours (as long as you don't drive traffic to your competition) is good practice. If you help others increase the ratings on their stories through your repostings and votes, they're more likely to return the favor. These practices establish your reputation as a fair-minded individual who's interested in the topic, not just in sales.

✦ **Be a courteous responder.** You make friends and influence people by responding to comments on your stories and commenting on others. Again, one good turn deserves another. Consider it as building your cyberkarma.

✦ **Become known as the go-to poster.** If you frequently post interesting material on one service, you may develop a reputation and a following, with readers watching for new items from you. They will happily rate or rank items you suggest.

✦ **Ask.** People who visit your site might be willing to let others know about it, but you need to remind them. Put a call to action or share button at the end of a story or post, reminding them to tell a friend or share your content publicly. If you've decided to focus on a particular service, display its icon with a link (see the later section "Using Social Media Buttons"). You might even include a call to action to install a toolbar.

Don't confuse *popularity* — a subjective and manipulated quantity — with the *quality* of leads that a bookmark or social news mention may generate. Popularity is a means, not an end. Ultimately, you're better off with fewer, but higher-quality, visitors arriving at your site.

Like exchanging reciprocal links to improve search engine ranking, exchanging bookmarks has become common practice. Like linking, bookmark swapping can be done honestly, but it has a darker side.

Follow the same principles that you do with links:

✦ Don't exchange bookmarks with spam-like junk sites — only with ones that offer value.

✦ Be suspicious of people who offer to sell bookmarks or votes.

✦ Look for relevance, including shared tags or search terms, as well as traffic rankings on the exchanging site.

Because submitting too many of your own pages to a bookmarking service can tag you as a spammer, you can participate in a service in which members bookmark each other. These are similar to some of the old link exchanges, banner exchanges, and web rings. Be cautious. Avoid anything that looks illegitimate.

If you have no friends or colleagues to help you out, you might examine the options of piqqus (`www.piqqus.com`) for exchanges among Digg and StumbleUpon, or LavaLinx (`www.lavalinx.com/social-bookmarking.lava`), which offers more comprehensive exchange services.

Avoid automated submission services or scripts. The safest way to participate in social bookmarking is the old-fashioned way: individually, by hand.

Using Social Media Buttons

Social media buttons have two functions: Follow Us buttons crosslink visitors to multiple elements of your web presence; share buttons enable visitors easily to share your content or website with others. Place buttons consistently near the top of a page or article, where you place key information.

When you repeat smaller versions of the buttons at the end of each post on your blog, users can share a specific item instead of the entire blog. Social media buttons can also be placed on e-newsletters and on multiple social media networks. Anecdotal evidence from some companies that tried organized campaigns shows dramatic increases in traffic on their social media sites.

Follow Us buttons

Follow Us buttons, shown in Figure 3-5 — sometimes called *chiclets* — link visitors to other elements of your web presence, such as to your Facebook profile, Twitter page, or blog. In Figure 3-5, the chiclets above the top navigation on every page of The Fat Finch's website (`www.fatfinch.com`) encourage users to link the user to the company's pages on Facebook, Twitter, Pinterest, Google+, YouTube, and their blog. Some services, such as the photo sharing site Flickr and the community-building site Ning, provide large, customizable graphical badges to promote a link to your alternative presence.

Follow Us buttons

Figure 3-5: On every page of its website, The Fat Finch includes chiclet links to its social media pages.

Almost all services offer free standard icons along with code to insert them. Alternatively, you can search for creative icons online at sites like

```
www.evohosting.co.uk/blog/web-development/design/
    more-free-social-media-icons
www.1stwebdesigner.com/freebies/amazing-free-social-
    media-icon-packs
```

and create your own link, or use a social bookmark links generator, such as Keotag (`www.keotag.com/sociable.php`).

Share buttons

Social share buttons from services like AddThis offer a drop-down list that gives the user sharing options, as shown in Figure 3-6. This approach lets visitors easily share content by linking them to the sign-in page for their own accounts on other social sharing services. In an interesting variation, Shareaholic (`www.shareaholic.com/publishers`) offers buttons that rise up as a user hovers on them. Several sources for other social share buttons are listed in Table 3-4.

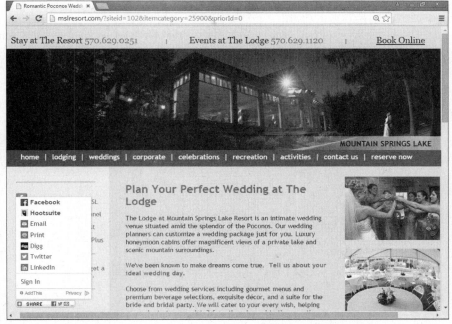

Figure 3-6:
Social share buttons encourage visitors to pass along your site or content through their own accounts.

Reproduced with permission of Mountain Springs Lake Corp.

Table 3-4	Sources for Social Share Buttons
Name	*URL*
AddThis	http://addthis.com
AddToAny	http://addtoany.com
HubSpot article titled "The Ultimate Cheat Sheet for Creating Social Media Buttons"	http://blog.hubspot.com/blog/tabid/6307/bid/29544/The-Ultimate-Cheat-Sheet-for-Creating-Social-Media-Buttons.aspx
Ridiculously Responsive Social Sharing Buttons	http://kurtnoble.com/labs/rrssb
Shareaholic	www.shareaholic.com
ShareThis	http://sharethis.com
Smart Addon	www.smartaddon.com
StrongView (paid service)	www.strongview.com/products/social

These free, easy-to-install buttons allow users to transfer content quickly to their own profiles, blogs, preferred social bookmarking service, instant messages, email, or text messages. You can even use a special, albeit paid, Social Notes widget from www.strongview.com/products/social that facilitates sharing of products from your e-commerce site, as shown in Figure 3-7. This is viral marketing at an epidemic level!

Figure 3-7: Widgets, like Social Notes from StrongView, enable users to recommend products directly from your online store.

Reproduced with permission of StrongView Systems, Inc.

Register for free analytics on sharing services that offer it to see how and where users elected to share your material or site. You can often find a toolbar add-on for each service on the site. You may want to install the ones you need in your browser and offer that option to your users in a call to action.

Always include Print, Email, and Favorites (for personal bookmarks) in your set of social share buttons. Some people like the convenience of the old stuff.

If you aren't comfortable inserting code on your site, ask your web developer or programmer to do it for you. Sometimes even your hosting company can help. Specify which Follow Us or share buttons you want to have visible and ask to have the buttons appear on every page of your site.

If all these tasks seem overwhelming, plenty of providers are willing to help you for a fee. Most SEO firms, press and public relations firms, online marketing companies, specialized social marketing ad agencies, and copywriters who specialize in online content now offer assistance with social bookmarking, social news, and other forms of social media marketing. Try searching for *social media services*, *social media agencies*, *digital media marketing*, or *social media marketing*.

We discuss more advanced methods for integrating social media into your overall marketing plans in Book VIII, Chapter 6.

**Book II
Chapter 3**

**Using Social
Bookmarks, News,
and Share Buttons**

Book III
Content Marketing

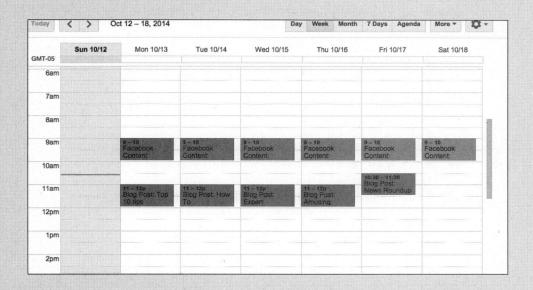

Find out about ten platforms to consider for your content marketing strategy at www.dummies.com/extras/socialmediamarketingaio.

Contents at a Glance

Chapter 1: Growing Your Brand with Content

In This Chapter

- ✓ Discovering the world of content marketing
- ✓ Considering your content platform choices
- ✓ Using content to sell your brand online
- ✓ Developing content that stands out from the crowd

*E*verything you see online is content — the written word, images, podcasts, radio, video, infographics, charts, and even social media updates on Facebook and Twitter. Content can amuse or teach, but it's also a powerful tool for catching the attention of the search engines and the people who are looking for whatever it is you do. Many businesses are achieving positive results by using different types of content to reach customers and raise brand awareness.

In this chapter, we discuss content marketing. In particular, we define content marketing and discuss the importance of having a content strategy in place.

Don't get overwhelmed thinking about all the different kinds of content you have to create. The important thing to remember is that you don't have to use every content platform available. Instead, master one or two platforms and see where that takes you.

Introducing Content Marketing

Today is a wonderful time to be in business. Thanks to the web, you can use endless tools to promote your business or brand, and many of them are free. If you have a way with words or a flair for the dramatic, you can sell your product or service online. All you need to do is tap into your creativity. Using online content to promote your personal or business brand can mean the difference between local and global recognition.

Understanding what content marketing is

If you're dabbling in social media to help market your business, you may have heard the expression *content marketing,* which is the practice of using blog posts, podcasts, videos, and images to promote your product or service. For example, if you own a farmer's market and you wish more people could find information about your market when they search online, you can create content that is attractive to search engines, making it easier to find your brand online.

For example, blog posts about how to choose the best strawberries or the time of the year when different fruits and vegetables are in season answer the questions people who shop at farmer's markets are searching for. While they read your blog posts, they'll see other links to more of your content, as well as your location, special events, sales, and other items of interest posted at your website. Content marketing drives people to a particular location, helping you achieve your goals.

Examining how content marketing can help your business

Content marketing serves several purposes — first and foremost to drive traffic and sales. Relevant content helps your business get a better ranking in search engine results. So if your business initially showed up on page ten of a Google search, content marketing, if done right, can help your business move to the first or second page for many different *search terms* — the words and phrases entered into the search engines.

Content marketing isn't only for the benefit of search engines, however. It's also a way to connect with your customers and community, and share expertise in order to build better brand recognition. When you create good content, something wonderful happens: People don't just read your content, they also leave comments to participate in the conversation, as shown in Figure 1-1.

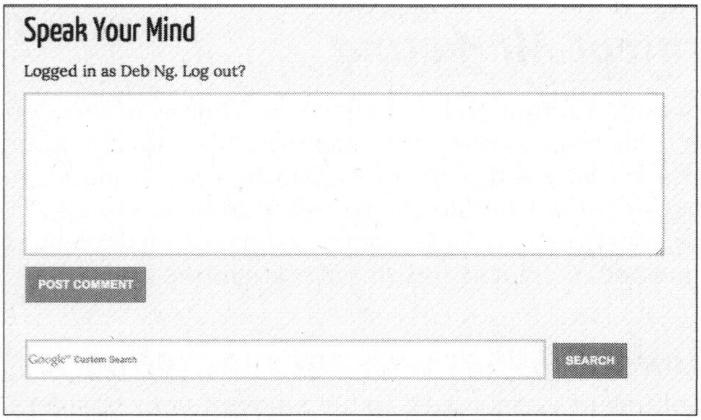

Figure 1-1: Use the comment area of your blog or social media platforms to have a conversation with customers and potential customers.

Speak Your Mind

Logged in as Deb Ng. Log out?

POST COMMENT

Google™ Custom Search   SEARCH

People also share your content with their own friends and online followers, as shown in Figure 1-2. Next thing you know, other people are reading, sharing, and commenting. Even though they're not actively promoting your brand, you're getting wonderful brand recognition because the more people who share your content, the more people are seeing your logo, brand name, and other recognizable features.

Here are some additional ways that content marketing can benefit your company:

✦ **Your company has a voice.** Content marketing allows you to present your business in a positive light. In addition to creating helpful educational content, you're also able to address customer concerns, competitor messages, and both bad and good reviews.

✦ **You establish expertise.** Are you really good at something, or is your brand known for being the foremost expert in its field? Content is an excellent way to share your expertise with others. When people think you're smart and transparent, they're more likely to trust you, which leads to sales.

✦ **You increase brand visibility.** The more content you share, the more your name is seen online.

✦ **Your local business can become global.** Online content helps a business that had only local connections grow to a place where more people can learn about what that business does. This access to a wider audience can mean national and even global exposure.

✦ **Content marketing can be inexpensive.** Creating and sharing content doesn't have to be expensive. If you or your team are creative, you can even handle content creation in-house. The types of content you create can be anything from a blog post, which doesn't cost anything, to a highly produced video, which can be costly. Both methods work.

Figure 1-2: When you create useful content, others will want to share it, which leads to better brand visibility.

Kindle Addicts shared a link.
October 4

Enjoy this weekend's list of free Kindle books!

Weekend Freebies: 20 Free Kindle Books for October 4, 2014 - Kindle Addicts
kindleaddicts.com
Today's list features a weekend's worth of free Kindle books to download. You shouldn't have any trouble finding a few good books to...

Like · Comment · Share

Maria Sanders-Wachholz, Stacey Haston Leopard, Dianne St Marie Griffin and 7 others like this.

✦ **Any business has the ability to use content marketing.** It doesn't matter what your business does, if you have an existing customer base, you can create content to communicate with them and reach even more customers.

✦ **People can find your business for as long as your content remains online.** However, creating content that's relevant both now and in the future means your brand's name will continue to come up in searches — both now and in the future. *Evergreen content* — content that people will always be searching for, such as instructions for how to do something — has staying power. We go into detail about evergreen content in Book III, Chapter 4.

✦ **Content allows people to make informed decisions.** The more information you share with people about your product or service, the better able they are to make purchasing decisions. Your content will enable customers and potential customers to make comparisons and purchase with confidence.

✦ **You can repurpose your content.** Content can be reworked and rewritten to add new information and make existing content more current.

✦ **Content inspires your team to be creative.** Your entire team can help plan the content and suggest ideas for blog posts, articles, videos, podcasts, and more.

People enjoy consuming content. They like to watch videos that teach and entertain, and they enjoy reading enlightening articles. If your content provides a valuable service and shares good information, it has the potential to be seen by many people.

Determining the Best Content Platform for Your Needs

There are plenty of content platforms to choose from, and it's easy to become overwhelmed if you're not sure which method to start out with. The important thing to remember is that you don't have to do everything at once, nor do you have to create content on every single platform or social network. In fact, it's better to pick a couple of platforms and build up content and community there over time, rather than spread content out in a million different places.

The content platform(s) you choose depends on several factors:

✦ **Goals:** What are some of the reasons you're creating content? Is it for SEO? Sales? Authority? Knowing why you want to attract customers will help you to determine which content and social media platforms to use.

✦ **Budget:** Some brands pull out all the stops to create a viral video, while others put very little money into a blog post. Figure 1-3 shows the

Figure 1-3:
Many
businesses
choose
blogs to
start their
content
marketing
strategy
because
they're
inexpensive
and easy
to do.

dashboard for a WordPress blog post, which has to cost only as much as you're willing to pay for web hosting. Interestingly, both blogs and videos can achieve the same result. Sometimes low-budget content goes viral, and sometimes high-budget content tanks.

✦ **Expertise:** If you create your content to teach, choose a platform that best illustrates your knowledge.

✦ **Talent:** Do you have a talented team of writers? Is someone on staff handy with a camera, or technically equipped to set up a podcast? Choose a platform that your team has the experience to use. You can still experiment, but your first effort should be something you and your team are comfortable doing.

✦ **Demographic:** The age and interests of your customers and community matter when choosing a content platform. Content should be tailored to that age and on a platform people in that demographic are mostly likely to use. For example, teens and people in their early 20s don't spend a lot of time on Facebook, and seniors don't often spend time on YouTube.

Don't dive into content creation blindly. Take some time to learn about your community and create a strategy. Marketers who have a plan in place are the ones who succeed. We talk more about content strategy in Book III, Chapter 3.

Selling Your Brand through Content Marketing

So how do you go about selling your brand online through your content? The secret is not to look like you're selling at all. People don't like pushy, and they're turned off by obvious sales pitches. However, when you share important information, you build trust with your readers and customers. They appreciate learning about what your brand has to offer, and next time they have a need for a product or service like yours, you're the one they'll call — not only because your brand is now familiar to them, but also because they know from your content that you're a resource that can be trusted.

Here are a few ideas to try selling through content:

✦ **Share information about your product or service.** Whether you're using blog posts or video, content allows you to show how your product works and how to get the best results. With content, you can go beyond the product label and discuss benefits, risks, and proven results.

✦ **Answer frequently asked questions.** Do your customers have questions? Do some questions arise more than others? Your content allows you to answer common questions your customers and potential customers have about not only your products and services, but also your competitors'.

✦ **Create links that lead to your product or service.** For every piece of content that you post online, you should, at the very least, also post a link to related sales pages.

✦ **Offer free content in exchange for a newsletter signup or registration.** The reason so many businesses use newsletters is because they're collecting email addresses so they can send their customers sales pitches. Many brands even use content to entice newsletter signups. For example, they'll give a link to download a free ebook for every registration.

✦ **Address known issues through your content.** If people are leaving negative reviews or comments about specific issues with products or services, you shouldn't ignore them. Use your content to talk about the issues and put rumors to rest.

✦ **Tell your brand's story.** People love history, and they especially enjoy feeling as if they're part of history. If you or your brand has a unique story, use content to share your history, your mission, and your goals. This type of honesty builds trust, and people shop where they trust.

✦ **Open up lines of communication.** Content enables you to have a conversation with your community. For example, any questions or comments posted to Twitter, Pinterest, or a Facebook page, or on blog posts or YouTube are an opportunity for you to have a conversation with your customers.

None of the above looks like selling. There is no call to action, nor is there an obvious sales page. However, your content took care of the hard part of the sales process: It got people to your website.

Not all content is created in the same manner. For example, blogs are usually text- or image-heavy, while podcasting and video require recording equipment and a little more technical knowledge. However, all are doable and easy to maintain, and all have the ability to drive traffic and sales, as well as raise awareness for your brand product or service.

Making Your Content Stand Out

All this content creation is for naught if no one is reading it. If you want to have the kind of content that people read or view, and then share, you have to take steps to ensure that your content stands out from the rest. Despite what you see on Facebook, you don't have to bring cats into your content for it to be well received.

In order for your content to stand out, it has to be useful and appealing. Answer this question: What value will your customers and potential customers receive from viewing your content?

What follows are some considerations for creating the type of content people respond to. Content should

✦ **Have a purpose.** Don't create content for the sake of creating content: otherwise, it will be bland, redundant, or confusing. Content should have both a plan and a purpose. For example, content should teach, or drive traffic or sales. Even content created solely to go viral has a purpose. When you understand why you're creating the content, it will be easier for you to write, photograph, or video tape.

✦ **Provide value.** If a video makes someone laugh, it has value. If a blog post teaches people something new, it has value. If a tweet breaks news, it has value. In other words, don't create content that doesn't offer anything to the viewer or reader.

✦ **Answer a question.** If someone is searching for information and lands on an article on your website, will they stay to read the whole thing, or will they move on after a quick scan? Your content should answer a question, even if the question is simply, "What am I doing here?"

✦ **Be unique.** What perspective can you give to your niche that no one else has covered? Content that stands out does so because it's different — not the same old, same old.

✦ **Be easy to relate to.** People like to read a blog post or watch a video, and then nod their head in agreement. For example, a funny video from a car-cleaning service that shows kids dropping food in the car or scribbling on the back seat with a permanent marker might have parents sharing the content because they've been in the same situation.

✦ **Be visual.** A vibrant or intriguing photo will catch the eye, and readers will want to know how it relates to the content.

✦ **Have variety.** Mix up your content! Some news, some timely, and some evergreen. Experiment with photos, videos, and written content, too.

✦ **Be entertaining.** Entertaining content doesn't necessarily mean it's slapstick or pet tricks. Entertaining can also mean it's educational, interesting, and intriguing. If content entertains, consumers will want to see more content from you and may even want to learn more about your product or service.

✦ **Be inspiring.** You want to create content that encourages reaction. Whether it's a call to action, a link to more information or a sales page, or an invitation to comment and share, your content should give readers and viewers the idea to do these things. It should make them want to take action.

✦ **Be scannable.** People consume content differently on the web than they do in print. Whereas they'll read books and consume newspaper and magazine articles in their entirety offline, on the web, most people have short attention spans. So break up all content into easily digestible pieces with images, headings, subheads, bullet points, and numbered lists. (Sort of like what we're doing here!) If you present the content in this way, people can scan it and still take something away from it.

✦ **Have an intriguing title.** You don't have to create a scandalous or shocking headline, but your content should have a title that will immediately capture attention and encourage readers or viewers to want to learn more.

✦ **Be shareable.** It's great when someone likes your content; it's even better when they like the content so much they want to share it with others. The more people who share your content, the more recognizable your brand. Shareable content is great marketing.

✦ **Be compatible.** Make sure content reads and views well across mobile platforms. Because so many people are consuming content via smartphones and tablets, it won't do to have content that doesn't work on every mobile platform.

✦ **Be published with some regularity.** You don't have to publish content every day, but if you're consistent with your posting, you give people something to look forward to. For example, if you post to the corporate blog every Tuesday, regular readers will stop by every Tuesday to see your new content.

The web is flooded with content that's inaccurate or fluffy and that doesn't really share solid information. By creating content that's valuable and that serves a purpose, you're cutting through the clutter and noise to become a trusted resource. This content creation may not seem like selling, but when it comes time to buy, potential customers will remember you for providing quality content and equate it with a quality product or service.

Chapter 2: Exploring Content Marketing Platforms

In This Chapter

↳ **Blogging for business**

↳ **Podcasting for professionals**

↳ **Diving into video**

↳ **Using images as content**

↳ **Getting social**

A s we discuss in chapter 1 of this minibook, content encompasses a wide variety of platforms, and every platform is beginner-friendly. After all, we all have to start somewhere. However, you may find you're more comfortable using some platforms than others, which is perfectly normal. Your content strategy can include one platform or all of them. As you become familiar with the different options, you can determine for yourself which are best for your needs.

Not to get ahead of ourselves, though — take a look at some of the different platforms available to you:

✦ **Blogs:** Informal, conversational, articles.

✦ **Podcasts:** Audio files akin to an online radio show. Podcasts can be a single person discussing issues or ranting, or it can be interviews, music, or news updates.

✦ **Video:** Videos can be used to promote, sell, entertain, and enlighten.

✦ **Images:** Use photographs in blog posts or alone to tell a story.

✦ **Social media:** Using Facebook, Pinterest, Twitter, Google+, Instagram, and/or other social networking sites as content — that is, to create your own post or to share relevant content that someone else created.

In this chapter, we explore some of the available platforms and talk about ways that you can use them all as part of your content marketing strategy.

Building a Blog

Blogs, such as the one shown in Figure 2-1, are no longer link-heavy, personal journals used to describe one's day or give a daily rant. Businesses use blogs as marketing tools to share updates and industry-related news and to offer tips, recipes, or ideas for using products and services.

Figure 2-1:
Use a blog to promote your business.

The good news is that even if your background isn't in writing or web design, you can easily maintain a regular blog. All you need is a way with words and the ability to write in a conversational tone; it's the conversational aspect that sets blogs apart from more newsy and antiseptic articles.

Understanding how blogging can benefit your business

The reason people enjoy reading blogs so much is because of the simple language and the ability to add their own comments. At the other end of the spectrum, blogs allow businesses to engage with their customers or community in a new way.

Additionally, blogging

✦ **Catches the attention of the search engines.** If you're looking for a heavier Internet presence, you most likely want people to be able to find you when they're searching Google, Yahoo!, or other search engines. Blogging is perfect for this purpose. With the right content and regular updates to your blog, there's no reason why you shouldn't land in the top results for any number of search terms.

✦ **Catches the attention of the people using the search engines.** With the right headlines, *keywords* (the words and terms people use when using the search engines), and images, web searchers are intrigued enough to land on one of your pages. If your blog is informative, they may even be intrigued enough to explore several different pages.

✦ **Is shareable.** When people find something they like online, they share it via email or on one of the social networks. When a blog post touches on an interesting or sensitive topic, your readers will likely want to pass it on.

✦ **Allows everyone to join the conversation.** Most blogs allow for comments at the bottom of each blog post. Readers love to comment because it gives them the opportunity to add their own thoughts and opinions and to share experiences.

✦ **Allows you to manage your reputation.** Sometimes people say something about a business or brand that isn't nice. Sometimes rumors fly. Sometimes you just need to set the record straight. Blogging allows you to speak to your community at a time when you need them most.

✦ **Builds expertise.** When you share tips on a regular basis, you're seen as someone who is knowledgeable in your field. You may even get a reputation as someone who really knows his stuff.

✦ **Can make you the go-to person for the subject matter.** With regular blogging, journalists, authors, conferences, and even other bloggers are likely to contact you for interviews and speaking engagements and to write articles or guest blog posts so that you can share your knowledge with their communities.

✦ **Enables you to grow your community.** When you have regular readers who comment on your blog and share your blog posts, they become your online community. Your community advocates for you and helps spread the word about your brand, product, or service. (We talk more about building an online community in later in this chapter.)

✦ **Is inexpensive.** Most blog platforms don't cost anything to use. Your biggest expense will be web hosting and possibly hiring someone to create a custom design or handle your blogging, if you decide not to do it yourself. However, blogging is one of the least expensive marketing tools you can use.

✦ **Allows you to update thousands of people at one time.** As your community grows and more people read your blog each day, it will become a place where you can update your customers on promotions, news, updates, and new product information.

✦ **Allows you to connect with other businesses, brands, and experts.** Blogs are wonderful networking tools. They allow you to link to people you respect and receive links back in return. You may even discover that influential people in your niche are following your blog and participating in your conversations.

✦ **Allows you to add personality to your business.** The beauty of blogging is the conversational tone. Because the writing is more casual than news articles, you can add humor and personality to your blog posts. Readers appreciate this lighthearted approach because they don't feel as if they're being talked down to.

✦ **Builds trust.** When you keep your community updated and use your blog as a two-way communication tool, you build trust among your customers and community. People won't feel you have something to hide if you're open and honest on your blog, which gives them a good feeling about using your product or service.

✦ **Is easy.** After you set up your blog and it's ready to roll, maintaining it is easy. In most cases, all you need to do is type the day's blog post and add the necessary links, images, or other bells and whistles.

What types of businesses can benefit from blogs? Just about anyone with a story to tell or a product to sell can benefit from having a blog, but some brands benefit more from this form of content than others. For example, blogs are perfect for product-oriented brands.

Some items that product-oriented brands can blog about are

✦ **Ingredients:** If you take pride in using wholesome ingredients, you should talk about it often. It's an important message and strong selling point. In fact, each individual ingredient can be turned into at least one blog post — probably more.

✦ **Recipes:** If you add two parts water to your household cleaning product, can it be used to clean stains off a rug? Can your brand of peanut butter be used as the base for a number of different dishes? Blog about it!

✦ **Uses for the products:** Vinegar has at least 100 different uses; how about your product? If your product can do a variety of different things, talk about it.

✦ **Launches and product news:** Do you have a new product on the horizon? Are you opening up shop in a new location? These items are worthy of a blog post.

✦ **A behind-the-scenes peek:** Your customers and community would love to know that you and the other people who work for your brand are real. Announce promotions. Take photos around the office. Show your employees hard at work or goofing off . . . er, team-building. Make your community feel as if they're in on a secret.

A common mistake brands make when blogging is to assume every update has to be a sales pitch or product-oriented content. The best blogs barely sell. Instead, they focus on the benefits of the product. Go beyond the obvious, and you'll have a blog people want to read.

Deciding if blogging is right for you

Any business or business person can benefit from regular blogging. If you have something to say, or something to sell, blogs are a simple, cost-effective solution to reach many people at once.

Building a blog takes time. You have to update it often and monitor it at least once per day for comments. You also have to promote new content on the social networks so that your community can learn when you share new blog posts. Don't expect to see massive traffic when you're just starting out, though. The best blogs have a slow, steady growth rate.

Setting up your blog

Before choosing a blog platform, decide whether you want to host the blog on your own domain or on a blog platform's subdomain. While a hosted blog through platforms such as WordPress or Blogger is free to use and maintain, most bloggers and business owners agree it's more beneficial to put out the money and purchase your own domain and hosting. Even so, it doesn't have to be an expensive endeavor, and it's well worth the investment.

Hosting on a blogging platform's subdomain means you have limited design and customization choices, and you may not be able to support advertising.

Setting up a blog can be as easy as you need it to be. Because you're using your blog for marketing purposes, I'm going to go ahead and assume you prefer to self-host your blog. A self-hosted blog means you pay for the hosting yourself and handle blog installation and design.

It's much better SEO to have traffic come to your own website (and brand) than someone else's, anyway. A self-hosted WordPress blog (as opposed to the free blog that is hosted on the WordPress subdomain) is the marketer's blogging tool of choice because it's so easy to use and adapt to your needs.

Some hosts — for example, Bluehost — allow you to easily set up a WordPress blog with very little effort. All you have to do is click a button, such as the one shown in Figure 2-2, and follow the simple step-by-step instructions. See www. bluehost.com/ for more details.

Install WordPress button

Figure 2-2:
Some
web-hosting
companies,
such as
Bluehost,
enable you
to set up
a blog on
WordPress
with the
click of a
mouse.

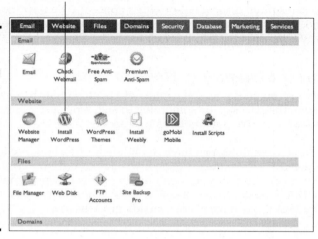

If you already have a website for your business, you'll want to host your blog there, with a link to the blog in the site's navigation menu. Your webmaster can install a WordPress setup in less than an hour. Or if you want to find out how to do it yourself, check out *WordPress Web Design For Dummies* by Lisa Sabin-Wilson (Wiley Publishing, Inc.).

As for design, you can look up WordPress themes online and upload one to your blog, or you can hire a designer for a more custom look. Most brands choose to have their blogs blend in with their website and match their logos, so they opt for a custom design.

Here's a look at the components of a successful blog:

✦ **Dashboard:** Your blog's *dashboard* is its control center. From here, you can choose to add a new post, upload plug-ins, customize the design, add a new static page, or take care of any blogging business.

✦ **Blog post:** A *blog post* is an individual article. Each time you create content for your blog, you're adding a blog post. The blog is the entire setup; the post is an individual article. In your dashboard, you can set up how many blog posts you want to appear on the blog's home page. Blog posts are generally listed in date order. Eventually, the oldest blog posts are no longer on the home page, but users can search the categories or the blog itself for older posts.

✦ **Static page:** Similar to a blog post, a *static page* is a page of content that stays in place, rather than falling off the home page when new content is added. The blog's navigation usually has a link to the static page. For example, a static page is an About page that lists information about your company or a sales page that offers a look at products and services, or a pricing menu.

✦ **Categories:** You can set up categories to make it easier for your readers to find specific content. For example, if your company is a dairy, your categories might be Products, Recipes, and Events. You can place categories in your blog's sidebar navigation.

✦ **Search:** A Search bar can help your readers and customers find specific content.

✦ **Comments section:** By enabling comments at the bottom of each post, you're inviting your customers and readers to share their own tips and anecdotes.

✦ **Sidebar:** Your blog's sidebar houses important information. For example, information about you and your brand, the menu of categories, the search bar, Follow buttons for Facebook and Twitter, and links to sales pages.

✦ **Share buttons:** Each of your blog posts should have share buttons so that readers can share the blog posts with their friends on Facebook, Twitter, and other social networks. You can set up a share button by downloading a plug-in and going to the plug-in's settings.

✦ **Plug-ins:** Plug-ins allow your blog to have some wonderful bells and whistles. For example, you can use plugins to keep spam out of your comments section, share your content, and configure advertising. To search for plug-ins, simply use the search function in the Plug-In section of your blog's dashboard.

The beauty of blogs is how easy they are to customize. You can do almost anything with a blog — you can sell products or tell a story, for example. You can even use a WordPress blog setup to create an entire website. Take some time to explore all the options to make your blog stand out from the competition.

Using Podcasts and Video on Your Blog or Website

Text isn't the only game in content marketing. Many brands are now taking advantage of creating podcasts and video blog posts to add a little variety to their written content. In the following sections, we explore the benefits of creating podcasts and video and how you can add them into your content marketing plan.

Deciding if podcasting is right for you

You don't have to podcast. With social media, you don't have to join every network or pontificate from every platform. Some people love podcasting, but others would rather type than talk. Is podcasting right for you?

Podcasting doesn't necessarily have to entail the use of a lot of expensive equipment. Many hard-core podcasters do have their own studios, while others get by with a simple microphone. Sound quality is important, however, and if you host hard-to-listen-to podcasts full of static and feedback, folks are going to stay away.

You don't want to spend lots of money on expensive equipment if you're not into podcasting. Definitely try podcasting a few times to be sure there's interest — not only from you, but from your community.

You also have to consider editing. All those perfect podcasts you watch or listen to aren't necessarily first takes, especially if you're just starting out. You're bound to have some fits and starts, and even a few "uhms." Your options are to leave them in or edit them out — and editing out can be time-consuming.

We don't mean to discourage you from podcasting in any way. However, we don't want you to enter into it blind. Here are a few things to consider before launching your first podcast:

✦ **Is podcasting something you want to do on a regular basis?** Will you want to record a podcast once a week and then edit and upload the podcast? For newbies, this process can take several hours.

✦ **Will you be able to handle the technical aspects?** Blog platforms are mostly intuitive, and most people can figure them out without much effort. Editing a podcast isn't difficult, per se, but it's not as easy as pressing a Send button.

✦ **Will you have listeners? Do you know people will tune in?** Will podcasting be worth the effort? Some communities aren't into regular podcasts. Also, the success of your podcast depends on the brand. For example, if you're a laundry detergent manufacturer, do you think you can come up with enough interesting material to bring in listeners each time you upload a podcast?

✦ **Will you be able to bring in listeners?** Though you're using podcasting as a marketing tool, you'll have to do a fair amount of marketing yourself in order to bring in listeners. Where will you find them, and how will you get them to listen?

✦ **What do you hope to achieve by podcasting?** Determine your reason for podcasting before you begin so that you can tailor your podcast to the right people. For example, if you're raising awareness for a cause, you wouldn't talk about the same thing as if you were selling a product.

✦ **Where will you host your podcast?** Will you post your podcast to your blog, website, or another area? If you host the podcast on your blog or website, your site will receive more traffic. If you host through iTunes, you may have more listeners. And there's nothing wrong with using a combination of both.

Not everyone has the time or even patience to read long, lengthy articles and blog posts. Having content that people can listen to at their convenience is another great option for spreading your message and can open you up to a whole new audience. Many people enjoy downloading podcasts to their smartphones and listening to them in the car or gym. Podcasting can be more convenient than text or video because you can listen much in the way you listen to music while you're going about your day. There's nothing to print, and you're not chained to your laptop.

Because your listeners hear your voice in a podcast, you build a different type of relationship. When they can hear your voice, and your emotion and passion as you talk about your favorite topics, you add another element of trust to your message. They laugh with you at jokes and know when you're dead serious. In text, your audience can easily misread tones and inflections. The content of a podcast is more engaging because it's more emotional.

Unlike written content, podcasts aren't scannable. Though people can fast forward as needed, most people are more focused when they're listening than when they're scanning a blog post.

Podcasts also allow you to expand upon your expertise. When you write a blog post, brevity is important. You have to say what you have to say in 500 to 1,000 words, or you run the risk of losing your reader. On the other hand, podcasts allow you to talk until the talking is done. Many podcasts run 30 to 60 minutes. Another beautiful thing about podcasts is how you can interview another person of interest and ask as many questions as you want.

For more information on podcasting, check out *Podcasting For Dummies* by Tee Morris, Chuck Tomasi, and Evo Terra (Wiley Publishing, Inc.).

Using podcasts to drive traffic and land sales

When you think about traditional marketing tactics, very few brands considered broadcasting regularly to appeal to more people. Perhaps they'd advertise on a popular program, but they didn't really want to commit staff or cover the cost for 30 minutes or an entire hour of programming. It's different today, though. Many brands are discovering how podcasting appeals to a whole different group of people. As long as your podcast isn't a long sales pitch, you definitely have the ability to drive sales.

Here's how podcasting drives traffic and sales for your brand:

✦ **Your host page always leads to an action page.** Whether you host your podcast on a blog or website, it should always be embedded on a page offering listeners an opportunity to take further action. It's not enough to embed your podcast. List bullets of the podcast's main points to draw in readers and offer a link to a More Information page for listeners who want to find out more.

+ **If you host a good podcast, others will recommend it.** If you have informative, actionable, engaging content, not only will new listeners come back, but they'll also tell others about it.

+ **The search engines pick it up.** Podcasting pages also catch the attention of the search engines. Use your search terms on your podcast's host page; folks looking for podcasts on your topic or to find out more about your topic will stop by for a listen.

+ **Choose buzzworthy content, which always brings in more listeners.** When you podcast an interesting discussion, with notable guests, you'll bring in regular listeners. Regular listeners also bring in new listeners, either with share buttons or word-of-mouth recommendation. This traffic, in turn, can lead to action, whether it's sales, awareness, or another goal.

+ **Get it on iTunes.** When you get your podcast on iTunes, you're opening yourself up to a whole new listener base. So many people browse iTunes each day to find new podcasts to listen to on their morning drive or while working out.

Creating viral videos

Sometimes videos go *viral* — that is, they're shared and viewed thousands (and sometimes millions!) of times on the web. Videos go viral for different reasons, and it's not always an accident. Some brands create videos in hopes that they'll catch the attention of the masses and the press.

 Just about every viral video has one thing in common: It's entertaining. Your video blog about Top 10 Reasons to Buy Organic isn't going to go viral because that's just not exciting or interesting to most people. Viral videos are funny or heartwarming, but more importantly, the people who view viral videos look at them and immediately want to share them afterwards.

Here are some more things that help to turn videos into viral sensations:

+ **They're parodies.** People like to see brands or celebrities poke fun at something, and self-deprecating humor always goes over well. When you poke fun at yourself, your brand, or your genre, people appreciate your ability to keep it real. Just be careful not to be mean and insult the people you're trying to reach.

+ **People can relate to them.** When people see a video that resonates with them, they're likely to share. Common household mishaps, children being children, bad acting or singing, and a humorous look at the things people go through during their regular routines are especially appealing.

+ **They appeal to our emotions.** Charitable organizations or campaigns to raise awareness often use unfortunate but real situations to tug at heartstrings and get people talking.

✦ **They're not too deep.** When people have to think about what they're watching or if they just don't get what they're watching, they're not going to stick around. If you have to touch on a deep or intellectual topic, try doing so with humor so that you don't lose your audience.

✦ **They're unique.** You know what makes a video not go viral? When it copies other viral videos. Come up with some ideas no one else is doing, and you'll have more viewers.

✦ **They show something remarkable.** Many viral videos show talented people. Singers, athletes, musicians, and others have gone viral.

✦ **They're not staged.** Videos that are staged to look spontaneous usually don't look anything close to spontaneous.

Though some brands or individuals create videos with the intention of them going viral, the truth is most viral videos weren't intended to be that way. They had a real quality to them that people appreciated and shared. What can you create that people will want to share?

Interviewing experts on camera

People love video interviews. They make more of an impact than text and even audio because viewers can see the faces of both the interviewer and interviewee and see reactions to questions. It's that trust thing again. Videos can show sincerity or catch someone in the middle of a lie. Plus, it's just nice to place faces with names and voices.

Because you're interviewing on camera, your flaws, imperfections, and mannerisms are open for scrutiny. If you're always smoothing your hair or rubbing your nose, it may be a source of embarrassment if you're not mindful of your quirks during the interview. Also, if you're not prepared for your interview, it's more difficult to wing it.

The following tips help you host an awesome video interview:

✦ **Do your research.** Know as much about your interview subject as possible so that when you're live on camera, you can get more personal, if needed.

✦ **Don't get too personal.** The last thing you want is to make the person with you feel uncomfortable. Not only will it lead to a bad interview, but your viewers may also be uncomfortable, and you may have problems finding future interview subjects.

✦ **If you're reading from notes, don't make it obvious.** Place bullet points off camera where you can sneak a glance, but don't spend your interview time reading. It looks unprofessional.

✦ **Be mindful of your "uhms."** Sometimes people don't notice their own little habits, but boy, do they show up on camera! It takes some practice, but do pay attention to throat clearings, "uhms," and other habits that don't show well on camera.

✦ **Make eye contact.** If you're not looking at the person you're interviewing, look at the camera. Looking off to the side or down at your lap makes you look distracted and not really interested in what's going on around you.

✦ **Talk into the camera.** If you're talking to viewers, look at the camera so that they feel as if you're talking to them.

✦ **Create your list of questions ahead of time and share it with your interview subject.** Always know what you're going to talk about ahead of time. Winging it sometimes leads to a lapse in the conversation and looks unprofessional. Also, if your interview subject knows what questions to expect, he can provide some good information, statistics, and other facts to help back up his point of view.

✦ **Don't let your interview subject take control.** If you're not careful, the person whom you're interviewing will take the lead and talk about only what she wants to talk about or start selling her latest book or blog post. After you lose control of an interview, it's hard to get back on the right track. Take the lead and keep the lead.

✦ **Ask to expand upon one-word answers.** Nothing turns off viewers more than a boring interview. You'll find most people enjoy talking about themselves or what they do. However, now and then, you'll come across someone who is shy or unpolished. They may even feel "yes" or "no" is an adequate response. It's up to the interviewer to bring out the best in the guests by asking open-ended questions and directing the conversation.

Sharing Images

Images are an important part of content creation. They help illustrate a point, break up text, and add more to the conversation. But using an image in your content isn't as simple as pilfering a photo from Google Images and adding it to your blog post. In addition to choosing a photo that helps to enhance your content, you also have legal and copyright considerations.

The following sections explore how to add great images to your content without breaking the law.

Using images for your online content

A picture doesn't always say a thousand words, but it often gives your content a little extra something-something. People like images; their eyes are drawn to them. If it's not the headline that makes them take notice, your image can be the one-two punch. Because online content works best when it's scannable, images give the reader another area to focus on, as well.

Images are also good search engine optimization. When you take the time to add keywords to your image and caption the photo, the search engines will pick up the search terms. Your images then show up in image searches, such as Google Images.

You can also use images for other reasons. For example, you can invite your community to Caption This on your Facebook Page or create a Twitter discussion by sharing a photo and inviting discussion. Images are a whole other way to provide content and bring in readers, build community, and (hopefully) drive sales.

Legalities: What you need to know about sharing images

Adding a photo to your blog isn't as simple as downloading an image, however. People who take photos own the copyright to them. Just because you see a photo online doesn't mean that you have permission to use it. Also, just because you don't see a copyright symbol doesn't mean that the image isn't copyright protected.

Some people feel that because something is posted on the web, it's in the public domain. This assumption isn't true, either. It's always important to check each and every image for the available rights and usage. You can tell whether you can use a photo by reading all the details around it. The different types of rights and usage are explained in the following list:

✦ **All Rights Reserved:** The photo isn't available for use unless you contact the author for permission.

If you receive permission to use the image, you may embed it into your blog post as long as you provide attribution. The photographer may also require a link back to the original content. Please note that this requirement usually means that you're granted only one-time usage for that specific blog post or content. You don't have permission to use the photo as often as you want.

In addition, most images require a fee to use: If you want to use an image more than once, you'll have to pay extra. Make sure that any agreement between the photographer and you is clear, and that you have a good understanding of how many times you can use the image and what other requirements she may have for its use.

✦ **Some Rights Reserved:** The agreement between you and the photographer isn't as strict, but it also means you should read all the fine print to find out exactly what rights you have when using the image. You may have unlimited use but have to attribute to the photographer each time. It also may mean that you can use the image on a personal blog but not for commercial use.

✦ **No Derivative Works:** You're not allowed to take the photo and alter it in any way and publically post it as your own. You can't add anything to the photo, nor can you change colors or retouch it using Photoshop.

✦ **Creative Commons:** You're welcome to use the photo, if you follow the listed guidelines, as shown in Figure 2-3. Although, in many cases, Creative Commons photographers allow others to share their photo, usually royalty-free, it doesn't mean that the images are free to use any way you like. Read all the fine print. The photographer may require specific credits, limited usage, and/or a link back to his original content.

Even if no specific requests are made, the right thing to do is to offer attribution to the photographer. Using a photo is the same as quoting another blogger on your blog or sharing someone else's text on your blog. If you post someone else's photo and pass it off as your own, even if that's not your intention, you're not only violating copyright laws, but you're sharing unethically.

Figure 2-3:
Always check for image rights and ask permission before using a photo.

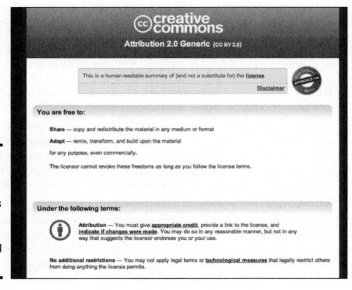

A good general rule for anyone looking to use a photo found online (or offline!) is, "When in doubt, ask." In some cases, photographers discovered years later that bloggers had used their images, and the photographers successfully sued for back royalties.

Finding images online

Don't let all this talk about rights and usage discourage you from finding photos to use for your content. Finding photos to use isn't difficult, and the rights are usually laid out for you below each photo.

Instead of punching keywords into your favorite search engine's image search, which can lead to confusion about rights, it's a better idea to become a member of photo sharing sites. Table 2-1 lists some popular photo sharing sites and indicates whether the sites are free or require a monthly or per photo fee.

Table 2-1	Popular Photo Sharing Sites	
Site		*Description*
123RF	www.123rf.com	Offers both free and paying options.
Bigstock	www.bigstockphoto.com	Requires a subscription fee.
Creative Commons	http://creative commons.org	Allows for the posting and sharing of Creative Commons works.
Dreamstime	www.dreamstime.com	Offers both free and paying options.
Flickr	www.flickr.com	Images often fall under Creative Commons, but check the right sidebar of each image page to view rights for each photo.
iStockphoto	www.istockphoto.com	Requires a subscription fee.
Morguefile	www.morguefile.com	Offers free photos that are mostly taken by amateur photographers and aren't always professional quality.

(continued)

**Book III
Chapter 2**

**Exploring Content
Marketing Platforms**

Table 2-1 *(continued)*

Site		*Description*
Pinterest	`www.pinterest.com`	Not a site where you can buy images, but you can search out images and contact the original photographer to find out whether you can buy a copy of the photo.
Shutterstock	`www.shutterstock.com`	Subscription-based service.
Free Images	`www.freeimages.com/`	Formerly called stck.xchng, Free Images offers a wide variety of free-to-use images; but be sure to check the restrictions.
Wikimedia Commons	`http://commons.wikimedia.org`	Offers royalty-free and free photos.
Wylio	`www.wylio.com`	A search engine featuring free images for bloggers. A nifty feature of this service is that you can format your image right on the website to cut and paste into your blog post.

Some sites allow you to use photos for free as long as you follow certain guidelines, such as notifying the photographer and giving attribution. Notifying the photographer, though, isn't the same as asking permission. If the site requires you to notify the photographer, it simply means the photographer has given permission already; he just wants to know where it's going to be used.

Also, some photographers won't allow their images to be used on certain sites — for example, pornography, political, religious, or any other sites where the image may be taken out of context or use of it will reflect poorly on the photographer. However, the photo sharing site you choose explains these limitations for each photo.

Many of the photos shared for free online, even on image sharing sites, aren't shot by professional photographers and can sometimes look a little rough or amateurish. However, you can still find plenty of professional-quality photos.

Most stock-image sites require you to pay a fee. It can either be a monthly fee, where you're granted permission to use a set amount of photos, or a per-photo fee. You may also be required to attribute the photo to the photo sharing site so that everyone knows where the image came from.

Sharing images on photo sharing sites

Images aren't useful only for illustrating your content. They're also handy as a marketing tool. When you share and upload your own images, you can reach a whole new audience. For example, if you like to photograph local architecture, you can post your images to a photo sharing site, such as Flickr (see Figure 2-4), and catch the eye of people who are also into architecture. They may end up following you on Twitter or Google+ because they enjoy your take.

When you allow others to use your images, you also create an opportunity for backlinks. When users attribute a photograph to you and link to your website, they're alerting the search engines, which is always a very good thing. Moreover, others will follow the attribution to your blog or website, and some may even become members of your community.

Sharing photos is also a way to establish expertise. For example, foodies often share images of their latest culinary creations or a wonderful dinner out. If your business is an auto dealership, sharing images based on the cars you sell can help bring in new business. If you sell cosmetics, sharing before and after makeover pictures can lead to sales.

**Book III
Chapter 2**

**Exploring Content
Marketing Platforms**

Figure 2-4:
Use a photo sharing site, such as Flickr, to help market your brand.

flickr Sign up Explore

Inspiring photography.
Introducing the all new Flickr app.

Share and connect with the Flickr Community.

Stunning photos made easy.

All your pictures in one place.

Download on the
App Store

GET IT ON
Google play

If you share images of people on your Facebook business page and tag them, your tags can show up in their friends' status updates, if their settings allow, which can also lead to new customers and community members.

Often times, when you post an image on a social network devoted to image sharing, others will comment. Those comments lead to a whole new way to grow your community.

Smartphone users enjoy using the Instagram photo sharing app to upload images to share on the social networks. When you take a photo with Instagram, you have the option to post a few words in the caption and share the photo on Facebook and Twitter. (See Book V, Chapter 5 for more on Instagram.)

When you share an image on photo sharing sites, make sure to leave contact information, just in case someone wants to share the image or find out more about you.

Using Social Media Platforms for Online Content

Most people don't usually think of social media updates such as Twitter or Facebook as "content." However, social media is a very important part of any content marketing strategy. (See Book III, Chapter 3 for the lowdown on developing your content marketing strategy.) Not only are all your posts and updates considered content, but you can also use social media as a marketing tool for your blog posts, videos, and podcasts.

Though we're going to cover the nitty-gritty details of how to use Facebook and Twitter later in this book, we'd be remiss if we didn't at least share here why you need to include social media in discussions about content and content marketing.

Why social media? Here are some reasons:

+ **Social media can be good SEO.** Public social media updates can appear in searches.

+ **Your customers and potential customers are on the social networks.** It makes sense to go where the people are. If your customers are using Facebook and Twitter, it's well worth your time to spend time talking to them on those platforms.

+ **Social media can help more people to see your content.** Not everyone will see your blog or video updates. Sharing on social media not only puts your content in front of more eyeballs, but your customers may also share that content, giving it even more exposure.

✦ **Social media is a good way to update customers and community.** If you have quick updates, using Twitter, Google+, or Facebook will share your news without having to invest a lot of time creating.

✦ **Social media is affordable.** The social networking platforms are all free to use.

Deciding which social media platforms to use

Social media encompasses a broad range of platforms. For example, blogs, video, image sharing, and podcasting all fall under social media's wide umbrella. Social media also includes the different social networks such as Facebook, Instagram, Pinterest, Twitter, and Google+.

Like all other content marketing platforms, you don't have to have a presence on every social media platform available. When brands sign on for too many platforms, at least one of them ends up in neglect, and it's much better to have a presence on a couple of platforms than to have dead space and old news on an existing platform. Try building up one platform at a time rather than spreading yourself thin on a variety of social networks.

How do you know which platforms to choose? Here are some questions to help you determine the best platform(s) for you:

✦ **Where are your customers?** Before you sign up for a social media platform, understand the platform's demographics and how that platform relates to your customers' and clients' demographics. For example, if yours is a brand that's hoping to attract teens, you have a better chance of doing so on Instagram than Facebook. If your brand manufactures crafting products, Pinterest is your game.

✦ **What platforms are your competitors neglecting?** Hopefully you're investigating your competitors' social media use. If so, there are two items to note:

 • Are they dominating a particular platform? This means that your customers are using that platform, too, and you want to get in on it.

 • Do you see an opportunity for growth and outreach on another platform that your competitors aren't using? It might be worth your while to consider testing the waters there, as well, so that you can be the dominant force for your niche.

✦ **Which platforms are you best equipped to handle?** Can you write better than you can take photos? Facebook or Google+ is probably a better place to begin than Instagram.

✦ **What is your budget? Can you spend money on your social media efforts?** You have a better chance of having your content seen on Facebook if you purchase an ad for your Facebook page. Twitter and LinkedIn also offer more visibility to those who pay to play. These aren't deal breakers, however, and you can still reach your customers and community in a smaller capacity without a big budget.

✦ **What kind of content will you be sharing?** If you prefer to share photos over words, you'll want to choose a more visual platform like Instagram or Pinterest. However, Facebook or Google+ lend themselves better to having a conversation around a video or blog post.

Don't spend too much time agonizing over a high friend or follower count on the social networks. The numbers aren't as important as making quality connections and cultivating existing relationships. The quality over quantity route is infinitely more rewarding than random follows just to up your numbers.

Creating and sharing content with social media

Social media serves a dual purpose in your content marketing strategy. You can use it as a way to create content, but also as a way to share content.

We'll start with using social media as a content-creation platform. What's interesting about the social networks is how many different things you can do with them. Here are some ideas:

✦ Use Twitter to tell 140-character stories about your brand.

✦ Use Instagram to create memes using your photos. Also, use Instagram to share tips, for example, when styling shoes, jewelry, or accessories with an outfit. (If yours is a brand that does this sort of thing.)

✦ Use Pinterest to share design tips and how to's. If you handle marketing for a hair or nail salon, or sell products to the same, use Pinterest to share different hair or nail style tips.

✦ Use Facebook to share product information, unique recipes, and photos of attractive place settings. Food product manufacturers would do well to share original recipes on Facebook.

✦ Use Google+ to share video demonstrations. Google+ hangouts are especially good for this.

✦ Use LinkedIn's blogging platform to share tips for professionals.

In addition to using social media as a tool for content creation, it's also a terrific tool for sharing content on different platforms. Every bit of content you post online should have the ability to be shared on the social networks as well. So if you publish a blog post, you'll also want to share the link on all of the social networks in which a brand has a presence.

You want to give your online community the opportunity to share your content as well. For example, you might notice blog and online articles have buttons near the top or bottom of the content where the author invites readers to share the post on Facebook, Twitter, YouTube, and Google+, and even LinkedIn. See Figure 2-5 for an example of share buttons.

Figure 2-5:
Use share buttons to make it easy for others to share your content.

Know someone who would love this? Please share!

f Facebook   8+ Google   P Pinterest   Twitter   StumbleUpon   Email

You'll find that when your brand has a loyal online community, they will want to share your content with others. Having share buttons allows them to do that with just a couple of clicks.

Understanding the importance of community

Many businesses and brands are now discovering the importance of cultivating an *online community*. Everyone who comments on your content, follows your brand on Twitter, and belongs to your Facebook pages and groups is part of your online community. How you decide to leverage your community is up to you.

It's important to consider your community when planning content because they are the people who will consume and respond to your online content. Without your online community, all your content marketing efforts will be for nil.

There's a difference, however, between customers and community. Customers are people who use your service or buy your product. On the other hand, community members rally around your brand. They feel good about you because they're spending time with you online, which can lead to some terrific brand advocacy and word-of-mouth marketing.

Online communities are important because they create trust. When a brand is interacting on a regular basis with the people who use their products or services, the people feel as if they're privy to something special — as if they're part of the brand. Plus, interaction and conversation don't feel or look like selling. Because your members are enjoying their time with you, they have a good feeling about buying your product or hiring your service.

Business is no longer local. Thanks to the Internet, you're global and your online communities can help spread the word even farther. Your members are your staunchest allies and advocates.

Your online relationships can lead to partnerships, collaborations, and fame. Even more important, online communities enable you to find out about the people who use your product or service and how you can improve. In fact, online communities are so important, one of your authors wrote an entire book devoted to their intricacies. Check out *Online Community Management For Dummies* by Deborah Ng (Wiley Publishing, Inc.).

Chapter 3: Developing a Content Marketing Strategy

All content needs a plan. It's not enough to write something and post it to your blog platform; you also want to take the time to plan out your content so it makes sense. If you're just posting without any clear direction, your content can become confusing, and your customers won't know what actions to take.

Having a clear content marketing strategy is even more important than the content itself. Without a plan, you won't be able to see the big picture, you'll be creating and posting without an end result in mind. Having a strategy in place allows you to focus on traffic, sales, and growth. A strategy helps you know what kind of content to create and how to achieve the desired growth with that content.

In this chapter, we talk about putting a content marketing strategy together in order to achieve your objectives.

Determining Content Goals

If you're reading this section, you're probably thinking about starting a blog, podcast, or video series, and you want to learn how to do so in order to achieve a particular result. Knowing why you're creating content is the first step — and the most important step — in your content marketing strategy.

Here's a look at many of the goals that businesses and business people hope to achieve with their content strategies:

✦ **Drive traffic.** Your content will help to bring new traffic to your blog or website.

✦ **Make sales.** If you have a product or service to promote, sales is probably your top reason for wanting to learn more about content marketing. Content is terrific for selling because you can drive traffic directly to your sales page or website.

✦ **Build brand recognition.** By putting out content regularly, you're growing a readership or viewership. After you have an audience, you're creating brand recognition. If you're recognized as sharing useful or entertaining content, people will know your brand and your logo. When it comes time to buy, your business will come to mind because you already have an online presence.

✦ **Establish expertise.** Content can be educational. You can use your content to share product information, details, and usage tips, or you can use your content to establish expertise for your personal or professional brand. If you share useful and important information, your community will see you as somewhat of an expert.

✦ **Improve your search engine rankings.** Plenty of good-quality content can help your business land on the first or second page of the top search engines.

✦ **Build trust.** Your content enables you to be transparent with customers and community. When you're honest about what you do and keep an open line of communication, people have trust in the brand. Trust equals sales.

✦ **Inspire customer loyalty.** Content that informs and rewards customers can also inspire customer loyalty. Not only will your customers make return visits to your content channels, but they'll share your content with others.

✦ **Generate subscriptions and registrations.** Content can lead to newsletter signups or website registrations. For example, you can direct traffic to a specific page or offer premium content (such as an ebook) in exchange for a signup or registration. We delve into how content can help drive sales and grow your mailing list a little more in the section "Collecting leads with your content," later in this chapter.

✦ **Engage customers.** Content allows your customers to chat with you. Whether it's friendly banter on Twitter or a more opinionated discussion on your blog, they'll appreciate having a voice.

✦ **Build links to your content.** A content marketing strategy is a link-building strategy. As long as you're providing valuable content to your consumers, other businesses and professionals will link to your content so that they can share it with their own communities. All those backlinks are good search engine optimization (SEO).

✦ **Generate leads or new opportunities.** Smart content leads to smart opportunities. For example, if you regularly blog on important topics in your industry, those blog discussions can land you new clients or speaking engagements.

Not everyone uses their content for the same purpose, so you can't count on doing what everyone else is doing online. Take some time to outline your goals before you begin.

In the following sections, we describe several of these content goals in more detail.

Driving traffic

Traffic is a top goal in most content marketing strategies. Businesses want to bring traffic to their websites that they can divert to sales or other signup pages, but they aren't sure how to drum up interest. By producing relevant, valuable content, you're catching the attention of the search engines.

When you're working out how to use your content to drive traffic, consider the following:

✦ **Guest blog posts:** Your content doesn't have to be only on your own pages or platforms. You can also consider writing a guest blog post for another blog. There are great benefits to guest blogging, including backlinks and creating brand visibility. Target the most influential blogs in your niche and read several posts before pitching to make sure you're a good fit. If you think that blogger's audience can benefit from your expertise, send the blogger a note describing the post you'd like to write and asking if he's interest.

✦ **Viral videos:** If you create a great video, hopefully others will want to share it on the social networks. You don't have to make a video that's a big sales pitch, but do put your company's information at the end of the video and link to your website or sales page in the video page's description. The interesting thing about viral videos is that if everyone is sharing it, they'll mention your name. "Hey, check out this funny video from XYZ brand."

✦ **How-to content:** People are always searching online to learn how to do things. If you create useful how-to content that includes descriptive steps to complete a certain task, people will find it online via the search engines and land on your website. If it's truly useful, they may even stick around and read a few more pages or see what you have to sell.

✦ **Lists:** List blog posts come in many shapes and sizes, and they serve a variety of purposes. You can create a list of influential professionals in your niche or list steps to achieving a specific goal. You can even create funny lists such as those you would see at BuzzFeed. The beauty of the list post is how it gets shared. If people enjoy your list or find it useful, it has the potential to go viral, which can lead to a lot of traffic and backlinks.

✦ **A call to action:** If you want to get people to take a specific action, lead them there with a *call to action* (or CTA). For example, if you're posting a link to your content on Facebook, give a call to action such as, "To learn more about building treehouses, see over 150 plans with step-by-step instructions for each at our website."

✦ **Optimized content, including photos:** Use your keywords to attract search engines. Don't do it in a way where the words are repetitious and annoying, but do insert key words and phrases, as needed. Save photos with keywords, as well, so that you can bring in traffic from users searching images online.

✦ **The social networks:** Sharing links to your content with a brief call to action will send traffic from Facebook, Twitter, and all the social networks you use to share with your community.

✦ **Easy sharing:** Using share buttons on all your content will inspire others to post your content to their Facebook walls or Twitter streams, or to email that content to friends who might have an interest.

✦ **Relationships with influential people:** Use your content to build relationships. For example, profile or interview influential people on your blog. They'll share that content in return, possibly giving you a few new sales.

 Content marketing isn't about advertising or spamming. Calls to actions shouldn't be overly "pitchy." The idea behind content marketing is that your content will be so interesting and useful, it will catch the attention of the search engines, as well as the people who can benefit from such content.

Making sales

Okay, to be honest, even though you don't want content to seem as if you're selling, you want sales — otherwise, you wouldn't be marketing so hard. People who consume your content know this. For example, people know a brand like Starbucks has a great social media presence in order to sell their products, and no one holds it against them. The only thing they would hold against a brand is obnoxious sales tactics.

So, how do you sell through content without being pushy? Here are a few ideas that might help:

✦ **Use a call to action.** Have a call to action (CTA) at the bottom or end of your content. For example, say your content is a how-to project for building a birdhouse, where you list all the materials and steps needed to create a beautiful birdhouse. At no time during the tutorial itself should you sell. However, when it's all over, you can post a relevant link with this call to action: "Stop by our website to purchase plans and materials needed to complete this project." You didn't sell at all, but you did give a suggestion at the end. Even if people don't buy that time, they now know where to go when it comes time for them to build their birdhouses.

✦ **Use newsletters.** Another way businesses use content to sell is through a newsletter signup. For example, through calls to action on blogs, websites, and the social networks, brands invite their customers and community to subscribe to their newsletters. Many businesses even offer something of value in exchange for the newsletter signup — for example, a coupon for significant savings or an ebook. Each week, the brand sends subscribers a newsletter that features tips and news, but also links to sales and discounts. Many of the discounts are offered only to subscribers.

✦ **Answer questions.** You can also try answering questions. If you notice customers or potential customers ask the same questions, address those questions in your content, giving your customers the ability to buy with confidence.

✦ **Follow the one-percent rule.** Content should follow a 99:1 ratio. That is, only one percent of your content should be a sales pitch. The rest of your content should focus on helping, educating, and entertaining. It's less pushy than constant in-your-face sales pitches, but your customers will prefer to support you by reading your content and buying your products or services, as needed, rather than to read spiel and jargon all the time.

✦ **Focus on your customers' needs.** Your content should have a purpose. For example, it can answer common questions that your customers may have. You can also use it to teach how the product or service works and establish expertise in a niche.

✦ **Provide proof.** People have to know that what you're selling is something that works. Create *infographics* (images listing facts) and case studies, or share reviews from existing customers.

Although traditional advertising and marketing still has its place, selling today is less about heavy block letters and a lot of exclamation points. Instead, people are inspired to buy after consuming content and feeling as if they can trust a person or brand.

Establishing expertise

Content marketing allows both businesses and individuals to share expertise within a niche or topic group. For example, an author or independent contractor can use content to prove to her potential readers or clients that she knows her topic.

Some of the methods used for establishing expertise include

✦ **Blog posts, articles, case studies, online reports, and white papers:** Text-based content is excellent for sharing tips, knowledge, facts, demographic information, and anything written that highlights your particular expertise.

✦ **Ebooks and traditional books:** Enable you to expand beyond the blog post. You can offer a book as a perk to entice people into buying, sell it to earn some side cash, or offer it for free to gain name recognition.

✦ **Videos:** You can use video for interviews, product demonstrations, case studies, and even mini-webinars. Video allows you an opportunity to really connect with your audience because they can hear your voice and see your facial expressions.

✦ **Guest blog posts:** Reach out to influential bloggers in your niche and ask them if you can offer a guest post for their blogs or if you can exchange blog posts with each other. Appearing in another person's blog gives you an opportunity to expand your reach.

If you want people to see you as an expert in your field, use content marketing.

Growing your online community

Another common content marketing goal is for online community growth and development. Your content gives you an opportunity to open up the channels and communication between you and your customers. Through your content, you also have the ability to foster loyal relationships, the kind that lead to word-of-mouth marketing. What follows are some ways content helps to grow your online community:

✦ **Have a dialogue.** Your content opens up a two-way line of communication. Through your content, you can address a variety of consumer or product-related issues, and through comment areas and social media, your customers can respond.

✦ **Collect and respond to feedback.** When you give your customers a chance to talk to you via your content, you have a wonderful opportunity to learn how they truly feel about your product or service. They'll share the bad and the good, which can help you improve. When your online community sees you responding to their comments and concerns, it builds trust. Trust equals sales.

✦ **Build brand loyalty.** All of the trust you establish means customers who really care about your product or service. That loyalty means they stay with the brand and recommend it to others.

✦ **Grow your social media presence.** When you share content online, your community will want to follow you on all the online platforms. You can also use the social networks to discuss content. For example, if you post an article to Facebook, your Facebook community can have a conversation about the article in the comments section of the same Facebook post.

✦ **Use your content to share promotions and discounts.** Through your content, you can offer special sales for your online customers, and also offer coupon codes and other discounts.

Collecting leads with your content

Your content has another important purpose — lead generation. Building your mailing list is an essential part of your content marketing strategy and should be one of your top goals.

Having customers and potential customers sign up for a newsletter or other type of online subscription can drive a lot more sales than if you had relied on content marketing without incorporating email contact. A database of email or even snail-mail addresses means you can share your content directly.

How do you get people to sign up or subscribe without a heavy sales pitch? By offering them something of value for free. For example, many brands create ebooks, white papers, case studies, and in-depth reports that they offer for free if their your customers register for their newsletter using a valid email address.

First, you have to convince your community that they will receive something of value. In addition to the free content, you'll give them a weekly newsletter in their email inboxes. Make sure these newsletters contain tips, ideas, news, and discounts — discounts that lead to sales.

Putting a Strategy on Paper

When you have a good idea about the types of goals you hope to accomplish with your content marketing strategy, put your strategy on paper in an order that makes sense to you and your team. If you don't take the time to list all your goals, as well as the steps needed to achieve those goals, you may forget an important step along the way.

Understanding the elements of a content marketing strategy

Components of a successful marketing strategy include

1. **Definition of goals:** Define goals so everyone who reads and uses the strategy has a clear picture of what you're hoping to achieve with content marketing.

2. **Core message:** What message are you trying to share with your customers and community? Is it a sales message? Are you trying to raise awareness for a cause? Do you want to share details for a new product? Keep your core message in mind while you plan your strategy.

3. **Target audience:** Knowing whom you're trying to reach can help you to focus on content and platform.

4. **Keywords:** Pinpoint the words and phrases people are using to lead to your website and your competitors' websites. Discuss ways you can use these keywords in your strategy.

5. **Content platform and types of content:** Your strategy should include a plan of action for each different platform, which can include blogs, websites, images, and the social networks.

6. **Editorial calendar:** An editorial calendar should list the content you're releasing each week, as well as deadlines for all. (We talk about putting together an editorial calendar in Book III, Chapter 4.)

7. **Task delegation:** A strategy is made up of tasks. Delegate tasks as part of the strategy, complete with deadlines, or nothing will get done.

8. **Reporting and analytics:** Keeping careful records is essential to any strategy so that you can know what works and what doesn't, and how to tweak next time around.

Doing a content inventory

What content do you have already, and what have you done with it? For example, do you have a blog? If so, are you only posting once a week and leaving it at that? Consider the steps needed to get people to view your content. Also, what do you have that's unpublished that might be useful to your community? For example, you can repurpose internal reports and demographic information into content to share with your readers.

Make a list of all the content that's available to use and the different ways you can use it. (A spreadsheet is especially handy for putting together these lists.) Using existing content can save time and resources, as compared to creating content from scratch.

You can format a content inventory on a spreadsheet as described in Table 3-1.

Table 3-1   Outlining Your Content Inventory on a Spreadsheet

Column	*Notes*
Type of content	Note whether it's an article, ebook, video, or other form of content. When you're planning your editorial calendar, mix around the types of content you're using. For example, don't release five videos in the same week. Having a list of the types of content available can help you avoid doubling or tripling up on the platform.
Name of content	When choosing a title for your content, think of something that is eye-catching, reflects the content itself, and has the type of keywords that will attract search engines. A good rule of thumb for headlines is "If I saw this, would I want to learn more?"
Date published, if published	You want to space out the topics so that you're not publishing a repurposed bit of content soon after you published the original.
Description of content	Arrange the list so that you can see, at a glance, what the content is about so that you can plan your editorial calendar accordingly.
Ways to repurpose original content	For example, if someone wrote up a blog post that wasn't used, how can you transform it into something that you can use? Also, what previously published content can you rework into something new? List all the different ways your content can be used — or used again.
Notes	Is there anything your team should know about the content? Do you have thoughts about how it should be published? Also, if it was previously published, note whether it was well received or poorly received.

Book III
Chapter 3

Developing a
Content Marketing
Strategy

Now that you have the components of your strategy and a content inventory, it's time to think about what's missing:

+ Do you want to cover a topic, how-to, editorial, or other type of content that you don't already have as inventory? If so, make a list so that it can become part of your strategy.

+ What are competitors doing that you're not? List all the ways you can take inspiration from people who have a similar business.

+ Is there content you want to create that, as far as you know, no one else is doing? It doesn't hurt to suggest taking a risk.

Taking steps to achieve your goals

A *strategy* is a plan you put into place in order to achieve your goals. It lists all the steps you need to complete, along with an explanation of why each step is necessary. You have to sell your strategy to your team, put ideas into place, and assign each task to the best person for the job.

Here's an example of how you might put your content strategy on paper:

1. **Give an overview of your content strategy.**

   You use your overview to sell your content strategy to your team or anyone who has a stake in the business. Talk about why the strategy is necessary and what you hope your end result will be. Discuss the problems you hope this strategy will solve and why you feel it would benefit the business and the community as a whole.

2. **Outline your goals.**

   List your goals for the strategy and how the strategy will help you to achieve your goals.

3. **Discuss your customers and community.**

   Who are you writing for? Profile typical members of your community and customer base. Discuss how your different types of content will appeal to the different demographic groups.

4. **Share your ideas for content.**

   List a clear plan for your content. Include titles, keywords for each title, a platform for each title, and how you plan to share each title on the social networks.

5. **Discuss how you'll share each piece of content.**

   For example, if you record a podcast that features an expert interview, you not only want to share it with your community, but you want to share it with the expert's community. Discuss a strategy for sharing on your pages and the expert's pages (with that expert's input) and targeting mutual influential friends who can also help share.

6. **Talk about cost.**

   Consider how much this will cost. Be honest about the investment involved, what you consider a necessary expense, and what kind of return on investment (ROI) you expect in the long run.

7. **Provide a call to action.**

   The most essential part of your content strategy is the call to action. Whether you're driving traffic, sales, or brand recognition, you need to guide people to the end result.

8. **Attach an editorial calendar.**

   Create an editorial calendar, and include it with your strategy so that your team can see what you have planned in the upcoming months. You'll probably need to tweak the calendar after everyone has a look because everyone will have suggestions and ideas. We discuss how to create an editorial calendar in more detail in Book III, Chapter 4.

9. **Set a follow-up date.**

   You're going to have to do a bit of reporting in three to six months to discuss the results of your content strategy. You have to prove it worked and discuss things that went well, things that didn't work, and how to move forward.

After you have your strategy in place, you or another person on your team will have to keep detailed records, including an analytics report to see whether campaigns and keywords are driving traffic, and a sales report to see whether sales did, indeed, go up.

Delegating tasks

If you're part of a team, and not handling the content strategy and all the tasks included on your own, be sure that tasks are matched to the correct person and that you have accountability in place to ensure that everything is done according to your calendar dates.

Sometimes, in social media, management feels tasks can be handed off to the intern because, after all, it's just a bunch of tweeting, isn't it? Although we think social media can be an entry-level position, you should hand the tasks surrounding content marketing to people who have the knowledge and experience to do the job correctly.

A content strategy can't work without the right people behind it. Here are some of the roles you may need to create when putting together your team:

✦ **Project manager:** Have a project manager in place to make sure that every task is being done properly and on time.

✦ **Content creators:** Choose content creators who are talented and know your audience. Writers should understand how to write clean copy in a tone that best represents your brand and your customers. Podcasters and video people should speak in a confident manner and know how to handle all the technical aspects of recording and video equipment. If script writers are needed, that's another task for delegation.

✦ **Correspondent:** You may also need to have a member of your team handle correspondence with industry experts so you can gather quotes and book interviews.

✦ **Editors:** You need editors to make sure writing is clean and coherent.

✦ **Marketing team:** Hand off promotion to the marketing team. They'll handle email marketing, social media marketing, advertising, and more.

You should distribute tasks with the utmost care. But it's not enough to assign tasks, however. You also need accountability. Project management software such as Basecamp (`https://basecamp.com`) or Teamwork (`https://www.teamwork.com`) can help you assign tasks, assign deadlines, request progress reports, and share files. Because everyone has access to the software and has their own accounts with tasks, reminders, and deadlines, no one can say they missed something.

Chapter 4: Getting Your Content to the Masses

In This Chapter

✔ **Planning content ahead of time**

✔ **Creating content with staying power**

✔ **Putting your content plan into play**

✔ **Sharing your content online**

✔ **Measuring results**

Think about content marketing like the old tree-falling-in-the-forest joke. If you put your content online and no one sees it, does it really matter that you took the time to create it? Why put all that time into writing or putting together an awesome video, just to let it languish?

Taking the time to put an editorial calendar into place, as well as a plan for sharing your content, can help to get as many eyes on that content as possible.

Content promotion is equally as important as content creation. Without promotion, no one will know about your blog posts, videos, and other content.

In this chapter, we talk about how to get your content seen. Some of the methods we discuss may not be visible to the public (that is, happening in the background) and may not seem as if they're important, but they really do make a difference.

Creating an Editorial Calendar to Keep Content Flowing

You might wonder what an editorial calendar has to do with getting people to view your content. The more organized you are, the better your strategy and your content will come together. An editorial calendar keeps your content team on track and ensures that fresh content is flowing on a regular basis, as shown in Figure 4-1.

Figure 4-1:
An editorial calendar can help keep your content organized and prioritized.

Exploring the benefits of an editorial calendar

Scheduling content ahead of time is important for several reasons:

✦ **Allows the marketing team to plan accordingly:** If your content is part of a particular campaign, or if a campaign is being created around your content, the team has enough time to work rather than plan a hasty, last-minute campaign.

✦ **Ensures you won't be duplicating content:** Seeing a month's worth of content on a calendar can help keep you from becoming repetitive and redundant.

✦ **Enables you to plan seasonal or timely content ahead of time:** If you're posting seasonal content, do it at least six weeks in advance to be available for search engine results. With an editorial calendar, you can set reminders to post seasonal content.

✦ **Gives everyone deadlines to meet:** With an editorial calendar, everyone can verify when content is due and when to post content online.

✦ **Enables you to post content with regularity:** Editorial calendars keep things consistent. You can see when you last put content online and how long it has been between postings.

Deciding what to include on your calendar

Here are some of the items to list on your editorial calendar:

✦ **Content:** The title of the content and a description, if you feel it's necessary.

✦ **Types of content:** Blog post, video, podcast, social media updates, newsletter, and so on.

✦ **Authors and producers:** Assign the tasks.

✦ **Editorial tasks:** If writing needs proofreading or videos need cleaning up, note it on the editorial calendar.

✦ **Marketing tasks:** Posting content or links to content on the social sites, creating email newsletters, and any other promotional tasks.

✦ **Deadlines:** The day the content is to be completed by the author or producer.

✦ **Reminders:** If you need to think about items such as seasonal content or a product launch, put those reminders on the calendar.

✦ **Date of publication:** What day will the content go live?

✦ **Publication location:** Where are you posting the content?

✦ **Reporting:** If you have to provide accountability to management, note the day reports are due on the editorial calendar.

You can use Google Calendar, which is free to use and stored online, as your editorial calendar. You can share the calendar, so your entire team has access to it, and you can allow others to add to it. Google Calendar also allows the user to set reminders so that she receives an email or pop-up message when she wants to see it.

Don't load your editorial calendar up with so many details it's hard to read. The calendar should act only as a reminder. You can go into greater detail in your content marketing strategy and with your project management program, if you're using one.

Finding the Right Mix between Evergreen and Timely Content

When you write a news analysis, do a product review, launch a product or service, or discuss an industry trend, this content gets more or less dated as time passes. It may bring in some eyeballs when the news first breaks, but after a while, searches for these news items or product news will trickle to a stop.

On the other hand, evergreen content has the potential to be searchable indefinitely. A blog post titled "How to Change a Tire" is a good example of evergreen content. Some other examples of evergreen content are

✦ How-to's

✦ Histories (even if it's the history of a certain product or service)

✦ Biographies

✦ Informational posts (for example, "The Health Benefits of Bananas")

✦ Etiquette (for example, "The Etiquette of Commenting on Blogs")

✦ Rules (for example, "Rules of Grammar")

Achieving a good balance with your content is important. You want both trendy and evergreen content. If not, you'll receive spikes in traffic here and there and not a steady rise, which is what you really want.

Many bloggers go for shocking headlines and controversial content in hopes of snagging the retweet crowd. This approach works sometimes, but your content and page traffic will spike and drop off. To keep traffic numbers high all the time, make the content consistent and appealing to searchers and readers for months, if not years, in the future.

Evergreen content is highly linkable as well. With the right kind of content, you'll always have something to link to internally. Plus, other content creators can use your content as a reference for their own blog posts. Also, consider how evergreen content works for all platforms: text, video, and audio.

If you write three blog posts per week, try writing one evergreen post once during that week. Soon, you'll see regular, steady streams of traffic rather than one-off spikes like you'd get with scandalous news or controversy.

Executing Your Content Strategy

After you receive approval for your content strategy, it's time to put the wheels in motion. What was once on paper now has to go to work in real-time.

Follow these steps to execute your content strategy:

1. **Schedule and assign tasks.**

Get your content strategy going:

- *Add all necessary items to your editorial calendar.*

- *Assign tasks in your project management system.*

2. **Make sure all aspects of your content strategy are working as planned.**

   Your strategy needs to be on target and on time:

   - *Request periodic updates or progress reports.* Check on each task half-way through. If you're using a project management system such as Basecamp, you'll find areas where you can communicate with your team, as well as receive notifications and reminders when something is due or past due.

   - *Make sure things are on track and on schedule.* Check to make sure everything is going according to schedule. If someone is falling behind, see what needs to be done to meet your deadlines.

     Be strict with deadlines; otherwise, no one will adhere to them.

3. **Make sure all your team's hard work is paying off.**

   Keep tabs on how things are going:

   - *Review your measurement tools.* You have to know whether all your team's efforts are working. Keep an eye on your analytics to see whether you're achieving your goals.

   - *Report any findings.* Keep records and set up regular reports — weekly, monthly, quarterly, and annually. Compare numbers and note trends.

   - *Make recommendations to improve your content strategy.* A content strategy isn't a static document. It's something that needs updating and reworking.

Don't rest on your laurels. As long as there's an Internet, you need to put out content. Keep repeating the cycle and tweaking as needed.

Sharing Your Content with the Public

You're going to have to do more than set it and forget it when it comes to your content. This is where the *marketing* part of the content marketing strategy comes in.

Social media is a wonderful tool for sharing. Don't be afraid to use the different platforms, but don't share only links to your own content. If you're overly promotional and only want to toot your horn, you'll lose friends and followers rather than earn new members of your community.

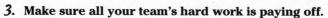

Here are some suggestions for sharing your content with the public:

- ✦ **Share your content with Facebook fans.** When you share your content on Facebook, it shows up in your fans' news feeds. If they like the content, they'll share it with their friends, and so on and so forth. This is how content goes viral. (Figure 4-2 shows how readers share content they feel is entertaining or informative.)

- ✦ **Share links to your content on Twitter.** Sharing links to your content on Twitter means the links will show up in your followers' feeds. If they like the content, they'll retweet it to their followers.

- ✦ **Share your content on other social networks, such as LinkedIn, Pinterest, and Google+.** You want your content to be seen by as many people as possible.

- ✦ **Share content in your regular newsletter.** Does your business have a regular newsletter? (If it doesn't, it should!) Include a brief excerpt, a paragraph or two, of new content with a link to the full article, video, or image.

- ✦ **Reach out to influential professionals.** If you know of influential professionals in your niche who have a good reach via social media or an email newsletter, see whether you can build up some sort of relationship in which you share each others' content.

- ✦ **Share and share alike.** When you share content from other people and brands, some will happily reciprocate.

Create the kind of content people want to share: People don't share boring content. Instead, they want to read or hear or watch content that educates, inspires, and entertains. Before publishing any content, ask yourself, "Would I want to share this?"

Figure 4-2:
Sharing your content on Facebook gives it the potential to go viral.

Pay special attention to activity times on the social network. For example, if you notice that you receive the most engagement on Facebook at 10 a.m., continue to post Facebook content at that time, while avoiding off-peak hours.

Measuring the Success of Your Content Strategy

An analytics program tells you how and why people are coming to your site. Without it, you know very little about your customers, your community, or the content they're consuming.

The type of analytics program you use depends on your needs, but most bloggers are comfortable with the free, tried-and-true Google Analytics (available at www.google.com/analytics to anyone with a Google account). Use Google Analytics to see how many visitors are coming to your pages and what they're doing after they arrive.

Analytics programs are easy to install and come with detailed, easy-to-follow instructions. Either it's a matter of uploading a plug-in or placing some code on your blog or website. We discuss analytics programs in more detail in Book IX.

Here is what you can discover from your analytics program:

✦ **How many people visit your content:** Your analytics program lists how many people visit on a given day, week, month, or even hour. This information enables you to pinpoint traffic trends. Knowing the most popular times of the day or week for readers can help you plan content and sales campaigns.

✦ **Your most popular content:** Your analytics program offers a rundown of how many people read your pages, letting you know which content went over well and what people weren't interested in reading.

✦ **Bounce rate:** The amount of time people spend on a page. A high bounce rate means people leave your site quickly. A low bounce rate means folks are staying for a while and consuming your content. If you have a high bounce rate, you want to work on having the kind of blog and content people want to read.

✦ **Keywords and search terms:** You need to know who's visiting your blog and why. Your analytics program can show you exactly which keywords people are searching for through the search engines before landing on your site. When you know these often-used keywords, you can use them in your content to attract even more readers.

✦ **Response to advertisements and sales pages:** Many analytics have heat maps that allow you to see specifically where most people are spending their time on each page. As a result, you can place ads in the right spots and see whether folks are reading and reacting to your sales pages.

✦ **Top traffic referrers:** Your analytics program shows you whether your Twitter or Facebook campaign is working. In fact, if anyone is sharing or talking about your content at all, you can follow the trail using your analytics program.

✦ **Page views:** You can discover how many people read a page and move on to read more pages, or if they leave after reading one page only. Page views are different from bounce rates in that page views tell how many individual pages each person spends time on at your blog or website, and bounce rates tell you only how long someone stays on your website before leaving.

✦ **Whether your content is driving sales:** Your analytics program shows you whether your content is leading folks to sales pages and how many people are taking action on those pages.

All this information can help you refine your marketing strategy because it gives you deeper knowledge about customers and online community. It's like you're spying on their habits, in a noninvasive way. When you know how, when, and why people are consuming your content, you're better able to tweak it for maximum potential. This knowledge can lead to more sales and visibility.

In addition to checking to see whether your content is driving more customers to your blog or website, you also want to notice other trends:

✦ **Sales:** Have you noticed higher sales since beginning your content strategy? Is your content driving people to the right pages? Note trends in sales, especially what's driving people to buy.

✦ **Signups and subscriptions:** Check the number of people who are signing up for a service, product demo, or offered freebies, as well as subscriptions to the company newsletter. Did your content lead people to take action?

✦ **Social media engagement:** Do you have more friends, fans, and followers? Are more people talking about your brand online? Are more people sharing your content and visiting your social media pages?

✦ **Visibility:** Is your personal or professional brand being talked about in a positive way?

There will always be people who want to read blog posts, listen to podcasts, watch videos, share images, and interact on the social networks. If you're looking to grow your business, it makes sense to go where the people are. Content helps you sell without looking like you're selling, while building trust among your customers and community.

Book IV

Twitter

See how to create a Twitter list at www.dummies.com/extras/socialmediamarketingaio.

Contents at a Glance

Chapter 1: Using Twitter as a Marketing Tool

In This Chapter

- ✔ Understanding the benefits of Twitter for your brand
- ✔ Embracing brevity
- ✔ Avoiding a reputation as a spammer
- ✔ Checking out other brands using Twitter
- ✔ Making every word count

Twitter took the world by storm in 2007. At first, the social media and blogging communities mostly embraced Twitter, but soon brands began appreciating its value. Today, Twitter is mainstream.

At first glance, Twitter looks like a lot of people dropping links and talking about nothing important. But before you write this microblogging site off as a lot of noise, consider the benefits of Twitter and how you can use it as a valuable marketing tool — because, make no mistake, Twitter can totally make a brand.

In this chapter, we discuss the benefits of Twitter and how you can use it to raise brand awareness and drive traffic and sales.

For more information, check out *Twitter For Dummies* by Laura Fitton, Anum Hussain, and Brittany Leaning, or *Twitter Marketing For Dummies* by Kyle Lacy.

Deciding Whether Twitter Is Right for You

Even if you've never used Twitter (see Figure 1-1), you've probably heard about this online social networking service. The Twitter icon, with its famous blue bird, is everywhere, from cable news broadcasts to your local supermarket. Everyone wants you to follow them on Twitter.

Before you post the Twitter icon on your blog or website, or add your Twitter handle to your business cards, you need to know what exactly Twitter is and whether it's the right marketing platform for you.

Twitter is a microblogging social network. We're going to get into the micro-blogging aspect more in the following section of this chapter, but suffice it to say that everything you post has to be short and simple. Believe us; com-municating in the short form isn't as easy as it sounds, especially if you want to get a message out. Still, millions of people are using Twitter, and many brands are finding success.

Different people use Twitter to

✦ **Build a community.** The best reason to join any social network is to grow a community of friends and advocates. Your community consists of the people whom you build trust and relationships with because they view you as being accessible. These people are the ones who will have your back.

✦ **Find new customers.** Thanks to the Internet, you now have the ability to reach a whole new global market. With Twitter, you have the ability to reach millions of new people. Each person you interact with has the ability to reach people, as well. You can leverage all that reachability into sales.

✦ **Have a conversation.** The best part of Twitter and other social networks is the ability to sell without sounding like you're selling. It's called *conver-sational marketing,* and it's exactly what it sounds like. When you have a conversation with your friends and followers, people get to know who you are and what you do. When they have a need for someone who does what you do, they're more likely to call on you. They may even like you so much that they decide to buy what you're selling just to support a friend.

✦ **Ask questions.** The best way to learn about your customers and potential customers is to ask questions. We're not saying that you need to have a Twitter poll (unless you want to), but there's nothing wrong with drop-ping a question now and then to find out about a demographic or habit (see Figure 1-2).

Figure 1-2:
Use Twitter to ask questions and learn about your brand's community.

✦ **Get customer support.** Many people like to reach out to their favorite brands on Twitter to ask questions about a product or service, or to ask for direction or technical support. Twitter is another way to be accessible to your customers. You can also use Twitter to search and make sure your customers aren't having issues.

✦ **Discover what people are saying about you.** It's important to receive feedback, especially unsolicited feedback. Sometimes folks are talking about your brand online, and you definitely want to know about it.

✦ **Promote your content.** Did you just write up a killer blog post? Are you releasing a new video? Do you want to let folks know about a new product launch? Twitter is an awesome tool for promoting new items.

✦ **Host Twitter chats.** Twitter chats allow you to discuss topics at length or bring in special guests. They're another way to interact with your community. See Chapter 5 of this minibook for an in-depth look at Twitter chats.

✦ **Promote brand visibility.** When people see your logo on Twitter and they see you communicating with customers and other Twitter friends, they feel confident in the brand. They like the human element and especially knowing that when they reach out to you on the social networks, you'll be there to respond.

✦ **Give out perks.** Some brands share Twitter-only discounts and freebies as a way to reward their followers. Lucky recipients will no doubt share these perks with their own followers.

Twitter is a commitment. Networking on Twitter isn't as simple as sending a tweet and expecting to bring in the masses; it's also a matter of building relationships, getting to know people, and holding a conversation.

Communicating in 140 Characters

Possibly the most challenging part of Twitter is the 140-character limit. This amount may seem like a lot at first — until you try to post something pithy or clever and realize you can't fit everything you want to say. Once you start deleting characters, your sentence can lose all meaning.

Don't fret and, whatever you do, don't break out the text speak (see Figure 1-3). Brevity is easier than you think.

Deborah Ng
View my profile page

31,397	**471**	**10,215**
TWEETS	FOLLOWING	FOLLOWERS

OMG! Did u c that? I want 2 do it 2! LOL!

99   Tweet

Figure 1-3:
Using text speak hurts the eyes and looks unprofessional.

You may notice that a lot of people use shortened words, such as "u" instead of "you" or "2" instead of "too" or "to." The problem is that using acronyms or abbreviations is unprofessional and hurts people's eyes. Ditto running words together to fit them in the space. A good general rule is that if people can't read your sentence at first glance, you'll lose them.

Here are a few tips for getting the most out of your 140 characters:

✦ **Make every word count.** Use words that show an action or make an impact. Avoid filler words, such as "that."

✦ **Use short words when at all possible.** Try short, eye-catching words over longer words. Just about every "big" word has a shorter counterpart.

✦ **Punctuation matters.** You may be tempted to skip your periods and commas in order to fit in more characters. Run-on sentences don't look very pretty, and they're hard to read. Do your best to use proper grammar and punctuation.

✦ **Use humor.** Do you know what gets lots of retweets and responses? A funny tweet. That isn't to say every post needs to be slapstick, but don't be afraid to say something funny now and again. Your community will enjoy it.

✦ **Get to the point.** Don't take the scenic route; get right to the point. You have only 140 characters to work with, so say what you have to say without mincing words.

✦ **Grammar counts.** Don't use poor grammar simply because you think it fits the tweet. Grammatical errors turn people off from wanting to do business with you because they feel you're unprofessional.

✦ **Use both upper- and lowercase.** All uppercase letters make people feel as if you're yelling at them, and all lowercase letters look as if you're too lazy to hit the Shift key. Make a good impression by rocking the upper- and lowercases.

✦ **Give value.** Being silly and fun on Twitter is okay, and it's fine to say something frivolous, as well. Just be sure to add value into the mix. If you're using Twitter to promote your business, share your expertise, as well.

✦ **Don't always make it about you.** Don't make every tweet about you or your business. Visit with your community. Participate in other conversations, ask questions, and share links to other people's stuff.

✦ **Don't break up your tweets.** Be careful dividing up tweets to continue a thought. A lot of people will see only the first or second half of the tweet and have absolutely no idea what you're talking about.

✦ **It's okay to use characters.** Even though we discourage text speak, feel free to replace the word "and" with an ampersand. Replacing a word with an accepted character isn't considered unprofessional.

Before you get started with tweets, research other brands that are having success using Twitter and observe how they're interacting with their communities. You may come away from the experience with some good ideas for interacting with your own communities. (See the upcoming "Researching Other Brands on Twitter" section.)

Promoting without Seeming Like You're Promoting

On the social networks, there's a delicate balance between promoting and spamming. If everything you do is calling attention to you or your business, you'll find yourself losing followers faster than you can bat an eye. The beautiful thing about conversational marketing is that you can talk to your friends and followers about anything in the world, and it still has the potential to drive business.

Your first course of action is to follow the right people (see Chapter 2 of this minibook). After all, why be on Twitter if you're not reaching people? Don't worry about starting out slowly at first; your numbers will grow if your tweets offer value, and you gain a reputation for being interactive and engaging.

The tricky part is to get people to dig what you do without turning them off with spam or over-the-top sales tactics.

You can easily be overly promotional on Twitter, especially when you see others do nothing but drop links. Because of the 140-character limit, many people feel it's more important to fit a link in than some interesting text. The problem is, many of the people who drop too many links either lose their followers, don't gain new follows, or end up ignored by their existing followers.

What follows is a list of do's and don'ts for promoting your brand on Twitter without looking like you're promoting your brand on Twitter:

- ✦ **Do follow the people who will receive the most value from your tweets and your brand.** You may be tempted to follow everyone you can simply to receive a follow-back in return, but this approach only leads to a cluttered, hard-to-follow Twitter stream with people who don't really care about you or your brand. Be selective with your follows for the best level of engagement. Go for quality over quantity.

- ✦ **Don't auto-follow everyone who follows you.** You may be considering paying for an *auto-follow program* — that is, an app that automatically follows everyone who follows you or who follows a specific Twitter account or keyword. An auto-follow program isn't a good idea because not only don't you know everyone in your Twitter stream, but people who auto-follow are very easy to spot because they have a high ratio of people they follow versus people who follow them. This ratio imbalance is usually the sign of a spammer, and it drives followers away.

- ✦ **Do search for specific keywords and topics.** By all means, use your search function to find the people who follow a specific keyword or talk about a particular topic.

- ✦ **Don't spam everyone who is talking about those topics and keywords.** Do you know what people who use Twitter regularly hate? They can't stand it when they mention a word, and then all these spammers come out of the woodwork. For example, mentioning "iPad" on Twitter leads to a flurry of hopeful sales people bombarding the unsuspecting tweeter with links to discounts on tablets. You'll find yourself reported as a spammer if you spam.

- ✦ Use keywords as a guide and a suggestion, but don't hit everyone who talks about or uses your particular keywords with a sales pitch.

- ✦ **Do ask questions.** Get some interaction going with your Twitter community by asking questions. Keep in mind that you won't get a response every time, but sometimes some great conversations ensue. Also, don't be afraid to use question time to solicit feedback — both positive and negative.

✦ **Don't respond to each question with a link.** If people reach out to your brand on Twitter, you may at times respond with links and at other times avoid them. For example, if they can't find a sign-up page for your newsletter, by all means respond with a link. If they ask a general information question falling within your area of expertise, don't respond with your latest blog post. That'll get old and spammy after a while.

✦ **Do be sure to inject your personality into your tweets.** Don't be afraid to use humor, slang (that isn't vulgar or offensive), or any other words that show off your personality. You want to show your human, endearing side. The people who are most successful on Twitter aren't afraid to show their personality and fun, playful side.

✦ **Don't rely solely on the scheduled tweet.** Scheduling your tweets, usually through an app such as Hootsuite, helps to make sure that you post announcements throughout your day. However, when all you post are announcements, links, or sales pitches, what you're doing is broadcasting and not interacting. If it helps, go ahead and schedule those announcements, but do stick around in case someone has questions. Try to have back-and-forth interaction through your tweets.

✦ **Do answer questions and respond to comments.** If folks are reaching out to you on Twitter, it's a good thing. It means they're putting their faith in you and find you accessible. Make sure to check Twitter throughout the day for questions and comments so that you can address everything in a timely manner.

✦ **Don't ignore a tweet because you don't want to draw light to negativity.** All feedback is good feedback, even the bad stuff. Answer questions even if they relate to a negative experience, especially because people are watching. If you'd rather not talk about such things with so many people in attendance, invite the tweeter to take it offline with a phone call or email.

✦ **Do share links to your stuff.** Have a great promotion? Share the link! Did you write a great blog post? Share the link! Does someone else have something cool to promote? Share the link! After all, if you're using Twitter as a promotional tool, you're looking for an end result for your ultimate goal, a goal which you can't meet without the link. Don't let all our warnings about spamming make you afraid to share

✦ **Don't only drop links.** If your Twitter stream is nothing but links and self-promotional spamminess, no one will care. You'll drive everyone away. Make sure that links are only a small percentage of what you're sharing on Twitter.

✦ **Do share links to other people's stuff.** The social networks aren't only about you. Highlight other people's achievements, and they'll be more likely to highlight yours. Remember, though, a "you scratch my back, and I'll scratch yours" mentality gets a bit old.

✦ **Don't share or retweet a link unless you know exactly what it's about.** Have you ever seen a popular tweeter share a link and instantaneously receive hundreds of retweets in return? It's a good bet many of those retweeters didn't even click the link to read what it's all about. Blind faith is cool and all, but what if the tweeter was linking to a post that is a lie or something offensive or inappropriate? A retweet is an endorsement, and it's in the best interests of your brand to know exactly what you're putting out there.

✦ **Do tweet every day.** Consistency is key to social media success. Put yourself out there every day so that you're a visible presence. When folks know when to expect your tweet, it's a good thing.

✦ **Don't let your Twitter account become a ghost town.** People feel better knowing that their favorite brands are socially engaged because it makes them feel as if they're really into what people think or want. When they look up a brand on Twitter and there haven't been any tweets since 2008, it tells everyone the brand isn't interested in what their community thinks.

✦ **Do take conversations private.** Not everything has to be out in the open. There's nothing wrong with offering to take an in-depth conversation offline or private. Sometimes, a one-on-one conversation is the best case because you don't want to exclude everyone else in your stream. Also, if you're dealing with a negative situation, there's only so much you can resolve in 140 characters, so taking the conversation private is the way to go.

✦ **Don't auto-DM.** Avoid sending auto private or direct messages (DMs), as shown in Figure 1-4. Some apps instantaneously send "thank you" or "follow this link" private messages as soon as someone follows you. Auto- and spam DMs are a sure way to receive an immediate unfollow. DMs are considered a private area, and most tweeters don't want their privacy invaded.

✦ **Do talk about yourself and your brand.** You're going to hear and read a lot about how the social networks aren't for self-promotion and how it's all about the conversation, and that's true. However, it's silly to think you're spending all your time on Twitter or Facebook and can't even promote your brand.

Figure 1-4:
Sending spammy auto-DMs to your new followers will cause most of them to immediately unfollow you.

✦ **Don't talk only about yourself and your brand.** It's all about balance. Go ahead and promote your stuff, but make sure that you have a good ratio of conversational tweets versus promotional tweets. Different experts have a good idea of what that ratio should be, but usually trial and error determine what works best for you. Try tweeting one to two promotional tweets out of every ten tweets.

✦ **Do find topics of interest.** Try introducing a different discussion topic or question to your community each day. See whether you find any news that will interest your niche, or talk about the latest tools and techniques. Find something discussion-worthy and go for it.

✦ **Don't be corporate and boring.** People don't always want to discuss the brand. While they do enjoy some transparency from time to time, you'll lose people if your tweets are all about the corporate shareholder meeting or yesterday's board meeting. Do share some company business, but all work and no play will make you a very dull tweeter.

✦ **Do talk to everyone.** If your Twitter account has 2,500 followers, 2,500 people are interested in learning about you or your brand. Of course, you can't reach out to everyone by name every day, but ensuring that many of your daily tweets apply to everyone is almost as good as reaching out to everyone. While at times you'll want to reach out to individuals, if your Twitter account is a hotbed of exclusivity, you'll lose followers.

✦ **Don't reach out to only the big names.** Many people feel that if they reach out to the big names on Twitter, they'll receive more attention. When someone with hundreds of thousands of followers retweets your link or mentions you on the social networks, you're bound to get more followers and interest in your brand. However, if you're only reaching out to the big names, it won't be long before you gain a reputation for pandering to the famous people. Your biggest advocates aren't the people with a huge following; they're the people who use your brand and interact with you every day. Collectively, they can have a bigger reach.

Many parts of this laundry list of action items and things to avoid make it sound as if you're not promoting at all, and that's the point. On the social networks, people don't want to be pitched to, unless they invite it. They want to enjoy a conversation and share interesting items they find online. If you turn it from a heavy sales pitch to a conversation between friends, you may find that you land more sales than if you did nothing but drop links.

Researching Other Brands on Twitter

Finding out more about how other brands are using Twitter can help you formulate your own Twitter marketing plan. Many brands are achieving success on the social networks because they're interesting and engaging, and there's nothing wrong with scoping them out and learning by their example.

First, get off Twitter and get on Google. Do a Google search to find the brands that have been successful on Twitter. So many case studies online talk about brands that are doing Twitter right. Read the case studies and follow the brands to see them in action. Note the following:

+ How often are they tweeting each day?
+ What are they tweeting about?
+ How are they handling customer comments, inquiries, and complaints online?
+ How often are they dropping links?
+ Are they offering discounts, freebies, or other perks to their followers?
+ In what way are they bantering good-naturedly with both brands and individuals?
+ What is setting their Twitter apart from the rest?

Next, you want to determine how brands that are similar to yours are using Twitter. You may love certain aspects of their community outreach and not agree with others. This contrast is good because it means you won't be tempted to flat-out copy their approach.

Finally, research cases of companies that made mistakes — and you can find plenty of these case studies and stories online. For example, some brands haven't reacted well to negative feedback, or a community manager dropped a personal tweet from the company account.

When you learn about the way others are using Twitter and learn from their mistakes, you'll become a positive case study yourself.

Knowing Quality Is More Important Than Quantity

Too many people on Twitter worry about numbers when they should really be thinking about other things. For example, sometimes brands don't feel as if they're successful unless they have tens of thousands of followers. True, it's great to have such a large reach, but the truth is, there's no way a brand can interact with all those people. By all means, strive for the big numbers, but don't obsess over them. Instead, worry about building up quality followers: the customers and members of your community who truly believe in the brand and will advocate for you online. Build a core follower base, and the rest will fall into place.

You may also be tempted to follow thousands of people right off the bat so that they'll follow you in return. Before you do so, keep in mind that all these people are going to show up in your Twitter stream. Adding thousands of people is much easier than removing them.

While there's nothing wrong with following so many people, sometimes seeing what people are saying in your Twitter stream is hard because so many people are talking at once. Following so many friends can make it very difficult to find the quality, conversational tweets through all the links and spam. Also, if Twitter feels you're randomly and blindly following people, they'll suspend your account pending further investigation.

By all means, continue to add new followers, but do so slowly so that you know whom you're following and are better able to have a conversation.

You may also be wondering how many tweets you should send out on any given day. While it's true no one wants to see nothing but you in their Twitter streams, it's also true that we can't give you a set-in-stone rule regarding the amount of tweets you should be sending out. Spontaneity is what leads to success, and if you're counting, planning, and scheduling tweets, you're going to lose a lot of the element of fun and surprise many successful brand accounts have. Do what feels right. If you're deep in conversation with others, you're going to be sending out more tweets than you would on a slow day. Also, if you're launching a new product, you're probably going to spend more time on the social networks than you would on a normal day.

**Book IV
Chapter 1**

**Using Twitter as a
Marketing Tool**

Finally, many brands and individuals are concerned about the number of links they share on a given day. Of course, you don't want to spam links all day; but, again, it depends on the day and what you're sharing. Always do your best to add balance and have more conversational tweets than link tweets because you don't want to be known only for dropping links.

Don't obsess over numbers. Succeeding on Twitter is more about tweeting out quality information to quality people than going overboard with followers or worrying about whether or not you tweeted enough in one day. Good, organic growth trumps big numbers every time.

Chapter 2: Using Twitter as a Networking Tool

In This Chapter

- ✔ Following people on Twitter
- ✔ Reaching out to others on Twitter
- ✔ Finding the right words
- ✔ Behaving properly on Twitter
- ✔ Tweeting up

The people who do nothing but drop links on Twitter are missing out on some amazing opportunities. That's because Twitter isn't just a useful promotional tool, but it's also an important networking tool.

Before the Internet, most people had to join professional organizations and attend networking events on a regular basis. While that's still the case now, the truth is, all that in-person networking can be expensive, too. Many people who are just starting out in their fields can't afford to put out the money to attend a lot of events or join many professional groups.

The beauty of Twitter and other social networks is the ability to reach so many people without spending a lot of money. With millions of people on Twitter at any given time, you have ample opportunity to reach out and be reached out to. Make no mistake, Twitter may force you into brevity, but the opportunity to grow your professional network is absolutely there.

In this chapter, we take a look at how to use Twitter as a networking tool and a few best practices for making the most of your experience.

Finding the Right People to Follow

The first step in your Twitter marketing journey is to spend time with the people who make up your community and enjoy their company. To do that, you have to build up a follower base.

The best way to find followers on Twitter is search Twitter for the people who are most likely to support your brand. Here are some ideas for getting started:

✦ **See how many of your existing customers are online.** If you're already in business, you probably have a list of people with whom you do business. They may also be on the social networks. Use your mailing lists to find people to follow on Twitter. Most business people now have their Twitter accounts on their business cards and email signatures. You can also use Twitter's search function.

✦ **Find your friends and followers from other social networks.** If you already have a Facebook, Google+, or brand page set up on one of the other social networks, see whether those same friends are on Twitter and give them a follow.

✦ **Follow other professionals you know from your respective space.** If you share tips or interact online with other professionals, follow them on Twitter, as well.

✦ **Use Twitter search to find people with similar jobs/brands to yours.** Use the search function located at the top of your Twitter page or Twitter app, or go to `http://twitter.com/search-home`. Search for similar brands and interests.

✦ **See who follows brands similar to yours.** When you find brands that do the same as or close to what you do, also follow their followers.

✦ **Use your keywords in Twitter search.** Take those keywords you use to optimize your pages and search for them.

Starting a Twitter follower base is as easy as following someone first. Once you start following people, most will follow you in return.

Be careful with randomly following dozens of people at once. Twitter has tools to detect a huge bulk following and can suspend your account pending further investigation. If Twitter checks your history and feels you're adding people only so they'll follow back so you can spam them, they'll close your account.

Finding Out Who Is Talking about You on Twitter

There's nothing voyeuristic or wrong about observing conversations on Twitter. Most people who tweet are hoping others will notice and join the conversation. If they didn't want a public conversation, they'd create a direct message (DM) or use some other form of communication. They also wouldn't mention or `@reply` you unless they wanted you to know what they're saying. So if you see a complaint or @reply (see Figure 2-1), it's in your best interest to respond, even if it's just to say, "Thank you."

As a brand (personal or professional), you always want to keep your ear to the ground. With Twitter, you can easily monitor the conversation and respond to comments and queries.

Figure 2-1: To get someone's attention on Twitter, use an @reply.

Many times, if someone is talking about or to you, he will @reply you. This means that person is putting an @ in front of your Twitter screen name in order to get your attention. Without the @, there's a chance you won't see the tweet, unless you do a search on your name, your company name, or specific keywords. Also, if you're reaching out to someone, you have to also put an @ in front of his screen name, or the tweet will get lost among the thousands of other tweets.

It's good customer service to find out what people are saying about you on Twitter. It gives you an opportunity to learn about problems or concerns and shows your customers and community you're accessible.

If it isn't on your daily schedule already, make time each day to explore Twitter and see who is talking and what they're saying. Don't shy away from criticism or critique. Instead, thank the other party and take it as valuable feedback.

Responding to Tweets

In order to monitor the conversation so that you can find out whether people are tweeting about you or your brand, keep a Twitter app, such as Hootsuite, Sprout Social, or TweetDeck, open on your computer's desktop. You can set up these apps to ping you every time someone @replies your name or posts a specific search term, including your name or that of your brand. (We cover apps in Chapter 3 of this minibook.)

You need to set up these searches in order to reach out or respond to the people who are talking about or to you. For example, if you work for a restaurant chain and someone tweets out a picture of one of your dishes and talks about how much she enjoyed her meal, you want to acknowledge the tweet by thanking the other party and encouraging her to visit again. If someone tweets that a meal was subpar, you want to respond with an apology and perhaps even offer a discount or coupon for another meal in order to make things right.

Avoid public negativity at all costs. If someone is saying negative things about you or your brand, do reach out to them publicly to ask if you can help, but also ask if you can take it private via phone, email, or IM so that you can discuss without feeling pressured to respond to the whole world. Be especially wary of trading barbs or disparaging remarks, or using rude language. This behavior can harm your brand beyond repair and lead to a public relations nightmare. A good rule of thumb is to never post anything online you wouldn't want to see on the front page of *The New York Times.*

When you `@reply` someone, the comment doesn't show up for the masses, only people you're both friends with. It's not a private conversation — anyone who is searching can find it — but it's not mainstream, either.

If you want everyone to see comments you make when you `@reply` people, put a period in front of it; now everyone can see it. For example, if you wanted everyone to see an `@reply` to Deb, it would read `.@debng` (see Figure 2-2).

Figure 2-2:
Put a period
in front of
an @reply
if you want
everyone
who follows
you to see it.

Searching on Twitter

Twitter is an excellent search tool. Not only can you use it to discover who is talking about you or your brand, but you can also use it as an awesome search engine to find people to follow or reach out to, to find similar brands, and to see what's going on with specific keywords, search terms, hashtags, and news items.

Twitter isn't a search engine, but that doesn't mean you can't treat it like a search engine. If you're looking for something, anything, there's a very good chance you'll find it on Twitter.

What follows are some of the ways to use Twitter's search function or the search engine at `http://twitter.com/search-home` as a search tool. You can find

✦ **People:** Search specific names, Twitter handles, professions, or hobbies. Don't forget to give them a follow so that you can connect.

✦ **Brands:** Use Twitter to search out similar brands to see how they're using the platform.

✦ **Clients:** Search terms will help you find potential clients. Also, consider the types of people you seek out offline in order to drum up business, and search out the same types of people online.

✦ **Jobs:** You can use a search engine, such as TwitJobSearch (`www.twitjobsearch.com`), to find work or follow one of the many accounts that tweet out jobs. You can also use these search engines to find clients.

✦ **Hashtags:** The Twitter search engines help you follow your favorite hashtags.

✦ **Search terms:** When you use a Twitter search for particular search terms and keywords, you'll find everyone who is talking about those words and phrases.

✦ **Your brand:** Discover what others are saying about your brand.

✦ **Your passion:** Search your favorite subjects.

✦ **News:** Whether you want to go local, international, or very niche-oriented, you can search out the latest news on Twitter.

Take advantage of Twitter's trending topics: There may be some discussions happening that can benefit you or your brand. Simply use the trending hashtag to ask questions or respond to people who are already chatting using that hashtag. Don't spam or get into hashtag-jacking. Be sure to stay on topic if you're getting involved in a hashtag conversation, and avoid sharing links unless they're specifically requested.

**Book IV
Chapter 2**

**Using Twitter as a
Networking Tool**

Tweeting Like a Pro

There's a difference in the way someone wanting to do business uses Twitter as opposed to a teen who only wants to tweet out to her friends. Just as you conduct yourself in a professional manner at offline networking events, you'll also want to conduct yourself as a professional on the social networks. People really do pay attention.

Articulating in 140 characters

Text speak, using abbreviations and shortened words in order to shorten a cellphone text message, is difficult to read and unprofessional when used while representing your brand on any platform. Because Twitter allows for only 140 characters, you may be tempted to use abbreviations or shortened words to fit in everything you want to say, but we don't recommend it.

What follows are some tips for making every character count:

✦ **Spell out every word.** The last thing you want is for people to mistake your message or get the wrong impression. When you're not spelling out entire words, some people may not understand what words you're trying to use. Also, some people may think you're lazy because you can't be bothered to spell. Still others might feel like they're talking with a kid. Keep in mind that every brand abbreviates words on their tweets, and while abbreviating is acceptable now and then, it's not recommended for everyday use.

✦ **Use punctuation.** Periods and commas make sentences neat and tidy and help others understand your intended message. Besides, it's more professional to post a real sentence. Run-on sentences or lack of punctuation can change the emphasis, inflection, and meaning of a sentence.

✦ **Practice the art of brevity.** There are always short words to use in place of big words. By choosing short words, you're adding the ability to create a longer sentence where the intended meaning comes through.

✦ **Let your personality shine through.** Don't get so caught up in professionalism that it takes your personality out of the equation. Quirkiness, humor, and even respectful sarcasm add personality to tweets and make you seem more human.

Using the social networks isn't a reason to forget you're a professional. When you're using your brand account, conduct yourself in the same manner in which you'd conduct yourself at an offline business event.

Using the hashtag

When you put a pound sign (#) in front of a keyword, you're using a *hashtag*. The hashtag makes it easy to follow a conversation centered on a keyword or topic. For example, if yours is a sausage brand and you want to create a recipe contest around your world famous kielbasa, you might use `#kielbasarecipes` as your hashtag. The benefits to using a hashtag over an `@reply` abound:

✦ **Hashtags catch the attention of others.** Sometimes people aren't necessarily part of a conversation but join in after espying a catchy hashtag in their Twitter streams.

✦ **Hashtags add longevity to a conversation.** An `@reply` can die in a busy Twitter stream, but following the hashtag will allow you to view all tweets in a conversation at one time.

✦ **Hashtags allow tweets to appear in a stream even if the other party doesn't `@reply` you.** Often during Twitter chats or hashtag campaigns, participants in the conversation don't use an `@reply` to catch your attention but instead rely solely on the hashtag. When you view a hashtag chat using an app such as Hootsuite or TweetChat, you can better view the entire conversation at one time.

✦ **You can measure the results of a hashtag.** Several apps and services, such as Radian6 or Hashtracking, not only have the ability to offer a transcript of a hashtag but also offer data from all the people who use the hashtag — for example, how many people viewed the hashtag (who didn't necessarily participate in the conversation), how many people clicked links, and who are the most influential people using the platform.

When you use hashtags, you can take your Twitter conversations to a whole new level. Hashtags allow you to have, keep track of, and measure a conversation, something very important to anyone marketing a brand.

Please see Book IV, Chapter 5 to discover the benefits and best practices of hosting a hashtag chat.

Sharing on Twitter

The beauty of Twitter is how awesome a tool it is for sharing. The people who use Twitter love to discover new articles, videos, and people. They're quick to offer a recommendation or review, and they especially enjoy when you ask for their opinions. If they like what you say, they'll even give you a retweet.

Knowing when to @reply and direct message

For the most part, your responses to other tweeters will be public unless someone specifically reaches out to you via direct message (DM). Sometimes, though, you want to take public messages private because you don't want to expose some things to the entire Twittersphere:

✦ **Long conversations between you and someone else:** Yes, Twitter is all about public conversations, but you also don't want to clutter up your friends' Twitter streams with a long conversation you're having with someone else. For something expansive, you may want to offer to take it private.

✦ **Complaints:** If someone has a complaint about your brand or is reaching out in a negative manner, let him know you're sorry for the inconvenience and offer to take it to a phone call, email, or DM so that you can better handle the situation. You don't want to sweep the complaint under the rug, nor do you want to ignore it. However, you don't necessarily want to air all your brand's negativity to the masses, either.

✦ **Personal details:** It should go without saying that private email addresses, phone numbers, addresses, and other personal details shouldn't be available to the public. If you need to share this information or need to request that others share it with you, it's best to take it private.

✦ **Information that isn't meant for public consumption:** Sometimes there are details you'd like to share with people but can't put it out to the public yet. By all means, use a Twitter DM.

✦ **Something that may embarrass someone:** Perhaps a negative situation is the result of customer or client error. The last thing you want to do is shame that person on the social networks. If you need to talk to someone because of a potentially embarrassing error, take it private.

For the most part, your Twitter updates are public. However, use your best judgment. Every now and then, you may need to take things private.

Retweeting and being retweeted

For many people on Twitter, getting retweeted is part of their marketing plan. It may not seem like much, but a retweet can go a long way. For example, if you tweet out a link to your latest blog post and someone else retweets it, more people are likely to view your blog post. The more retweets you get, the further your reach.

If you're on Twitter for any length of time, you may notice that certain famous tweeters and those with the most followers get retweets every time they post something. What follows are some tips for retweeting other people's tweets and also for writing the types of things people will want to retweet:

✦ **Say something people want to share.** If you're tweeting links to your food or talking about the weather, your content isn't very shareable. The type of content people share is usually funny, unique, profound, or interesting.

✦ **Share something others want to share.** Don't share for the sake of sharing; share because you think an item has interest or value. Before tweeting a quote or link, ask, "Will this interest my community enough that they want to share it with others?" Think about why you felt compelled to share it and whether your community will feel the same way.

✦ **Don't write for the retweet.** Usually people who try hard to think of something clever or funny to tweet fall flat for trying too hard. Retweetable tweets are usually organic and spontaneous, not forced or flat.

✦ **Don't retweet just because someone famous said something.** Many people retweet well-known people in hopes of catching their attention. If you retweet celebrities all the time, it tells your community you don't really care about them as much as you do famous people. If the Kardashians have nothing to do with you and your community, and the celebrities aren't saying anything all that great, maybe save your retweet for someone more deserving.

✦ **Say "thank you" for retweets.** When people retweet something you said or share links to your blog posts, be sure to say, "Thank you." It shows them you appreciate the community effort.

Avoid the *vanity retweet* — when someone tweets something nice about you and you retweet it. For example, if someone tweeted "@debng is the most brilliant blogger in the world" and I retweeted it, I'd look like a fool. Most people think a vanity retweet looks like bragging and roll their eyes at those who do it.

Blocking people

It's going to happen. There are going to be people on Twitter who are so abusive or spammy that you have no recourse but to ban them. First, don't feel guilty. We all have a list of blocked tweeters, even if we don't talk about them. Second, understand that no one has to put up with abuse.

What does it mean to *block* your tweets? Simply, it means the person you block shouldn't be able to see or respond to your tweets.

Here are some reasons you might want to block people from viewing your tweets or participating in your conversation:

✦ Every time they respond to a question or comment, it's with a link to a sales page.

✦ Every time you post, they respond with something snarky.

✦ Someone uses vulgarity and profanity on a regular basis, and that's not your thing.

✦ Someone is abusive to you and your followers.

If someone isn't being very nice on Twitter, or if someone is using your conversations as an excuse to sell stuff or drive traffic to her site, go ahead and block that person. Your community will probably applaud you.

Creating a successful Twitter campaign

Your Twitter campaign takes careful planning. It's not enough to shoot out a tweet every now and then. You also want to put a strategy in place. If you don't go into it with a specific plan and goal, your tweets may be sporadic and haphazard, and you won't achieve the success you hoped for.

Here are some tips for creating a successful Twitter campaign:

✦ **Plan a follower strategy.** Determine the types of people you want to follow and have follow you in return. Consider a mix of people who are customers, have the potential to be customers, who work in similar jobs, and also brand accounts that may have a tie in with your community. (For more on this topic, see the section "Finding the Right People to Follow," earlier in this chapter.)

✦ **Plan a content strategy.** Think about the types of tweets you want to post each day. Consider a mix of humor, news, questions, retweets, and a few promotional tweets with or without links.

✦ **Plan a hashtag strategy.** Hashtags can be a lot of fun. You can have a regular hashtag chat (see Book IV, Chapter 5 to learn more about hashtag chats) or use a hashtag in contests, news, and updates about your brand and more. Plan for at least a couple hashtag updates per day. (See the earlier "Using the hashtag" section for details.)

✦ **Don't make every tweet a sale.** Plan a balanced content strategy so that your tweets feature more than selling. Perhaps publish two links or sales for every ten tweets.

✦ **Don't make every tweet about your brand.** Share non–brand-related thoughts and ideas so as not to make everything about you.

✦ **Ask questions.** Ask questions not only about your products and services, but also about news items, trending topics, and topics geared toward individual members of your community.

✦ **Share other people's stuff.** Share links to blog posts, images, news articles, and videos by a variety of people.

✦ **With all that said, don't be afraid to share your own stuff.** There's no shame in sharing your own blog posts, news, and even links to sales and discounts. Again, it's all about balance.

✦ **Think outside of the box.** Think about ways to reach your community on Twitter that are different from the same old, same old. Plan content or campaigns that no one is, or very few people are, doing. Research some unique ways brands are using Twitter, and then put your own spin on them. (For more on researching brands, see Chapter 1 of this minibook.)

✦ **Use Twitter in conjunction with other platforms.** Plan content and campaigns that span the platforms. Use teaser tweets to draw attention to blog posts or Facebook content, for example. (For more on marketing with Facebook, see Book V, Chapter 1.)

✦ **Call out your community.** If someone in your community has a milestone, offer public congratulations. Wish happy birthdays and anniversaries, and offer condolences or congratulations. Don't forget to use the @reply so that the other party knows you're offering good wishes.

✦ **Seek assistance.** If you have any technical questions or would like recommendations on the latest gadgets and gear, reach out to your community. Try to have at least one question per week because your community appreciates seeing your human side.

✦ **Create discount codes for your community.** While you don't want to be spammy, offering perks to your community is a nice gesture. Why not create discount codes for your Twitter members only to thank them for their support? Try for at least one discount per month.

✦ **Be transparent.** Be honest with your community. If you're asked questions, don't tap dance around an issue or fudge numbers — it's sure to backfire on you later.

Using keywords in your tweets

With 140 characters, you need to choose your words wisely, so we don't always recommend that you use keywords in your tweets. However, you can make your Twitter content more searchable by using keywords in some of your tweets. Don't use the types of words and phrases that don't make any sense or don't work in a sentence, but do use words that you know others are searching for online. Try writing your keyword tweets ahead of time,

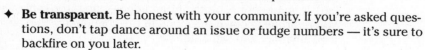

playing with the words so that they make sense. If you're using keywords to make announcements, perhaps take an hour or two to write up a list of tweets that are appropriate. When you try to tweet keywords off the cuff, it often doesn't come out as intended.

To make your tweets even more searchable, use your keywords as hashtags. Using hashtags makes it easy to refer back to them later to see who else is using them. A hashtag is different from a keyword; a hashtag is used to hold a conversation rather than make your tweet visible in a search.

Don't use keywords for every tweet. If your community feels as if you're using Twitter only to drive traffic or sell something, you're sure to lose followers.

Following the Twitter Rules of Etiquette

Like everything else online, there are certain unwritten rules of behavior on Twitter.

What follows is a list of accepted Twitter practices. Most of these items are common courtesy, and some are things that aren't so intuitive to the new Twitter users. While most of these items won't get you booted off Twitter, not following certain rules of etiquette can cost you some followers:

✦ **Don't spam.** If a potential follower takes a peek at your Twitter stream and it's nothing but preprogrammed links, she's going to turn tail and run. If you post sales or traffic driving links all day, you're going to lose community. If you talk only about yourself, your brand, or your product, you'll never enjoy a good conversation. Balance your promotional tweets with conversational tweets.

✦ **Be positive.** There's a time and place for negativity, and Twitter usually isn't it. Avoid rants, profanity, and depressing woe-is-me type topics. If you're bringing down the mood of the community, they won't feel the love anymore and will unfollow.

✦ **Don't use all caps.** TYPING IN ALL CAPS IS CONSIDERED YELLING. It hurts the eyes, too. Avoid it at all costs.

✦ **Leave space for retweets.** Try to make all your tweets retweetable. Because you're allowed only 140 characters, try typing no more than 120 characters so that others have room to retweet your tweets. If it's too much work for them to edit your tweet to add their own commentary, they won't do it.

✦ **Don't swear unless you're sure that your community isn't easily offended by profanity.** Though some people don't mind a little cursing, most people do. If you're going to go the edgy route, make sure that your community is comfortable with it.

✦ **If you're joining a Twitter chat, let your community know.** When you participate in a Twitter chat, you generally have more tweets in your stream than usual. Give a tweet before beginning to let everyone know that you're joining a chat and will tweet more than normal for the next hour or so.

✦ **Don't feel you need to follow everyone who follows you.** Not everyone who follows you is a good fit for you. Don't feel compelled to follow everyone who follows you first. By the same token, don't be afraid to unfollow someone who doesn't sit well with you or your brand's message and tone.

✦ **Give credit where it's due.** If you're sharing a tip, quote, or link you saw someone else share, give that person credit. You don't want a reputation as someone who steals everyone's thunder.

✦ **Don't hijack someone else's hashtag.** Don't use someone else's hashtag to promote your stuff. It's wrong and will turn off both old and new followers.

✦ **Don't respond to a tweet with a sales push.** If someone is reaching out to the community for assistance, don't respond with a link to something promotional. It makes you look insincere. Instead, reach out with genuine, helpful information.

✦ **Avoid private jokes.** If you can't share with everyone, don't share at all.

When using Twitter, follow your best practices for business in the offline world. Sure, it's a more casual form of communication, but you're still looking to make a good impression.

Hosting a Tweet-Up

Enjoying Twitter? Feel like taking your show on the road? Why not grow your community offline with a tweet-up?

Tweet-ups are Twitter community get-togethers. You see them at many blogging, business, and social media conferences, though they're also held often in cities, as well. They don't take much effort to plan, they don't have to cost much money, and promoting them is as simple as getting everyone you know to tweet.

Many brands host tweet-ups in order to meet their community offline. They invite the people who follow them on Twitter to join them at a pub or restaurant to meet them face to face. Sometimes the brand buys a round of drinks or provides food, and other times it's up to individuals in attendance to provide their own refreshments. It's usually more about the people than what's being served.

Tweet-ups are easy to set up. Just follow these steps:

1. **Plan a time and place for your tweet-up.**

2. **Contact the venue in advance to make sure that it can accommodate a small gathering.**

3. **Start tweeting out the details of the tweet-up at least two weeks in advance.**

4. **Invite your community to share the details with their friends.**

5. **Show up at the designated date and time, and meet and greet your community.**

Tweet-ups can be low-maintenance gatherings, or you can invest money in putting on a full-fledged spread. Either way, your community will be happy to spend time with you.

Chapter 3: Finding the Right Twitter Tools

In This Chapter

✔ **Personalizing your page**

✔ **Creating your profile**

✔ **Using Twitter apps**

✔ **Tweeting from your devices**

Twitter has evolved over the past few years to highlight the user and his interests. Visitors to your Twitter home page now find an eye-catching header image that draws the attention to your avatar and bio. This setup is especially helpful for users who want to find people to follow who have common interests. The Twitter page now allows users to add personality and passion to their profiles.

Despite a striking header image, you don't have to spend all your time at Twitter.com itself. Tools and applications, or apps, enhance your experience and take your page from ho-hum to something that's intriguing, personal, and unique — and the best part is that you don't have to be on Twitter to use them.

In this chapter, we discuss the tools that can help make your Twitter experience even better, and we also suggest ways to take your Twitter profile page to a whole new level.

Customizing Your Twitter Profile Page

Don't overlook customizing your Twitter profile page, or else it's just a page with no personality, giving others no reason to follow you. You see, unless potential followers know you, they don't have much to go on. So they want to click your profile page and know immediately whether you're worthy of a follow.

On your website, you take the time to create an About page that's representative of you and your brand (see Book III, Chapter 2). Your Twitter profile page, shown in Figure 3-1, should be no different.

Figure 3-1:
Your Twitter profile page offers little space to make a big impression.

The following elements make up your Twitter profile page:

✦ **Header photo:** A large background image that best represents you or your brand

✦ **Avatar:** A photo or logo that you feel best represents your brand

✦ **Bio:** A few lines telling who you are and what you do

✦ **URL:** A link to your blog or website

✦ **Location:** Where you're based

Your profile page also lists the number of people you follow and how many people follow you. These numbers tell people how popular your Twitter account is and can indicate whether you're a spammer.

As we mention in Book IV, Chapter 2, following more people than you have followers is usually an indication that you're spammy or heavy into the sales because it's a sign of someone who uses auto-follow software. People tend to stay away from those who don't organically grow their followers.

Your most recent tweets are also listed on your profile page. The number of recent tweets is important because it shows potential followers that your account is still active.

The following sections explain how to add a header photo and avatar to your Twitter profile page.

Creating a header photo

Generic Twitter pages are boring. By creating a custom header photo (see Figure 3-2), you're offering a better opportunity for potential followers, customers, and members of your community to find out more about you. A picture is worth a thousand words, right? You're also proving you're a real human being and not some spammy bot. People who make up accounts for the purpose of pushy selling or spamming don't take the time to create a custom header image because they know they'll probably be banned soon. Your background not only represents you as a brand, but it also tells folks you're legit.

Figure 3-2: A header photo can highlight personality and passion.

Use the space in your Twitter header image to define your brand and entice people into wanting to learn more about you.

Before you create your header image, take a look around. Visit other people and brands to see how they're customizing their Twitter pages and get some ideas. If you're technically challenged and not sure that you can create the right type of header image, you can also hire someone to put together something representative of you or your brand. If you're representing a personal brand — for example, if you're a freelancer — your photo should say something about you and your interests or expertise. If you're placing a header photo on a brand page, the image should be representative of your brand and customers.

Deciding what to include in your header

Consider putting these elements into your background image:

✦ **Your brand's logo:** It doesn't have to be front and center, but having a logo incorporated somehow helps with brand recognition.

✦ **An image representative of your brand:** For example, if you work for a beer company, consider a frosty mug of one of your premium beers as a header image.

✦ **Your fans and community:** Showing how people who are passionate about the brand are using the brand is a great sales tactic.

Uploading a header image

After you create a header image, you're ready to upload to your Twitter page:

1. **Click your avatar in the upper-right corner of your Twitter profile page and select Settings from the pop-up menu that appears.**

   The Settings page opens.

2. **Select Profile in the left sidebar.**

   The Profile Settings page opens, where you can upload both your avatar and header image.

3. **Click Change Header and select Upload Photo from the pop-up menu that appears.**

4. **Click Save Changes.**

   You now have a custom Twitter header that shares information about you and your brand, and hopefully reflects the message you're trying to share.

Creating a custom Twitter avatar

Your Twitter *avatar* is the small image next to your @name that your followers see every time you tweet. If yours is a personal brand, you may want to use an image showing your likeness. If you're managing a professional brand, consider using a logo for your avatar.

Uploading an avatar is simple. Just follow these steps:

1. **Click your small avatar in the upper-right corner of your profile page and select Settings from the drop-down list that appears.**

2. **In the Settings page that opens, choose Profile from the left sidebar.**

   The Profile Settings page opens, where you can upload photos for both your avatar and header image.

3. **Click Change Photo, and select Upload Photo from the pop-up menu that appears.**

   You can instead opt to take a photo right then and there by selecting Take Photo from the pop-up menu. If you decide to take a photo, skip Step 4 in this list.

4. **In the File Upload pop-up window that appears, select the image you want to use as your avatar.**

5. **Click Save Changes.**

Feel free to change your header to reflect the seasons or holidays, but you want your avatar to remain familiar to your community. If you change your avatar more than people change shoes, your brand isn't going to be very recognizable on Twitter.

Pinning Tweets

Did you tweet something especially important, amusing, or newsworthy? Is your brand currently running a promotion? Twitter now offers the ability to *pin* tweets to the top of your Twitter profile page so they remain there, even after you add other tweets. As Figure 3-3 illustrates, the pinned tweet stays at the top of your profile page, so it's the first thing people read when they access that page.

To pin tweets, follow these steps:

1. **Open your profile page.**

2. **Select the tweet you want to highlight.**

   That tweet appears in its own page.

3. **Select the More option (which looks like an ellipsis).**

4. **Select Pin to Your Profile Page from the pop-up menu that appears.**

Keep in mind that if you have a tweet that is already pinned, you will have to unpin it first. Twitter only allows you to pin one tweet at a time.

To unpin a tweet, follow the preceding steps, but choose the Unpin option in Step 4.

Figure 3-3:
Pinning tweets keeps them at the top of your profile page.

Using a Twitter Application

Twitter applications (or apps) help enhance your experience. They allow you to manage multiple accounts or see several different search terms or hashtags at a glance. They can also tell you whether you're using Twitter effectively and how well your followers are responding to your tweets, and even help you upload images to your account.

If you're looking to spend any amount of time on Twitter to market your brand and interact with your customers and community, a Twitter app is essential.

Exploring Twitter desktop applications

Twitter applications are programs and websites that allow you to do more things with your Twitter account. For example, an app like Hootsuite or TweetDeck enables you not only to see all your followers' tweets and the messages you tweet, but also to see direct messages and any search terms or hashtags you follow, all at the same glance.

Here are some Twitter apps to consider:

✦ **TweetChat** (http://tweetchat.com): Allows you to keep up with busy hashtag chats.

✦ **Hootsuite** (http://hootsuite.com) and **TweetDeck** (www.tweetdeck.com): Enable you to see all your followers, as well as search terms and hashtags. You can also manage several different Twitter accounts at a time, follow and update your Facebook accounts, and even schedule your tweets. Hootsuite also offers a premium (paid version) where you can access reports and statistics.

✦ **Sprout Social** (http://sproutsocial.com): A tool that allows you to handle multiple Twitter, Facebook, Google+, and other social accounts. In addition to scheduling tweets, Sprout Social offers insights and analytics so that you know how well your social media campaigns are working.

✦ **Twitterfeed** (http://twitterfeed.com): Allows you to attach your blog's feed to your Twitter account so that the URL for your latest posts are automatically fed to the masses every time you update.

✦ **TweetCaster** (http://tweetcaster.com): Manage multiple accounts from your smartphone.

✦ **Buffer** (https://bufferapp.com): Schedule your tweets so you can have them go live at a specific time, even if you're not online.

✦ **Instagram** (`http://instagram.com`): Although it's a separate social network on its own, the Instagram app on your smartphone can also post your photos to your Twitter account, if you're so inclined. (See Book V, Chapter 5 to learn more about using Instagram.)

Literally thousands of Twitter apps are available. To find out more about Twitter apps, do a web search — you can find plenty of roundups of the available tools. Just be sure to check the date on the reviews because some of the tools from, say 2012, aren't available today, and many new ones have been added to the mix. Also, ask your friends and followers for recommendations. Everyone has favorites.

Tweeting from a gadget

Thankfully, we don't have to stay chained to our desks anymore. We can still market our brands online from the beach, grocery store, or coffee shop using our favorite gadgets. In fact, you can use some of the same apps for tweeting online to tweet from your devices.

You can download Hootsuite or TweetCaster for your iPhone or Android app, enabling you to manage several accounts at once and still follow keywords and hashtags.

Instagram, the popular photo-sharing app for smartphones, allows for sharing on Twitter, leading to more visual engagement with your community.

What's important to remember is that thumb typing isn't an excuse for poor business practices. Some people feel that because they're not typing on a full-size keyboard, they have carte blanche to misspell words or use text speak, which isn't the case. These things are considered unprofessional no matter where you're tweeting from.

If you're marketing your brand, treat your mobile tweeting seriously, just as if you were working from your home or office computer. Don't just broadcast, engage. Because sending links from a full-size keyboard is easier, schedule these types of tweets if you'll be away from your desk for an extended period of time and use your mobile devices to have conversations with your followers.

Here are a few tips for tweeting from a mobile device or tablet:

✦ **Proofread.** People tend to make more typos from gadgets.

✦ **Set up notifications.** If you're away from your desk, your notifications will let you know whether people are engaging, and you can respond in kind. You can set your notifications up to make noise or just to send an email.

✦ **Install an app for easy tweeting.** Try using a Twitter management app, such as Hootsuite, for your mobile tweeting. You can use this app in conjunction with your regular Twitter account and pull all your stats together.

✦ **Use an app that allows you to manage several different accounts at once.** If you have more than one Twitter account (for example, business and personal), find an app that will manage both accounts. This way, you don't have to do a lot of logging on and off.

✦ **Check back as often as you can.** We're not saying that you should tweet from a wedding or funeral, but if you're not in the middle of an important obligation, do check your mobile Twitter app several times a day to be sure you're not missing out on an engagement.

Chapter 4: Supplementing Online Marketing Tools with Twitter

In This Chapter

↙ **Using Twitter to gain traffic**

↙ **Sharing your content on Twitter**

↙ **Linking Twitter to Facebook**

*I*f you're on Twitter for more than just fun and entertainment, you most likely use other social media. You might have a website, a blog, and a presence on Facebook and other social networks, and these social media channels are possibly feeding content to each other. In this same way, you can use Twitter to draw attention to your Facebook page, your blog, and your website.

In this chapter, we show you how to seamlessly dovetail Twitter into your other forms of social media.

Blogs and Twitter make a formidable tag team because each can bring new readership to the other. You can drive traffic to your blog using Twitter and also send new followers to your Twitter account using your blog for a double whammy. That's the beauty of using content to market your brand — you can use one platform or a combination of all.

Using Twitter to Drive Traffic to Your Content

It's not a good idea to do nothing but drop links to your blog posts or sales pages on Twitter. To market properly, you also need to create engaging conversation, ask questions, and field customer service inquiries. The links and traffic are the gravy on the proverbial potatoes. If you do the rest of it right, people have no problem following your links, which will help you to reach your end goal.

Here are some tips for using Twitter to drive traffic to your blog:

✦ **Create a discussion topic around your blog posts.** Instead of simply tweeting a link and leaving it at that, start a discussion around your blog topic. Ask questions and respond to responses. Not only are you engaging with your community, but other people who can see their streams may become intrigued enough to want to see what you're talking about.

✦ **Analyze your most productive Twitter times.** Take some time to analyze your Twitter traffic to find out when your community is most engaged.

✦ **Create the type of content people want to share.** If you tweet only to talk about your brand or to sell something, you're going to drive people away rather than to your blog. Create content that teaches, inspires, or engages. Take a look around on Twitter to see what kind of tweets people are sharing or retweeting. These are probably some good examples of engaging tweets.

✦ **Thank everyone who shares your content.** People appreciate appreciation. Taking time to say "thank you" encourages your loyal followers to continue recommending your content to others. You can do this publicly or via a direct message; either way is appropriate.

✦ **Use a logo as your profile image.** A recognizable logo and regular presence can inspire trust, which can in turn encourage others to visit your blog and also share your content.

✦ **Be friendly.** Your online attitude is everything. If you have a reputation for being friendly and helpful, you'll grow a wonderful community of supporters.

✦ **Be consistent.** Have a regular presence on Twitter. There are many people who won't subscribe to your blog's RSS feed but instead will wait to see you tweet the links. If you're not sharing, they're not visiting.

Schedule your blog posts for the same time every day, as shown in Figure 4-1, and use your Twitter feed to broadcast the links to your followers. Your regulars will appreciate seeing and expecting updated content at the same time each day.

Figure 4-1: Schedule your blog posts for the same time each day for consistency.

Sharing Content with Buttons

To make sharing more intuitive for your followers, you can add share buttons to your content.

Several different types of share buttons are available for Twitter. (See Figure 4-2.) For example, you can place icons in your blog's sidebar that encourage readers to follow you on Twitter. The sidebar buttons won't enable readers to share links, but these buttons will help you to build your follower base.

To install Twitter share buttons on your blog or website, go to `https://twitter.com/about/resources/buttons`. On that page you'll find several options for the type of button you can use for your blog or website. Select the button that best suits your needs. Once you choose your button, you'll be taken to a form asking you to fill out information including your Twitter handle, the size of the button you want to use, and your language. After entering that information, you can grab the HTML code that is provided.

Your webmaster will know exactly where to paste the code so it will appear in the area where it will do the most good. However, if you have a blog, for example on the Blogger or WordPress platform, you can post the code in a text widget located in the blog's theme designing function so the button appears in the blog's sidebar.

Figure 4-2: Creating a custom Twitter share button adds a cohesive and professional look to your blog.

Custom share buttons

You can also install plug-ins that appear at each individual post so readers can share the links to that post with their Twitter followers. When a reader clicks the button to share on Twitter, the blog post's title and a shortened link are tweeted through that reader's account.

The most popular WordPress plug-ins for sharing blog posts on Twitter are

✦ AddThis

✦ DiggDigg

✦ Easy Social Share

✦ Shareaholic

✦ Jetpack by WordPress

✦ ShareThis

✦ Sharebar

In this section, we use TweetMeme as an example of how to install a share button plug-in to your blog posts.

You may have to pay for some of the preceding sharing tools. Don't commit to a charge until you're sure that you know what you're paying for and why it's worth the expense over the free sharing tools.

To install one of the share buttons just mentioned, head to your WordPress dashboard and follow these steps:

1. **Click the Plugins icon (it looks like a little plug) in the left sidebar and choose Add New from the pop-up menu, as shown in Figure 4-3.**

   The Install Plugins Search page appears.

Figure 4-3:
The Plugins function allows you to search for any plug-in you need.

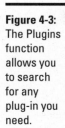

2. **Type the plug-in's name in the Search text box, as shown in Figure 4-4, and then click the Search Plugins button.**

   The Install Plugins Search Results page provides a list of results with the name, version, user rating, and description of each plug-in.

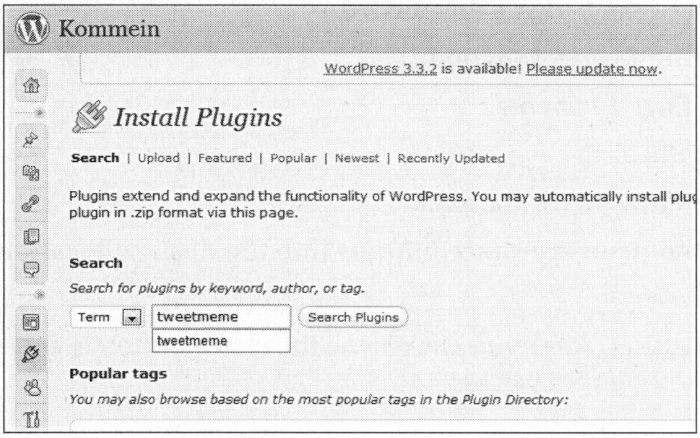

Figure 4-4: When you enter the plug-in's name into the Search box, the plug-in will appear in the results.

3. **Find the desired plug-in in the list of results, and then click its Install Now link, as shown in Figure 4-5.**

Figure 4-5: When you select the desired plug-in, it installs automatically.

After your plug-in is installed, you need to return to your WordPress Dashboard's Plugins page (click the Plugins icon in the left sidebar and then choose Plugins; refer to Figure 4-3), select the plug-in, and configure it. Enter your desired Twitter handle in order to receive retweets. Also, determine where to place the button, such as at the top, bottom, or side of your posts. Most people find success having the Retweet button at the top of their blog posts or floating along the left sidebar.

If you own a Blogger blog, some of the button options mentioned earlier aren't available as plug-ins. However, Blogger's template editor has several drag-and-drop options for Twitter share buttons.

To install a Twitter share button on your Blogger blog, follow these steps:

1. **Sign in to your blog's dashboard.**

2. **Select the Design function.**

3. **Select Page Elements.**

4. **Click Edit.**

5. **Select Show Share Buttons.**

6. **Drag and drop the share buttons into the desired location.**

7. **Click Save.**

   You're all set. After you click Save, the share button is saved to your blog and ready to use.

Linking Twitter to Your Facebook Page

If you have fans on Facebook who aren't Twitter users, you can post your tweets on your Facebook Wall for your fans to see. After you do this, every public tweet you send on Twitter also shows up on your Facebook Wall.

Follow these steps to add your Twitter feed to your Facebook brand page:

1. **Log in to your Twitter account.**

2. **Click your avatar in the upper-right corner and select Settings from the pop-up menu that appears.**

   The Setting page opens.

3. **Click Profile in the left sidebar, and in the Profile Settings page that opens, click the Connect to Facebook button.**

   You might have to scroll down to see the Facebook section.

4. **In the Log in with Facebook pop-up window, click the Okay button.**

   You'll need to enter your Facebook information in order to sync the two accounts.

5. **Select the My Facebook Page option to post your tweets on your Facebook page as opposed to your personal profile.**

   A listing of all your Facebook pages appears. Select the one you want to add your feed to.

6. **Click Save Changes.**

If you're a heavy tweeter, your Facebook fans may not appreciate every single tweet appearing in their Facebook News Feeds, and they might Unlike you if you're too prolific. Think very carefully about whether linking your Twitter and Facebook accounts is appropriate for you, given the way you tweet.

Chapter 5: Hosting Twitter Chats

Twitter chats are a way for people with similar interests to come together and discuss relevant information regularly. Generally, Twitter chats happen at regular intervals (usually weekly). Twitter chats, when done well, are an excellent way to build and maintain community.

This chapter helps you determine whether a Twitter chat matches your business goals and needs, explains how to choose the best hashtag for your chat, and introduces you to tools to help you manage your chats effectively. If you're concerned that no one will show up to the chat, don't worry, we also share some ideas about where to find guests and how to promote your chat so that more people will come (and tell their friends). Finally, we give you a complete step-by-step run-through of how to host a Twitter chat.

Benefiting from Twitter Chats

Many brands are hosting Twitter chats as a way to connect with their communities. Hosted regularly, usually once per week, Twitter chats allow for a brand to discuss issues everyone in the community has to deal with, or share tips and ideas.

Twitter chats have many benefits:

✦ **Create brand awareness.** When you have an engaging presence on Twitter, people remember you.

✦ **Get people talking about you.** Not only will your hashtag get people noticing what you're talking about, but if your community has a good time at your regular chat, they'll share with others.

✦ **Help others learn about your community.** Twitter chats enable you to interview guests or pose questions to your community. This way, you find out about their likes, dislikes, and needs, even if you aren't directly surveying them about a product or service.

✦ **Allow a conversation among like-minded people.** If you're a real estate professional and host a Twitter chat to share tips and ideas and discuss issues pertaining to real estate professionals, you're not only establishing your name and expertise, but you're also allowing those in your profession to rally around a specific topic.

✦ **Grow your follower base.** When people participate in a Twitter chat, the hashtag shows up in their Twitter streams, which attracts the attention of others who might also follow your brand and participate.

✦ **Provide valuable networking opportunities.** Through your Twitter chats, you can meet other professionals, customers, clients, collaborators, and friends.

Hosting a regular Twitter chat is a commitment because you have to provide value every week at a designated date and time, so don't enter into them lightly. First, try having a Twitter party, a one-off hashtag chat to see whether there's interest on both ends. If you enjoy the experience and you have a decent turnout, you can then determine whether it's worth it to continue the effort.

Coming Up with a Hashtag for Your Chat

The hashtag, the most important part of the Twitter chat, appears next to each and every post and on all promotional tweets, blog posts, and Facebook updates. Everyone who participates in the chat will use the hashtag, which means it has the opportunity to be viewed by millions. Take your time and determine the best hashtag for your chat.

Don't go overboard trying to figure out something hip. If you overthink your hashtag, you'll fall short. The most popular Twitter chats use obvious hashtags. For example, #blogchat is a chat about bloggers and #speakchat is a chat for public speakers.

Something important to keep in mind is the 140-character limit on Twitter. The last thing you want is for your hashtag to take up so many characters that you can't have a conversation. If you want to represent your brand, do so with brevity. For example, Community Manager Chat, the Twitter chat by online community managers for online community managers, uses #cmgrchat as their hashtag because spelling out the whole title wouldn't leave any room for conversation.

Having a short hashtag also enables you to leave room for retweets. People enjoy quoting others during Twitter chats by retweeting, which they can't do if the original tweet has too many characters. To make a tweet retweetable, try using 120 characters or fewer.

You also want your hashtag to be more reflective of your niche or your brand. For example, if yours is a soap manufacturer, do you want your hashtag to be #soapchat or #sudschat, or would you rather it was #JoesSoapChat? Be careful, though. While it's a good thing to throw branding in there, a long hashtag takes up precious character space.

By the way, in case you haven't already noticed, make sure the word **chat** is attached to the end of your hashtag so that folks on Twitter know a chat is in session (see Figure 5-1).

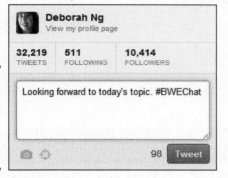

Figure 5-1: Attach *chat* to the end of your hashtag word.

> **Deborah Ng**
> View my profile page
>
> **32,219** TWEETS   **511** FOLLOWING   **10,414** FOLLOWERS
>
> Looking forward to today's topic. #BWEChat
>
> 98   Tweet

Keeping Track of Who Says What

If a lot of people are participating, your Twitter chat will go by fast. You won't just be interviewing a guest; everyone who participates will be talking at once. All this conversation can be a lot to keep up with, and your usual Twitter app won't do.

Some tools can help make your Twitter chat experience work a little better. For example, TweetChat is a platform allowing you to view only the tweets for one particular hashtag at a time so that all the other conversations on Twitter don't get caught up in a confusing stream. TweetChat also allows you to respond and retweet to everyone who is taking part.

A platform such as TweetChat, shown in Figure 5-2, is much more manageable than using Hootsuite because TweetChat updates quicker and shares every tweet by everyone who's using the hashtag. You can also set it to refresh every five seconds or slow it down so that the tweets aren't coming at you so fast.

Figure 5-2:
A Twitter
chat
management
platform,
such as
TweetChat,
can help
you follow a
busy chat.

Not all of your followers will enjoy watching you participate in a Twitter chat, especially if you're a prolific chatter. While most people gain followers after a Twitter chat, you may also find you lost a few regular followers, as well, because you're taking up too much of their Twitter stream. It's customary to let your followers know that you'll be participating in a Twitter chat for the next hour and apologize in advance for excessive tweeting.

Another important Twitter chat tool is Hashtracking, shown in Figure 5-3. With Hashtracking, you can generate a transcript of the chat to share with others, plus you'll receive statistics for each chat so that you know how many people participated, who the most influential people were in the chat, and how many people you reached through the chat.

Figure 5-3:
Use a
transcript
tool to
share the
chat with
members
of your
community
who can't
make the
chat.

Before hosting your Twitter chat, take some time to research the best tools for your needs. They'll make a world of difference.

Finding Guests for Your Twitter Chat

Twitter chats can take on a couple of different formats. You can host a town-hall type format where it's just you and your community, or you can invite special guests to participate. We get in to how to host both types of chats in the section "Hosting Your Twitter Chat," later in this chapter. For now, we focus on how to find guests for your chat.

The beautiful thing about the online social media world is how many people fancy themselves experts and have something to promote. Authors, bloggers, independent musicians, online talk show hosts, podcasters, and a variety of professionals are interested in sharing their knowledge online. What follows are some ways to find these people:

✦ **Social networks:** The people whom you follow on the social networks, or who follow you, have interest in your topic. How many of them are experts or have something to share or promote to your community? Many times, you don't have to look further than the friends, followers, customers, and brands who are sharing with you online.

✦ **Public-speaking networks:** Speakers love to share their expertise both online and offline. Many of them are happy to participate in Twitter chats.

✦ **Publishing companies:** Book publishers want their authors to succeed. See who has anyone of interest. Many times, if you follow publishers on Twitter or Facebook, you can see which authors they're promoting. See who is a good fit.

✦ **Brand pages:** Similar brands also have experts who like to share. Don't be afraid to reach out — it can be the start of a beautiful collaboration.

✦ **Colleges:** Teachers and professors are a gold mine of information and enjoy sharing with others. Invite them to take part in your Twitter chats.

✦ **Web search:** Search Google or Yahoo! to see who the movers and shakers in your world are and invite them to chat.

✦ **Crowd sourcing:** Ask your community members who they'd like to see as a #chat guest.

When you interview anyone for anything or invite them to participate in a community project, it's always a good idea to let them know what's in it for them. If you can present your chat as something of value, they're less likely to say no.

Here are some of the ways to sell a Twitter chat:

✦ **Visibility:** Let your guests know your community has great reach. Each person who participates in your chat has the ability to reach hundreds of people, depending on her number of followers. Estimate all your participants by the number of people who follow each, and the number of people who view the hashtag can number in the thousands — the bigger chats average millions of views.

✦ **Promotion:** Let guests know that you'll allow time at the end of the chat for them to plug books, products, services, and so on. Sometimes your guests may even have special discounts or offers for your Twitter chat community.

✦ **Stats:** If you use a service such as Hashtracking to put together your Twitter chat stats, share some of these stats with potential guests so that they can see the value. Let them know the average number of participants, the reach, and how many new followers you gain after each track.

✦ **Influential participants:** Every niche has their influential members. If you have influential regular participants, do share this information with your guests. But don't look like you're name-dropping, as that can be a turnoff.

If you can't find a guest for a particular week's chat, don't sweat it. You can find plenty of things to talk about with your community. Sometimes the community-driven chats are livelier than those involving guests.

Promoting Your Twitter Chat

Twitter chats are easy to market and promote. If you have a network and a platform, you have the ability to tell people about your chat:

✦ **Blog:** Use your blog to announce each Twitter chat. Touch on the discussion topic and announce any special guests. Be sure to link to your guest's blog, website, or Twitter account, which will catch her attention and encourage her to share the link with her own community.

✦ **Twitter:** Announce your chat at least once or twice per day. Although you're limited in characters, try to name the topic and guest, and don't forget the hashtag, as shown in Figure 5-4.

Figure 5-4:
Promote
your chat on
the social
networks.

> **Blog World & New Media Expo**
> 19 hours ago
>
> Join us at 2:00 EST for #BWEChat. Our guest, Tamsen
> McMahon will tell you how to sell social to skeptics.
>
> Like · Comment · Share

✦ **Facebook:** Try announcing the time, hashtag, and date at least once per day.

✦ **Google+:** Share with everyone in your circles.

✦ **LinkedIn:** Career-oriented chats are especially of interest to the folks on LinkedIn.

✦ **Your community:** Ask your community to help spread the word. Don't spam them, but do say "please share" when tweeting, blogging, or putting it out on the other social networks.

✦ **Your guests:** Ask your guests to help promote the event to their communities.

✦ **A community calendar:** Create a shareable calendar listing all the #chat dates, topics, and guests. Plan at least a month in advance.

Promote your Twitter chat in the same way you promote your business. Share it with your community without being pushy, smarmy, or spammy. Invite them to participate and share with their communities.

You're not going to get the same interest in every topic every week, but you'll find that you do have at least a couple of loyal community members who show up each time. Use participation to gauge the types of things your Twitter community enjoys talking about.

Hosting Your Twitter Chat

Most Twitter chats follow the same format. The host asks questions, the guest and community respond, and conversation ensues. However, put forth in that manner, chaos will also ensue. That's why Twitter chat hosts follow a numbered format for questions and answers. Twitter chats can be fast and busy. If they're not organized, no one will be able to follow the chat, and you won't gain a very strong community of participants.

Try following this format for hour-long Twitter chats:

1. **Welcome community members to your chat and invite them all to share a little about themselves.**

   Allow about three to five minutes for this.

2. **Introduce the format.**

   For most Twitter chats, each question will be prefaced with a `Q1` for Question 1 (see Figure 5-5). Those who answer the question will respond `A1` for Answer 1. This way, there's no mistake about which questions are being answered because some people come late but start at the beginning.

Figure 5-5: Following a numbered format will help keep your chat more organized.

When questioning your guest, always `@reply` their name — for example, `@debng, Q1. What is your favorite ice cream flavor?` If you have no guests, don't worry about the `@reply` unless you reach out to a specific person. (Refer to Figure 5-5.)

3. **Retweet your questions, as well as the guest's answers.**

4. **See what responses your community is sharing and retweet the best of those, too.**

5. **After about 10 or 15 minutes, ask the next question.**

   Most hosts share four to six questions. Just time them accordingly so that you have enough space for responding.

6. **(Optional) Save the last ten minutes for the community to ask questions to the guests.**

7. **Three minutes before the hour is up, thank your guest and ask him whether he has anything to plug or promote.**

8. **End the chat with any announcement you need to make, including the next week's guests.**

Don't be afraid to ask questions of your community when you see opportunity during the discussion. If you'd like for people to expand upon their answers or to keep the chat flowing between numbered questions, it's fine to throw out some non-numbered questions for your participants.

Here's a bonus tip for you: If you're intrigued by the idea of starting your own Twitter chat, check out some of these popular chats to see how they're handled:

✦ **#BlogChat:** For bloggers; hosted every Sunday night at 9 p.m. EST

✦ **#CmgrChat:** Devoted to online community management; hosted every Wednesday afternoon at 2 p.m. EST

✦ **#CMWorld:** Devoted to content marketing; every Tuesday at noon EST

✦ **#MMChat:** For marketers; Monday nights at 8 p.m. EST

✦ **#BrandChat:** About digital marketing and promotion; Wednesdays at 10:00 a.m. CT.

**Book IV
Chapter 5**

**Hosting
Twitter Chats**

Book V
Facebook and Instagram

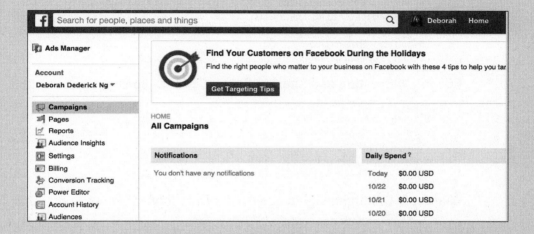

Contents at a Glance

Chapter 1: Using Facebook as a Marketing Tool

In This Chapter

✔ Using Facebook Pages

✔ Setting up your Facebook presence

✔ Making the most of Likes

✔ Using Facebook Events

*F*acebook is the world's most popular social network, where people of all ages, professions, and backgrounds gather to stay in touch and share cute cat photos with friends, present and former colleagues, old classmates, and family.

Having millions of people gathered in one place is the perfect opportunity for any brand to raise awareness and grow a community of customers and advocates. If you're not on Facebook already, you're missing out on a huge opportunity. Simply put, Facebook is where the people are, and to succeed in business, you also have to be where the people are.

In this chapter, we explore how Facebook Pages work and how you can make them work for your brand.

For more in-depth coverage, find a copy of *Facebook Marketing All-in-One For Dummies* by Andrea Vahl, John Haydon, and Jan Zimmerman (Wiley Publishing, Inc.).

Understanding the Appeal of Brands on Facebook

People who *like,* or give a thumbs-up to, a brand on Facebook are more likely to buy from that brand. *But they're not liking you to buy from you.* They're liking you to find out more about you and to receive updates and news regarding products and services. They might have had a positive experience with the brand and want to engage more. In any event, it's important to know why people are so willing to like a business on a social network.

Everyone knows plenty of people who like brands on Facebook. Friends and family come to Facebook each day to enjoy the company of others, but not necessarily to engage in a lot of deep reading or thinking. So why are people following brands on Facebook? Here are a few reasons:

✦ **Seeking a discount:** The majority of people liking your brand's Facebook Page are hoping to receive some sort of benefit. This doesn't mean you have to give discounts and freebies every day, but if people know at some point they'll receive coupons, codes, or other perks, they're more likely to sign up and remain active members of your Facebook community.

✦ **Looking for updates and news:** Fans follow television shows, bands and musicians, and other forms of entertainment to learn about show times and dates, new releases, and more.

✦ **Interacting with like-minded people:** People enjoy following local businesses, news stations, politicians, movies, television shows, and other businesses on Facebook to talk about those things with other enthusiasts.

✦ **Because their friends are doing it:** When someone likes, shares, or comments on a brand's Facebook Page, many of that person's friends will see that action. The power of suggestion can lead others to like a brand Page, if only because they know other friends are fans, as well.

✦ **Following a recommendation:** When people feel good about a brand, they leave positive comments on their Timelines and tell their friends, hoping that the friends then enjoy the same positive experience. If their friends also enjoy the experience, those friends in turn invite their friends and family, and so on.

✦ **Expressing their loyalty:** Customers who enjoy the brand offline often seek out the brand to enjoy online. In addition to receiving freebies or updates, they're mostly interested in showing support to a name they believe in.

✦ **Wanting entertainment:** If your content is stale with only the occasional business-like updates, you're not going to keep your Facebook fans. However, if your content is entertaining and fun, and keeps folks coming back to see what you're going to talk about each day, your community will continue to grow.

✦ **Needing a question answered:** Your community has many questions, but they may not want to call a customer service line and wait on hold. Being able to reach out via Facebook gives people a way to connect without having to invest a lot of time.

✦ **Giving feedback:** Many people follow a brand on Facebook so they can leave feedback regarding a product, service, or experience.

Many people who like your Facebook Page won't interact further on it. They'll read your updates on their News Feeds and may even take advantage of discount codes or calls to action, but they won't comment or communicate. That's fine; marketing to the silent members of your community is still important.

If your brand's Facebook Page is engaging and the person running it is funny, knowledgeable, and patient, your Facebook community will evolve into something wonderful. Some followers will comment on posts, others will vote in polls — and, yes, a number of folks will buy when you have sales or offer discounts.

Although this chapter explores all the ways a brand can benefit from using Facebook to reach its customers, remember that Facebook is continuously evolving and changing its algorithm. It's not as easy for brands to reach their Facebook fans as it used to be, and social media marketers are encouraged to stay on top of Facebook updates and changes. If you don't keep apprised of Facebook news, your brand can be penalized for not following specific rules or understanding how specific changes will reflect upon the brand's Facebook Page. Also, you may not receive as much traffic to your page if you don't know how the latest algorithm works. This is why it's important keep apprised of Facebook news and updates. Checking the Facebook section of Google News (under Technology) will alert you to any changes and recommendations for handling said changes.

Branding with Facebook Pages

You may think you know Facebook pretty well because you have a personal account, but Facebook Pages for brands (formerly called *fan pages*) and your Facebook profile have major differences. Facebook Pages have to follow specific rules to avoid coming across as overly spammy. For example, you have to follow specific guidelines for selling or running contests. (For more on these guidelines, see Book V, Chapter 2.)

The purpose of the Facebook Page is simple: to promote a brand. The goal of most brands is to have as many individuals like them as possible in order to best get their message to the masses. Some brands (such as Coca-Cola, with over 90 million followers) can reach more people with one Facebook update than with a television commercial — and it's cheaper, too. So a major brand's goal is to make their Facebook Page as interactive as possible to get those Likes.

After your brand has accumulated fans and followers, a variety of interactions can occur. A representative of the brand posts an update in hopes of getting as many Likes, comments, and shares on that post as possible. When an individual likes a post, comments on that post, or shares a status update or image, that content appears in that person's status updates, which means it's exposed to even more people.

If a brand's update gets liked and/or shared by hundreds of thousands of people, it has the potential to be seen by millions of people. This visibility leads to higher brand recognition, even if the people who viewed the update didn't share it in return. You want as many people as possible to at least know about your brand on Facebook.

If your Page is truly interactive and offers some cool perks, your community will be inspired to invite others to like the brand, as well. So another purpose of the Facebook Page is to create a community of brand advocates and word-of-mouth marketers.

Facebook Pages are a way to humanize your brand and make you seem more real to your customers or community. If you take the time to answer inquiries, post updates, and make them feel as if they're part of the brand, too, your fans will put their faith and trust into you and are more likely to support your efforts.

Brands are taking advantage of Facebook Pages because they're a way to reach people honestly and effectively. The most successful brands on Facebook aren't shouting out, "BUY ME!" or posting only product updates. They're having conversations with their communities, and it's working.

Examining the Components of a Facebook Page

A Facebook Page has several components, which you'll want to be familiar with before launching your own Page:

✦ **Profile photo:** Most brands use this space to post their logo or something that's regularly associated with the brand. Your profile photo isn't the biggest photo on your Page, but it's visible at eye level for whoever visits your Page. (See Figure 1-1.)

Figure 1-1:
Use your brand's logo for the profile photo.

Make sure that you properly prepare your graphic so it doesn't end up distorted when Facebook places the image into its pre-sized box. Facebook recommends the image be at least 180 pixels wide.

✦ **Cover photo:** The biggest photo on your Page, this cover photo can be a touching, amusing, or scenic image that best represents your brand and what it stands for.

✦ **About:** Includes your company's message, mission statement, or a brief bio of who you are and what you do. Your About page should be compelling and written in an engaging style. For more on your About page, see the section "Filling Out What You're About," later in this chapter.

✦ **Contact info:** This section, found on the About page, should list all the ways people can get in touch with you. At the very least, it should include email addresses where your community can offer feedback. You should also include your Twitter handle, blog, or website.

✦ **Posts to Page:** Posts to the brand page by others in your online community. You can delete posts if they're inappropriate, highlight them if they're something you feel everyone should see, or disable this feature so that no one else is publishing to your page. If you do nothing, posts by others will remain in a small, out-of-the-way area, in the sidebar.

✦ **Liked By This Page:** Brand Pages that your brand's Page follows in order to show support to another brand.

✦ **Settings Page:** Your Settings Page (see Figure 1-2) is also your admin panel and is where you discover how many new Likes you have each week, how many people are sharing on your Page, what countries people are visiting from, and more. From your Admin Panel, you can learn about your community, and you can also update the content and design of your Facebook Page.

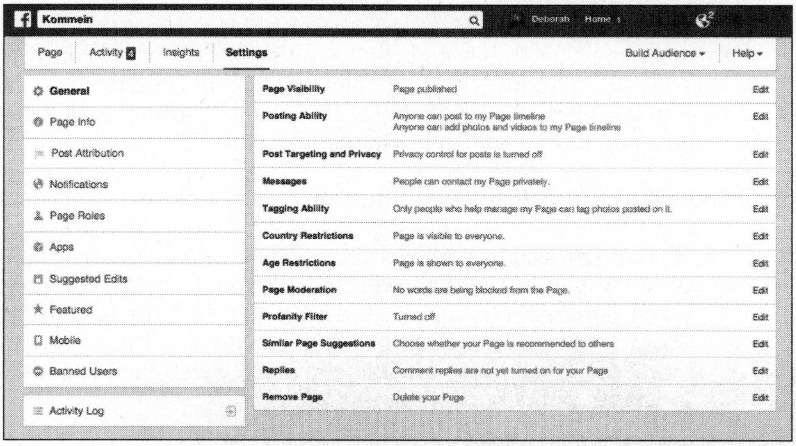

Figure 1-2:
Your Setting Page is your Facebook toolbox.

✦ **Wall:** Your brand's Facebook Wall, shown in Figure 1-3, is where you post content.

✦ **Pinned posts:** Posts you want to keep front and center on your Timeline.

✦ **Tabs:** Extras your community can click to engage with the brand. Polls, quizzes, photo albums, video, as well as hundreds of apps and other fun items are accessed through tabs.

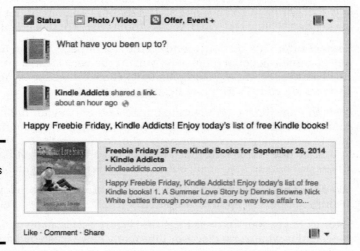

Figure 1-3:
Your Wall is where you and your community interact.

Making the Most of Your Facebook Page

Setting up your Timeline is simple and can take as little or as much time as you want, depending on how many bells and whistles you add to your profile.

Because the Timeline is so visual, it's the perfect opportunity for you to share your company's story. In fact, with your Timeline, you can go back in time to your brand's beginning and share milestones, articles, photographs, videos, and more — all in chronological order.

Some interesting features of the Timeline include

✦ **Private messaging:** Allows your community to reach out and ask questions privately and then receive a personal response in return. Please note, some brands turn off the messaging feature because they'd rather not receive private messages. You can turn off the private messaging feature, but you'll miss valuable community feedback because not everyone wants to publicly post to your Wall.

✦ **Notifications:** A number on the Admin Panel tab, shown in Figure 1-4, shows all your new notifications so that you can welcome new members by name, see who's messaging you, know who's posting to your Wall, and find out who's talking about you on their own Walls.

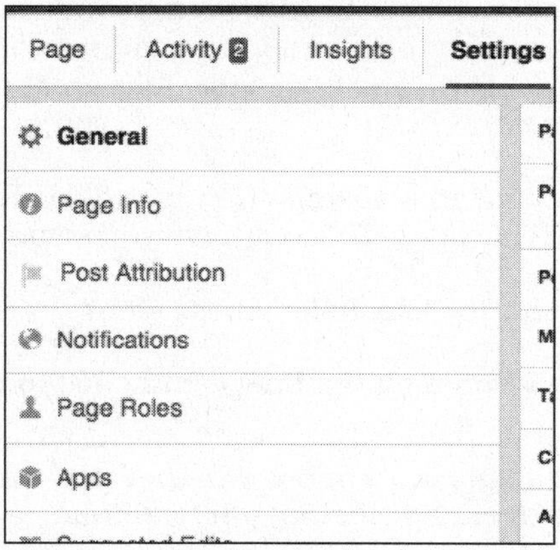

Figure 1-4:
A number
on your
Admin Panel
signifies
new
interactions
and
updates.

Page	Activity 2	Insights	**Settings**	
⚙ **General**				P
ℹ Page Info				P
▷ Post Attribution				P
🌐 Notifications				M
👤 Page Roles				T
🎛 Apps				C

✦ **The ability to pin key events and photos:** You can make certain content "sticky" to highlight key dates, milestones, and events.

✦ **Your fans can post:** Allowing others to post on your Wall enables your brand to interact with its customers and community.

Adding a profile picture

To set up your Timeline, the first step is to upload a profile picture. Your profile picture is the small photo on the left, usually a brand logo. To upload your profile photo, follow these steps:

1. **Hover on the profile image area and click the Update Profile Picture function that appears.**

A pop-up window appears, enabling you to choose from a variety of options.

2. **Choose the Upload Photo option.**

Alternatively, you can choose a photo that's already been uploaded to Facebook or take an image using Facebook's camera function.

3. **Assuming that you're going to upload your brand's logo, choose Upload Photo and choose the file you want to upload from the File Upload window that appears.**

4. **Save your profile photo.**

Adding a cover photo

Your next step is to choose your cover photo. This is the large background photo appearing at the top of your Timeline (refer to Figure 1-1) and the first thing people will see when landing on your brand's Page. Your cover photo is more than just a picture; it's a representation of your brand. You have a wonderful opportunity to illustrate your brand, product, or service in any way you want — and you want to make a lasting impression. Many top brands, such as Ben & Jerry's, Ford, and Coca-Cola, take great care in designing their Timeline images.

Before you get started, take time to research other brands on Facebook to see how they're using their Timelines. This may give you some good ideas.

To add a cover photo to your Timeline, follow these steps:

1. **Select the camera icon located on the image and click to change your cover photo.**

2. **In the pop-up menu that appears, choose whether you want to upload a new photo or a photo from an existing photo album.**

   • *Choose from Photos:* If you want to use a photo that already resides in your Page's Photo Albums, choose this option.

   • *Upload Photo:* If you want to upload an image from your computer, choose this option.

   After you choose a photo, you can reposition it by clicking the image and dragging it up or down.

3. **Click Save Changes.**

   This helpful link has information for working with the cover photo: `www.facebook.com/help/timeline/cover`.

Keep in mind that your Timeline cover image doesn't have to be a permanent thing. You can change it as often as you see fit. Change with the seasons or to coincide with product launches.

To change your Timeline cover image or profile photo, follow these steps:

1. **Select the camera icon located on the photo.**

2. **Choose where you want to get your photo from.**

   You have these choices:

   • *Choose from Photos:* If you want to use a photo that already resides in your Page's Photo Albums, choose this option.

- *Upload Photo:* If you want to upload an image from your computer, choose this option.

- *Reposition:* You can keep your current cover photo and simply reposition it by clicking and holding the cover photo, then dragging it to its new position.

- *Remove:* You can remove the cover photo completely with this option. You don't have to remove the current cover photo in order to change it. Instead, you can just choose one of the first two options.

3. **Click Save Changes.**

Adding finishing touches

If you went through the steps in the preceding sections, your Facebook Timeline is pretty much set up except for a little tweaking. From here, you can

✦ **Pin content.** Make certain posts or images *sticky,* meaning they'll stay in the same location until you unpin them. Pinning content is a good way to highlight sales events, announcements, and promotional campaigns. The pins last for only a week, unless you unpin or pin another item before the seven days are up. Please note, Facebook allows you to pin only one item at a time.

To pin a post: Once you post an update, select the arrow located at the upper-right side of the published post. You will see a drop down menu. Select Pin Post to pin the post to the top of the page.

✦ **Share your brand's story.** Because Facebook's Timeline allows you to upload content in chronological order, you can now go back to the day your brand launched, even if it was 100 years ago. Scan old newspaper articles, advertisements, photos, and more. Give your community a transparent look into your brand's past.

✦ **Explore apps.** Make your brand's Page even more interactive with apps that allow you to poll your community, share videos, share slides from presentations, post testimonials from customers, connect your Twitter account, share your blog posts, and so much more.

Don't go overboard with the bells and whistles. When you have too many items pinned to your Timeline, or if your Page is nothing but Twitter updates and blog feeds, your brand's account becomes too cluttered and confusing. Take the time to research the best apps for your community and use them in a way that doesn't assault the senses.

Understanding Your Facebook Administrative Functions

Facebook allows you to have a detailed look at the activity on your brand's Page with several administrative features. The features include settings and Insights, which give you the information needed to provide your Facebook community with a positive user experience.

Here are some of the things you can discover when you access your Adminstrative Functions.

✦ **New Likes:** The number of new Likes for the current week are posted in the right sidebar next to your cover photo.

✦ **Post reach:** Under your new Likes, you'll find the *post reach,* which tells you how many people viewed your Facebook posts for the week.

✦ **Private messages:** If you choose to have the messaging option available, your fans can send you messages that no one else can see.

✦ **Notifications:** When there's new activity on your page, a red button appears at the Activity link at the very top of the page. The button also displays a number indicating how many activities have occurred.

The following are features of the Insights area of your Administrative Functions (to find out how to best use your Facebook Insights, see Chapter 3 of this minibook):

✦ **Activity on the page:** Any new likes, shares, comments, messages, or other activities.

✦ **Advertising insights:** A rundown of how many people saw your brand's Facebook ad and what actions, if any, they performed.

✦ **Activity insights:** Analyzes your Facebook content, helping you to determine the best types of content to post, as well as the best times of day and days of the week to post.

✦ **Settings:** Helps you to set up your Facebook page just the way you like it.

Before launching your brand's Facebook Page, take some time to explore all of the administrative features and learn how to use them. The last thing you want to do is fly blind.

Filling Out What You're About

Your About page, the spot where you share a brief story or description about your brand, is essentially your business profile. You should be able to tell people what your brand is about while not overwhelming them with details.

Your Facebook Page is a vehicle in which to drive traffic to your website or sales page. Keep your profile information brief but intriguing so that readers seek out more information from your home page.

Here are some important details to include in your brand's business profile:

✦ A brief explanation of what your company does and perhaps your mission statement. This information shouldn't be a sales pitch; focus more on what you believe and what your brand can offer the community.

✦ A link to your blog and/or website.

✦ Links to other social media profiles — for example, Twitter and Google+.

✦ Contact information.

The purpose of your brand's Facebook Page is to engage with your community and share your brand's story. Therefore, don't make the About section of your profile a long, historical manifesto. Instead, keep it brief so that you don't lose anyone before they get to a link where they can learn more.

Using a Custom URL for Your Page

You have the option to have a custom URL for your brand's Page. A recognizable URL means better search engine optimization, and people are more likely to remember this address over an address featuring a lot of random numbers and letters.

To create your custom URL, follow these steps:

1. **Go to your Page's About section.**

2. **Scroll down to a Facebook Web Address ad and click the link that asks Create a Web Address for This Page?**

3. **Select the Page you're working with from the drop-down menu, type the name you want to have in the URL, and select Check Availability.**

4. **Click Check Availability.**

   If that name is available, you're all set (see Figure 1-5). If the name is taken, you'll have to choose another name.

Figure 1-5:
Choose
your brand's
name for
your custom
URL.

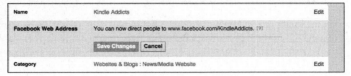

Name	Kindle Addicts	Edit
Facebook Web Address	You can now direct people to www.facebook.com/KindleAddicts. [?]	
	Save Changes Cancel	
Category	Websites & Blogs : News/Media Website	Edit

It should go without saying that it's a good idea to choose your brand name as your username. However, if your brand name is rather common, someone may have already beaten you to the punch. See whether you can add another word to your brand name so that you still have that recognizability.

Choose wisely! You can go back and change your custom URL only once. Thus, the name used on your custom URL should be something you're comfortable using well into the future.

Inviting People to Join Your Community

The most important aspect of having a Facebook Page isn't compelling About information or the perfect Timeline cover photo. Instead, it's the community of people who will become your biggest advocates. If you're like most brands, you want to have as many people interacting on your Wall as possible.

Before you begin inviting folks to join your community, keep in mind a couple of things:

✦ You can invite only people you're friends with. (We discuss how to attract people who aren't your friends in the section "Getting Likes from others," later in this chapter.)

✦ Facebook frowns upon blatant attempts to get Likes on specific posts and takes measures to make sure you're not *Like-baiting* by having people like your page in exchange for a perk.

Inviting friends to like your Page

When choosing friends to invite to like your Page and participate, take care to choose those who will really appreciate being part of that community. When you randomly and regularly invite people who don't care to be a part of the brand, they might get annoyed at having their Facebook experience interrupted with brand messages, and this can cost you a Facebook friendship

To invite friends to like your Facebook Page, follow these steps:

1. **Locate the Build Audience pop-up menu at the top-right of your Facebook Page, as shown in Figure 1-6.**

2. **Select Invite Friends.**

   A list of all your friends appears.

3. **Choose the Search All Friends option.**

4. **Click the Invite button next to each friend's name.**

   Your friends receive an invitation to like your brand's Page. Not all will accept your invitation, so please don't take it personally. Some people simply don't want to follow brands on Facebook.

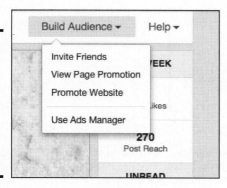

Figure 1-6: Use the Build Audience menu to invite friends to join your community.

Getting Likes from others

In addition to inviting friends to like your brand on Facebook, you can also try some of these methods for raising brand awareness and getting Likes:

✦ **Use your brand's Twitter, Google+, and Pinterest accounts to bring in new community members.** Without spamming, invite people to join your Facebook Page from time to time. If space permits, also share the benefits of becoming a member of your Facebook community.

✦ **Invite your community to share.** Although Facebook frowns upon contests and events in which people have to like a Page to participate, there's nothing wrong with inviting your community to share content they like.

✦ **Create the type of content your community will share.** Have you ever logged in to your personal Facebook account to find that your friends are sharing a funny video, provocative image, or informative article? This is the type of content people enjoy sharing on their Walls. If your brand's Facebook Page is nothing but brand updates, that's not very compelling. Instead, share informative or fun items with your community, and not only will they share in return, but they may also inspire others to like your brand.

✦ **Place share buttons on your blog and website.** If you want people to share your content, you have to give them a way to share. Having a Facebook share button, like those shown in Figure 1-7, on your blog or website will encourage readers to like your Page. You can also place individual share buttons on the bottom of each post so people can share your content.

Figure 1-7:
Use share buttons on your content.

Follow Kommein!

✦ **Be consistent.** If you post engaging or compelling content every day, folks are more likely to like your brand. If you're sporadic and haphazard with your content, you won't receive many Likes in return.

✦ **Place share information in offline content.** If you have offline content — for example, if yours is a supermarket brand with a weekly flyer or a retail shop with posters on the windows — be sure to let shoppers know how they can follow your brand on the social networks. If you're a restaurant, add the URL for your social networking channels on the back of your menus or have postcards handy for customers.

Unlike the popular movie tagline, if you build it, they won't necessarily come. You have to give everyone a reason to want to show up each day. Everyone has a favorite brand of detergent or applesauce, but very few people love these brands so much that they want to receive updates from them every day. It's not enough to have a presence; give everyone a reason to like you.

Liking Other Brands

One step you shouldn't overlook in your Facebook marketing campaign is to like other brands, even competing brands. Many people are afraid to like competitors because they feel they'll lose community to someone else. This fear isn't true at all. People who like brands on Facebook like many different brands, even if some are similar.

Here are some of the benefits of liking brands on Facebook:

✦ **Using your brand account, you can participate in discussions happening on other Pages.** Your comments may inspire others to check out your brand's Page and like you.

✦ **It puts you on the other brand's radar, which may be a good thing.** They may want to use and recommend your product or service one day or collaborate on a promotion.

✦ **It creates brand awareness.** The more people who see your logo, the better. When people see your logo on the social networks, it instills trust. They feel you're more accessible.

✦ **It helps to establish your expertise.** When you participate in discussions and respond to comments and inquiries in a knowledgeable manner, people see you as an authority and are inspired to follow you on the various social media channels.

 Be sure to follow the rules of social media etiquette and avoid dropping links on another brand's Page unless you're invited to do so. The last thing you want is to have a reputation as a spammer. Also, if Facebook feels you've been spammy, you could lose your account.

Creating Facebook Events

The power of community is a wonderful thing. A tight-knit community will rally around the brand for all occasions. They'll comment on blog posts and social networking updates, respond to promotions and discounts, and attend events. In fact, a good way to gauge community interest is to create an event.

What is an event? Events can include

✦ A sale

✦ A party

✦ A tweet-up (a real-world meet-up organized on Twitter)

✦ A conference

Events can also be online affairs, such as

✦ Webinars

✦ Contests

✦ Twitter chats

When you create an event using Facebook, you have the opportunity to invite everyone who likes your brand's Page to attend.

Creating events doesn't take much time at all, and they're simple to set up. Just follow these steps:

1. **Select Offer, Events, + located in the area where you type in updates or share links on your Facebook page.**

A pop-up menu opens.

2. **Select Event.**

3. **In the box that appears, enter important information, such as the event name, date, time, and location, and a few words about the event.**

4. **In the box that appears, select guests whom you would like to invite to attend.**

5. **Click Create Event.**

Invited guests will receive their invitations, and everyone who subscribes to your Page will see the event on their own news feeds. Also, the event will appear on your events tab and on your Timeline.

You also have the option to select whether you want your invitation page to show who has been invited to the event. Most people like to see who will be attending events, so it's a good idea to check this option. People can also see who has declined and who's a maybe. Because you don't want to have an invitation page filled with declines, don't create events for every move your brand makes. Instead, send invites to events you know will receive a positive response.

Don't use events as invitations to spam. If you send out invitations every other day to drive traffic and sales, you're going to lose your community and possibly your Facebook account.

Chapter 2: Creating and Sharing Content on Facebook

In This Chapter

↙ **Planning a Facebook content strategy**

↙ **Developing a Facebook Timeline for your brand**

↙ **Coming up with shareable content**

↙ **Creating a community**

↙ **Taking groups private**

Your brand's Facebook Page, just like everything else you do for your brand both online and off, requires a strategy and a set of goals. Plan out what you hope to achieve with Facebook, as well as how you hope to achieve it, before you make your first post or upload your brand's cover photo. Just as you would take time to plan a marketing or advertising campaign, so should you also think through your Facebook campaign.

Facebook may look like a random bunch of comments and images, but it's much more than that. For your brand Page, it's a way to create the type of content people want to both digest and pass along to others. However, creating simply interesting content isn't your most important objective if you're on Facebook to sell or raise brand awareness.

In this chapter, we discuss how to create the type of content that inspires your Facebook community to react.

See Book III, Chapter 3 for a more in-depth look at planning and implementing a content strategy for all platforms, including Facebook.

Creating a Facebook Content Strategy

Many brands set up a Facebook account without any idea of what to do with it. Just like with a blog, website, or even a Twitter account, you have to have a plan. To just randomly post topics and hope they stick will lead to inconsistency and confusion.

Facebook is constantly changing the rules for brands and brand Pages, and to enter into it blindly without any planning and research on your part can mean Facebook will penalize your page — or even your personal account. A poorly executed brand Page can even reflect badly on you, as a social media marketer, and on your brand from the public's perspective.

Take some time to put together a plan before you get started. If you already have a Facebook account for your brand and need an overhaul, pretend you're starting from scratch and plan a strategy anyway.

The first item to check off your list is your goal. What do you hope to achieve with your Facebook account? You won't be able to plan the right types of content without listing your goals first. For most brands, the goal is to build a community of advocates, which will lead to traffic to the main company website and, hopefully, sales.

After you know your brand's goal, you want to plan the type of content that will help lead to that goal. Now, this doesn't mean if you're looking for sales, every Facebook post should be selling something. However, it also doesn't mean you shouldn't post with sales and the people who help you achieve your ultimate goal in mind. (For more on creating content, see the section "Creating Content That Sings," later in this chapter.)

What follows are some ideas for the types of goals you might want to achieve with your Facebook Page, as well as the content to help you best achieve each goal:

✦ **Drive sales.** Your content should inspire a sale but not necessarily be a sales pitch. For example, has one of your customers been in the news as a result of using your product? If so, share that story. Do the ingredients in your products have health benefits? If so, talk about them and share other healthy living tips. Do you offer a business-oriented coaching service? If so, use your Facebook Page to share tips and best practices. In this manner, you're not exactly selling, but you are putting the idea of the sale in people's minds.

✦ **Grow your community.** Your updates should be more conversational. The people who join your Facebook Page will do so because of the engaging content, which will help to establish trust. This trust leads to community growth and sales through customer loyalty and word-of-mouth marketing.

✦ **Grow your mailing list.** Do you want more people to sign up for your newsletter? If so, offer sneak peeks of what they'll receive if they sign up.

✦ **Create brand awareness.** When you share news and updates regarding your brand, it shows up in News Feeds belonging to the people who are Facebook fans of your brand. When they like or comment on your public posts, those actions can show up on their friends' and family's News Feeds, as well. When people share your content, it helps to turn your brand into a household name.

✦ **Establish expertise.** Use Facebook to share facts and drop tips. This approach is especially useful in selling books, providing informational products and services, or promoting blogs.

✦ **Receive feedback.** Use Facebook to create polls, ask questions, and pick the brains of the people who use your product or service. Just be sure you're ready to receive some brutally honest answers.

✦ **Drive traffic.** Link to your blog posts and web articles, and create discussions around the day's topics.

✦ **Have multiple goals.** Most brands have multiple goals for their Facebook Pages. Mixing and matching content to serve many different purposes is okay. Be mindful of sharing too many links, however, because it can be perceived as spammy.

You may not necessarily see your Timeline cover photo as a sales tool, but as the first thing people see when they land on your Facebook Page, that's exactly what it is. The photo may not be of your product or service, but it should inspire the sale. You're not allowed to use your Timeline cover photo as a call to action, but that doesn't mean it can't inspire action. (For more on setting up your Timeline cover photo, see Book V, Chapter 1.)

Take time to understand your community. Watch them interact on the various social networks and watch how they interact on Facebook with you. Use your Facebook insights and analytics to observe the types of content they best react to and what they shy away from. When you know your community, you can plan the most successful types of content.

Sharing Your Brand's Story

Facebook's Timeline for brands is created so you can share your brand's story from the very beginning. This chronological approach is a beautiful opportunity for your customers to find out more about all your milestones and feel connected to your history.

Your community enjoys being made to feel as if they're part of the brand, even learning some secrets about your brand or being regaled with tales from back in the day. When your customers feel connected to you, they're more likely to share your stories — and products or services — with their friends and family. The more stories you share, the more brand loyalty is inspired.

Some items you may want to include on your Timeline are

✦ **A brand logo:** Use your logo as the profile photo — it helps to promote brand awareness.

✦ **A cover photo representative of your brand:** Your Timeline cover photo is designed to catch the eye of anyone landing on your Page.

✦ **A blurb describing your brand:** You have the opportunity to grab the attention of potential customers with a couple of impactful sentences under your profile photo.

✦ **A longer brand description in the About section:** Use your Timeline's About section to tell potential customers what you do and how your product or service will benefit them. For more on penning descriptive text for your About page, see Book V, Chapter 1.

✦ **Links to your website and social media pages:** Your Facebook community isn't network-exclusive. Many of your customers enjoy interacting at your blog or on Twitter, too. Be sure to include links to all the different places folks can follow you.

✦ **Contact information:** Include your email address in your Timeline's About section. Also, consider including other important contact details, including a customer service phone line and address.

✦ **Milestones:** In the area where you post status updates, there's also an option called Offers, Events, +. When you select the + function, you can opt to create a milestone. For example, if you want to note the day you opened for business on your Page, you click the Milestone function and add the date and name of the milestone.

✦ **Events:** Are you having a special sale? Throwing a gala? Having a Twitter chat? If so, use the Events function. You can invite people individually, and also have the event show up in your Timeline. Use events sparingly, however. No one wants to be hit up with an event invite every day.

✦ **Photos and videos:** Your online community is especially receptive of photos and videos. You can share images of your team and offices, old historic photos, and even videos of your company's old television commercials. The options are endless. Photos and videos are shared more often than any other content, as well.

✦ **Tabs:** You can create a variety of tabs for your Facebook Timeline, including events, polls, FAQs, and so much more. To learn more about tabs, see the section "Creating polls, quizzes, and contests," later in this chapter.

Creating Content That Sings

If you create a Facebook content strategy, then you should have some idea of what to talk about with your Facebook community. Planning content in advance by using an editorial calendar or spreadsheet can help to keep you from posting stale updates because you don't know what to say.

Before creating content for your Facebook Page, visit some successful Pages to see how those brands are handling content. Seeing how other brands are engaging their communities can inspire you to do some pretty neat things of your own. Also, visit competitors to see what they're doing right, and also what they're missing. There may be an opportunity to fill a void with some much-needed content.

Your content isn't about the sale, but rather the conversation and engagement that may lead to the sale. Make sure to provide a mix of fun questions, photographs, videos, and informative articles and blog posts.

What follows are some tips for creating good content for your Facebook Page:

✦ **Don't make everything serious and deep.** It's best to keep brand interaction light. Although thought-provoking questions and discussions are part of a good content strategy, don't forget to add humor to the mix.

✦ **Brevity counts.** Although you can be wordier than when using Twitter, Facebook isn't your blog. Keep updates brief. Too many words, and people lose interest. Write for the short attention span.

✦ **Stay on topic.** When you write about a mishmash of different things that have nothing to do with your niche, people get confused. If yours is a cereal brand, your community expects topics centered around cereal — for example, nutrition and recipes. If you start talking about cross-country skiing or barbecue grills, people are going to wonder what any of that has to do with your brand.

✦ **Try to create content that's open-ended.** Give your community opportunity to respond. Ask questions or talk about the sorts of things that provoke a discussion. Make sure everything you post is inviting a response.

✦ **Let your comments be your guide.** What kinds of questions does your community ask on your page? What posts do they most respond to? When they do respond, what do they say? Look to your community for topics. If certain topics stir up more interest than others, plan more of those types of topics.

✦ **Proofread everything you post.** When you don't take the time to read over everything and eliminate errors and typos, it tells your community you don't care enough about them to communicate error-free.

✦ **Look to your blog or website traffic for ideas.** If people are using search terms, phrases, and certain topics to land on your content, use these same topics when creating content for your Facebook community.

✦ **Be careful of TMI:** Although you should use a personal touch on a brand Page, there's such a thing as too much information. Avoid making your brand Page about you as a person, unless the brand Page is for your personal brand.

✦ **Don't be afraid to court controversy.** You don't want to always have negativity and squabbles on your Facebook Page, but the occasional controversial topic does wonders to create a discussion.

When you post too many controversial topics or allow a lot of negativity on your brand Page, eventually the only people who come around are those who thrive on drama and negativity. A positive attitude, with positive content, will inspire positive results.

Sharing and Being Shared

Sharing is an important part of brand Page interaction. Creating the right types of content means that same content may be seen by thousands of eyes. When your community and others share your content, it generates brand recognition and word-of-mouth marketing. If you're known for creating interesting and creative content, you gain even more fans on your Facebook Page, which means more potential sales.

Be careful not to write for Facebook, an inanimate thing, instead of people. Too many brands make the mistake of creating content for its ability to go viral, as opposed to making content that resonates with people. When all your content is obvious click-bait, your fans will grow wary of all the shocking headlines and exclamation points.

People like to feel as if they discovered something wonderful. Sharing items with their friends and family sometimes can make them feel as if they created that content themselves.

When someone clicks the Share button below something you posted, it means your content is going to show up in the News Feeds of that person's friends, as well. If a dozen fans with 200 friends each share your content, your post has the potential to be seen by 2,400 people. Out of all those people, it would be terrific if ten new fans like your Page as a result. However, even if they don't, sharing is creating brand recognition.

If you're recognized for putting out shareable content, not only will more people follow and use your brand, but your brand will be seen as a respected authority in your field.

Posting content that followers will want to share

So what types of content do people want to share?

✦ **Photos:** People share more photos than anything else. Make sure that your photos are relevant, thought-provoking, discussion-worthy, and even amusing, but please don't make them offensive. People see photos before they see words, so put some thought into the photos you share.

✦ **Funny or amusing content:** People like to share content that makes them laugh. There's nothing wrong with posting tasteful but amusing photographs, blog posts, or videos.

✦ **Heartwarming stories:** People love a good success or comeback story. They enjoy hearing tales of folks who beat the odds. People share inspiration.

✦ **Relatable content:** Ever read an article and think, "Oh my gosh. This happens to me all the time!"? People respond well to content they can relate to. Create content based on experiences everyone in your community may share.

✦ **Discounts:** Most people who follow brands do so in hopes of receiving special perks that they can share with their friends and family.

✦ **Viral videos:** Admit it; you love to share a funny video. That's how videos go viral. Post relevant, fun videos on your Page for more shares.

✦ **Lists, tips, and how-to's:** People enjoy sharing learning experiences. Share tips or steps to success.

Say thank you to the people who share your content. When they're called out in a positive manner, they're more inclined to continue with the support. If another brand Page shares your content, try to do the same for continued cross-promotion.

Don't sit around waiting to be shared, however. Do some sharing of your own. Take some time each day to visit other Facebook accounts and find content relevant to your community to share. This goodwill toward other brands puts you on their radar, and they may want to reciprocate. In addition, your community will appreciate your finding discussion topics or images to share with them. This especially works if you switch your Facebook identity to that of your brand Page and not your personal account.

You don't have to limit shared content to Facebook posts or your own content creation. Sharing blog posts, images, videos, and podcasts by others will help create goodwill among different communities and will bring in more awareness of your brand Page.

Sharing your tweets (or not)

You can set up your Facebook Timeline to include all your Twitter updates. Then every time you tweet, your Facebook fans can see it, too. Sharing your tweets may sound like a fun way for folks to see another side of you, but the downsides may be stronger than the positives. (For more on marketing with Twitter, see Book IV.)

Most people don't want to see Twitter on Facebook. Before you make the decision to post your Twitter feed on Facebook, strongly consider why we don't recommend it. Introducing your Twitter feed to your Facebook fans is sort of a culture clash. They're used to seeing occasional updates from brands and friends, not a constant barrage of a one-sided conversation from Twitter.

If you're a heavy tweeter, each and every item you tweet appears on your Timeline. Your tweets also appear on the News Feeds of everyone who likes you. However, most people don't want to receive a whole lot of updates from any one person or brand. If you tweet a lot, many people may opt to unfollow or hide your updates so that they don't have to see a prolific brand in their News Feeds. Moreover, you're carrying only your own Twitter feed, so if you have a conversation with someone, your Facebook community sees only your comments and not the person or people you're talking to.

Another downside is that if people are seeing all your updates on Facebook, they have no reason to follow and discuss on Twitter. If you want to build up your Twitter community, you may want to share your tweets only there.

When you're posting on Twitter, you're using language that's native to Twitter. For example, if you're using *RT* for retweet or participating in a hashtag chat, many members of your Facebook community may have no idea what your tweets are about at all. Posting something to your Facebook Page makes no sense if your entire community doesn't understand what you're talking about.

There's no rule against posting your Twitter feed on Facebook, but some people do consider it an unwritten breach of etiquette. There's also no rule saying you can't share or repurpose some of your Twitter posts to appeal to your Facebook community. For example, if you're tweeting to invite your Twitter community to take part in a survey, you can post the same information on Facebook. However, do take care to not use the same abbreviations and language you use to fit Twitter's 140-character limit.

With all that said, it's not unheard of for brands and individuals to post Twitter feeds to their Facebook Pages, and there are certainly apps enabling you to do so. You can also share your Twitter feed without your updates appearing on your community's news feeds.

After reading all the above, why would you want to post tweets to your Facebook Page? Here are a few reasons:

✦ Not everyone uses Twitter. By allowing your tweets to syndicate to your Facebook Page, you're allowing more people to see them.

✦ Your message gets through to more people. For example, if you're sharing a discount code on Twitter, your Facebook followers can use it, as well.

✦ Seeing your Twitter feed on Facebook may inspire others to follow you on both networks, which means your message sinks in twice.

You can access Facebook's Twitter app from `https://apps.facebook.com/twitter`. When you click the Go to Your Twitter Profile Settings to Start button, the app asks for permission to access your Twitter account. After you grant permission, the updates appear in your Timeline.

Investigate apps that appear as a tab on your Timeline — you can add one so that interested parties can click to read your tweets rather than have all your tweets appear on the Timeline. TwitterTab is one such app that can help: `https://apps.facebook.com/twittertab`.

Using hashtags in your posts

Hashtags make topics searchable without having to use a search bar or search engine. When you use a hashtag in your Facebook post, it's visible to all who search for the topic used in your hashtag. For example, if you're posting a healthy recipe using the grain quinoa, you can use the hashtags #quinoa, #recipes, or even #healthy. Now everyone who's searching for that same hashtag will see your post.

Here are some best practices for using hashtags:

✦ **Use hashtags sparingly.** Too many hashtags hurt the eyes. Try for one or two — any more than three is too many and makes your update look cluttered and confusing.

✦ **Hashtags should make sense.** Don't use a hashtag because it's popular or trending. Use one that works with the content. The last thing your brand wants is to be accused of *hashtag jacking,* or spamming a hashtag with your irrelevant content.

✦ **Hashtags are all one word.** Avoid spaces and hyphens when using hashtags. They're all one word, usually all lowercase.

✦ **Do a search before using a hashtag.** If you have a hashtag you want to use, do a search of that hashtag first. It could be in use or could have previously held inappropriate content.

✦ **Don't worry about upper- or lowercase.** Hashtags are usually all lowercase. Don't worry about making sure words are separated by capital letters.

✦ **It's okay to use a unique hashtag.** Don't be afraid of making up your own hashtag. A unique hashtag can help your brand stand apart.

Bringing Your Community into the Mix

Every tip you read about Facebook will come to nil if you don't have a positive, productive community. The more people who like your brand Page, the more people you have responding to and commenting on your posts and campaigns. You want your community members to feel good about participating, and when they feel good, they share and they buy.

The last thing you want is a Timeline filled with random updates. Take some time to explore the different Facebook apps to find out how to better interact with people. When you share in different, unique ways, your community will grow, and so will sales and brand recognition.

Selling on Facebook

Most of the people on Facebook aren't there because they want to buy or find a good bargain. They're there to visit with their friends. This mindset shouldn't discourage you from selling, however. With the right campaign, Facebook can become your community's equivalent of the supermarket impulse-item aisle. People aren't on Facebook to buy, but it doesn't mean they can't be enticed to do so. Although they may not have been interested in a sale, seeing that you have some products on display couldn't hurt. Facebook offers the perfect social shopping opportunity because people can socialize, shop, and share. In fact, people are more likely to buy something they see their friends buying.

Facebook has specific rules about what brands can present to their communities, especially when it comes to selling, promoting, and holding contests. If not kept in check, Facebook can become a haven for spammers, so regulations are necessary. It's a good idea to familiarize yourself with Facebook's Terms of Use for brands before selling in your Facebook updates. You can find the terms of use at `www.facebook.com/page_guidelines.php`.

Facebook requires the use of specific apps for selling and promotion to keep spammers out of the mix and ensure that all opportunities are legitimate. So, although it's absolutely possible to sell on Facebook, you have to do so the right way.

Here are a couple of apps to help you sell on Facebook:

✦ **Facebook Store:** This feature gives you the opportunity to create a shopping experience on your Timeline. The app appears as a tab and allows you to display merchandise or sell products and services. Your store can have as many items as you like.

✦ **Facebook Marketplace:** This app allows your advertisement to appear in classified-advertising format. Because most Facebook users don't really know about this app, you may find it results in a low level of buying and engagement. However, some brands have found success.

Facebook advertising is a terrific way to sell products and reach people who share similar likes and interests. Check out Book V, Chapter 4 for more about using Facebook advertising.

Not all your selling on Facebook has to be via apps and widgets. You can also create action terms and phrases to post on your Timeline that lead your community to your website. Sharing news about a sale, new merchandise, or a discount is fine, as long as you're not spamming.

Creating polls, quizzes, and contests

For a truly interactive experience, you have to give your Facebook community the tools to really get the party going. Asking questions or posting links is only a small part of growing your Facebook network. To truly tap into the power of the people, create some other fun experiences.

Polls

Polls can be fun and frivolous, or you can use them to collect information about the consumer. People like to participate in polls because they feel as if they're part of a campaign. Plus, creating a poll isn't a big-time commitment; a simple click of the button, and you have the user's vote.

Facebook's poll app, available at `www.facebook.com/simple.polls`, allows participants to add comments about why they voted as they did, and you can also configure the poll to allow participants to add their own items for folks to vote on.

Test out a free app such as the one found at `https://apps.facebook.com/my-polls` to see how your community responds to Facebook polls. Sometimes polls just aren't a good fit, and you'll want to play around a bit before investing money.

Polls are best advised for bigger, active Facebook communities. When smaller communities put out polls and have a poor showing, they may receive only a couple of responses. The last thing you want is to promote something publicly and have a poor showing.

Quizzes

For even more community interaction, try creating quizzes. Quizzes aren't necessarily a way to gather information from your community, but if the quizzes are entertaining, the people who take them will share them with others in the community.

Facebook features several quiz-building apps such as QuizMaker, and they're intuitive enough that even the most technically challenged people can create a quiz. See whether you can put something together representative of your brand. For example, if you're representing an Italian restaurant, create a quiz seeing how many Italian words and phrases your community recognizes. If yours is a car brand, list the parts of the car and see whether your community knows what each part does or where it's located. At the end of the quiz, have a ratings score for expertise. These quizzes are frivolous, but fun and extremely shareable. They're also great community-building tools.

Contests

Contests are another way to perform community outreach and raise awareness of your brand. However, like with selling, Facebook has specific rules about contests. You don't have to download a special app to host contests, but Facebook does have specific rules as to what is and what isn't allowed.

 Before running a contest on Facebook, read Facebook's promotions policy. Check the policy each time you run a contest because the rules often change, and you don't want to be caught unawares. See Facebook's Terms of Use for Pages at `www.facebook.com/page_guidelines.php#promotionsguidelines`.

 When planning fun content for your Facebook Page, keep in mind that Facebook is cracking down on *Like bait,* or the practice of asking Facebook fans to Like, share, or comment on posts. Facebook is also cracking down on *click bait,* or the practice of using sensational headlines to bring Likes and shares to specific posts. For example, be careful using headlines that say ". . . and you won't believe what happened next!" as a way to draw in readers.

Offering discounts to your community

One of the main reasons people follow brands on Facebook is because they're interested in receiving bargains, freebies, or discounts. In fact, these types of perks are a terrific way to reward your community for their loyalty.

When you offer discounts and perks that are available only to your Facebook community, it makes people feel special and inclined to share your brand with others. Discounts are what fans share the most when it comes to brands.

You can offer discounts in a variety of ways:

✦ Set up a unique code for your Facebook community only.

✦ Link to discounts on your website.

✦ Use the Facebook Offers feature, which enables you to post your discount and an image (and they then appear in your fans' News Feeds). This feature is found in the status update box when you select the Offers, Events, + function.

Do be careful not to spam your Facebook Page with discount codes and sales pitches. Although your community is very interested in receiving bargains, they're not interested in reading spiel and jargon every time they see an update from you. Balance your discounts with other content and don't post sales or discounted items more than once per day.

Using Closed or Secret Groups

Facebook enables users to create Closed groups and Secret groups for more intimate discussion. There are times people want to share their opinions but aren't comfortable doing so because liking or commenting on a public page can mean their Facebook friends might see what they're doing. Closed and Secret groups allow Facebook groups to participate without having to worry that friends and family are watching.

Closed versus Secret groups

Both Closed and Secret groups are private. However, they do vary in a couple ways:

✦ **A Closed group shows up in a Facebook search, and anyone can request membership.** The group's administrator can approve membership requests or set the group up so that anyone can approve new members. With Closed groups, you can also see a list of all members of that group, even though you can't see any of the messages, images, or other interaction.

✦ **A Secret group doesn't show up in a search, and members must be invited to join.** You (or another member) have to be Facebook friends with a person to invite him to join a Secret group, and all membership is approved by the group's administrators. In fact, many families use Secret groups to keep in touch and share photos without having to worry about outsiders viewing their personal family details. If you're not a member of a Secret group, you can't see that group's updates or member list, and you can't access the group at all without an invitation from a friend.

Although Secret groups are great for private interaction and they keep out spammers, some feel they promote exclusivity and cliquishness because only select people are part of the group, which may not be a good idea for a popular brand.

Content posted to a Secret or Closed group isn't available for public search (for example, on Google), nor can it be shared outside of the group.

Brand Pages and groups are different in that Pages are for fans to have conversations and learn about a brand, whereas groups allow like-minded people to interact and have conversations on a more expansive basis. Although you wouldn't have dozens of conversations going each day on your brand Page, in a group, where members can opt in, you can have many conversations going at the same time. The downside to groups is that Facebook caps the amount of people who can join to 5,000 members, whereas your brand's Facebook Page can host millions.

Creating a Facebook group

To create a Facebook group, follow these steps:

1. **Click on the Groups function located in the left sidebar of your Facebook profile.**

2. **Click Create Group.**

   The Create New Group dialog box appears.

3. **Determine your Group name, invite members, and select your privacy options.**

4. **Click Create, and you're good to go.**

Don't create a group unless you already have people to invite. Facebook won't allow you to create an empty group.

After you start your group, you can do a few things to make it interactive and appealing. For example, you can upload a cover photo that's representative of the group. You can also pin a welcome message or group rules to the top of the page.

Groups allow you to share photos and even upload documents and files, so be sure to spend some time exploring all the different features.

When creating separate discussion groups on Facebook, don't allow them to turn into cliques. If members feel excluded, they won't feel as strongly about your brand. Continue adding members to your groups to keep the interaction fresh. See Book III, Chapter 2 for more on creating communities, not cliques.

Chapter 3: Gaining Insights about Your Facebook Community

In This Chapter

✔ **Getting stats with Facebook Insights**

✔ **Looking over the numbers**

✔ **Using the data to your benefit**

*F*acebook continues to evolve, with the rules for brands changing all the time. Although some social media marketers aren't thrilled with many of the changes, most are reluctant to move away from Facebook because it's still where most of their customers converge.

No matter how they feel about Facebook's changes to both algorithm and rules for brand Pages, marketers can't deny the benefit of using Facebook's *Insights,* or analytics panel, to learn more about their customers and online community.

Take advantage of all Facebook has to offer for brand Pages. By using the tools available to you, you can better interact with your Facebook community and learn more about the people who are supporting your brand. The more you know about them, the better you can tailor your content and campaigns to suit their wants and needs.

In this chapter, we explain how to analyze your Facebook Timeline to better promote and sell your brand. We also talk about how to handle some of the administrative tasks that come with having a Facebook Timeline.

The more you use Facebook Insights to analyze your Page's content, the more your Page will grow. The information on your Facebook Page offers a valuable look into your Facebook community's habits. When you know how they behave while they're on Facebook, you can create the type of Facebook content that they will best respond to. When you plan your Facebook content strategy, make sure to allow time to analyze all the data that comes with Facebook Insights.

Getting the Scoop on Your Fans through Insights

Facebook Insights is an analytics tool for your brand Page, which allows you to see what your community is up to, as well as to keep track of things like Likes, unlikes, and comments. You can even access downloadable reports for in-depth analysis. In short, Facebook Insights gives you a peek into what people are doing when they land on your Page.

Through Insights, located at the top of your brand page with your Settings, you can determine your Facebook Page's success. You can find out the following information about your visitors:

✦ **How many people like your Page each day, week, and month:** In addition to finding out how many people like your Page on a daily, weekly, and monthly basis, Insights also breaks down the Likes by demographics. A downloadable spreadsheet shows these numbers over time, enabling you to gauge growth and loss.

✦ **How many people unlike your Page:** Don't just measure Likes. Learning how many people unlike your Page is important, too. It helps you determine how your Facebook community is reacting to your content and the amount of updates you're serving up each day.

✦ **Organic Likes versus paid Likes:** Learn whether the Likes you received were achieved via people who landed on your Page on their own or who were brought in through paid advertising. If you find most Likes are via paid advertising, analyze your content to see why it might not be bringing in many organic views.

✦ **Where your Likes happened:** Insights tells you whether Likes were achieved via a computer or mobile device. If more people are viewing your brand's Page through their smartphones, be sure to provide the type of content that's easy to view on a smaller device, and maybe offer some sort of coupons or perks for people who might be on the go.

✦ **Your Page's reach:** Because Likes, shares, and comments can be seen by people who aren't fans of the Page, each post has the ability to reach many people. Insights will let you know your Facebook Page's true reach.

✦ **Engagement per post:** Insights breaks down each post and lets you know how many comments, Likes, and shares it received.

✦ **Types of posts:** You can find out which types of posts do better than others — for example, if a humorous image gets more engagement than a link to a blog post or straight-up text.

✦ **Pages you watch:** You can watch Facebook Pages via your brand's Facebook Page. That is, you can keep an eye on competitors' Pages and see how their most popular Pages are performing by using the Pages to Watch feature in the Overview section of Insights.

**Book V
Chapter 3**

Gaining Insights
about Your
Facebook
Community

✦ **Information about external referrals:** Insights details which outside websites are sending people to your Facebook Page, such as if you're receiving traffic to your Page from a search engine or link from a website.

✦ **Details on demographics:** Facebook Insights offers a variety of demographics, including age, gender, and location.

Putting Your Insights Data to Good Use

Now that you have all this information about your Facebook community, what are you going to do with it? The reason Facebook provides Insights for Pages is because they know how important it is for you to see whether Facebook offers good *ROI,* or return on investment. By analyzing the data offered in Insights, you can make any needed improvements and drive even more traffic and engagement to your Facebook Page.

Take some time each week to check out your Facebook numbers and make note of the following:

✦ **If your Likes are going up:** You're doing something right! When people like your Page, it means they're interested in your brand. It also means the promotion you're doing on behalf of your Facebook Page is working, and you're creating the type of content folks are responding to and sharing. Continue doing what you're doing — but don't be afraid to add different types of content to see what your Facebook community best responds to.

✦ **If your Likes are going down:** If you're losing Facebook fans, it can be for a variety of reasons. It might mean you're updating too many times in a day. Two to three times per day is optimal. Any more than that, and people are going to tire of seeing you in their News Feeds. It can also be that you're not offering the type of content they find interesting. Experiment with different types of content to see what they react to most.

✦ **If your Likes aren't doing anything at all:** This isn't a bad thing because people aren't unliking your Page, but it's not an ideal situation, either. You want your Page to receive new Likes daily, and if this isn't happening, you have to step up your game. Try changing your Timeline photo to see whether you can find one more appealing to your community. See what you can do to find the type of content or images that appeal at first glance to the people landing on your page.

✦ **If people are responding well to certain types of content:** Take note. If people are commenting, liking, and sharing certain content on your Facebook Page, this is the type of content you want to continue to provide. Do still create a good mix of different types of content, but give the people what they want, as well.

✦ **If your demographic is made up of people of a certain age:** If your community is made up of 20- or 30-year-olds, you want to tailor most of your content to appeal to people in these age groups.

✦ **If specific types of content receive more engagement:** If you notice photos and videos get more shares and comments than a simple post with a few sentences of text, add more visual content to your Facebook Page.

✦ **If no one is responding to certain types of content:** If you post certain types of content and no one is responding, it means your community isn't interested. Avoid posting this type of content in the future.

Facebook provides Insights so that you can better understand the people who are interacting on your Page or show interest in your brand. When you know how they react to your content, you can plan the types of campaigns they best respond to. Because you're given the additional benefit of demographics, you can also appeal to gender, age, and even locale.

Chapter 4: Advertising on Facebook

In This Chapter

↙ **Paying to reach more people**

↙ **Choosing specific people to target**

↙ **Boosting your Facebook posts**

↙ **Understanding if advertising is working for you**

With recent changes to Facebook's algorithm, marketers have noticed an increase in traffic to and engagement with their Facebook Pages. Facebook has made changes to the way brands operate for a few reasons, the first being that they don't want brands to spam the Facebook community. So, although they don't mind brands selling on Facebook, they don't want sales pitches and pleas for interaction to make for an unpleasant experience for users.

Facebook is also a free service, which means they have to make their money somehow. Brands who pay for advertising on Facebook can find they reach more people, achieve more interaction, and even drive traffic to their websites.

In this chapter, we cover the basics of Facebook advertising so that you can determine whether it's worth it for you to pay for more fans and interaction.

Reaching More Fans with Ads

Should you pay to play on Facebook? Many brands are asking this very question. Because of the aforementioned changes to Facebook's algorithm and the changes in brand Page management, fewer fans are seeing your Facebook posts in their News feeds. If you're trying organic methods for growing your fans and interactions (for example, viral or more visual content), and those methods aren't panning out, advertising might be worth looking into.

The good news for small businesses is that it's really not very expensive to advertise on Facebook. You can invest as little as $5 in an ad or boosted post, or as much as hundreds of dollars, as shown in Figure 4-1. The more you spend, the more people you reach.

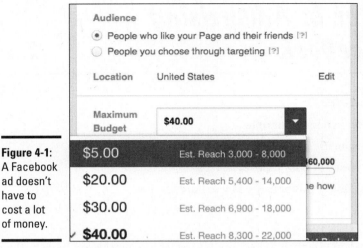

Figure 4-1: A Facebook ad doesn't have to cost a lot of money.

TIP

If you're wary of spending money on a Facebook ad, try testing the waters with a small amount. Boosting a post (we talk about that in the section "Targeting your fans," later in this chapter) for as little as $5 or $10 is a good way to gauge if you want to advertise on Facebook on a more regular basis without putting out a large investment.

Facebook offers different ad choices, so it's important to put money into the right campaign for your needs. Just as it's important to have a Facebook content strategy (see Chapter 2 of this minibook), it's equally as important to have a plan for advertising.

Deciding whether you want to invest in an ad

First, you need to determine what you hope to achieve with your Facebook ad. What follows is a look at some of the reasons people invest in Facebook advertising:

✦ **More engagement on your brand page:** If you have fans but no one is communicating via Likes, shares, or comments, they might not be seeing your page in their News Feeds. An ad can help to reach more people and up the engagement.

✦ **More Likes to your brand's Page:** Sometimes a brand needs a boost to get started. Using Facebook advertising is a good way to gain new fans who wouldn't have known your brand has a Facebook Page otherwise.

✦ **More traffic to your website:** When your posts appear in more fans' News Feeds, more fans will click on your blog posts, articles, and other shared web pages.

✦ **More people to attend your event:** Facebook advertising can help your events reach more people.

Taking out a Facebook ad means more visibility for your brand. On your own Facebook News Feed, much of the brand content isn't shared by your friends — you're seeing it because that Page's manager used advertising. Advertising can be targeted to people who have similar interests or friends of fans, which means more views and actions on your Facebook Page.

Choosing the right Facebook ad for you

Consider the different types of Facebook ads and the benefits of each:

✦ **Boosted post:** When you *boost* a Facebook post by clicking Boost Post, as shown in Figure 4-2, that post appears higher in your fans' News Feeds. A single post or update can have a wider reach than a post you didn't boost. For example, if a single post normally gets 200 views, you can boost a post so it receives 2,000 views.

✦ **Click to website:** These ads are geared towards driving traffic to your website. A specific article or page on your website is highlighted, so when the reader clicks to learn more, she's taken to your website instead of your Facebook Page.

✦ **Events:** Create invitations and share them with your fans. Paying for the ad makes sure the invite gets in front of more eyes than if you created a Facebook event invitation without an ad.

✦ **Page post engagement:** Like a boosted post, these ads give a little push to single posts so they're seen by more people, but they're designed so they receive more Likes, shares, or comments. For example, instead of seeing an advertised post in your News Feed, there will be a call to action to Like the post or the page.

Figure 4-2:
You can boost a post on Facebook to give it more visibility.

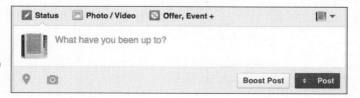

✦ **Page Likes:** Page Like ads advertise the page itself, with a Like button included so viewers have the ability to Like directly from their News Feeds. You can choose to target this (and other) ads to a specific demographic or send it to friends of fans.

✦ **Offer claims:** When you use Facebook's Offer function on your brand's Page, you can also pay to boost that offer so more people can take advantage of it.

The cost of a Facebook ad is up to you. Whether you choose to spend $5 to put your ad in front of several hundred people, or pay hundreds of dollars to have your ad put in front of thousands of people, you set a cost you can live with.

Before investing in a Facebook ad, take some time to familiarize yourself with Facebook's guidelines for advertisers. You can find guidelines at `https://www.facebook.com/ad_guidelines.php`. The last thing you want is to have your ad pulled or declined because it wasn't in compliance.

Creating an ad with Facebook's Ads Manager

Facebook's Ads Manager, shown in Figure 4-3, is sort of your one-stop shopping destination for Facebook ads.

To create an ad by using the Ads Manager, follow these steps:

1. **Access the Ads Manager at** `https://www.facebook.com/ads/manage/accounts/.`

You're greeted with a dashboard like the one in Figure 4-3, featuring Create Ads buttons so that you can set up your ad, as well as analytics for past and future advertising.

Figure 4-3:
Facebook's
Ads
Manager
dashboard
can help
you get
started.

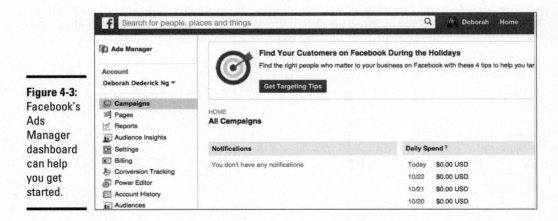

2. **Click the Create Ad button.**

   A menu page appears, listing options for advertising, including a variety of scenarios to choose from.

3. **Choose an objective for your ad.**

   For example, you can choose to reach more people who are already fans, boost an existing Facebook post, or add to your existing fan base. When you select a scenario, you're taken to a window where you're asked to perform a series of actions. For example, if you're selecting the option to boost a post, you then select the brand page account you want to use and the post you want to boost. You're also asked to name your campaign, select various demographics to target your ad to, and choose your budget.

4. **After you have filled in all the required information about your campaign, select the option at the very bottom to review your order.**

5. **If everything is to your liking, click on the Place Order button.**

After you create your ad, you can use the Ads Manager to access analytics, print reports, and see your page history, among other functions. For example, you can see at a glance how many ads you've purchased and how each is performing.

Targeting your fans

One of the nicest features about Facebook advertising is the ability to target fans — or potential fans. For example, if you want to boost a post, you can target your audience as follows:

1. **After you create your post, click the Boost Post button, located to the left of the Post button on your status update (refer to Figure 4-2).**

   A dashboard of sorts appears.

2. **In the upper-right corner of the Boost Post dashboard, select an audience option.**

   You can choose from People Who Like Your Page and Their Friends if you want to reach existing Facebook fans, or People You Choose through Targeting if you want to reach new people, as shown in Figure 4-4.

3. **If you select the People You Choose through Targeting option in Step 2, select the country you want to target, as well as gender, age, and interests, as shown in Figure 4-4.**

4. **Click Set Budge for a drop-down menu of price options.**

5. **From the drop-down menu, set your budget with the amount of money you want to spend.**

Audience

○ People who like your Page and their friends [?]

◉ People you choose through targeting [?]

Location   [Country ▼]

[United States ▼]

Age   [18 ▼] - [65+ ▼]

Gender   [**All** | Men | Women]

Interests [?]   [Add 4-10 interests...]

[Clear] [Set Budget]

Figure 4-4:
To reach the right people, target your ads.

6. **Next to Duration, you can select the amount of time you want the ad to run from a drop-down menu.**

7. **Click Set Budget to publish your post.**

Your ad won't start running immediately. Facebook has to review the ad first to make sure it's in compliance. This review doesn't take long, and in most cases, your ad will run within a couple of hours.

Measuring Your Ad's ROI

It's important to know how well your Facebook ad is performing, and Facebook has the tools to help you with this. Whether you use your Page's Insights dashboard (described in Book V, Chapter 3) or the Ads Manager dashboard, you can determine whether your investment is working.

What follows are a few of the ways to determine your ad's return on investment:

✦ **Regular posts versus paid posts:** When you select Posts on your Insights dashboard, you receive an overview on how your posts are performing. You can also see whether a post is paid or unpaid, enabling you to make a comparison.

✦ **Likes:** When you select Likes on your Insights dashboard, you can compare Likes achieved during paid campaigns with organic Likes.

✦ **Reach:** When you select Reach on your Insights dashboard, you can see at a glance how much of a boost a paid post received and how many people were reached as a result of that boost.

✦ **Engagement:** On your Ads Manager dashboard, you can see a list of your advertising and how much engagement each received. You can even see the cost per engagement.

✦ **Number of impressions:** The Reporting function in the Ads Manager gives you a rundown on how many impressions your ad received or the number of times your ad was served.

✦ **Clicks:** The Ads Manager Reporting function also shares how many times people clicked on your ad, as well as how many clicked through to your website. It also measures unique or first-time clickers.

So how do you put all of this together to determine ROI? First, it depends on your goals:

✦ **If your goal was to receive Likes to your Facebook Page or to have more people see a specific post,** you can analyze the numbers and determine whether you achieved the results you were hoping for. If you spent $100 and received one Like, your campaign probably didn't work for you. But if you spent $100 and received 50 Likes, you have to determine if spending $2 per Like is a worthwhile investment for you.

✦ **If you wanted to drive traffic to your website,** you can easily measure your success through the Ads Manager's click-through reporting, and also your own website's analytics. On days you purchased advertising, how much traffic did it send to your website, and was the amount of traffic worth the money spent? Moreover, how many of the people who came to your website as a result of the ad will continue to visit in the future? Do measure traffic over time and see whether you have a nice steady rise and repeat visits as a result of your ad.

You can also measure sales. If you receive traffic and no sales, it could be the ad needs to be reworked or retargeted — or it can mean Facebook ads aren't a good fit. In this case, consider trying more than once, just to make sure. However, if you notice a rise in sales as a result of your Facebook ad, continue with this investment.

It's important to determine whether a Facebook ad campaign is worth the investment. If you don't take time to analyze the numbers and determine whether you're meeting your goals, you're just throwing away money.

Chapter 5: Getting Started with Instagram

In This Chapter

↙ **Using Instagram for branding purposes**

↙ **Getting set up with Instagram**

↙ **Choosing photos to share**

↙ **Making your photos searchable with hashtags**

↙ **Creating a community on Instagram**

Have you ever noticed how people tend to react more to imagery than text on the social networks? That's because they see photos before they read text. So it's always in a brand's best interest to accompany great text with a great photo. Many times, though, the photo speaks for itself, and few words are needed. In fact, brands can find their community is very receptive to hanging out with them on a more visual platform, and that's where Instagram comes in.

Instagram is a social network based on photos, not words. Although Instagram allows hashtags, likes, and comments, you won't see text-heavy updates or link sharing. Instead, both individuals and brands alike let their photographs do the talking. In fact, many people prefer Instagram to other social platforms because there's less chatter.

Instagram gives you an opportunity to show your brand's creative side and think outside of the proverbial box. Instead of attracting people with viral videos or discount codes, you're using color and light.

In this chapter, we talk about how to set up an Instagram account and share photos with your community.

Promoting Your Brand on Instagram

Instagram is a mobile platform. Although you can view Instagram photos online via your regular web browser, you're very limited with what you can do. The majority of people using Instagram to view photos and interact are doing so with smartphones and tablets.

You can't set up an Instagram account or upload photos to your Instagram account from your computer; you can only view and like photos from your computer. If you want to sign up for an Instagram account or share photos with your community on Instagram, you must use a mobile device.

Here are a few examples of how brands use Instagram in creative ways, while still staying within their comfort zones:

✦ The Starbucks account shares images of their customers, their baristas, and even members of the executive team trying new flavors and blends.

✦ Red Bull Energy Drink uses their Instagram account to appeal to adrenaline junkies by posting photos of skydivers or skateboards high in the air.

✦ Nike shares photos of athletes doing what they do best.

Be creative with your Instagram photos. The best Instagram strategy is to keep it simple. Oftentimes, the best photos are the ones closest to home. You don't need to take a trip to Europe in order to take photos to share with your community, because your brand has enough interesting things going on in your own backyard.

Almost every brand can present a more visual side to its community by using Instagram, although you might not immediately see what your brand should highlight. In the section "Determining What Is Photo-Worthy for Your Brand," later in this chapter, we throw out some suggestions for photogenic moments.

Creating and Using Your Instagram Account

Is your mobile device in hand? Good. In the following sections, we discuss how to set up an Instagram account, upload photos, and control notifications.

Setting up your account

Follow these steps to set up an Instagram account:

1. **Locate the Instagram app on iTunes or Google Play and download it to your mobile device.**

2. **Choose to register either with your Facebook account or with your email account, as shown in Figure 5-1.**

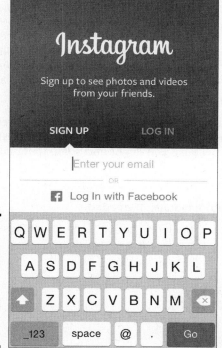

Figure 5-1:
Use either
Facebook or
your email
address to
create an
Instagram
account.

3. **If you elected to register with your Facebook account, enter your Facebook login information.**

   If you elected to register with your email account, enter your email address and the password you want to use for the site and select Next.

4. **Create your username, fill out your profile, and upload your profile shot. Also, you have the option to enter your full name and phone number. After you enter all the desired information click Done.**

   Now you're ready to take and share photos.

Sharing photos

You can share photos on Instagram by following these steps:

1. **Open the Instagram app on your mobile device and select the Camera option.**

   The Camera option looks like a square with a circle inside.

2. **Either select a photo from the photo album or click the blue button to take a photo.**

3. **When you have the photo you like, tap Next.**

   You see the photo you want to display, along with various filters, as shown in Figure 5-2. The filters are fun ways to highlight your photo, for example, with different borders and tones, or even in black and white.

4. **(Optional) Choose a filter, if you want.**

   If you like the photo as-is, don't worry about a filter. However, do take some time at some point to familiarize yourself with Instagram's different filter options because you might find some that make your photos look awesome.

5. **Tap Next.**

6. **Write a caption and add hashtags, if needed.**

   For more on hashtags, see the later section "Using Hashtags in Your Instagram Posts."

Figure 5-2:
Instagram comes with a variety of filters you can use to enhance your photos.

7. **(Optional) Tap on Facebook, Twitter, and other social networks to share, as shown in Figure 5-3.**

   You can upload your Instagram photos to both Facebook and Twitter at the same time you're Instagramming. Your photo gets increased visibility when you share it on multiple channels, which means more opportunities for others to like, share, comment, and recognize your brand.

   When you post the same content on every platform, people may not feel the need to follow you on every platform. You may gain more Instagram followers if you don't share the same images on Facebook, Twitter, and other platforms.

   If you're not logged into these social networks, you may be taken to a screen at those social networks so you can log in.

8. **Tap Share, located at the bottom of the screen.**

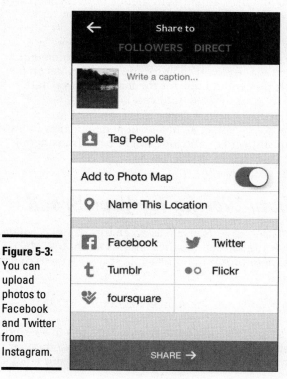

Figure 5-3:
You can upload photos to Facebook and Twitter from Instagram.

Controlling notifications

You can set your account up so that you can receive Instagram notifications on your mobile device, even when you're not using the app. To do so, follow these steps:

1. **Select Options in your profile account.**

You can find your profile at the lower-right corner of your Instagram screen. It looks like an ID card — a rectangle containing a circle and three lines.

2. **At the top-right of the profile screen that appears, tap the wheel to open a drop-down list.**

3. **Scroll down and, below Preferences, select the Push Notification Settings option you want.**

You can choose to turn on notifications from friends or everyone, or to turn them off completely.

If you find your phone is always beeping and buzzing because you're receiving Instagram notifications every time someone likes or comments on a photo or sends a friend request, you can turn the notifications off in your smartphone's notification center. Look for the Instagram app in the notification center and select your desired notification settings.

If you received a like, you were tagged in an image, or someone new followed you, a red heart notification appears on the lower-right of your Instagram app screen.

Determining What Is Photo-Worthy for Your Brand

You may be thinking your brand isn't as visual as an energy drink or coffee brand. The truth is, very few brands can tell their stories in photos. Most, however, can find some ways to present photos while staying true to their brand's focus and mission.

Here are some of the ways brands can share on Instagram:

✦ **Teamwork:** Fans love to see the behind-the-scenes workings of a brand. Don't shy away from showing the team at meetings, in the cafeteria, or chatting it up in the hallway. It shows your community that your team is human.

✦ **Test kitchens and factories:** Who doesn't love to see how products are made or served to the public? Taking the mystery away (without giving away company secrets) will endear you to your fans.

✦ **Products and ingredients:** Show what goes into a product. For example, if yours is an organic food brand using only wholesome ingredients, share photos of some of your suppliers, like farms and farmers markets. Showing what goes into a product is also a great tool for selling. People like to know what they're eating.

✦ **Outings:** Share photos of the team picnic or conference.

✦ **Ideas for using the product or service:** What are some of the things people make with your products? Share how others use what you do.

✦ **Sightings "in the wild":** If you spot people using your products on the street, share photos on Instagram — but do get permission first.

With Instagram, the possibilities are endless. You don't need expensive equipment or a degree in photography. You only need the ability to understand what your community responds to.

Before taking photos, do a search and see how other brands and individuals are using Instagram. If you tap the Explore button, shown in Figure 5-4, random images from Instagram users appear in a grid on your screen. A search bar also appears, which you can use to search out other brands that are on Instagram and see how they're doing it. You're sure to get inspiration from others, and you also can see how the brands are interacting.

Figure 5-4:
Use the Explore button to view random photos or search for other Instagram accounts.

Explore

Using Hashtags in Your Instagram Posts

Hashtags help to make a photo searchable. For example, if you post a photo of shoes on Instagram, and use the hashtags #shoes, #style, and/or #fashion, that photo will show up in the streams of others who are looking for items by using that same hashtag. When someone clicks on that hashtag, it will bring up public images that have been labeled with that hashtag.

Your content has a limited shelf life when hashtagged, especially with a popular hashtag. So if it's a trending or popular topic, it may be visible at the top of the search for only a few minutes or hours. Sometimes an image will have longer visibility on a less popular hashtag because it's not pushed to the bottom of the search by more current entries. Play around with both popular and less trendy hashtags to see where you receive the most engagement.

Here are some hashtag best practices:

+ **Use two or three hashtags at most.** Using too many hashtags makes a post too busy. Sure, your post appears on many different searches now, but most people prefer to look at photos with less clutter.

+ **Make up your own hashtag.** Make up a hashtag that suits your brand and share it with your community. Now when they use your product or take part in a related activity, they use your brand's hashtag, giving you more visibility and prompting others to try the same.

+ **Keep an eye out for trending hashtags.** Hashtags don't have to be brand related. Plenty of hashtags relate to holidays, current events, and television shows. Don't spam a hashtag with irrelevant content, but if you have an image appropriate for trending hashtags, don't be afraid to use it.

+ **Think of popular things people like to do or buy.** Some hashtags that are popular on Instagram are #food, #shoes, and #cats. Familiarize yourself with popular hashtags but keep in mind that your content won't stay at the top of a very popular hashtag for long.

+ **Take part in hashtag memes.** Try having fun with your Instagram account by taking part in a meme. For example, you can use #ThrowbackThursday or #TBT to share photos of your business in its early stages or #outfitoftheday to show what your staff is wearing.

+ **Hashtags work best with public accounts.** Brands shouldn't have private accounts because it limits the brand's audience: Hashtags are seen only by people who have access to the account. If yours is a private account with 50 followers, it has the potential to be seen by only 50 people. If your account is public, your image has the potential to be seen by hundreds, if not thousands.

If you want to make your account private so only people you choose to be friends with can see your photos, follow these steps:

1. **On your profile screen, select Edit Profile.**
2. **Scroll down to the bottom of the page to the area where it says Posts Are Private.**
3. **Flip the little toggle switch to the right.**

Keep in mind that with a private account, you have to manually approve any friend request. With an account that is public, anyone can follow and view your photos.

People come to Instagram for the visual. Although you should give the photo a little caption or description, don't write an essay or you'll lose people.

Finding Friends and Fans on Instagram

What good is having an Instagram account if you have no friends to share your photos with?

To search for people or brands to follow, follow these steps:

1. **Tap the Explore button.**
2. **In the search text box, shown in Figure 5-5, type the person's or brand's name or Instagram handle.**

   You can also search hashtags for topics related to your business. For example, if you restore classic cars, you can use hashtags #classiccars, #classiccarspotting, and #classiccarsdaily, which are the most popular hashtags in that topic. Now you can see who some of the classic car enthusiasts are on Instagram. Follow them, and they may follow you in return to see photos of your restorations.

3. **When you find an account you're interested in, click the Follow button to follow that account.**

   Unless you follow people or brands that have private accounts, after you click the Follow button, their photos automatically appear in your feed. However, if you want to follow someone who has a private account, you have to request permission to follow her. Many of the people you follow will follow you in return.

Figure 5-5:
The search
text box
enables
you to
search both
users and
hashtags.

Don't follow random people just to get followers. Make sure you're following the right people. Online communities are made up of like-minded people. It's a waste of time to follow people who have no interest in what you do. Find people with whom you have a common interest for a mutually beneficial relationship.

Make sure to tell your Facebook, Twitter, and blog communities that you're now on Instagram. If people follow you on one social media site, they'll likely follow you on another.

Book VI

LinkedIn

Contents at a Glance

Chapter 1: Promoting Yourself With LinkedIn

In This Chapter

✔ Using LinkedIn as an online résumé

✔ Highlighting your career

✔ Endorsing and being endorsed

✔ Private messaging with LinkedIn

LinkedIn sometimes gets a bum rap because people aren't sure how to use it, or because they don't see the same type of interaction as they do on Facebook, Twitter, or Pinterest. However, different social networks serve different purposes, and thus they're used differently. Don't write LinkedIn off just because it's more about business than cat photos. If you use it on a regular basis, it can be a formidable part of your marketing plan — not just in finding work, but in making important connections.

LinkedIn isn't merely a place to post your résumé. Use it to connect with old business associates and meet new associates. You can share your achievements, recommend colleagues, find jobs, and join discussion groups filled with like-minded people. You can also use LinkedIn to promote your brand with brand pages or groups. Many businesses are using LinkedIn to connect with a more professional crowd.

In this chapter, we show you how to set up a profile that attracts the attention of potential employers and clients, while highlighting your expertise. We also show you how others can help highlight your achievements and how you can recommend others in return.

Exploring the Benefits of Using LinkedIn

LinkedIn has many features for the brand and social media marketer. You can establish your expertise through the LinkedIn content platform (you find out more about blogging with LinkedIn in Book VI, Chapter 4), interact with your community via brand pages and groups, and reach out to others via LinkedIn messaging.

Also, LinkedIn offers opportunities to network every day. You can expand your business connections through LinkedIn far more than by using Facebook or Twitter.

You need to be on LinkedIn for the following reasons:

✦ **Recruiters and Human Resources professionals are on LinkedIn.** People who are hiring are looking at your profile on LinkedIn. In fact, if you're not on LinkedIn, it may lead them to speculate why. For example, are you not Internet savvy? If you're looking for a job, it's expected you'll be on LinkedIn.

✦ **LinkedIn has extensive job listings.** If you're looking for work, you can take advantage of LinkedIn's job search engine. Many top brands are using LinkedIn as a way to find suitable candidates through job listings, and there are plenty of listings exclusive to LinkedIn.

✦ **Receive (and give) endorsements and testimonials.** LinkedIn enables your peers to endorse your skills and write up recommendations, and you can do the same for them. People who are searching for networking connections or job candidates will take these recommendations into consideration. (We discuss endorsements and testimonials in more detail in the section "Understanding Endorsements and Testimonials," later in this chapter.)

✦ **Make important business connections.** You get to choose whom to connect with on LinkedIn. For example, you can connect with past co-workers, employers, and Fortune 500 executives. You never know who will accept your invitation.

✦ **Join professional groups that include like-minded people.** LinkedIn hosts thousands of online groups, enabling professionals to network within their respective niches.

✦ **Reach out to the people who are viewing your profile.** LinkedIn tells you who's viewing your profile, which opens the door when it comes to meeting new people and making important connections. For example, if someone you're interested in working with has viewed your profile, you can contact him, saying, "I noticed you viewed my profile. I'd love to chat." We talk more about contacting the people who view your LinkedIn profile in Chapter 4 in this minibook.

✦ **Updating an online résumé is easier than continuously updating a paper résumé.** With LinkedIn, you don't have to worry about hiring a professional résumé writer or formatting documents. You just have to click the Edit button and enter your desired information. The formatting is done for you. (However, you still have to worry about spelling and grammar.)

✦ **Establish your expertise by using the LinkedIn content platform.** LinkedIn invites users to create content, as well. Posting articles on LinkedIn can help to establish your expertise.

✦ **Read news from your connections.** Your connections post news, tips, and updates, which you can look over to stay current on industry trends and timely topics.

✦ **Research other businesses.** A lot of businesses are on LinkedIn. If you're interested in working with a particular business, you can use LinkedIn to read its business profile, connect with people who work for that business, and more.

✦ **Introduce others to your books, websites, blogs, and more.** Your profile has spots where you can list books you authored and links to your blog, website, or other online content. This drives more traffic (and sales) to your interests.

On LinkedIn, your community members aren't called friends or followers; instead, they're considered *connections.* You have varying degrees of connections: The closer you're connected to a person, the more ways you can interact with him or her. For example, you can't send a private message to someone who isn't a 1st-degree connection. We really get into connections, levels of connectivity, and how to connect to others in Chapter 4 of this minibook.

Creating an Online Résumé

Something interesting is happening in the world of hiring. Many employers are now accepting LinkedIn profiles instead of résumés. In fact, many online job applications even offer an option to link to a LinkedIn profile rather than to upload your résumé.

Even if you're not looking for work, someone may be looking for you. Recruiters visit LinkedIn daily, throughout the day. They are always looking for fresh prospects, and LinkedIn enables them to see new, qualified people.

LinkedIn is also a way for sales people, customers, and potential clients and job candidates to learn about a business.

Keep your LinkedIn profile updated because you never know who's going to come calling.

Projecting a professional image on LinkedIn

LinkedIn isn't your usual social network. Most people aren't on LinkedIn to find friends; they're looking for professional connections, so how you present yourself is very important. Whereas you may be a little more casual with your profile photo and bio on Facebook, for example, the type of photo you use on LinkedIn and the information you share on your profile should be of a more professional nature.

Here are a few things to consider before creating your LinkedIn profile:

✦ **Your title or headline is front and center.** Your title is the second thing people view after your headshot. Choose a title that represents you and what you do in the most professional manner. If you want to attract clients, for example, use a title that best highlights both you and your business.

✦ **Participate in groups.** Many people say they're not on LinkedIn to socialize; rather, they want to have an online résumé. Don't discount the importance of joining groups, however. Not only are they important networking tools, but when you join a group, those groups show up on your profile. Group membership shows potential connections that you're looking to continuously learn and network.

✦ **Make sure your career summary is professional, but personal.** Your summary should sum up your career in a businesslike tone but should also feature elements of your personality. For example, there's nothing wrong with adding elements of humor, as long as you aren't raunchy or over the top.

✦ **Spelling and grammar matter.** You wouldn't hand out a paper résumé that contained misspellings, and neither would you want people to view your online résumé if it's riddled with errors. Clients want to know you'll take care with their product or service. A résumé with errors says you don't pay attention.

✦ **Ask for recommendations.** Your colleagues and former colleagues can give testimonials as to how you work. Don't be afraid to ask them to recommend you on LinkedIn — and don't forget to reciprocate.

✦ **Use relevant keywords.** Keywords help recruiters and potential employers, clients, and connections find you.

✦ **Decide whether you want to browse LinkedIn publicly or anonymously.** When you view another member's profile, that action shows up in the person's Who Viewed Your Profile section. You may not mind making it known you looked at someone's profile, but it can lead that person to contact you to see whether she can help with anything or to make a connection. However, if you go anonymous, you can't see who viewed your profile, or any of the statistics LinkedIn offers regarding the people who viewed your profile.

✦ **Check your privacy settings so that your activities aren't broadcast to the world.** When you update your résumé or add experiences, your connections may receive notifications of those updates. This can be a problem if you don't want your current employer or clients to know you're in the market for something new. Adjust your LinkedIn privacy settings, as shown in Figure 1-1, if you don't want others knowing you're making changes.

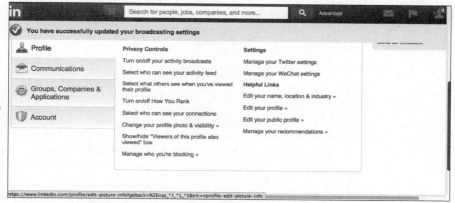

**Book VI
Chapter 1**

Promoting
Yourself
With LinkedIn

Figure 1-1:
Pay
attention to
your privacy
settings.

✦ **Add media to your profile.** You can add video, images, and presentations to your LinkedIn profile. Take advantage of these tools to show off your creative side.

✦ **Reorder skills so the most important skills are at the top.** You can set up your skills so they're in the order you feel goes from most to least important.

✦ **List places you volunteer.** Clients, employers, and other connections like to know the people they work with are doing some good in the world. List your charitable endeavors.

✦ **Don't skimp on the achievements and accolades.** You may find it to be a humble brag to talk about the great things you do, but it's perfectly acceptable in your LinkedIn profile. Go ahead and list all your important achievements and awards received.

Choosing and uploading a profile photo

According to LinkedIn, a profile with a photo receives 14 times more views than a profile without a photo. It also holds true many professionals won't connect with anyone on LinkedIn unless he has a photo on his profile. Photos add an element of trust. It also tells others you care enough about your professional profile to make sure you have all the necessary elements. If you can't take the time to present yourself in the best light, how can a business trust you to present them in the best light?

Choose the right type of photos for your LinkedIn profile. Because your photo is the first view of you people see on LinkedIn, if you choose a completely inappropriate photo, a potential client may wonder what other bad choices you make. Thus, take the utmost care with your LinkedIn profile photo.

Choosing a profile photo

Here are a few guidelines for choosing a profile photo:

✦ **Headshots are fine.** Most professionals on LinkedIn choose to go with a headshot. Some even have headshots done professionally for their LinkedIn and other professional social profiles. You don't have to break the bank to post a headshot on LinkedIn, but fancy backgrounds and photos of your entire body are unnecessary. Although it's important to have a photo on LinkedIn, most people just want to see your face, like the profile photo in Figure 1-2.

✦ **Avoid party or vacation photos.** Your LinkedIn profile isn't the place to post personal photos. Don't post an image of you in a bikini or with beer in hand. Neither type of picture portrays you as a professional and can even cost you a job.

✦ **Choose a simple background.** If you have a photo with a white background, or with nothing going on in the background, it's a better choice than a photo that has a lot going on.

Figure 1-2:
Choose a photo that portrays you in a positive, professional manner.

✦ **Avoid photos with others.** Don't post group photos or photos with a significant other, kids, or friends. It's not professional, and people won't know which person is you.

✦ **Choose a photo that's up to date.** The photo should reflect what you look like now. This way, if professional connections see you in real life, they can recognize you instantly. For example, if your profile shot has you with long brown hair, but you now sport a bright pink Mohawk, that might be a deal breaker for an image-conscious employer who wouldn't have invited you in for an interview had he or she had known you what you really look like.

✦ **No selfies.** There's a time and place for selfies. LinkedIn isn't it. Selfies aren't considered professional.

✦ **No wedding photos.** You may be over-the-top blissfully happy because you're a newlywed, but if you choose a profile photo in a wedding dress, it might lead to a potential client or connection feeling you're too focused on the wedding or marriage to concentrate on anything else.

✦ **Avoid pets or objects.** Using a photo of pets or objects, instead of a photo of yourself, will lead others to wonder why you're being vague about your professional appearance. Do you have something to hide?

✦ **Don't opt for no photo at all.** LinkedIn connections like to get a feel for whom they're dealing with — or might potentially deal with. If you don't upload a photo, they're likely to pass you over in favor of someone they can get a feel for.

✦ **Avoid blurry images.** A blurry profile photo indicates you don't pay careful attention to what you're putting out there.

✦ **Avoid a logo unless you're setting up a brand page.** Logos are fine for brand pages, but few people will want to ask you to represent their brand if your own brand is front and center.

Your LinkedIn photo is the first thing people see when they access your LinkedIn profile. Choose wisely. As the old saying goes, you never get a second chance to make a good first impression.

Uploading a profile photo

To upload a photo to LinkedIn, follow these steps:

1. **Click Profile, and then select Edit Profile from the drop-down list that opens.**

   Your profile page opens.

2. **Hover over your profile photo and click where it says Change Photo. You will also see a camera icon.**

3. **In the Edit Photo pop-up window that appears, click Browse.**

   A File Upload pop-up window appears.

4. **Select the photo you want to use and click Open.**

5. **Click and drag to position the photo as desired.**

6. **Click Save.**

Uploading a background photo

You can elect to have a background image on your LinkedIn profile. This should be an image that's representative of you as a professional or of your brand. The background photo appears underneath the text on your profile.

To upload a background photo such as the one shown in Figure 1-3, follow these steps:

1. **From your profile page, click the camera icon located just above your profile.**

2. **In the Upload File pop-up window that appears, choose an image and click Open.**

3. **Click and drag to reposition the image, if you want.**

4. **Click Save to add this picture as your background photo.**

   You can instead select Change Image or Remove Image if you've changed your mind. Selecting Change Image reopens the Upload File pop-up window in Step 3. Remove Image leaves you with no background image displayed.

Figure 1-3: Choose a background photo that says something about you as a professional.

Filling out your profile

What should you include in your LinkedIn profile? Considering it's an online résumé, include your work history, achievements, accolades, and anything that portrays you and your career in a positive light.

To fill in all the appropriate items on your LinkedIn profile, hover your mouse over the sections you want to edit, as shown in Figure 1-4. You'll notice a pencil icon next to each item that is available for editing. Click the pencil, and you're now in edit mode for that item. Make your changes and updates, and then click Save. You'll also notice you have to click the appropriate pencil to edit each individual section and save those sections separately as you finish updating the items you want to edit.

**Book VI
Chapter 1**

Promoting
Yourself
With LinkedIn

Figure 1-4:
Hover
over each
section you
want to edit.

You can edit the following profile sections:

✦ **Summary:** Summarize your experiences and achievements. This is often the second place people look after your photo. What you say in your summary can determine whether a LinkedIn connection or potential connection will read on or look for another candidate.

✦ **Experience:** Just like you would on your résumé, list your employment history. Click Add Position to add a new job. You can also use the arrows to arrange your past and present jobs in date order, with the most current job first just as you would list it on a paper résumé.

✦ **Projects:** If you're working on something amazing in your spare time or took part in an important project, list it here.

✦ **Publications:** Where authors can list and link to their books, articles, or other publications.

✦ **Skills:** Your skills come from your endorsements (we talk about endorsements in the following section).

✦ **Education:** List high school and college education, and all degrees and honors.

Don't set up your LinkedIn profile once and forget about it. Just like you evolve in your career, so should your online résumé. Take care to keep it updated.

Understanding Endorsements and Testimonials

LinkedIn offers the opportunity to receive accolades and recommendations from your peers:

✦ **Endorsements:** Like check marks attesting to your skills. LinkedIn occasionally asks your peers whether they'll endorse you for particular skills. If they agree, they only have to click a button to endorse you. Their LinkedIn profile photos show up next to the skills they endorse you for.

Having many people endorse you for your individual skills helps to establish your expertise. Moreover, it has benefits for the person who endorsed your skills, as well, because when her profile photo shows up in your Skills area, others can click it to see her profile.

✦ **Recommendations:** Like job references. People you work with can write a few paragraphs to attest to your skills and expertise. Having testimonials backs up what you write in your LinkedIn profile and acts as proof that you can do what you promise.

The beauty of endorsements and testimonials is that they save you from having to keep files of references to hand over to potential clients and employers.

In the following sections, we cover the benefits and basics of testimonials and endorsements so that you can have social proof of all your career achievements.

Receiving recommendations

Don't underestimate the importance of LinkedIn testimonials. It's essential to back up your experience with other peoples' experiences in working with you. A potential client or employer can look at testimonials on LinkedIn, saving himself a lot of time researching your skills and helping him see that you're someone who's trustworthy, and that you can get the job done.

Recommendations aren't visible in public LinkedIn pages. Instead, they're visible to only 1st-, 2nd-, and 3rd-level connections who are logged in. Therefore, people who aren't familiar with your industry and don't have many of the same connections in common can't just stumble upon your testimonials.

Here are some tips and best practices for receiving testimonials:

✦ **Don't be afraid to ask.** Just like you ask employers, clients, and co-workers for reference letters, don't be afraid to ask them for testimonials on LinkedIn.

✦ **Request many testimonials.** The more testimonials, the merrier. If you have many stellar references, it means many people appreciate your work. Get as many on your LinkedIn profile as you can.

✦ **Do some back scratching.** Offer to trade testimonials. Give a testimonial to get a testimonial.

✦ **Offer to write it yourself.** Sometimes people don't have time to write a testimonial. Offer to write up a testimonial that the person can approve and post at her convenience.

✦ **Use LinkedIn's Ask to Be Recommended feature.** LinkedIn offers a way for you to ask your connections for testimonials. When you select this option, shown in Figure 1-5, your connections receive a message asking for a testimonial.

Don't request a testimonial from a client or colleague with whom you may have had a stormy relationship. Even though you might have done stellar work, bitterness can show through in a testimonial.

**Book VI
Chapter 1**

Promoting Yourself With LinkedIn

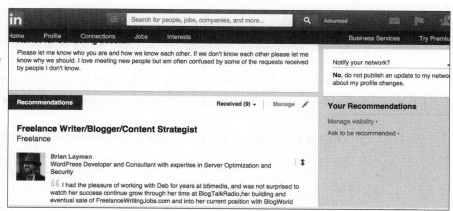

Figure 1-5: LinkedIn makes it easy to ask your connections for recommendations.

Giving recommendations

You should also give testimonials to deserving colleagues and connections. They'll appreciate the recommendations because it makes their LinkedIn profiles look good.

Recommending others strengthens your relationships with those people, and it also helps to add more visibility to your profile because your recommendation will appear in other profiles.

To give a recommendation to a LinkedIn connection, follow these steps:

1. **Go to the profile of the person you want to recommend.**

2. **Hover over the down-pointing arrow next to Send a Message.**

3. **Choose Recommendation from the drop-down list that appears.**

4. **In the Recommendations screen that appears, enter your recommendation in the Write a Recommendation text box and click Send.**

5. **(Optional) Create a personalized message for the person you're recommending in the Your Message to *Connection* text box.**

   You can also just leave the standard message that LinkedIn provides.

6. **Select an option from the What's Your Relationship drop-down list.**

7. **Select from the What Were Your Positions at the Time drop-down lists for both you and the connection you want to recommend.**

8. **Click Send.**

You can also recommend someone from your LinkedIn profile, using the Recommendations section. Follow these steps:

1. **Scroll down your profile to the Recommendations area.**

2. **Hover your mouse over this section and select Manage when it appears in the upper right of the Recommendations section.**

3. **Select Give Recommendations, located just below Recommendations.**

4. **In the Who Do You Want to Recommend text box, type the person's name.**

5. **Fill out the appropriate information and write the testimonial.**

6. **Click Send.**

Don't wait to be asked to give recommendations to people whose work you respect. You can recommend anyone at any time. Providing recommendations gives your profile more visibility and sets you up as an influential person. You're also doing something nice for someone else.

Asking for endorsements

Endorsements (see Figure 1-6) are a way for your connections to attest to your skills without having to write out a recommendation. They can respond to a prompt generated by LinkedIn asking if you're good at particular skills, they can respond to a request from you, or they can even offer an endorsement out of the goodness of their hearts.

Figure 1-6: More endorsements mean more people are attesting to your skills.

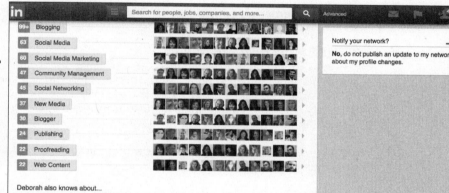

The most popular way to receive endorsements is when LinkedIn prompts your connections to do so. For example, every now and then when you log into LinkedIn, a prompt appears at the top of your page listing several of your connections and asking you if those people are skilled in a particular topic. You can endorse by clicking Yes to answer the question, or click X or skip to not respond.

Endorsements show others that you have the skill-set to back up your profile. Make sure that the skills listed and endorsed on your profile are the best representation of you.

Adding skills to your profile

You can add endorsements so that your contacts know for which skills you want an endorsement. To add skills to your profile, follow these steps:

1. **On your profile page, scroll down to the Skills section.**

2. **Select the Edit function (which looks like a pencil) that appears when you hover your mouse over this section.**

   The Skills and Endorsements Settings screen appears.

3. **Type the skill into the What Are Your Areas of Expertise text box.**

   A drop-down list appears with options that match the text you enter.

4. **Select the desired skill from the drop-down list.**

   Alternatively, if you don't see the desired skill, simply finish typing it into the text box.

5. **Click Add.**

6. **Repeat Steps 5 through 8 for each skill you want to add.**

7. **After you enter all your skills, click Save.**

Removing skills from your profile

It's good to show you're well rounded on your LinkedIn profile with a lot of skills and endorsements. Sometimes, though, LinkedIn will generate skills that aren't appropriate, but your friends may endorse them anyway. Fortunately, you can remove skills from your profile if you don't feel them to be a good fit, or if they aren't what you want to be known for.

To remove skills from your profile, follow these steps on the Skills and Endorsements Settings screen:

1. **In the Add & Remove section of the screen, click the X to the right of each skill that you want to remove.**

2. **Click Save.**

Reordering skills

You can also reorder your endorsements so that the most appropriate and important skills appear on top of your skills list, and the stuff you're not as great at appears at the bottom.

To reorder skills, follow these steps on the Skills and Endorsements Settings screen:

1. **Click and drag the skill you wish to move to the desired location in the group of skills.**

2. **Repeat, as necessary.**

3. **When you have your skills in the order you want, click Save.**

Opting out of endorsements

You may not even want to have endorsements on your LinkedIn profile. Although they're nice to have, they're purely optional.

To opt out of receiving endorsements altogether, follow these steps on the Skills and Endorsements Settings screen:

1. **For the I Want to Be Endorsed option, select the No radio button.**

2. **Click Save.**

Using LinkedIn Messages

LinkedIn provides a way to send and receive private messages that you can access in your LinkedIn mailbox. You can send and receive private messages only with 1st-degree connections. However, other levels of connections can choose to pay for a LinkedIn Premium account to use InMail, which runs upwards of $39.95 per month. So anyone can send you a message if he wants to badly enough. Fortunately, you mostly receive messages from connections.

Why would you want to send a personal message to a connection? Maybe you don't have that person's email address and need to get in touch with her. Or you might want to request an endorsement or testimonial, which you can do via private message. You can also reach out to someone from a group you participate in to further a discussion or ask to connect.

To send a LinkedIn message, follow these steps:

1. **Click the Messages icon at the top-right of any LinkedIn page.**

   The icon looks like a little envelope.

2. **Click New on the left side of the Messages dashboard that appears.**

3. **Type your connection's name in the To text box.**

4. **Enter the topic of discussion in the Subject text box.**

5. **Enter your message in the Type Your Message field.**

6. **Click the Send Message button when you're done writing your message.**

For a more in-depth look at using LinkedIn, check out *LinkedIn For Dummies,* 3rd Edition, by Joel Elad (Wiley Publishing, Inc.).

Chapter 2: Promoting Your Business with LinkedIn

In This Chapter

✔ Using a LinkedIn Company Page

✔ Showcasing products with LinkedIn

✔ Putting together a Showcase Page

LinkedIn isn't merely a social network for job seekers to get their résumé to the right people. It's also a wonderful marketing tool for businesses. LinkedIn Company Pages enable you to connect with a different kind of audience — a more businesslike audience.

The people who network on LinkedIn are professionals — some of whom are, yes, looking for work, but also many are looking to meet and learn from other professionals. These same professionals are also using LinkedIn to research businesses either because they either want to work for or with the brand, or because they want to become a customer of the brand. You don't want to miss out on an important opportunity because you didn't start a Company Page on LinkedIn.

In this chapter, we delve into some of the things you can do with a LinkedIn Company Page so that you can gain better brand visibility, highlight your products and services, grow your business, and drive traffic to your website and sales pages.

Exploring the Benefits of a Company Page

A Company Page on LinkedIn is different from a Brand page on Facebook or Google+, especially in the content being shared. Everything on LinkedIn is geared towards businesses and professionals, which presents a whole different atmosphere than other social media sites. You also have a unique opportunity to create specific pages that showcase your different products, services, events, and brands.

Why does your business need a LinkedIn Company Page? Here are a few reasons:

✦ **Share job openings.** You can set up your LinkedIn Company Page so that it lists open positions with your business. In addition to viewing the listings, candidates can also learn more about your business from the information you put forth on your Company Page.

✦ **Use Showcase Pages.** You can create special pages for products, services, and events. These Showcase Pages enable you to share in-depth information and engage with a target audience.

✦ **Share content.** Share blog posts, articles, and more with the LinkedIn community.

✦ **Share news.** You can share news — for example, product launches — with your LinkedIn community through your Company Page.

✦ **Increase your searchability.** Increase your business's visibility on both LinkedIn and the search engines.

✦ **Engage with your community.** Use your Company Page to chat with your followers.

✦ **Increase opportunities for your team to network.** People who list your business as their place of employment on their LinkedIn profiles will also show up on your Company Page as working for your brand, which gives them more opportunities to network.

Creating a LinkedIn Company Page

A LinkedIn Company Page gives your brand a strong presence on an important business and career-oriented social network. As such, you don't want to just slap together any old page and be done with it. Put time and care into your page — it's well worth the effort.

Here are some tips and best practices for your LinkedIn Company Page:

✦ **Choose a background image that represents your brand.** Just as with Facebook and Twitter, your LinkedIn Company Page encourages the use of a large cover image, in addition to a smaller profile shot, such as a logo. Choose an eye-catching background image that shows off your company in the best possible light.

✦ **Ask your team to give recommendations.** Is your company a great place to work? If so, ask the people who work with you or for you to give your brand a recommendation. Showcasing your brand as a good place to work is good for business, as well.

✦ **Take advantage of the Career Page.** If you have job openings within your company, you can highlight them on your Career Page. Those jobs have the potential to appear in front of many more qualified professionals than if you simply took out an ad. Your page will show up in a job search on LinkedIn, adding even more brand visibility.

✦ **Optimize your page for search.** Use relevant keywords to attract searches in- and outside of LinkedIn.

✦ **Check your Company Page every day.** Engage with your community on a daily basis. Posting new content each day ensures traffic every day, as well.

✦ **Use image and video.** Mix up your content to keep interest going on your page.

✦ **Stay on topic.** Make sure to share content relevant to your brand.

Before setting up your LinkedIn Company Page, look around to see how other brands are using LinkedIn. You may walk away with some good ideas for your own page, as well as see how your competitors are interacting with the community.

Setting up your brand's profile

A Company Page on LinkedIn is an important marketing tool. Because people will be researching your brand and interacting with you online, you definitely want to take advantage of the opportunity to connect with others on LinkedIn.

You have to have an existing personal LinkedIn account to create a Company Page. If you make up a fake account and LinkedIn suspects you're using a fake account, you receive notification and your page may become unpublished.

It doesn't take much time to set up a LinkedIn Company Page. Just follow these steps:

1. **Select Interests, located at the top of any LinkedIn page.**

2. **From the drop-down list that appears, select Companies.**

3. **In the right sidebar, click the Create button in the Create a Company Page section.**

   The Add a Company screen appears.

4. **Fill in your company name and your business email address in the appropriate text boxes, as shown in Figure 2-1.**

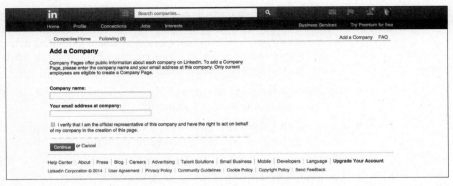

Figure 2-1:
Use your
company
information
to set
up your
LinkedIn
Company
Page profile.

5. **Select the I Verify That I Am the Official Representative of This Company check box.**

6. **Click Continue.**

7. **In the text box that appears, fill in your company information.**

8. **Click Save.**

Adding and removing administrators

You may want to appoint an administrator or two for your LinkedIn Company Page. Most businesses let the marketing or social media department handle LinkedIn updates.

You must be connected to the person whom you're appointing as an administrator. Invite that person to connect if you haven't done so already.

To add an administrator, follow these steps:

1. **On your Company Page, click the Edit button at the top-right of the page.**

2. **On your company's Overview page that appears, scroll down to find the Company Pages Admin function on the left side of the page.**

3. **Type the name of the person who will be handling the Company Page in the Designated Admins section.**

   If you want to remove someone as an administrator, in the Designated Admins section, click the X to the right of the person's information.

4. **Click Publish, located at the top right of the page**

Sharing your brand's content

Of course, you can't have a Company Page and not do anything with it. Just like you would on Facebook, Twitter, and Google+, you should share content on LinkedIn.

Some types of content that do well on LinkedIn include

+ **Company news:** Share new hires, product launches, event announcements, promotions, and anything of note happening with your company.

+ **Industry news:** Share news of interest or related to your niche.

+ **How-to's and tutorials:** Show how to use your product or service, or offer tips for others in your industry.

+ **Business-oriented images and videos:** Don't forget to add visual elements to your Company Page.

+ **Blog posts and articles:** If your business has a blog, share posts on LinkedIn. Also, share related content from other brands.

Book VI
Chapter 2

Promoting Your
Business with
LinkedIn

WARNING!
Be mindful of how often you post. If you batter your LinkedIn community with a constant barrage of updates, they'll consider you too spammy to follow. Most brands update one to three times per day at most, with updates spaced out several hours apart.

Selling and Promoting with LinkedIn Showcase Pages

LinkedIn provides you with the perfect opportunity to highlight products and services with Showcase Pages. *Showcase Pages* are stand-alone pages that you can use to announce product launches, websites, events, and any kind of product, service, or opportunity (see Figure 2-2).

Basically, you have individual LinkedIn pages where you can engage your community and share a particular aspect of your business. For example, if your company is umbrella to several smaller brands, you can use a Company Page as your main page with the smaller brands highlighted in the Showcase Pages.

Highlighting your products and services

People enter Showcase Pages through the right sidebar of your Company Page or via a link on each individual Showcase Page. For example, each Showcase Page links to all of your brand's other Showcase Pages (if you have more than one). So people can see at a glance what's being showcased

Figure 2-2:
Use
Showcase
Pages to
highlight
individual
products,
events, or
services.

whenever they visit any of your pages. Best of all, people can follow the pages that interest them without having to follow all pages.

What are the benefits of Showcase Pages? Use them to

✦ **Share in-depth information about your brand.** Rather than a brief status update, Showcase Pages enable you to share any and all necessary information with your LinkedIn community.

✦ **Share with a target audience.** Because people follow only the Showcase Pages that interest them, you're interacting with people who truly want to be there. The audience is more targeted, and you don't have to sell as much on your Company Page.

✦ **Answer questions and receive feedback regarding the showcased element of your business.** When people have questions regarding your product or service, they can ask on the appropriate Showcase Page. Talking with you or your team can increase their confidence with the brand, making them more likely to buy. Moreover, you can use this opportunity to receive valuable feedback.

✦ **Increase engagement.** Multiple Showcase Pages mean multiple opportunities for having a conversation with your now well-informed LinkedIn community.

You can create ten Showcase Pages for each Company Page. However, you can delete a Showcase Page if you need to make room for another. If your brand has a lot of things going on, choose the most important items to highlight. You might want to save one or two pages for new product launches or events, instead of using all ten at once.

Showcase Pages

Only a Company Page administrator can create Showcase Pages. Before you begin, you need to know the following:

✦ The name of the Showcase Page

✦ A short and sweet description — up to 200 characters

✦ The industry your page falls under

✦ The name of at least one Showcase Page administrator assigned to each page.

You also need to have a *hero image* (meaning a cover image) for your Showcase Page, preferably one highlighting the showcased item, as well as two logo images.

Here are the specifications for your Showcase Page's images:

✦ **Hero image:** A minimum of 974 x 300 pixels; PNG, JPEG, or GIF format. You can play around and crop the image after you upload it.

✦ **Logos:** 100 x 60 pixels. If you're a little off, LinkedIn will resize it to fit.

To create a Showcase Page, follow these steps:

1. **While on your Company Page, select the down-pointing arrow located next to the Edit button.**

2. **From the drop-down list that appears, select Create a Showcase Page.**

3. **Enter the Showcase Page's name (for example, the name of the item you're showcasing) and the person who will be administrator in the appropriate fields.**

4. **Click Create.**

   You can now see what the page will look like. If you're happy, go on to the next step. Otherwise, make any necessary edits.

5. **Click Publish to make the Showcase Page go live.**

Unfortunately, you can't easily unpublish a LinkedIn Showcase Page. To remove a Page, you have to contact LinkedIn and ask them to remove it for you. Choose wisely when it comes to the products and services you're showcasing because you can't delete at will.

LinkedIn provides you with some wonderful tools to promote your business and drive sales. Don't miss this opportunity to reach a whole new audience.

Chapter 3: Starting a LinkedIn Group

In This Chapter

✔ Engaging with like-minded people through LinkedIn groups

✔ Growing a LinkedIn community around your brand

✔ Moderating LinkedIn groups

A LinkedIn group is much different than a Company Page or individual profile. A group is less about your brand and more about growing a community and engaging people about a specific topic or niche. Creating a group doesn't promote your business in an obvious way, nor does it give you a place to sell — however, a group can be a wonderful place to learn more about your online community and your niche, which can help with the sales process.

LinkedIn groups provide you with a way to extend your brand's reach without selling. When you spend time with your online community, you gain their trust, and trust leads to sales. In this chapter, we talk about how to rock a LinkedIn group so that it's the place everyone wants to be.

Exploring the Benefits of LinkedIn Groups

LinkedIn groups are like forums where the members of your group can ask and answer questions and share ideas. You can have up to 20,000 members of your LinkedIn group, so it gives you an opportunity to reach tens of thousands of people.

The benefits of a LinkedIn group abound:

✦ **Establish expertise.** By participating in discussions, you're showing off your knowledge.

✦ **Learn about the people who are interested in your brand or niche.** Having ongoing discussions outside of your Company Page gives you an opportunity to learn about the people who are part of your online community.

✦ **Understand what questions your community might have.** Knowing what people have questions about can help you shape your content, as well as your products and services.

✦ **Drive traffic to your website and sales pages.** By putting a link to your website in the group description, you're driving traffic to your interests.

✦ **Create subgroups.** LinkedIn offers the ability for groups to break off into subgroups. You can use this feature to focus on specific topics without having those topics dominate the entire group.

✦ **Send weekly messages.** Group owners can send messages once a week to everyone in the group. For example, you can create a newsletter especially for your LinkedIn group community, sharing company information, content, and product updates. Consider your LinkedIn group to be an extension of your mailing list.

✦ **Make new connections and expand your reach.** The people who participate in groups may want to connect with you — and vice versa.

✦ **Hold in-depth discussions.** A group enables you to delve deeply into topics, rather than simply putting a quick update on your Company Page.

Growing a Community with a LinkedIn Group

Business people like to network. They want to have career-related discussions with others and ask questions while also establishing their own expertise and making new connections. By participating in a LinkedIn group, they're helping to make that happen.

In the following sections, we discuss how to set up a LinkedIn group, as well as how to set guidelines and restrictions for it.

Setting up a LinkedIn group

You can set up your LinkedIn group in a matter of minutes. Follow these steps to create your group:

1. **Select Interests at the top of any LinkedIn page and select Groups from the drop-down list that appears.**

   The Your Groups page opens.

2. **Select Create a Group in the upper-right of the page.**

3. **Fill in all necessary information about your group, including Group Name, Group Type, Summary, and Description. Also, upload a logo or photo if desired.**

Be as descriptive as possible about the purpose of the group, so you have the right type of networking happening in the group.

4. **Enter your email address in the Group Owner Email text box.**

5. **In the Access section, select a radio button.**

   You can choose from two options:

   - *Auto-Join:* Group members don't need approval to join the group.

   - *Request to Join:* Members must be approved before they can join the group.

   We discuss these options in more detail in the section "Approving or preapproving group members," later in this chapter.

6. **Fill in the remaining fields and select the check box to agree to the Terms of Service.**

7. **Click the appropriate Create a Group button.**

   You can create two kinds of groups, depending on the option you select:

   - *Create an Open Group:* Click this button to create a public group.

   - *Create a Members-Only Group:* Click this button to create a private group.

Book VI
Chapter 3

Starting a
LinkedIn Group

You can change your Members-Only group to an Open group at any time. However, once you change it, you can't change it back to Members Only. So make sure this is a change you want to make. If you do choose an Open Group, you can set it up so that anyone who wants to join the group requires approval before he or she can participate. You can find this option in the Group Settings located in the left sidebar of the group.

We discuss open and closed groups in detail in the following section.

You can also opt to have any posts that contain links be held in moderation, and to not approve anyone who has few or no connections. Take some time to familiarize yourself with the group's administration settings, located under Manage Group in the right sidebar before inviting members to join the group.

Choosing an open or closed group

LinkedIn offers two options for types of groups:

✦ **Open group:** If you have an open group

   - Discussions can be viewed by anyone on LinkedIn, even if they're not a member of the group.

   - Discussions show up in search engine results.

✦ **Members-Only group:** For a Members-Only group

- Discussions don't show up in search engine searches.
- Only members can view discussions.
- Closed groups are indicated by a padlock icon.

Basically, an open group is a public group, and a closed group is a private group. Keep in mind that having an open group can be a good thing because it's more visible and more people can see brand interaction. However, the downside is some people might shy away from participating in a public group.

You can share conversations that you have with open groups with your other online communities. For example, if your group is having an interesting discussion, you can post a link to it on your Facebook page and invite your community to join the discussion. This link can lead to additional membership. With a closed group, you're less likely to see additional membership because anyone who isn't a member can't access the link.

Both open and closed groups have their benefits, and some top online brands have no problem managing either.

To edit your LinkedIn group settings so that your group is open or closed, follow these steps:

1. **While in the group, select Manage, located at the top of the group.**

   You see a menu in the left sidebar with all your group administration options.

2. **Select Group Settings from the left sidebar.**

   You're taken to the Group Settings page, which has a variety of options for managing your LinkedIn group.

3. **Check either the open or closed group option.**

4. **Scroll to the bottom of the page and select Save Changes.**

Setting group permissions and restrictions

Your LinkedIn group is only as good as its moderation. If you aren't careful, you can let in spammers who hit everyone up with a hard pitch or drop links every chance they get. If you allow one person to post a link, soon everyone will be posting links, and you'll be stuck with a link farm instead of a group filled with discussion topics.

You can set up your LinkedIn group so certain types of situations are put into moderation. For example, you can make sure someone who has no connections is held in moderation for your approval before being allowed to join the group.

To manage permissions and restrictions for your group, follow these steps:

1. **While in the group, select Manage to be taken to the group administrations page.**

2. **In the left sidebar, select Group Settings.**

You're taken to a page featuring permission options for your group.

The available Permissions and Restrictions settings appear, as shown in Figure 3-1.

3. **Make your selections, and then click Save Changes.**

You can set up permissions so that members can post anything, including discussion topics, promotions and jobs, and comments; or you can hold everything in moderation. Remember, though, holding everything in moderation will probably turn off members who would rather have a conversation than constantly wait for topics to be approved.

Also, you can hold new members in moderation. This process helps ensure that prospective members aren't spammers. For example, you can request all new members be held in moderation for three days so that you have to approve everything they post. After three days, if it's established they're not spammers, they're free to interact with others and not have to worry about being held in moderation.

Book VI
Chapter 3

Starting a
LinkedIn Group

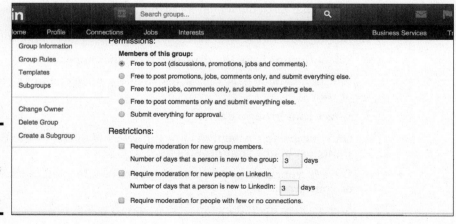

Figure 3-1:
Setting permissions helps keep down spam.

Establishing group guidelines

Something you can't overlook in your LinkedIn group are your group rules. The group rules set some guidelines for the members so they know what's expected and what behavior won't be tolerated. For example, LinkedIn groups can be a hotbed of spam if not moderated properly. Members always want to share links to their blog posts and articles, and this can be a turnoff to other members because your group will soon resemble a spammy link farm. So, in your group rules, you can let everyone know where you stand on allowing members to post links.

You can set up your group rules by clicking the Group Rules function in the left sidebar of your LinkedIn group. Type in your rules, and click Save Changes.

You might also set a few gentle guidelines for how members treat each other. For example, if you'd prefer not to have members swearing in their comments, you can mention this restriction in your group rules.

If you're already a part of some existing LinkedIn groups, read their group rules for ideas about what to include in your own group rules. If you're not a member of any groups, check out a few open groups to see how they handle group rules.

Growing Your Group

After you create a group, you need members. You can grow your membership by inviting connections or approving requests to join.

Inviting others to join your group

To invite other LinkedIn members to join your group, follow these steps:

1. **Hover your mouse over Interests at the top of any LinkedIn page.**

2. **Select Groups from the drop-down list that appears.**

   The Your Groups page opens, displaying a menu of groups you belong to or own.

3. **Select your group's name.**

4. **On your group's page that appears, select Manage, located at the top right, just below your group's title.**

5. **Once in your group, select Send Invitations, located in the left sidebar of your group.**

   A prewritten invitation appears, as shown in Figure 3-2.

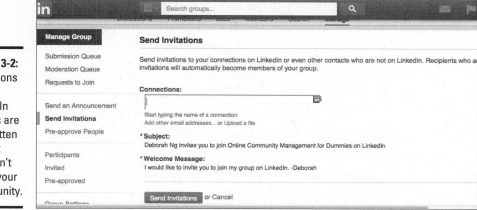

**Book VI
Chapter 3**

Starting a
LinkedIn Group

Figure 3-2:
Invitations
for
LinkedIn
groups are
prewritten
so that
you don't
spam your
community.

You can't customize a LinkedIn group invitation. LinkedIn has it set up this way in order to protect its members. It's a gentle invitation, not a hard sell, so no one feels harassed or pressured into joining a group.

6. **Click the In icon to the right of the Connections text box and select the name of the person you wish to invite from the list of connections that appears.**

   Alternatively, you can enter in the text box the email address of anyone to whom you're not connected.

   Take care in selecting connections to invite to your LinkedIn group. Not everyone to whom you're connected will want to join your group; select only those who you feel will have an interest.

7. **Click Send Invitations.**

   The invited person will see a notification at the top right of his LinkedIn page, indicating an invitation. If his email is set up to sent LinkedIn notifications, he will also receive an email invitation.

Everyone you invite either via a LinkedIn invitation or via email is already pre-approved to join your group. No further approval is necessary for these connections.

Approving or preapproving group members

In addition to receiving an invitation, potential group members can find your group by doing a search on LinkedIn for groups within a particular topic. You can set up your group for Auto Join, where group members don't need approval to join the group. However, this setting opens the door for spammers and abuse.

You can and should set your group so that individual membership has to be approved, which helps you keep out spammers and fake accounts. For example, if a profile has only vague information, few or no connections, and/or no headshot, it may be a fake account, and you can elect not to allow that person in the group.

To edit your group settings so that members can join automatically or have to request to join, follow these steps:

1. **While in your group, select to be taken to your groups administrative options.**

2. **Select Group Settings, located in the left sidebar.**

   You see a menu of items for managing group permissions.

3. **Scroll down to select either the Auto-Join or Request to Join radio button, as shown in Figure 3-3.**

4. **Scroll to the bottom and select Save Changes.**

Don't be afraid to share your group on your other social channels. Many people with whom you're not connected via LinkedIn might follow you on another social network. If they follow you on Facebook or Twitter, or subscribe to your newsletter, they might be interested in joining your LinkedIn group, as well.

Figure 3-3:
You can set up your group to preapprove members or to require new members to request to join.

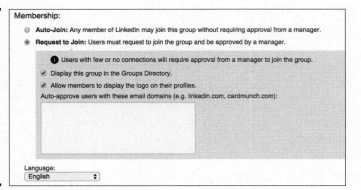

Membership:

- ⚪ **Auto-Join:** Any member of LinkedIn may join this group without requiring approval from a manager.
- 🔘 **Request to Join:** Users must request to join the group and be approved by a manager.

    ⓘ Users with few or no connections will require approval from a manager to join the group.

    ☑ Display this group in the Groups Directory.

    ☑ Allow members to display the logo on their profiles.

    Auto-approve users with these email domains (e.g. linkedin.com, cardmunch.com):

Language:
English

Moderating Your LinkedIn Group

Have at least one person in place to moderate or manage your LinkedIn group. Without someone in charge, anarchy can ensue. Managers can make sure that your community members are treating each other respectfully and that no one is spamming with links and sales pitches.

Appointing a manager or moderator

Before you appoint someone to watch over your LinkedIn group, understand the roles available for managing LinkedIn groups:

✦ **Owner:** The person who created the group. Controls moderators, membership, and all aspects of group administration. Ownership can be transferred if the group owner is moving on.

✦ **Manager:** Can perform the same duties as the owner, except the group manager can't transfer ownership.

✦ **Moderator:** Can feature discussions as Moderator's Choice (located in a feature box at the top of the group), moderate conversations, and manage posts that are being held in moderation.

Smaller groups might not require heavy moderation, but if your group has thousands of members, you might want to appoint at least a couple of people in moderation or manager roles so that nothing falls through the cracks.

In order for someone to become a member or moderator, he must already be a member of the group.

To appoint a moderator or manager, follow these steps:

1. **While in your group, select the Manage option at the top of the group.**

2. **In the left sidebar, select Participants from the left sidebar.**

   You're taken to a page with several tabs including Members, Administrators, and Blocked.

   The Participants options shown in Figure 3-4 appear.

3. **Select Members.**

4. **Select the check box to the left of the member you want to add as moderator or manager, and then click Change Role.**

   When you click Change Role, you see a drop-down menu with two options: Manager and Moderator.

5. **Select your desired role.**

   The new manager or moderator will receive notice that she has been promoted within the group.

6. **Click Save.**

Managing a moderation queue

At the top of your group, in the top-right corner of Manage, a red number appears (as shown in Figure 3-5), telling you how many notifications your group has, if it has any. Notifications let you know if a post is being held in moderation, usually because it contains links.

Here's how to manage your moderation queue:

✦ **To handle a post that's held in moderation:** Check the box to the left of the post, and then choose the link to approve, delete, or move to a different area.

✦ **To handle requests to join:** Click the Requests to Join function in the left sidebar, which takes you to a list of anyone who's waiting on approval. Check the box next to people's names, and then click the link to approve, decline, or block those people from your group.

✦ **To delete a post because it doesn't fall within your group's guidelines:** Click the down-pointing arrow at the top right of the post and select Delete from the drop-down list that opens.

You don't have to be militant in your moderation. Just make sure people are following the rules. Most group members are happy to comply. However, if a member does drop a link, delete the offending post and send him a nice message in private to let him know you did so and why. Most are testing the waters and probably will be apologetic. If you establish that links aren't allowed, your group members will comply.

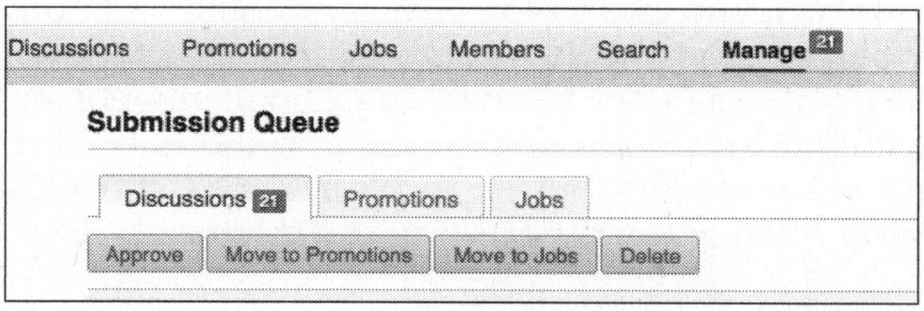

Figure 3-5:
If there
are items
in your
moderation
queue, a
notification
number
appears
at the top
of your
dashboard.

Highlighting community members with Manager's Choice

A nice way to highlight some community discussions is to feature them in the *Manager's Choice,* a carousel featuring links to interesting discussions, which you can find above the group's discussion topics. The Manager's Choice carousel highlights the member who started the discussion and the discussion itself. Because the carousel is front and center at the top of the group page, more people see it, and thus more people participate in the discussion.

To add a discussion to the Manager's Choice carousel, click the down-pointing arrow to the top right of the chosen topic and select Add to Manager's Choice from the drop-down list that appears. That discussion stays pinned to the top of the group until you remove it.

Some managers like to highlight a few different discussions each week so that each member has a chance to be featured.

Adding a Promotions or Jobs tab to your group

You can add Jobs and Promotions tabs to your group to create sections for members to post promotions (about their business, blog, or whatever they might want to promote) or jobs that their business currently has available.

Promotions tab

Because members want to promote themselves, they want to share links to events, products, or other fun things — but you don't want them to spam. This is where the Promotions tab comes in.

Promotions enable your members to share links within a specific area, without annoying the rest of your community. You can determine what goes into the Promotions tab when you set up your group rules. For example, people may try to share each and every blog post they create in hopes of driving traffic to their blog. You probably want to discourage this kind-of-spammy practice. However, if a member is launching a book or webinar, you can let her announce it by using the Promotions tab. Promotions allow members to toot their horns without being pushy, and they can post discussions on the Promotions tab the same way they post in the discussion area.

If someone posts content to the group that you feel would be better off in the Promotions tab, click the down-pointing arrow to the top right xxx of the original post, and select Flag for Promotions from the drop-down list that appears. The promotional post goes to the correct area, the Promotions tab. Meanwhile, also privately notify the person who posted the content so he knows it's been moved and why.

Jobs tab

You can allow your members to post relevant jobs in the Jobs tab. You have to police this area because, again, it can be a haven for spammers; but your community may appreciate your allowing job opportunities to be posted. Jobs are posted just like you would post a discussion topic — it's just in a different area.

Just like with the Promotions tab, if someone posts a job in the main group, you can choose to delete or move it to the Jobs tab — just click the down-pointing arrow in the upper-left of the post and select Flag for Jobs from the drop-down list that appears.

Sending a weekly email to your group

Many Company Page managers see the option to send a weekly email, or *announcement,* to group members as a way to reach potential customers. Some brands think of it as a weekly newsletter, but others use it only if they have something particular to share. These announcements are sent via email, not LinkedIn messaging.

Group managers can send announcements to

✦ **Highlight discussions or group members.** Sharing links to the week's discussion is a way to bring some members back to the group because not everyone checks out your LinkedIn group every day.

✦ **Share news.** If something important is going on with your brand, you can share it in your weekly announcement.

✦ **Launch products or events.** Share new releases.

✦ **Link to blog posts.** If you have a company blog, you can share links to blog posts and articles in the weekly announcement.

✦ **Reiterate group rules.** It doesn't hurt to give reminders from time to time. (We talk about group rules in the section "Establishing group guidelines," earlier in this chapter.)

Because you can send only one email each week, make note of the time and date you send the email. If you sent the last email at 4 p.m. on Friday, you can't send another email until the next Friday at 4 p.m.

Avoid turning your weekly announcement into spam. Try to mix up the content so it is pertinent to the group and highlights some of the goings-on of your business, or your group's niche or interest area, in addition to news and links.

To send a weekly announcement, follow these steps:

1. **Click Manage (located at the top of the group) to access your groups administrative area, and select Send an Announcement in the left sidebar.**

A page with the Send an Announcement text window appears, as shown in Figure 3-6. LinkedIn adds a generic subject line to your announcement automatically.

2. **(Optional) Change the subject line, if you want, by clicking in the Subject text box and entering your subject.**

We recommend you change the subject line to something more engaging and personalized.

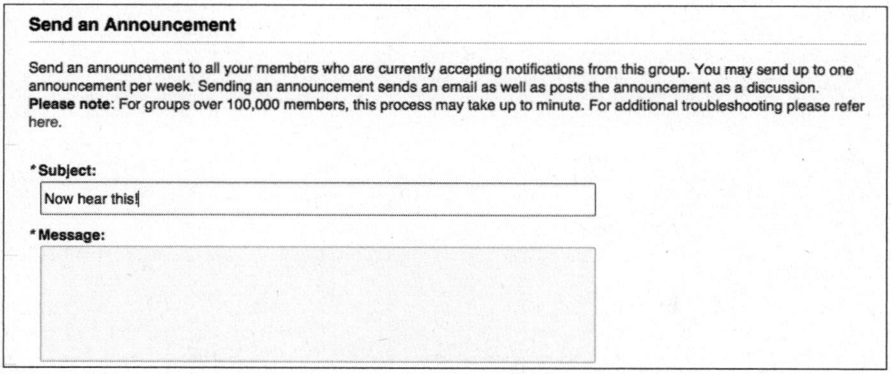

Book VI
Chapter 3

Starting a
LinkedIn Group

Figure 3-6:
LinkedIn
allows you
to send one
announce-
ment per
week to
your group.

Send an Announcement

Send an announcement to all your members who are currently accepting notifications from this group. You may send up to one announcement per week. Sending an announcement sends an email as well as posts the announcement as a discussion. **Please note:** For groups over 100,000 members, this process may take up to minute. For additional troubleshooting please refer here.

* **Subject:**

Now hear this!

* **Message:**

3. **Type or paste your message into the Message text box.**

   You can't anchor a link to text to create a hyperlink for that text, but you can post a link that will be active to recipients.

4. **(Optional) If desired, check the Send Test box to receive a test email.**

   You can use this test email to see how it arrives in your own email, give it a last proofread, and check formatting before sending to everyone.

5. **If you're satisfied with your message, click Send Announcement.**

Don't send an announcement just to send an announcement. If you don't have anything of interest to share with your community, you can skip a week or two — or more, if necessary. Your community would rather receive sporadic announcements that offer something of value, rather than a boring email or just spam with links every week.

Keep in mind that this chapter touches only on the basics of a LinkedIn group, and you can do so much more with LinkedIn groups (such as creating subgroups for different topics). For information on using LinkedIn groups for business, see *LinkedIn For Dummies,* 3rd Edition, by Joe Elad (Wiley Publishing, Inc.).

Chapter 4: Using LinkedIn as a Content Platform

In This Chapter

✓ **Using LinkedIn as a content platform**

✓ **Sharing your LinkedIn content across platforms**

*L*inkedIn is now offering members the opportunity to showcase their expertise by publishing long-form content on the LinkedIn platform. Even if you have a blog or a website where you share content, you might still want to consider writing on LinkedIn, at least occasionally.

Having a post on LinkedIn enables you to reach a new, more professional social network — and what could be a whole new audience.

You may not yet have the ability to publish a post on LinkedIn. Although they're rolling out this feature for everyone, it hasn't reached all members yet. However, if you're invited to publish on LinkedIn, you receive notification via email and your LinkedIn home page.

In this chapter, we discuss the benefits of using LinkedIn as a content platform, plus a few of the basics for posting and promoting your content.

Blogging on LinkedIn

With all the content platforms available, why publish on LinkedIn when you can use your own blog or website, keeping all the traffic to yourself? Although you don't receive direct traffic to your website when you publish to LinkedIn, it does provide you the ability to drive traffic. If you share informative content, people will want to learn more and look up your website, blog, and other projects.

Some of the benefits of using LinkedIn as a content platform are

✦ **Your posts appear on your profile.** As you can see in Figure 4-1, when you publish a post, it's listed on your professional profile. Therefore, anyone who views your profile may also click through to read your content.

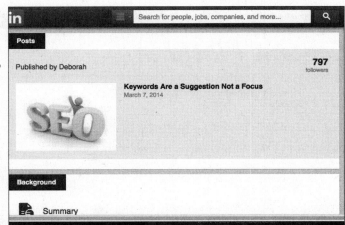

Figure 4-1:
Your published posts appear in your profile, further establishing your expertise.

✦ **Your posts can be seen by your entire professional network on LinkedIn.** When you publish a post, your connections receive notification via the flag icon at the top of their LinkedIn pages. The bigger your network, the more people can potentially view your content.

✦ **People with whom you're not connected can see your posts, leading to new connections.**

✦ **If you don't already have a blog, you can use the LinkedIn platform.** Everything is already set up for you, and it's free.

✦ **LinkedIn members can follow your content without having to follow you.** People can read your content without having to connect with you.

✦ **You increase the chances for engagement with other professionals.** Readers can comment or like your posts.

Creating your first post

You can create your first or any post from your LinkedIn home page. Follow these steps:

1. **Click Home at the top-left of any LinkedIn page.**

   Your LinkedIn home page appears. This page includes updates from connections and a space for you to add your own updates, as shown in Figure 4-2.

2. **At the top of the page, click the pencil icon in the Share an Update text box.**

   A blogging dashboard like the one shown in Figure 4-3 opens.

Figure 4-2: You can access your LinkedIn blogging dashboard from your home page.

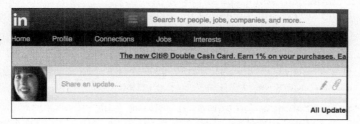

Figure 4-3: You can start writing your post directly in the LinkedIn blogging dashboard.

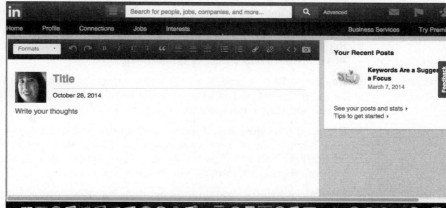

3. **Fill in your title, and then write or paste content where it says Write Your Thoughts.**

   You can use the formatting buttons as needed.

4. **Click Publish located at the top of the page when done.**

Preview your post before publishing by clicking Preview instead of Publish in Step 4 of the preceding list. Giving your post a read-through and format check before publishing ensures that you have no spelling, grammatical, or formatting errors; those mistakes can come off as unprofessional.

Writing in a professional voice

Because LinkedIn is considered a platform for professional, career-oriented people, you have to write in the proper tone. Although you can still use a casual, blogging style, do be mindful of your words and topics. For example, most marketers would never even think of using profanity on LinkedIn because it's unprofessional.

What follows are some tips and best practices for writing in a professional voice and successful blogging on LinkedIn:

✦ **Stay within your area of expertise.** Stick with topics you know well so that you can establish yourself as an expert. If you talk about things you're unsure of, someone may comment to prove you wrong, which can make readers lose faith in your expertise.

✦ **Solve problems and answer questions.** What do people want to know about your industry and what you do? Make sure your content serves a purpose. Readers like posts that teach and guide.

✦ **Give advice to others starting out in your profession.** Young professionals are reading your posts on LinkedIn. What can you tell them that you wish you knew when you were just starting out?

✦ **Brevity counts.** Word count should fall between 500 and 800 words. Anything more than that, and people begin to lose interest.

✦ **Respectfully disagree.** If you're writing to disagree with another blogger or writer, be respectful in your disagreement. Make your points without finger-pointing, name-calling, or accusation.

✦ **Respond to comments.** If readers ask questions, share tips, or add to your discussion, do be sure to respond. If they know you're likely to respond, and they feel as if their opinion matters, they're more likely to become regular readers and even share your content.

✦ **Link thoughtfully.** Add links as needed, but only if they add to the discussion. Don't write a post that contains nothing but links.

✦ **Know your demographic.** Understand who you're writing for. You may have to do a little research and learn more about your connections, the people who visit your LinkedIn Company Page, or those who use your product or service.

✦ **Think carefully about your headline.** Try to avoid overly inflated headlines. Keep them brief and professional. If it looks like it belongs to a tabloid, you're on the wrong platform.

✦ **Use rich media.** Don't forget to add a visual element to your posts. LinkedIn enables you to use images, as well as embed videos from YouTube and presentations from SlideShare.

 If you're still not sure about whether to write on LinkedIn's platform, take some time to look at some other blog posts there. Seeing how well it works for other professionals may inspire you to create some content. At the very least, try one post to test the waters.

Promoting Your LinkedIn Posts on Other Social Channels

Almost every content platform offers a way to share your newly created content with others, and LinkedIn is no different. In fact, it provides share buttons for LinkedIn, Facebook, Twitter, and Google+ right on your published post so that you can share as soon as you publish.

To share a post, follow these steps:

1. **Click the share button for the content platform you want to use, as shown in Figure 4-4.**

   A window appears for that social network.

2. **Fill in some brief descriptive text in the text window.**

3. **Click Share.**

4. **Repeat Steps 1 through 3 for each platform on which you want to share.**

> **TIP**
>
> Don't share your post more than once per platform; otherwise, it can be considered spam.

Creating content on LinkedIn is another way to tell your brand's story, share tips and news regarding your industry, and grow your personal and professional brand visibility. The best part is, your posts have the potential to be seen by a vast professional community. How could you not take advantage of the opportunity?

**Book VI
Chapter 4**

Using LinkedIn as a Content Platform

Figure 4-4: LinkedIn allows you to share your posts on other social networks.

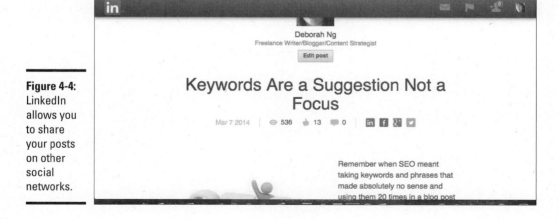

Deborah Ng
Freelance Writer/Blogger/Content Strategist

Edit post

Keywords Are a Suggestion Not a Focus

Mar 7 2014 | 👁 536 👍 13 💬 0 | in f g+ ✆

Remember when SEO meant taking keywords and phrases that made absolutely no sense and using them 20 times in a blog post

Book VII
Pinterest

Contents at a Glance

Chapter 1: Pinning Down Pinterest

In This Chapter

- ✔ **Understanding Pinterest**
- ✔ **Setting up your Pinterest account**
- ✔ **Creating boards**
- ✔ **Pinning pins**
- ✔ **Following other pinners**

*W*hat is it about Pinterest that's so attractive? Is it the mouthwatering food images, the inspiring island-getaway shots, or the humorous jokes?

The answer is all of the above. Pinterest is a social network that enables you to share content, but with a twist: You can't see the text beyond the caption that the pinner adds when pinning the image to his board. Because Pinterest pulls only the images from blog posts and web articles, the site is very visually appealing. It's not an eye-catching headline that pulls you in, but rather colors and creativity.

One complaint people have about the various social networks is that everyone is sharing the same things across all the networks. They're making the same comments and sharing the same links and videos. Pinterest takes that sharing to a whole new level. It's not the same old, same old. It's more visual, so instead of seeing nothing but links, you're seeing vibrant, enticing images.

Pinterest is the perfect place to plan a vacation, redesign a kitchen, or landscape a backyard. By creating boards for all your interests, you're also saving images you might want to refer to later.

In this chapter, you find out about Pinterest, why it's so popular, and why this social network is so different from all the others.

What Is Pinterest?

Pinterest is a social network based on images. Users upload photos (called *pins*) to create *boards*, or groups of images centered on a common theme. Members of the Pinterest community use Pinterest for different reasons. Some just like to share pretty photos or recipes, and others share images in hopes that those viewing the photos will click through and drive traffic to their blogs or website. Because it's a visual site, it's perfect for product-based retailers who are hoping to drive sales.

Pinterest is the perfect social network for clothing retailers, interior designers, foodies, landscapers, travel professionals, and members of any profession who can benefit from telling a story with an image. Although the U.S. user base is primarily female, men are also using Pinterest to share funny images, sports-related photos, gadgets, and the great outdoors. Knowing how the different demographics are using Pinterest is important, especially if you're reaching out to a global market.

Before you dive into the Pinterest deep end, be familiar with these common Pinterest terms:

✦ **Pin:** An image or video that you or someone else has uploaded to a board on Pinterest, such as the one shown in Figure 1-1. When you enter a URL or upload an image to one of your boards, you're pinning to that board.

✦ **Boards:** Each time you add a pin, you assign it to a category of your creation called a *board.* In essence, you're creating virtual pin boards. For instance, you can create a board named Funny and pin images that make you laugh, or you can make a board named Knitting Patterns to Try and pin images from relevant how-to articles.

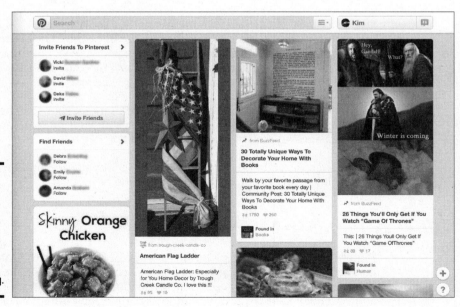

Figure 1-1:
Each pin includes buttons for sharing or repining, liking, and commenting.

✦ **Pinner:** Someone who uses Pinterest.

✦ **Repin:** When someone shares one of your pins, or you share one of theirs. When you *repin* something, you add something pinned by some-one else to one of your boards. (The Pin It button appears at the top of a pin when you hover your mouse pointer over that pin.)

✦ **Comment:** You can discuss pins by commenting in the area below the pin.

✦ **Like:** If you enjoy someone's pin but don't necessarily want to repin it, you can show approval by liking it. Hover your mouse pointer over the pin and then, in the top-right of the pin, click the Like button (which looks like a heart) to like that pin.

Getting Started

Before launching your Pinterest account, take some time to see what a few brands are doing on Pinterest. Whole Foods Market, shown in Figure 1-2, is a great example of a business that effectively uses Pinterest. Their boards tell the story of who they are without being overly promotional.

To search for a specific brand on Pinterest, follow these steps:

1. **Type any company name into the Search box at the top of the page, and then press Enter.**

You see a drop-down menu with suggestions and items with that brand's name.

You can choose the brand itself from the drop-down menu. Or you can choose one of the keyword options. If you do this, a results page appears, displaying every pin that uses that search term.

Figure 1-2:
Type the
name of the
brand you're
searching
for in
Pinterest's
search
engine.

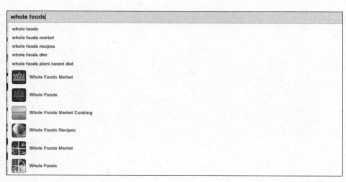

At the very top of the page, you see more keywords. Choose one if you want, or browse the pins to see if one of those has what you are looking for.

2. **Click any button that appears above the search results to focus your search.**

   These buttons include

   - *All Pins:* Shows all pins that contain the search term. This is also the page you land on by default.

   - *Your Pins:* Shows pins you added to Pinterest that fall within the search term.

   - *Boards:* Shows all boards that have a title that includes the search term.

   - *Pinners:* Shows all users who have that search term in their username or profile description.

   You can see the examples of keywords, as well as the four ways to sort your search results, in Figure 1-3.

3. **Click the Boards link to see the boards and the pins they contain.**

   Check out boards that have a good variety of pins and start thinking of ways your brand can incorporate pinning. If you're looking at brand examples for inspiration, it's probably best to check out boards the brand itself is pinning to, rather than pins about the brand.

Figure 1-3:
The four ways to sort your search results.

Sort buttons

Pinterest For Dummies and *Pinterest Marketing For Dummies,* both by Kelby Carr (Wiley Publishing, Inc.), are also great resources for getting up and running on Pinterest.

Joining Pinterest

You can create a Pinterest account more easily these days than you could when Pinterest first arrived on the scene. You no longer need to request an invitation from Pinterest or ask a friend with a Pinterest account to invite you.

Just head to `http://pinterest.com` and follow these steps to create an account:

1. **On the Pinterest home page, type your email address and desired password in the appropriate text boxes, and then click the red Sign Up button, as shown in Figure 1-4.**

2. **Alternatively, you also have the option to sign in using your Facebook account. Click on the Facebook icon to do so.**

   When you log in with Facebook, you also have the option to follow your friends from that network after you provide your profile details.

   Next, a page appears that asks you what you're interested in, with many options to check off as interests.

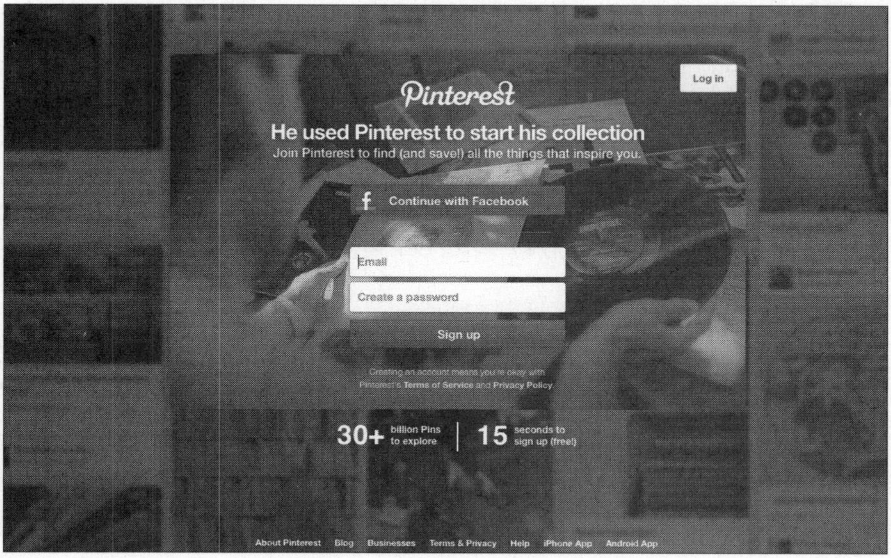

**Book VII
Chapter 1**

**Pinning Down
Pinterest**

Figure 1-4:
Sign up for
Pinterest.

Pinterest

Log in

He used Pinterest to start his collection
Join Pinterest to find (and save!) all the things that inspire you.

f   Continue with Facebook

Email

Create a password

Sign up

Creating an account means you're okay with
Pinterest's Terms of Service and Privacy Policy

30+ billion Pins
to explore | 15 seconds to
sign up (free!)

About Pinterest   Blog   Businesses   Terms & Privacy   Help   iPhone App   Android App

3. **Check off the categories you like the most.**

   Don't worry, though, you can tweak and fine-tune your account any time.

4. **If you're signing in with email, you're taken to a screen where you're asked to add your name, select whether you are male or female, and type in your age. Because this is about brand pages, instead of continuing on to create a personal account, select the link below the red Continue button that says Continue as a Business.**

5. **Type in your email address, password, and business name, and select your business type from the drop-down menu. You can also list your business URL. Then click Create Account.**

   You're taken to a visual menu where you can choose topics that interest you.

6. **Choose a minimum of five categories — but you can choose as many as you like.**

7. **Click Follow.**

   Now you have some pins to look at.

After you get an account, the easiest way to log in is by using the same method you used to create the account. Click the icon to sign in via Facebook. You can also log in using your email address. After you log in, you can get started.

You can choose to have your pins show up on Facebook. Many people who use Pinterest as a personal account enjoy sharing pins with their Facebook communities. However, it's different for a brand account. As we mention in Book V, Chapter 2, a brand's community doesn't want to receive a ton of updates and may become turned off if a brand's pins are showing up all day on their Facebook News Feeds.

Navigating Pinterest

You have to know your way around Pinterest so that you can pin like a pro. Whenever you log in, you see the most recent pins added to the boards you follow.

Your Pinterest home page is organized as follows:

✦ **Search box:** At the very top of the page is a Search box. Type a search term to open a page that lists pins that fall with your search term. You can also choose to narrow down your search to the following: All Pins, Your Pins, Boards, or Pinners. Find out more about searching on Pinterest in the section "Getting started with Pinterest," later in this chapter.

✦ **Following:** The images you see on your Pinterest page are from all pinners whom you follow. For each pinner, you can follow specific boards or all her boards.

✦ **Plus sign (+) button:** Clicking this plus-sign (+) button, located in the lower right of your screen, opens a pop-up menu that you can use to add pins to your own boards. You can select the options Upload a Pin (which opens the Upload an Image pop-up window, which you can use to locate an image file on your computer), Add from a Website (which opens the Add a Pin from a Website pop-up window), or Create a New Pin Board (which opens the Create a Board pop-up window).

✦ **Categories drop-down list:** Directly next to the Search box is the Categories button (the button with three lines). When you click it, a drop-down list appears, displaying the available categories, which range from Animals and Architecture to Women's Fashion and Videos. Select a category that interests you to see the most recent pins in that category by anyone and everyone on Pinterest. Figure 1-5 shows the layout of the Categories drop-down list.

Book VII
Chapter 1

Pinning Down
Pinterest

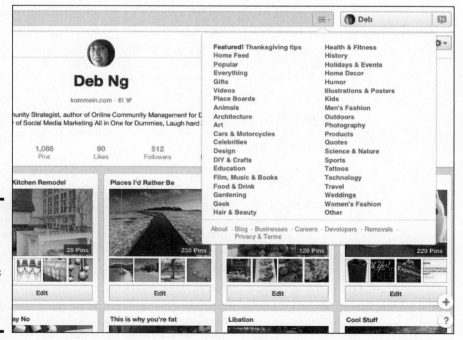

Figure 1-5: The Categories drop-down list contains a variety of options and features.

Here's a rundown of some of the areas you might want to explore in the Categories drop-down list:

✦ **Everything:** The most recently pinned and repinned images made by anyone on Pinterest.

✦ **Popular:** The most popular *viral pins,* meaning the pins that have the most people sharing, liking, and repinning them.

✦ **Gifts:** Pinterest can also be used as a handy shopping tool. When you click the Gifts link, you go to a page of the most recently pinned images that have price tags on them. We talk more about gifts in Chapter 3 of this minibook.

✦ **Seasonal or timely tips:** For example, around November, a link appears at the top of the Categories drop-down list offering Thanksgiving Tips (refer to Figure 1-5).

✦ **Links to other areas of the site:** The options located at the bottom of the Categories drop-down list give you more information about Pinterest:

• *About:* Learn more about Pinterest.

• *Careers:* Looking for a job and can't get enough of Pinterest? Maybe they have an opening for you!

• *Removals:* If someone is using an image of yours without permission and posting it on Pinterest, it's a copyright violation. Use this section to learn how to remove a photo from Pinterest.

• *Blog:* Find out what's new and happening in the world of Pinterest.

• *Privacy & Terms:* This legal stuff tells you what you can and can't do while using the site. It's definitely worth a read to make sure you stay within the rules.

• *Business:* This is for people who have personal pages and want to start a business page.

• *Developers:* This offers a variety of bells and whistles for your blog or website. It includes code to add a Pinterest share button to your blog or website, or to have your blog or website's images show a Pin It button when visitors hover over those images.

Creating your Pinterest profile

As with any social network, a first impression is important. It's especially important if you're using the social network as a marketing tool. Your Pinterest profile page is where pinners stop by to find out more about you. To get to this page, click your username in the top-right corner of any Pinterest page. The profile page contains your profile image and a few words about you and displays your boards. You can also add your website address (if you have one) and your Facebook profile page.

Before you get started on filling out your profile, get to know the elements of the Pinterest profile page, as shown in Figure 1-6:

✦ **Profile image:** The image you want to display that best represents your brand. Most brands use their logo or a photo of their product.

✦ **The profile itself:** The profile page shows your business name, information about your business, your location, and a link to your website.

✦ **Edit Profile button:** Enables you to add your profile photo, bio, and links.

✦ **Settings button:** When you click the Settings button, which looks like a gear icon, you see a variety of options including Account Settings, Promoted Pins, Tips for Your Business, and Analytics.

✦ **Boards:** All of your boards appear on your profile page, and you can see how many boards you have at the top of your profile page.

✦ **Pins:** Shows how many pins you have.

✦ **Likes:** Shows how many pins you *liked* (meaning you clicked the Like button for those pins).

✦ **Followers:** The number of people who follow your boards on Pinterest.

✦ **Following:** The people and boards you follow on Pinterest.

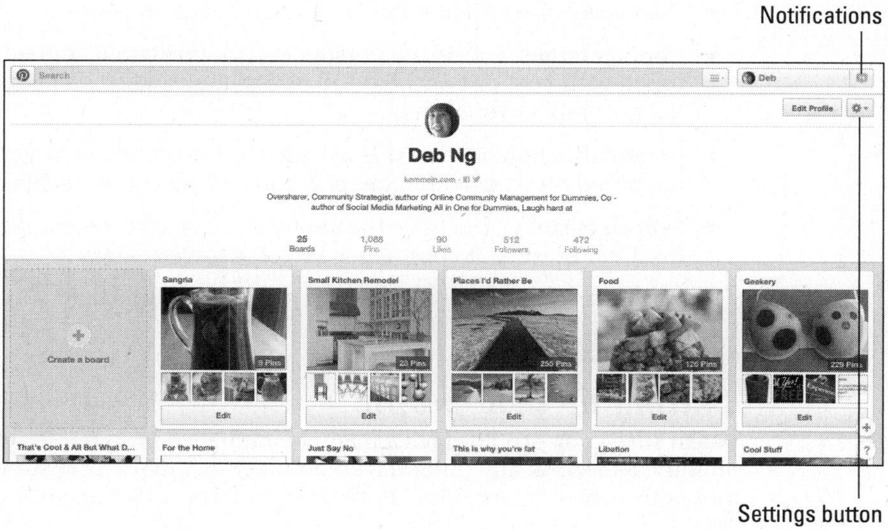

Book VII
Chapter 1

Pinning Down
Pinterest

Notifications

Figure 1-6:
Your
Pinterest
profile page.

Settings button

✦ **Notifications:** The red Notifications button shows a number to tell you when people follow you or like your pins. (See Figure 1-7.) It also notifies you if someone has repinned your pins or added your pins to other boards.

Figure 1-7:
The
Notifications
button.

Setting up your business account basics

Under your settings, there is a section called Business Account Basics. This section contains the following:

✦ **Language:** You can choose the language in which you're most comfortable using.

✦ **Country:** The country where you do business.

✦ **Business Type:** What do you do?

✦ **Business Name:** What name do you do business under?

✦ **Contact name:** This is the person who Pinterest will contact to get in touch with you, or to send email notifications when someone follows, likes, or repins your pins.

✦ **Personalization:** Pinterest is asking if it can show you targeted advertising based on your search history. You can accept or decline.

✦ **Search History:** You have the ability to clear your recent search history from Pinterest so no one sends targeted advertising.

✦ **Account:** Click the Deactivate Account button to delete your Pinterest account.

Setting up your profile

Make sure your profile gives a positive impression to your Pinterest community, as well as any potential community members or customers, by filling out your profile information. Follow these steps to set up your profile page:

1. **Click your name at the top right of any Pinterest page and then click the red Edit Profile button located under your name.**

The Edit Profile page window appears, as shown in Figure 1-8.

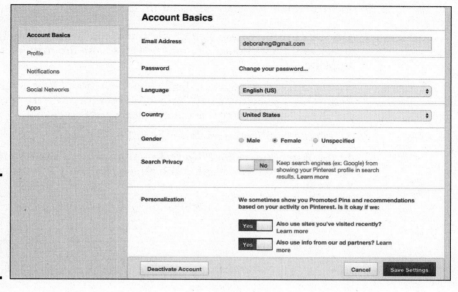

Figure 1-8:
Fill out the
Edit Profile
page to tell
everyone all
about you.

2. **Fill in your name and write up a brief bio.**

   You can also add website links and links to your social media account.

3. **In the Picture section, click the Change Picture option.**

4. **In the Change Your Picture pop-up window that appears, click Choose File to upload your photo.**

   You can choose a photo from your computer files in the File Upload dialog box that appears.

   If you're using Twitter as a marketing tool for your brand, you may want to consider a logo instead of headshot for better brand visibility.

5. **Click Open.**

   Congratulations! Your Pinterest account has a face.

6. **Click the Save Profile button at the bottom of the page.**

Setting your email notification preferences

After you fill out your profile, you should determine what kind of email notifications you want to receive.

By default, you receive notifications for every pin, repin, comment, and follow associated with your account — and if your account is very active, that can add up to a lot of notifications.

To set what email notifications you want to receive, follow these steps:

1. **On your Profile page, click the Settings icon (which looks like a gear), and then choose Account Settings from the drop-down list that appears.**

   The Settings page appears, displaying the Account Basics tab, shown in Figure 1-9. The Settings page provides you with a variety of options for setting up your Pinterest account just the way you like it.

2. **Select the Notifications tab on the left of the page.**

3. **In the When You're on Pinterest section, select a radio button to specify whether you want notifications from only friends or from everyone.**

   You can elect to receive notifications only regarding people you follow.

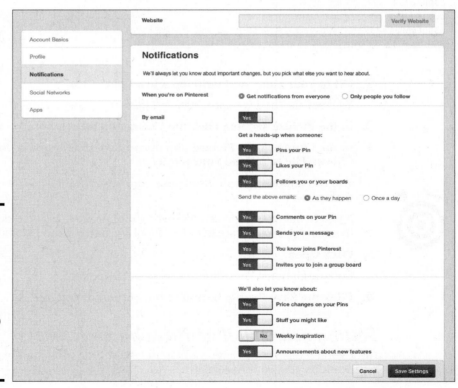

Figure 1-9: Your account settings enable you to set notifications, link to the social networks, and more.

4. **In the By Email section, set the options for Group Pins, Comments, Likes, Repins, and Follows to Yes or No (which reflects whether you'll receive notifications about those things).**

   Think twice about opting in to receive notifications every time someone repins or comments on one of your pins or follows you. If your Pinterest account is active, your inbox will become very full very quickly!

   At the very least, be notified when someone comments on or repins what you've pinned because you can check to see what they said and have a conversation if you'd like. You can always test different settings out to see what works best for you. However, if you stop by Pinterest once a day as part of your marketing strategy, there really isn't much of a need for notifications.

5. **In the On Your Phone section, click the Edit Push Notification Settings button.**

   The Push Notifications pop-up window opens.

6. **Uncheck any option for which you don't want to receive push notifications on your cellphone; then click Save Changes to close the pop-up window.**

   If you select the option to receive notifications on your smartphone, you receive a ping for every notification. This can get a bit old after the first few days of constant pinging.

7. **When you finish, click the Save Settings button in the lower right of the screen to save your email or cellphone preferences.**

If you're a heavy pinner who has many friends, think long and hard about whether you want to have push notifications on your smartphone. You'll receive notifications throughout the day and night, which can get busy, noisy, and annoying for you and others. In fact, if you visit Pinterest throughout the day, you don't really need phone notifications because the red Notifications button appears at the top of Pinterest pages when you're logged in to your account.

The social networks

On the Settings page, you can also opt to sign in with Facebook, Twitter, and a variety of other social networks and email accounts and also to have pins appear on your timeline.

If you want to sign in to Pinterest with another social media account, scroll down until you see Social Networks and then click the switch to the right of Sign In with Platform option so that it reads Yes. Here are your choices:

1. **On the Settings page, scroll down until you see Social Networks.**

   Alternatively, select the Social Networks tab on the left of the page.

2. **Determine whether you want to have the ability to sign in to Pinterest with one of the social network or email options:**

   - If you do, click on the Log In with *(name of the social network or email account)* and toggle the option to Yes to select this option.

   - You're then taken to a sign-in screen for that account. After Pinterest is signed in to that account, you return to the original screen.

   - If you don't want this ability, click the Log in with Facebook button so that it reads No.

3. **When you're finished, click Save Settings.**

Getting on Board

Boards, such as those shown in Figure 1-10, are the way Pinterest organizes its users' content, in a manner that resembles a series of bulletin boards hanging on a wall, with each board having its own label. Boards organize your pins into categories of your choosing. However, if you treat your Pinterest boards as mere categories, you end up with a bunch of random, generic groupings. If you treat boards as a marketing tool for your product, brand, or business, you can create content that people want to follow, encouraging them to find out more about what your brand is all about.

Figure 1-10: Pin images that have a common theme on their own board.

Basic boards can accomplish any number of goals, such as

✦ **Showing steps in a process:** For example, create a craft project and visually list the instructions.

✦ **Reflecting different elements of planning:** For instance, for party or wedding planning; kitchen and bath renovations; or food, drink, table settings, and theme ideas.

✦ **Providing an industry overview:** Perhaps pin the clothing styles, designers, and fabrics of the fashion world.

✦ **Showing how something works:** For example, point out all the moving parts of a vehicle and how they come together to make the vehicle go.

✦ **Offering recipes:** Provide pins illustrating the process of food preparation, from beginning to end.

✦ **Highlighting the departments of a business:** You could include images from meetings or production facilities, as well as news items, awards, accolades, and online mentions.

Planning your initial boards

Before you start pinning, you want to have several boards in place. You'll create new boards while you progress on Pinterest, but do plan out the first few. What follows are some suggestions for your first boards:

✦ **History of your brand:** Go back to where you began and show how things have changed throughout the years. Pin promotional material or product labels from prior years to show how they've evolved.

✦ **History of your products:** Have your products received a makeover over the years? Has the packaging changed? Or maybe you have an archive of print ads spanning back through the decades. Use these items to create historic boards. When viewers see how long your product has been around, it tells them you have a product and a name worthy of their trust.

Kodak has a great example of how to feature your product in this manner at `http://pinterest.com/kodakcb/historic-photography`, and Blockbuster's Old Hollywood board tempts viewers to rent an old black-and-white movie at `http://pinterest.com/blockbuster/old-hollywood`.

✦ **Brand showcase:** Entice people into buying by showing them how they can use your product or service. You can even pin unusual or uncommon uses. Additionally, community members love it when they're highlighted on brand pages. Ask your community members to send photos of themselves using your product or service.

✦ **Who you are:** A Pinterest board can make a great About page. Use it to highlight team members, your location, your mission, and what you're selling. A couple of great examples of boards that tell about a brand can be found at New Media Expo's Pinterest account, where they feature team members (`http://www.pinterest.com/newmediaexpo/meet-the-nmxtbex-team`) and brief bios of all the speakers at their events (`www.pinterest.com/newmediaexpo/nmx-2014-speakers`).

✦ **Tips, how-to's, and DIYs:** Use your pins to teach. For example, if you're a writer, give tips for creating headlines and hooks; if you're a carpenter, share tips for creating projects that don't look homemade.

✦ **Gift ideas:** Product-oriented brands can benefit from pinning gift ideas. Take it even further by pinning a series of gift boards. We talk more about gift boards in Chapter 3 of this minibook.

✦ **Books:** Recommend books to your community that relate to your field. Lead a discussion in the comments section.

If you're at a loss as to the types of boards you can create, go through your company's archives, photo albums, and old files. You might find some literature from back in the day, memos and announcements, storyboards, and all kinds of inspiration.

Creating your first board

To create a board, follow these steps:

1. **Click the plus-sign (+) button located in bottom-right of any Pinterest page.**

A pop-up menu appears, which you can use to upload an image to pin, pull a pin from a web page, or create a board. (See Figure 1-11.)

2. **Click the Create a Board option.**

The Create a Board pop-up window appears.

3. **Fill in the Name text box.**

Choose a name that will describe what your board is about, but in a way that catches the eye so other pinners will want to learn more.

4. **Fill in a description of your board in the Description text box.**

Add a brief paragraph or two describing your board and what makes it so unique.

5. **Select an option from the Category drop-down list.**

Your category options range from Architecture to Photography, from Art to Wedding & Events. Choose the one most representative of your board and your brand.

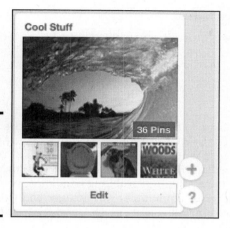

Figure 1-11:
Use the +
button to
pin images
or create
boards.

You can also choose Other if you don't see a suitable category on the menu. Do your best to choose a descriptive category, however. You want to be as specific as possible to catch the attention of people who are searching on Pinterest.

6. **If you want to add a map, click the Add a Map option so that it displays Yes.**

   For example, if your brand is a restaurant and you're featuring some of your delectable entrees, you might want to add a map to your board so that local diners can find you.

   This option is set to No by default.

7. **If you want to keep your board a secret, click the Keep It Secret option so that it displays Yes.**

   This option is set to No by default. If you're using Pinterest as a marketing tool, you most likely don't want yours to be a secret board that no one can see. However, if you're using Pinterest for research or to plan an event and don't want the world to know, you can select this option to make a secret board.

8. **In the Who Can Add Pins text box, enter the name or email address of a person you want to give access to pin on the board, then click Add.**

   If you want to be the only pinner, don't change a thing.

9. **Repeat Step 8 to invite more people.**

   A collaborative board is a wonderful way to find out how others see your brand or niche and to get people excited about what you do. We talk more about collaborating on boards in Chapter 2 of this minibook.

10. **Click the Create Board button.**

    You arrive at your newly created, and sadly empty, board. Go add some pins!

Pinning on Pinterest

Pinning can be addictive. Many pinners admit to spending hours pinning and finding items to like and repin. From a brand perspective, it may not look or feel like marketing because you're not doing something like creating eye-catching headlines. (You *will* need a way with words for your descriptions, however.) But instead of those attention-grabbing headlines, you're capturing the attention of the Pinterest community with images and videos. That's why your content has to be appealing and colorful, and it needs to make folks want to learn more.

Pinning an image

Pinterest is a huge traffic driver. Funny and vivid images can capture the attention of thousands of people. To start, go ahead and pin something.

To pin an image from a blog or website (which, by the way, also pins a link back to the blog), follow these steps:

1. **To pin something, click the plus-sign (+) button located at the bottom-right of your page.**

   A pop-up menu appears, with three options: Upload a Pin, Add from a Website, and Create a Board.

2. **Click the Pin from a Website button.**

   A dialog box appears, containing a text box where you can enter a URL.

3. **Enter the URL of the item you want to pin, and then click Next.**

   Pinterest automatically pulls images from the website and displays them in the Choose a Pin page that appears.

4. **Click the arrow to cycle through the images to choose the one you want to pin.**

   Make sure you select a photo that's eye-catching and properly showcases what you're trying to show.

5. **Hover over the picture you want to pin and click the Pin It button that appears.**

   The Pick a Board dialog box opens.

6. **Select the board you want to pin to from the Board drop-down list.**

   Alternatively, you can create an appropriate board. We discuss creating new boards in the section "Getting on Board," earlier in this chapter.

7. **In the Description text box, create a description of up to 500 characters.**

   We talk more about creating meaningful descriptions for your pins in Chapter 2 of this minibook.

8. **Click the Pin It button at the bottom of the dialog box.**

   Your pin now appears in the feed on your main page, as well as on the feeds of everyone who follows that particular board.

Some websites and blogs have blocked the ability to download or share their images because they don't want them reposted on Pinterest. If you come across a photo that has sharing disabled, seek permission before pinning the image. The last thing you want is to violate a copyright.

Pinning the right images

At first glance, Pinterest might seem like a random bunch of images. On a typical Pinterest feed, most users see dozens of photos, and many of the same pins are repinned over and over.

Being random and repetitive might be okay for personal users, but a brand must make sure its pins are well thought out. Keep these points in mind when selecting an image to pin:

✦ **Images shouldn't conflict with the message you're trying to send.** You want the viewer to be clear, not confused, about what you pin. For example, it wouldn't make sense for a ravioli manufacturer to post pictures of vehicles — unless they were delivery trucks or made out of ravioli.

✦ **Images should make people feel good or evoke emotion.** You want people to see the images and react with a comment, a like, or a repin. Just like with Facebook posts or Twitter tweets, you want to know your Pinterest community is paying attention.

✦ **Images must be eye-catching, engaging, and unique.** You want your content to stand out, and you have only a small number of seconds for your pin to catch someone's attention. If a viewer's response isn't positive and immediate, chances are your pin won't get a second look.

✦ **Images should support your goals.** If you want to drive sales, create pins with sales in mind. Create a board of images showing happy people using your product or the end result of your service.

If you want to drive traffic to a particular website, create one board with pins that link to the site. If every board you create and every image you pin is a link to your blog or website, you'll lose followers — fast — because they want to view wonderful images without feeling like they're being sold to all the time.

The rest of your boards should represent what you do without pushing sales or traffic.

Pinning the wrong images

You can come up with many ideas for what to pin, but there are plenty of types of pins you need to avoid. Because Pinterest is visual and pins appeal to emotions, pinning one of the following can lead to unfollows:

✦ **Photos that are out of focus:** Images should be sharp and vivid.

✦ **Photos that have no rhyme, reason, or purpose:** Although not every pin should be about your brand, if you have too many pins that are off topic, you might confuse your followers.

✦ **Repins that everyone is repinning:** If you pin the same things everyone else is pinning, Pinterest users have no reason to follow you.

✦ **Photos that are rude and offensive:** Be considerate of your community. Leave swearing and vulgarity out of it, lest folks get the wrong message about you and your brand. If you wouldn't say something to a customer in person, don't say it on Pinterest.

✦ **Constantly spamming with sales messages:** Very few people use Pinterest to receive sales messages. Avoid pitching to the Pinterest community. Instead, let your images be your pitch. If you're known for making it all about the sale, no one will want to follow you.

✦ **Bait-and-switch images:** Don't mislead your followers. If you pin an image and it refers to an article called "10 Reasons to Paint Your Bedroom Purple," that's what people should see. Don't reference one thing on Pinterest only to have users click through to something completely different, such as a sales page.

Whenever you repin someone else's pin, make sure the pin is legitimate: Test the pin by clicking through to the website. There's nothing worse than to repin something only to find out later that it's one of those hated bait-and-switch pins.

Considering the use of watermarks

Watermarking is the act of putting your name or brand name on your original photos. Many people who share photos on Pinterest want to be sure they get credit for their photographs, which doesn't always happen when people repin a photo on Pinterest. By watermarking, they also hope to prevent people from using their images without proper authorization.

Many people who watermark photos don't mind if the photo is shared on Pinterest, as long as pinners can click through to the original source — but do check first before repinning. The problem begins when folks don't link to the original source and instead upload the photo as their own original pin. Or worse, they take the photo and add it to their own content (for example, a blog post) without proper attribution. Passing off someone else's image as your own is completely unethical and a copyright violation.

Should you watermark your photos? Consider the following:

✦ **When you watermark, you'll receive proper credit for your photo.** Even though it's considered good Pinterest etiquette, not all people offer attribution. Many photos are repinned dozens of times, and the original photographer doesn't receive any credit for the image or the original pin. Watermarks ensure that the original photographer receives the proper attribution, even though the images have been pinned many times over.

✦ **Watermarks can sometime distract or take away from the beauty of the image.** In watermarked photos, the eye is often drawn to the watermark rather than the subject of the image. There's no mistaking who the photographer is, but now the photo isn't as aesthetically pleasing. If you watermark a picture, add the watermark to the lowest part of the image, where it's less likely to be noticed.

If you decide to add watermarks to the bottom of images, someone may still crop out the watermarks by using one of the many photo-editing programs out there. Keep that in mind when deciding where to place your watermark.

✦ **Watermarking helps to protect you from copyright theft.** When you watermark a photo, you're deterring others from passing your image off as their own. If they post the photo in their own content, your watermark appears. Also, if people enjoy your photos and see your watermark, they might search for more of your images.

Watermarking has its pros and cons. It provides protection, but it doesn't guarantee you'll receive credit for your photography.

Several tools are available that can help you watermark your photos. For instance, you can use photo-editing software, such as Photoshop Elements or PaintShop Pro. Each software comes with its own set of instructions, and you can also find tutorials online.

You can also find plenty of free photo-editing tools online, such as Pixlr Express (`http://pixlr.com/express`) and FotoFlexer (`http://fotoflexer.com`).

Try using a semitransparent watermark so that your name is visible but less distracting than if you used a solid color.

Pinning a video

Pinterest isn't just for static images. You can also upload videos. Videos have their own category on the main Pinterest page, so the people who want to find in-depth experiences or how-to's know exactly where to go.

To pin a video from a video site such as YouTube or Vimeo, follow these steps:

1. **Click the plus-sign (+) button, located on the bottom-right of your Pinterest page.**

   You're presented with two choices: Select Pin from a Website, and Create a Board.

2. **Select Pin from a Website.**

   The Add a Pin from a Website dialog box, where you can enter the URL of the item you want to pin, appears.

3. **Navigate to the site hosting the video you want to upload, copy the URL from the top navigation bar, paste it into the URL text box, and click the Next button.**

   Your video shows up in the search results page.

4. **If a snapshot of your video isn't visible on the results page, scroll to locate it; then hover your mouse over the snapshot and click the Pin It button that appears.**

   Whether you need to do this step depends on where you're uploading the video from. If it's from sites like YouTube or Vimeo, you typically don't have to do it. However if the video is from a blog or other website, you may have to pick the right image. You may get something from the website not related to the video at all.

5. **In the Pick a Board dialog box that appears, select a board from the Board drop-down list and add a description in the Description text box.**

   Properly categorize your video by choosing the correct board, and write a compelling description — these clues will entice the viewer to click and watch your video.

6. **Click the red Pin It button at the bottom of the dialog box.**

Voila! You pinned a video.

Be sure to include the word *video* in your description to let people know they're going to be viewing a video (and it also helps those who are searching specifically for videos).

Creating conversational pins

When you first start with Pinterest, it may be frustrating to wait for people to comment on your pins. It takes a while to grow a community and start receiving comments. With that said, you can work to create the types of pins people feel inclined to comment on:

✦ **Appeal to emotion.** Whether it's laughing out loud or choking back tears, people talk about pins that inspire emotion. Before you pin something, ask yourself how you feel about it. If the answer is indifferent, consider finding something more thought-provoking.

✦ **Pin items your target audience can relate to.** It's important for you to stay on topic with your Pinterest community. For example, if you're marketing to parent bloggers, your pins should reflect items of interest to parents. If you're an automotive dealership, consider posting photos of cars or funny street signs. You want your community members to relate to you. If you go off topic, that only confuses people. If they're relating to your pins, they'll comment to tell you why.

✦ **There's nothing wrong with controversy from time to time.** Don't post negative pins, but don't shy away from discussion-worthy topics simply because they're hot topics.

✦ **Be different.** There may be times when you look at your feeds and notice that everyone is repinning the same thing. It's great for the original pinner if something goes viral, but after a while, seeing the same image over and over again gets boring. Go against the grain and find something different. Search Pinterest for pins that are compelling and unique, or create unique content and share that.

✦ **Find out what people are responding to.** Take a ride around Pinterest. Which types of pins are getting the most comments and why? Is it the type of pin? The types of friends? How is the pinner interacting? Take notes.

Tagging

Tagging on Pinterest is similar to tagging on Facebook or Twitter. You *tag* people, or type their name so it links to their account, to call their attention to your pins. For example, you can tag someone if he's in the photo you're pinning or if the topic is of interest to him. When you call someone's attention to your photos through tagging, she might be inclined to share your pins with her communities too.

Here's how you tag someone on Pinterest: In the description area of the pin, put an @ symbol in front of the name of the person you want to tag. If that person is a friend (see the following section for a discussion of following people on Pinterest), a menu of pinners' names appears from which you can select. If that person isn't a friend, you can't tag him.

When a person is tagged, she is notified that you've tagged her in a pin. Tagging is a great way to call a person's attention to a particular pin. For example, suppose you have a client who loves Italian food. If you're connected to him on Pinterest, you can let him know you posted a delicious recipe for him to consider. He'll appreciate that you were thinking about him!

Following on Pinterest

What fun is it to create boards and share pins when there's no one to share them with? To make friends, you have to first follow others. Following is similar to friending on Facebook. When you *follow* someone, it means you're choosing to have her boards and pins show up in your feed, which can help you find people you want to know more about and inspire others to follow you in return.

Determining the types of people you want to follow and want to have follow you requires some strategy. Although your ultimate goal is to reach a wide variety of people, you also want to target the people who will do the most good. And by good, we mean those who will follow through with liking, commenting on, and repinning your content.

Following friends

Because you're representing a brand, you definitely want to appeal to the people who already follow your brand on Facebook, Twitter, and other social networks. However, you don't want to solely rely on your loyal, existing online community to make up your Pinterest community. The reason you join any social network is to grow your community, and you can't grow it by following (and being followed by) the same people on every platform.

Definitely announce on your blog, Twitter, Facebook, Google+, and other social media services that you've started a Pinterest page, but to build up the number of pinners you follow and who follow you, also contact social networking connections directly and let them know you want to connect on Pinterest.

To invite Facebook friends to follow you on Pinterest, follow these steps:

1. **Go to your main Pinterest feed page.**

   This is the page where you see all the pins from people and boards you follow. In the upper-left corner, a Find Friends option appears.

2. **Click Find Friends.**

   The right side of the Find Your Friends page that appears displays the friendly faces of all your Facebook friends who are on Pinterest. On the right, you see Facebook friends who aren't yet on Pinterest. (See Figure 1-12.)

3. **Invite friends to follow you on Pinterest.**

   You can use any of the following methods:

   - *For friends who are your Facebook friends and already have Pinterest accounts:* On the left side of the Find Your Friends page, click the icon of each friend you wish to add (a check mark appears, confirming the follow).

   - *If you want to invite a Facebook friend who isn't yet on Pinterest:* In the Facebook tab on the right side of the page, click the Invite button to the right of that friend's name and picture.

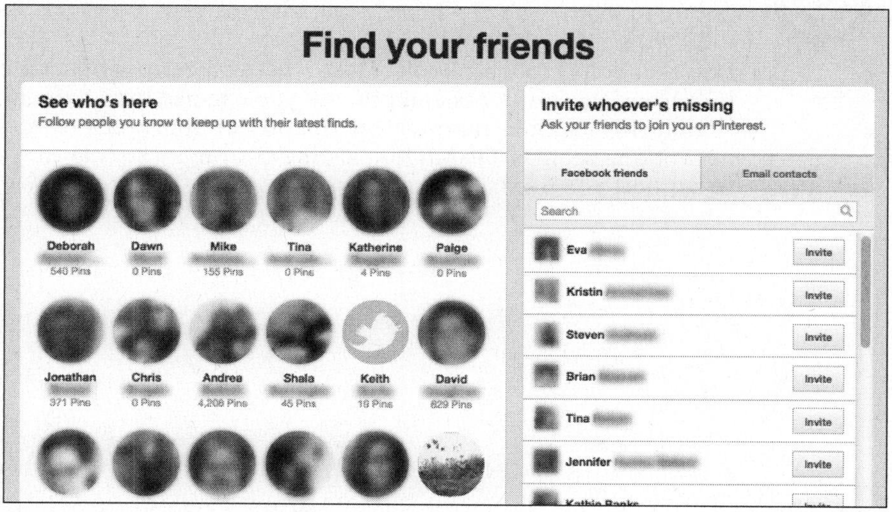

Book VII Chapter 1

Pinning Down Pinterest

Figure 1-12: Invite Facebook friends and email contacts to follow you on Pinterest.

Find your friends

See who's here
Follow people you know to keep up with their latest finds.

Deborah — 540 Pins
Dawn — 0 Pins
Mike — 155 Pins
Tina — 0 Pins
Katherine — 4 Pins
Paige — 0 Pins

Jonathan — 371 Pins
Chris — 0 Pins
Andrea — 4,208 Pins
Shala — 45 Pins
Keith — 19 Pins
David — 629 Pins

Invite whoever's missing
Ask your friends to join you on Pinterest.

Facebook friends | Email contacts

Search

Eva — Invite
Kristin — Invite
Steven — Invite
Brian — Invite
Tina — Invite
Jennifer — Invite
Kathie Banks —

- *If you want to invite friends via email:* Click the appropriate tab (either Gmail or Yahoo!) on the right side of the screen to search for contacts on Gmail or Yahoo! Mail. You see a list of names of your contacts for those accounts. Click the check box next to each person you want to invite, and when you're done click Invite at the bottom of the page.

- For friends who are using a different email platform, type an individual email address in the Email Address text box and click Send Invite.

Following folks you don't know

After you exhaust all your known contacts, it's time to branch out to make new friends to follow. To find new friends whom you aren't already connected to, use the Search box located at the top of any of your Pinterest pages. You can also use the Categories drop-down list located above the Pinterest feeds, and then browse the categories that appear to find pins and pinners that would be a good fit for your community.

Before randomly following everyone who pins, make sure you share common interests and that your brand page fits the types of pins they post and the interests discussed in their personal profiles.

Also, before you begin following others, have some boards already created. This way, when people follow you in return, they have something to look at, as well.

If you're worried about being overwhelmed by too many images in your feed, you don't have to follow every board by a particular pinner. You have the option to follow only the boards that interest you.

Don't randomly follow people. Make a list of the types of people you want to follow and the keywords and phrases you can use to find them, including the search engine optimization terms you use for your website or other social networking profiles. Search for existing customers so that they can continue to support you by sharing your pins.

Chapter 2: Marketing with Pinterest

In This Chapter

🗸 Sharing content on Pinterest

🗸 Using keywords in your descriptions

🗸 Building a community on Pinterest

*P*interest is more than a social network for people who like to share recipes or photos of their latest home improvement projects. On Pinterest, the marketing element is subtle — you can tell your brand's story and direct traffic to your business without using a single marketing term — but effective. Viewers don't see promotional copy or a sales spiel; instead, their eyes are drawn to images, and if the images are compelling, the viewers will want to learn more.

In this chapter, you find out how to effectively share content to drive traffic and grow your community using Pinterest.

Sharing on Pinterest

Many marketers who were skeptical about Pinterest at first now admit it's a great source for sharing information about brands, products, and services. With the right image and the right descriptive text, a picture really is worth a thousand words.

Here are just a few of the ways brands are sharing their content on Pinterest:

✦ **Wedding planners:** Use Pinterest to pin images of flowers, gowns, table settings, and limousines in order to catch the attention of brides-to-be.

✦ **Catering companies:** Pin recipes with mouthwatering images of food.

✦ **Yarn suppliers:** Pin images of scarves, hats, and sweaters, as well as supplies such as needles and knitting bags.

✦ **Travel agencies:** Pin images of island getaways, luggage, and luxurious hotel suites.

✦ **Interior designers:** Share photos of finished rooms and individual design elements.

✦ **Home contractors and supply brands:** Show off finished rooms done with their products and services.

✦ **Fashion brands:** Pin images of complete ensembles, including accessories and shoes.

✦ **Businesses:** Create boards featuring team members.

✦ **Book publishers:** Highlight books and authors.

What all these types of brands have in common is that they're not using their boards to post logos or product sales and information. In fact, many times, their pins come from external sources. They're providing an appealing look into what they do. This is what helps them to gain more followers, more interest, and greater brand recognition.

Check out *Pinterest Marketing For Dummies,* by Kelby Carr (Wiley Publishing, Inc.), for more tips on building and nurturing a following on Pinterest.

Choosing what to share

What to share isn't a decision to take lightly. If you repin only the most popular pins, pins that everyone on Pinterest has already seen ad nausea, you're not giving any incentive for anyone to follow you. If you share only obvious sales ploys, people are going to consider you a spammer. However, if you're known as someone who posts interesting, intriguing, shareable content, you'll have followers galore.

What sort of things you should share depends on your goal with Pinterest, the type of business you run, and who your customers are. Consider your brand and your message, and then brainstorm unique ways to share your brand's story. Before posting anything, ask yourself, "Is this image representative of my brand?"

Here are a few things to consider:

✦ **Make your content shareable.** Find images people will enjoy and talk about.

✦ **Images should appeal to the senses.** Make them mouthwatering, thought-provoking, funny, or the stuff that inspires fantasy.

✦ **Try to find images no one else is sharing:** The more unique your pins and boards, the more followers you will have for those pins and boards.

✦ **People prefer images to text.** Funny sayings and infographics are fun from time to time, but they can get old if that's all you post.

If you run a product-based company, consider putting a price tag on some of the items you sell, which places the items in the Gifts section. We cover the Gifts feature in Chapter 3 of this minibook.

Sharing other people's pins

When you share another person's pin in your feed, you *repin* it. Similar to a Facebook share or Twitter retweet, a repin tells the original pinner you liked what she posted so much, you also wanted to share.

To repin a pin that you like, follow these steps:

1. **Hover your mouse pointer on the pin that you want to share and click the red Pin It button that appears in the top-left of the pin.**

   The Pick a Board window pops up with the pin on the right, as shown in Figure 2-1. The Description section automatically populates with what the original pinner wrote.

Figure 2-1: Click the Pin It button to share someone else's pin with your community.

I call this my "Hail Mary" sangria. Not planned, made with items foraged from the cabinets - and saying a prayer it will taste ok. Syrah, ginger brandy, triple sec, orange juice, tangerines, green apple slices, lemon, and lime. Fizzy water courtesy of my Soda Stream. It's delicious - cheers!

Uploaded by Deb Ng

Book VII
Chapter 2

Marketing with Pinterest

2. **From the Boards drop-down list, select the board you want to repin the image to.**

   You have the option to select a board you already have or create a new board. We cover creating boards in Chapter 1 of this minibook.

3. **If you want to change the description, you may do so at this time.**

   If it's helpful information, such as the name of a particular food dish, we recommend leaving it as-is.

4. **Click the Pin It button.**

   The pin gets added to the board you selected, and it shows up in your feed and in the feeds of all the people who follow your board.

Note: You can also click the pin, which takes you to the pinner's page and to the pin itself. You can like the pin from there in the same manner. Click the pin image one more time to be taken to the original website where the image came from.

Using share buttons

Ultimately, you want others to share your content on Pinterest. The ideal situation is for other people to read your blog or view one of your photographs and pin it, inspiring dozens of repins. However, you have to make it easy to do so.

Most people who read content online won't share the same content if sharing isn't made easy for them. Though it doesn't take more than a few seconds to cut a link and paste it into the Pinterest Add function, the truth is, it's too much trouble for most. They want to be able to share at the click of a button and not have to leave their current page.

Share buttons enable the people who consume your content to share it without even visiting Pinterest. All the user does is click the Pin It button, fill in the description, and choose a board, and then your content is pinned to his board. If you're not logged in to Pinterest already, you're taken to the login screen so you can do so first.

Here are a few features and plug-ins to look into:

✦ **Pin It:** Available from Pinterest at `http://pinterest.com/about/goodies`, the Pin It button enables you to embed code on your blog or website so that others can pin your content. Pin It is available for WordPress blogs and even Flickr so that you can share your photos with others.

✦ **Follow Me on Pinterest:** You can add this button to your blog or website. Grab the code at `https://business.pinterest.com/en/widget-builder#do_pin_it_button` and paste the code where you feel it will do the most good. Most people like pasting the code into their right side-bars at eye level. Share buttons should never be difficult to find.

✦ **DiggDigg:** This WordPress plug-in (`http://wordpress.org/extend/plugins/digg-digg`) features a variety of share buttons for Twitter, Facebook, Google+, and many other social networks, including Pinterest. When you install this plug-in, the share buttons appear on the side of your content so readers can share the content if they're so inclined.

✦ **ShareThis:** Another plug-in that enables social share buttons. When you activate this plug-in, share buttons appear at the top or bottom of the page. You can find it at `https://wordpress.org/plugins/share-this`.

Although DiggDigg and ShareThis aren't specific to Pinterest, these popular share buttons are used to share content on Pinterest and other social networks. People who use one of these plug-ins, such as the ShareThis plug-in, shown in Figure 2-2, have the option to tweet, pin, post on Facebook, and so on. Because DiggDigg and ShareThis feature all the social networks, the majority of bloggers who use share buttons on their content use these plug-ins rather than installing a bunch of individual ones.

Figure 2-2:
Use Pinterest share buttons on your content.

Driving Traffic with Pinterest

Did you know that Pinterest drives more traffic to individual blogs and websites than YouTube, Google+, and LinkedIn combined? That's a force to be reckoned with, and it's why Pinterest, unlike some of the other emerging social networks, is something anyone marketing a brand needs to take seriously.

Here's how the traffic flow works. If you're following proper Pinterest etiquette, you're sharing a good mix of content (which can be both images and video). Some of that content is from your own sources, such as your blog or website. The rest of your content is from other content, including repins and other people's blog posts or videos. In fact, most of the items you pin shouldn't be your own content. Unless an image is uploaded directly, most images are links from external sources. Most people who are marketing with Pinterest do so because they want pinners to click their links.

However, it isn't as simple as sharing a link and hoping people visit your website; you have to be strategic about it.

What follows are a few things to consider when creating and sharing content on Pinterest:

+ **Select images with Pinterest in mind.** Your most important goal when creating pin-worthy content is to select an image that represents the article and entices others to click through to the originating site. Don't go through the motions and select some random stock photo. Use colorful, thought-provoking, and awe-inspiring photos. Pinterest automatically gives image options when you're preparing to pin something from a site, so take advantage of that opportunity to select the best pin! Photos that tell a story will inspire others to click to learn more.

+ **Be descriptive.** On Pinterest, brevity is essential. With that said, you should write a description worthy of the image. It's not exactly a headline but, similar to a headline, you want to use the description to capture attention. Share one or two sentences describing the image but leave most of the details to the imagination.

+ **Tag when at all possible.** There's really no reason to tag all your friends every time you post a pin; that gets kind of annoying. However, if a pin reminds you of someone or if you want to give credit to a particular pinner, do tag. The person being tagged, more often than not, will like or share your pin, and that helps get your brand on other people's radars.

+ **Give others the opportunity to pin your content.** Use share buttons on your blog posts, articles, images, and videos so that others can share with their friends.

+ **Take advantage of the Gifts option.** We cover ways to sell on Pinterest in Chapter 3 of this minibook, but the Gifts option is a way to sell without annoying people with spam or a sales pitch. You can add a price tag to a sales item, and it will appear on the Gifts page.

+ **Use keywords and search terms.** In your descriptions, use the words and phrases that people are searching for. People also search for images online, so optimize your photos for search to help others find them. We're going to talk about keywords in the section "Using keywords," later in this chapter.

+ **Grow your community.** Keep finding new people to follow and interact with. While you grow your Pinterest community, you also grow traffic.

We talk more about community later in this chapter, in the "Building Your Pinterest Community" section.

✦ **Be consistent.** Pin on a regular basis. If people never see anything new from you, they have no reason to continue to follow your pins.

✦ **Get nichey.** Cater to your niche. Appeal to the people who are most likely to use your products or services.

✦ **Use humor.** People love to share funny pins, and humor is a great way to break up the themes of your regular pins now and again.

✦ **Pay attention to your board categories.** Don't be generic. Your boards should be as eye-catching as your images. Take special care with the names you use for your boards. Pinterest suggests names, but those are only suggestions. Don't be afraid to change them. Be creative and imaginative, and explore how other brands are using boards. We dive into how to use boards to your advantage in Chapter 1 of this minibook.

✦ **Be strategic when arranging your boards.** Don't have a random mishmash of boards. Arrange them in an order that puts the most important boards first. If your goal is to sell, place the board with pins relating to your products or services first. To find more about planning boards, see Chapter 1 of this minibook.

When we talk about sharing content and arranging boards, not every pin has to be your content or from you. You can use other people's content on your boards and in your pins.

Being descriptive but brief

The descriptions you include with pins are just as important as the images. It's not the image that brings in search traffic, but the words you use to describe the image.

If you're a travel agent and are posting a photo taken in Bora Bora, for example, you should let the viewer know where the image was taken, but you also need to tell the viewer that you can arrange vacations there. Write a description such as, "This gorgeous vista is Bora Bora. Now doesn't it make you want to plan your next tropical getaway there?" With this description, you also appear in searches for *Bora Bora*, *tropical*, and *getaway*. Did you notice that we didn't state directly that we can plan the vacation for the viewer, though? Drive traffic with your pin but avoid appearing too "selly" to the viewer. You want the viewer to come to you.

Pinterest doesn't allow descriptions to break text into paragraphs, which means descriptions can become one long-winded block of text if you're not careful. Make sure your message comes across in a few clear, concise sentences.

Book VII
Chapter 2

Marketing with
Pinterest

Finding the right words

Because you're using Pinterest as a sales or marketing tool, you want to be visible to search engines. You also want to create a description so enticing that pinners click through to your website when you pin your own items.

What follows are a few best practices for creating the best descriptions for your pins:

✦ **Use search engine optimization (SEO).** We talk about SEO a lot in this book because it's so important to catch the attention of the search engines. By all means, use search terms in your pin descriptions, but don't make it obvious. The terms you use should flow naturally. Think about what words people use, or words you want them to use, to land on your brand in Pinterest. Use those words or terms in a way that doesn't look silly.

✦ **Use words that paint a picture.** A description should, well, describe. If you pinned an image of a hen holding a flag, avoid stating the obvious. *This is a hen holding a flag* is descriptive but kind of boring. Calling the hen *patriotic* is less boring and describes the hen without insulting the intelligence of the reader.

✦ **Use words that stimulate discussion.** Try to string together words so they're open ended. When you ask questions, request more information, or make a statement that leaves room for interpretation, you're more likely to receive comments.

✦ **Use titles if they benefit you.** If you're pinning from a link to an article or a blog post, there's nothing wrong with using the original title as your description. However, there's also nothing wrong with *not* using the title and instead describing the image using words that benefit your brand and bring searchers to your board or pin.

✦ **Let your personality show.** Don't be afraid to be funny, perky, or anything else that helps you and your brand shine. Avoid bland, general terminology and Internet slang. Use words that show your personality instead.

✦ **Avoid negativity.** Don't use words that evoke negative images or connotations. Always go for a positive point of view. But it's important to be appropriate and authentic. If your business sells Goth items, for example, "dark" words might be expected by the audience.

Finding pinners to emulate

You can get help from the top pinners in your community to see which pins are receiving the most attention. Just click the Categories button (which displays three lines) at the top of any Pinterest window, and then select the

Popular link from the pop-up menu that appears; or simply look closely at your feed. Each pin shows how many likes and repins it receives. If a pin is going viral — you see the pin more than once — look for its original source.

Note the types of posts getting the best reactions in terms of the most repins and positive comments, too.

Using keywords

After you find the top pinners (discussed in the preceding section), read a sampling of their pins. Think about the descriptive words and phrases you would use to find them. Are they using the same keywords? For example, if a bedroom set has gone viral, read the description to note if it's a *girl's bedroom set* or a *blue bedroom set*. Those descriptive terms are keyword phrases. Consider the words and phrases people are using to find pins and use those words and phrases in your own pins.

What follows are some best practices when using keywords on Pinterest:

✦ **Keywords and phrases should sound natural.** People don't type information into search engines in the same way they speak. For example, they would type *wet iPhone* instead of *How to dry a wet iPhone*. When pinning, use phrases that sound natural. Pinterest is a visual platform, and the words should be as pleasing as the photos.

✦ **Avoid creating pins with keywords in mind.** Write for the people, not the platform. Definitely use keywords in your pins, but don't put up any old photo just because you want to use a keyword.

✦ **The keyword or phrase should match the pin.** Don't use a keyword unless it describes the pin. You'll lose followers if you're known to bait and switch.

✦ **Use keywords for board titles.** Rather than using Pinterest-suggested titles for your boards, use your own titles that include keywords. This way, both boards and pins will appear in a search.

✦ **Research keywords within your niche.** Use a keyword tool to see what the popular keywords are for your niche. There are some free tools you can use — for example, Google's keyword suggestion tool located at `https://adwords.google.com/KeywordPlanner`.

Do some Pinterest searches within your niche and see what keywords are being used in the most popular results. This information gives you a good idea of keywords to use for your own pins.

Book VII
Chapter 2

Marketing with Pinterest

Building Your Pinterest Community

Even though you're using Pinterest as a marketing tool, make no mistake: Building up a community on any of the social networks is more about others than it is you. Your Pinterest community is made up of people who share like-minded interests. They visit Pinterest for their own reasons. They may be pinning to promote books, learn about particular topics, or market their own businesses. They want you to be part of their communities, too. That's why interaction and participation are so important.

A variety of people make up your Pinterest community. As with the other social networks, you follow and are followed by friends, co-workers, family, new friends whom you met online, and strangers. When you harness the power of your community, you're turning online friends into loyal customers and creating word-of-mouth marketing.

Driving traffic isn't about typing *CLICK ON MY LINKS* in big, bold letters. It's about giving people a reason to want to learn more about you. Driving traffic is more about creating the right types of content and building your community than it is using a sales pitch. When you take on a warm tone over marketing speech, you have a better chance of winning them over.

Collaborating with group boards

A great way to connect with your community is to collaborate on boards. Pinterest lets pinners participate in *group boards*, where like-minded people add pins around a common theme. For example, crafters can contribute to a board featuring current projects, or LEGO enthusiasts can pin their latest creations.

Here are a few reasons pinners are collaborating:

✦ **Exposure:** You're marketing your brand, and others are doing the same. Having pins on a collaborative board means more exposure. Moreover, some of the pins you share will lead to your blogs and websites.

✦ **Community:** If you consistently post intriguing pins, others will want to see more of your Pinterest pins and boards. Group boards are a terrific community-building tool.

✦ **Camaraderie:** Some pinners just enjoy planning boards around a theme in the spirit of fun collaboration.

To create a group board, you essentially follow the steps to create a regular board that you can find in Chapter 1 of this minibook. Follow these steps:

1. **Click the plus-sign (+) button located on the bottom-right corner of any Pinterest page.**

2. **Select Create a Board from the pop-up menu that appears.**

3. **Enter the board name and category in the Create a Board pop-up window, as described in Chapter 1 of this minibook.**

   Near the bottom of the pop-up window, the Who Can Add Pins section appears, which contains your name below a blank text box.

4. **In the Who Can Add Pins text box, start typing the name of a pinner you want to invite to your group board.**

   Here's the first catch: The person has to be a member of Pinterest for you to invite her. And here's the second catch: You also have to be following the person before you can invite her to your group board.

   As you type, potential matches appear in a drop-down list.

5. **When you see your invitee listed, select the person's name and then click the Add button.**

   The person is added below your name.

6. **Repeat Steps 4 and 5 to add all the people you want to invite to the group board.**

7. **Click the Create Board button.**

   After the group board is created, those who are invited to collaborate receive a notification and can begin pinning immediately.

**Book VII
Chapter 2**

**Marketing with
Pinterest**

Check your notifications, as outlined in Chapter 1 of this minibook. Otherwise, you'll receive a notification any time someone in your group pins to the group board. This can be a little distracting if yours is a large group of pinners.

Here are some additional things to consider about group boards:

✦ **Invite people you trust.** Instead of inviting random pinners you don't know, invite friends. Be sure group pinners have your best interests at heart and won't spam the boards.

✦ **Invite people who are knowledgeable about the topic.** When you plan a board, choose people who know the subject matter. If you don't, your board will be a mishmash of items instead of a visually, informative resource.

✦ **Establish clear guidelines.** You want to establish some guidelines for pinning to your group board so there's no inappropriate content. You can provide this information in an email before you invite pinners — in either a heads-up that an invite is on the way or, better, a request asking whether it's okay to send the invite.

✦ **Stay on topic.** If the board is meant to share the architecture of New York City and someone pins an image of the St. Louis's Gateway Arch, you'll probably want to alert the pinner to remove it unless it's germane to the discussion.

Liking pins

The fun isn't contained to only your boards. Showing approval for other people's boards and pins by liking them tells the pinner that he's on the right track. And if you like pins by people you don't know, they might want to look at your pins and subsequently follow you in return.

Likes show the Pinterest community you do more than pin and that you're not just on Pinterest to pimp out your own stuff. When others land on your page and see that you like a lot of images, they might be inclined to friend you so that you can like their stuff, too. When people see photos with a lot of likes to them, they want to see what all the fuss is about and click through for more information.

To like a pin, hover your mouse pointer on the pin's image, as shown in Figure 2-3. The Pin It, Send, and Like buttons appear. Click the Like button (which displays a heart) to show the pinner you like her pin.

Like

Figure 2-3: Hover your mouse over the desired pin to see the heart icon, which indicates a like button.

The Rock of Cashel, Ireland-BREATHTAKING. Where St.Pat converted the people of Ireland to Catholicism...

We cover the Pin It button in the "Sharing other people's pins" section, earlier in this chapter. You find out how to comment in the section that follows.

Commenting on pins

You may think the fun is in the pinning, but that's not it at all. The fun is in the conversation.

Don't wait for people to make remarks on your pins to engage with your community. Go ahead and comment on other people's pins. Do you have an opinion on a particular image? Tell the pinner how you feel! (See Figure 2-4.) Does an image evoke emotion? Share that emotion with the person who pinned. Do you have questions or concerns? Share those, as well. Conversations ensue when others comment.

Figure 2-4:
Take some time to comment on pins.

To comment, click the pin. That pin now fills your entire window. Scroll down to the bottom of the page where you see your picture or logo. Right next to that is a text box for commenting. Because it's white on white, the text box can get lost on the page; but if you remember it's next to your picture towards the bottom of the page, you'll find it. Type in your comment and press Enter.

Always be polite in your comments. Some people on the Internet are looking to start fights by posting rude and negative comments. Don't give them the pleasure of knowing they've gotten under your skin by responding. Take the higher road.

Playing nice

Every social network has its own set of etiquette rules, and Pinterest is no exception. Most social networking etiquette is in place so you don't annoy others, but most of it is common sense and courtesy.

Keep in mind that etiquette isn't made up of hard-and-fast rules; rather, it's a series of best practices most pinners follow to keep Pinterest free of spammers, trolls, and people who make the experience more difficult by causing arguments. Here's a list of Pinterest etiquette tips:

✦ **Give credit where credit is due.** If you're sharing another person's pin, always give a shout-out to the original source. For example, if I upload a pin and you share it in your feed, type *via @debng* at the bottom of your description.

When sharing online content, some photographers or websites want you to ask permission before posting their images on Pinterest. You may feel you're doing a third party a favor by linking to their work, but because Pinterest pulls the image and you gave Pinterest permission to use your content, the original source may want compensation or recognition.

Be safe; follow the intellectual property rules laid out in the About Pinterest page. To open this page, click the Categories button (which displays three lines) at the top of any Pinterest page and select About at the bottom of the pop-up menu that appears — the About Pinterest page opens in its own tab. And if you link to content someone else owns, be very sure they're okay with you doing so.

✦ **Fill out descriptions for all your pins.** It's not always easy to tell what the pin is about. For example, not everyone will know the name of a recipe or the location of an island scene. It's a nice courtesy to your friends to let them know what you're pinning.

✦ **Avoid over-pinning.** We know that pinning is addictive. However, don't flood your friends' streams with dozens of photos at once. Pace yourself. If they see only your pins all the time, and everyone else's pins are lost, your friends are going to stop following you.

✦ **Don't spam.** Mix up your pins so they provide a variety of content. For example, share other people's blog posts, web articles, and images (if you have permission). Don't make everything link back to your own website or sales page.

✦ **Keep your pin descriptions brief.** If your description is filled with all the details that are in the pin's original link, why would anyone click through to the pin's site for more information? See the earlier "Driving Traffic with Pinterest" section for tips on writing a tantalizing pin description.

Most rules of etiquette are good common sense. If you think something you do might make others uncomfortable, it probably will.

Chapter 3: Driving Sales with Pinterest

In This Chapter

✔ Setting up shop

✔ Selling without annoying others

✔ Setting up a Pinterest brand page

✔ Being honest about your affiliations

*P*interest offers a unique opportunity for brands to sell their products because not too many social networks allow you to display your products and pricing. Whether your brand is a product or a service, you can use Pinterest boards as catalogs or gift guides so that pinners can browse your wares and, we hope, buy. In this chapter, we talk about selling on Pinterest, ethically and responsibly.

Showing Off Your Wares

You might be surprised to find out you can't set up an actual shop on Pinterest. Though it's the perfect social network for displaying your products, you can't use Pinterest as an online store. Pinterest is, first and foremost, a social network. Although many opportunities for sales exist, you can't actually hang an Open for Business banner in your storefront window.

Then how is Pinterest better at driving sales than Facebook or Twitter? There are several reasons:

✦ **Pinterest has a large female base.** Many women plan their family's menu, home design, kids crafts, and other visually appealing projects.

✦ **Pinterest is a visual site.** Products and services are displayed in an aesthetically pleasing manner. Pinners are enticed into buying because of the photos, rather than a sales spiel.

✦ **Pinterest offers great product placement opportunities.** Because you're drawing in buyers via images rather than a written sales pitch, you can display your products in ways that best highlight their usefulness.

✦ **Images are shareable.** When pinners like what they see, they repin. Your products have the ability to reach thousands of people, which would cost thousands of dollars using traditional advertising methods.

According to a social shopping survey at Steelhouse.com, 59 percent of Pinterest users have purchased an item they saw on the site, whereas only 33 percent of Facebook users purchase items they find on brand pages. Moreover, even though Facebook users are more likely to click on product images to learn more about them, the majority of them don't go much further than that. Pinners click and often buy.

Selling without Looking Like You're Selling

Here's the thing about selling on any social network: People get very touchy if they feel they're being pitched to. The majority of people online are doing their social networking during their downtime as a way to relax. They don't want advertisements and spiels to be front and center. However, that doesn't mean they're not interested in buying. All you have to do is post the content that makes people say, "I want that."

What follows are some tips for selling on Pinterest:

✦ **Use images that paint the product or service in a positive light.** When adding any item directly to Pinterest — or even to a blog, website, sales page, or online catalog — use the best, most enticing shots possible. Remember that people can pin content from your blog and other web pages, so you want all your content to look good! If it's in your budget, consider getting a professional photographer to take the photos — she'll know the best lighting and setups to ensure that your products shine.

✦ **Make it easy for pinners to buy.** If you pin a link to an enticing product, people need to know where to go to buy it. If you can't lead to a sales page, make sure the page the pin does lead to offers details on where to find the product.

✦ **Pin shareable content.** Pin the types of images people like to share. Make sure they're pleasing to the eye and evoke emotion. Look around Pinterest at which pins are the most popular or viral. See whether you can pin down (pun intended) the common denominator among the most popular pins.

✦ **Use enticing words and phrases.** Be descriptive without selling. If you're pinning food, use words that make people hungry, such as *succulent* or *mouth-watering*. If you're pinning clothes, use words that make the potential wearer feel as if the style will look good on him, such as *flattering*.

✦ **Don't spam.** If you spam or push sales in a heavy way, you'll gain a bad reputation. Don't tag random people in your pins and say things like,

"Hey! Have you checked out our great new thing-a-ma-bob?" The quickest way to lose followers is to be a spammer.

✦ **Share images of influential people using your product.** Do famous people use your product or service? Gather photographs and pin them. Nothing inspires people to buy more than knowing their heroes use a product.

✦ **Make sure pinners know where the original photo came from.** If possible, add the name of your brand to your pin. This way, folks can come to your website or research your brand for more information. Even better, link back to the product page on your website or blog.

Major brands are on Pinterest, and they're selling in a big way. They're able to do so because Pinterest offers a unique opportunity to sell using images instead of words. Most people will agree that marketing lingo and smarmy sales tactics are a turnoff. However, a strong visual can help viewers picture themselves using the product or service.

Pinterest gives you a chance to show, rather than tell. And everyone knows a picture is worth a thousand words.

Setting Up a Business Page on Pinterest

Pinterest recently introduced the ability to sign up as a business instead of an individual. So if you are marketing a brand instead of yourself (as a professional), you can set up a Pinterest business page.

There aren't huge differences between a business page and a personal page; you can still follow the same steps and practices as you would a personal account. However, business pages do come with a few perks that are of interest to businesses:

✦ **Analytics:** Pinterest offers analytics for verified business pages. Analytics can tell you about your Pinterest community and the activity on your pins. For example, you can see which pins received the most activity in terms of shares, repins, and likes. You can also discover demographic information about the people who visit your Pinterest brand account.

✦ **Rich Pins:** If you want to include pricing, maps, ingredients, and a direct link to your website on Pinterest, you can do so using *Rich Pins*. Pinterest offers five types of Rich Pins: movies, recipes, articles, products, and places. To learn more about Rich Pins, see `https://business.pinterest.com/rich-pins`.

✦ **Verified accounts:** To take advantage of the extra options you receive with a Pinterest business account, you have to verify your website. This verification just makes sure you're not faking a brand page or pretending to be from a brand you're not affiliated with. You don't have to verify your website, but if you don't, you can't receive as many business perks like analytics.

✦ **A business name:** If you want to use a brand account, you can log in with your brand name — if that's the name you used to create an account — instead of your personal name.

If you already have an existing personal account and you'd rather it was a business account, you can make a change. Mind you, the account doesn't use your name anymore; it uses your brand. So if you have personal pins or pins inappropriate for a business on your personal account, remove them before making the change.

To convert your personal account to a business account, do the following:

1. **Log in to your personal Pinterest account.**

2. **Go to** `https://business.pinterest.com/en` **and click the Convert Now link located below the red Join As a Business button.**

3. **On the next screen, enter your business name, select your business type from a drop-down menu, and type in your website address if desired.**

4. **Click the red Convert button.**

You now have a business account instead of a personal account.

If you want to keep business and personal accounts separate, log out of your personal account and follow these steps to create a business account:

1. **Go to** `https://business.pinterest.com`**.**

2. **Click the red Join as a Business button, shown in Figure 3-1.**

The Create a Business Account pop-up window appears.

Figure 3-1: You can set up a business page on Pinterest.

3. **Fill out the required information about your business, as well as the information for the person who will be running the business account.**

   You can always change this later if you want.

4. **Read the Terms of Service for a Pinterest business page.**

5. **Click Create Account.**

Creating Gift Guides

If your brand sells products, you can create boards as gift guides. For example, if you specialize in wedding gifts and accessories, you can create a board for bridesmaid gifts, one for gifts for the groom, one for wedding favors, and more. What follows is a look at some of the types of gift guides you can create on Pinterest:

✦ **Your catch-all gift guide:** Some brands don't sell a wide variety of items. If you sell just one type of thing, you might need only one gift guide on which you can pin items you have for sale.

✦ **Holiday gift guides:** This technique works especially well for brands that have particular holiday significance. For instance, are you marketing floral arrangements? Create separate boards to display Valentine's Day bouquets, Christmas arrangements, Thanksgiving centerpieces, and so on.

✦ **Seasonal gift guides:** Create four boards, one for each season, and fill them with appropriate gifts. If you sell fashion wear, for example, you could pin the sundresses on the Summer Gifts board and the sweaters on the Winter Gifts board.

✦ **Pricing gift guides:** You can divide your merchandise into your own preferred price ranges. For instance, if you sell children's toys, consider dividing categories by price so Uncle Fred can buy a gift that's in the $5-to-$10 range, and grandma and grandpa can find a deluxe toy in the $50-to-$100 range.

✦ **And more:** You have a lot of options. Check out what other brands are doing for gift guides, particularly brands that you compete with.

REMEMBER

Put your gifts into specific gift guide categories that make sense for how your followers want to shop.

We cover planning and creating boards in Chapter 1 of this minibook. The only difference in creating a gift board is that you want to make sure you reflect that in the title of the board — for instance, Easter Basket Gift Guide, Jewelry Gifts for Geeks, or Baby Dresses under $20.

**Book VII
Chapter 3**

**Driving Sales
with Pinterest**

It's not enough to create a gift guide and leave it at that. Find creative ways to promote your guide. For example, advertise it on your blog or website, or share it on Twitter and your brand's Facebook Page. Don't wait for people to find it. Also, make sure you promote often enough that it gets fresh views, but not so often that you're spamming.

Disclosing Affiliates

If you're going to be selling on Pinterest as an affiliate for a brand, you have to disclose this information. The Federal Trade Commission (FTC) has strict rules for affiliate sales online, and if you're going to be earning money by selling someone else's products, you have to let people know.

According to the FTC, the following needs to be disclosed:

+ If someone gives you a free product in order for you to review that product

+ If you receive money every time someone clicks a link

+ If you write about a product and receive money in return

+ If you push a product that belongs to someone who advertises on your blog or website

Now, if you wrote up a product review and you're pinning the review to a Pinterest board, you might want to say in your description that you're reviewing a product. When people click through to the review to learn more about the product, they can read your disclosure there.

However, if you're directly selling a product on Pinterest (for example, in a gift guide), let the Pinterest community know you're receiving money in exchange for that product. Also, it's misleading if you pin an affiliate or sales link without letting others know your intentions.

Some pinners simply type *affiliate link* or *sales page* at the bottom of their description. This satisfies the FTC guidelines and shows that you're honest about your intentions. People who want to find out more will click through.

However, although Pinterest doesn't have anything in its Terms of Service specifically banning the use of affiliate links, they have recently been removing affiliate links from pins. It's probably better to sell on your website using an affiliate link, and then link to the website post from your Pinterest account.

When it comes to selling online, always disclose your intentions. It keeps you out of trouble and builds trust between you and your customers and community.

Book VIII
Other Social Media Marketing Sites

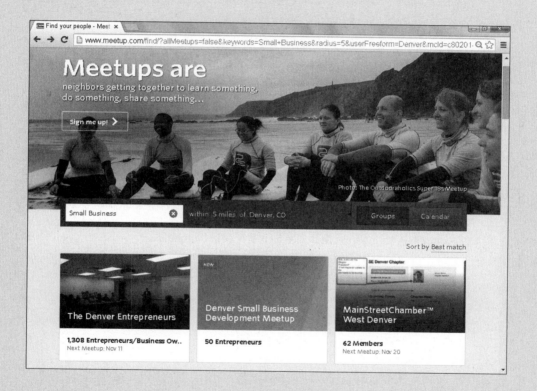

Visit www.dummies.com for great Dummies content online.

Contents at a Glance

Chapter 1: Weighing the Business Benefits of Minor Social Sites

In This Chapter

↳ Reviewing goals for social media marketing

↳ Conducting social media marketing research

↳ Assessing audience involvement

↳ Choosing minor social communities strategically

*W*ithout a doubt, Facebook, Twitter, LinkedIn, and Google+ are the elephants in the social marketing zoo, at least in terms of the largest number of visits per month. But this is one big zoo, as shown in Figure 1-1, which displays only 35 of more than 300 significant social sites. Among these sites, you'll find lions and tigers and bears, and more than a few turtles, trout, squirrels, and seagulls.

You have to assess your business needs, research the options, and select which (if any) of these minor social marketing sites belongs in your personal petting zoo. In this chapter, we look at methods for doing just that.

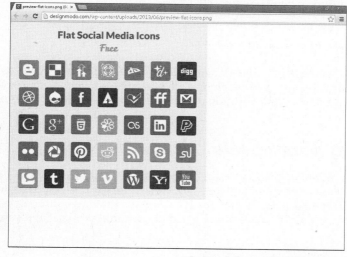

Figure 1-1:
The zoo of social media sites is vast. Your time, however, is limited.

With the exception of the community building site, Ning (described in Chapter 4 of this minibook), and free-standing blogs (which can become your primary web presence if you use your own domain name), these smaller sites are best used to supplement your other social marketing efforts.

Reviewing Your Goals

In Book I, we suggest that you develop a strategic marketing plan. If you haven't done so yet, there's no time like the present. Otherwise, managing your social networks can quickly spin out of control, especially when you start to add multiple smaller sites for generating or distributing content.

Marketing is marketing, whether offline or online, whether for search engine ranking or social networking. Obviously, your primary business goal is to make a profit. However, your goals for a particular marketing campaign or social media technique may vary.

As we discuss in Book I, social media marketing can serve multiple goals. It can help you

✦ Cast a wide net to catch your target market.

✦ Brand.

✦ Build relationships.

✦ Improve business processes.

✦ Improve search engine rankings.

✦ Sell when opportunity arises.

✦ Save money on advertising.

Your challenge is to decide which goal(s) apply to your business and then to quantify objectives for each one. Be sure that you can measure your achievements. You can find additional measurement information in Book IX.

Researching Minor Social Networks

Doing all the necessary research to pick the right mix of social networks may seem overwhelming, but, hey, this is the web — help is at your fingertips. Table 1-1 lists many resource websites that have directories of social networking sites, usage statistics, demographic profiles, and valuable tips on how to use different sites. The selection process is straightforward, and the steps are quite similar to constructing an online marketing plan, as described in Book I, Chapter 3.

Table 1-1	Social Network Research URLs	
Site Name	*URL*	*What It Does*
Alexa	`www.alexa.com/siteinfo`	Ranks traffic and demographic data by site
Experian Marketing Services	`www.experian.com/ marketing-services/ online-trends-social- media.html`	Presents the top ten social sites by visits per week
Display Planner by Google	`https://adwords.google. com/da/DisplayPlanner/ Home`	Compiles traffic data, demographics, and device use by site; requires a Google account
Google Toolbar	`www.google.com/toolbar`	Installs Google Toolbar with Google PageRank (not available for all browsers)
HubSpot	`http://blog.hubspot. com/blog/tabid/6307/ bid/33663/7-Targeted- Social-Networks-Niche- Marketers-Should-Try.aspx`	Describes seven attractive niche social media sites

Ignite Social Media	`www.ignitesocialmedia.com/ social-media-stats/2012- social-network-analysis- report`
	
	`www.ignitesocialmedia. com/social-media-stats`
		Compiles traffic and demographic data for 2012; other interesting social media statistics available

(Continued)

Table 1-1 *(continued)*

Site Name	URL	What It Does
Mashable	`http://mashable.com`	Presents social media news and web tips
	`http://mashable.com/category/social-media`	Lists stories and resources about social media
	`http://mashable.com/category/social-network-lists`	Lists of older social media sites by topic
Quantcast	`www.quantcast.com`	Compiles traffic and demographic data by site
Moz	`http://moz.com/beginners-guide-to-social-media`	Beginners Guide to Social Media
SitePoint	`www.sitepoint.com/social-networking-sites-for-business`	20 Social Networking Sites for Business Professionals
Social Networking Watch	`www.socialnetworking-watch.com/all_social_networking_statistics`	Aggregates social net news and stats
Wikipedia	`http://en.wikipedia.org/wiki/List_of_social_networking_websites`	Directory of more than 200 social networking sites

Follow these general steps to get your research under way:

1. **Review the strategy, goals, and target markets for your social marketing campaign, as described in Book I.**

   If your B2B business needs to target particular individuals during the sales cycle, such as a CFO, buyer, or project engineer, be specific in your plan.

2. **Decide how much time (yours, staff's, or third party's), and possibly budget, you want to commit to minor social networking sites.**

Don't underestimate how much time social media marketing can take. After you're comfortable with Facebook and (if they fit) Twitter or LinkedIn, it's okay to start with just one or two minor sites and slowly add services over time.

3. **Skim the directories and lists of social media in (refer to Table 1-1) to select possibilities that fit your goals.**

For more ideas, simply search using terms for your business area plus the words *social network* or *social media* (for example, *fashion social network*).

4. **Review the demographics and traffic for each possibility by using a site such as Alexa, Google's DisplayPlanner for ads, or Quantcast (as discussed in Book I, Chapter 3), and then cull your list to keep only those that fit your target market and marketing objectives.**

Figure 1-2 displays the relative market share, according to StatCounter Global Stats (http://gs.statcounter.com/#all-social_media-US-monthly-201406-201408-bar), for the seven top-ranked social media services in the United States from June 2014 to August 2014. Market share is ranked not by traffic to the sites themselves, but rather by the amount of traffic they refer to other sites. This approach may be valuable for business analysis because it discounts personal users who stay on social media sites to communicate with their friends. The Other category in this figure encompasses LinkedIn, Delicious, Digg, Google+, and many more sites.

5. **Review each network (see suggestions in the following bullet list) to make sure you feel comfortable with its web presence, user interaction, Google PageRank, features, ease of use, and ability to provide key reports. Prioritize your sites accordingly.**

6. **Enter your final selection in your Social Media Marketing Plan (described in Book I, Chapter 3), and set up a schedule for implementation and monitoring on your Social Media Activity Calendar (see Book I, Chapter 4).**

7. **Implement your plan. Modify it as needed after results come in.**

Wait at least a month before you make changes; gaining visibility within some social network sites can take time.

For leads to other social networks that appeal to your audience, look for a section named Other Sites Visited (or similar wording) on one of the statistical sites.

Book VIII
Chapter 1

Weighing the
Business Benefits of
Minor Social Sites

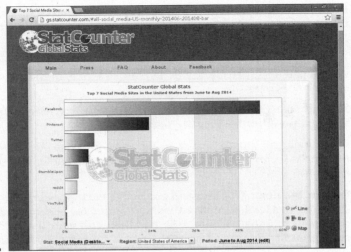

Figure 1-2:
Factor in relative market share, using data such as that from StatCounter Global Stats.

Keep in mind these words of caution as you review statistics for various minor social networks in Steps 3 and 4 of the preceding list:

✦ **Not all directories or reports on market share define the universe of social media or social networks the same way.** Some sources include blogs, social bookmarking sites such as Delicious, or news aggregators. Small social networks may come and go so quickly that the universe is different even a few months later.

✦ **Confirm whether you're looking at global or U.S. data.** What you need depends on the submarkets you're trying to reach.

✦ **Determine whether the site displays data for unique visitors or visits.** A unique visitor may make multiple visits during the evaluation period. Results for market share vary significantly depending on what's being measured.

✦ **Repeat visits, pages per view, time on site, and number of visits per day or per visitor all reflect user engagement with the site.** Not all services provide this data, whose importance depends on your business goals.

✦ **Decide whether you're interested in a site's casual visitors or registered members.** Your implementation and message will vary according to the audience you're trying to reach.

✦ **Check the window of measurement (day, week, month, or longer) and the effective dates for the results.** These numbers are volatile, so be sure you're looking at current data.

Regarding social media or everything else, consider online statistics for relative value and trends, not for absolute numbers. Because every statistical service defines its terms and measurements differently, stick with one source to make the results comparable across all your possibilities.

Assessing the Involvement of Your Target Audience

After you finish the research process, you should have a good theoretical model of which minor social networks might be a good fit for your business. But there's nothing like being involved. Our advice in the preceding section recommends visiting every site to assess a number of criteria, including user interaction. If you plan to engage your audience in comments, reviews, forums, or other user-generated content, you *must* understand how active participants on the network now interact.

Start by signing up and creating a personal profile of some sort so that you can access all member-related activities. The actual activities, of course, depend on the particular network.

Lurking

Spend time watching and reading what transpires in every interactive venue on the site, without participating. In the olden days of Internet forums and chat rooms, you were *lurking*. You can make a number of qualitative assessments that can help you determine whether this site is a good fit for you:

✦ **Quality of dialog:** Do statements of any sort float in the ether, or does interaction take place? Does a moderator respond? The site owners? Other registered members? Is there one response or continual back and forth? If you intend to establish an ongoing business relationship with other participants on the network, you want to select a site where ongoing dialog is already standard practice.

✦ **Quality of posts:** Are posts respectful or hostile? Do posts appear automatically, or is someone reviewing them before publication? Do they appear authentic? Because you're conducting business online, your standards may need to be higher than they would be for casual, personal interaction. Anger and profanity that might be acceptable from respondents on a political news site would be totally unacceptable on a site that engages biologists in discussion of an experiment.

✦ **Quantity of posts compared to the number of registered users:** On some sites, you may find that the same 20 people post or respond to everything, even though the site boasts 10,000 registered members. This situation signals a site that isn't successful as a social network, however successful it might be in other ways.

Responding

After you have a sense of the ethos of a site, try responding to a blog post, participating in a forum, or establishing yourself as an expert on a product review or e-zine listing. Assess what happens. Do others respond on the network? Email you off-site? Call the office?

Use this side of the lurk-and-response routine to gain a better understanding of what you, as a member and prospective customer, would expect. Will you or your staff be able to deliver?

If a site requires more care and feeding than you have the staff to support, consider dropping it from your list.

Quantifying market presence

In addition to assessing the number of unique visitors, visits, and registered members, you may want to assess additional components of audience engagement. Sites that provide quantitative information, such as Quantcast, help you better understand your audience's behavior, learn more about their lifestyles and brand preferences, and target your message. You can learn about these concepts:

✦ **Affinity:** A statistical correlation that shows the strength of a particular user behavior, such as visiting another site, relative to that of the U.S. Internet population as a whole — for instance, whether an Instagram user is more or less likely than the general Internet population to visit YouTube

✦ **Index:** The delivery of a specific audience segment, such as women or seniors, compared with their share of the overall Internet population

✦ **Composition:** The relative distribution of the audience for a site by audience segment, such as gender, age, or ethnicity

✦ **Addict:** The most loyal component of a site's audience, with 30 or more visits per month

✦ **Passer-by:** Casual visitor who visits a site only once per month

✦ **Regular:** A user partway between Addict and Passer-by; someone who visits more than once but fewer than 30 times per month

Choosing Social Sites Strategically

It may seem ridiculously time-consuming to select which minor social marketing sites are best for your business. Why not just throw a virtual dart at a list or choose randomly from social sites that your staff likes to visit?

Ultimately, you save more time by planning and making strategic choices than by investing time in a social media site that doesn't pay off.

If you're short of time, select sites that meet your demographics requirement but on which you can easily reuse and syndicate content, as described in Book II, Chapter 1. You can replicate blog postings, for instance, almost instantly on multiple sites.

If you truly have no time to select one of these sleek minor critters, stick to one of the elephants and add others later.

Somebody's Mother's Chocolate Syrup, shown in Figure 1-3 and described in the nearby sidebar, uses multiple social media channels to achieve its marketing goals.

Even the smallest social network sites can be valuable if they have your target market. All the averages mean nothing. It's about *your* business and *your* audience. Niche marketing is always an effective use of your time. Fish where *your* fish are!

Figure 1-3:
Somebody's Mother's Chocolate Sauce generates traffic to its website from a variety of social media, as shown by the chiclets in the lower-right corner.

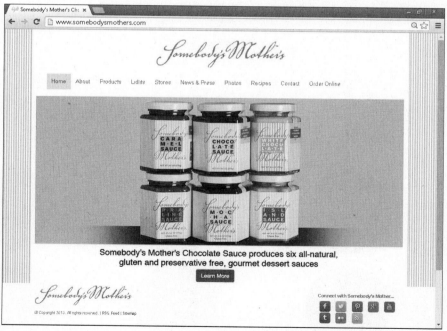

Reproduced with permission of Somebody's Mother's Chocolate Sauce

Somebody's Mother's says, "Try social media!"

Owner Lynn Lasher started Somebody's Mother's in April 2005 to teach her three children how to start a business, to assume responsibility for their own financial well-being, and to take matters into their own hands. One weekend when she was out of work, she asked someone who was demonstrating salsa in a neighborhood grocery store how he got his product on the shelves. Thus inspired, she decided to sell her mother's chocolate sauce. Within two days, her company was born. Now, almost 10 years later, she has created a profitable business without incurring debt, made (and learned from) her inevitable mistakes on a smaller stage, improved product quality, and earned a very loyal customer following. (Plus, two of her children have already become entrepreneurs themselves.)

For Lasher, both homemade foods and mothers are very special. Her product, her website, and her social media presence all reflect that. Because mothers "are almost never validated or recognized, much less compensated," Lasher says, she began using quotes about mothering or parenting on the jar lids of her products, as seen in the nearby screenshot.

Reproduced with permission of Somebody's Mother's Chocolate Sauce

Audrey Marshall, the VP of Online Marketing and PR for Somebody's Mother's, explains that the company started with a website immediately and began utilizing social media in 2008 with the channels available at that time: Facebook, Twitter, and Myspace. Seeing social media as an opportunity to reach new online audiences for the brand, Marshall has since adopted additional platforms, including YouTube, Pinterest, Tumblr, and Flickr.

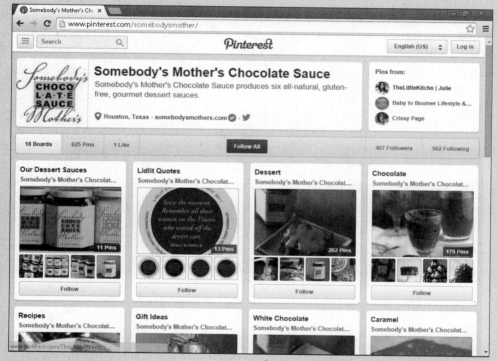

Reproduced with permission of Somebody's Mother's Chocolate Sauce

"It was never our goal to sign up for all the social media platforms available," she explains. "Rather, it's about knowing our target audience, where they exist online, and how best to engage with them." Their posts primarily target mothers and *foodies* (people who are interested in cooking or baking, and trying out new recipes).

For Marshall, each social media platform requires a slightly different focus, even when she's posting the same content. "For example, on Tumblr and Pinterest, visual media is incredibly important, whereas on Twitter and Facebook, you can have more of a dialogue with your community. It's important for us to have a consistent brand identity in all of our posts, with the opportunity for sales conversions as appropriate."

(continued)

**Book VIII
Chapter 1**

Weighing the Business Benefits of Minor Social Sites

(continued)

Somebody's Mother's posts to each social media platform at least several times per week. Rather than adhering to a rigid schedule, she takes her cues from their audience, based on tent-pole events (such as holiday seasons), specialty food news, trending topics, and so on. In total, she spends one to two hours a week on social media: prepping posts, responding to comments, and engaging with the audience.

Currently, she uses a tool called Buffer to schedule posts, and Google Analytics, Facebook Insights, and other platform analytics to track visits, user engagement, and similar metrics. To track incoming visits from sites such as TasteSpotting, StumbleUpon, or reddit, she primarily looks at Google Analytics. Finally, Marshall checks Alexa to monitor Somebody's Mother's site ranking.

She cross-promotes the company's social media profiles, linking to all of their profiles from the website (refer to Figure 1-3), and between the others, as appropriate.

Based on her experience, Marshall adds a note of caution about submitting products to review sites. She recommends knowing your target audience and your community before asking for a review. When the audience match is right, product submissions are more likely to result in sales conversions and click-throughs.

Marshall offers one more important reminder: "You can never stop learning about social media. Rather, you have to learn to grow with it and update your strategies as the platforms evolve."

Somebody's Mother's web presence:

- www.somebodysmothers.com
- www.facebook.com/somebodysmothers
- www.twitter.com/somebodysmother
- www.pinterest.com/somebodysmother/
- http://plus.google.com/+somebodysmothers
- www.youtube.com/somebodysmothers
- http://blog.somebodysmothers.com
- www.flickr.com/photos/somebodysmothers
- www.somebodysmothers.com/feed (RSS)
- http://instagram.com/somebodysmothers

Chapter 2: Leaping into Google+

In This Chapter

✔ Understanding how Google+ works

✔ Bringing your Google+ page to life

✔ Using Circles for sharing

✔ Developing a Google+ community

✔ Getting the hang of Hangouts

*F*ree Google+ pages are spots on the Google+ social network where companies of all sizes and in all industries maintain a presence in order to share information and interact with their current and (hopefully) future customers. Whenever we reference a company's page in this chapter, we're talking about its Google+ page.

Conceived in 2011 as Google's answer to Facebook, Google+ is a social network on Google steroids: Your Google+ community can show approval for your content with +1s, share your content, and join in video chats. They can even interact with people who have similar interests when you use Google+ Circles for market segmentation.

Because Google automatically creates Google+ pages for existing business accounts, it appears to have millions of active accounts. Alas, the degree of actual engagement and viewer participation is less certain.

When you consider the extra search-engine-optimization value that comes with Google indexing any public updates, we believe that Google+ has tactical value for marketers, even though it may not be the best place for finding prospects or building loyalty. In this chapter, we address the challenge of leveraging this free social network successfully.

Exploring the Benefits of Google+

You may not feel like dealing with yet another social network profile. When you create a page, you want to do it right, and maintaining it involves a time commitment. Is your time better spent cultivating the networks you're already a part of, or finding new ways to reach out to customers and clients and grow your online community?

Only you can determine whether you need Google+. Google+ hasn't replaced Facebook or Twitter as the social media weapon of choice for many brands, but companies such as TOMS, Cadbury, and Financial Times have embraced Google+ in addition to other social networks, and they're finding success with it. You, too, may find that Google+ offers you a little something different than the usual social networks.

Check out Jesse Stay's *Google+ Marketing For Dummies*, Portable Edition (Wiley Publishing, Inc.), for more information on Google+.

In the following sections, we take a closer look at why you should consider using Google+.

Determining whether Google+ is worth the effort

When marketing a brand, you need to be careful about the content you put out in social media for the world to see. As important as it is to have a strong social media presence, if you promote your Google+ presence and then never use it, the resulting account quickly falls out of date. That doesn't look good for you or the brand — it looks like you either don't care about the account or can't find the time for it, and the brand appears to lack relevance and popularity. So before you take on Google+, be sure you have the time to devote to your web presence there and keep your page from becoming a virtual ghost town.

If you decide not to spend much time developing or promoting your Google+ presence, set up a dashboard like Hootsuite or Netvibes (see Book II, Chapter 1). Then Google+ will update automatically when you post to Twitter or Facebook. At least your Google+ page won't look abandoned.

Here are several reasons to consider using Google+:

✦ **A better presence on the search engines.** Google's search engine will search content you post on your Google+ page. Each post ends up with a unique URL. Hashtag searches on Google will also report in search results Google+ posts that use that hashtag.

✦ **To improve your likelihood of appearing in the Local Carousel, which spotlights local search results.** The Local Carousel has different criteria for ranking than general search results, including the number of +1s on a business's Google+ page. Both the quantity and quality of Google+ reviews are critical to determining ranking on the Local Carousel.

✦ **To improve your appearance in the Local Knowledge Panel, which shows up on mobile searches and on the right side of search results pages.** If you don't post actively to your Google+ page, Google may display competitors that have active Google+ pages at the bottom of the

Local Knowledge Panel instead of your Google+ page. That's another reason to post regularly on Google+ — or at least set up a dashboard to auto-post to your page.

Being a part of the Google+ community means your brand is weighed heavier in the top-secret algorithm Google uses to determine where a company or site lands in search engine results. Using Google+ is an easy way to get closer to the top.

✦ **Additional ways to interact with your existing customers and community.** Sure, you may be on other social networking sites such as Facebook, Twitter, and LinkedIn, but if you have the time and resources, why not add another service to the mix? By trial and error, you'll find the social networks that produce the best results for your brand. And by best results, we mean more visibility and interaction with current and potential customers. Who wouldn't want that?

✦ **To share engaging content or updates with your community without starting a separate blog.** Google+ allows you to share your content with people who don't have a Google+ account by entering their email addresses in the Share menu. They, in turn, can share your content with others.

Individual users are no longer automatically forced into creating a Google+ page when they sign up for a Gmail account. A Google+ page is created only when someone signs up for Google My Business (www.google.com/business) or another (non-Gmail) Google product.

✦ **An easy way for customers and potential customers to contact you.** Sure, your customers can access you via phone, email, or your website, but Google+ adds yet another way they can communicate their thoughts by commenting on your posts or adding their own posts via the Join the Discussion box that you can add to the top of your page. The About section of your Google+ profile also allows you to add further contact information, so be sure to provide your customers plenty of ways to reach out to you.

Some obvious and not-so-obvious perks set Google+ apart from other social media services, as described in the following sections.

Recognizing the Google factor

Google is a search engine giant, and you want your brand front and center in the search engine race. Google+ can help you in that race because public profiles and updates are indexed for Google's search function and appear in search results for your brand. Therefore, someone using a Google search to seek more information on your brand could land on your Google+ page and see a lot of engagement. And, keeping in line with Google's uncluttered look, Google+ has no ads running. In other words, there's nothing to pull your fans' attention away from your content!

Seeing the way clear with Google+

Isaac Porter, MD, an ophthalmologist specializing in LASIK, cataract, and cornea surgery, owns Lowry Porter Ophthalmology in Raleigh, North Carolina. He's also an early adopter of social media (as you can see from the list of social media sites at the end of this sidebar) and an enthusiastic expert in Google+.

Lowry Porter Ophthalmology was founded in 1983 by his former partner (now retired), who created the firm's original website in 1998. In 2014, Dr. Porter oversaw the release of a new website, www. eyeporter.com, seen in the nearby figure.

Reproduced with permission of Isaac Porter, MD

When Dr. Porter first joined the practice in 2010, its only social media presence was on Facebook. He soon changed that. First, he created a YouTube channel to post his video blog, "A State of Sight," where he shares the latest information in ophthalmology and eye care. Then, in 2011, he created a Twitter account. "I was attending many Internet and marketing events in Raleigh that had a heavy Twitter presence. I think Twitter is the best social channel at this time for meetings and events," he explains.

His introduction to Google+ occurred at a Google promotional event held at the Marbles Museum in Raleigh in September 2012. It was the early days of Google+, but Dr. Porter was hooked and has been using it ever since to extend the practice's reach beyond its original target market, which was within a 100-mile radius of Raleigh. (See the nearby figure for the Lowry Porter Ophthalmology Google+ page.)

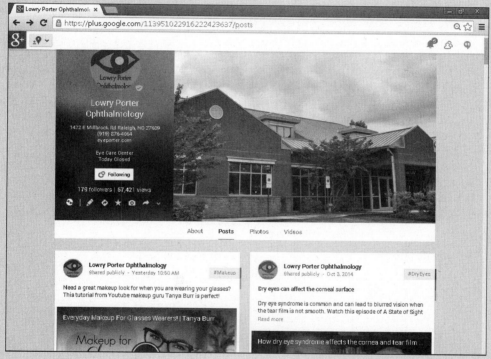

Reproduced with permission of Isaac Porter, MD

**Book VIII
Chapter 2**

**Leaping into
Google+**

"This extended reach has helped me build my personal brand and authority, and also helped me share valuable eye information," says Dr. Porter. He estimates that their Google+ following falls into the 30- to 60-year-old age range, which is the middle segment of their business demographics. (Lowry Porter sees patients of all ages, with younger patients for LASIK and older patients for cataract surgery and medical eye problems like glaucoma and macular degeneration.)

Porter's top marketing goal is to obtain more new patients for the practice. Building on the interaction between Google+ and Google's other products, he notes that Google+ helps new patients

(continued)

(continued)

find them in searches, while at the same time helping both existing and potential patients find information about eye problems and eye health.

Initially, Porter was the sole manager for the practice's Google+ page. Now he has team members who help post on all the company's social sites, but he still handles all the posts from his personal Google+ and Twitter accounts. The team, which aims for two to three Google+ posts per week, spends one to two hours per week posting or reviewing content. In 2014, they started using a content calendar to help the team plan and post regularly, while Porter reviews and approves the content.

For the practice, new patient visits are the most important metric. All new patients are asked how they learned about the practice. If they visited any of its social sites, the team tracks the information in a spreadsheet. In an unusual marketing effort, the office has a few small signs in the reception area and in the exam rooms that list their social sites with QR codes in case patients would like to follow them.

"I enjoy participating in a few communities, including ones for eye doctors, healthcare marketing, and Internet marketing," says Dr. Porter. "I have been in a few Hangouts and think they are a great way to interact and share content. I would like to have more Hangouts with eye specialists or patients from around the world so I can share their experiences."

Dr. Porter offers solid advice to any business owner. He urges companies to claim and completely fill out their listing on Google+/Google My Business. "This lets the public know that you are active online and welcoming new customers. Then, by adding content or posting regularly, you can gain interest in your business and engage with your followers."

Lowry Porter Ophthalmology's web presence:

- ✔ `www.eyeporter.com`
- ✔ `https://plus.google.com/113951022916222423637`
- ✔ `https://plus.google.com/+IsaacPorterMD`
- ✔ `http://youtube.com/isaacportermd`
- ✔ `https://twitter.com/eyeporter`
- ✔ `www.facebook.com/eyeporter`
- ✔ `www.eyeporter.com/blog`
- ✔ `https://foursquare.com/v/lowry-porter-ophthalmology/4cc584883d7fa1cd7712b25f`
- ✔ `www.pinterest.com/eyeporter`

Interacting via Google+ Features

You have several ways to interact with the people you are connected with on Google+. When using the social network, the following features enhance your experience with your friends or fans:

✦ **Circles:** Your Circles are how you arrange the customers or fans you follow on Google+. Circles are like lists you can use to direct content to specific people; if those people choose to follow you back, they see your content on their home pages. For example, you can have separate Circles for team members, vendors, clients, and customers. This feature is great for ensuring that the information you share with a specific Circle doesn't get seen by others for whom the content wasn't intended. You can find more about Circles in the section "Socializing in Circles," later in this chapter.

✦ **+1:** The +1 feature is a great way for users to find interesting content to read and share. Similar to a Facebook Like, the +1 says you like the content someone posted. The writer of the post and the people who originally received the post will see your +1. When a post has a lot of +1s, more people are likely to read the post. We talk more about +1 in the section "Maximizing use of the +1 feature," later in this chapter.

✦ **Hangouts:** Google+ allows users to host *Hangouts* — video conversations with up to ten people at one time — so getting a group of people together for a video chat is easy. Maybe you want to hold a meeting of colleagues, but a few are traveling. Hangouts are a great way to get some face-time without having to be in the same location.

✦ **Hangouts On Air:** Hangouts On Air allow an unlimited amount of people to view your Hangout live. Hangouts On Air are excellent tools for discussion groups, focus groups, and reaching out to your community. We provide more information about Hangouts On Air in the section "Creating a Google+ Hangout on Air," later in this chapter.

✦ **Hashtags:** *Hashtags,* which are a keyword (or phrase without spaces) preceded by the hash sign (#), help people find or join conversations about a topic. You can place any hashtag you want anywhere in the body of a post, including on images and video. The tag will also appear in the top-right corner of your post. By clicking the hashtag in either location, you can browse other posts that share the same hashtag.

To explore trending hashtags or search for specific ones, viewers use the search box at the top of most Google+ pages, or they can navigate directly to `https://plus.google.com/explore`, as shown in Figure 2-1.

TIP Not sure what hashtag to use? Google+ can generate hashtags automatically. These tags appear *only* in the top-right corner of a post. Turn this functionality on or off by going to Settings. Check or uncheck the Add Related Hashtags from Google on My Newly Created Posts option.

#SmallBusiness hashtag

Search box   Share box   Share icon

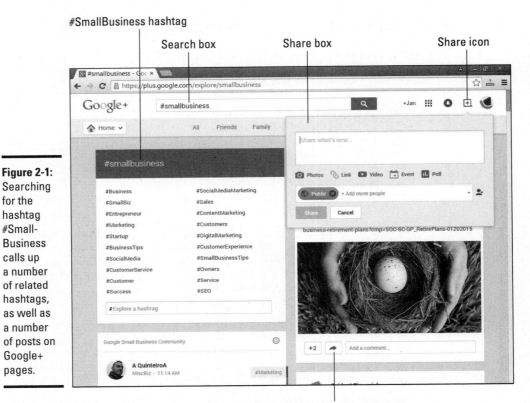

Figure 2-1:
Searching
for the
hashtag
#Small-
Business
calls up
a number
of related
hashtags,
as well as
a number
of posts on
Google+
pages.

Click the Share icon to share a post.

✦ **Share:** You can share your content with the easy-to-use Share function:

- *Sharing a link:* Click the Link button the pop-up that appears when you click the Share icon (the box with the plus sign) in the top navigation. (Refer to Figure 2-1 to locate this option.) Then enter or paste your link in the text field that appears. Select Public (anyone can see the link) and/or enter specific recipients for your link; click Share to finish. (You can share a specific post simply by clicking the curved Share arrow that appears directly below each post.)

- *Sharing photos:* Click the Photo button in the pop-up that appears when you click the Share icon (the box with the plus sign) in the top navigation. (Refer to Figure 2-1 to locate this option.) When the pop-up expands, drag your images as indicated, or upload them from your computer. Select Public (anyone can see the images) and/or enter specific recipients for your images; click Share to finish.

- *Sharing events:* To share an event, click the Event button in the pop-up that appears when you click the Share icon (the box with the plus sign) in the top navigation (refer to Figure 2-1 to locate this option). Enter all the required information in the pop-up that appears, including the people you want to invite. Then click the Invite button in the lower-left corner of the pop-up to share the event. To invite people to an existing event, share it from the Event page itself.

- *Sharing polls:* To add a poll, click the Poll button in the pop-up that appears when you click the Share icon (the box with the plus sign) in the top navigation. (Refer to Figure 2-1 to locate this option.) In the pop-up that appears, enter your poll question and answer choices. Specify how you want to see the poll. Click the Share button to finish.

- *Sharing videos:* Click the Video button in the pop-up that appears when you click the Share icon (the box with the plus sign) in the top navigation. (Refer to Figure 2-1 to locate this option.) In the pop-up that appears, select the source for your video by clicking the tabs on the top (Enter a URL, Your YouTube Videos, Record Video, or Upload Video) and taking the action required. (Alternatively, you can enter a keyword to search YouTube for videos.)

  Click the Add button at the bottom when you've identified your video. Another pop-up then appears below the Share icon with an image of your video. Specify who should be allowed to see it; click the Share button in the pop-up to finish.

✦ **Mentioning:** To grab someone's attention when you share in Google+, mention that person in a post using the plus sign (+) or at sign (@). Depending on that user's notification settings, she may receive a notice of her mention and a copy of the post.

✦ **Edit status updates:** An extremely attractive element of Google+ is that you can edit your posts, even if you already hit Enter. Everyone makes a spelling error or wants to reword something at one point or another. On Google+, you can do so without having to delete the entire post.

 Before getting started on Google+, take some time to get your bearings. Look around and see how other brands and individuals are using this network. Look at what people are sharing and what they're talking about, and take some time to notice the posts that receive the most +1s and shares.

Book VIII
Chapter 2

Leaping into
Google+

Creating a Google+ Page through Google My Business

Google My Business (www.google.com/business) is Google's latest attempt to create a rational, coherent portal for all Google's business-related products, from YouTube and Analytics to AdWords and Google+. Now that Google has integrated Google+ with its new Google My Business feature, marketers automatically get a Google+ page when they register their business with Google My Business.

Exploring Google My Business features

With the free Google My Business dashboard, you can

✦ Create and modify your current business information in one place for use with all Google business products, including Google Search, Local Search, Maps, and Ads.

✦ Build your Google+ page and track engagement using Google+ Insights.

✦ Create and track Google ads with easy-to-use AdWords Express campaigns.

✦ Review Google Analytics for your site and YouTube channel.

Google My Business replaces the Google+ Pages dashboard and Google Places for Business. If you already had either of those accounts, your dashboard has been automatically moved and upgraded. In that case, skip the following section and proceed directly to the section "Filling Out Your Google+ Page," later in this chapter.

Getting on Google My Business

To sign up for a Google My Business account, go to www.google.com/business.

If you already have a Google or Gmail account, click Sign In in the top-right corner, as shown in Figure 2-2; then follow the steps in the following step list.

If you don't have a Google or Gmail account, follow the steps in the nearby sidebar, "Creating a brand-new Google business identity."

1. **Sign in with your existing Google account credentials.**

   After you sign in, the introductory Google + dashboard screen (shown in Figure 2-3) appears.

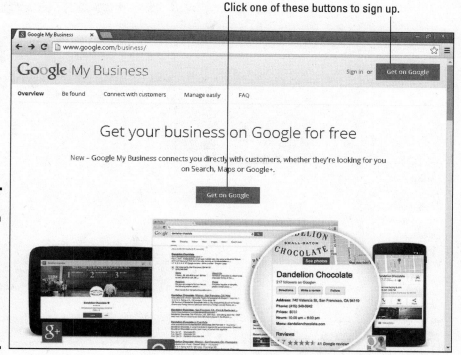

Click one of these buttons to sign up.

Figure 2-2:
Sign up for a
Google My
Business
account
to access
many
Google
business
products.

2. **For a new Google+ page, click the blue Get Your Page button, shown in the top-right corner of Figure 2-3, and continue to Step 3.**

   If you want to continue with the page that Google has set up for you, click the Manage This Page button and follow the directions in the later section, "Filling Out Your Google+ Page."

3. **Select your business type.**

   Your options, shown in Figure 2-4, are Storefront (meaning restaurant or store), Service Area (for example, plumbing, taxicabs, or graphic design), or Brand (such as the name of your product, cause, or team; this is generally used for an online-only business, or a company or organization with a national or international service area).

   If Google has already found and created a page for your domain name, click the Manage This Page button on the screen that appears. In this case, proceed to one of the next sections according to your page type: "Customizing Storefront and Service Area pages" or "Customizing Brand pages." Otherwise, continue to Step 4.

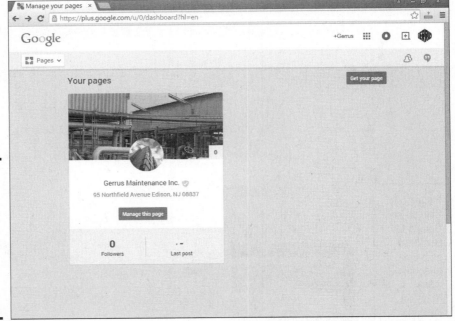

Figure 2-3:
You can have more than one Google+ page, as well as pages of several types.

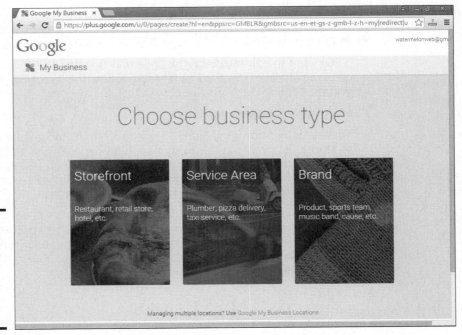

Figure 2-4:
Select your business type: Storefront, Service, or Brand.

Creating a brand-new Google business identity

To create a brand-new account, follow these steps:

1. **Go to www.google.com/business (refer to Figure 2-2).**

2. **If you don't already have a Google account — not even a Gmail account — click either of the two Get on Google buttons on that page.**

3. **Click Create an Account below the log-in box that appears. Fill out the required information on the new page that follows.**

   Next, you see a world map asking for the location of your business.

4. **Google may offer a list of businesses it finds with a similar name. If you see your company name, select it from the list.**

5. **After you identify the location, click the Not a Local Business link next to the gear icon in the top-right corner of the map only if you are *not* a local business (for example, you don't have a physical space or serve customers within a specific area).**

   In that case, your Google+ page will be designated as a Brand page. If you don't designate yourself as a local business, your company won't show up on local Google maps; be careful before making that selection.

6. **When you finish listing your locations, click the Create New Page button, which takes you to a page to enter basic business information. Complete the fields and click Submit.**

   Google then builds a Google+ page for you. You can proceed to the directions in the later sections, "Customizing Storefront and Service Area pages" or "Customizing Brand pages."

---

4. **If you chose Storefront or Service Area in Step 3, proceed to Step 5 because your business has a physical location.**

   If you chose Brand (for online-only businesses), the Create Your Google+ Page page appears. Skip to Step 8.

5. **Enter the name or address of your storefront or service business in the text field.**

   Google tries to locate your business on its map.

6. **If your business appears in the drop-down list below the text field, click it and proceed to Step 9.**

7. **If you don't see your business in the drop-down list, click the Add Your Business button. Then enter your address and phone number. Proceed to Step 9.**

   If you have multiple business locations, click the Google My Business Locations link. It takes you to a page that makes it easier to enter multiple locations.

   You can see a typical Service page in Figure 2-5.

8. **On the Create Your Google+ Page, enter your page name, its URL, and the type of page it is.**

9. **When you're finished, click the Create Page button.**

   See Figure 2-6 for a typical Brand page.

   That's it. You've created your Google + page, and your Google My Business dashboard overview appears, as shown in Figure 2-7.

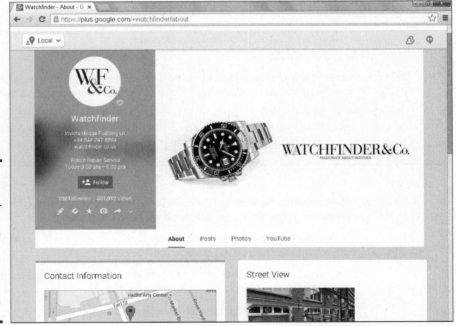

Figure 2-5:
An example of a Google+ Storefront page, which includes the physical location for mapping purposes.

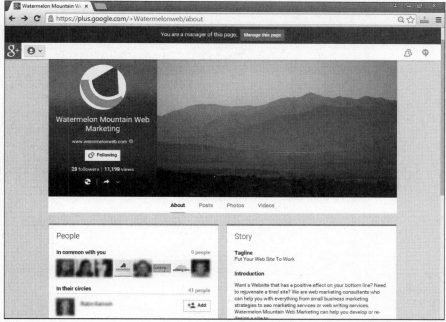

Figure 2-6:
An example of the About tab on a Brand page with sections for People and Story.

Reproduced with permission of Watermelon Mountain Web Marketing, www.watermelonweb.com

If you have a brick-and-mortar location, your business information will not appear on Google+, Search, Maps, or Mobile until you verify your business. Google wants you to prove that you have a real, live business at a specified location.

Start by claiming your listing on the Storefront or Service Area page (discussed in the section "Customizing Storefront and Service Area pages," later in this chapter). This is *not* the same as the website verification process that requires you to insert a line of code into the source code for your home page. Choose whether you want verification by postcard, phone, or instantly online. (The online option is available only if you have already verified your website using Google Webmaster Tools.)

Whichever choice you make, you will receive a verification number that you must enter on your Google My Business dashboard. For more information, see `https://support.google.com/business/answer/2911778?hl=en`.

Figure 2-7:
The Google+
dashboard
overview
screen.

Reproduced with permission of Watermelon Mountain Web Marketing, www.watermelonweb.com

Filling Out Your Google+ Page

Your Google+ page is an important resource. Because Google+ indexes pages for search, your page is immediately available to those seeking more information about your products or services. Moreover, it's also an important first look at your brand by the people who are seeking you out on the search engine and Google+ itself.

After you sign up for your Google+ page, as described in the preceding section, Google deposits you on your Google My Business dashboard (refer to Figure 2-7). You want to add information to your page to give your fans a better idea of who you are and what you or your business can do for them. You see different fields to fill out depending on which type of Google+ page you choose.

Customizing Storefront and Service Area pages

To customize Storefront and Service Area pages, follow these steps:

1. **Click the red Edit button in the top-right corner of your dashboard (refer to Figure 2-7).**

   Your Business Info Edit page appears.

2. **Fill in any missing Business Info highlighted in yellow.**

   Because Google integrates this information with its search function, it's important for you to complete all fields. Hover over each field until the pencil icon appears in the upper right; then click the field and enter your information.

3. **Write the tagline and introduction that will appear in the Story block on your Google+ About page.**

   For search engine purposes, include some of the same search terms you use on your home page, as well as the text of your Page Description metatags. (See Book II, Chapter 2 for more on search terms and metatags.) The What You See Is What You Get (WYSIWYG) tool lets you format text and insert links; take advantage of this feature to link to your home page and other key pages of your website.

New content for these pages doesn't appear until you've verified your site, as discussed in the section "Getting on Google My Business," earlier in this chapter. Nor will you have access to Reviews or Insights. Even after verification, edits to previously approved business information may be subject to review before they appear.

Customizing Brand pages

To customize Brand pages, click the red Edit button in the top-right corner of your dashboard. Your Business Info Edit page appears, displaying a notice that you can edit below each section. Fill in these sections:

✦ **Story:** When you click Edit below the Story section, a pop-up window appears where you can enter a ten-word marketing tagline and your introduction. As with Storefront and Service Area pages, we recommend that you use the same page description and some of the keywords used on your website. Don't forget to link to your home page or other key pages on your website.

✦ **Links:** When you click Edit below the Link section, a pop-up window appears where you can enter multiple links with a label. Be sure to link to your home page, other key product pages on your site, and multiple custom links, such as to all your other social media pages.

✦ **Contact Information:** When you click Edit below the Contact Information section, a pop-up window appears where you can choose access devices from a drop-down list. Choose all the means of access that you're able to support. The list offers options for phone, mobile, email, fax, pager, chat, or mailing address.

Although some fields allow you to choose Private or to restrict availability to certain Circles, leave as much information public as possible. You're in business — you need to be found. One exception: home-based businesses may want to hide their locations, although that means your business won't appear on Google Maps.

Adding profile and cover pictures

Your profile picture appears in the left column of your Google+ page; the cover image is the large header graphic on the right side that you want people to see when they land on your Google+ page.

To brand a business, use your logo as your profile photo. For the cover, try a resized version of the header graphic on your website, or specific images of your storefront, products, or services.

Log in to your Google+ page and follow these steps to set up your profile photo:

1. **Hover over the existing profile photo or space set aside for it.**

A camera icon appears.

2. **Click the camera icon to change the profile photo.**

A new screen appears with the Upload tab underlined.

3. **Drag the image you want to use or click the Select a Photo from Your Computer button.**

The usual directories appear, so you can select the image you want.

4. **When you're satisfied, click the Set as Profile Photo button in the lower-left corner.**

For the profile photo, choose a square image that's at least 150-x-150 pixels and in JPG, GIF, or PNG format.

To change your cover graphic, go to your Google+ page and follow these steps:

1. **Hover over the existing cover graphic until the Change Cover button appears. Click on the button.**

A new screen appears with the Gallery tab underlined.

2. **If you want, click one of the images that appear on this page and then click the Select Cover Photo button in the lower-left corner.**

3. **If you don't want one of those images, click the Upload tab at the top.**

4. **On the ensuing screen, drag the image you want to use or click the Select a Photo from Your Computer button.**

   The usual directories appear, so you can select the image you want.

5. **When you're satisfied, click the Set Cover Photo button in the lower-left corner.**

The cover graphic must be at least 480 x 270 pixels. The larger the better, but keep the rectangular format.

There you have it. Your Google+ page is set up and ready to go.

Adding managers

If you're not going to be the only person maintaining your Google+ page, you may want to add others as managers or communication managers. Google allows you to have up to 50 of them!

Deciding whether to add a manager

The owner of your Google+ page (that's probably you) is the only person who can delete the page or transfer ownership of the page to another individual.

Managers can make posts, edit a profile, change your account information, start a Hangout On Air, or manage videos on YouTube, but they can't delete the page or manage access. Communications managers can only enter and edit posts.

It's a good idea to have more than one manager just in case someone can't sign in for whatever reason. That way, your Google+ page won't be silent!

Maintaining a social network for a brand is an important responsibility. Be sure the people you appoint for this task are up for the responsibility because everything they post on your behalf reflects you, your business, and your brand. Be sure your managers are aware of the type of comments and content you consider acceptable.

Inviting a manager

If you don't have any managers, you must first issue them an invite, and then wait for them to accept. To add managers, follow these steps:

1. **Sign in to your Google+ page by navigating to www.google.com/ business.**

   The Your Pages dashboard appears.

2. **Choose the page for which you're adding a manager by clicking the blue Manage This Page button.**

   The Dashboard Overview page appears.

3. **Click the gear icon in the top-right corner of the Dashboard page and select Settings from the drop-down list that appears.**

   You arrive at your Google+ Settings page. (Settings also happens to be the name of the default landing tab.)

4. **Click the Managers tab at the top of the page.**

   A list of the managers you already have and the roles they play appears, as shown in Figure 2-8. Your profile always shows up at the top of the list with the word Owner under your name, even if you don't have any other managers.

5. **Click the blue Add Managers button in the top-right corner of the page.**

   The Invite New Managers pop-up window appears.

6. **In the pop-up text box, enter the name (if the manager you wish to add is already on Google+) or the email address of the person you want to invite to be a manager of the page.**

7. **Select Manager or Communications Manager from the drop-down list in the bottom-left corner of the pop-up window.**

8. **Click the Invite button to send the invitation.**

   After you invite the person, he is automatically added to the Managers list. The page displays Invited below the person's name or email address until he accepts the invitation. At that point, Invited disappears from his name in the Managers list.

Setting notifications

If you have an active Google+ stream, you don't necessarily want to receive notifications for every little thing that takes place. For example, if you don't adjust your notifications, you'll receive an email every time someone tags you in a photo, mentions you in a post, comments on your posts, comments on posts you commented on, puts you in Circles, and more.

Managers and roles

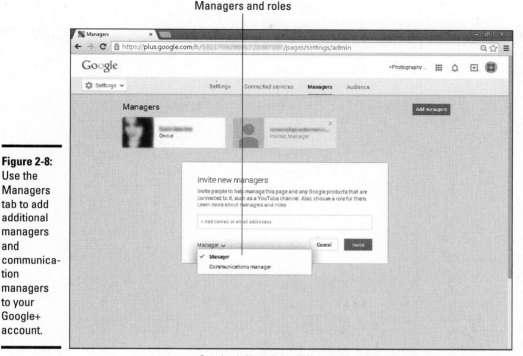

Figure 2-8:
Use the
Managers
tab to add
additional
managers
and
communica-
tion
managers
to your
Google+
account.

If your role with your brand requires you to know about all community interaction and engagement, receiving notifications is important. Determine which notifications are most important to receive and set your notifications accordingly. You can choose from multiple options for posts, Circles, photos, events, and communities.

By default, notifications are delivered to the page owner's email address. On your Google+ Settings page, scroll down to Notification Delivery. Click Change to use a different email address; for example, you could have notifications sent to the communications manager for a page.

To avoid receiving so many notifications, follow these steps:

1. **On the Google+ Settings page, scroll down to the Receive Notifications section, as shown in Figure 2-9.**

2. **Click the sideways arrow next to each option to expand the number of choices. Deselect the check boxes for the notifications you want to stop receiving.**

**Book VIII
Chapter 2**

**Leaping into
Google+**

Settings tab   Notifications

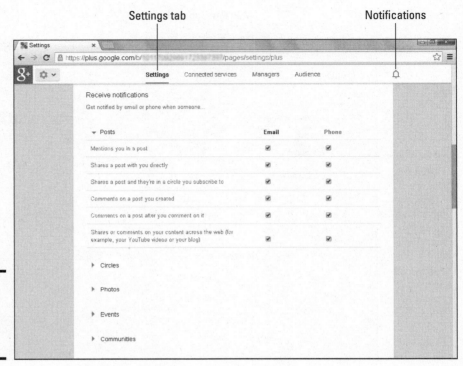

Figure 2-9:
You can adjust your notification settings.

To stay on top of what your followers are saying to and about you, keep the Posts settings selected, as well as any setting that deals with someone commenting on what you've posted.

Even if you turn off all notifications, you still see activity. When you access any of your Google accounts, whether it's Gmail or Google+, the bell icon on the top right of your browser window shows the number of notifications available for you to view.

Socializing in Circles

Google+ has some loyal members who prefer to interact on Google+ over other online communities. Therefore, you have the opportunity to reach different groups of people than those on other social media networks. You can also take advantage of Circles to communicate selectively with groups of prospects, clients, or customers.

Introducing Circles

On Google+, interaction occurs in *Circles,* which are user-created categories that group friends, customers, clients, brands, and so on. For example, if someone follows your brand, she might add you to one of her personal Circles, which she might call something like Brands I Like or Businesses I Follow.

When you first create your Google+ page, people may not yet have listed you in their Circles.

You will need to promote your Google+ page, let people know you have an account, and ask friends and fans to add your page to their Circles. (Google thinks of signing up for Circles as akin to people opting in to receive email newsletters.) Read the later section, "Adding people you know to your Circles," for ideas on how to kickstart sign-ups for your Circles.

Start by going to your new Google+ page and click the down arrow next to My Business in the top navigation. From the drop-down menu that appears, select People (see Figure 2-10).

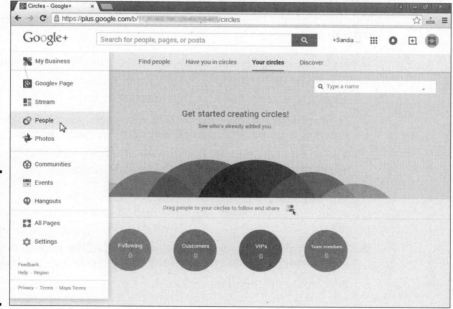

Figure 2-10: Google+ starts with four default Circles, but you can add as many as you want.

Under the Your Circles tab, Google provides four default Circles to segment your audience:

✦ Following

✦ Customers

✦ VIPs

✦ Team Members

You can edit the name of a Circle or delete any of the default Circles by right-clicking on that Circle's name and selecting the option you want from the pop-up menu that appears. To add a new Circle, click the large plus sign (+) to the left of the four circles. (In Figure 2-10, the + sign is hidden beneath the drop-down menu.)

No matter how you initially find people for your Circles, the best way to hold on to them is to create compelling content. Then those who already have you in their Circles will be inclined to share and encourage others to follow you, as well.

Adding people you know to your Circles

It's always easiest to start with people you already know. To add people you know to one of your Circles, follow these steps:

1. **From the same Circles dashboard page, click the Find People tab in the top navigation (refer to Figure 2-10).**

   A new page appears with a different display.

2. **In Search for Anyone box on this new page, search Google+ users by entering a name, city, school, company, or email address.**

   If names, email addresses or companies are already in Google+, They appear in a drop-down list the search box as you type.

3. **Click on the entry you're interested in.**

   A Google+ page opens with a red Add to Circles button below the profile photo.

4. **Click the Add to Circles button, and then in the pop-up that appears, select which Circle(s) they belong to, or create a new Circle.**

   People can belong to more than one Circle.

If you enter a general term like a city to the search box, you may need to click the magnifying glass to get results. Thumbnail images of multiple Google+ pages appear to the right of the search box. Below each thumbnail, click the Add or Follow button to add them to one or more of your Circles.

TIP

The pop-up that appears allows you to choose which Circle(s) to use or to create a new Circle.

Do you have a list of customer emails? Use this search process to see if they're on Google+.

The downside is that you can search only one field at a time.

Discovering new people to add to your Circles

Another way to add people to your Circles is to find Google+ users you don't know who already participate in categories that pertain to your business; just use Google's Discover function by following these steps:

1. **From the Circles dashboard page, click the Discover tab in the top navigation.**

The Discover page appears, displaying users and pages sorted by interest category, as shown in Figure 2-11.

Selected category

Click this tab to see users and pages by category.

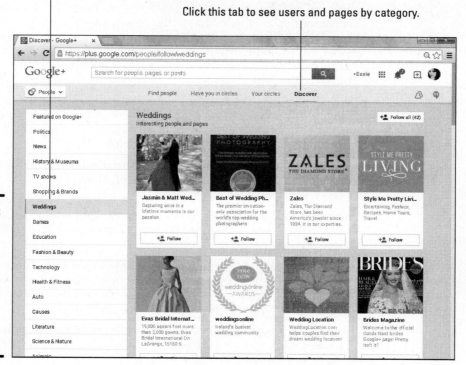

Figure 2-11:
A Discover page sorted by Weddings, the interest group selected in the left navigation.

2. **In the left navigation, click the interest category that best fits your business, and then click the Follow button at the bottom of the thumbnail for each user or page you want to follow.**

Getting on users' radar screens

Building your Circles might take some time. The trick is to get on people's radars so they'll add you to their Circles, and you can then circle them in return. Start by taking part in the conversations of people you discover; this activity also helps you promote your Google+ page.

Here are some suggestions to get you going:

✦ **Use your personal Google+ account.** If you have a personal Google+ account, use it to promote your business account. Tag or highlight your brand page by using the plus sign (+) or at symbol (@) in front of the name used for your Google+ account. Also, share some posts from your brand Google+ page on your personal Google+ page. When people in your personal Circles see cool stuff shared from private Circles, they might be inclined to add your brand to their Circles, as well.

✦ **Use your social networking accounts.** You can promote your Google+ account on your other social networking accounts. From time to time, encourage your other communities to join in on your discussions there. Let them know what you're talking about and how much you value their input. For example, "We're recommending books today on our Google+ page. Won't you come by and tell us about your favorites?" Don't forget to link to the page.

✦ **Include Google+ chiclets on your websites.** Your blog, website, and other channels should have a link or button that will lead your community to your brand's page on Google+, as shown in Figure 2-12. To learn more about chiclets, see Book II, Chapter 3.

✦ **Include +1 buttons on your content.** These buttons let visitors quickly recommend your brand and your content. Include a call to action to remind users what to do.

✦ **Include share buttons:** Provide an easy way for people to share your content with their circles. See Book III, Chapter 2 for more information on share buttons.

✦ **Take advantage of Google plug-ins:** Ask your programmer or web developer to add Google+ plug-ins to your website. These plug-ins make it easy for visitors to find and follow you on Google+ without having to leave your website. Your programmer can choose from

• *Badges:* These large buttons let people follow your Google+ page with one click.

Google+ chiclet

Figure 2-12: When you add a Google+ chiclet to your blog or website, it encourages others to visit your page and add you to their Circles.

- *Embedded posts:* Display public Google+ posts on your web pages so visitors can +1, comment, and follow from there.

- *Snippets:* Customize the appearance of the text and image that other people see when your content has been shared.

✦ **Ask.** Ask your friends and fans to help share your page. If they like what you do, they'll recommend it to their own friends and family.

✦ **Participate in as many conversations as possible.** When you add people to your Circles, you'll see their posts in your stream. Participate in as many of these discussions as possible. When people see a brand page actively engaged in the community, it reminds them to follow the page. Also, if you're productive in conversation, it will encourage others to add you to their Circles.

✦ **Optimize your brand updates for search.** When you use this technique, people searching for topics, products, or services similar to yours have a good chance of landing on your Google+ profile and adding you to their Circles. For more information on search engine optimization, see Book II, Chapter 2.

It may take a little time for others to add your brand's page to their Circles. Just continue updating as if you already have a thriving community. Because Google+ is indexed for search, the more you update, the better it is for brand visibility.

Building Community through +s, Shares, and Comments

Unlike Facebook, your Google+ updates are seen by everyone who has you in their Circles, and unlike Twitter, you can have a conversation using more than 140 characters.

Because many of the people who are using Google+ are on that social network to avoid some of the drama other social networks offer, they're more focused on a positive, intelligent conversation. Here's your chance to reach some old friends, as well as a whole new audience.

In the following sections, we take a look at sharing content with your Google+ community and using the +1 feature to help you get your content noticed by others who aren't Google+ members yet.

Sharing your Google+ content

Everything brands do online must be strategic. If you don't map out a plan and follow a strategy, your presence on Google+ (and other social networks) is going to be a confusing mishmash rather than a series of well-thought-out, discussion-worthy posts. The outcome of everything you post should benefit your community and your brand. You want followers to become likely to share your content or even add their two cents.

If you haven't refined your marketing plan for social media marketing purposes yet, check out Book I, Chapter 1. Book III, Chapter 1 provides information on choosing content that meets your needs.

Remember these strategies when sharing on any social media network:

✦ **Mix it up.** Use a variety of content so your community doesn't get bored. Ask questions, tell jokes, create short stories, or share photos and videos. People enjoy seeing beyond the same old, same old, so don't be afraid of originality.

✦ **Provoke intelligent discussion.** Although it's definitely important to keep your tone light, you also shouldn't be afraid of providing more thought-provoking questions or topics. Give your community a chance to weigh in. Ask open-ended questions or encourage opinions. Make it clear that your followers' voices matter.

✦ **Establish a routine.** Post as much as you can, but if you can't post multiple times every day, at least keep a consistent schedule. For example, if you find that Mondays and Wednesdays are the busiest days of your week, consider setting a schedule that runs Tuesday and Thursday. But make sure you stick with it, no matter what. The more followers check back to see what you're up to, the better.

✦ **Participate often.** Community isn't a one-way street. You also have to get out among the people. Visit the people in your community and comment on their posts and updates. Not only will others view you as accessible, but it may encourage others who don't already follow you to add you.

✦ **Avoid hard selling.** Of course you want to drive sales, but if everything you post is perceived as a pressure tactic, your community will tire of it and no longer follow you.

✦ **Determine who will be posting and when.** If more than one person is running your account, coordinate efforts so they don't post the same things at the same time. Set up a schedule or follow an editorial calendar.

✦ **Use search engine optimization (SEO).** SEO is a must when it comes to online content. People will have trouble finding your content if the search engines bury it in their search results pages because you didn't use enough or the correct keywords in your content. Book II, Chapter 2 has more information on SEO.

Your public Google+ posts have the ability to catch the attention of the search engines — most importantly, Google, the top search engine in the world. Make sure all your content is optimized for search. Use search terms in your posts and when labeling your photographs or videos.

Maximizing use of the +1 feature

The Facebook Like button is one of that network's most popular features. Users like it because they can show their approval for content without having to commit to a comment or full-fledged discussion. Google+'s +1 feature works in a similar manner. Instead of a thumbs-up button, Google+ offers a +1 button next to every comment and below every post. Simply click the button to show your approval. Plus, when you post content, your community will reciprocate by +1-ing the items they like best. And you can use the number of +1s on a given post to determine the type of content your community likes best.

The more useful and meaningful content you post, whether it's links to articles or text updates asking your community's opinions on a hot topic, the more likely you are to receive approval for your information in the form of the reader clicking the +1 button. When a community member +1s your content, it will be shared in his activity stream for others to see. This is an amazing way for your content to be shared with the Circles of others and will lead to you being able to expand your own Circles, which also increases your brand awareness. The more Circles you're added to, the more it shows that your content is trusted and worthwhile. See how it all comes full, er, circle?

Clicking the +1 button doesn't have to happen on just your Google+ page, however. When someone stumbles across one of your blog posts, for example, if you have the +1 button code installed on your website, they can click it directly at the source.

Don't forget to show approval for comments left on your posts, or posts and comments left by other people. Use the +1 button to show others you appreciate their comments. Unfortunately, +1s no longer show up in Google search.

Introducing Google Hangouts

Google+ allows users to take their interaction to a more visual level with Hangouts. Hangouts are video chats involving two or more people. They're easy to set up and maintain, and you can record them to share on your website or a video sharing site. All you need is a webcam, a working internal or external microphone, headphones or ear buds to minimize background noise, and you're ready to go!

In the following sections, we tell you what Google+ Hangouts are, why they're cool, and how to use them.

Why Hangout?

The benefits of Google+ Hangouts abound. Here are some things you can use Hangouts for:

✦ **Put a face to the brand.** Hangouts add a human element and personal touch to the brand name. This adds trust between you and the people who are your costumers or part of your community.

✦ **Receive feedback.** Hosting Hangouts to find out what people think of your brand is a terrific way to discover the wants and needs of your customers.

✦ **Interview guests.** Bring in experts to help your community learn, grow, and further benefit from interaction with your brand.

✦ **Give how-to presentations.** Use Hangouts to teach everyone how to use your product or service to its maximum potential.

✦ **Create focus groups.** Send active members of your community product samples, and gather the members later to collect their thoughts.

✦ **Have a book or movie discussion.** Not everything has to be business related. Use Google+ for discussion groups that have nothing to do with your brand. Off-topic Hangouts once in a while are not only acceptable, they're fun!

✦ **Answer questions from your community.** Host a town hall and invite your community to ask questions.

✦ **Share documents and slides.** Hangouts enable you to share more than your smiling face. Use them to host full-fledged presentations.

✦ **Share your screen with others.** Use live examples to illustrate a point by sharing your screen.

✦ **Show rather than tell.** Video allows you to add a new dimension to your content. When you offer video, people can see the expression on your face, hear the passion in your voice, and see exactly how to do whatever it is that you're sharing.

✦ **Talk live with people around the world.** Hangouts allow you to reach an international audience in a cost-effective manner. Hangouts on Air, in particular, allow you to reach a bigger audience than Google's Video Hangouts, Group Video Chat on Skype, or Apple's Facetime.

✦ **Hangout publicly or with only a few people.** Open your Hangouts to everyone or invite only a few people for a staff or client meeting.

Video Hangouts versus Hangouts On Air

Hangouts come in the following two flavors:

✦ **Video Hangouts:** Video Hangouts allow for up to ten participants at a time, including the host. Anyone who doesn't make it in has to wait until someone leaves in order to view the Hangout. Video Hangouts are now integrated with Google Voice. The feature, which comes built into all Android devices with GooglePlay, can be considered an alternative to group video chats on Skype or Apple's Facetime. Hangouts are available to apps users, even if they don't have a Google+ account.

✦ **Hangouts On Air:** This variety of Hangout allows ten people at a time to participate actively in a video chat, but an unlimited number of people can watch the action in broadcast mode and participate via chat as they would in a webinar.

Hangouts On Air are recorded to YouTube so that you can share the video with anyone who couldn't make it to the live event. The YouTube presence gives you the opportunity to share this content with people for years to come. If you don't already have an account with YouTube, you're prompted to set one up before starting your Hangout On Air.

Public hangouts are considered Listed events. They are widely publicized on Google+ and searchable on Google+ or YouTube. Non-public events, called Unlisted events, are found only by people whom you have invited or to whom you have sent the link to watch the video.

Many people who host Video Hangouts and Hangouts On Air choose the Extended Circles option as an alternative to Public distribution. Sometimes disruptive people come out of the woodwork and interrupt a public Hangout or act rude.

If you're unfamiliar with Hangouts, sit in on a few first. See how they work and how others participate, and then you can decide whether it's something you'd like to try with your community.

To watch a live public Video Hangout or Hangout On Air, visit `https://plus.google.com/hangouts/active` and click the tab for either Hangouts on Air or Video Hangouts.

Which type of Hangout you select is based on your projected audience size and the business purpose of your event. You can make either option as public or private as you like. Both allow you to share documents and screenshots.

Video Hangouts work well for client conferences, team meetings, and small group training sessions that you don't need — or want — to archive. Because of their nature, most Video Hangouts are not publicly distributed.

Hangouts On Air are perfect for large group discussions, lectures, presentations with Q&A sessions, training sessions, sales meetings, or product demonstrations. Because many companies use Hangouts on Air to generate leads or demonstrate the company's expertise, they designate their Hangouts as Public and widely publicize the recorded sessions on YouTube.

It makes sense to restrict Hangouts on Air to Circles or other members of your community only if you need to include more than ten participants for an essentially private event, or if you have already identified a large target audience for your Hangout.

While you have the option to schedule a Video Hangout, you can host one whenever the urge hits. Unscheduled Video Hangouts are useful for training clients or for holding an ad hoc meeting with team members, for example. In contrast, most people schedule Hangouts on Air in advance to allow time to promote the event to a larger audience and to provide notice for attendees to add the event to their schedules.

Setting Up Google+ Hangouts

It doesn't take much hardware to set up Hangouts. In addition to your computer, all you need are these three things:

✦ An external webcam, if one isn't already built into your laptop or monitor

✦ A working internal or external microphone

✦ Headphones or ear buds to minimize background noise

The computer setup is a bit more involved. Here's your checklist:

1. **Set up your Google My Business account.**

2. **If you don't already have one, create a YouTube channel through Google My Business.**

Your Hangouts On Air will be recorded and saved automatically to your YouTube channel.

3. **If it isn't already connected, connect your Google+ profile or page to your YouTube channel.**

Google connects new YouTube channels automatically to Google+. If your existing channel isn't connected to Google+, connect it now to a Google+ profile or a Google+ page. For more information about doing this, visit: `https://support.google.com/plus/answer/3470295?hl=en`.

4. **Set up your computer or mobile device.**

Here are some common setups:

• *Gmail:* Turn on Hangouts in Gmail. It's automatically turned on in Google+, so don't worry about that.

• *Chrome browser extension:* Download a Hangouts Chrome extension from `http://bit.ly/chromehangoutextension`. You must have the Chrome browser or Chrome OS device. Windows 8 Metro Mode is not supported.

• *Chrome desktop app:* Download the Hangouts Chrome desktop app from `www.google.com/hangouts`. The app is supported on Windows and Chrome OS, but not on Mac or Linux.

• *Mobile device:* On an iOS or Android device, download the Hangouts app. Also, download the Hangouts Dialer to turn on optional call capability.

Once you've got those basics in place, follow the directions in the following sections to create a Video Hangout or a Hangout On Air.

Creating a Google+ Video Hangout

Before you host a Video Hangout, determine whom you want to invite. It's appropriate to invite specific individuals or members of a small group, such as your client's staff or your sales team. A narrowly targeted audience will help keep your video chat focused on the business task at hand.

Follow these steps to set up your own Google+ Video Hangout:

1. **Log in to your Google+ page. From the drop-down menu below the My Business tab, click on Hangouts.**

2. **On the Hangouts Overview page that appears, click the Video Hangouts tab at the right of the top navigation (see Figure 2-13).**

3. **On the page that appears, click on the button labeled Start a Video Hangout (see Figure 2-14).**

   The Video Hangout pop-up window appears, displaying fields for you to fill out, as shown in Figure 2-15. Remember to click the Allow button at the top of the screen to permit the use of your camera.

Figure 2-13: Choose between Video Hangouts and Hangouts on Air on the Hangouts Overview page.

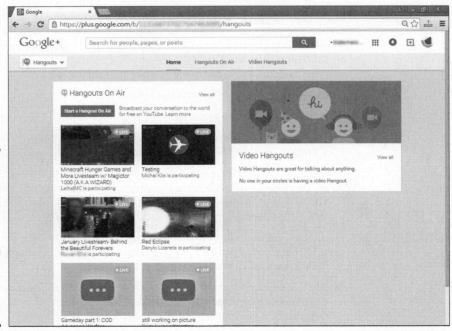

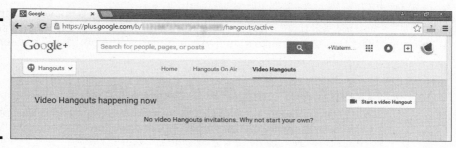

Figure 2-14: Click the Start a Video Hangout button to begin.

Link to share

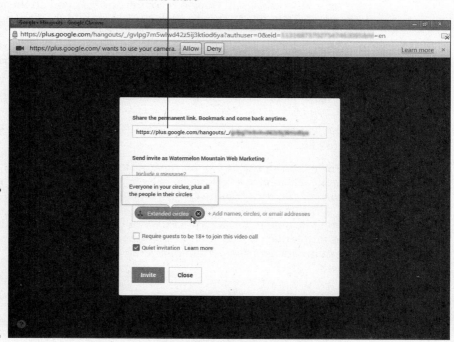

Figure 2-15: Fill out the Video Hangout pop-up window and designate your audience.

4. **Click the Invite button.**

   Your Video Hangout starts immediately.

Before opening a Hangout to the people in your Circles, do a few trial runs by yourself or with a trusted friend or team member. Make sure you know how to handle the basics before going live.

As soon as others show up, you can start talking. Whoever is currently talking will have a larger image on display, one that's front and center. The rest of the participants are arranged at the bottom of the screen with a thumbnail-size image.

Creating a Google+ Hangout On Air

With Hangouts On Air, you can broadcast live discussions and performances to the world through your Google+ page and YouTube channel. You can also edit and share a copy of the broadcast after it's over.

In preparation, follow the same steps listed in the preceding section to prepare for a Video Hangout. Google recommends that you do the following for a Hangout On Air, in addition to what's listed for a Video Hangout:

✦ Make sure your browser, operating system, processor, and bandwidth meet the system requirements at `https://support.google.com/hangouts/answer/1216376`.

✦ Download and install the latest version of the Hangouts plug-in from `https://tools.google.com/dlpage/hangoutplugin`.

✦ Check that your webcam drivers are up to date and that your webcam is working.

✦ Connect headphones to your device. Headphones with a built-in microphone will improve your video-call experience since you don't need to worry if you turn your head away from the mic.

You won't be able to broadcast a Hangout On Air if your YouTube channel has any active copyright strikes or global blocks on videos, or if you're trying to broadcast from certain restricted countries.

Now you're ready for action. To create a Google Hangout On Air, follow these steps:

1. **Log in to your Google+ page. From the drop-down below the My Business tab, click on Hangouts.**

2. **On the Hangouts Overview page that appears, click the Home tab in the top navigation. Then click the blue Start a Hangout On Air button at the top of the left panel.**

3. **In the Hangout On Air pop-up window that appears, enter a name and description in the appropriate text boxes, as shown in Figure 2-16.**

   Both items deserve careful thought. Try to brainstorm a name that will create some buzz. Include benefits in the description to encourage people to attend and tell their friends. Definitely include a few good keywords in your title and description.

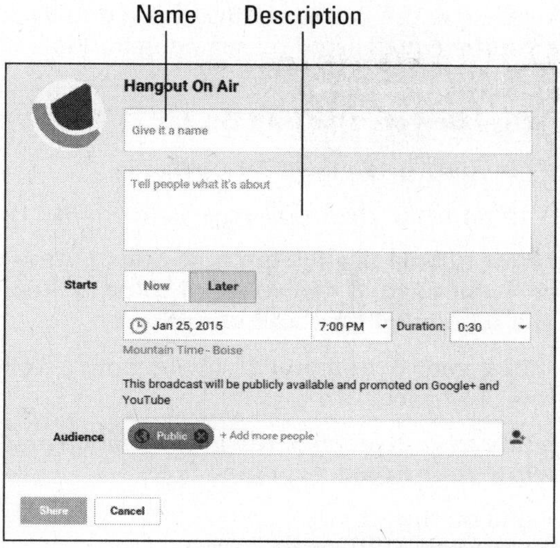

Name   Description

Figure 2-16:
Setting up
your Google
Hangout On
Air.

*Reproduced with permission of Watermelon Mountain
Web Marketing, www.watermelonweb.com*

4. **Choose a start time.**

   You have two options:

   - *Now:* Starts the Hangout On Air immediately after you create the Event page.

   - *Later:* If you select this option, fill in the date and time when you want your Hangout On Air to start. A date scheduled at least a week later makes more tactical sense for most Hangouts on Air. This gives your target audience advance notice to schedule this event on their calendars, and gives you time to promote it and encourage sign-ups.

5. **The Audience box includes Public by default. You can keep that choice if you want. Otherwise, click X to close that option. Then click in the Audience box to reveal a drop-down list of your Circles.**

   Specify your audience by choosing one or more Circles, or by entering a name in the Audience text box; repeat for everyone or every circle you want to add.

   The specified audience sees a Google+ Event page that announces the Hangout On Air. Add additional people and/or Circles to ensure that they're notified.

For maximum reach, use the Public setting. If you don't want broad publicity, make your event Unlisted by selecting multiple Circles and/or individuals.

6. **Click Share to schedule your Hangout On Air.**

   The Event page for your Hangout On Air opens.

   The easiest way to return to the Event page is to choose Home ⇨ Events.

7. **If you selected Now in Step 5, click the blue Start button on your Hangout On Air Event page. If you selected Later in Step 5, visit the Event page at the scheduled time and click Start.**

   After you click Start, you're prompted to invite more people and to agree to Google's Terms of Service.

8. **When you're ready to go live, click the green Start Broadcast button that appears below your broadcast video feed.**

   Now you're live and on the air.

After you finish your Hangout On Air, it's posted immediately to both your YouTube channel and your Google+ page. From your home page, you'll see directions to edit the video if you want. The edited version replaces the original in both locations and becomes the recording that others view.

Share the link to your recording liberally to keep the conversation going. For more tips, visit www.socialmediaexaminer.com/google-hangout-on-air-tips.

If your audience isn't Google+ savvy, you can embed your Hangout on Air recording on your website using the code you obtain from your YouTube channel. That way, your viewers won't have to go to Google+ or even YouTube. They can join you right from your familiar website.

For more information on Google+ Hangouts and other aspects of Google+, see *Google+ Marketing For Dummies* by Jesse Stay.

Hyping a Google+ Hangout-On-Air Event

Brand your event! To change the generic header that Google provides for a Hangout on Air, go to your Hangout's Event page and click Edit Event. Edit your theme to match your branding by clicking Change Theme. Upload your brand image or logo and then click Save to return to the Event page.

For the best results, upload a theme image that's 1200 x 300 pixels. An image that size appears full-sized on the Event page but shows up as a thumbnail in the general Google+ stream.

Use the event page URL to announce your Hangout On Air to all your other social media pages and profiles, as well as in your email newsletter. For mobile users, you might want to promote the YouTube page URL because YouTube resizes automatically for a mobile display.

If your creative juices are really flowing, you can promote your Hangout with a short, enticing video trailer. Shoot a one- to two-minute promotional video and host the trailer on your YouTube channel.

Add the trailer by clicking the Trailer button on your Event page. Then select your trailer from the list of videos on your YouTube channels. When you start your Hangout On Air, Google automatically switches from the trailer to the live stream of your event. Cool, huh?

You can also embed the same trailer on your website, and Google performs the same trailer-to-stream magic trick. The embed code for the trailer appears in the Details box of your Hangout On Air's Event page.

Running Your Hangout

You're in control of your Hangout, so it's up to you to take the lead. In essence, as the host, you're a moderator for a discussion, and you're also there to pose topics and ensure that there's no dead space or long pauses in the conversation.

Engaging with others

Here are some tips and best practices for hosting Google+ Hangouts:

✦ **Talk first.** As people file in to the Hangout, say, "Hello" and make small talk. When you feel it's time to begin, start. Don't wait for someone else to get the ball rolling if it's your Hangout.

✦ **Ask participants to introduce themselves.** When it's time to get started, encourage participants to introduce themselves. They'll participate more often if they also see it as a marketing opportunity.

✦ **Use the Mute button (shown in Figure 2-17) to silence background noise.** Sometimes you might hear unintentional background noise coming from someone's mic — for example, planes, trains, kids playing, and road noise. You can mute the participants with particularly noisy backgrounds while still enjoying the chat — simply click the Mute button that appears below that person's name.

✦ **Use the Block button (shown in Figure 2-17) if someone is causing a disturbance.** Sometimes people forget their etiquette and play music or talk to others while a Hangout is going on. If you have attendees who are creating a negative experience for everyone, use the Block button to delete the offending party from your view. Just click the gear icon in the top navigation first, and then select the Block User option from the dropdown that appears.

✦ **Although it's your Hangout, don't dominate the entire discussion.** Make sure everyone gets to participate so that all points of view are represented.

Click Settings to access the Block button.

Google Drive

Mute

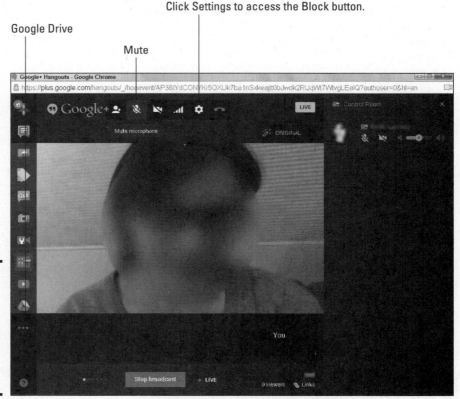

Figure 2-17: The dashboard, that you see while streaming a Hangout On Air.

✦ **Be prepared.** Before the Hangout, write out a list of what you plan to talk about so that you don't lose track of the day's topic. Make a list of questions and comments geared toward provoking discussion.

✦ **Offer perks.** Surprise participants with coupon codes for discounts or free stuff. If word gets around that you offer perks or swag to the people who participate in your Hangouts, you'll attract more participants, and more people will add you to their Circles.

✦ **Minimize noise.** Using a headset or ear buds can help to control background noise, feedback, and echoing.

Don't try to wing it in a public Hangout on Air. Because you're using this for business purposes, it's not the same as holding a small Video Hangout with friends or family. Although it's okay to be off-the-cuff and ad-lib, it's best to plan in advance. Don't choose topics you know nothing about or think you can fill an hour-long Hangout on Air without printing out a list of talking points. You can't rely on others to fill the void.

Sharing documents, photos, and your screen

To share a document that you have stored on your Google Drive account, click the Google Drive icon (the triangle at the bottom of the left navigation of your streaming Hangout on Air; refer to Figure 2-17). Select the document you want to share from the pop-up window that appears. From that pop-up window, you also have the option to upload a new document or image to Google Drive, and then share it in your Hangout.

You can also share what's on your screen at the moment with your Hangout attendees: a slide deck for a presentation, a website, or an online video, for example. In the Hangout window, click the Screenshare icon in the left navigation (refer to Figure 2-17). In the pop-up window that opens, select the screen you want to share (for example, your desktop, an open window on the Internet, or a Google Doc). When you click the Share Selected Window button, your selection opens in a new window. When you finish, close the window of your shared screen to return to your Hangout screen.

Your Hangout attendees will see everything on your screen in real-time, so make sure you have closed any sensitive information or Internet windows!

The merry-go-round of changes in Google+ are enough to make your head spin! Among the recent ones giving marketers the greatest concern are Google's decision to remove authorship and Circle counts from its own search engine results, and making Google Hangouts available as an app, even to users who don't have a Google+ account. It's possible that Google will make the same conversion with its Google+ photo service, too. The best thing for you to do is watch sources like www.marketingprofs.com and www.mashable.com for the latest news.

Chapter 3: Maximizing Stratified Social Communities

In This Chapter

✔ Valuing stratified social communities

✔ Making business connections online

✔ Searching for networks by industry, demographics, and activity type

✔ Examining geolocation services for Foursquare, Twitter, and Facebook

✔ Organizing meet-ups and tweet-ups

✔ Starting a social coupon campaign

Social networking communities, like other marketing outlets, can be sliced and diced many ways. They can be sorted vertically by industry or horizontally by demographics, such as age, gender, ethnicity, education, or income. By doing a little research, you can *stratify* (classify) them according to other commonly used marketing segmentation parameters, such as life stage (student, young married, family with kids, empty nester, retired) or *psychographics* (beliefs or behaviors).

If you want to delve even further into niche sites, you can find social media channels that are driven by type of activity, geographical location, or by types of social offers. In this chapter, we discuss how you can find these smaller, niche sites and then how you can get value from them.

Making a Bigger Splash on a Smaller Site

Stratified sites may have much smaller audiences than sites such as Pinterest or Twitter. However, if you choose correctly, the users of these sites will closely resemble the profile of your typical client or customer, making them better prospects. Compare it to the difference between advertising at the Super Bowl versus distributing a flyer at a local high school football game. It all depends on where your audience is.

Your business can also make a much bigger splash on smaller sites. Frankly, it's so difficult to gain visibility and traction on a large social networking site that you almost need a marketing campaign just for that purpose (for instance, to acquire 2,000 Likes on Facebook).

On a smaller site, your business becomes a big fish in a small pond, quickly establishing itself as an expert resource or a source of great products or services.

The August 2014 CMO survey conducted by Duke University's Fuqua School of Business found that businesses already spend 9 percent of their marketing budgets on social media marketing, with that figure predicted to grow to 13 percent in the next 12 months and to 21 percent in the next five years. To maintain your market share, you need to decide how you will communicate just as effectively across numerous platforms. Fortunately, all it takes is time.

Taking Networking to the Next Level

From your own experience, you know the importance of offline networking to find vendors, employees, and customers. From tip networks to trade associations, networking is a mantra for business owners. Social media marketing is, first and foremost, a method of networking online.

Business connection sites have proliferated in the past several years. These sites are generally appropriate for soft selling, not for hard-core marketing. Although referrals are used primarily for making business-to-business (B2B) connections, especially when targeting those with a specific job title, you never know when a referral will bring you a customer.

Make a habit of including a link to your primary website on every profile, and using some of your preferred search terms within your profile title and text. These techniques increase your inbound links and may help with search engine ranking, as described in Book II, Chapter 2.

Table 3-1 lists cross-industry directories. Visit the ones that seem appropriate, using the tactics described in Chapter 1 of this minibook to make your selections.

Be selective. Participating in multiple sites productively is time-consuming. Keep clear records of all sites that have your business profile. If your situation changes, you probably have to update your profiles individually.

Table 3-1	Business Networks	
Website	*URL*	*What It Is*
Biznik	`http://biznik.com`	Community of entrepreneurs and small businesses
Chief Financial Officer Network	`www.linkedin.com/groups?gid=51826`	Network of high-level CFOs, financial executives, and accounting leaders (requires LinkedIn account)
Data.com Connect	`https://connect.data.com`	Community of B2B professionals
Doostang	`www.doostang.com`	Career community for professionals seeking new jobs
EFactor	`www.efactor.com`	Global network and virtual marketplace for entrepreneurs and investors
MeetTheBoss TV	`www.meettheboss.tv`	Video network and roundtables for high-level business leaders
Naymz	`www.naymz.com`	Networking platform for professionals that has tools to measure and manage your reputation
PartnerUp	`https://plus.google.com/communities/105088976956808519330`	Google+ community for small-business owners
PROskore	`www.proskore.com`	An online business network that measures professional reputation

(continued)

Table 3-1 *(continued)*

Website	URL	What It Is
Spoke	www.spoke.com	Company and business-professional informational database
StartupNation	www.startupnation.com	Entrepreneurial business advice and networking
Talkbiznow	www.talkbiznow.com	Business services and collaboration network
TheFunded.com	http://thefunded.com	Community of entrepreneurs who rate and compare investors and funding sources
Women About Biz	www.womenaboutbiz.com	Online resource center for women entrepreneurs
XING	www.xing.com	Global networking for professionals
Yammer	www.yammer.com	Free networking tool for networking within a company

Figure 3-1 shows a networking profile for PatentPlaques.com, a company that makes patent award and recognition products on Spoke. In this case, the company takes advantage of a professional networking audience to showcase its products at www.spoke.com/companies/patentplaques-com-3e122f809e597c1003388881. This Spoke page offers a full profile, which links to PatentPlaques.com's website, and it's loaded with keywords.

You can syndicate content postings (see Book II, Chapter 1), but you usually can't syndicate profile entries.

You may want to submit your profile to several likely sites on a one-time basis, but commit to only several in terms of community participation. Otherwise, you may go into overload!

Figure 3-1:
Patent-
Plaques.
com uses
the business
directory
on Spoke
to promote
its patent
recognition
and award
products.

Selecting Social Networks by Vertical Industry Sector

Whether you're marketing B2B (business-to-business) or B2C (business-to-consumer), you can find dozens of industry- or interest-specific social networks. Search online for communities in your industry, using the strategies described in Chapter 1 in this minibook. As long as the social network is large enough to support your time investment and continues to attract new users, you should enjoy enough of payback to make your effort worthwhile.

Vertical industry sites, other than shopping, are particularly appealing for B2B marketers. If you use some adroit maneuvering, you can intersect with the sales cycle, reaching the appropriate decision-maker with the right message.

For the retail community, the growth of social shopping sites is a new avenue to reach consumers who want to spend after they see what everyone else is buying. Users flock to these sites for the latest product reviews, real-time deals, and news about the hottest items.

Track results so that you can decide which sites work best for you. If a site doesn't produce leads or sales after a few months, find another.

**Book VIII
Chapter 3**

**Maximizing
Stratified Social
Communities**

If you want to promote your products or services to more than one online community, customize your profiles and messages accordingly. For instance, a sporting goods store might promote camping gear on a social network for backpackers and running gear on one for joggers.

The list of vertical market social networks seems endless and ever changing. You'll find more at `http://blog.hubspot.com/blog/tabid/6307/bid/33663/7-Targeted-Social-Networks-Niche-Marketers-Should-Try.aspx`. Table 3-2 provides a sample of some of these networks just to give you an idea of the range. This list does not include blogs, bookmarking sites, or news aggregators.

Table 3-2	Vertical Market Social Networks	
Website	*URL*	*Description*
Art		
ArtSlant	`www.artslant.com`	Contemporary art network with profiles for artists, art professionals, art organizations, and art lovers
deviantART	`www.deviantart.com`	Post and share original artwork
Imagekind	`www.imagekind.com`	CafePress-owned community for buying, selling, and creating art
Independent Collectors	`www.independent-collectors.com`	Global network for contemporary art collectors
Auto		
CarGurus	`www.cargurus.com`	Automobile community with reviews, photos, and opinions
Motortopia	`www.motortopia.com`	Community for lovers of cars, motorbikes, planes, and boats
Books		
Goodreads	`www.goodreads.com`	Book recommendations to share
LibraryThing	`www.librarything.com`	Book recommendations and online catalog

Website	URL	Description
Design		
Design Float	www.designfloat.com	Web design-related content sharing, advertising, digital art, and branding
Environment		
Care 2	www.care2.com	Eco-friendly lifestyle site
Make Me Sustainable	www.makemesustainable.com	Environmental community
TreeHugger	www.treehugger.com	Environmental topics at interactive community
Entertainment, Film, and Music		
CreateSpace	www.createspace.com	Creation, collaboration, and distribution for writers, musicians, and filmmakers
Fanpop	www.fanpop.com	Network of fan clubs for television, movies, music, and more
Flixster	www.flixster.com	Movie lovers community
Last.fm	www.last.fm	Music community
Mediabistro	www.mediabistro.com	Careers and community for media professionals
Myspace	www.myspace.com	Social networking site for music entertainment
Pandora	www.pandora.com	Music community
Spotify	www.spotify.com	Music community
Medical		
PatientsLikeMe	www.patientslikeme.com	Patients, healthcare professionals, and industry organizations making connections
Sermo	www.sermo.com	Physician community
Legal		
lawyrs.net	www.lawyrs.net	International social networking community for lawyers and law students

(Continued)

Table 3-2 *(continued)*

Website	URL	Description
Philanthropy and Nonprofits		
Care2	www.care2.com	Online community for people passionate about making a difference
ChangingThePresent	www.changingthepresent.org	Nonprofit giving community
Pets		
Critterlink	http://critterlink.net	Social networking for all animals everywhere
Uniteddogs	www.uniteddogs.com	Social networking for dogs and their owners
WellPaw	www.wellpaw.com	Social pet community
Shopping, Fashion, and Collecting		
Curiobot	www.curiobot.net	Collection of the most interesting items for sale on the Internet
Gilt	www.gilt.com	Flash sales on women's apparel
Kaboodle	www.kaboodle.com	Product discovery, recommendations, and sharing
Polyvore	www.polyvore.com	Product mixing and matching from any online store
Rue La La	www.ruelala.com	Flash sales
Stylehive	www.stylehive.com	Stylish people connecting
ThisNext	www.thisnext.com	Product discovery, recommendations, and sharing
UsTrendy	www.ustrendy.com	Discover and shop indie fashion
Wanelo	www.wanelo.com	Discover and bookmark products
Sports		
Athlinks	www.athlinks.com	Database with all types of sports race results and athlete community

Website	URL	Description
Sports		
BeRecruited	`https://new.berecruited.com`	Connecting high school athletes and college coaches
Science and Technology		
ResearchGate	`www.researchgate.net`	Social network for scientists to connect and make their work more visible
ScienceStage.com	`http://sciencestage.com`	Hub for research scientists

As always, include a link to your primary website and use some of your preferred search terms within your postings and profiles. If these sites have blogs or accept photos, video, or music, you can syndicate that type of content to many sites simultaneously.

Selecting Social Networks by Demographics

No one ever has enough staff and time to do everything. You already know that the more tightly you focus your marketing efforts, the better the payoff from your investment. If you created a strategic plan in Book I, Chapter 1, return to it to analyze and segment your markets demographically into smaller, niche markets that you can reach with a coordinated campaign.

Think online guerrilla marketing. Go after one niche market online at a time. After you conquer one, go after the next. If you scatter your efforts across too many target markets at one time, your business won't have enough visibility in any of them to drive meaningful traffic your way.

Table 3-3 describes some sites that are primarily demographically and geographically stratified. You can find many, many more. As usual, qualify the sites for your business by following the concepts described in Chapter 1 of this minibook.

As usual, customize your message and profile for the audience you're trying to reach. Be sure to include a link to your primary website and some of your key search terms in any profile or posting.

Figure 3-2 shows how businesses can take advantage of demographically targeted sites. The advertisement to work from home that appears at the top of a page on MommySavers clearly targets stay-at-home moms.

Table 3-3   Demographically and Geographically Stratified Sites

Website	URL	Description
Ethnic		
Black Business Women Online	`www.mybbwo.com`	A social network for black women in business, women entrepreneurs, and bloggers
BlackPlanet.com	`www.black planet.com`	African American network that includes a job section by way of Monster.com
MiGente.com	`www.migente.com`	Largest Latin American community; includes a job section by way of Monster.com
High School and College		
Classmates	`www.classmates. com`	Networking with members of your graduating class at all levels
MeetMe	`www.meetme.com`	Networking site for high school and college students and grads
Generational		
20 Something Bloggers	`www.20sb.net`	Community for 20-somethings
Club Penguin	`www.club penguin.com`	Disney site for children under 12
More	`www.more.com`	Community for women over 40
ThirdAge	`www.thirdage. com`	Community for Baby Boomer women
Local		
Citysearch	`www.citysearch. com`	Localized directory with reviews and comments
Kudzu	`www.kudzu.com`	Local business directory with reviews and daily deals
Local.com	`www.local.com`	Local business directory with deals, events, and activities listings

Website	URL	Description
Manta	www.manta.com	Local business directory for small businesses
MerchantCircle	www.merchantcircle.com	Find, review, and comment on local businesses
Nextdoor	https://nextdoor.com	Private social network for neighborhoods
tribe	www.tribe.net	Local-resident connections for advice and sharing about local resources
TripAdvisor	www.tripadvisor.com	Reviews of flights, hotels, vacation rentals, restaurants, and things to do
Urbanspoon	www.urbanspoon.com	Restaurant listings and reviews from critics, food bloggers, and friends
Yelp	www.yelp.com	Local business reviews and comments
Yext	www.yext.com/products/social	Power-listings for business profiles across multiple websites, all from one website
International		
Badoo	http://badoo.com	Popular international social networking and dating site
Nexopia	www.nexopia.com	Canada's largest social networking site for young people
Sonico	www.sonico.com	Latin American social networking site
Zorpia	http://en.zorpia.com	International friendship network
Moms		
CafeMom	www.cafemom.com	Largest social networking, blogging, and community site for moms and parenting

(Continued)

Table 3-3 *(continued)*

Website	*URL*	*Description*
MommySavers	`www.mommy savers.com`	Money-saving community and tips for moms
LifetimeMoms	`www.lifetime moms.com`	Parenting resource for moms
Seniors		
Grandparents.com	`http:// community.grand parents.com`	Social networking and news site for grandparents
Wealthy		
ASMALLWORLD	`www.asmall world.com`	Private international community of culturally influential people

Ad

Figure 3-2: Mommy-Savers is an example of a demographically targeted social network.

Selecting Social Networks by Activity Type

We can imagine what you're thinking. Why in the world would you want more than one service of a particular type, such as video sharing or blogging? The answer is simple: to improve search engine rankings and inbound links from high-ranking sites. When your content appears on multiple sites, such as those listed by activity in Table 3-4, you're simply casting a wider net and hoping to catch more fish.

Table 3-4	Social Networks by Activity Type	
Website	*URL*	*Description*
Networking and Profiles		
FriendFeed	http://friendfeed.com	Create personal networks to share with friends, family, and co-workers
hi5	www.hi5.com	Social entertainment for the youth market over 18 worldwide with personal profiles
MocoSpace	www.mocospace.com	Cellphone-compatible online community
Image Sharing		
Flickr	www.flickr.com	Well-known photo-sharing site
Gentlemint	http://gentlemint.com	A site "to find and share manly things"; similar to Pinterest but with a male demographic
HoverSpot	http://hoverspot.com	Free social network with good photo-sharing capabilities
Instagram	http://instagram.com	An image-sharing and photo-manipulation site, especially for images taken on smartphones
Photobucket	http://photobucket.com	Free image hosting, and photo and video sharing
Picasa	http://picasa.google.com	Google's photo-sharing site
Pinterest	www.pinterest.com	Visual bookmarking site

(Continued)

Table 3-4 *(continued)*

Website	*URL*	*Description*
SlideShare	www.slideshare.net	Presentation sharing site
TasteSpotting	www.tastespotting.com	Food and recipe image-sharing site; a visual potluck
Video Sharing (YouTube Alternatives)		
Dailymotion	www.dailymotion.com	Video-hosting and -sharing community
Jing	www.techsmith.com/jing.html	Video-hosting and -sharing tool
Livestream	http://new.livestream.com	Platform for live, interactive broadcast video
Ustream	www.ustream.tv	Platform for live, interactive broadcast video
Vimeo	http://vimeo.com	Video-hosting and -sharing community
Vine	https://vine.co	Six-second looping video platform
Unique Services		
eHow	www.ehow.com	Content submissions on how to do things
HubPages	http://hubpages.com	Publish content on thousands of topics on which you happen to be an expert
Mahalo	www.mahalo.com	Content submissions on how to do things
Meetup	www.meetup.com	Local-group organizing for face-to-face meetings
Ning	www.ning.com	Build your own multifaceted community
Plurk	www.plurk.com	A Twitter-like alternative for events
Quora	www.quora.com	Group-sourced answers to questions

TIP

The secret to keeping this situation manageable is syndication, via a dashboard like Hootsuite or Netvibes, or by using really simple syndication (RSS), as discussed in Book II, Chapter 1. You post an image, a video, or a blog entry to your primary site, and your distribution service automatically updates other services with the same content.

Even with syndication, use some common sense. It doesn't help to drive the wrong fish to your website and dilute your conversion rate. Of course, if you've monetized your site by showing ads by the impressions, then the more eyeballs, the merrier.

Because setting up multiple accounts can be time-consuming, you may want to stagger the process. Of course, by now, you automatically include in any profile or posting a link to your primary website and some of your key search terms.

For example, The Karen Martin Group (www.ksmartin.com) takes advantage of SlideShare (see Figure 3-3) to establish credibility and provide evidence of its expertise. By viewing any of her 79 presentations or 60 videos, prospective clients can get a very good sense of the skills and services her company provides. The company profile on the left links to her website and displays a number of relevant tags (keywords) for search.

Figure 3-3:
The Karen Martin Group uses SlideShare to establish credibility, experience, and expertise.

Book VIII
Chapter 3

Maximizing Stratified Social Communities

Yelping to the Melting

Daily Melt (see the nearby figure) was officially born in 2011 when the company's two principals, Gregg and Kevin Lurie, saw a kiosk in Boston serving only grilled cheese sandwiches. Upon returning to Miami, the Luries began assembling a team to create a chain of quick-serve restaurants based on a grilled-cheese menu. Currently, Daily Melt has three locations with ten employees each.

Reproduced with permission of Jean De Boyrie

According to Jean De Boyrie, Director of Marketing, social media profiles were developed at the beginning for Facebook, Twitter, and Yelp. "We wanted to create a conversational online presence that would reflect the style of our food: comfortable, hip, no frills. For each individual store, we target specific segments," explains De Boyrie. "Some [segments] are college students, others are office employees from nearby businesses. Facebook is such a powerful tool that we focus most of our efforts on that network. Twitter and Instagram are mostly used for the hashtags and communicating with customers."

Daily Melt now tries to schedule two to three posts per day on Facebook and one to two posts per day on Twitter, but they've found that social media works well with spur-of-the-moment posts, as well. "What we are trying to do now is move the conversation from a hard sell every single time to speaking a bit more of who we are as a company and our culture," says De Boyrie.

In an original approach, the company partnered with Yelp to have a Yelper party that created a great buzz about the new restaurant. As De Boyrie describes it, the Yelp event was a way for Daily Melt to reach out to the increasingly involved food community in South Florida. With the event open only to Elite members of Yelp, Daily Melt used the party to introduce them to the restaurant concept. "We are actually planning another one very soon for our new location. We saw a great increase in positive reviews and organic searches to our locations on Yelp."

Reproduced with permission of Jean De Boyrie

Of course, Daily Melt posts their social media handles on everything from flyers to business cards to its main website. Even at events, Daily Melt encourages people to post on its social media.

The one common obstacle that De Boyrie faces with his social media campaigns is the difficulty of tracking ad spending and ROI. For data, they rely on Google Analytics, Facebook Insights, store

(continued)

**Book VIII
Chapter 3**

**Maximizing
Stratified Social
Communities**

(continued)

analytics, and general reporting. "Sometimes it works and sometimes it doesn't, but we are now able to work past that [issue] with better targeted campaigns with specific strategies associated with each," he says.

Daily Melt's web presence:

www.dailymelt.com

www.facebook.com/dailymelt

https://twitter.com/followdailymelt

www.yelp.com/biz/daily-melt-miami

http://instagram.com/dailymelt

Finding Yourself in the Real World with Geomarketing

Location, location, location: It's the mantra of real estate and yet another feature of successful social media marketing. The convergence of mobile devices (smartphones and tablets) with GPS and social media offers a great opportunity for marketers. You can inform potential customers that you offer exactly what they're looking for, when they're looking for it, and provide directions to get them there from their current location.

In this book, we use the term *geomarketing tools* to refer to social media services that incorporate knowledge of users' locations or that bring people together in a specific, real-world space.

Several location-based services, including *social mapping* (identifying where people are) and location-based marketing games, are available for geomarketing, though the number of independent vendors has diminished in favor of check-in and location-tagging options on Facebook, Twitter, and Google+.

Before you undertake geomarketing, follow the directions for local optimization in Book II, Chapter 2 to improve your success rate.

Going geo for good reason

The techniques we describe in this section apply to businesses that exist in the physical world with their own storefront, or that offer events that bring people together face-to-face. Pure cyber-businesses may not find these ideas as useful, but you never know what creative idea will hit you. Although geolocation services are particularly appropriate for business-to-consumer

(B2C) operations, we also offer some intriguing business-to-business (B2B) applications in this chapter.

For most businesses, geomarketing involves a teaser deal that attracts residents or out-of-town visitors who "check in" online or with a mobile device when they arrive at the establishment. This concept is particularly attractive for events, tourist sites, restaurants, and entertainment venues. Almost all these services notify their subscribers by email or text message, or on their mobile apps, whenever an offer is available nearby.

According to the Pew Center on the Internet and American Life, the number of smartphone owners who used check-in location services dropped modestly from 18 percent in 2012 to 12 percent in 2013. Of those, 39 percent used Facebook, 18 percent used Foursquare, and 14 percent used Google+.

Although the number of geomarketing vendors may be down, a recent analysis by MDG Advertising claims that 72 percent of consumers would respond to calls to action received when they are within sight of a retailer. Alas, less than 25 percent of retailers take advantage of this opportunity.

Deciding whether geomarketing is right for you

Geomarketing isn't for every business. Whether you should use a geomarketing service depends on the nature of your business, whether your customer base already is using it, and which location-based activities consume your prospective customers' time. Mull over these factors before you take the leap:

✦ **Don't reinvent the wheel.** Many cellphone apps already offer a location-specific tool — for example, a weather report, road conditions, a list of gas prices at stations around town — and then add a sponsor. If all you're trying to do is reach the on-the-go consumer who is ready to buy, do you need more than that? Maybe a pay per click (PPC) ad on a mobile search engine solves your needs.

✦ **Numbers matter.** Enough people living near or planning to visit your location have to use a particular geomarketing application to make it worth the effort. This issue is nontrivial because most services don't publicize this data. Try to research the number of users in your area with both the service provider and a third-party source, such as Alexa. The numbers can fluctuate widely and are difficult to find.

After you estimate the size of the potential audience (the *reach*), remember that only a small percentage of the audience is likely to become customers. Your best bet: Ask existing customers whether they use Foursquare, Facebook check-ins, or other services.

To get an idea of the number of members, try creating a user account. Then scan the list of places in your area (sometimes called places, locations, or venues) for the inclusion of neighbors and competitors, and look at the maximum number of check-ins at those locations. For instance, even if you don't ordinarily serve Foursquare fanatics, a high-tech conference that draws a huge number of users may be a one-time opportunity worth taking advantage of.

✦ **Prospective customers must be willing to participate.** You must take privacy issues into account. Although about 30 percent of all users include location tagging on their posts (so their friends know where they are), the percentage declines with age.

✦ **Local is not always enough.** No matter the size of the total user base for your neighborhood, you may draw a large audience of Foursquare users only if you happen to own the pizza place across the street from the computer science building at the local college, not if you offer a deal to seniors at a local retirement community who show up for early-bird specials.

✦ **Demographics are fluid.** Be cautious: The demographics and statistics of users may fluctuate.

✦ **The temptation is great to "go geo."** Don't jump into geomarketing just because it's cool or trendy.

For a summary of geolocation services, see Table 3-5.

Table 3-5	Geolocation Services	
Geolocation	*Site URL for Businesses*	*Number of User Accounts & Notes*
Everplaces	`https://everplaces.com`	A mash-up of Pinterest and Foursquare
Facebook Location	`https://www.facebook.com/about/location`	More than 1.3 billion worldwide monthly active users (undetermined number who use check-in or tag location)
Findery	`https://findery.com/`	A place-sharing site and travel community
Foursquare	`http://business.foursquare.com`	50 million worldwide

Geolocation	Site URL for Businesses	Number of User Accounts & Notes
Instagram	`https://help.instagram.com/236245819849257`	200 million active users, many of whom share locations from Instagram app to Foursquare, Facebook, and Twitter; location is not automatically tagged
Twitter Geolocation	`https://support.twitter.com/articles/78525-about-the-tweetlocation-feature`	284 million monthly active users; geo-tags available on all tweets but turned off by default
Yelp	`https://biz.yelp.com/support/what_is_yelp`	139 million monthly unique visitors

Focusing on Foursquare

Because Foursquare remains the primary, independent, location-based loyalty program that offers rewards to consumers for patronizing particular retailers, the following sections focus on Foursquare's social media and advertising value.

Foursquare claims more than 55 million total users worldwide for its computer implementation and its mobile app called Swarm. Much of this traffic may be international because sources outside Foursquare indicate 4 million unique U.S. users per month in 2014. According to its own numbers, Foursquare has seen more than 6 billion check-ins to date, and nearly 2 million businesses have claimed their locations over the years.

Featuring teaser deals

For most businesses, Foursquare involves a teaser deal that attracts residents or out-of-town visitors who "check in" with a mobile device when they arrive at the establishment, as shown in Figure 3-4. This concept is particularly attractive for events, tourist sites, restaurants, and entertainment venues.

Subscribers can choose to be notified by email or through the mobile app whenever "something great" is available nearby, or when other engagement actions occur.

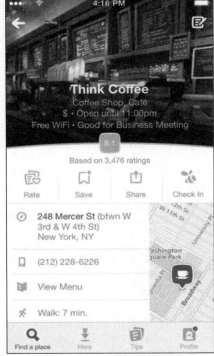

Figure 3-4:
A typical
Foursquare
check-in
page on a
smartphone.

Foursquare offers some temptations to marketers:

✦ It works on multiple smartphone, tablet, and desktop platforms, so end-user device limitations aren't a concern.

✦ The audience for Foursquare skews to younger men. Sixty percent of users are male; 42 percent are 30 to 43 years old. If your product or service fits this demographic base well, Foursquare might be up your alley.

✦ Some businesses may see only limited benefits, but the cost is also minimal. Unlike group coupons (see the following section), these offers are generally inexpensive, so merchants face no significant losses.

✦ Companies have found Foursquare useful for informing neighborhood residents about their existence, introducing new products, getting the word out about complementary products, and building repeat business.

✦ Foursquare is another way to encourage customers to post online reviews.

✦ Hospitality businesses, entertainment venues, and restaurants can create a special offer for slow times of day or off-season occupancy. This approach can turn down-times into profitable opportunities.

Claiming your Foursquare presence

Any business can easily claim its Foursquare location. It's free, and it's another inbound link, even if you don't use it. Anytime a Foursquare user checks into a claimed business, its location will be broadcast to all the user's friends on Foursquare and may be published on the user's Twitter or Facebook page as well.

Once you claim your business, you can change the header graphic on your listing, update business information, enter offers and events, and use Foursquare analytics.

To claim your business, follow these steps:

1. Go to `http://business.foursquare.com`.

2. **Enter your business name and its city, state, and country (optional) to see whether Foursquare already has a listing for it.**

   In some cases, a drop-down list of similar business names appears below the Business Name field.

3. **If your business appears in the drop-down list below Business Name, click its name. If your business is not listed, click Search.**

   The page that appears next depends on whether Foursquare found your business.

4. **If Foursquare found your business, click Claim My Listing and skip to Step 9. If Foursquare didn't find your business, click Add My Business.**

5. **Either log in with your Facebook credentials or follow the steps to create a Foursquare account.**

   After you log in, you see the Add a Place to Foursquare page.

6. **Complete the form on the page, including adding your Twitter handle and business category. Place a pin on the map to indicate your location.**

7. **Click Save when you're finished.**

   On the next screen, you can review and edit your information.

8. **If the information on the screen is correct, click the Claim It Now link on the right.**

   At this point, the claiming process converges for "found" and "new" businesses.

9. **Select the check box to agree to the terms of use and click the Get Started button to complete the two remaining verification steps.**

10. **On the next screen, start validating your ownership by entering a phone number at which you can be reached immediately.**

    Foursquare places an automated call to that number, while displaying a four-digit code number on the screen.

11. **Follow the prompts on the verification phone call and enter the code when requested using your telephone keypad.**

    The word Confirmed appears on the screen in place of the code number.

12. **Choose one of the following options:**

    - Expedited (immediate) verification for $20, which you pay for with a credit or debit card

    - Postcard verification, which is free but takes 3 to 4 weeks

13. **Click Continue.**

14. **After you receive your six-character verification code, enter it at `https://foursquare.com/venue/verify`.**

15. **Click the Verify button to finish the process.**

Monitoring your Foursquare success

The Foursquare merchant dashboard lets business managers monitor such metrics as unique and first-time customers at your venues, total check-ins at your venues, and people who liked your venues.

For more information, visit `https://support.foursquare.com/hc/en-us/articles/201064250-How-to-view-analytics`. To see your stats, follow these steps:

1. **Log into Foursquare.**

2. **Mouse over your profile picture in the top-right corner of the screen and select Settings from the drop-down menu that appears.**

    Or, go directly to `https://foursquare.com/settings`.

3. **On the next screen, indicate that you're the manager of your claimed business page. Or if you have already designated yourself as the manager of your business page, simply mouse over your profile, select Switch Accounts from the drop-down menu, and then choose whichever business listing you want.**

    You are then directed to the Manager home page.

4. **On the Manager home page, scroll down to the Your Business Listing section and click the See Customer Stats link to view analytics for each of your locations.**

    The View Stats page, shown in Figure 3-5, appears.

5. **Select the statistics you want and click View Report.**

Alternatively, you can choose to download your data in .csv format from the right-hand column.

Foursquare offers self-service tools for business owners to create, manage, and track offers. Make it worth the effort for people to visit your business often. Offer something appealing enough to make people want to earn a reward.

Start with the Manager home page. From there, choose the listing to which you want to add a Special. Select the link to Manage Your Specials under the Your Business Locations section. For more information, see `https://support.foursquare.com/hc/en-us/articles/201064270-How-to-create-a-special`.

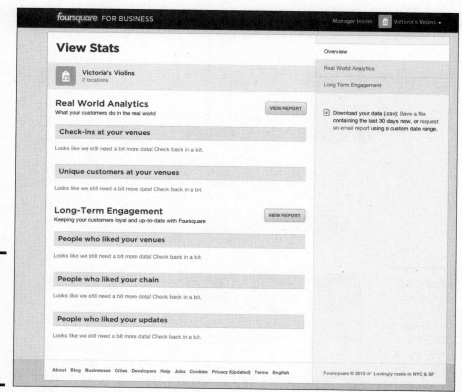

Figure 3-5:
Foursquare allows you to monitor visitors who check in to your business.

Getting merchant mileage from the Swarm app

Swarm, now a separate mobile app for Foursquare, still retains some of the popular features of the prior version of Swarm on Foursquare. People still use Swarm to find and notify their friends, check in, and receive alerts that your business offers a Foursquare check-in whenever they're nearby. However, Swarm no longer designates a group event the way it used to.

In particular, the Swarm app offers the Foursquare honorific of *mayor*, awarded to the Foursquare member who has checked into a particular place on the most days in the past two months. The mayor receives an online golden sticker (shown in Figure 3-6) and usually something special from the business owner. For more information, see `https://support.foursquare.com/hc/en-us/articles/202005800-Swarm-for-Merchants`.

Foursquare Golden Sticker

Figure 3-6:
A Golden Sticker is awarded to the mayor of a Foursquare location.

Users who are into virtual badges can award themselves two other badges. They can add a mood sticker to any check-in or a category sticker based on the type of business they are in.

Swarm offers users several ways to rate the places they visit. They can rate them on a scale of 0 to 10, or simply indicate if they like a place, have mixed feelings, or don't really like it.

To improve the rating of your business on Foursquare, use a call to action to remind customers to leave a tip or to like your listing.

Businesses promote their Foursquare participation in many ways: on their own social media feeds, counter-cards at cash registers, and sandwich boards in the streets. Be sure to promote your Foursquare/Swarm participation in as many ways as possible on your other social media accounts and websites.

Watching the rise of advertising on Foursquare

The rapid growth in mobile marketing (see Chapter 5 of this minibook) has accelerated the development and deployment of Foursquare advertising products so much that the company expects to generate $40 to $50 million in ad revenue in 2014, up from $12 million in 2013.

You might want to consider Foursquare's advertising option as a good channel to reach a locally-targeted market making impulse decisions based on where they are. Your ads will appear when Foursquare users search with their phones for somewhere to go (for example, pizza places near their location), or on search results if users habitually visit businesses like yours. For more information, see `https://support.foursquare.com/hc/en-us/articles/201066900-About-ads`.

Spacing Out with Twitter

The importance of integrating social media with location hasn't been lost on Twitter.

Tagging on Twitter

Twitter's Tweet with Your Location feature allows users to opt-in to include *geotags* (geolocation information) with their tweets; it's off by default. After it's enabled, Twitter attaches your specific location to your tweet if you're using the Twitter app. (We do mean specific — it can send you street intersections!) If you're using Twitter's website, it attaches your pre-specified general location, such as a city or neighborhood, to your tweet.

Twitter also uses geotagging within its Twitter Ads products to help advertisers target audiences in a particular place, assuming that users have turned on the location feature on their mobile devices.

Searching real space with Twitter

The search function can help you estimate the number of local Twitter users within a city or radius. Go to https://twitter.com/search-advanced. In the Places section, enter a neighborhood, city, or latitude and longitude; then click search. By default, Twitter searches within a 15-mile radius. To enter a place in Advanced Search, you must enable the location capability on your mobile device.

To change the search radius, use the search operators in the Near This Place text box, such as **Coliseum near: Los Angeles within: 5 miles**.

One third-party developer offers a handy app based on the locations listed in user profiles. Twellowhood (www.twellow.com/twellowhood) gives you a list of tweeters in a specified area, which can be very useful for targeted marketing.

Finding Your Business on Facebook

Facebook offers its users four ways to relate to the real world: geotagging, Places Nearby, check-ins, and Offers.

Geotagging on Facebook

On both its desktop and mobile app versions, Facebook allows users to add a location to any post, whether text, image, or video. If someone else tries to tag a post that names another Facebook user who isn't a friend, the second person must approve the geotag before it appears. For more information, see www.facebook.com/about/location.

Getting close with Places Nearby

Places Nearby appears as an option only when you use the Facebook app on mobile devices with location turned on. Users find places by tapping Nearby on the app menu. Facebook, being Facebook, doesn't just list everyone within 100 feet. Instead, it displays Places Nearby based on check-ins, Likes, and friends' recommendations. The Places that a Facebook user sees vary based on how many engagement actions she and her friends have taken.

Checking in on Facebook

To enable check-ins at your business, you must choose Local Business as the category for your Facebook Page and add your business address. If you already have a Page, you can change its category. (Log in as the Page Administrator. Click the About tab below your header photo. On the page that appears, click the Edit link in the Category row and select Local Businesses from the drop-down choices.)

You can also set up Facebook ads to generate check-ins, which are available only to people using the Facebook app on mobile devices with location turned on. From their News Feeds, users must tap the Check-in icon and select their location. They can add a description of what they're doing and then tap Post to share their location with their own friends.

Post a counter-card at your business to remind people to check-in. For more information on check-ins, see www.facebook.com/help/343548832389235.

Results for check-ins are visible on your Facebook Insights page (see Book IX, Chapter 4) but only after 30 people have checked in at your business. To understand any of these Facebook geomarketing options in more detail, see Book V or read *Facebook Marketing All-in-One For Dummies* by Andrea Vahl, John Haydon, and Jan Zimmerman (Wiley Publishing, Inc.).

The local review site Yelp (www.yelp.com) has a location-based check-in feature on its Android and iOS devices. Instagram and Snapchat also offer optional geotags. Users must always turn on geotags; geotags default to Off on all social media for security and privacy reasons.

Making a Facebook Offer they can't refuse

If you want to improve traffic from Facebook users when they are close by, use Facebook Offers to entice folks with a discount or other special offer on your Facebook Timeline or in a mobile ad. While there's no charge to write an offer as a simple post, Facebook will charge if you decide to boost your post or advertise your offer. For more about Facebook advertising and boosted posts, see Chapter 6 of this minibook.

To create an offer, you must have at least 50 Likes. All offers must comply with Facebook's Terms and Conditions.

First, you must create an offer either directly from your Facebook Page or from the Ads Create tool. To do this from your Page, follow these steps:

1. **On your Page's Timeline, click the Offer, Event+ tab at the top of the right column below the header graphic. Select Offer from the drop-down list below the tabs.**

2. **On the pop-up that appears, fill out the fields for Title, Description, Image, Expiration Date, and Claims Limit (the maximum number of offers you'll accept).**

3. **Click the down arrow to the right of More Options to reveal choices for Start Date, Online Redemption Link, or additional Terms and Conditions. Make your selection and then click Create Offer.**

   After you click the Create Offer button, you return to your Page, and the offer now appears at the top of your Timeline.

4. **Choose one of two ways to inform Facebook users know about your offer:**

   - *Boost the post.* To boost the post, continue to Step 6.

   - *Advertise the offer.* For advertising directions, skip to the following numbered list. You'll find more detailed directions and suggested tactics for both boosting posts and advertising on Facebook in Chapter 6 of this minibook.

5. **Below the offer, click the Boost Post button.**

   A new pop-up appears. In the left panel, click whether you want your boosted post to appear in desktop and/or mobile newsfeeds.

6. **Complete the fields in the right panel for Audience, Total Budget, Duration, and Account.**

   The Total Budget is the amount you're willing to spend to promote your offer during the entire time frame you specify in the Duration field. The values in the Estimated Reach field are supplied by Facebook based on the Audience you define and the budget you set.

7. **After you fill in all the fields, click the Boost button in the lower-right corner to implement your promotion plan.**

For more information on creating an offer from your business Page, go to www.facebook.com/help/410451192330456.

Alternatively, you can create the offer using the Ads Create tool by following these steps:

1. **Log in as the Page administrator.**

2. **Click the down caret at the far right of the top navigation to open a drop-down list. Then select Create Ads.**

3. **On the Objectives screen that appears, choose Get People to Claim Your Offer from the list.**

   The screen expands to the right.

4. **Choose the offer from the list in the right panel and click the Continue button.**

   If you don't already have an eligible Offer to advertise, you're prompted to create one by clicking the + icon to the right of the prompt. This takes you to the pop-up screen described in Steps 2–4 of the preceding list. Follow the directions to fill out all the required fields. After you preview and edit your offer to perfection, click Create Offer.

5. **After you click Continue, the screen expands below the Objectives section. Keep scrolling down to view the options for targeting your market, setting your budget, and selecting text and links.**

6. **Now go through the standard steps of the Ads Create tool to promote your offer with an ad.**

   See Book V or Chapter 6 of this minibook for more information about creating an ad, defining a target audience, and setting a budget.

For location-based offers that people will redeem in your store, be sure that the Mobile News Feed option is selected in the Text and Links section.

For more information on creating an offer by using the Ads Create tool, go to www.facebook.com/help/102534329872055.

Making Real Connections in Virtual Space

Meet-ups and tweet-ups bridge the gap between the cyberworld and the one we live in. These services make it easy for people who have similar interests to organize meetings for fun, advocacy, learning, or simply to meet one another.

Meeting through Meetup

Meetup (www.meetup.com), which has been around since 2002, bills itself as "the world's largest network of local groups," claiming that more than 19 million members attend nearly 500,000 meetings per month held by more than 180,000 local groups located in 45,000 cities in 177 countries.

Meetup charges organizers a fee ranging from $10 to $40 per month for using its platform Meetup pages (as shown in Figure 3-7) to help people find or start a group located near them. The system includes an easy-to-use interface to identify either groups or meet-ups (via calendar view) within a certain distance.

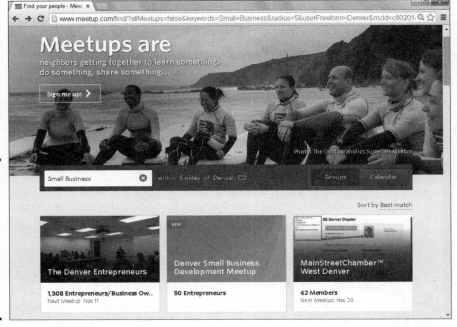

Figure 3-7:
A Meetup search for small-business activities near Denver produces several results.

Click on a group or on a meet-up to find directions to future meet-ups and check out the history of a Meetup group. Meetup lets you easily invite your Facebook friends to join you at a meet-up or see whether you have friends participating in other Meetup groups.

In an inevitable mash-up, Meetup now allows Groupon fans (described in the section "Comparing LivingSocial and Groupon," later in this chapter) to hook up at official and self-organized events through `http://groupon.meetup.com`. What an easy way to find your target market in a location close to you!

Tweeting for meeting in real space

The term *tweet-up* has been part of the Twitter lexicon for a long time; it describes a live meeting of Twitter users or, more generally, any face-to-face event organized by way of social media.

Although there isn't yet a nationwide site that facilitates connections the way Meetup does (see the preceding section), local sites exist. For example, in addition to its feed at `https://twitter.com/bostontweetup`, Boston TweetUp maintains a calendar and reviews technology-oriented events at its website `http://bostontweetup.com` (shown in Figure 3-8).

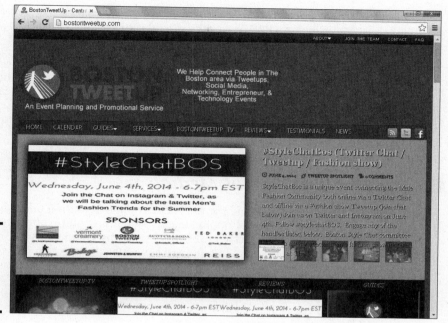

Figure 3-8:
Boston is serious about its tweet-ups.

Reproduced with permission of Joselin Mane

Twitter is already influencing traditional gatherings, such as large conferences and seminars. Small groups with a particular interest or agenda can now more easily meet with each other socially or in a *rump session* (the "meeting" after the meeting). And many attendees have started tweeting questions and commentary during presentations, using the hashtag (#) to mark tweets related to a particular session. This technique can either unnerve or energize presenters. Some tech-savvy people read the tweet stream as the session goes on and respond to questions on the fly.

In either case, a tweet-up is definitely another way to take networking to the next level.

Marketing with meet-ups and tweet-ups

Meet-ups and tweet-ups offer you an exquisite opportunity to reach out to new customers, even if they're only complementary to your primary business. Contact meeting organizers to see whether you can

✦ Host an event at your restaurant or another event location. For example, a company selling kitchen countertops could offer to hold cooking classes in its showroom.

✦ Offer a discount to members or for the event.

✦ Give a presentation or teach a class at a future meeting, which is an excellent way for a B2B or service provider to establish expertise in an area.

✦ Provide information to members.

Attending a meeting first is helpful (but not required) to make sure that the makeup of the group fits your target audience and to meet the leaders.

You can gauge interest by using Meetup to estimate the number of members in similar groups in your location(s).

Making Deals on Social Media

A group of friends hitting the mall is the offline definition of *social shopping*. Online, though, social shopping means something quite different: A group of folks (sometimes, strangers) saves money by volume buying with a group coupon. The group coupon emerged several years ago as a way to aggregate new buyers, usually in specific cities, by offering a half-off, one-day promotion online or by email. The underlying assumption was that by attracting a high volume of customers, a business could still make money on a highly discounted deal, buy goodwill and exposure, or fill their businesses during off-times or off-season.

The best-known and oldest of these coupon services are Groupon (www. groupon.com), which went public in fall 2011, and LivingSocial (www. livingsocial.com). (Groupon and LivingSocial are described in the section "Comparing LivingSocial and Groupon," later in this chapter.) Both companies have expanded to offer specific tourism-related deals, as well as deals on goods, tickets, and national brands.

Seeing an opportunity for profit, dozens of other companies — some national, some regional or local — have entered the group-coupon frenzy. The competition has had several consequences:

✦ With more coupon vendors to choose from, merchants have more leverage negotiating deals on favorable terms.

✦ Familiarity has taken the bloom off the discount rose.

✦ Some customers, who have come to expect major discounts as a matter of course, pressure merchants to bend the rules in their favor by threatening bad online reviews.

Using high-discount coupons can indeed bring new and repeat customers. On the downside, businesses may be exposed to significant financial risk and bad publicity. Many companies are now rethinking the shared coupon experiment or taking advantage of less costly local sites, offering daily deals.

In the following sections, which primarily address the needs of business-to-consumer (B2C) companies, you can assess the risks and benefits of high-discount group deals. With this information, you can decide whether a deal strategy makes sense for your particular business.

Offering savings, gaining customers

Offering a discount to attract customers is an obvious B2C technique used for ages by service and product companies: bars and restaurants, tourist destinations, health and beauty salons, events, recreation, personal services, and more.

Generally, customers who sign up for a deal service receive a daily email offering some product or service for an average 57 percent off, though deals may range from 30 to 90 percent off.

In the past, a minimum number of deals had to be purchased during a specific time period. If the minimum wasn't reached, the deal didn't go through. Most of the deal sites have now eliminated the minimum requirement, finding that they were able to sell enough deals without any problem.

Most, but not all, daily deal sites are set up geographically, with users signing up to see deals near their homes or watching for deals they can use on their next vacation. For an example of a typical deal like this, DailyDealOmaha (`www.dailydealomaha.com/deal/omaha`) offers high-discount deals weekly.

So that's how it works for users. To see how online coupons affect your end of the rope as a business, see the section "Making an attractive offer," later in this chapter.

Consider these points before you decide whether to pursue a high-discount deal strategy:

✦ **Ultimately, the coupon companies select which businesses participate at which time and set the schedule for featuring offers.** You may not get the time frame that you want.

✦ **A link to your site will appear in the offer.** In preparation, you should be willing to create a separate landing page on your website for the offer.

✦ **Some sites offer national deals, particularly for large, web-based retailers, online shopping, and travel.** For a national reach, you might target multiple individual cities within your national audience with separate offers. This approach works for participating franchises or branches in several cities.

✦ **Confirm that the deal service you select reaches your city.** Because tourists and local residents are your primary audience, a service must have enough email subscribers interested in a specific geographic area to make your deal workable.

You can make online couponing work for a business-to-business (B2B) audience, but it's a little more complicated. A successful B2B deal depends on the size and quality of the email list that the coupon service maintains, an attractive offer on a product or service of wide interest (payroll services or office supplies, perhaps), and on recommendations from employees to employers. For example, Rewardli (`www.rewardli.com/offers`) and BuyerHive (`www.buyerhive.com`) focus on the B2B deal market.

Making an attractive offer

Sometimes, you just want people in your door, virtual or otherwise. If you offer a *loss leader* (a sale below cost), try not to sell too far below cost. Selling hundreds of $4 ice-cream cones for half-price is one thing as long as you cover your cost of goods and service; on the other hand, discounting hundreds of $40 haircuts at half-price may leave you short on the rent.

If you're in a position to handle a potential loss, there are some viable reasons to consider online deals as a tool in your marketing arsenal:

✦ **There are no upfront payments.** That's a good thing for your cash flow (if you get paid promptly by the coupon service).

✦ **There are backloaded payments.** The coupon company gets paid from revenues only if the minimum number of offers is purchased — and usually you can set the minimum and maximum number of coupons sold (more on that in a bit).

✦ **Coupon deals often provide a stream of new customers in a relatively short length of time.** Compare the result to how long it takes other forms of advertising to produce new business. If you just opened a new business, coupons may be a good technique.

✦ **Word-of-mouth works.** Buyers might bring their friends to share the experience.

✦ **Factor estimated add-on purchases, as well as lifetime-customer value (the value of estimated repeat purchases from the same customer), into your calculation.** Obviously, new customers who make multiple, repeat purchases are more valuable than customers who buy only once — for example, tourists. Try to make your offer something worth a repeat buy or set the offer low enough that you can generate an up-sale from most buyers.

Setting Terms for Your Coupon Campaign

You have many ways to refine and tailor your coupon campaign, within limits. You do want customers, but you don't want to lose your shirt, either. To limit your discount-exposure, you may be able to tweak the coupon vendor's share of revenue, the time frame during which the offer will be honored, the maximum number of deals, and more.

Be sure to read the fine print before you sign with a coupon service. Each company has different rules.

The depth of the discount

Typically, the buyer receives 30 to 50 percent (or more) off the standard price. Then, the coupon service gets its slice: sometimes as high as an additional half of how much the buyer pays. So, as the merchant, you receive only 25 percent of your list price.

30-minute parasailing adventure	$100
Customer coupon discount (50% off)	$50
Coupon service's cut	$25
Merchant's final take	$25

The percentages vary by company and by the nature of the offer, but thanks to the competition for deals, you may sometimes be able to negotiate better terms on the coupon service's cut, especially with some of the smaller deal companies (or if you're a huge multinational corporation).

The scope of the deal

Consider how you will establish the parameters of an offer to best meet your goals and objectives:

✦ **Assess your net return.** The coupon company takes its cut off the revenue first. The coupon firm collects payments from customers by credit card and sends you a check for your share afterward. The schedule of payments varies by coupon company.

Watch the schedule of payments carefully. Delayed payments from the coupon service can create a totally unnecessary cash flow crisis for your company.

✦ **Set the maximum number of deals you will offer.** Set a maximum number of deals to limit both your financial and service exposure. A cap makes sense, especially for event organizers and service providers. For example, your small theater company may have a fixed number of seats, you may have room for only a certain number of people in a dance class, or you may have enough stylists to handle only a certain number of haircuts per day.

✦ **Determine how long the offer will last.** You specify the time frame over which buyers can exercise a deal, usually several months to a year. Plan ahead, keeping in mind how much product, space, and staff you'll need to fulfill your end of the deal.

Some deal companies require you to honor a group deal forever.

✦ **Timing is everything.** Schedule the term of your offer so you don't have buyers showing up on your doorstep all at one time — unless the offer is for a scheduled event or you intentionally set a short period for redemption. Most merchants see a peak in redemptions the first 30 days after an offer and the last 30 days before expiration.

Grappling with the gotchas

Watch for landmines like these before signing up for a deal:

✦ **Fashionably late?** The fine print on some deals (and the law in some states) allows buyers to receive a discount equal to the amount they paid for their coupon — even if the deal itself has expired. For instance, suppose someone saved $6 on a pound of coffee costing $14 with a deal that expired on 12/31/14. Even if they come into your store a year later, you may have to give them $6 off a pound of coffee, whose price has now increased to $16. However, you don't have to honor the original discounted net price on the product that they buy. (In the previous example, you wouldn't have to sell the $16 pound of coffee for $8, (its price with the original deal), but you'd have to sell it for $10.

Be cautious when making offers that include a percentage discount; a fixed-dollar discount is better.

✦ **Special package deals.** Many companies create a unique package or service just for their deal offer. You are usually not required to continue to offer that product or service beyond the term of the deal. For instance, say your company usually offers only hour-long dance lessons for couples and prices them at $40 per hour. For the deal only, you offer a ½-hour dance lesson for couples valued at $20 but sold at $10. After the offer has expired, coupon buyers may be able to get $10 off the $40 price, but you aren't required to offer the ½-hour lesson anymore.

✦ **Bookkeeping nightmares.** These deals can leave you with a record-keeping headache, from tracking outstanding and redeemed offers at the register to holding potential entries on your books, even for expired coupons. Talk to your accountant about the impact on your financial statements for these ongoing liabilities.

✦ **Where's my money?** Payment isn't swift, either. Some coupon services divide your payments into three installments paid over 60 days, which could create cash flow problems for you if large numbers of buyers redeem their coupons quickly.

✦ **Price-gouging customers.** Nasty deal-seekers may threaten to write bad reviews if you don't meet their demands to provide more than the deal offered. They may demand a higher-priced product or service at the same discount, a greater quantity than you offered, or a deeper discount.

✦ **Be prepared.** If you can't provide high-quality service to meet the demand with the staff or space you have, you may lose not only the customer but also your reputation, if poor reviews appear online. Depending on the deal you're offering, protect yourself from unhappy customers by requiring appointments, stating "subject to availability" (say, for a massage or a haircut), and allowing adequate time to redeem the offer.

Measuring success

Good coupon sites offer detailed analytics, similar to newsletters, stating the number of offers emailed, number and percent of offers opened, number and percent of viewers who clicked for details, and the number and percent of viewers who purchased the deal. Additionally, they can provide how many viewers purchased more than one deal, total number of deals sold, and total dollar value received. Copy this information to a spreadsheet so that you can

✦ Assess whether the offer was financially successful for your business.

✦ Obtain clues about what factors might have affected an offer that didn't draw buyers.

✦ Compare the success and parameters of offers that you have sent out through the same company to see which offers are the most successful.

✦ Compare what happens with the same offer distributed through different companies.

If you can't figure out how to analyze results from your coupon site, ask your bookkeeper or accountant. They eat numbers for lunch.

Do the math. What percentage of customers might convert or upgrade their purchase? What's a reasonable lifetime-customer value for each one? How does it compare to the cost of acquisition? Get help from your accountant, if needed.

Seller beware! Small businesses with shallow pockets sometimes can't handle the pressure of serving so many customers. Many companies, especially restaurants, now report a loss in revenue whenever existing customers snap up their coupon deals. Receiving less than half the full price for a meal or service can turn coupon deals into an expensive loyalty program for existing clientele.

Further leveraging your deal

Many companies offer extra options to their coupon buyers in the hope that deals will go viral:

✦ **Opportunities to share opinions and photos:** Coupon buyers, for example, may have the opportunity to share on Facebook or Twitter, entering comments about a company that's offering a deal. Other sites encourage participation in a social activity, such as ranking a service or posting photos. These actions are often perceived as testimonials by other prospective buyers and encourage them to purchase coupons. Almost all deal sites provide share buttons that facilitate users sharing deals with others on their own social media pages.

✦ **Easy-to-share links to send deals to friends:** If three or more friends share a deal, the referrer receives a freebie. Include this element as an allowance in your revenue calculations. If someone organizes a share campaign, total revenues may decline.

This share-this-deal functionality encourages people who receive a daily coupon email, or people who visit your site, to tell their friends about the deal on Facebook and Twitter, and by email.

✦ **Affiliate options:** Recommending a deal to others or signing up to promote offers on a commission basis usually generates internal *deal bucks* (additional discounts, not cash). Groupon, for instance, offers bucks to first-time buyers who make referrals, and a 10 percent commission for members of Groupon's Affiliate programs. LivingSocial lets users earn deal bucks if they make purchases with its branded Visa card.

✦ **Easy integration with Facebook, Twitter, and email to share deals:** Most services offer mobile apps for iPhone, iPad, Android, and BlackBerry.

After the offer appears, you can promote the deal in your newsletter, on your social media outlets, and elsewhere, although you may not have much notice.

More upsides and downsides

As a merchant, you gain brand awareness, a direct appeal to locally targeted markets, word-of-mouth advertising, and high visibility to a new customer stream. The low-cost offer supposedly reduces customers' perceived risk of trying something new. It's your job to turn these one-time experimenters into loyal repeat customers.

In theory, compared with how long it takes other forms of advertising to produce new business, your business benefits from this approach by obtaining a stream of new customers in a relatively short length of time. The concept assumes (but this assumption doesn't always prove to be true) that when an offer brings prospects in the door, satisfied customers will proceed to spend more money through these avenues:

✦ **Impulse buys and add-ons:** Hey, you got them in the door, right? Time to exploit customers' good moods for your deal. See whether you can get them to cough up a little more cash. Say your buyers get 50 percent off a specialty burrito. You can then entice them to spend their savings on drinks, sides, or a take-home purchase: "This cupcake from the offer was so good that I'm buying a dozen to take home."

✦ **Repeat customers:** This is worth repeating (pun intended). Deliver quality on your discount deal, and you'll likely build a solid client base. One great massage, and that client may be yours every two or three weeks for years.

✦ **Word-of-mouth:** Worth repeating, too. Buyers might bring friends.

Human nature being what it is, customers cashing in your deal don't always generate gold:

✦ **One-hit wonders:** Many people who use these deals are there only for the discount and have no intention of returning. That's life — and why you have to remember to price your deal with a profit margin/loss you can live with.

✦ **Cannibalizing existing customers:** Loyal patrons who would have paid full price or happily taken a 5 or 10 percent discount are now receiving a product or service at half-off, causing a loss in regular revenue.

✦ **Customer service versus aggressive customers:** Here's an ugly side of human nature: Regardless of conditions in the deal, some deal redeemers can be unreasonable and sometimes unpleasant. They demand to use more than one coupon per purchase, want to buy an item that's not on the offer, or otherwise take advantage of merchants who don't want to have anyone making a scene in their business.

✦ **Succumbing to greediness:** An overwhelmed business that can't meet the demand of a deal's sales are toast. When a business is pressured into selling more deals than it can manage, everyone — staff, customers, and business owners — has a bad experience. Unhappy customers threaten to post negative reviews on sites like Yelp, and some actually do.

To be fair, Groupon is aware of the criticisms and has tried to address them by offering less price-driven deals and additional, pro-business tools. In October 2014, it launched Groupon Pages, a new listing directory for local businesses. It hopes that Pages will offer merchants an additional online presence to increase reach and sales.

**Book VIII
Chapter 3**

**Maximizing
Stratified Social
Communities**

Comparing LivingSocial and Groupon

LivingSocial and Groupon reach fairly similar U.S. audiences demographically, and both have expanded into the international market. For a more detailed comparison, see Table 3-6.

Table 3-6	Comparing Groupon and Living Social
Groupon	*LivingSocial*
74% female.	70% female.
24% have a household income greater than $100,000.	56% make more than $75,000.
71% have a college education; 14% have a graduate degree.	76% have a college degree.
57% are 18 to 44 years old.	70% are between ages 25 and 54.
85% of customers say they are likely to return to the merchant again.	70% plan to return to the business, frequently within three months.
79% of customers have referred someone to the business.	55% refer others to local businesses after visiting.
77% of customers spend beyond the value of the Groupon (no value given).	The average LivingSocial customer spends $26 above the voucher amount on their first visit.

Sources: http://files.shareholder.com/downloads/AMDA-E2NTR/0x0x777786/82A1AD1E-5C03-4175-9DCF-F125D369ED28/Groupon_Q2_2014_Public_Fact_Summary.pdf and http://corporate.livingsocial.com/run-a-deal-with-livingsocial/

In the following sections, we discuss these two services in more detail.

Digging into Groupon

Like Don Vito Corleone in *The Godfather,* Groupon makes "an offer you can't refuse" to 200 million daily email subscribers and site visitors in more than 500 markets in 48 countries. Groupon is far and away the largest of the group coupon sites, claiming that more than 44 million unique customers purchased at least one Groupon offer in 2013. By comparison, LivingSocial, its closest competitor, claims 70 million members worldwide. For a typical Groupon offer, see Figure 3-9.

In addition to its featured deals in 10 topical categories, Groupon classifies deals in sections called Goods for products and Getaways for travel. In its "Best of Groupon" section, you'll find a collection of Kids & Family deals. Groupon also offers an affiliate program and in-house credits for referring deals to friends.

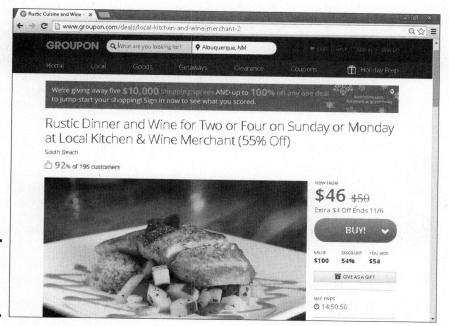

Figure 3-9: A typical Groupon offer.

After your offer appears, you can promote the deal in your own newsletter, blog, social media outlets, and elsewhere, although you may not have much notice. The share-this-deal functionality encourages people who receive your daily Groupon email, or those who visit your site, to tell their friends about the deal on Facebook, Pinterest, and Twitter, and by email.

Demographics

According to studies by Forbes and comScore, Groupon users represent a coveted demographic profile: educated, young, single, working women who have a fair amount of discretionary income:

✦ Female users outnumber males by almost three to one.

✦ The majority of users are relatively young: 57 percent were 18 to 44 years old.

✦ Almost one-quarter of Groupon users have a household income over $100,000.

✦ 71 percent have a college education; these are not subsistence shoppers.

Merchant satisfaction

Groupon contends (on www.grouponworks.com) that its merchants are more than satisfied, with more than 71 percent of featured merchants wanting to make an offer again. According to Groupon, 93 percent of businesses report getting new customers, 77 percent claim customers spend more than the face value of their coupon, and 84 percent say the promotion increased their visibility. About 85 percent of Groupon users say they are likely to return to the merchant who offered the deal.

Independent studies, which are hard to find, don't always concur with this rosy assessment.

Speak with your accountant about how to handle revenue from Groupon and similar deals. Prepaid income is usually treated as a liability on your balance sheet until you fulfill the obligation or until the time expires to exercise the offer. (Think gift cards.) You may also encounter state-by-state issues regarding sales tax.

LivingSocial

The second-largest competitor to Groupon, LivingSocial (www.livingsocial.com) offers enticing coupon deals, with a focus on local travel and events. Launched in August 2009, LivingSocial says it now reaches more than 7 million subscribers around the world in almost 200 cities in 27 countries. For a typical LivingSocial offer, see Figure 3-10.

The benefits are the same as with other deal sites: brand awareness, direct appeal to locally targeted markets, word-of-mouth advertising, high visibility to a new customer stream, and easy results tracking. LivingSocial, which has long offered travel deals under LivingSocial Escapes, also has categories for family deals, nationwide deals, at-home deals, online shopping, coupons, and gifts.

Like Groupon, LivingSocial is trying to get out of the daily deal grind. Instead of relying on random deals delivered by email, it's trying to shift to a website and mobile app that allow shoppers to browse for offers from local businesses.

LivingSocial integrates with Facebook, Twitter, and email, and has apps for both the iPhone and Android. Like Groupon, it offers an affiliate program and in-house rewards for referrals.

Figure 3-10:
A typical
Living Social
travel offer.

Diversifying Your Daily Deals

Many businesses have discovered smaller daily deal sites that are far less risky for the merchant. Some of these are local sites; some are national online opportunities targeting a particular product or market. Table 3-7 provides several examples. For sites in your area, try searching for your city or your product, plus the words *daily deals* or *group coupons.*

Ask other local merchants about their experiences before you sign up with any deal sites.

Table 3-7	Group Coupon and Daily Deal Sites	
Name	*URL for Media Kit and Advertising Information*	*Notes*
Facebook Offers	`www.facebook.com/business/offers`	Provides a way to create an offer users can claim and share with their friends
Gilt City	`https://vendornet.giltcity.com`	Offers local deals in selected cities to reach an affluent market
HauteLook	`www.hautelook.com/about`	Daily discounts on top fashion and lifestyle brands
RapidBuyr	`www.rapidbuyr.crowdsavings.com/get-featured`	An online customer acquisition program for local merchants
Rue La La	`www.ruelala.com`	High-style, short-lived, online flash sale boutiques; runs nationwide to members
Yelp for Business Owners	`https://biz.yelp.com/support/deals`	Deals promoted on Yelp, a consumer-rating site
Yipit	`www.yipit.com`	Compiled deals and coupons from multiple, partnered sources offered by location, interest, and brand
ZOZI	`www.zozi.com/businesses`	Deals on adventure travel, tours, and outdoor activities
Zulily	`www.zulily.com/index.php/vendor`	Promotes daily deals targeting moms, babies, and kids

Chapter 4: Profiting from Mid-Size Social Media Channels

In This Chapter

✔ Using Ning to build communities

✔ Growing visually famous with Snapchat

✔ Building business with music on Spotify

✔ Topping off a rich-media blog with Tumblr

✔ Vying for video with Vimeo and Vine

*N*ew social media channels and apps seem to spring up faster than weeds. Minor channels may burst on the scene and die quickly, or grow up to become the next blockbuster innovation in social marketing. In this chapter, we look at some of the mid-size social media channels.

These channels aren't quite large enough to justify their own chapters yet, but their user bases qualify them as reaching more than niche markets, discussed in Chapter 3 of this minibook. Some you may have heard of; others may elicit the reaction, "I don't have a clue."

Take a look to see whether any of them make sense for your business. With adroit marketing, you can gain an edge in brand visibility and reach, long before the channel becomes crowded with marketing copy-cats. In particular, if you're looking for younger audiences, you can establish your social credibility by being there first.

Deciding Whether to Invest Time in Mid-Size Social Media Channels

Consider each of these minor-league social media channels through the lens of your business. Can you piggyback on their moment of fame — bringing some glory to your business — before they become so bloated with competing businesses that your company becomes just another ant in the anthill? The criteria are simple:

✦ Is there enough online buzz about the new channel for you to leverage their publicity for your own benefit as a pioneer?

✦ Does the channel reach your desired audience?

✦ Is the social space (whether music, images, blogs, or communities) a good fit for your company and its marketing goals?

✦ Do you have an innovative spirit and the ability to act quickly?

✦ Can you think of a clever way to use the technology to get attention, grow your brand, or gather leads while you're still a big fish in a small pond?

✦ Can you experiment for a reasonable price or level of effort?

✦ Can you extricate yourself quickly if something doesn't work without damping your enthusiasm for trying something else new another time?

If the answers are yes, go for it! See if you can become the equivalent of the first company to accept a tweeted takeout order or the first company to reply to a disappearing photo with a disappearing coupon.

Building Your Own Network with Ning

Ning has been around since 2005, but don't discount its power. An easy-to-use platform, Ning lets businesses and nonprofits create their own custom social networks. It claims to have hosted more than 2 million social networks since its founding, with millions of combined active users accessing those sites each month.

Ning offers many of the features of Facebook, plus privacy! Community features include message forums, blogs, photo and video sharing, Like and Comment engagement options, email broadcast capability, customizable member profiles, and unlimited groups. To top it off, Ning sites are already smartphone and tablet compatible, and they integrate with Google Analytics.

You have to pay a fee of $25 to $99 per month, based on the size of your membership. If you want to build an interactive community, using Ning is far more cost-effective than paying a developer to build a new online community from scratch.

For an example of an active Ning community site, see the National Peace Corps Association "Community Builder" site (`http://community.peacecorpsconnect.org`), shown in Figure 4-1. Nothing obviously indicates whether a site has been built using a Ning platform except for an optional "powered by Ning" tagline.

On the revenue side, creators of Ning sites can charge and collect membership fees for their organizations. You can also offer advertising through Google and provide other services (including a store) through other third-party partners with Ning.

Book VIII
Chapter 4

Profiting from
Mid-Size Social
Media Channels

Figure 4-1:
Building
a site on
the Ning
platform
is a cost-
effective
way to
build your
own online
community.

Link to main website

Ning tagline

Follow these steps to set up an account with Ning:

1. **Go to www.ning.com and click the Get Started for Free button.**

2. **Select whichever plan you want to test on.**

   The Create Your Account pop-up window appears.

3. **Fill out the Full Name, Email Address, Re-Type Email, and Choose Password text boxes.**

   Optionally, you can also include a phone number in the Phone Number text box.

4. **Enter a title (or name) for your Ning site in the Name Your Social Site text box.**

5. **In the Choose Your Ning URL, enter the address you want to use.**

   For the free trial, your URL will be a subdomain in the form of `http://yourname.ning.com`. Later, you can purchase your own domain name, and you should! For directions on buying or using your own domain name, see `www.ning.com/ning3help/use-your-own-domain`.

6. **Click Check Availability.**

   Ning checks your name for availability.

7. **If your selected name is available, then click Submit.**

   If someone is already using that name, try another until you find one that's available.

8. **Enter your credit card information, and then just follow directions to build your site.**

   If you need help setting up your site, go to `www.ning.com/ning3help`.

Take advantage of the 14-day free trial to see how easy it is to build a Ning site using their templates. Ask your graphic designer for help with colors and fonts to give your Ning templates some extra zing. If you want, you can create your own design instead of using theirs, or work with one of their certified providers.

Snapping the Future with Snapchat

Snapchat is like the instant-coffee version of Instagram. It's another photo messaging app that's downloaded to smartphones. Users can easily send *Snaps* — photos, videos, comments, or drawings — to a select list of recipients. Snapchat has one unique feature — the Snaps disappear quickly after they're opened.

To maintain promises of anonymity and privacy that make the app more appealing to its predominantly young users, Snapchat lets users set a time limit of 1 to 10 seconds for how long a recipient can view an image, at which point the image is supposed to self-delete. (The self-deletion feature, unfortunately, turns out to be not quite true; recipients can save the Snaps.) If she wants a longer time frame, a user has the option to Add a Story, which keeps an image visible for 24 hours and combines multiple Snaps into a simple story.

Founded in September 2011, the rapidly growing company claims that its more than 100 million active monthly users circulated more than 400 million Snaps per day by November 2014. Those users are 70 percent female and 71 percent under 25 years old. In other words, Snapchat is snapping up the very users who are leaving Facebook.

Those user numbers are enough to make Snapchat an attractive target for acquisition (both Facebook and Yahoo! are rumored to have made offers) or an initial public offering. Stay tuned as Snapchat starts to develop a revenue stream.

Advertising on Snapchat

In October 2014, Snapchat announced that it started placing ads in the Recent Updates box on the app. The ads, which may be static or include a series of Snaps edited to look like a Snapchat Story, will appear in the box sometimes, but not always. Users can choose to view the ad, after which it will go away, or it will disappear by itself within 24 hours.

Still in beta with only a limited number of advertisers at this time, Snapchat's advertising potential remains an unknown. How much will advertisers pay for an ad with a limited lifetime?

Getting started with Snapchat

Getting started with Snapchat is the same for all users, whether you're setting up a business or personal account. Follow these steps:

1. **Download the Snapchat app from the Apple App Store or Google Play.**

2. **On the Sign Up screen, enter your email address, password, and birthday (you must be at least 13 years old!).**

3. **Enter your brand-related username and verify your cellphone number.**

4. **Follow the directions to create a list of people to whom you wish to send Snaps and those you will allow to send Snaps to you.**

   Building these lists may be time-consuming unless you choose the option on this screen that allows the app to use your contact lists.

5. **Take a photo or video from the Snapchat app and send it off.**

Until promoted Snaps or advertising are more widely available, stick with creative marketing. Try to build on Snapchat's short visual time limit to convey urgency with your calls to action. For inspiration, look at other techniques that companies have come up with, from GrubHub's week-long scavenger contest (see http://blog.grubhub.com/food-and-fun/potluck/the-snaphunt-is-o) in Figure 4-2, to Karmaloop's reply Snaps that display promo codes, as shown in Figure 4-3. In both cases, the companies used Snapchat to reach their target markets without resorting to expensive paid advertising.

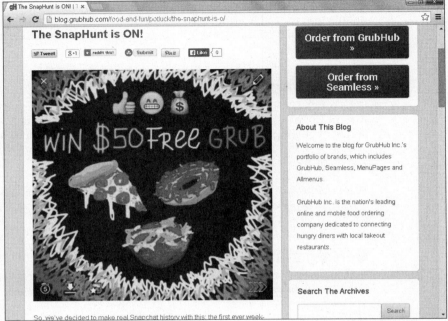

Figure 4-2:
GrubHub uses Snapchat for a scavenger contest.

Figure 4-3:
Karmaloop uses Snapchat to send promo codes for use on its website.

Spotting Your Audience with Spotify

A commercial music streaming service, Spotify accesses more than 20 million songs and allows users to create their own customized playlists. Because Spotify playlists are easy to share with other social media channels, its influence extends beyond the site itself.

Founded in 2008 in Sweden and available in the U.S. since 2011, Spotify has more than 50 million active users per month, of which 12.5 million are paid subscriptions. Demographically speaking, Spotify appeals to younger users — 40 percent are 18 to 24 years old — and its mobile user base is growing rapidly.

If you're in a creative business or trying to reach users who enjoy certain types of music, Spotify may be a valuable social media channel for you. Consider running contests or starting a collaborative playlist to interact with prospective customers.

A recent comScore study found that people who stream music are more likely to be strong brand advocates than those who don't. According to the study, Spotify users are especially likely to recommend something to friends and pay more for brands they value.

Spotify offers a broad menu of advertising options, which are detailed on `www.spotify.com/us/brands/formats`:

✦ **Sponsored session:** Sponsor a 30-minute, ad-free session in exchange for users viewing your short video (shown in Figure 4-4).

✦ **Video takeover:** An advertising break dedicated to your brand, including video and display ads.

✦ **Audio:** A cross-platform ad that includes an audio spot, cover art, and a link.

✦ **Display:** Run-of-site (ROS) leaderboard ads (the large banners at the top of a page) seen when users interact with Spotify.

✦ **Homepage takeover:** A full day of dedicated advertising on the Spotify home page.

✦ **Branded playlist:** Customized user-generated playlists with your logo, text, and a link to your campaign.

✦ **Advertiser page:** A complete, multimedia, microsite that appears between screens of the Spotify player.

To get started with advertising, fill out the contact form at the bottom of `www.spotify.com/us/brands`.

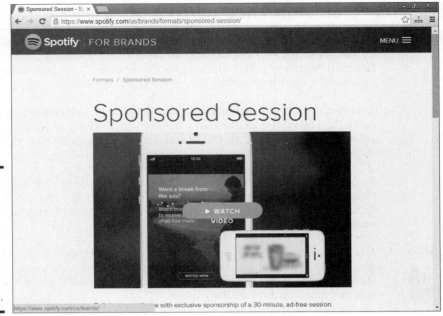

Figure 4-4:
Spotify offers a variety of advertising options, including a sponsored session.

Turning Up New Prospects with Tumblr

Tumblr is a microblogging platform and social networking website that allows users to post multimedia and other content to a short-form blog (see Figure 4-5) from a desktop or mobile app. Many users take advantage of the Tumblr dashboard to find and reblog content they find there.

Founded in 2007 and acquired by Yahoo! in June 2013, Tumblr boasted more than 200 million blogs and more than 95 billion posts by Fall 2014. Like with many of the channels in this chapter, Tumblr has great appeal to a younger audience (46 percent of users are 16 to 24 years old), fairly evenly divided by gender.

With 30 to 50 million active users per month, the site may well be worthwhile for branding, mining for prospects, and increasing customer loyalty with content and customers.

Setting up an account

Getting started as a contributor is easy. At Tumblr.com, follow these steps:

1. **Enter your email address, password, and a username in the text boxes, and then click Sign Up.**

2. **In the How Old Are You text box that appears, enter your age, and then select the Terms of Service check box. Click Next.**

3. **A CAPTCHA appears — in the text box, just enter what you see in the picture, then click Almost Done.**

   The Welcome to Tumblr page appears.

4. **Select five blogs that you want to follow. (If you can't be bothered, click Skip in the bottom right of the page.)**

   Your Tumblr dashboard appears, where you're invited to create your own Tumblr blog.

5. **First, you have to verify your email address by clicking a link in a message that Tumblr sends you.**

6. **When you're offered a choice in Settings, select your own domain name, which can be a subdomain of your existing website.**

   That's it.

Figure 4-5:
An easy-to-use blogging platform, Tumblr offers another route for branding and lead generation.

**Book VIII
Chapter 4**

**Profiting from
Mid-Size Social
Media Channels**

Advertising on Tumblr

Tumblr offers a wide variety of advertising options, all native to the channel. (Scroll down to the advertising options on `www.tumblr.com/business/`). According to one study, "Tumblr is ranked #1 in social sentiment toward brands," with users highly likely to recommend brands they follow to others. Options include

+ **Sponsored posts:** Promoted on a cost per engagement (CPE) basis (*engagement* means when a viewer likes or shares the post); targeting offered by interest, location, or gender.

+ **Sponsored video posts:** Charged on a cost-per-view (CPV) basis. These posts auto-play with muted audio on user dashboards; you can reuse videos from other sources, such as Instagram and Vine.

+ **Radar posts:** The ad appears above the fold on the dashboard.

+ **Trending blogs:** Promote your blog in the Trending tab that appears in Tumblr's mobile apps.

+ **Sponsored Posts + Yahoo!:** Syndicate your sponsored post through the Yahoo! ad network to reach a combined potential audience of 800 million unique visitors.

For more advertising information, email `sponsors@tumblr.com`.

Analyzing Tumblr results

Tumblr offers access to content and advertising analytics only to advertisers. Their analytics package breaks down results into paid and organic engagement numbers. To reach these results, click Analytics in the right column of the dashboard.

As an alternative, you can connect your blog to Google Analytics.

If you don't plan to advertise, be sure to select a blog theme that will allow you to paste a Google Analytics ID number into the Appearance section of the Customize Theme page. (See Book IX, Chapter 1 for more on Google Analytics.) You'll need to set up your Google Analytics account first to get the ID number. If your blog is already set up, try connecting it to Google Analytics by clicking the Settings icon (which looks like a gear) at the top of your dashboard. Then click your chosen blog on the left side of the page, and finally, click customize in the Theme section.

Promoting Video with Vimeo

Vimeo, a social media community geared toward visual artists, filmmakers, and videographers, was originally created in 2004 as an outlet for creative work, compared to the more popular, trending, and commercial use of YouTube. Users can upload, view, share, and comment on videos, as shown in Figure 4-6.

The demographics are attractive: 100 million registered users as of Fall 2014, with 170 million video views worldwide. The audience skews to a college-educated, high-income population with a 2:1 ratio of men to women.

If you're in a creative profession (including graphic arts, advertising, music, dance, theater, comedy, or other performance arts), Vimeo is an excellent and cost-effective showcase for promoting the quality of your work to an appreciative audience and maybe picking up a few gigs!

Figure 4-6: Vimeo is an excellent platform for Voortex Productions to showcase its skills.

Reproduced with permission of Charley Voorhis, Voortex Productions, www.VoortexProductions.com

Signing up for a Vimeo PRO account

With the creation of PRO accounts for businesses (at $17 per month or $199 per year), Vimeo recognized that it needed financial support from business subscribers to avoid having to run banner advertisements on uploaded videos. (Vimeo offers both free and Plus accounts for $60 a year to individuals.)

According to Vimeo, the PRO account gets businesses the following:

✦ Up to 20 gigs of video storage per week

✦ Unlimited HD plays

✦ No caps on video bandwidth or time

✦ A customizable player, including your company colors and logo above your videos

✦ Mobile compatibility

✦ Ability to embed videos on your own site

✦ *Vimeo On Demand,* an option to receive payment for your video content through distribution directly to fans

✦ Advanced statistics

Vimeo PRO has some downsides, of course. Vimeo obviously has less traffic than YouTube, and it may be at risk of being eliminated from Google search results pages. (Nothing keeps you from posting your videos in both locations, however.)

Go for community and relationship building on Vimeo by interacting with the people who leave comments. This interaction may encourage your fans to return to view future work. Good relationships are like planting seeds. You never know when they may sprout into qualified leads, or even a collaborative effort.

Advertising on Vimeo

Most businesses advertise on Vimeo simply by creating a PRO account and uploading their work. You're not permitted to upload commercial videos any other way. To create an account, go to `http://vimeo.com/business` and click Join Now. In the Create Your Vimeo Account window that appears, enter your email address, username, and password; then click Continue. In the Checkout page that opens, supply your credit card information, and then click Place Order. For information about more elaborate "brand channels," see `http://vimeo.com/about/advertisers`.

All PRO accounts come with an Advanced Statistics package that goes beyond what you see above your videos. You can find more information on `http://vimeo.com/stats`. For videos embedded on your site, you can also integrate with Google Analytics by using a plug-in.

Visualizing Marketing Success with Vine

Vine is a mobile app and social sharing site that allows you to record and share six-second looping videos from your mobile device. It's become an attractive outlet for branding and for showing companies' products and services. Vine's short videos have a great reputation for going viral.

Founded in 2012 and now owned by Twitter, Vine claims 40 million registered accounts, although it's not clear how many of those accounts are active. The largest age cohort for users is 18 to 20 years old, and the population skews slightly female (57 percent).

Currently, Vine doesn't offer advertising other than an account, and has only limited statistics. Vine pages display loop counts (the number of times viewers have looped a video on Vine and wherever else it's been embedded on the web). It also displays how many followers you have and how many Vine accounts you follow, as shown in Figure 4-7.

Alas, Vine doesn't integrate with Google Analytics. However, if you want more than loop counts, try third-party sources for Vine stats, such as `http://simplymeasured.com/freebies/vine-analytics`.

To get started, download the Vine app from the Apple App Store, Google Play, or the Windows Phone store. After installing Vine, sign up with an email address or your Twitter account. For the web version, go to `https://vine.co`.

After logging in, you can find people to follow, create a channel, post your own videos, or view other Vines. You can leverage your smartphone's address book and the people you follow on Twitter to increase your reach on Vine. Simply tap the People icon on your Settings page to start searching for potential followers.

Use the Explore section (the eye icon on the far-left corner of the navigation) to find Vines you might like, or start with Popular Now (the star icon), the vines Featured In various categories, Trending Tags, or the list of Vine channels. Alternately, use the search bar at the top to locate specific people or hashtags.

Statistics

Search box

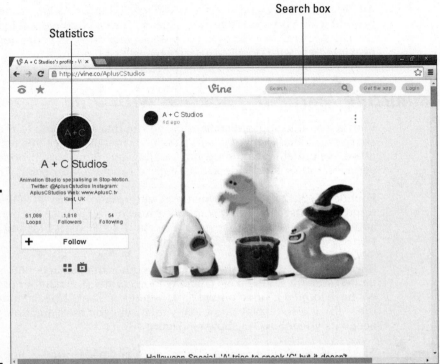

Figure 4-7:
Vine offers
animation
businesses
like A+C
Studios a
unique way
to promote
their
creative
capabilities.

Chapter 5: Making Social Media Mobile

In This Chapter

✔ **Understanding mobile media users**

✔ **Reaching people on the go**

✔ **Marketing with social media sites on smartphones**

✔ **Marketing with social media sites on tablets**

✔ **Advertising on mobile social media**

Social media is no longer confined to a standard computer of any size. The proliferation of smartphones and apps, 4G networks, more affordable data plans, built-in web browsers, and mobile-ready websites have all contributed to the growth of mobile social activities. Most devices (except old feature phones) can use either a cellular network or Wi-Fi for wireless Internet access.

The integration of social media with mobile devices creates more opportunities to reach your target audience in addition to challenges for managing and integrating your marketing campaigns.

As a social media marketer, try to tap the potential that these mobile devices offer: incredible marketing opportunities to reach both retail and business prospects at the moment they seek information about the product or service you offer, wherever they are. You don't have to wait for them to get back to their desktop computers. Of course, the social media marketing techniques you select may depend on the platforms that your target market uses. In this chapter, we look at how rapidly advancing mobile technology allows you to use social media to reach people on the go.

Mobile social marketing gives you many new ways to reach with your message. The challenge, of course, is that everyone else is trying to do that, too. Your efforts have to cut through an increasing amount of clutter.

Understanding the Statistics of Mobile Device Usage

To understand why mobile social marketing is so important, you must first acknowledge the explosive growth in the use of mobile devices. StatsCounter Global Stats estimates the usage of mobile devices for Internet access ballooned by 67 percent worldwide between August 2013 and August 2014.

Overall, the rate of use of mobile platforms and apps has already surpassed the use of desktops and laptops for web access, as shown in Table 5-1.

Table 5-1 Changes in Platform Usage for Web Access in the U.S.

Device Usage	March 2013	March 2014
Desktop	53%	40%
Mobile	47%	60%
Mobile App	40%	52%

Source: www.comscore.com/Insights/Presentations-and-Whitepapers/2014/The-US-Mobile-App-Report (page 5)

With 56 percent smartphone penetration of the U.S. market by population in January 2014, consumers increasingly use smartphones to search for local information, research products, and make purchases, as shown in Figure 5-1.

Exploring mobile use of social media

According to *Business Insider,* more than 60 percent of the time users spend on social media is now on mobile devices, not desktops. *ExactTarget's* research shows that 75 percent of consumers access social media at least once a day on their smartphones, as do 64 percent of tablet owners.

As you would expect, the increased use of mobile devices means that social media channels are seeing significant growth in mobile usage. According to ComScore, Facebook and Twitter enjoy majority usage on mobile platforms, while newer social networks like Vine, Snapchat, and Instagram are used almost exclusively on mobile platforms (see Figure 5-2). Only LinkedIn and Tumblr are still used primarily on desktops.

Generally speaking, Apple's iOS and Google's Android operating systems are highly competitive. Android led with a 52.5-percent market share April 2014, as shown in Figure 5-3.

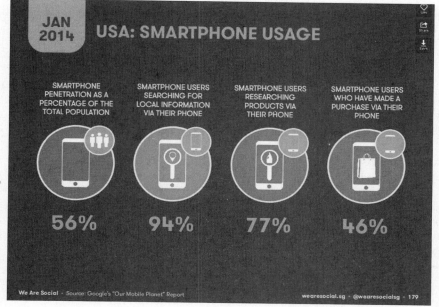

Figure 5-1:
How people
in the U.S.
used their
smartphones
in January
2014.

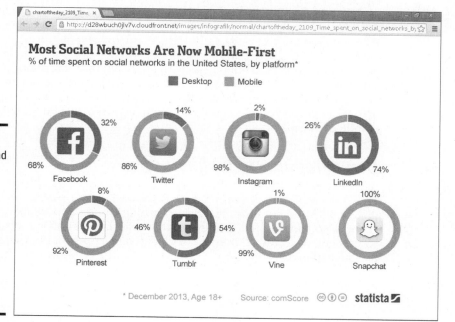

Figure 5-2:
Users spend
more time
on social
media
channels
in the U.S.
from their
mobile
devices
than from
desktops.

**Book VIII
Chapter 5**

Making Social
Media Mobile

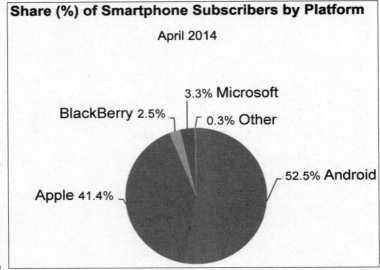

Figure 5-3: Market share for smartphones by operating system.

In terms of social media marketing, the question of platforms affects only the development of mobile apps, which need to be created for specific operating systems. Mobile sites, mobile advertising, and social media channels are generally operating-system neutral from a marketer's point of view (unless you're marketing your own app to users of a specific platform).

Why bother your marketing head with all this mobile information? You need to get your social media message across on the specific social media channels that your target audience uses, no matter how they access those channels. Your social content should be optimized visually and for ease of use on mobile platforms.

Demographics of mobile users

A 2014 study by the Pew Center (www.pewinternet.org/fact-sheets/mobile-technology-fact-sheet) showed that 61 percent of U.S. adult men and 57 percent of women owned a smartphone as of January 2014. The report also showed that the smartphone user population is racially diverse: 53 percent of whites, 59 percent of blacks, and 61 percent of Hispanics now use smartphones.

The biggest variation in smartphone use is by age, with 83 percent of those age 18 to 29 using smartphones; 74 percent of 30- to 49-year-olds; 49 percent of those ages 50 to 64; and 19 percent of those 65 and older.

Household income is a second differentiator: Only 47 percent of households earning less than $30,000 annually have a smartphone, but 53 percent of those earning $30,000 to $49,999 have one, as do 61 percent of those earning $50,000 to $74,999 and 81 percent of those earning more than $75,000.

Getting a handle on mobile activities

Mobile users check email, weather, traffic, maps, directions, and headlines. They also search for companies and products (especially local ones), compare prices, review entertainment schedules, access social media sites, watch videos, check review and ratings sites, sign up for alerts and coupons, and play games online. In other words, they are avid users of just about every social media channel.

Going Mobile

With the rapid growth in the use of mobile media, you really don't have a choice about creating a mobile version of your website. If you haven't already done so, ask your Web developer or programmer to create a mobile site as part of your web presence. That mobile site should link seamlessly to your social media presence on mobile media.

As you can see by comparing the regular website for HoardingNJ.com (see Figure 5-4) with its mobile version (see Figure 5-5), the regular website is too wide to navigate on a small screen. The mobile site has a different layout and focuses on fast, easy navigation.

You have several options for creating a mobile version of your website:

✦ Reformat an existing website so that it automatically resizes to fit various mobile platforms using a process called responsive design.

✦ Build a new website that's designed from scratch to work on desktops as well as on multiple mobile platforms of various sizes.

✦ Create a completely separate, new mobile site that has a mobile-friendly layout.

✦ Combine both a responsive design version of your primary website with a new mobile-friendly site and link between them.

✦ Develop a unique mobile app for your site, which users must download from an app store.

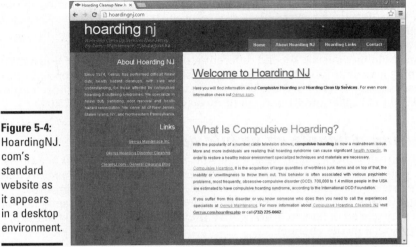

Figure 5-4:
HoardingNJ.
com's
standard
website as
it appears
in a desktop
environment.

Reproduced with permission of Gerrus Maintenance, Inc.

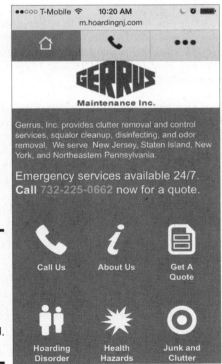

Figure 5-5:
The
dedicated
mobile
website for
http://m.
HoardingNJ.
com.

Reproduced with permission of Gerrus Maintenance, Inc.

You can have your Web programmer or developer build a mobile site or app from scratch, but many template-based sites allow you to build a mobile site yourself, or they will automatically convert your site into responsive design at a much lower cost than custom development. Some of these tools are listed in Table 5-2.

Table 5-2	Tools for Building Mobile Sites, Apps, and Ads
Name	*URL*
AdMob (mobile app promotion run by Google)	www.google.com/ads/admob/index.html
bMobilized (mobile site creator)	www.bmobilized.com
DudaMobile (mobile site creator; free and low-cost template and responsive design versions)	www.dudamobile.com
goMobi (mobile site creator; free seven-day trial)	http://gomobi.info
InMobi (mobile advertising network for games)	www.inmobi.com
MobGold (mobile advertising network)	www.mobgold.com
Mobify (mobile shopping platform)	www.mobify.com
MoPub (mobile ad network owned by Twitter)	www.mopub.com
Wadja (mobile SMS service)	www.wadja.com
Webhosting Search (mobile website tools and resources)	www.webhostingsearch.com/articles/30-best-tools-to-create-mobile-website.php

To decide the best type of mobile presence for your business, you must first decide the goals for your mobile site, just as you establish goals for any other marketing effort. Conduct some basic research to see whether content, content length, writing style, calls to action, navigation, and/or user behavior should be different in a mobile environment compared to desktop use to meet those goals.

Making the choice for responsive design

Responsive design makes the most sense when the content and functionality of your primary site and your mobile site will be basically the same. All you need to do is re-arrange the layout a bit. For example, if your site is compatible with it, responsive design may be a quick, first answer to obtaining a mobile presence. And it's inexpensive if you use one of the automated conversion sites.

Responsive design works particularly well when you have a small, information-based site. Keep in mind that some sites designed for desktop use don't convert well to responsive design. Carefully test sites like these:

+ Text-intensive sites with long scrolling pages

+ Image-intensive sites with graphics spread out around a page

+ Sites with so many images that it may take too long to download to a smartphone

+ Sites with many tables, which generally need to be reformatted

+ Sites supported by banner advertising

+ Sites with multiple columns of information

On the positive side, when you change content on a primary site built with responsive design, it changes on the mobile platform, as well. With responsive design, you don't need to set up redirects; people on a mobile environment automatically see the mobile version.

Making the choice for a new mobile site

Creating an entirely new mobile site has some distinct advantages:

+ You can break free from older technologies you used to build your website long ago or that you selected to remain compatible with older versions of desktop browsers.

+ Users generally have a better experience with newer technologies, and those technologies reduce your maintenance costs.

+ Third, you can reduce the download time by reducing the amount of content, such as using fewer, smaller images.

Mobile-only sites are particularly valuable when you want to create a teaser advertisement, using only a few screens to tell your story and drive people elsewhere online for additional activity.

There are some downsides to a mobile-only site, of course:

+ Depending on the application, some users will prefer a consistent experience between their desktop and mobile environments.

+ Whenever you have two separate sites, you need to update both.

✦ With two sites, you must offer obvious ways to link between them, and you must insert simple code so that mobile users are automatically redirected to your mobile site.

Making the choice for a mobile app

An app is a different animal altogether. Apps, by definition, involve more than the presentation of information with simple links; they require programming so that users can enter information or must supply information in response to a query, as the Foursquare app does in Figure 5-6.

Most apps are done with custom programming. Generally, this custom programming makes an app more expensive to develop than a mobile site, and it will take longer to launch. Because new versions of operating systems are released frequently, apps usually don't have as long a lifespan as a mobile site or one with responsive design; they will need to be updated and tested to keep pace with changes in operating systems. And because apps are platform-specific, they don't have as broad a reach as mobile sites that can be seen on any smartphone.

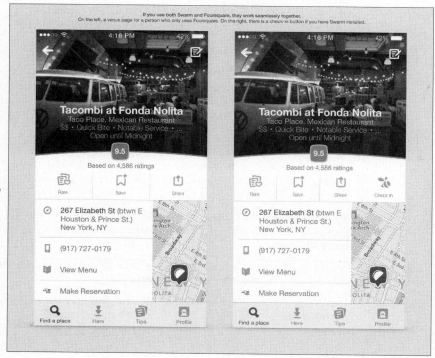

Figure 5-6: Foursquare, a location-based social media channel, exists as an app in a mobile environment.

Table 5-2, earlier in this chapter, includes some sources for less expensive, automated app-development services. Sometimes these apps work, sometimes they don't. Test thoroughly!

Choosing the app route

An app is the preferred solution if your mobile activity involves

✦ Interactive gaming

✦ Frequent, personalized usage, requiring that the app pull up specific records

✦ Inserting entered data into calculations, reports, or charts, such as financial records

✦ Accessing functionality that isn't mobile-specific, such as a separate camera or additional processing power

✦ Accessing content or functions without a wireless connection

Like with responsive design and mobile sites, apps have some downsides. Consider these drawbacks:

✦ Users can't instantly access apps via a browser on multiple devices; they must download and install each app (and each new update) from an app store such as iTunes or Google Play.

✦ Apps aren't compatible across platforms the way mobile sites are; you must create separate versions for each platform and make them available for each type of device. This incompatibility extends to ongoing support issues because you'll need to do upgrades and testing on multiple platforms over time.

✦ Mobile sites are more practical than apps for public communications or marketing because they're easier to change. Updated content or features are immediately available on mobile sites, but changes to apps require that users download new versions.

✦ You can more easily integrate mobile sites with other mobile technologies, such as GPS and QR codes, than you can integrate apps with these technologies.

✦ Search engines can't find apps (you have to publicize them to users), nor can search engines index the content of apps.

✦ Users can't share apps with a simple link, the way they can share a mobile site.

Reaching People on the Move with Social Media

Almost all social media services now automatically reconfigure their sites for mobile devices (responsive design). However, most also have their own app optimized for mobile usage (both smartphone and tablet), as shown in Table 5-3.

In either case, you don't have to worry about the mechanics of changing your page or post. But you do have to think about how you can benefit from reaching people who are using mobile devices and how your posts and profiles will appear in these formats.

Table 5-3	Mobile Apps for Social Media		
Name	*URL to Download App*	*Mobile Site (Responsive Design)*	*Vanity URL*
Digg	https://itunes.apple.com/us/app/digg/id362872995?mt=8 https://play.google.com/store/apps/details?id=com.diggreader&hl=en	http://m.digg.com	None
Facebook	https://itunes.apple.com/us/app/facebook/id284882215?mt=8 https://play.google.com/store/apps/details?id=com.facebook.katana	https://m.facebook.com	www.facebook.com/mobile
Flickr	http://itunes.apple.com/us/app/flickr/id328407587?mt=8 https://play.google.com/store/apps/details?id=com.yahoo.mobile.client.android.flickr	https://m.flickr.com	www.flickr.com

(continued)

Book VIII Chapter 5

Making Social Media Mobile

Table 5-3 *(continued)*

Name	URL to Download App	Mobile Site (Responsive Design)	Vanity URL

Foursquare	`http://itunes. apple.com/us/ app/foursquare/ id306934924?mt=8`
	
	`https://play.google. com/store/apps/ details?id=com. joelapenna. foursquared`
		None	`https:// foursquare. com/download`

Google+	`http://itunes.apple. com/us/app/google+/ id447119634?mt=8`
	
	`https://play.google. com/store/apps/ details?id=com. google.android.apps. plus`
		None	`www.google. com/mobile/+`

LinkedIn	`http://itunes.apple. com/us/app/linkedin/ id288429040?mt=8`
	
	`https://play.google. com/store/apps/ details?id=com. linkedin.android`
		`https://touch. www.linkedin. com`	`www.linkedin. com/mobile`

Myspace	`http://itunes.apple. com/us/app/myspace/ id284792653?mt=8`
	
	`https://play.google. com/store/apps/ details?id=com. myspace.spacerock`
		None	None

Name	URL to Download App	Mobile Site (Responsive Design)	Vanity URL
Pinterest	http://itunes.apple.com/us/app/pinterest/id429047995?mt=8 https://play.google.com/store/apps/details?id=com.pinterest	None	None
Twitter	https://play.google.com/store/apps/details?id=com.twitter.android	https://mobile.twitter.com	https://twitter.com/download

For example, the mobile version of Facebook focuses on interactivity. Users can view their News Feeds and post their own updates, comments, videos, and images.

Even Twitter, which has cellphone DNA in its genes, has revamped its mobile appearance with an app. The app offers an easy-to-use layout, with navigation that allows you to visit your Timeline, discover trends or people, view your own profile, search for people or tweets, and of course, send out a tweet.

So what does all this mean for your business while you develop social media messages for users who are always on the run? Keep in mind the following points:

✦ Pin your posts to the top of the newsfeed stream because only the first several posts will be displayed on mobile screens.

✦ Use analytics to make sure your posts are relevant to the demographics and behavioral patterns of the users of that particular social channel.

✦ Before publishing, always double-check the appearance of your posts and other content on smartphones and tablets to be sure everything looks right.

✦ If you have links, be sure they go to mobile-friendly pages; links to your website should go to a mobile-specific site or to a page built with responsive design.

✦ Make it easy for users to share your content from their mobile devices via text, email, and/or share buttons.

Compare the mobile app version of The Lodge at MSL Resort's Facebook Page in Figure 5-7 with the desktop version of that Facebook page in Figure 5-8.

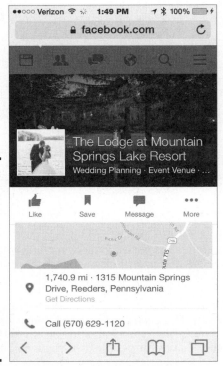

Figure 5-7:
Compare
the mobile
app version
of the
Facebook
page for
the Lodge
at MSL
Resort with
the desktop
version in
Figure 5-8.

Reproduced with permission of Mountain Springs Lake Corp.

Figure 5-8:
The desktop
version
of the
Facebook
page for the
Lodge at
MSL Resort.

Reproduced with permission of Mountain Springs Lake Corp.

Also check your Facebook Page, LinkedIn profile, and Twitter stream on various smartphone and tablet operating systems to see how they appear; adjust as needed.

Harvesting Leads and Sales from Social Mobile

You can find as many applications for marketing via mobile social media as you can imagine. Keep in mind the areas described in this list, whatever the device or market segment you target:

✦ **News and updates:** Distribute this type of information to your Twitter, Facebook, and LinkedIn followers, as well as to people on your prospect list and your newsletter subscribers. (See Figure 5-9 for an example of news updates distributed on the mobile version of Twitter.)

✦ **Emergency information:** Warnings range from product recalls to weather hazards.

✦ **Comparison shopping:** Provide information so that Facebook, Twitter, and Pinterest shoppers can compare by price and feature and learn about sales.

✦ **Local business announcements:** Announce coupons, deals, and special offers across all your social media channels.

✦ **Customer service improvements:** For instance, use Twitter to let customers place a pickup order and find out when their order is ready. Use QR codes so people can quickly determine your competitive products, features, and prices.

QR codes are the two-dimensional versions of bar codes. Able to hold about 350 times more information than a bar code, QR codes usually appear in print or online as a square or rectangle with black-and-white dots. Viewers can use their smartphones to scan a QR code, which then links them directly to a web page with additional information.

✦ **Event publicity:** On Twitter and Facebook, consider providing real-time logistical information.

✦ **Integration of mobile marketing and social media:** Post updates on the fly and use geo-marketing services, such as Foursquare (described in Book VIII, Chapter 3), especially if your business targets younger, local customers. (Refer to Figure 5-6, earlier in this chapter.)

Don't let the obvious business-to-customer (B2C) value of mobile devices blind you: Mobile marketing has a place in business-to-business (B2B) strategies, as well. For example, sales people are using the technology for competitive research, tracking sales calls, and demonstrating their products and services to prospective customers. In fact, according to the 2013 AT&T Small Business Technology Poll, 98 percent of small businesses have already incorporated some form of wireless devices into their operations.

Figure 5-9: Distributing news updates on Twitter's mobile version makes a lot of sense for the Strand Bookstore.

Reproduced with permission of Strand Bookstore, Inc.

Mobile messaging turns to gold

Founded by Scott Swerland in 2004, Seattle Sun Tan has grown rapidly to a staff of 275 handling 38 tanning salons throughout the Pacific Northwest.

The company started immediately with a website, allowing its social media presence to evolve organically. It adopted Facebook, Twitter, Tumblr, Pinterest, Vimeo, and Instagram, in that order. Now in the process of redeveloping the Seattle Sun Tan website with responsive design, Stewart Kelpe, Director of Marketing, notes how critical this has become. "With so many different devices in use today, it is imperative that we update our site with responsive design to give the end user the best experience possible when interacting with our brand. . . . Our analytics have shown a dramatic platform shift from desktop to mobile over the past year." (View the mobile version on a smartphone in the nearby screenshot.)

Reproduced with permission of SST Group LLC

The company is devoted to mobile marketing in many more ways, taking advantage of mobile media for advertising as well as text messaging. "Mobile provides incredible opportunities for us to reach and engage with our target demographic, primarily women 18 to 54, who are extremely active in the mobile space," explains Kelpe.

For example, when Kelpe discovered that Pandora Internet radio was one of the biggest drivers of new traffic to the website, he used Pandora to leverage a 30-day text campaign that generated more than $62,000 in revenue.

(continued)

(continued)

Kelpe first decided to incorporate text messaging (short message service, or SMS) into his marketing strategy in February 2013. He knew that everyone who would receive a text message would already have prequalified by opting in. "Text messaging (SMS) provides us with an affordable, direct line to share our campaigns or brand message with our customers, unlike email, where the open rate can be substantially less."

He selected Tatango, an SMS provider, for assistance, distribution, and analytics. His in-house staff creates and executes the campaigns, which generally involve sending one to two text messages per month. Kelpe uses both the website and social pages to promote the text campaigns and for social cross-promotion (as seen in the nearby screenshot), as well as direct in-store marketing and email campaigns.

Reproduced with permission of SST Group LLC

For instance, one on-site promotion to encourage opt-ins offered clients a $20 credit to join Seattle Sun Tan's Mobile VIP club. Kelpe deliberately chose the $20 amount because "it's a great value for the client and for us; it functions very well with our business model." Since he launched the text message campaign a little over a year ago, Seattle Sun Tan has gained nearly 15,000 users and garnered more than $975,000.

Other offers on the website have different goals; some are geared toward customer acquisition, others toward platform growth or increased sales. Kelpe integrates SMS with other marketing channels, from radio, direct mail, store events, community outreach, billboards, and in-store point-of-purchase to Internet radio, pay-per-click ads, and SEO. "Text messaging," he explains, "integrates so well with other platforms." To illustrate his point, Kelpe describes how someone searching for tanning deals online might click on Seattle Sun Tan's PPC ads. The click takes them to a specific landing page based on the keywords they used in the search request. Instantaneously, the keyword generates an offer specifically tailored to the user's search term. From the landing page, users can print the coupon or send the offer to their mobile devices.

Kelpe encourages other companies to follow Seattle Sun Tan's lead. "SMS is absolutely within reach of small business. [It] can be a very affordable way to reach your customers with messaging that is direct and to the point. . . . Be sure not to be overbearing with the frequency of your messaging, but rather aim for quality messaging over quantity."

Seattle Suntan's web presence:

✔ `http://seattlesuntan.com` (website)

✔ `www.facebook.com/seattlesuntan`

✔ `https://twitter.com/seattlesuntan`

✔ `http://vimeo.com/user9989824`

✔ `http://seattlesuntan.tumblr.com`

✔ `www.pinterest.com/seattlesuntan`

✔ `http://instagram.com/seattlesuntan`

Measuring Your Mobile Marketing Success

As with all analytics, which elements you measure depend on your goals and objectives. Of course, your choices depend on whether you're measuring intermediate performance indicators (for example, the number of Likes on your Facebook Page from mobile versus desktop users) or your return on investment in a mobile advertising campaign, a new mobile app, or increased foot traffic to your brick-and-mortar store.

You can segment mobile visitors by using the available tools within Google Analytics to track behavior on a mobile site or on your regular website (or both). You might want to set up a separate conversion funnel for mobile users. Watch for variations between mobile and web visitors on traffic to your social media pages, links to your mobile website, qualified prospects, and leads that turn into sales.

See Book IX, Chapter 5 for additional information about analyzing mobile social metrics and comparing them to metrics for social media in a standard environment.

Counting on Tablets

Use of e-readers, iPads, and other tablet computers is exploding. Given the convergence of high technology with usability, portability, mobility, and affordability, it may represent a true paradigm shift in computing.

By January 2014, roughly 44 percent of U.S. consumers owned tablet computers, and 69 percent of small businesses were using them. Social media channels are now omnipresent on both Apple iPads and Android-based tablets.

Like with smartphones, tablet owners use their devices for many purposes: research, shopping, news, customer reviews, and yes, social media. Once again, the Pew Research Center Internet & American Life Project comes through with essential insights:

✦ Tablet use doesn't differ much by gender or by race and ethnicity any more. The percentage of American adults hovers at roughly one-third in each group.

✦ The highest adoption rate is by users ages 30 to 49 (52 percent), followed closely by the younger cohort of 18- to 29-year-olds (48 percent). Both have significantly higher usage than 50- to 64-year-olds (37 percent) and those over 65 (25 percent).

✦ As you might expect, the higher their education level, the more likely it is that adults own a tablet: 59 percent of college graduates, 45 percent with some college, and 29 percent of those without any college education.

✦ Also quite predictably, ownership rises with household income, ranging from 25 percent of those with less than $30,000 in annual income, to 45 percent with annual income in the $30,000-to-$50,000 range, and 65 percent for those with a household annual income of $75,000 or more.

As smartphones become larger and tablets become smaller, the challenge of developing sites that will work in both environments may become moot.

Obviously, larger high-resolution tablets make viewing videos on tablets more appealing than viewing them on smartphones, leading to even greater popularity for video-sharing sites like YouTube and Vimeo. Figure 5-10 shows a YouTube site on a tablet.

Figure 5-10: The YouTube page for Mountain Springs Lake Resort displays well on a tablet.

Reproduced with permission of Mountain Springs Lake Corp.

Although many social media channels have apps that work for all mobile devices, regardless of size, others have versions designed specifically for tablets. Some of these apps appear in Table 5-3, earlier in this chapter.

Using Mobile Social Media for Advertising

In Chapter 6 of this minibook, we show that the overall social advertising market is projected to grow to $11 billion by 2017. Suffice it to say that mobile social media has more than a minor share of that advertising. More than half of Facebook's advertising revenue now comes from ads that appear on Facebook's mobile pages; one quarter of YouTube's advertising revenue comes from mobile views.

Facebook, Twitter, and other social media channels now mine their huge populations of users to deliver extremely targeted audiences for advertising based not only on search terms, but also on behavior and likely action. As an advertiser, you can now follow users as they research products, compare prices, and make purchases in near real-time from their mobile devices.

Facebook's own mobile advertising network publishes ads not only on Facebook mobile pages, but also on third-party Facebook apps. For more information on Facebook mobile advertising, see *Facebook Marketing All-in-One For Dummies* by Andrea Vahl, John Haydon, and Jan Zimmerman (Wiley Publishing, Inc.), or visit `www.facebook.com/help/714656935225188` to get started.

Twitter, which acquired the ad network MoPub in 2013, has taken a similar approach, allowing you to target your audiences by device, as well as by behavior or interest area. For more about Twitter mobile advertising, visit `https://business.twitter.com`. Pay special attention to the use of mobile advertising to encourage people to download your apps directly from a tweet at `https://business.twitter.com/solutions/drive-app-installations-or-engagements`.

Chapter 6: Multiplying Your Impact

In This Chapter

✔ Integrating social media with e-newsletters

✔ Incorporating social media into press releases and public relations

✔ Leveraging social media with website features

✔ Using paid advertising on social media

A volatile debate rages in marketing circles: Has social media become so prohibitively popular — and social media companies so desperate to monetize their sites and satisfy their investors — that it's no longer possible to be successful with only free posts and content?

Statistical analysis by *The Guardian* (`www.theguardian.com/media/2014/sep/15/pay-to-play-the-end-of-free-social-media-marketing`) shows that *organic* (unsponsored) reach for brands on Facebook and Twitter has plummeted to the point that less than 10 percent of your followers even see your content. Instead, promoted posts, ads, and posts from friends squeeze out your attempts to communicate for free.

You can address this problem in two ways: beat 'em or join 'em. In this chapter, we talk first about beating 'em by combining social media with email, press releases, or websites to increase reach.

If those methods don't work, you can always join 'em by paying to promote your posts, tweets, and pins to reach the audience you want. We discuss a range of advertising possibilities on four primary social media channels: Facebook, Twitter, LinkedIn, and Pinterest.

Thinking Strategically about Social Media Integration

For many businesses, social media marketing adds to the richness of the company's marketing mix with a purpose of its own. Others see it as a low-cost boost to standard press release distribution, email newsletter subscribers, loyalty programs, or other forms of marketing.

These more traditional marketing efforts can go viral when you take advantage of social media integration to

✦ Increase newsletter subscriptions.

✦ Broaden the audience for event announcements.

✦ Maximize the distribution of press releases and other news.

✦ Drive traffic to your hub website to encourage users to take advantage of special features.

✦ Cross-post content in all these venues to increase reach.

We discuss simple integration techniques in Book II, Chapter 3, such as displaying chiclets to invite people to follow your company on social media outlets and implementing share buttons to encourage viewers to share your pages with others.

Keep in mind that a social media campaign may take six months to a year to reach maturity. Don't stop using other tactics that now reach your target markets successfully. Wait for results from metrics showing that social media perform at least as well before you abandon a current technique. And you can't know what to measure unless you first set goals for your integration efforts, which we discuss in Book I, Chapter 1. Sometimes you're after sales, sometimes leads, sometimes brand recognition, or sometimes just your 15 minutes of fame.

Whatever you're planning, take advantage of the measurement tools we discuss in Book IX to establish baselines for traffic, click-through rate (CTR), conversion rates, and return on investment (ROI) for existing marketing methods so that you can detect any lift (or drop) that integration brings.

In its *Social Media Marketing Industry Report 2014,* Social Media Examiner asked businesses whether they integrated their social media with other marketing techniques. An amazing 83 percent of respondents replied affirmatively, as shown in Figure 6-1. Consider their experiences while you move forward with your own plans for social media integration.

Include your integrated marketing tactics on your Social Media Marketing Plan (see Book I, Chapter 3) and schedule activities on your Social Media Activity Calendar (Book 1, Chapter 4).

To define the specific form your integration methods will take, who will execute them and when, and how you will measure the results, create a block diagram showing how content will flow as part of your integration plans (see Book I, Chapter 3).

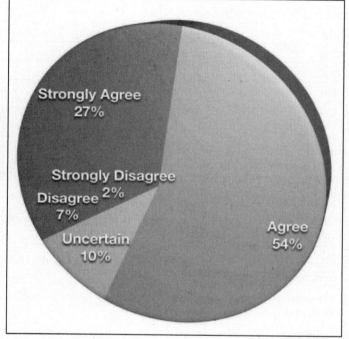

Figure 6-1:
More than 80 percent of marketers say they have integrated social media with traditional marketing efforts to some degree.

Integrating Social Media with E-Newsletters

As Table 6-1 shows, social media sharing now outpaces email sharing, especially on mobile devices. However, there are still good reasons for maintaining and cross-posting between social media and your e-newsletter campaigns.

Table 6-1	The Top Ways Consumers Share Content
Method	*Percent of Shared Links by Source*
Sharing to Facebook	26%
Address bar sharing	21%
Facebook Like	15%
Twitter	12%
Email	7%

(continued)

Table 6-1 *(continued)*

Method	Percent of Shared Links by Source
Printing	6%
Pinterest	2%
All other sources	11%

Source: http://cache.addthiscdn.com/site/report/addthis_quarterly_report_formatted_042814.pdf

Be cautious with summary numbers. Sources for sharing may differ significantly by content. For instance, Pinterest may appear as a lowly sharing source overall, but it's the top source for sharing food content! Sharing behavior may also vary significantly by age and ethnicity.

The following list provides a few indicators of the popularity of combining social media with e-newsletters:

✦ Fifty-six percent of companies incorporate social media sharing with e-newsletters.

✦ Forty-nine percent of companies find it easy to install social sharing buttons on their newsletters.

✦ Twenty-nine percent of companies find it simple to use a Facebook registration tab to gain newsletter subscribers.

✦ By 2014, the number of companies integrating social media into their email marketing campaigns grew to 91 percent from 60 percent in 2012.

More than three times as many people have email accounts than Twitter and Facebook accounts combined. Email open rates, which average in the 20- to 30-percent range, make an email message five times more likely to be seen than the same post in Facebook, where organic reach has dropped to 6 percent. And the click-through rate for email, which generally hits about 3 percent, is six times that of the click-through rate for tweets.

With numbers like these, you have every reason to integrate social media with email to attract new subscribers, promote your newsletter, obtain content ideas, and identify issues to address in your email newsletters, not to mention increasing the reach for your social media posts. For more information on email marketing, see *E-Mail Marketing For Dummies*, 2nd Edition, by John Arnold (Wiley Publishing, Inc.).

Gaining more subscribers

Wherever and whenever prospects discover your presence on social media, try to provide them with other opportunities to find out how you might be able to solve their problems. Your online newsletter is certainly one of those opportunities. Follow these guidelines to gain more newsletter subscribers:

✦ **Include a link for newsletter subscription on your blog, all your other social media pages, and your email signature block.** Constant Contact (`https://marketplace.constantcontact.com/Listing/applications/constant-contact-labs-facebook/PML-0239`) and MailChimp (`https://apps.facebook.com/mailchimp`), among others, have apps you can add to your Facebook Page to allow individuals to sign up for your newsletter directly (see Figure 6-2). You never know — you might reach dozens, hundreds, maybe thousands of new prospects.

✦ **Treat your newsletter as an event on social media networks.** Add a preview of topics or tweet an announcement of your newsletter a day or so in advance. Include a linkable call to action to subscribe in both cases.

Join Our List tab

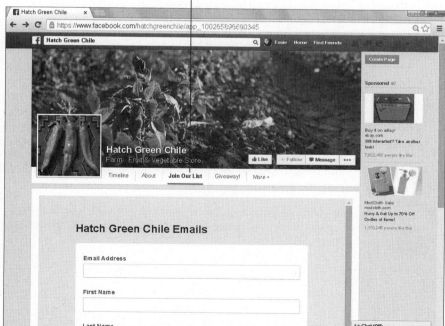

Figure 6-2: Hatch Green Chile solicits e-newsletter subscribers directly on a Facebook tab labeled Join Our List.

Book VIII Chapter 6

Multiplying Your Impact

✦ **Post a teaser line in your social media outlets with a linkable call to action.** You might say, for example, "To learn more about healthcare reform for small businesses, sign up for our newsletter."

✦ **Post newsworthy findings.** Use material from your newsletter on social news services like Digg and reddit (see Book II, Chapter 3) to attract more readers.

✦ **Include edited versions of social media posts in your newsletters.** This increases reach for important items.

✦ **Link to a sample newsletter or newsletter archive from your blog, website, or from the About section or a tab on your Facebook Page.** Prospective subscribers can see your newsletter's usefulness. Of course, also indicate the frequency with which you email newsletters.

Finding more followers and connections

Email integration with social media works both ways: You can drive people from your newsletter to social media services or use social media services to gain subscribers. Here are some guidelines for finding more followers and connections:

✦ Use your newsletter to drive traffic to your social media outlets with social media chiclets, as wedding and events supplier Koyal Wholesale does in Figure 6-3.

✦ Include share buttons in every issue of your newsletter.

✦ Add options for signing up for social media on the email registration page on your website (if possible).

✦ Use your e-newsletter to make an offer or run a contest for social media participants. For example, Koyal Wholesale also combined a Facebook photo contest with an email campaign to launch its summer product line. (The new products became prizes for the contest.) The happy marriage of old and new marketing techniques increased revenue by 16 percent. In the process, Koyal increased its number of Facebook Likes and shares, as well as newsletter subscribers.

Cross-promote your email newsletter on all your social media channels. Remember to post all your social venues, not just your hub website, in your email signature block.

Social media chiclets

Figure 6-3:
Use chiclets on your newsletter to drive traffic to multiple social media outlets, as well as to your website.

Reproduced with permission of Marketing Sherpa

Finding and sharing content

Writing content continuously for newsletters and social media is always a challenge. However, you can exploit the easy interaction between the two to lighten your writing burden:

✦ **Take advantage of social marketing capabilities from your email service provider.** Many companies now let you easily send your email directly to Facebook and other social networking pages.

✦ **Mine social media for content.** Read related information on social news sites, listen to hot topics that come up in LinkedIn and Facebook groups, and watch for trending topics. Pay attention to comments on your own and other people's forums, message boards, and social communities. Those comments may clue you in to concerns, trends, or industry news.

✦ **Use Google Alerts, Social Mention, Twitter Search, and other search functions for mentions of your company.** You can turn positive comments into testimonial content on your newsletter, social media outlet, or website (with permission), or respond to many people at a time who may have read a negative comment.

✦ **Create a Q&A section in your regular newsletter.** Respond to questions that are common across social media venues.

✦ **Use keywords and tags to identify social news and content related to your industry.** In turn, be sure to include keywords in any newsletters or newsletter announcements that may be reposted on the web.

✦ **Pursue market intelligence even further by using the advanced Twitter Search features.** Sort tweets geographically through an advanced search to see which topics are of interest locally, in locations where you have offices, or wherever large clusters of your customers or prospects live or work. Then segment your mailing list accordingly, if appropriate. Follow these steps:

1. *Go to* `https://twitter.com/search-home`*.*

2. *Enter your search term and then click the blue Search button.*

3. *In the left navigation of the returned search results, click Advanced Search.*

4. *Under Places, enter location information in the Near This Place text box.*

   If you enter a zip code or city, the search results will automatically be set to a 15-mile radius.

5. *Click the blue Search button to see the geographic subset of search results. Because trending topics may vary by region, this approach lets you discover topics that are of interest to prospects or customers in different locations.*

Use Google Trends (`www.google.com/trends`) to figure out the day of week and time of year when users are most likely to use specific search terms, such as *Christmas tree ornaments* in November or December. Use that information to schedule your topical email blasts. There's nothing like having information show up in someone's inbox just when he's looking for it! You'll be way beyond top of mind.

Integrating Social Media with Press Releases

The reasons for dealing with public relations and press release distribution haven't changed since the explosion of social media — just the methodology and relative prominence. Where once you worried only about the care and feeding of a small covey of journalists, now you must nourish a veritable horde of bloggers, individual influencers, authors of e-zine articles, editors of online publications, and individuals who will recommend your article on a social news service.

In companies that view social media primarily as a public relations vehicle, the public or community relations person (or contractor) may be the one who coordinates the social media marketing strategy.

All these venues, not just standard media, open a door to public attention. Take advantage of them all as a cost-effective way to achieve these goals:

✦ **Broadcast announcements of products, appearances, and events.** Alerting target markets to new products and services is one of the most traditional uses of publicity.

✦ **Build brand recognition.** Whether it's acknowledgment of your participation in community events, awareness of your position within your industry, or simply the frequent repetition of your name in front of your audience, press coverage brings you publicity at a relatively low cost.

✦ **Ask journalists, authors, or bloggers to write about your company.** Stories about your firm — at least, the positive ones — boost your credibility, extend your reach, and provide you with bragging destinations for links from your site. Trade press is especially critical to business-to-business (B2B) companies.

✦ **Drive traffic to your website.** Online press releases almost always have at least one link to your central web presence, and often more. Social media offers a mechanism for distributing linkable press content around the web that others may embed. The accumulation of long-lasting inbound links obviously has a greater impact than a one-time release.

✦ **Improve search engine ranking.** You can gain many inbound links to your site when your release posts on multiple press outlets. Press sites generally transfer their high page rankings to your site; Google, in particular, weighs mentions in blogs and press sites (and other rich content) highly. Your visibility on preferred search terms may also rise, especially if you optimize your press releases and sub-heads for keywords (within reasonable constraints).

To counteract spammers' attempts to use press releases to goose SEO rankings, Google's Panda update discounts anonymous authorship in favor of clearly sourced articles. Beware of using template-based releases that are too short or that appear to be stuffed with keywords. Watch for news of other algorithm updates that filter out fake Likes, reviews, and other social media content. Many press release sites are now using human reviewers to ensure quality content.

Setting up an online newsroom

If you haven't already done so, set up an online newsroom (media page) for the press on your primary website. Use this newsroom to present any press releases you create, provide writers with downloadable logos and images, link to articles and posts written about your company, and let writers sign up for really simple syndication (RSS) feeds for future release.

Also consider setting up this newsroom as a separate section in blog format (another way to integrate social media!) to aggregate queries, moderated posts, and trackbacks from individual releases. Give each release a unique URL, and place your headline on the page title.

Cultivating influencers

Identifying influencers is one key way to get into a conversation. Influencers are people whose blogs, tweets, or Facebook Pages drive much of the conversation in a particular topic area. They often have a loyal following of readers who engage in dialog, and repeat and amplify discussions the influencer began. In the olden days, press folks would cultivate public relations and press contacts the same way you now cultivate influencers.

Here's a quick checklist for finding these key figures to approach with a request for coverage:

✦ **Find conversations on blogs, Twitter, Facebook, forums, message boards, communities, and industry-specific social media by using keywords relevant to your company, brand, product, industry, and competitors.** You can find such searches on Meltwater's IceRocket (www. icerocket.com) or Topsy (http://topsy.com).

✦ **Use search tools on particular networks and aggregator searches, such as Social Mention or mention.** Those who post most often, or who have a lot of connections or followers, may be the experts or influencers you seek. Monitor the conversations for a while to be sure that you identified the right folks.

✦ **Use standard search techniques to locate trade publications or related newsletters.** Publication sites may include links to their own social media sites. Or you can identify specific writers and editors whose interests sync with yours and search for their individual blogs and social networking accounts.

✦ **Become a contributor who answers questions on related subjects in various social media venues.** You can (and should) identify yourself, without promoting your company or products in your comments. Before you ask for anything, engage in the conversation and offer links to related posts and articles. Because links are the currency of social media, link from your site to influencers' sites, blogs, and tweets, and become a connection or follower.

To track your contacts, bookmark the conversations you find, organizing them in subfolders by the name of the influencer.

Distributing your news

Frankly, the more sites, the merrier. Although you'll pay a penalty for duplicate website content in search engines, press releases don't seem to suffer.

Place identifying tags on links in different press releases so that you can tell which releases generate click-throughs to your site. If you create only one release a month, this isn't essential; however, if you have an active campaign with numerous press mentions or other types of postings on the same source sites, these identifying tags are absolutely critical.

Table 6-2 shows a partial list of press and PR online resources.

Table 6-2	Publicity and PR Resources	
Name	*URL*	*Description*
24-7 Press Release	www.24-7pressrelease.com	Disseminates news to online media, print media, journalists, bloggers, and search engines
BuzzStream	www.buzzstream.com/social-media	Fee-based social CRM and monitoring service
Business Wire	www.businesswire.com/files/whitepapers/press-release-optimization-guide.pdf	"A Guide to Press Release Optimization"
Amanda Spann's blog	http://breakingthebrand.com/2014/05/10-websites-offering-free-press-release-distribution	"10 Websites Offering Free Press Release Distribution"
ClickPress	www.clickpress.com	Paid press-release posting on-site
Free Press Release	www.free-press-release.com	Free press release distribution; includes social media for paid subscriptions
Help a Reporter Out (HARO)	http://helpareporter.com	Matching reporters to sources

(continued)

Table 6-2 *(continued)*

Name	URL	Description
iNewsWire	www.i-newswire.com	Submits press releases and other content to news, social media, and media outlets. Free account offers one press release/month; fee versions starting at $79/month
PitchEngine	www.pitchengine.com	Social PR platform, social media release creation and distribution; paid versions starting at $19/month for one pitch; pay-as-you go for $20 per pitch
Press About	www.pressabout.com	Paid press release distribution in the form of a blog
PRLog	www.prlog.org	Free basic distribution for press releases; paid versions with wider distribution for $49 or $349 per release
PRWeb	http://service.prweb.com/learning/article/press-release-grader	Free press-release grader service
ReleaseWire	www.releasewire.com	Syndicated press release distribution to more than 400 media sites and search engines; fees starting at $39.95/month
reddit	www.reddit.com	Social news site that accepts links to releases
The Open Press	www.theopenpress.com	Paid on-site press-release posting
Tiny Pitch	http://tiny.pr	Free service; turns a press release into a web app that can be shared on social networks and with your contacts

Posting on your own sites

Post your release, at minimum, on your own website and blog. You can, however, easily add releases to your other social networking profiles, if it's appropriate. For instance, an author might post a release for each book she writes, but wouldn't necessarily post a press release for everyone hired at her company.

To simplify your life, use syndication tools such as Hootsuite, TweetDeck, Netvibes, or Sprout Social (see Book II, Chapter 1) to post press releases and newsletter content on your blog, Facebook Page, and elsewhere. Of course, then the content will be identical.

Using standard press distribution sources

Many paid online press-release distribution sources exist. Among the most well-known are Business Wire, Vocus, PR Newswire, PRWeb, and Marketwired. Sometimes, distribution services offer levels of service at different prices depending on the quantity and type of distribution, geographical distribution, and whether distribution includes social media, multimedia, offline publications, or other criteria.

Table 6-2, earlier in this chapter, includes several options for free distribution. Many free services don't distribute your releases — except perhaps to search engines — but, rather, simply post them on their sites for finite periods. Whether they're free or paid, be sure to read carefully what you're getting.

Perhaps the most straightforward example of integrating press releases with social media is the distribution of a release announcing your social media activities. SideChef distributed the press release shown in Figure 6-4 through PRWeb, one of many paid press-release distribution services.

Post linkable event announcements on calendars all over the web, as well as Event pages on Facebook and other social media. Calendars may be an old-fashioned, pre–social media technique, but many high-ranking calendar pages feed page rank value until your event occurs and the listing expires.

Using bloggers as a distribution channel

You've laid the groundwork by identifying appropriate bloggers and other influencers and participated on their publications. The next step is to get them to post your news. The most discrete way is to email it (or a link to it) with a cover note to see whether the recipient wants to share the article with readers or comment on its content.

Figure 6-4:
SideChef's press release announced its participation in Social Media Week to promote its award-winning app.

Because you're "pitching" the bloggers, include in your cover note why you think readers of the blog would be interested and also a descriptive paragraph about your company. It's considered bad form to submit your press release as a post on most blogs — bad enough that a moderator probably would exclude it.

If you include a product sample with your release, implicitly asking for an independent review, the blogger now has to disclose that fact. In October 2009, the Federal Trade Commission (FTC) published final guidelines for endorsement and testimonials; The FTC updated the guidelines in June 2010. For more information, see www.ftc.gov/news-events/press-releases/2009/10/ftc-publishes-final-guides-governing-endorsements-testimonials or www.business.ftc.gov/documents/bus71-ftcs-revised-endorsement-guideswhat-people-are-asking.

Using social news services and other social networks

You can send similar emails to individuals and influencers you have identified as participating in key discussions about related products or issues, including a short notice about the press release on Twitter and a mention to groups and professionals on sites like Facebook and LinkedIn.

You can submit your release to the few social news services, such as reddit, that permit you to submit your own link to your press release. In other cases, you may need to submit to social news and bookmark services from another identity, or wait until the story appears on a blog and submit the blog post instead.

Of course, you can always link to press releases on your own site from your other social media, as news aggregator GreenAir Online does with shortened URLs from its Twitter feed (see Figure 6-5).

If your press release includes multimedia or you've created a video or audio release, be sure to submit it to relevant directories, such as www.podcast directory.com, www.digitalpodcast.com, or www.ipodder.org/ directory/4/podcasts.

Emphasizing content

As always, content, tone, and interest level are the keys. Keep your release to about 400 words or fewer if you're including multimedia, but don't go below 100 words lest your release is viewed by search engines as spam.

Keep your headline to about 80 characters and use an `<h1>` HTML header tag.

Shortened link

Figure 6-5:
For extra mileage on press releases, link from your Twitter feed to releases on your website.

GreenAir Online
@GreenAirOnline

Independent reporting on aviation's impact on the environment and climate change. Retweets don't necessarily mean we agree with them!

London
greenaironline.com
Joined March 2009

10 Photos and videos

| TWEETS | PHOTOS&VIDEOS | FOLLOWING | FOLLOWERS |
| 2,862 | 10 | 342 | 1,621 |

More ∨   Follow

Tweets   Tweets & replies

GreenAir Online @GreenAirOnline · Oct 6
NATS looks for long-term solutions for the problem of false radar returns from wind turbines shar.es/1mm7hX @natspressoffice

GreenAir Online @GreenAirOnline · Oct 3
Hong Kong International's new runway plan gets green light from government's environmental advisors shar.es/1aSrZr @hkairport

Combine anchor text (see Book II, Chapter 2) with the URL in parentheses right next to it (to cover all bases), but don't use the same anchor text twice. On some press distribution services — and, of course, on social media — you have a chance to submit keywords or tags, which is an essential process for leveraging your press release for search engine optimization (SEO) purposes.

Be sure that some or all the keywords or tags that you identified are also included in the headline or first paragraph of the release. Try to use at least some of your primary set of search terms, as described in Book II, Chapter 2. For instance, in Figure 6-4, earlier in this chapter, good keywords or tags appearing in a headline, subhead, or lede paragraph might have been *food technology*, *social media week*, *cooking app*, or *sidechef*.

Pressing for attention

Given the visibility available through social media, you need to decide whether press releases are worth the effort. A Marx Communications survey in March 2013 showed that social media may be eating traditional PR for lunch, at least as far as B2B companies are concerned. The survey revealed the following information:

✦ If they could use only one promotional technique, 45 percent of respondents would prefer social media to 24 percent who would write a press release.

✦ Ninety-four percent of companies already use social media for announcements, but 71 percent use press releases (some do both).

✦ Seventy-five percent post their releases on their websites, but 68 percent send releases to reporters.

For more information about online publicity techniques, download the HubSpot PR guide at `http://offers.hubspot.com/newsworthy-guide-to-inbound-public-relations`.

One possible way around this mash-up between social media and publicity is to create a socially friendly press announcement that you can post easily on multiple social media and encourage engagement. PitchEngine has a free app called Tiny Pitch that will convert content you create on any device into just such a format, complete with a logo, images, Likes, a message feature, and a share button, as shown in Figure 6-6.

Figure 6-6:
A press release in a social media format called Tiny Pitch.

Reproduced with permission of PitchEngine, Inc., Jason Kintzler, President & CEO

Measuring results

The same social monitoring tools that you use to find influencers can be applied to track key performance indicators for your press efforts, such as Google Alerts, Social Mention, and Twitter Search. Assessing results from your publicity is a good place to use all that qualitative data, as well as advertising measurements, for online brand awareness and equity. (See, for example, www.questionpro.com/brand-awareness.html or http://covalentmarketing.com/blog/2013/07/10/measuring-brand-awareness.)

Measure baselines before you begin your press campaigns, and be sure that before-and-after results span comparable time frames. Here are a few key performance indicators that you might find relevant:

✦ Number of online mentions of company, brand, product or service line, and/or individual products or services anywhere online, including social media, during a specific time frame.

✦ Number and location of media placements; where and when mentions occurred, a press release was published, or an article about your company or product appeared on a recognized media outlet, whether online or offline.

✦ Site traffic generated from press releases and other linkable press-related mentions; see referrer logs in your web stats software for number of inbound links from each source. Include comparative click-through rates (CTRs) and conversion rates, if available. To make this process easier, tag links with the identifiers related to the topic or date of the press release.

✦ Social media campaign participation and sentiment using monitoring tools; see Book II, Chapter 1.

✦ Average frequency of the product, company, or brand conversations related to the release compared to the frequency of conversations before the release.

✦ Estimated costs (hard dollars and labor) that were spent. Be sure to include costs for paid distribution, if used. To compare ROI for publicity to other methods, you compare costs to the value of sales that can be traced back to the release (if any). If you can't trace back sales, you might be able to compare brand engagement.

Integrating Social Media with Your Website

Any website can incorporate a myriad of features that integrate with social media, going well beyond the obvious and oft-repeated reminders to include Follow Us On and share buttons everywhere, including product pages within stores. You can get clever: Include links to your Help forum or YouTube video tutorials as part of the automated purchase confirmation email you send to buyers.

And, of course, this integration can work the other way: integrating your social media with your website. In Figure 6-7, Pure Fix Cycles (www.pure fixcycles.com) uses links throughout its Facebook Page to drive viewers to its website for additional information about the company and its products. Links on the Shop tab take users to product pages on the website for Pure Fix Cycles.

In some cases, old-fashioned versions of social media — on-site forums, chat rooms, product reviews, and wikis — effectively draw repeat visitors to the hub site, avoiding any integration with third-party social media sites.

More advanced sites have already implemented social media techniques on-site, including blogs, communities, and calls for user-generated content — photos and videos of people using your product or suggesting creative new designs and applications, as well as ratings.

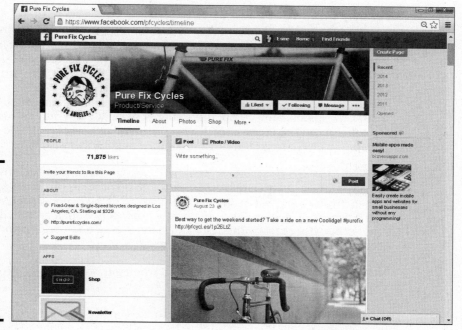

Figure 6-7:
Pure Fix
Cycles
links to its
website
from its
Facebook
About
tab and
Timeline.

Several strategic factors may affect your decision whether to implement such techniques on-site or off:

✦ The cost of development, storage, support, and ongoing maintenance versus costs off-site

✦ SEO and link strategies

✦ Plus-and-minus points of managing a more centralized and simplified web presence

A few on-site techniques, like loyalty programs, work just as well on social media (for example, special offers for those who like you on Facebook). Three other popular methods practically cry out for integration: coupons, discounts, and freebies; games and contests; and microsites (more about these methods in the following sections). For more information about on-site and other forms of online marketing, see *Web Marketing For Dummies*, 3rd Edition, by Jan Zimmerman (Wiley Publishing, Inc.).

Brainstorm ways that an integrated website/social media campaign might succeed for you. Diagram it and figure out what you'll measure to assess your accomplishments.

**Book VIII
Chapter 6**

**Multiplying
Your Impact**

Coupons, discounts, and freebies

It doesn't take much monitoring of Facebook, LinkedIn, and Twitter, as well as social news, bookmarking, and shopping streams, to see how frequently they're used to offer time-limited deals, coupons, special promotions, discounts, and free samples.

The sense of urgency in certain social media environments catches viewers' interest. Just like the competitive energy of an auction may cause bidders to offer more than they intend, the ephemeral nature of real-time offers may inspire viewers to grab for a coupon they might otherwise have passed up.

The upside and downside of real-time social media is precisely the immediacy of these offers and how quickly a chain of other posts extinguishes them from awareness. You have a chance to move overstock quickly, bring in business on a slow day, or gain new prospects from a group you might not otherwise reach without making a long-term, and perhaps too-expensive, commitment.

Here are some points to keep in mind when offering coupons, discounts, and freebies:

✦ Pin your offer and contest posts to the top of your Facebook Timeline to make sure they continue to be seen. Consider paying to boost these posts to promote your specials.

✦ Preplan and schedule your posts, repeating them frequently enough throughout the day to appear in real-time search results and near the top of chronologically organized posts on any social media site that doesn't permit pinning them to the top.

✦ Always link back to your primary website or blog, not only to explain the details of the offer, but also to enjoy the inbound link value, offer additional goods and services, and capture prospect information.

✦ Be sure to use a unique promotion code for each offer and tag your links with identifiers to track the source of click-throughs and conversions.

Most of the hundreds of online coupon sites already have a presence on Twitter, Facebook, Digg, and elsewhere. You can use their services or simply create a coupon of your own.

Whether you offer a discount through your website, social media, or any other form of advertising, be sure to include the impact of the discount in your cost analysis. Giving away a free soda may cost a business only 10¢ (mostly for the cup!), but if it gives away 1,000 drinks, the discount costs $100.

In Chapter 3 of this minibook, we discuss the group-purchasing model for coupons, which is dependent on volume use reaching a critical mass.

Contests and games

Your imagination is the only limit to contests and games that you can post on your site and cross-promote via social media. As usual, make sure that viewers link back and forth among your sites, ensuring that an inbound link to your primary web presence exists. The goals of your contest may vary:

✦ Branding and name recognition

✦ Building relationships through entertainment

✦ Obtaining feedback and building community through customer-generated content

✦ Locating hard-to-find resources, clients, or vendors

✦ Cross-promoting

✦ Acquiring testimonials

✦ Getting input into your own brainstorming process about where your product or service should go

Like with special offers, be sure to include the cost of prizes and the labor involved in running the contest in your analysis of ROI. Depending on the goal of the contest, you may be looking for new visitors, repeat visitors, leads, or sales.

Figure 6-8 provides an example of a social media contest that helps draw traffic to a site. Tires Plus (`http://tiresplusdequeen.com`) uses a Facebook photo-caption contest to encourage a regional audience to win free oil changes for a year. They cross-promote their contests on their site, Facebook, and Twitter.

You can find ideas for creating more effective contests and games at `www.socialmediaexaminer.com/six-ways-supercharge-contests-social-media`.

Microsites

Microsites are branded environments specific to a particular product, line, or brand. Created like any other free-standing websites with their own domain names and only a few pages, microsites are usually dedicated to a specific product or service. Often used in conjunction with a new product introduction or special promotion, microsites may facilitate social media–style activities specific to that project. Often, user conversations or user-generated content contributions are incorporated into the site.

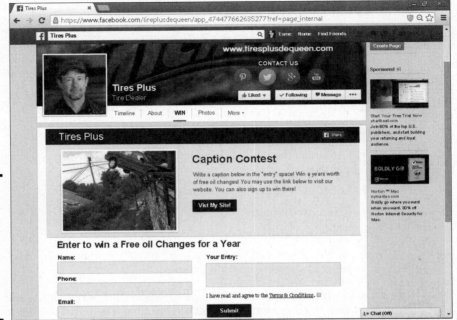

Reproduced with permission of Marty Hooker; Carmen Tedder-Internet Marketing

Figure 6-8:
Tires Plus uses a photo-caption contest on Facebook to generate leads.

Many microsites incorporate highly focused presentations to launch a new product, turn a sale into an event, provide how-to instruction, or target specific demographic groups.

A microsite is an excellent way to branch out from the design of your main site and show off your style and skills. It might portray your brand in a new light — one that connects more closely to users and makes a creative impact on them. And beyond the aesthetic design, an easy and engaging interaction will make the experience more enjoyable and beneficial for your users.

Integrating Social Media with Paid Advertising

Social media has the advertising world in ferment. As applications from social media companies mature, audiences grow, and technology improves, the companies expand their advertising opportunities to make money for their investors — everyone is just trying to make a buck, especially through mobile advertising.

Advertising on social media sites

Many social media sites, especially blogs, have long accepted advertising that you can incorporate into your plans for paid advertising (if any). Some large channels (like Google+, Blogger, and YouTube) and many smaller social media venues display standard PPC, banner, and/or multimedia ads from Google AdWords or Yahoo! Ad Solutions. Other social media channels offer their own advertising programs.

Later in this chapter, we discuss four of the major ones: Facebook, Twitter, LinkedIn, and Pinterest. Table 6-3 lists other popular social media sites offering paid advertising, which we encourage you to explore on your own.

Table 6-3	Social Media Sites That Offer Paid Advertising	
Name	*URL for Media Kit or Advertising Information*	*Resources*
Facebook	`www.facebook.com/advertising` `https://www.facebook.com/business/products/ads`	`www.facebook.com/help/458369380926902`
Instagram	`http://instagram.com/about-ads`	`https://help.instagram.com/1415228085373580`
LinkedIn	`www.linkedin.com/advertising`	`http://help.linkedin.com/app/answers/detail/a_id/1015/ft/eng`
reddit	`www.reddit.com/advertising`	`www.reddit.com/wiki/selfserve`
Pinterest	`https://ads.pinterest.com`	`https://business.pinterest.com/promoted-pins`
Snapchat	`http://blog.snapchat.com/post/100255857340/advertising-on-snapchat`	Contact Business Development to be included: `https://support.snapchat.com/co/bizdev`
Spotify	`www.spotify.com/us/brands`	`http://www.spotify.com/us/brands/formats`

(continued)

Table 6-3 *(continued)*

Name	URL for Media Kit or Advertising Information	Resources
Twitter	`https://ads.twitter.com` `https://business.twitter.com/ad-products`	`https://support.twitter.com/groups/58-advertising`
Vimeo	`http://vimeo.com/about/advertisers`	`http://vimeo.com/help/faq/vimeo-membership/vimeo-pro#can-i-use-vimeo-pro-to-upload-videos-that-contain-ads`
YouTube	`www.youtube.com/yt/advertise`	`www.youtube.com/yt/advertise/resources.html`

Plan ahead. All the major social media advertising channels review and approve ads before allowing them to post. Allow 24 hours for turnaround, although sometimes it takes much less time, and occasionally it takes much longer.

Exploring the growth in social advertising

The increased advertising offerings on social media channels could be interpreted as attempts to overcome consumers' acquired *banner blindness* to ads appearing in predictable online locations — and a deep desire to cut into Google's share of total online advertising revenue.

eMarketer (`www.emarketer.com/Article/Mobile-Growth-Pushes-Facebook-Become-No-2-US-Digital-Ad-Seller/1010469`) showed Google garnering almost a 40 percent share of the U.S. digital advertising market at the end of 2013, compared to Facebook's 7.4 percent share — more than five times as much. Even with the projected growth in digital marketing, eMarketer expects Google to hold onto a 42.3 percent share in 2015, compared to Facebook's 9 percent. eMarketer foresees both companies' shares growing at the expense of other digital ad providers.

But there's more than Google envy at play. The growth in social advertising is also driven by the greater reach, better analytics, higher click-through rates, and higher degree of engagement with mobile ads. Mobile ads not only catch people who seek something specific, but they catch them at the very moment they're on the move and interested in a purchase.

As shown in Figure 6-9, social ad spending reached $5.1 billion in 2013, and is anticipated to grow to $15 billion by 2018, at which point, mobile-ad revenues are projected to exceed desktop-ad revenues.

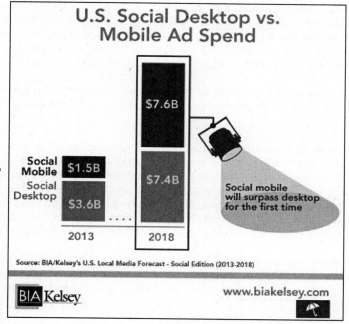

Figure 6-9: A comparison of social media revenues from mobile versus desktop advertising.

Reproduced with permission of BIA/Kelsey

 WARNING!

Demand for mobile advertising will likely drive up costs while performance and targeting improve. If mobile ad space becomes scarce, competition for it will increase. Don't expect social media channels to increase the number of ads they show to a particular user. They can simply raise their prices, in effect slamming shut the advertising window for small businesses that have limited budgets.

For more information on online advertising, see *Local Online Advertising For Dummies* by Court Cunningham and Stephanie Brown (Wiley Publishing, Inc.).

**Book VIII
Chapter 6**

Multiplying Your Impact

Maximizing your advertising dollars

You can and should take advantage of targeting your audience as closely as the tools allow, selecting by geography, demographics, education, and interest area whenever possible. Some folks object to the targeting: Older women seem to receive a disproportionate number of ads for skin creams and diets; those who change their status to Engaged are quickly deluged with ads from wedding service providers.

You can evaluate advertising placements on these sites just as you would evaluate advertising placed anywhere else. Using the advertising metrics discussed in Book IX, Chapter 6, consider cost per click (CPC), cost per 1,000 (CPM) impressions, click-through rate (CTR), and the resulting conversions to decide whether any of these ads pay off for you.

Sometimes, social media advertising is less expensive than traditional pay-per-click (PPC), banner, or retargeting ads through search engines, but not always.

Results so far indicate that display ads appearing on social media pages generally perform about the same as display ads on other sites. The average CTR in 2013 was 0.10 percent for standard web banners compared to 0.11 percent for Facebook banner ads, according to www.marketingcharts. com/wp-content/uploads/2013/03/MediaBrix-Social-Mobile-Gaming-Ads-Mar2013.png. What's interesting is that the CTR on mobile banner ads (from any source) is about eight times greater at 0.86 percent.

So many variables affect CTR — ad size, placement, quality of the ad, match to audience, and value of the offer — that it's hard to predict exactly how your ad will perform. Compare your CTR to the numbers in the preceding paragraph.

Averages are averages. The range at both ends may be extreme. Like so much material on the web, the only metrics that matter are your own.

Although you can test the same ad in several places at the same time to see which publishers yield the most bang for your advertising buck, also take into consideration whether the audiences on different social channels respond to a different message.

Advertising on Facebook

Facebook offers several forms of advertising, each of which can appear in three places: in the right-hand column of a desktop Facebook Page, within a user's Desktop News Feed, or with Facebook's mobile News Feed. The first two options are visible in Figure 6-10.

Sponsored ads

Figure 6-10:
Facebook advertising runs within a viewer's News Feed or in the right column.

News Feed ads are much more visible to viewers because they appear in the middle of posts from their friends and others, and because they almost always involve large, eye-catching graphics. Right-column ads are often ignored, so you might want to save those for branding.

Like Google AdWords, pricing is done on a bid basis, where you can set your daily maximum, campaign duration, and a variety of other options.

Getting started

Facebook recently restructured its program to increase advertiser success. To start developing an ad campaign, log in to your Facebook Page and then follow these steps:

1. **To start advertising, go to** www.facebook.com/ads/create **in your browser address bar.**

   Alternatively, select Create Ads from the drop-down list that appears when you click the down-pointing arrow in the top-right corner of the blue toolbar at the top of your Page.

2. **On the screen that appears, establish an objective for your ad by selecting an option from the Choose the Objective for Your Campaign list.**

Choose the objective that comes closest to your needs. Don't worry — you can always change your mind later! Facebook distinguishes the following objectives:

- *Send people to your website:* Drive traffic to your website (away from Facebook).

- *Increase conversions on your website:* Promote specific actions (conversions) on your website, such as a newsletter signup, whitepaper download, or purchase.

- *Boost your posts:* Promote a specific post on your Timeline to increase reach; this is an internal Facebook objective.

- *Promote your Page:* Increase traffic or Likes to grow your brand or audience; this is an internal Facebook objective.

- *Get installs of your app:* Encourage downloads of your apps.

- *Increase engagement in your app:* Encourage people to use your desktop app.

- *Reach people near your business:* Use geographically localized ads to draw people into your brick-and-mortar store or reach nearby prospects for a service business, such as tax return preparation.

- *Raise attendance at your event:* Get more people to attend your events.

- *Get people to claim your offer:* Offer discounts, promo codes, or coupons for buyers to use on your site, in your storefront, or when purchasing a service.

- *Get video views:* Get more people to view your videos.

After you select an objective, a panel opens to the right of the list.

3. **Choose the page you want to promote by entering the URL, or select it from the drop-down list that appears when you place your cursor in the Choose Page field.**

4. **Click the Continue button.**

5. **Make selections appropriate for your choice of objective. Scroll down and follow the steps to target your audience, select your spending level, upload images, and write the text for your ad.**

   Facebook recommends everything from image size to text.

Boosting or promoting a post

Boost Your Posts (a Facebook advertising objectives mentioned in the preceding section) is also available as a shortcut from each post on your

Timeline so you don't have to go through the Ads Create tool. Follow these simple steps:

1. **Go to any recent post.**
2. **Click the Boost Post button at the bottom of the post.**
3. **In the pop-up window that appears, choose your audience, budget, and how you want the Boost Post campaign to run.**
4. **Click Boost.**

There are minor differences between boosting a post directly from the post and Boosting Your Posts through the Ads Create tool. The latter is a bit more time-consuming, but it offers more targeting options and greater budget flexibility.

Whether a post has been boosted from your timeline or through the Ads Create tool, it has two special characteristics:

✦ It appears higher in viewers' News Feeds, so it attracts more attention.

✦ It gets a much broader distribution than an ordinary post. You can boost any post, including status updates, photos, offers, or videos.

> Only 6 to 8 percent of your followers or Likes may actually see a specific, un-boosted post in their News Feeds. There's simply too much material for Facebook to show everyone everything. By boosting a post, you ensure wider distribution to your Likes and to followers who may not yet have liked your page, thus dramatically increasing the reach for that post.

Starting in January 2015, Facebook implemented a new policy to reduce the number of free, organic posts in News Feeds that Facebook deems to be "too promotional." This includes posts that only push a product purchase or app installation; posts that only ask viewers to enter a promotion or sweepstakes; and posts that duplicate the content of a paid ad. Whether you want to or not, you will soon need to pay for a Boosted Post or an obvious advertisement in a News Feed to distribute this type of information. You can expect free distribution of these types of posts in viewers News Feeds to decline over time.

Paying for your Facebook ads

Facebook offers a bid-based ad auction. You specify the amount you're willing to pay, but the winning bid may vary constantly based on the number of competing ads and the quality of your ad performance.

As with online advertising elsewhere, Facebook generally offers several options for pricing ads:

✦ **Cost per click (CPC):** You pay for the ad only when someone clicks on an ad that takes them to either an external link or another internal Facebook Page. The minimum bid for a click is one cent.

✦ **Cost per thousand (CPM) impressions:** Your cost is based on how many thousands of people see your ad, whether they click or not; this type of pricing makes more sense for branding ads.

✦ **Flat fee (available only for boosted posts):** You set a flat fee to boost a post that will last for the length of time you set for your boost campaign; charges, which are calculated by impression, are deducted from that budget.

No matter what option you select, Facebook will never charge more per click than you enter, or charge more than the lifetime or daily budget you specify when you set up your ad campaign.

For more information on Facebook advertising, see *Facebook Marketing All-in-One For Dummies,* 3rd Edition, by Andrea Vahl, John Haydon, and Jan Zimmerman (Wiley Publishing, Inc.), or visit `www.facebook.com/advertising`. (For more about Facebook, in general, see Book V.)

Advertising on Twitter

Twitter has exploded with new advertising offerings to help you reach its more than 284 million monthly users. The Twitter Ads product line now includes

✦ **Promoted Tweets:** Promote specific tweets in the feeds of targeted non-followers to build your brand, increase reach, and generate leads.

✦ **Promoted Accounts:** Promote your entire account, not just a specific tweet, for branding purposes and to increase the number of followers interested in your business.

✦ **Promoted Trends:** Promote an idea or concept in the left column of Twitter pages to help you introduce a new product or build your brand.

✦ **Twitter Cards:** Attach photos, videos, and other rich media to tweets to drive traffic to your website.

✦ **Twitter remarketing:** Target users on Twitter who have already visited your website and who have seen one of your Promoted Tweets or Twitter Cards.

✦ **Twitter engagement campaigns:** Similar to some of the objectives in Facebook, Twitter now offers campaigns designed to increase followers, leads, clicks to your website, or app installs.

We talk about each of these products in greater detail in the following sections. If you're already convinced, get started at `https://biz.twitter.com/start-advertising`, or visit `https://ads.twitter.com`, `https://blog.twitter.com/advertising`, or `https://support.twitter.com/groups/58-advertising` for more information. You can also follow Twitter's advertising news on Twitter @TwitterAds or @TwitterSmallBiz.

Promoting your tweets

Promoted Tweets, like organic tweets, may include hashtags, rich media, and links to your website, and they offer the same forms of engagement: replies, favorites, and retweets.

Unlike organic tweets, however, you can target non-followers by demographics, interests, keywords, geography, device, similarity to current followers, and more. You pay only when someone engages with your tweet. Whether you promote an existing organic tweet or create a new one, you can reach a new audience to grow your Twitter presence.

As you can see in Figure 6-11, Promoted Tweets are clearly marked. According to Twitter, "Only one Promoted Tweet will appear in a user's timeline at any given time." That's true at the time of this publication, at least!

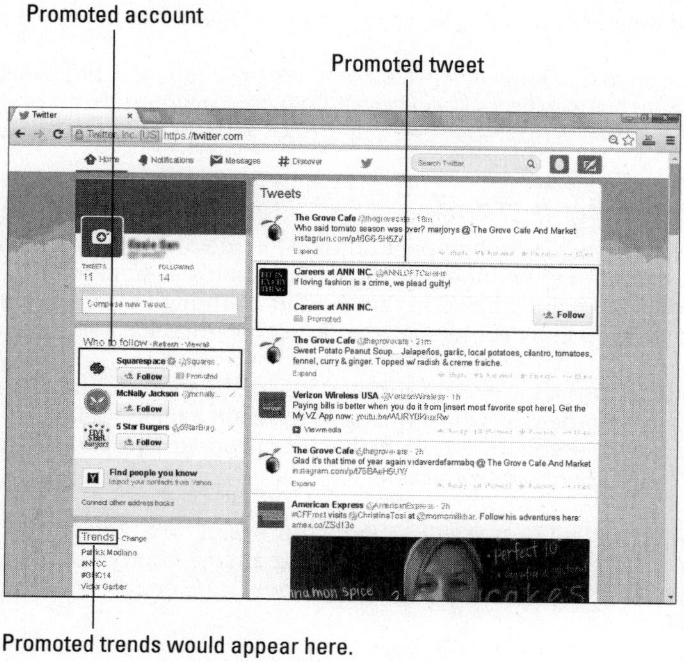

Promoted account

Promoted tweet

Figure 6-11:
Both
Promoted
Tweets and
Promoted
Accounts
expand
your reach
to targeted
non-
followers.

Promoted trends would appear here.

Promoted Tweets may appear other places besides viewers' timelines, including in search results for terms or trends, on Twitter's mobile products, and syndicated to some third-party clients, such as Hootsuite.

Pretest your content or look at results of existing organic tweets to select one for promotion that already performs well. According to BI Intelligence, a good engagement rate for a Promoted Tweet would be about 3 percent.

For more information, see `https://biz.twitter.com/en-gb/products/promoted-tweets`.

Promoting your account

Like a Promoted Tweet, a Promoted Account can be targeted to your desired audience. However, it differs from a tweet in content and format. A Promoted Account ad includes a short, vivid description of the benefits of following your business on Twitter, plus your company logo and a call to action.

For this type of promotion, you might want to target users who are similar to your existing followers, are similar to influential figures in your industry, or share an interest in the products, services, issues, or concepts relevant to your business.

Promoted Accounts appear in somewhat different places than Promoted Tweets. In addition to the timeline, they appear in the Who to Follow widget, which appears on multiple pages (refer to Figure 6-11).

This advertising choice is priced on a cost-per-follow (CPF) basis. You pay only when new visitors choose to follow your account. For more information, see `https://business.twitter.com/solutions/promoted-accounts`.

Promoting a trend

Trending topics, which appear on the left side of a viewer's home page show topics of interest in different countries during a 24-hour window. Promoted Trends, if any, are labeled in this module. Although trends are updated every 24 hours, you can promote a trend for several weeks if you want.

Promoted Trends are fairly subtle. They make sense for large corporate branding campaigns, when you need to reach a mass (relatively untargeted) audience, or if you want to launch a new product line — say to promote the next Apple iPhone introduction.

They generally boost tweets about your brand for about two weeks. Think of them as a top-of-funnel feeder, getting a large number of people to at least hear about you. (To learn more about conversion funnels, see Book I, Chapter 1.)

For more information, see `https://biz.twitter.com/products/promoted-trends`.

Dealing Twitter Cards

Twitter Cards allow you to attach photos, videos, and other rich media to tweets, as shown in Figure 6-12. And guess what: Twitter Cards are free.

Figure 6-12:
A Twitter Player Card that includes a video.

Your clue that this is a Twitter Card.

Twitter offers the following types of Cards:

✦ **Summary Card (default):** Includes title, description, thumbnail, and Twitter account information

✦ **Summary Card with Large Image:** Same as the default Summary Card, plus a large photo

✦ **Photo Card:** One photo only

✦ **Gallery Card:** Four photos

✦ **App Card:** Info about a mobile app, including a download link

✦ **Player Card:** Offers video, audio, or other rich media as part of a tweet

✦ **Product Card:** Displays optimized product information

Because most Twitter Cards interact with your website, your Web developer will need to add a few lines of HTML code to your site. When users tweet a link to your content, their tweet will include a Card that their followers can see. For more information, send your developer to `https://dev.twitter.com/cards/overview` or `https://dev.twitter.com/cards/getting-started`.

Remarketing with Twitter

Like remarketing products on other platforms, Twitter remarketing lets you target only Twitter users who have already visited your website. Twitter visitors who see one of your Promoted Tweets or Twitter Cards will then see a reminder ad to help keep your company top of mind.

For more information, see `www.marketingprofs.com/articles/2014/26159/twitter-remarketing-what-it-is-and-how-to-use-it-to-target-audiences`.

Engaging your Twitter audience

It does sometimes seem that social media platforms are spending more time watching their competitors than developing new ideas of their own. That certainly seems true of those Twitter Ads products that have started to copy Facebook's advertising objectives. Or perhaps it's the other way around. In any case, you can now use Twitter engagement ads to

✦ **Increase traffic or conversions on your website.** Follow Twitter's targeting options for keywords, location, or interest to drive a more qualified audience to your website.

✦ **Increase the number of installations of your app or engagement with it.** Create campaigns specifically designed so that Twitter users can download and open your app from a tweet.

✦ **Increase your Twitter followers.** Target Twitter users who are most like your current followers or who match the profile of those you seek as followers.

✦ **Improve lead generation.** Add a special Lead Generation Card (`https://business.twitter.com/solutions/lead-generation-card`) to your tweet. This allows prospects to share their contact information with two simple clicks instead of leaving Twitter or filling out a form. Then, all you have to do is follow up.

For more information, see `https://business.twitter.com/solutions/grow-followers` or `https://business.twitter.com/solutions/tweet-engagements`. (For more about Twitter, in general, see Book IV.)

Pricing and bidding on Twitter

Twitter's ad prices are based on actions other than clicks. You bid a price for a specific action based on the type of advertising you choose. You're charged a flat price only when a viewer takes that action, whether it's submitting information through your campaign, following you, or retweeting.

Twitter doesn't charge for organic tweets or engagement actions.

Follow these steps to bid:

1. **Go to `https://biz.twitter.com/start-advertising` to set up your account.**

2. **Using the drop-down menus, indicate the country where your business is located and whether your monthly budget will be less than or more than $5,000.**

3. **Click the Let's Go button at the bottom of the screen.**

4. **Click the Create New Campaign button in the top-right corner of the screen.**

   A drop-down menu with advertising objectives appears.

5. **Select your objective from the six choices on the list (Followers, Website Clicks or Conversions, Tweet Engagements, App Installs or Engagements, Leads on Twitter, Custom).**

   A new screen appears for the objective you selected.

6. **Scroll down the screen as Twitter leads you through the appropriate steps for creating a Twitter ad to match your objective.**

   These sections include campaign settings, composing your tweet, targeting your audience, and setting your budget.

7. **In the budget section, set a daily spending maximum, a maximum bid per action, and the pace at which your ads are shown.**

   No matter where you set your maximum bid, Twitter won't charge more than a penny above the next highest bid until you reach your maximum price. You'll receive information about what other advertisers are bidding so you can optimize your spending.

   Set a total budget (optional) for the duration of your campaign. Your ads will stop showing as soon as your budget has been met.

8. **Click the Save Campaign button at the bottom of the screen to start advertising. You'll be prompted to enter a payment source.**

Check back for results to adjust your bids or budgets.

For more information on Twitter advertising, see *Twitter Marketing For Dummies,* 2nd Edition by Kyle Lacy (Wiley Publishing, Inc.), or visit `https://support.twitter.com/groups/58-advertising`.

According to a 2014 analysis by The Hub (`www.thehubcomms.com`), "Fourteen percent of Twitter users never see an ad (and that number is growing)." The Hub claims the source of this problem is that users who access Twitter through third-party apps are invisible to Twitter's targeting algorithms. Keep your eyes open to see whether Twitter addresses this issue.

Advertising on LinkedIn

Without a doubt, LinkedIn is the best social media channel for reaching professionals and business-to-business prospects. Although its user population is smaller than many of the other, broader B2C social media channels, LinkedIn still offers opportunities for advertising to reach targeted populations.

Be cautious about creating too narrow a target market for your advertising in LinkedIn. You can quickly exhaust the potential reach for your ad if the base is too small.

Like Facebook, LinkedIn now offers a combination of externally focused ads that appear in the right column of various pages (see Figure 6-13), and promoted posts that appear within viewers' news feeds to drive people to a specific post you've created.

Ads may appear on the profile pages of other LinkedIn members, on a user's own home page, in a user's message inbox, on a search results page, or on LinkedIn group pages.

Targeting your LinkedIn ads

Not surprisingly, the categories available for targeting an audience on LinkedIn are somewhat different from the categories you see on Facebook or Twitter. LinkedIn collects many strictly business-oriented items that other social media simply don't ask about for their profiles.

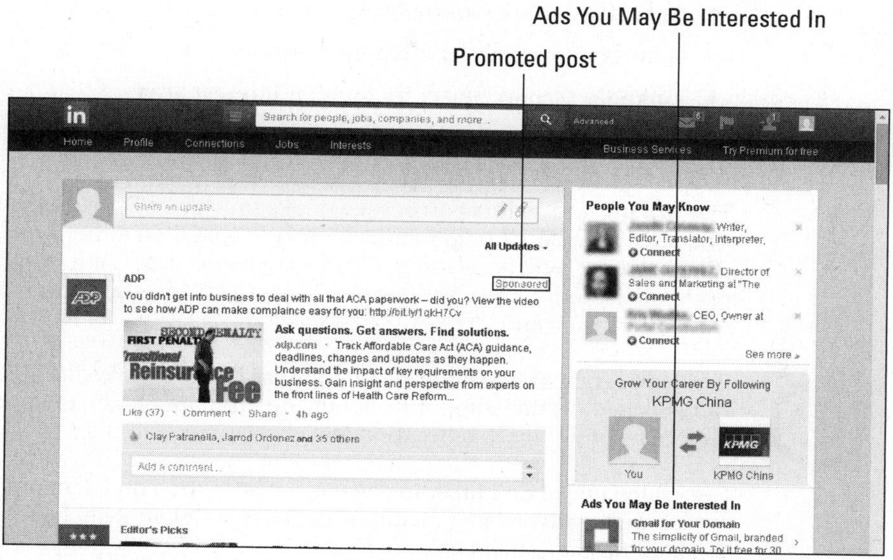

Ads You May Be Interested In

Promoted post

Figure 6-13: Sponsored (paid) posts on LinkedIn appear in the news feed; other ads appear in the right column.

Because members supply most of the information in their own profiles, business pages, and showcase pages that LinkedIn uses for targeting, you have to accept that self-revealed information may not always be accurate. LinkedIn generally allows you to select multiple items within a category or offers you the chance to drill down so that you can narrow a field. Categories include:

✦ **Job Title:** Choose C-suite executives, purchasing agents, members of technical staff, and more.

✦ **Job Function:** Select from engineers, human resources, or marketing, for example.

✦ **Industry:** Select from dozens of drill-down categories.

✦ **Geography:** Select up to ten geographical areas, drilling down within international, national, regional, state-wide, or local metropolitan areas.

✦ **Company Size:** Based on the number of employees.

✦ **Company Name:** Great for targeting everyone on LinkedIn who works for a large multinational corporation — for example, everyone who might need your travel services.

✦ **Seniority:** Position in firm, such as owner.

✦ **Age:** Standard demographic choices.

✦ **Gender:** Standard demographic choices.

✦ **LinkedIn Group:** Select by topic or interest area.

Pricing and bidding

The pricing and bidding structure works much like Facebook and Twitter. You specify a daily budget and a bid price based on either cost per click (CPC) or cost per thousand (CPM) impressions. Like with other advertising options, LinkedIn must approve your ads. You can start and stop your ads whenever you want.

LinkedIn requires a $10-per-day minimum budget. LinkedIn will suggest a bid range based on the competition, but the ultimate choice is up to you. It also charges a one-time $5 activation fee.

Generally, clicks on LinkedIn are more costly than on Facebook and other social media advertising channels because it delivers such a coveted and detailed target audience.

For more information, see www.linkedin.com/ads/start or http://partner.linkedin.com/ads/info/Ads_faqs_updated_en_US.html. (For more about LinkedIn, in general, see Book VI.)

Advertising on Pinterest

As we discuss in Book VII, Pinterest has now accumulated tens of millions of users who have posted more than 30 billion pins. In 2014, Pinterest finally released an advertising option called Promoted Pins (see Figure 6-14), which allows you to target non-followers with pins of interest and drive those users directly to your website.

Pinterest will soon allow advertisers to place conversion pixels on their website to track from click-through to purchase. Your programmer will need to place a tiny piece of code on your site, probably on the thank-you page following a purchase.

Based on information provided by its users, Pinterest lets you target your audience by geography, demographics, devices, and search-term use. It also allows advertisers to supply coded identifiers that can be matched to Pinterest users to define a target audience. For example, the email addresses of your newsletter subscribers can be cross-matched to the database of Pinterest users.

Women's Fashion

Figure 6-14: Promoted Pins on Pinterest are a new advertising option.

Promoted Pin

Pinterest has established some fairly specific rules for what constitutes an acceptable Promoted Pin and reviews all Promoted Pins. In particular, Pinterest specifies, "There can be no promotional information, calls to action, service claims, price listing or deceptive content in the pin image. Ads must be accurate, and lead to a relevant landing page with no signup requests."

Pricing and bidding

Charges for Promoted Pins are based on a cost per click (CPC). As usual, you specify a daily budget, duration, and a CPC bid. You're charged only when someone clicks from your Promoted Pin to your website.

As of this writing, Pinterest is still rolling out Promoted Pins to selected advertisers while it works out any kinks. To apply for inclusion, go to `https://business.pinterest.com/promoted-pins`.

For more information, see `https://help.pinterest.com/articles/advertiser-sharing` or `www.socialmediaexaminer.com/use-pinterest-promoted-pins`. (For more about Pinterest, in general, see Book VII.)

Engagement ads

Users have obviously started to tune out banner ads online, even when the ads spill all over content and refuse to close, irritate eyeballs with annoying animation, or interrupt concentration with surprising bursts of unwanted sound. New forms of advertising that incorporate user information from social media are beginning to populate pages all over the Internet.

The fuse was lit for this form of innovation, and social media technologies ignited it, for good or ill. The marriage of advertising message with individual user information — with the potential of turning every viewer into a shill — has serious implications for privacy. Although the Interactive Advertising Bureau (IAB) has published best practices for user opt-in and privacy protection (`www.iab.net/socialads` and `www.iab.net/sm_buyers_guide`), it isn't clear how well they will be followed. The IAB defines these engagement ads, sometimes called *social banners,* as

> *a type of banner that incorporates social or conversational functionality within it. . . . The key to success is for social banner ads to enable consumers to have a real interactive experience within the unit, as opposed to just passively viewing the content within the ad.*

Comment-style ads seem to work well for entertainment, new products, cars, and clothes, although virtual gift ads seem to attract consumer product and entertainment advertisers. Clicking the Like button on an ad now turns viewers into connections for that brand. This call-to-action ad works well for any established brand, luxury products, and products or entertainers that have a passionate following.

More complex engagement ads draw content from a social network: the photo image and name from a profile (presuming an emotionally effective brand endorsement) or user-generated phrases from tweets, blogs, or RSS feeds. Users review the modified ads; if they agree to allow it, the ads are then distributed to their personal networks. For these complex ads to operate, the user must already be connected to her social network. (One could imagine using these ads to play an interesting game of rumor.)

Interactive engagement ads probably require involvement from tech support or your web developer.

Like Promoted Tweets, marketers currently hypothesize that engagement ads have an enhanced value based on factors other than click-through rates (CTRs), such as how long consumers spend interacting with an ad or how often consumers share the ad with their friends. If the sharing results in a cascading effect of recommended impressions to presumably qualified prospects, who just so happen to be friends, all the better for you.

Promoting engagement with Promoted Tweets

Chegg (www.chegg.com) is one-stop shop for high school and college students. Whether they need a tutor; homework help; assistance with SATs; or information about colleges, career choices, or scholarships, students can find time- and money-saving services on the site or on the Chegg blog (see nearby art). Chegg also acts as a huge textbook online swap meet, allowing students to rent, buy, or sell textbooks at great prices.

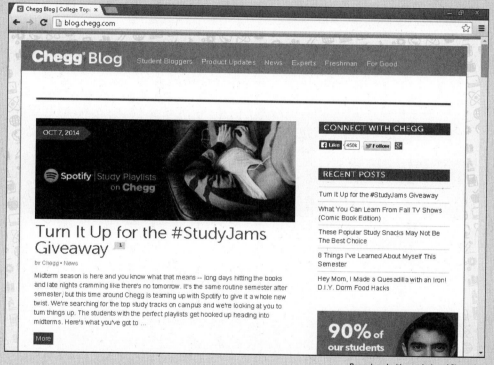

Reproduced with permission of Chegg, Inc.

Founded in 2005, Chegg has moved fast to build a successful community; it reported annual revenue of more than $255 million in 2013.

According to Usher Lieberman, VP of Corporate Communication, Twitter just happened to be the first social channel Chegg used, simply because that was where their student customers could be found. Chegg's first tweet in 2008 — We rent textbooks for really cheap — was a serendipitous success. "Today, there is very much a master plan for how we leverage social

(continued)

Book VIII Chapter 6

Multiplying Your Impact

(continued)

channels. . . . We utilize a lot of sophisticated tools and we listen to our students and are engaged in an ongoing dialogue with them. Our customer support team monitors these channels closely and responds, usually within minutes, to customers who reach out," Lieberman notes. "We do track sales against social media performance, but our primary metric is brand engagement."

To meet the needs of a company its size, Chegg uses two full-time staff leaders devoted to social media and a customer support team for added resources, especially during busy seasons. "We operate off of an editorial calendar and generally plan our posts several weeks in advance. That said," he indicates, "we have the flexibility to respond in real-time and engage our audience via all of our social channels."

Chegg took advantage of Promoted Tweets on Twitter (see the nearby figure) and Promoted Posts on Facebook to run a two-week seasonal campaign during one of their busiest sales seasons — the textbook rush in Winter 2014. "Promoting the posts (Facebook and Twitter) was critical as it allowed our message to rise above the noise in organic messaging," says Lieberman.

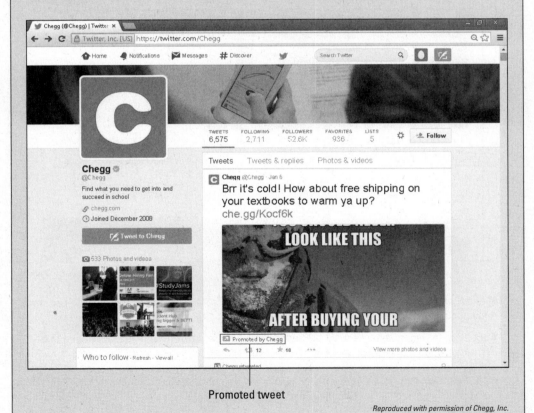

Promoted tweet

Reproduced with permission of Chegg, Inc.

The Promoted Tweets ran concurrently with other messages and didn't affect the frequency with which Chegg handled its myriad other social activities.

Lieberman stresses that he utilizes promoted options strategically and sparingly. "We use promoted tweets and posts when we feel a message really needs to be seen by a maximum audience. This isn't something we do all the time. In fact, it is the exception. We also advertise on Facebook, but generally do not have spends on other networks."

He offers succinct advice to businesses seeking cost-effective advertising. "Test, test, test, and know your audience. It doesn't matter how much you spend promoting your message; if it doesn't resonate with your audience, you are not going to get the results you want or need. . . . [You need to know] what are their challenges, what problems are you trying to solve for them right now, what can you possibly say that will get them talking. . . . Don't start a campaign thinking how much you can spend, think about what you have to say, then figure out how much it will cost to get your audience talking about your message."

Chegg's web presence:

- `www.chegg.com`
- `https://twitter.com/chegg`
- `www.facebook.com/chegg`
- `http://instagram.com/chegg`
- `http://blog.chegg.com`
- `https://www.linkedin.com/company/chegg-inc.?trk=company_logo`
- `http://www.youtube.com/user/cheggchannel`

Book IX

Measuring Results;
Building Success

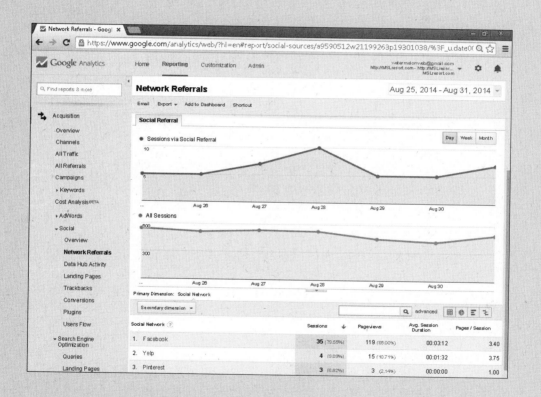

Find out how to access basic Pinterest data with ease at www.dummies.com/
extras/socialmediamarketingaio.

Contents at a Glance

Chapter 1: Delving into Data

Web analytics is the practice of analyzing performance and business statistics for a website, social media marketing, and other online marketing efforts to better understand user behavior and improve results. Some might call web analytics more art than science; to others, it's black magic.

The amount of data that can be acquired from online marketing efforts vastly exceeds the amount available using traditional offline methods. That statement alone makes online marketing, including social media, an attractive form of public relations and advertising.

In the best of all possible worlds, the results of your marketing efforts should appear as increased profits — in other words, as an improved bottom line with a nice return on investment (ROI). You're more likely to achieve this goal if you make analytics part of a process of continuous quality improvement.

Before getting mired in the swamp of online marketing data, assess the performance of your hub website. If you aren't making a profit from that core investment, it doesn't matter whether you fill the conversion funnel (see Book I, Chapter 1) with fantastic traffic from social media, exhibit a soaring click-through rate, or tally revenues through the roof. If you aren't sure how your hub site is performing, use the tools in this chapter and ask your web developer and bookkeeper for help.

Planning a Measurement Strategy

The basic principle "You can't manage what you don't measure" applies doubly to the online universe. Do you know whether Facebook or LinkedIn drives more traffic to your site? Whether more people buy after reading a blog post about pets than after reading a blog post about plants? If not, you're simply guessing at how to expend your precious marketing dollars and time.

To make the most of your effort, return to the goals and objectives you established on your Social Media Marketing Goals statement (see Book I, Chapter 1 or download it from www.dummies.com/extras/socialmediamarketingaio).

Ask yourself what you need to measure to determine your accomplishments. Would interim measurements help you decide whether a particular aspect of a social media campaign is working?

For instance, if one of your goals is to substitute social media marketing for paid advertising, compare performance between the two. If you initiated social media activities to improve a ranking on Search Engine Results Pages (SERP), you must measure your standing by keywords at different times. In either case, of course, you might want to track visitors to the site who arrive from either a social media referral or from natural search to see whether they continue to a purchase.

Fortunately, computers do one thing extremely well: count. Chances are good that if you have a question, you can find an answer.

Because computers count just about everything, you can quickly drown in so much data that you find it impossible to gather meaningful information, let alone make a decision. The last thing you need is a dozen reports that you don't have time to read.

Unless you have a very large site, monitoring statistics monthly or quarterly is usually sufficient. You might check more often when you first initiate a specific social media campaign or another online marketing activity, if you invest significant amounts of money or effort into a new campaign, or if you support your site by way of advertising (in which case, monitoring traffic is the sine qua non of your existence).

On your Social Media Marketing Plan (see Book I, Chapter 3, or download it from www.dummies.com/extras/socialmediamarketingaio), add your choice of measurement parameters and analytical tools, as well as the names of the people who will be responsible for creating reports. Schedule the frequency of analytical review on your Social Media Activity Calendar (see Book I, Chapter 4).

Monitoring versus measuring

For the purposes of this book, we discuss only quantitative data as part of the measurement process. Use monitoring tools to review such qualitative data from social media as

+ The degree of customer engagement

+ The nature of customer dialog, sometimes called *sentiment*

+ Your brand reputation on a social network

+ The quality of relationships with your target market

+ The extent of participation in online conversations

+ Positioning in your industry versus your competitors

If you have no monitoring tools in place yet, turn to Book II, Chapter 1.

"Real people" usually review subjective monitoring data to assess such ineffable qualities as the positive or negative characteristics of consumer posts, conversational tone, and brand acknowledgment. Notwithstanding Hal in the movie *2001: A Space Odyssey,* we don't yet have analytical software with the supple linguistic sophistication of the human brain.

Setting aside the squishy qualitative data, you still have two types of quantitative data to measure:

+ **Internal performance measurements:** Measure the effectiveness of your social media, other marketing efforts, and website in achieving your objectives. Performance measurements include such parameters as traffic to your social pages or website, the number of people who click-through to your hub presence, which products sell best, and *conversion rate,* or the percentage of visitors who buy or become qualified leads.

+ **Business measurements:** Primarily dollar-based parameters — costs, revenues, profits — that go directly to your business operations. Such financial items as the cost of customer or lead acquisition, average dollar value per sale, the value assigned to leads, the break-even point, and ROI fall into this category. For more about measuring ROI, see Book I, Chapter 2.

Deciding what to measure

Most of the key performance indicators (KPI) and business criteria you measure fall into one of the following categories:

+ **Traffic:** You must know the number and nature of visitors to any of the sites that are part of your web presence.

✦ **Leads:** Business-to-business (B2B) companies, service professionals, and companies that sell expensive, complex products often close their sales offline. Online efforts yield prospects, many of whom — you hope — will become qualified leads as they move down the conversion funnel.

✦ **Financials:** Costs, sales, revenue, and profits are the essential components of business success. Analytics let you track which sales arrive from which sources and how much revenue they generate.

✦ **Search marketing:** As discussed in Book II, Chapter 2, optimizing social media can improve visibility in search engine results. Not only do many social media sites appear in search results, but your hub site also gains valuable inbound links from direct and indirect referrals.

✦ **Other business objectives:** You may need customized analytics to track goals and objectives that don't fall into the other categories.

Book IX, Chapter 6 discusses KPIs in depth.

Don't plan on flying to the moon based on the accuracy of any statistical web data. For one thing, definitions of parameters differ by tool. Does a new visitor session start after someone has logged off for 24 minutes or 24 hours? For another, results in real-time tools sometimes oscillate unpredictably.

If a value differs from what you expected, try running your analytics again later or run them over a longer period to smooth out irregularities.

Relative numbers are more meaningful than absolute ones. Is your traffic growing or shrinking? Is your conversion rate increasing or decreasing? Focus on ratios or percentages to make the data more meaningful. Suppose that 10 percent of a small number of viewers to your site converted to buyers before you started a blog, compared to only 5 percent of a larger number of viewers afterward. What does that tell you?

Figure 1-1 shows what most businesses are measuring online. You can find a lot of research about typical performance on different statistical parameters. Though it's nice to know industry averages for benchmarking purposes, the only statistics that matter are your own.

Regardless of how you go about the measurement process, you must define success before you begin. Without some sort of target value, you can't know whether you've succeeded. Keep your handy, dandy Social Media Marketing Goals (see Book I, Chapter 1) accessible while you review this chapter.

A good measurement strategy determines how much data to leave out, as well as how much to measure. Unless you have a huge site or quite a complex marketing campaign, you can focus on just a few parameters.

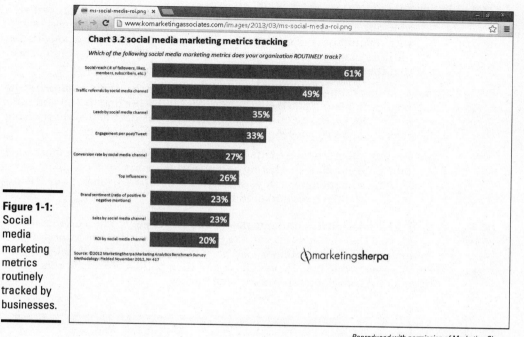

Figure 1-1:
Social
media
marketing
metrics
routinely
tracked by
businesses.

Establishing responsibility for analytics

Chances are good that your business isn't large enough to field an entire team whose sole responsibility is statistical analysis. Even if you aren't running an employment agency for statisticians, you can still take a few concrete steps to ensure that the right data is collected, analyzed, and acted on:

1. Ask your marketing person (is that you?) to take responsibility for defining what needs to be measured based on business objectives.

   Consult with your financial advisor, if necessary.

2. Have your programmer, web developer, or go-to IT person select and install the analytics tools that will provide the data you need.

   Make ease of use, flexibility, and customizability important factors in the decision.

3. If it isn't part of the analytical package, ask your IT person to set up a one-page *dashboard* (a graphical "executive summary" of key data).

   Try the Google Analytics dashboard, shown in Figure 1-2, or the HubSpot dashboard for multiple media, shown in Figure 1-3. Dashboards display essential results quickly, preferably over easy-to-change time frames of your choice.

4. Let your marketing, IT, and content management folks work together to finalize the highest priority pages (usually landing pages and pages within your conversion funnels). When possible, set up tracking codes for links coming from social marketing pages. IT should test to ensure that the data collection system works and adjust it as needed.

5. Your marketing person can be responsible for regularly monitoring the results, adjusting marketing campaigns, and reporting to you and other stakeholders. Have your IT person validate the data and audit tracking tags at least twice a year — they can easily get out of sync.

6. Always integrate the results of your social media and online marketing efforts with offline marketing and financial results for a complete picture of what's happening with your business. Compare against your business goals and objectives and modify as needed.

Aggregate all analytics into one place. You're unlikely to find a premade dashboard that includes everything you need to measure for your specific campaigns. Your programmer may have to export data into Excel, PDF, or email format; save it all in one place; and then build a custom spreadsheet to generate combined reports for your review.

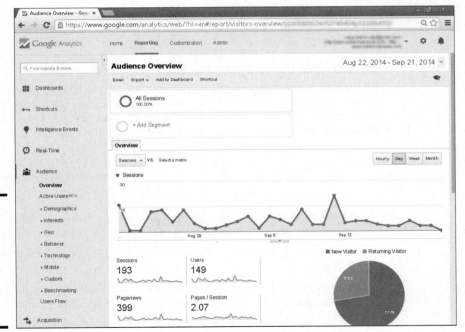

Figure 1-2:
A typical Google Analytics dashboard displays key web statistics.

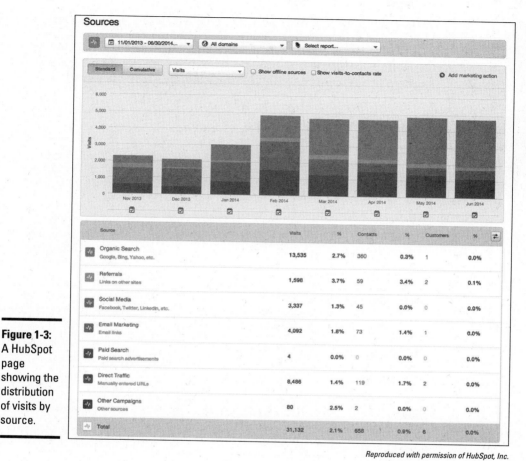

Figure 1-3:
A HubSpot page showing the distribution of visits by source.

Selecting Analytics Packages

Ask your developer or web host which statistical packages are available for your site. Unless you have a fairly large site or need real-time data, one of the free packages in Table 1-1 should work well. Review your choices to select the best fit for your needs. In many cases, Google Analytics is the best answer.

If your developer or web host tells you that you don't need statistics, find another provider. It's nearly impossible to measure success without easy access to statistics.

The specific suite of statistical results that a package offers may influence your choice of tools. Unfortunately, you can't count on getting comparable results when you mix and match different tools. Each one defines parameters differently (for example, what constitutes a repeat visitor). Consequently, you need to watch trends, not absolute numbers.

Table 1-1   Free Analytics Packages

Name	URL	Notes
AddFreeStats	`www.addfreestats.com`	Graphical display; real-time, adjustable time frame
AWStats	`http://awstats.org`	Log analysis tool
Clicky	`http://clicky.com`	All the basics for a single website; 3,000 daily page view max; offers paid options
eXTReMe Tracking	`http://extremetracking.com/?free`	Free version limited to one tracker on one page per site
GoingUp!	`www.goingup.com/features`	Customizable dashboard with graphs and charts
Google Analytics	`www.google.com/analytics`	Can include social media
Piwik	`http://piwik.org`	Open source analytics
Site Meter	`http://sitemeter.com`	Basic analytics tool with graphs and charts
SiteTrail	`www.sitetrail.com/analysis`	Used for quick estimates on social media
StatCounter	`www.statcounter.com`	Accepts and analyzes traffic from many blogs and other social networking websites
Webalizer	`www.webalizer.org`	Simple graphical display that works well with small sites
Yahoo! Web Analytics	`https://help.yahoo.com/l/us/yahoo/ywa`	Can create a segment to identify social media sources, comments, and shares

If you have a large site with heavy traffic or extensive reporting requirements, free packages — even Google Analytics — might not be enough. You can find dozens of paid statistical programs in an online search; Table 1-2 lists 15 of them. Several are fairly inexpensive, but the ones marked Enterprise-Level Solution in the Cost column of Table 1-2 can escalate into real money.

Table 1-2	Paid Statistical Packages	
Name	*URL*	*Cost*
Adobe Analytics	`www.adobe.com/ solutions/digital- analytics.html`	Enterprise-level solution; includes social media
Chartbeat	`http://chartbeat. com`	Starting at $9.95 for standard real-time web analytics for five sites
Clicky	`http://clicky.com/ compare`	Paid options start at $9.99/ month for 1 million page views/month
eXTReMe Tracking	`http:// extremetracking.com`	$4.50 per month
IBM Enterprise Marketing Management	`www-03.ibm.com/ software/products/ en/category/ enterprise- marketing- management`	Enterprise-level solution; includes social media
Log Rover	`www.logrover.com`	$99 to $499 flat fee
Lyris	`http://lyris.com/ us-en/services/ analytics-services`	Aggregated stats for marketing optimization; individual level for segmentation and targeting
Sawmill LITE	`www.sawmill.net/ lite.html`	Lite version $99 for 1 profile; $199 for 5 profiles. Professional level starts at $199; Enterprise level starts at $599 based on the number of profiles.

(continued)

Table 1-2 (*continued*)

Name	URL	Cost
Site Stats Lite	`www.sitestats.com`	Cost varies by page views and features; Lite version starts at $15 per month; Professional at $20 per month; Enterprise at $30 per month.
Site Meter	`http://sitemeter.com`	Premium starts at $6.95 per month
uberVU (now part of Hootsuite)	`www.ubervu.com`	Pricing is based on number of items monitored; contact for custom quote
VisitorVille	`www.visitorville.com`	Real-time 3-D statistics; from $19.95 per month
Upsight	`www.upsight.com`	Analytics for mobile and social apps. Free for up to 50K active monthly users; enterprise level priced on custom basis
Webtrends Social Measurement	`http://webtrends.com/solutions/digital-measurement/social-measurement`	Enterprise-level solution; includes social media
Woopra	`www.woopra.com`	Starts at $79.95 per month

Not all marketing channels use the same yardstick — nor should they. Your business objectives drive your choice of channels and therefore your choice of yardsticks.

Some paid statistical packages are hosted on a third-party server. Others are designed for installation on your own server. Generally, higher-end paid statistical solutions offer several benefits:

✦ Real-time analytics (no waiting for results)

✦ Sophisticated reporting tools by domain or across multiple domains, departments, or enterprises

+ Customizable data-mining filters
+ Path-through-site analysis, tracking an individual user from entry to exit
+ Integrated traffic and store statistics
+ Integrated qualitative and quantitative analytics for multiple social media services
+ Analysis of downloaded PDF, video, audio, or another file type
+ Mapping host addresses to company names and details
+ Clickstream analysis to show which sites visitors arrive from and go to

Don't collect information for information's sake. Stop when you have enough data to make essential business decisions.

Reviewing analytical options for social media

Depending on what you're trying to measure, you may need data from some of the analytical tools available internally from a particular social media channel or statistics from social bookmarking sites such as AddToAny (www.addtoany.com) or from URL shorteners, which we discuss the following section.

Table 1-3 summarizes which social media services integrate with Google Analytics for traffic monitoring purposes and which also offer their own internal performance statistics. See Chapters 2 through 5 in this minibook for a detailed discussion of analytics on specific social media services.

Register for free optional statistics whenever you can.

Selecting a URL-shortening tool for statistics

One type of free optional statistics is particularly handy: traffic generated by shortened URLs, as described in Book II, Chapter 1. Be sure to select a free shortener that offers analytics, such as

+ **Bitly (http://bitly.com):** A free account (registration required) to track statistics from shortened links

+ **Google URL Shortener (http://goo.gl):** Google's free URL shortener

+ **Ow.ly (http://ow.ly):** Hootsuite's free URL shortener

+ **Snipurl (http://snipurl.com):** Stores, manages, and tracks traffic on short URLs

Table 1-3	Analytics for Specific Social Networks		
Website	*URL*	*Integrates with Google Analytics?*	*Own Analytics Package?*
Facebook Page Insights	`www.facebook.com/ help/336893449723054`	Yes	Yes
Google+ Platform Insights	`https://developers. google.com/+/ features/analytics`	Yes	Yes
LinkedIn Analytics Tab	`http://help.linkedin. com/app/answers/ detail/a_id/26032/~/ analytics-tab-for- company-pages`	Yes	Yes
Meetup Group Stats	`http://help.meetup. com/customer/portal/ articles/868781- meetup-group-stats`	Yes	Yes
Ning (uses Google Analytics)	`www.ning.com/ ning3help/ set-up-google- analytics`	Yes	No
Twitter Analytics	`https://analytics. twitter.com`	Yes	Yes
YouTube Analytics	`www.youtube.com/ analytics`	Yes	Yes (must have an account with a channel)

To access a shortcut to results for links shortened with Bitly, paste the short URL into a browser, followed by the plus sign (+) (for example, `https:// bitly.com/Xv1TDI+`). A page appears showing how many clicks the short URL received. After you sign into your Bitly account, you can see additional metrics, such as those shown in Figure 1-4.

You can use a dashboard tool like Netvibes to see all your stats in one convenient place. See Book I, Chapter 4 for more details about dashboards.

Figure 1-4:
After you log into your account, Bitly offers several displays for traffic statistics for a shortened URL, `https:// bitly. com/ Xv1TDI+`.

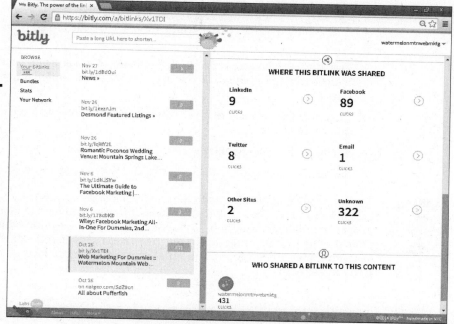

Getting Started with Google Analytics

Google Analytics is so popular that it justifies some additional discussion. This free, high-quality analytics tool works well for most website owners. It now incorporates many social media services as part of its analysis and scales well from tiny sites to extremely large ones.

Start with the free Google Analytics and switch to an enterprise-level solution when and if your web effort demands it.

Among its many advantages, Google Analytics offers

✦ More in-depth analysis than most other free statistical packages

✦ Plenty of support, as shown in Table 1-4

✦ Easy-to-set specific time frames to compare results to other years

✦ Many of the more sophisticated features of expensive software, such as path-through-site information

✦ Customization of the dashboard display

◆ Conversion funnel visualization, shown in Figure 1-5

◆ Analysis by *referrer* (where traffic to your site has linked from) or search term

◆ Tracking of such key performance indicators as returning visitors and *bounce rate* (percentage of visitors who leave without visiting a second page)

◆ Customizable reports to meet your needs that you can have emailed automatically to you

◆ Social analytics capabilities

◆ Seamless integration with AdWords, the Google pay-per-click program

Google provides steps for installing Analytics at `www.google.com/analytics`. This task definitely isn't for anyone who is faint-of-programming-heart. Get help from your developer. For detailed information on installing Google Analytics, refer to the help sites listed in Table 1-4 or go to `https://support.google.com/analytics/?hl=en#topic=3544906`.

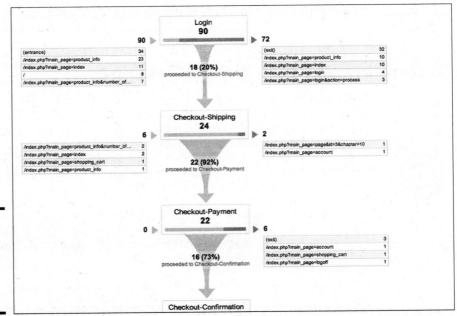

Figure 1-5: A sample conversion funnel for Google Analytics.

Table 1-4	Helpful Google Analytics Resource URLs	
Name	*URL*	*Description*
Analytics Academy	`https:// analyticsacademy. withgoogle.com/explorer`	Google Analytics Academy courses
Google Analytics Blog	`http://analytics. blogspot.com`	Google blog for all things analytics
"How to Set Up Goals in Google Analytics"	`http://blog.gumroad. com/post/87921227603/ how-to-set-up-goals- in-google-analytics`	Setting up goals
About Social Analytics	`https://support. google.com/analytics/ answer/1683971?hl= en&ref_topic=1316551`	Guide to the features of Google's social media tools
Analytics Help Center	`https://support.google. com/analytics/?hl=en# topic=3544906`	Google Analytics support
"15 Google Analytics Tricks to Maximize Your Marketing Campaign"	`www.forbes.com/sites/ jaysondemers/ 2014/08/20/15-google- analytics-tricks- to-maximize-your- marketing-campaign`	Useful Google Analytics tips and tricks
KISSmetrics 50+ Google Analytics Resources	`https://blog. kissmetrics.com/ google-analytics- resources-2014/`	Collection of Google Analytics guides
"How to Prepare for Google Analytics IQ"	`https://support. google.com/analytics/ answer/3424288?hl=en`	Online Google Analytics training

You must tag each page of your website with a short piece of JavaScript. The tagging task isn't difficult. If your site uses a template or a common server-side include (for example, for a footer), you place the Analytics code once, and it appears on all pages. You should start seeing results within 24 hours.

Integrating Google's Social Media Analytics

To be sure, you can still identify traffic arriving at your site from social media services simply by looking at All Referrers under Acquisition in your Google Analytics account.

However, Google's Social Media Analytics makes it much easier to integrate statistical results from social media services into your reports and to assess the business value of social media. Take advantage of the Social option to pre-filter for social-site referrers only.

Start by clicking Acquisition in the left navigation, as usual. Then click again to expand the Social option, as shown in Figure 1-6, and select Network Referrals. As shown in Figure 1-6, Google Social Analytics compares sessions from social media to all sessions in the graphs and lists traffic from individual social media sources below the graphs.

Alternatively, below the Social options in the left navigation, click Users Flow. In the Select Segment drop-down list (at the top of the Social Users Flow page), select Referral Traffic. The resulting display, shown in Figure 1-7, appears.

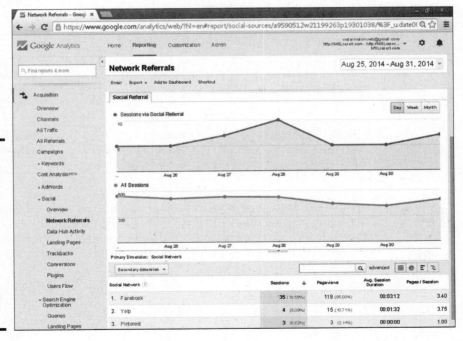

Figure 1-6: The Social section of Google Analytics makes it easy to collect and compare referrals from social networks.

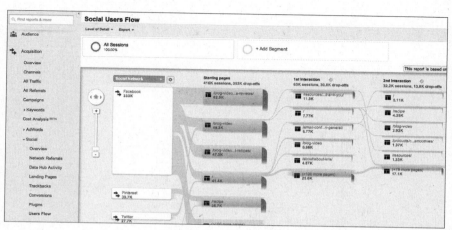

Figure 1-7:
The Social Users Flow page displays the path taken by visitors who arrive at your site from various social media.

https://megalytic.com/blog/social-insights-from-google-analytics

Some social media services, such as Ning, Facebook, and Meetup, make it easy to integrate their data with Google Analytics by enabling you to place Google Analytics tracking code on your social media pages. Of course, the Google-owned Blogger, Google+, and YouTube, as well as the RSS service FeedBurner, are already compatible with Analytics.

Web analytics, from Google or anywhere else, are valuable only if you use them to improve users' experience on your site and your bottom line.

The URLs for funnel and goal pages don't need to have identical domain names, as long as the correct tracking code appears on the pages. The thank-you page for a purchase is sometimes on a third-party storefront, for instance. Or perhaps you want to track how many people go from a particular page on your main website to post a comment on one of your social network sites or blog.

Chapter 2: Analyzing Content-Sharing Metrics

In This Chapter

✔ Using standard analytics to evaluate content-sharing success

✔ Evaluating internal metrics for blogs, videos, podcasts, and photos

✔ Estimating ROI for content sharing

You've built a blog, updated hundreds of photos, created a podcast, or shot a series of videos. You've nurtured and fed your effort with multiple posts and episodes. You've promoted your creative endeavor, and now you want to know how many people have visited, how engaged they were, and most of all, whether they shared your content with others, giving your efforts maximum exposure.

Developing good content is hard work. Like with any of your other marketing efforts, you need to understand your return on investment (ROI). In this chapter, we show you how to figure out your ROI and evaluate the effectiveness of your content-sharing social channels.

Measuring the Effectiveness of Content Sharing with Standard Analytics

If you use content as a marketing tool, how do you know whether your message is getting out there? How do you measure your results? How viral is your content? Are viewers or readers recommending your content to people other than those you reached directly through your own efforts? Your website stats reveal the most information, but you can also glean effective information from specific statistics for each type of content sharing.

Maximizing website stats

You can find an amazing amount of information about the effectiveness of your content simply by using the program that tracks your website statistics, whether that's Google Analytics or any other program we mention in Chapter 1 of this minibook. Table 2-1 summarizes which of the primary content-sharing sites integrate with Google Analytics and/or offer their own.

Perhaps the easiest solution is to install Google Analytics on every content-sharing platform for which it's offered.

Review your general statistics to find the following types of information:

✦ **The number of visitors who land on the home page of your blog or other content site:** Watch for variations in the number and timing of visits, as well.

✦ **The number of visitors seeking specific posts, videos, or podcasts:** This information tells you that visitors found the post through an external link or perhaps a specific set of keywords in a search engine. Most analytics enable you to search content results to the page level.

✦ **How visitors arrived at your content-sharing site:** Someone might have used a search engine, entered the URL for your social-sharing presence, or linked from another website.

✦ **How long visitors remain on a specific post page:** If the duration of a visit is shorter than the potential length of time spent reading the post and pondering its contents, the post wasn't effective. You can infer the effectiveness of a post from the bounce rate.

Capitalize on effective posts by creating similar posts. When you analyze your web statistics, you'll know which posts are effective.

✦ **The number of unique visitors to your content-sharing site compared to the number of visitors to your website:** For instance, content posts can consist of unique information about your products or services. The more unique visitors you have to specific content posts — or to your content, in general — the better your information is received. If your blog attracts more unique visitors than your site does, consider creating links in your blog posts to related information on your website. If your site receives more hits than your blog, add some links from the specific products or services you offer to blog posts about these specific items.

✦ **The number of people who linked to your website from one of your content-sharing pages.** The more people link from a content-sharing site, the more effective that channel is for your marketing.

✦ **The geographical location of your content visitors:** If the majority of visitors are from a country or area other than your target market, change your message.

✦ **The direction of traffic:** After you have an established content-sharing presence, your traffic rate and number of incoming links to your website should increase. If they aren't increasing, consider shaking things up a bit by offering different content. Look at which posts have been popular in the past. Expand on those topics or put a new spin on them, and carefully monitor the results.

Table 2-1	Analytics Availability on Content-Sharing Sites			
Website	*URL*	*Description*	*Google Analytics Integration?*	*Own Analytics Package?*
Image Sharing				
Flickr	www.flickr.com	Well-known photo-sharing site	No	No
Instagram	http:// instagram.com	Popular app used to share photos and videos from mobile device on social media sites	Yes	No
Picasa	http://picasa. google.com	Google's photo-sharing site	Yes	Yes
Pinterest	www.pinterest. com	Share and collect photos on visual scrapbooks	Yes	Yes
Video/Audio Sharing				
Spotify	www.spotify. com	A digital music service where you can listen to millions of songs	No	Yes
Ustream	www. ustream.tv	Platform for live, interactive broadcast video	No	Yes
Vimeo	https:// vimeo.com https:// vimeo.com/ upgrade?v=c	Created by filmmakers and videographers to share creative work; commercial accounts available on Pro version	Yes	Yes
Vine	https:// vine.co	Capture and share short video loops	No	Yes (loop count only)
YouTube	www.youtube. com	Well-known video sharing site	Yes	Yes

(continued)

Table 2-1 *(continued)*

Website	URL	Description	Google Analytics Integration?	Own Analytics Package?
Blogs				
Blogger	www.blogger.com	Google's blog platform	Yes	Yes
Tumblr	www.tumblr.com	Share text, photos, links, music, videos, and more	No	Yes
Typepad	www.typepad.com	Inexpensive blog platform	Yes	Yes
WordPress.com	https://wordpress.com	Blog/website platform with hosting	No	Yes
WordPress.org	https://wordpress.org	Blog/website platform without hosting	Yes (with plug-ins)	Yes

✦ **Which pages are most frequently used to enter or leave the site:** If visitors are entering and exiting the home page and spending only a short length of time on your site, they're skimming only one or two posts before getting out of Dodge. If you're facing this situation, it's time to rethink your message. Visitors entering your site on a specific page, however, have honed in on a specific post from either a search engine result or an incoming link. If you have a lot of these kinds of visitors and they're spending a fair amount of time on your site and exiting from a different page, you have an effective content-sharing site.

Tracking comments

Beyond statistics, one of the most valuable ways to assess the success of your content-sharing sites is by tracking how many and what type of comments people leave. Look for the following information in the Comments section on blogs, YouTube, podcasts, and any other content-sharing sites that permit comments, reviews, rankings, or Likes/Unlikes.

Third-party social alert and monitoring sites may help you analyze comments for sentiment (an assessment of the positive or negative feelings found in comments). See Book II, Chapter 3 for helpful tools to use when the number of comments becomes overwhelming.

Here are some metrics to watch when assessing comments:

✦ **Number of comments on each blog post:** This information is important if your goal is to stimulate interaction with potential customers. If certain blog posts are drawing more comments than others, the information in those posts is more relevant to your subscribers.

✦ **Comment length:** If you've written a lengthy post and you receive lengthy comments, you've struck a chord with subscribers and presented useful information. If comments are sparse, however, which indicates that you haven't given your user-base food for thought, consider changing the nature of your posts or the type of information you post.

✦ **The tone of comments on your posts:** If comments on the majority of your posts sound positive and you receive a lot of comments, you're sending the right message. You can be somewhat controversial at times and stir up provocative comments, but unless you're a shock jock, make it the exception and not the rule. If, on the other hand, the comments aren't flattering, you know what you need to do.

If the number of comments for new posts is decreasing, you're losing your audience — and you probably need to review your messages. Be sure that you're inviting responses with an open question like, "What do you think?" You may need to provide explicit directions about where to click to make a comment.

If you're receiving comments on individual podcast episodes, people are downloading the podcast from your website rather than using a subscription. Analyze which episodes reward you with the most comments — and then include that type of information in future podcasts.

✦ **Number of visitors versus the number of comments:** If you have a fairly high ratio of comments to visitors, you're creating interesting material that gets visitors thinking.

Evaluating Blog-Specific Metrics

Each of the primary blogging sites provides analytics information such as that seen in Figure 2-1. Blogger, WordPress, Tumblr, and Typepad all integrate with Google Analytics. However, Blogger (which is owned by Google) and Typepad (`http://help.typepad.com/overview_and_stats.html`) offer their own proprietary tools, in addition or as an alternative to Analytics. WordPress.com, the hosted version of this popular blog software, does offer its own statistical package at `http://support.wordpress.com/stats`.

If your blog is your only online effort, internal statistics may be enough. However, if you want to be able to compare and contrast multiple components of your web presence, you need Google Analytics or another package.

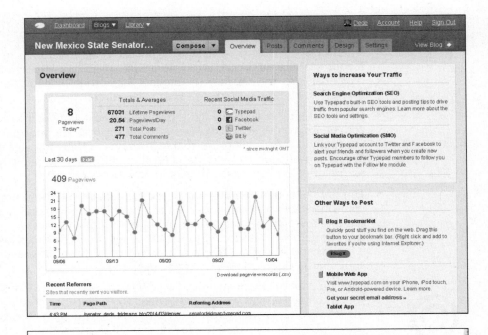

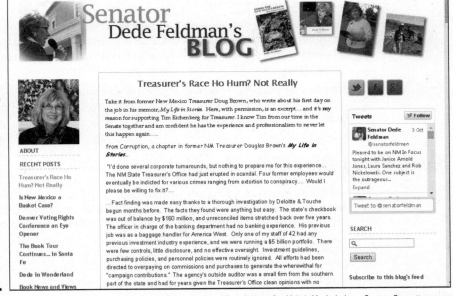

Figure 2-1: Typepad stats (top) for the blog run by retired New Mexico State Senator Dede Feldman (bottom).

Reproduced with permission of Dede Feldman Co., Melody Mock, designer; Suzanne Prescott, manager

Of course, you'll watch for the number of incoming visitors in your blog dashboard. You also want to look at the number of people who have decided to *follow* you — by subscribing through the service, getting email notifications, or using RSS.

Visualizing Video Success

After you post a video to a third-party site (such as YouTube or Vimeo), you can look there for some stats about views, click-throughs, and more.

After logging into YouTube, type `www.youtube.com/analytics` into the address bar to get to the screen shown in Figure 2-2. The Overview display shows how many subscribers you have and the total number of views for your channel.

The left navigation column of this dashboard offers a Views Reports option, which deals with traffic metrics in greater deal, and an Engagement Reports option, which deals with comments, subscribers, and shares. (See Figure 2-2.)

For more information on YouTube analytics, see `http://blogs.constantcontact.com/product-blogs/social-media-marketing/youtube-analytics`.

As an alternate path to Analytics, start by clicking My Channel in the left navigation after you log in. If the left navigation is not visible on your screen, click the three-bar icon next to the YouTube logo in the top-left corner to extend the navigation. Then click Video Manager below the top search box (above the center graphic), followed by a click on Analytics in the left navigation.

On Vimeo, you need to subscribe to the PRO option (the paid version for commercial customers) to see statistics. Log in and hover over the My Videos icon in the top navigation bar. When you click My Stats in the drop-down list that appears, a graph appears, displaying comment quantity, Likes, total downloads, and total plays by date, as well as statistics for embedded videos.

Statistics on Vine are minimal, but free. You can see only the number of times a loop has been viewed. The number appears in the top-right corner above your video.

Views Reports   Engagement Reports   Top 10 Videos

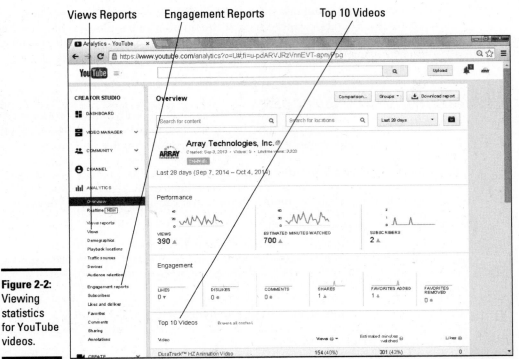

Figure 2-2:
Viewing
statistics
for YouTube
videos.

To assess the performance of your video content, the important metrics to watch include:

✦ **Number of subscribers:** At YouTube, you find this information on your channel in the top-left corner of the screen. If you're creating relevant videos, you should notice a steady increase in subscribers with each new video you upload.

✦ **Growth in the number of subscribers:** You should experience steady growth as you regularly add new videos to your channel. If you notice a significant spurt after you post a video, analyze its content to determine why the video caused the growth spurt. Chances are good that you did something different or found a topic of particular interest to your subscribers. If, on the other hand, you notice a decline in new subscribers or a decrease in subscribers after posting a video, figure out what you did wrong and refrain from posting similar videos.

✦ **Number of people viewing individual videos:** You can find this information by visiting your home page. On Vimeo, you can see the number of plays for each video by clicking My Videos in the top navigation. To view metrics on a specific video, on your YouTube channel, scroll down to the list of videos on your Analytics page and click on the video you want. You can toggle between Top 10 Videos and Browse All Content.

Understanding Podcast Metrics

Like with blogs, you need to watch several primary statistics on your podcasts:

✦ **The number of people listening to your live podcast:** This tells you how effective your marketing efforts are. When you have a lot of visitors, you've created informative media that's in demand.

✦ **The number of unique page views for your podcast:** You can figure out which posts are being received well. Use this information for planning future episodes of your podcast.

✦ **The number of people who subscribe to follow your podcast.** This measure of engagement indicates whether your content is helping you develop a loyal following of listeners.

✦ **The number of people who rate your podcast highly and/or refer it to others.** High ratings and referrals indicate that others are helping share your message.

Include a social media share button (see Book II, Chapter 3) whenever possible to encourage your readers, viewers, and listeners to post the link to your material on their own social media pages.

When you make your podcast available from the iTunes store (whether for free or for a fee), you're out there with the heavy hitters — and have access to additional analytical information. You have no way, at least for now, to find out how many iTunes users subscribe to your podcast, but you can find out the popularity of your podcast by following these steps:

1. **Enter** `https://itunes.apple.com/us/store` **in the address bar.**

The iTunes store appears.

2. **Click the More button (which looks like an ellipsis) in the top-left navigation, and then select Podcasts from the pop-up menu that appears.**

New & Noteworthy podcasts, as well as Editor's Choices, appear in the center of the screen. In the right column are lists of Top Episodes and Top Podcasts. If your podcast appears on this screen, congratulations — no need to go any further in this list. If it doesn't appear on this page, continue to Step 3.

3. **At the top of the right column, click the down arrow next to the words All Categories.**

   From the drop-down list that appears, select the category for your podcast. The screen with generic results covering all categories is replaced by a screen showing a revised set of New & Noteworthy podcasts and other subcategories relevant to each topic area. A list of Top Episodes and Top Podcasts within your chosen category appears in the right column. If your podcast still doesn't appear, continue to Step 4.

4. **Enter a keyword that's associated with your podcast in the Search Store text box in the top-right corner of your iTunes window, and then click Search (which looks like a magnifying glass).**

   Because this function searches the entire iTunes Store, add the word *podcast* to your keyword. For example, if you've created a photography podcast, *photography* might be the keyword, and the complete search term would be *photography podcast.*

   The most popular podcasts appear in a table, which includes a Popularity column. The small, individual bar graphs in this column show the relative popularity for each podcast.

5. **Analyze the resulting list to see where your podcast appears.**

   If your podcast doesn't appear in the list, click the See All button at the top right of the table. When you find your podcast on the resulting screen, click on it.

   You can also sort podcast episodes by podcast name, episode name, time duration, popularity, or price by clicking on the desired column title to re-sort the table. You're looking for popularity: When you see bars extending all the way across the Popularity column, you know that the episode is quite a popular one.

Take advantage of iTunes to rank the relative popularity of multiple podcast episodes. This information is useful in planning future episodes. To rank podcasts by popularity, follow these steps after you enter the iTunes Store and select Podcasts from the More pop-up menu:

1. **Enter the name of your podcast in the Search Store text box in the top-right corner of the iTunes window.**

   Your podcast thumbnail appears.

2. **Click your podcast thumbnail.**

   A new page appears, displaying information about your show. The Details tab displays a table listing all your episodes, as shown in Figure 2-3.

View star ratings   Read reviews   Search box

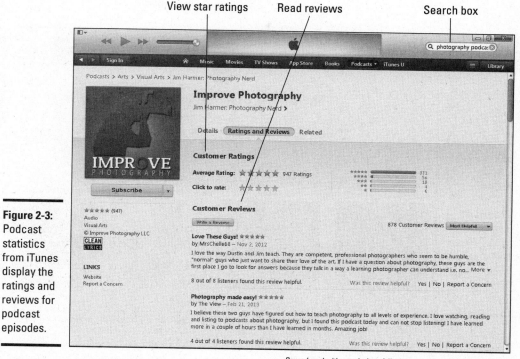

Figure 2-3:
Podcast
statistics
from iTunes
display the
ratings and
reviews for
podcast
episodes.

Reproduced with permission of Jim Harmer - ImprovePhotography.com

3. **Click the tab for Ratings and Reviews in the top navigation.**

   You can see your star rating and read reviews left by listeners for individual episodes. You can also see your overall star rating in the left pane
   of your podcast page. (Refer to Figure 2-3.)

Measuring Your Results from Pinterest

When it first launched, Pinterest offered only the briefest of statistics on the
number of Boards, Pins, Likes, Followers, and Following running across the
page horizontally below your header image, as shown in Figure 2-4.

All viewers, including your competitors, can see these statistics, Of course,
you can see the basic statistics showing how your competitors perform on
Pinterest, too.

Now Pinterest offers useful, private analytics that show how users interact
with your pins, your profile, and your website. You can also use Pinterest
Analytics to find out more about the demographics of your audience.

Statistics

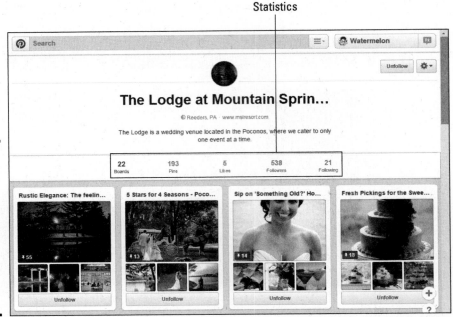

Figure 2-4: Basic statistics on pins and followers are visible to everyone who visits your Pinterest site.

Reproduced with permission of Mountain Springs Lake Corp.

To access Pinterest Analytics, you must first create a business account, as described in Book VII. From your business account, go to your Profile page and click the Settings icon (which looks like a gear). Then select Analytics from the pop-up menu that appears, as shown in Figure 2-5.

You can easily convert a personal account that you've been using for your business into a business account, as described in Book VII.

After you're in Analytics, the screen shown in Figure 2-6 appears, displaying a running summary of activity for the past 30 days, including Impressions, Clicks, Repins, Likes, and Pin Type (these data appear below the graphs).

For additional detail in each category, select a tab from the top navigation for Your Pinterest Profile, Your Audience, or Activity from *Your Website*.

For more information, see `https://business.pinterest.com/blog/ how-use-pinterest-analytics-change-way-you-pin` and `https:// help.pinterest.com/articles/pinterest-analytics`.

Settings

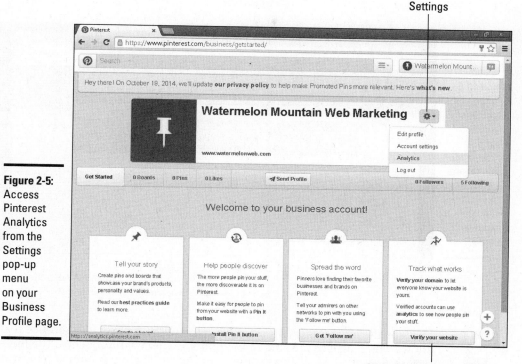

Click to verify your website.

Reproduced with permission of Watermelon Mountain Web Marketing, www.watermelonweb.com

Figure 2-5:
Access
Pinterest
Analytics
from the
Settings
pop-up
menu
on your
Business
Profile page.

Discovering details about your Pinterest profile

After you log in and reach the Analytics page of your Pinterest profile
(`https://analytics.pinterest.com`), select the Your Pinterest Profile
tab at the top of the page. Profile information is divided into four sections:

✦ Impressions

✦ Repins

✦ Clicks

✦ All-Time

You can filter data by time frame using the date range settings. Or you can
choose to filter by device (for example, mobile versus website) with the All
Apps option. If you want to conduct further analysis offline, export these
average daily metrics to a `.csv` file with the Export Data button.

Analytics tabs

Figure 2-6:
Pinterest's analytics provide valuable information about users and how they interact with your pins and profile.

Summary of activity

Source: https://help.pinterest.com/sites/help/files/help-center-analytics-1dashboard.jpg

Perhaps the most important measure is the number of repins, because that shows which images are shared by others — their "viral" quality. The more others share your pins, the greater your Reach. The top repinned pins are available in the detail section.

For more information about profile analytics, visit `https://help.pinterest.com/en/articles/your-pinterest-profile-analytics`.

Finding out about your Pinterest audience

As with all marketing, it's helpful to understand the demographics of your audience and to compare the demographics of Pinterest users to those of your desired target market and also to users on your other social media channels. After you log in and reach the Analytics page (`https://analytics.pinterest.com`), select the Your Audience tab at the top of the page.

The Your Audience tab offers self-provided details about your followers and viewers, and those who interacted with your content (for example, with a Repin, Comment, or Like). As you can do with Pinterest's Profile analytics (see the preceding section), you can filter data by device or by date range to view trends over time. Use the All Audiences menu to filter data to show only the characteristics of your followers. Unlike the Profile data, Audience data is aggregated monthly, not daily.

Additional audience information is further divided into two sections: Demographics and Interests. You can take advantage of this information to guide your selection and organization of future pins and boards.

Distinguishing demographics and interests

The following details are available about your followers and viewers:

✦ Monthly average number of the unique impressions for your pins

✦ Monthly average for the number of people who repinned, clicked, liked, or otherwise engaged with your pins

✦ Demographic information about country, language, metropolitan area, and gender is compiled based on information entered by Pinterest users in their own settings.

Interpreting interests

The Interests view provides insight into three aspects of followers' activity:

✦ **Interests:** What subject areas your followers are exploring

✦ **Boards:** A visual collection of boards that contain your pins; shows how your audience organizes your material and assesses your brand

✦ **Businesses:** Other business accounts that your audience follows

For additional information on audience analytics, visit `https://help.pinterest.com/en/articles/your-audience-analytics`.

Analyzing interactions between your website and Pinterest

You can use the Activity from *Your Website* tab to discover which content receives a Like and which content people click on to visit your primary website. In this section, you can find daily averages for the number of impressions, repins, and clicks for those pins that link to your site, and track how people have used any Pin It buttons you placed on your website. To see this option, you must first verify your site, as we describe in this section.

Verifying your site

To get Pinterest analytics for website interactions, you must first verify your domain ownership by following these steps:

1. **Click the Settings icon (which looks like a gear) on your Profile page and select Analytics from the pop-up menu that appears.**

2. **Click the Verify Your Website button in the lower-right corner of the Analytics page that opens (refer to Figure 2-4).**

   Alternatively, you can click the Verify Your Website button in the Analytics Summary page. This button appears in place of the Activity from mlsupply.co graph on the right side of Figure 2-6.

3. **When the Verify Your Website pop-up window appears (as shown in Figure 2-7), copy the metatag in the How to Verify text box, and then paste it into the `<head>` tag on the index page of your site.**

   You may need to ask your programmer to assist.

   Alternately, click the Verify by Upload link.

4. **After adding the verification file or metatag to your site, click the Complete Verification button in the pop-up window to finish the process.**

   The Activity from *Your Website* graph should now appear on your Analytics Summary page. If it doesn't appear, click the Refresh button on your browser.

Figure 2-7: You need to verify your website before you can view website analytics related to Pinterest activity.

Verify Your Website	✕
Why verify?	Verified sites show up on profile and in search results
How to verify	`<meta name="p:domain_verify" content="4b1e045754868e81!`
	Add this meta tag to the <head> of your index.html file or equivalent
Can't use a meta tag? Verify by upload	Do This Later Complete Verification

Verify by Upload option   Click to finish verification.

Analyzing Website Interaction

Once you've verified your site, it's easy to view the data for website interaction. Log in, access the Pinterest Analytics page (`https://analytics.pinterest.com`), and select the Activity from Your Website tab at the top of the page.

As with other Pinterest analytics, you can select the desired time frame for analysis by using date range setting.

For more information, see `https://help.pinterest.com/en/articles/activity-your-website`.

Look at referrers to your primary website in Google Analytics to compare how much traffic to your site comes from Pinterest or other image-sharing sites versus traffic that arrives from websites, other social media, advertising, or search engines.

Third-party Pinterest analytics

In addition to the comparative data you find in the Social section of Google Analytics, you can obtain Pinterest information from Tailwind (www.tailwindapp.com/features), a third-party provider of Pinterest tools.

As part of its Pinterest marketing and management suite, Tailwind measures the progress of pins and boards over time, helping you assess the value of Pinterest in terms of Return on Investment (ROI). It offers a free trial, with paid versions starting at $9.99 per month. Among its metrics, Tailwind allows you to

+ Archive historical data.

+ Analyze pin performance by #hashtag, keyword, board, or category, including changes in the performance of specific pins over time.

+ Compare the viral value and engagement levels of your Pinterest content against that of your competition.

+ Integrate with Google Analytics.

+ Analyze revenue and site traffic generated from Pinterest.

Comparing Hard and Soft Costs versus Income

Smart business people don't spin their wheels. If something doesn't gain traction, they do something else. After analyzing the number of visitors that your content-sharing effort receives, consider your ROI to see whether the effort is really worthwhile. (For more on ROI, see Book I, Chapter 2.)

Unless you're selling your content, this is a subtle number to figure out. You need to derive sales results indirectly.

Remember to consider two types of costs in your evaluation:

+ **Hard:** The number of man-hours needed to create content for your podcast, blog, photos, or videos. Also, the cost to host any media online, which would be web hosting fees and any fees you pay to a designer to get your media online. If you're paying for premium video hosting such as Vimeo Plus, factor in this cost, as well.

✦ **Soft:** The amount of time you personally spend creating content. Did that time take you away from any other profitable activities, such as hobnobbing with the rich and famous, or other potential clients?

TIP

Include a question at your online checkout that asks buyers which forms of social media they use. If you aren't using a social media network that attracts your customers, you may want to modify your social media efforts to see whether you can increase your business.

Cultivating the vineyard with analytics

vineyard vines®, a company best known for its whimsical neckties and smiling pink whale logo, was founded in 1998 on Martha's Vineyard when brothers Shep and Ian Murray left corporate America behind to start making ties that represented the "good life." The company now offers a variety of clothing and accessories for men, women, and children through more than 600 specialty and department stores worldwide, more than 40 free-standing stores, a seasonal catalog, and their website (www.vineyardvines.com). With more than 175 employees at its main office and more than 1,000 in retail stores, the "good life" has spread around.

vineyard vines has built its brand by engaging with customers. Because fan photos and content were always part of vineyard vines' online presence, social networking has been a natural fit. At this time, the company's social tentacles spread across eight social media channels, each used for different purposes.

For instance, content on Instagram and Tumblr focuses on crafting a brand message and high-lighting a few key products, but Facebook content tends to be a mix of branded content, blog posts, and promoted posts. Pinterest has become an especially useful platform for vineyard vines to engage with both fans and new customers.

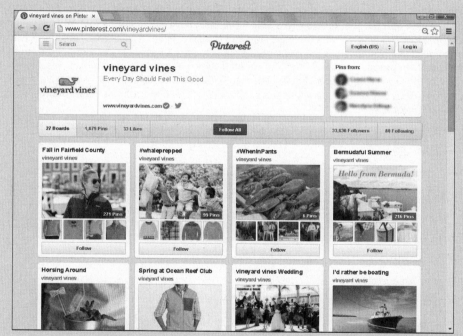

Reproduced with permission of vineyard vine

In one particular example, Pinterest results actually affected the company's product mix. vineyard vines had pinned one particular belt design when it was a new product. The pin gained a lot of traction and quickly became a top performer. Its top-pin performance persisted for weeks, even after the product sold out. Marketing staff brought this data to the merchandising team, who quickly brought the belt back into production to meet demand. This is a classic case of how paying attention to data and customer feedback can directly affect sales.

(continued)

(continued)

Data analysis is handled in-house and in conjunction with their social media agency. vineyard vines uses Pinterest Analytics to measure performance of different types of content (such as in-context photography versus web shots), while relying on Google Analytics to measure how much traffic, revenue, and new users each pin drives.

The company develops its social media strategy partly from these analytics, but it's definitely influenced more by its branding goals. vineyard vines wants to extend its brand through these social channels by delivering relevant, engaging content that stimulates conversation and promotes its brand lifestyle.

The marketing team emphasizes the importance of focusing on the basics of communication, and on creating content that meets users' expectations. "It's easy to get caught up in the analytics and make decisions based off driving traffic and sales; however, you have to remember why your customers are on these social media platforms. They are engaging with everyone from friends and family to brands and celebrities. . . . For platforms that are revenue-focused, it's important to identify those opportunities and then deliver the appropriate content that helps drive those conversions. That being said, not every social channel will lead to traffic or sales and that is okay," the team stresses.

vineyard vines web presence:

✔ www.vineyardvines.com

✔ http://pinterest.com/vineyardvines

✔ www.facebook.com/vineyardvines

✔ http://instagram.com/vineyardvines

✔ https://twitter.com/vineyardvines

✔ www.youtube.com/user/vineyardvines

✔ www.vineyardvines.com/blog

✔ http://vineyardvines.tumblr.com

✔ www.flickr.com/photos/vineyardvines

Chapter 3: Analyzing Twitter Metrics

In This Chapter

✔ Checking inbound website referrers and followers

✔ Using Twitter's own analytics programs

✔ Following your Twitter metrics with third-party options

✔ Keeping tabs on your Twitter presence

✔ Getting the right follower-to-following numbers

After your Twitter marketing campaign has been rolling for a while, you need to check out both your performance metrics and the return on your time investment. You can do this in many ways:

✦ By using an analytics program such as Google Analytics

✦ By using Twitter Analytics (`https://analytics.twitter.com/about`)

✦ By using Twitter's TweetDeck tool (`https://about.twitter.com/products/tweetdeck`)

✦ By looking at the information on your Twitter page

We discuss all these methods in this chapter.

Tracking Website Referrals with Google Analytics

If you already utilize Google Analytics (as discussed in Chapter 1 of this minibook), you can easily track the number of referrals from Twitter to your website or blog. This information is quite useful if one of your marketing goals is to drive more traffic to your website by way of Twitter.

 If you use Twitter's Web Intents JavaScript Events (`https://dev.twitter.com/web/javascript/events`) to measure user interaction, you can actually track far more than referrals, including the number of tweets and follows generated from your website. For more information on tracking and integration with Google Analytics, see `https://developers.google.com/analytics/devguides/collection/gajs/gaTrackingSocial#twitter` and

www.optimizesmart.com/social-interactions-tracking-through-
google-analytics.

To most easily see how much traffic comes to your website from Twitter,
use Google Social Analytics (Chapter 1 of this minibook). Simply log into
your Analytics account and click Acquisition in the left navigation. Choose
Social➪Network Referrals. Your Twitter numbers appear as part of Social
Referrals, as shown in Figure 3-1.

Figure 3-1:
Referrers
from social
media are
accessible
through
Google
Analytics'
Social
feature.

Tracking Shortened Links

You can easily track shortened links from Twitter back to your website if
you use Bitly or bit.do to shorten your URLs (as we discuss in Chapter 1 of
this minibook and Book II, Chapter 1). With Bitly, simply add a plus sign (+)
to the end of the URL to track the source of links to your site. With bit.do,
add a minus sign (–) to the URL to obtain free statistics in real-time.

Twitter's own link-shortening service, found at `http://t.co` for logged-in
users, works only on links posted on Twitter.com. Because it was set up
primarily to avoid spamming, it doesn't work as a general shortening service
for other sites or apps.

Using Twitter Analytics

Twitter now offers its own analytics program with four distinct dashboards (`https://analytics.twitter.com/about`). Twitter Analytics offers more than merely statistics on tweet activity, engagement, and followers. By paying attention to these statistics, you can learn how to make your tweets more successful, while discovering essential marketing information about your followers, such as demographics, geographic location, and interest areas. Take advantage of each of these dashboards:

✦ **Twitter Activity dashboard:** This overview dashboard displays how your tweets perform in real-time, as shown in Figure 3-2. You can compare month-over-month results for impressions, retweets, and engagement levels. Clicking on an individual tweet brings up a details page with additional information about engagement for that tweet: "retweets, replies, favorites, follows, link clicks, and embedded media clicks." For additional information, see `https://support.twitter.com/articles/320043-tweet-activity-dashboard`.

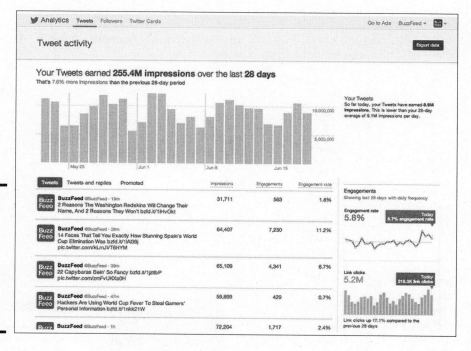

Figure 3-2:
The basic Twitter Analytics Content dashboard displays tweet activity.

✦ **Followers dashboard:** Discover more about your followers' gender, location, interests, age, and other details. You can choose to display your growth in followers over time, as shown in Figure 3-3.

✦ **Websites dashboard:** This dashboard allows you to track how often multiple URLs have been mentioned in tweets and how many clicks those sites have received.

✦ **Twitter Cards dashboard:** Unlike the other dashboards, this one is also a management tool. It allows you to incorporate rich media into your tweets, and then provides information about how the media has been shared. By paying attention to your results, you can learn how to improve such metrics as app installs, clicks, and retweets. Figures 3-4 and 3-5 show examples of Twitter Cards displays.

Implementing Twitter Cards is a multi-step process. Ask your programmer to follow the directions at `https://dev.twitter.com/cards` and then request approval at `https://dev.twitter.com/docs/cards/validation/validator`. Alternately, ask her to add the following metatag to your web pages:

```
<meta name="twitter:site" content="@yourusername">
```

In both cases, Twitter Cards analytics will become available 24 hours after you tweet links to your content.

Figure 3-3:
The Twitter Followers dashboard tracks the growth of followers over time.

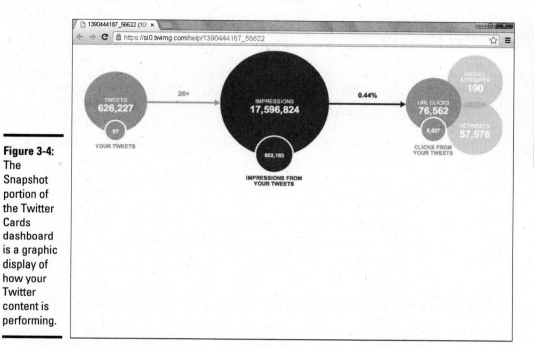

Figure 3-4:
The
Snapshot
portion of
the Twitter
Cards
dashboard
is a graphic
display of
how your
Twitter
content is
performing.

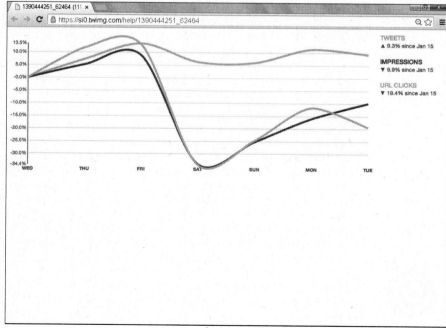

Figure 3-5:
The Time
portion of
the Twitter
Cards
dashboard
displays
how tweets,
impressions,
and URL
clicks vary
over time.

Using TweetDeck

TweetDeck used to be a third-party application for managing and analyzing Twitter activity. Twitter modified TweetDeck's functionality after purchasing it in 2011. For more information, see `https://about.twitter.com/products/tweetdeck`. Here are the most useful applications for TweetDeck:

✦ Monitor multiple Twitter accounts with one interface, including tweeting and following from one, some, or all accounts.

✦ Schedule tweets for the future on multiple accounts.

✦ Set up alerts.

✦ Filter searches on multiple accounts.

✦ Create multiple custom timelines from various accounts to insert on your website(s).

Using Third-Party Twitter Analytics Applications

Several good third-party applications are devoted to Twitter analytics. Enter your username to find all sorts of information, such as the subjects you tweeted about, the hashtags you used, the number of tweets per day, and the extent of your reach. Here are a few analytic programs you might want to try:

✦ **TweetStats** (`http://tweetstats.com`) creates graphs showing what you've been up to on Twitter. See the number of tweets sent per hour, day, or month; a tweet timeline; reply statistics; a review of people you retweet; and more (as shown in Figure 3-6). TweetStats, which offers free and premium versions, provides helpful visual displays by time frame.

✦ **TwitterCounter** (`http://twittercounter.com`) claims to track more than 94 million Twitter users, providing information about the number of followers of your account, the number of accounts you're following, tweets, top 100 Twitter users, worldwide rank of your Twitter feed, and much more. It's excellent for comparing metrics such as followers versus following, which don't appear in Twitter Analytics. You can set up your account to receive regular updates and notifications or use their new browser-based Tweet Stats plug-in, which allows you to receive stats, grading, and recommendations for each tweet straight from your Twitter feed. For more information on the Tweet Stats plug-in, see `http://twittercounter.com/pages/plugin`.

You can find more Twitter tools at `http://twittertoolsbook.com/10-awesome-twitter-analytics-visualization-tools`.

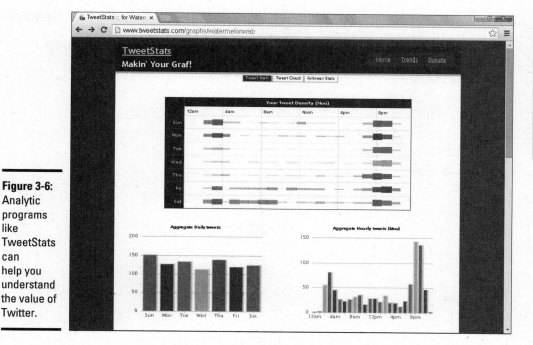

Figure 3-6:
Analytic programs like TweetStats can help you understand the value of Twitter.

Tracking Account Activity with the Notifications Tab

Your Twitter account's Notifications tab provides a running review of retweets and favorites. To view this tab, log into your Twitter account. Notifications and Mentions both appear at the top of the left column, as shown in Figure 3-7. Clicking on Notifications displays that information in the right column.

One of the most important things to track is the number of messages that are *retweeted* (copied by others and sent to their followers), compared to all the messages you've sent yourself. That's the best metric for assessing whether your messages are going viral. No hard-and-fast rule applies to what constitutes a good ratio, but a high percentage of retweets means that you're sending the right stuff. You'll find this information in the Engagement columns on the right side of the Twitter Activity Dashboard.

Use Twitter Analytics (refer to Figure 3-2) or TweetDeck to find aggregated information about retweets, mentions, and replies in statistical format during a specified time period.

Figure 3-7:
You can monitor retweets, favorites, mentions, and replies from the Notifications tab.

Checking your retweet ranking

If you're adventurous, you can see your rank regarding retweets compared to all Twitter users by using a tool called Retweet Rank (www.retweetrank.com).

Enter your username in the Twitter Username text box and click Go to see the results. If you log in with your Twitter handle, you can also see a variety of recent Twitter stats on a weekly dashboard. For longer-term records, you need the paid version of Retweet Rank. The paid version also helps you see exactly which tweets strike a chord with your followers and which followers retweet most often.

Monitoring the Mentions tab

The Mentions tab filters out the stream to display only replies and mentions. You access the Mentions tab just as you do the Notifications tab we describe above. Any tweet that's created as an @reply to one of your posts will appear in the Mentions stream with @username at the beginning of the tweet.

When you start a tweet with `@username`, that tweet's reach is limited to only your own and the addressee's followers. To reach a broader audience, use something other than the at symbol (@) as the first character. This can be as simple as the word `Hi`, a single character of punctuation, or any other short character string that you want.

By comparison, a *mention* is defined as a tweet that includes `@username` anywhere in the body of the tweet (refer to Figure 3-7).

To see other users' mentions (perhaps a competitor's), search for all tweets mentioning their `@username` in the Search text box.

Gleaning meaning from direct messages

Hmmm. We know what you're thinking: Why would you want to analyze your direct messages? After all, you know to whom you send direct messages — but which of your followers sent direct messages to you, and what was the subject matter of those messages? The answer to this two-part question tells you which followers are engaging you as a source of information and tells you the type of information they're requesting. If the same topic shows up in several direct messages, you can tweet about it and write blog posts about it.

To review your direct messages, click the envelope icon to the left of the search bar in the top navigation (refer to Figure 3-7). Note which subjects prompted direct messages and expand on those subjects in future tweets. Whenever you receive a direct message regarding one of your tweets, it's a good sign that the topic is worthy of further embellishment.

Using the Hashtag as a Measurement Mechanism

As we discuss in Book IV, when people want to make sure the word they're searching for is the main subject of the post and not just randomly added, they use the hashtag symbol (#).

The use of hashtags in conjunction with your Twitter username is another way to measure your popularity on Twitter. If a lot of people, including those who don't follow you, take the time to precede your username with a hashtag, you're being directly referenced in a Twitter post. You can easily find out whether your username or brand is hashtagged.

Go to `https://twitter.com/search-home` and enter *#yourusername* (where *yourusername* is your actual username) in the Search field. The Twitter search engine returns a list of tweets with your username preceded by the hashtag. In the results, you'll probably see some other usernames you recognize and some you don't for people who have hashtagged you in their tweets. You may also see some bad press. Monitoring hashtags is a wonderful way of finding out who's talking about you and what they're saying. You may also find some people you want to follow.

FollowFriday, or #FF, is a Twitter hashtag tradition. Users incorporate this hashtag in their Friday tweets to give someone a shout-out by recommending a company or individual that others might want to follow. Fridays are a good day to check the use of your name or brand as a hashtag.

Calculating the Twitter Follower-to-Following (TFF) Ratio

The Twitter Follower-to-Following (TFF) ratio is calculated by dividing the number of followers of your username by the number of people you follow. This valuable information is public for any Twitter user who stops by your piece of the Twitterverse. If you're following a lot of people and not many people are following you, it may look like you're simply trying to sell something, especially if almost all your tweets are about your own company, brand, or products.

There's no official number for TFF, but as a rule of thumb, your marketing goal is to have at least one and a half times the number of followers as the number of people you follow. Strive for a ratio of two or three! This ratio should provide a good balance for generating, receiving, and sharing content.

Include linkable calls-to-action on your website and other social media to remind visitors to follow you on Twitter.

Chapter 4: Analyzing Facebook Metrics

In This Chapter

✔ Keeping tabs on users with Facebook Insights

✔ Using Facebook Insights to improve content

✔ Downloading Insights data

✔ Understanding the Insights Overview Dashboard

✔ Diving into Insights detail pages

You've created a spiffy Facebook Page, added a couple of bells and whistles, posted regularly to your Timeline, responded to comments, and recruited Likes. One of your goals was probably to drive more traffic to your website. But how do you calculate the fruits of your efforts? Almost all analytical packages provide this information — typically, in a section called Referrers or Traffic Sources.

In this chapter, we show you some ways to measure the effectiveness of your Facebook presence using Facebook's own analytics package, called Insights. For more information on Facebook for marketing, see Book V.

If you've enabled Google Analytics for your website, you can find more about incorporating Facebook metrics in Chapter 1 of this minibook.

Monitoring Facebook Interaction with Insights

Facebook offers four forms of analytics, which it calls Insights:

✦ **Page Insights:** Shows performance of your Facebook page, including engagement, reach, and demographics

✦ **Domain Insights:** Explores the interaction between your website and Facebook

✦ **App Insights:** Displays performance for your web and mobile applications

✦ **App Events:** Shows actions taken by app users; also profiles those app users so that you can improve the targeting of your custom audiences and increase reach.

In this chapter, we discuss only Page Insights because those analytics are critical to all Facebook marketers. For more information about Domain Insights, App Insights, or App Events, send your programmer to `https://developers.facebook.com/docs/platforminsights`.

For additional analytical information, see `www.facebook.com/insights` or *Facebook Marketing All-in-One For Dummies,* 3rd Edition, by Andrea Vahl, John Haydon, and Jan Zimmerman.

Using Page Insights

If you're looking for standard measurements for regular Timeline posts, the recently expanded Page Insights feature provides valuable, free, content-focused metrics.

Your Facebook Page must have 30 Likes before you can access Page Insights.

By analyzing user growth, demographics, and engagement with content, you can better focus on content that helps you hold onto people in your audience, and encourage them to share your material with their friends.

Gathering data for data's sake doesn't make sense. You need to take advantage of the data to modify your content stream. The principle is the same as with all marketing: If it works, keep doing it; if it doesn't work, stop.

Accessing Insights

As usual, Facebook provides multiple — and sometimes confusing — ways to accomplish a task.

First, log in as administrator; then follow one of these three methods to access Insights for a particular page (see Figure 4-1 for the Insights Dashboard Overview page that appears):

✦ In the left navigation, select the page you want to review (in the Pages section). When that page opens, click Insights in the row of navigation above the cover photo.

✦ Type `www.facebook.com/insights` into the address bar of your browser. In the Page Insights section, click the thumbnail for the page which has the Insights you want to see.

✦ Click the ellipsis button (. . .) below your Page's cover photo and choose View Insights from the pop-up menu that appears.

REMEMBER

Facebook sometimes uses the word Fans in Page Insights and elsewhere as a synonym for people who like your Page.

Figure 4-1:
The Insights Dashboard Overview page provides basic traffic and user information.

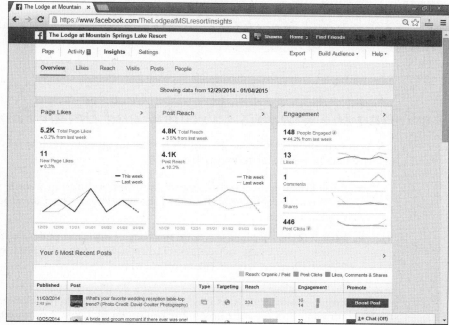

Exporting Insights

To download the data in Insights, click the Export tab in the top-right corner of the dashboard, as shown in Figure 4-2. (This may not work with all browsers.) You can specify

✦ The date range for which you want to get data

✦ Whether you want data in Excel or CSV (comma-separated values) format

✦ Whether you want to see data at the Page level, or for each post or video

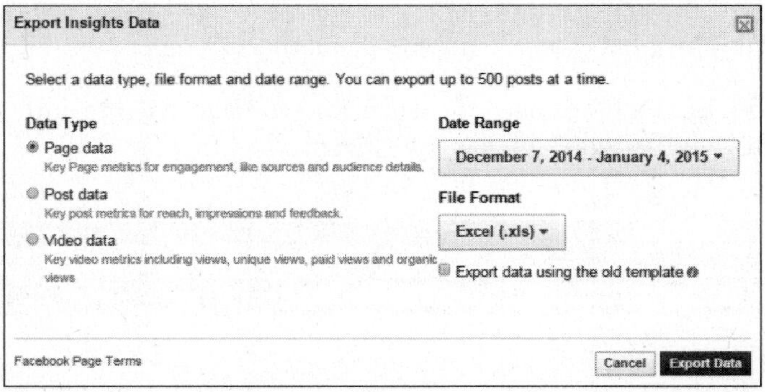

Export Insights Data ⊠

Select a data type, file format and date range. You can export up to 500 posts at a time.

Data Type

⦿ Page data
Key Page metrics for engagement, like sources and audience details.

○ Post data
Key post metrics for reach, impressions and feedback.

○ Video data
Key video metrics including views, unique views, paid views and organic views

Date Range

December 7, 2014 - January 4, 2015 ▾

File Format

Excel (.xls) ▾

☐ Export data using the old template ❷

Facebook Page Terms   Cancel   **Export Data**

Figure 4-2:
The pop-up window for exporting Insights.

Exploring the Insights Overview and Detail Pages

You can find the following insights on the Insights Overview Dashboard at the Page level (refer to Figure 4-1):

✦ **Page Likes:** Shows both the total number of different people who have liked your Page over all time and the number of new Likes for the past week.

✦ **Post Reach:** Displays the total number of different people who have viewed any of your content (including ads) during the past week and the week before, as well as the subtotal of just those who have viewed your page posts.

✦ **Engagement:** Indicates how many different people have taken some social action on your posts, broken down by Likes, Comments, Shares, and Post Clicks during the past week.

✦ **Your Five Most Recent Posts:** Below the three graphs, a table offers details for your five most-recent posts. The columns show the Published date and time, the Post, and the post's Type, Targeting, Reach, and Engagement. The Promote column on the far right displays the amount (if any) you spent promoting your post or a shortcut button to Boost a Post directly from Insights. (See Book VIII, Chapter 6 for information about promoting or boosting posts on Facebook.)

TIP

Take advantage of competitor research! If you continue scrolling past the table of Your 5 Most Recent Posts, you see the Pages to Watch section (see Figure 4-3). This section compares your Page and posts to other Pages on Facebook so that you can see how you match up against your competition. Click the Add Pages button to select other companies' Facebook Pages to monitor. In the ensuing pop-up, enter the name of the company in the search field, labeled Search for a Page to Watch. From the list that appears, select the Pages you want by clicking the button labeled +Watch page. Repeat the process until you finish adding Pages. Then click the Done button or close the window.

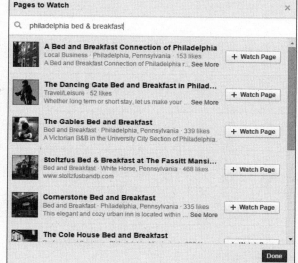

Figure 4-3:
Take advantage of the Pages to Watch feature to keep tabs on your competitors' performance.

If you click a right-pointing arrow to the right of a graph's title (refer to Figure 4-1), additional information for each of these categories appears in a detail page. On each detail page, click the tabs in the second row of navigation to view the other detail pages, described in the following sections.

Likes

The Likes detail page allows you to view Likes by the day, instead of by the week, as well as Net Likes (Likes minus Unlikes), as shown in the lower graph in Figure 4-4. It also distinguishes paid from organic Likes.

For additional information about Unlikes and how they decrease your reach, click the Unlikes link below the word Benchmark to the right of the graph.

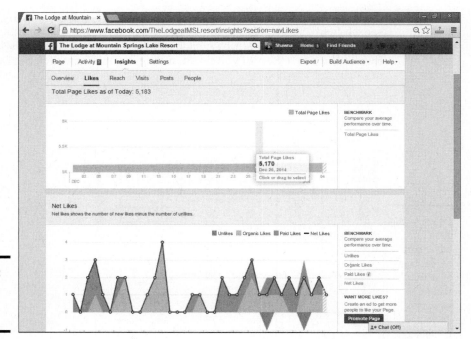

Figure 4-4:
The detail
page for
Likes.

Post Reach

The Post Reach detail page displays post reach by day, distinguishing paid from organic post distribution in the top graph (see Figure 4-5). The lower graph shows how many Likes, comments, and shares your posts received daily. Click the labeled links in the right column below Benchmark to drill down further in each of these categories. If you correlate your content with this graph, you can tell which types of posts draw the most traffic and engagement. Then you can create similar posts to ensure future success.

The Post Reach detail page tells you how many people have seen your content, and whether they found your content through paid or organic means:

+ **Organic:** The number of unique people (fans or non-fans) who saw any content about your Page in their News Feeds as a post or shared by their friends, or on your Page.

+ **Paid:** The number of unique people who saw a Facebook ad or Promoted Post that pointed to your Page.

Figure 4-5:
The Post Reach detail page.

Because people may see your post in more than one way, the sum of reach through paid and organic channels may exceed your total Page reach. Total Page reach eliminates the duplication.

Recent studies show that shorter posts (40 to 80 characters) increase engagement on Facebook. So, to keep your fans coming back for more, break a popular subject into several small tidbits, and use a URL shortener that also offers analytics, such as Bitly. For more on shortener analytics, see Chapter 1 of this minibook.

Visits

In the Visits detail page, the top graph, Page and Tab Visits, breaks down which parts of your Facebook presence viewers have seen (for example, your Timeline, Photo tab, Info tab, reviews, or other tabs), as shown in Figure 4-6. The bottom graph distinguishes how viewers arrived at your Facebook Page. (This graph varies for each Facebook Page based on which referral sources viewers happen to use.)

https://www.facebook.com/TheLodgeatMSLresort/insights

Figure 4-6:
The Visits
detail page.

Posts

The Posts Detail page has two parts: a graphic display with three options at
the top (as shown in Figure 4-7) and a detailed table below the graph that
displays your entire post performance history, similar to what appears for
Your 5 Most Recent Posts at the bottom of the Overview Page in Figure 4-1.

The graphic portion of the Posts detail page offers three tabs: When Your
Fans Are Online, Post Types, and Top Posts from Pages You Watch. Select
the tab you want. You can use the information about the day and hour that
your fans are online to decide the best time to schedule new posts.

Figure 4-7 displays the average reach and engagement by Post Type. You can
use this information to decide which type of post (for example, link, photo,
or video) works best for your audience.

To assess how well your messages are received, look at the number of comments left in individual posts and see which posts your readers pass along
to their friends. There's a summary of this information in the Engagement
column (see Figure 4-7). To drill down into the results for an individual post,
view the pop-up that appears when you click on the content of the post in
the second column of the table in Figure 4-7.

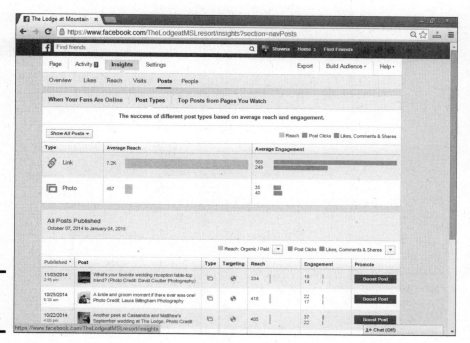

Figure 4-7:
The Posts
detail page.

You want to have at least twice as many comments as you have posts. The higher the ratio of comments to posts, the better.

People

The People detail page includes multiple sub-tabs to help you better understand the demographics of your fans (people who liked your page), people reached, people who have engaged with your site, and people who have checked in. These data are presented for the past 28 days on a rolling basis. You can view gender, age range, country, city, and language for each category. Gender and age for your audience are also compared to the total Facebook audience. This information, which is shown in Figure 4-8, helps you target your audience more tightly to yield greater engagement.

For more information about how to take advantage of the Insight Details pages, see www.verticalresponse.com/blog/a-definitive-guide-to-using-facebook-insights-for-your-business or go to www.facebook.com/help/336893449723054.

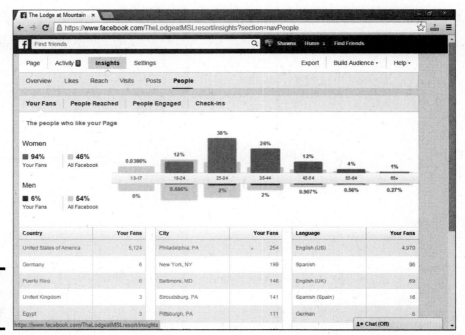

Figure 4-8:
The People
detail page.

Chapter 5: Measuring Other Social Media Networks

In This Chapter

✔ Tracking social plug-in results

✔ Analyzing Google+ metrics

✔ Measuring LinkedIn success

✔ Mixing it all up with social mobile metrics

A t this point, social media performance metrics are probably dancing in your head, having replaced sugar plums as your object of desire. The newer and less popular sites have fewer metric options, but they are important if you've selected any of them as part of your social marketing mix. Therefore, in this chapter, we look at performance measurements for social plug-ins like share buttons and chiclets, as well as for Google+, LinkedIn, and the mobile versions of your social media pages.

Plugging into Social Media

The term *social plug-ins* refers to social media chiclets, share buttons, and other tools that allow your social media services to interact with your website and each other. In Google Analytics, you can find reports on the performance of plug-ins by going to Acquisition ⇨ Social ⇨ Plugins in the left navigation (see Figure 5-1).

Select a Primary Dimension option below the graph to determine which statistical sorting method will be applied first to the analysis of your social media plug-ins (Social Entity, Social Source, or Social Source and Action). In the row below that, you can select one of the two remaining sorting methods as an optional secondary dimension from the drop-down list. The definitions for these choices are

✦ **Social Entity:** The default setting; the page URL that was shared

✦ **Social Source:** The social media channel on which the social action occurred (for example, Facebook or Pinterest)

✦ **Social Source and Action:** The social media channel and the action that occurred (for example, Facebook with a Like, share, or comment)

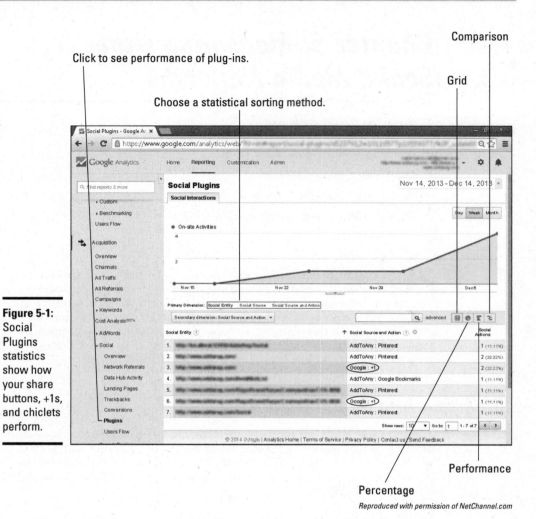

Figure 5-1:
Social
Plugins
statistics
show how
your share
buttons, +1s,
and chiclets
perform.

In Figure 5-1, the primary dimension is Social Entity (the default choice), and the secondary dimension is Social Source and Action.

If you just love data, you can change its appearance in the report simply by clicking one of the four buttons to the far right of the Secondary Dimension drop-down list (refer to Figure 5-1). For each primary dimension, you may select Table (grid icon), Percentage (pie chart icon), Performance (bar graph icon), or Comparison view (positive and negative bar graph icon).

Analyzing Google+ Success

Metrics for Google+ is, on some level, a no-brainer. Google+ is part of Google's suite of tools, so of course Google has integrated statistics for Google+ into Google Analytics.

Because Google+ is search engine–based (unlike other social networks), it may actually be more useful to SEO than it currently seems to be to real human beings. In any case, as discussed in Book VIII, Chapter 2, Google+ is useful for search engine optimization (SEO) and should be part of your social media suite. Watch the statistics for your site to see whether it produces traffic, engagement, and/or sales.

You can see traffic for your Google+ profile and compare it to referrals from other social media by going to Google Analytics and selecting Acquisition ⇨ Social ⇨ Network Referrals, as shown in Figure 5-2. For more on Google Social Analytics, see Chapter 1 of this minibook.

Click to see Google+ traffic as a social network referral.

Figure 5-2: Google+ traffic appears as a social network referral when you drill down within the Social section of Google Analytics.

Google+ stats

+1 rankings

The whole point of +1 rankings is to see which pages of your website and other pages of your web presence get the most votes (refer to Figure 5-1 for an example). In theory, if you write more pages and posts similar to those with the most +1 points, your site is more likely to produce greater engagement. We're a bit skeptical of that conclusion in all cases, but test it yourself.

After you have the +1 plug-in working — which Google will do for you automatically — ask your developer to set up plug-ins for other social media. For more on the +1 plug-in, direct your developer to

```
https://developers.google.com/analytics/devguides/
    collection/analyticsjs/social-interactions
```

or to the prior implementation of Google Analytics at

```
https://developers.google.com/analytics/devguides/
    collection/gajs/gaTrackingSocial
```

To simply install the +1 button on your website, go to `https://developers.google.com/+/web/+1button`.

You don't need to do any separate setup to track Google +1 interactions that occur on your own site; Google Analytics does the setup for you. Similarly, the reports for +1 interactions in Google Analytics (refer to Figure 5-1) include only the +1 interactions that occur on your own website, not elsewhere online.

Google+ internal performance metrics

For the most part, you can analyze your Google+ profile performance by using standard reports in Google Analytics. Just enter the URL for your profile in the Content section's search box. Drill down to In-Page Analytics to analyze results in greater detail.

However, Google+ now offers these separate internal statistics through your Google+ Insights Dashboard:

✦ Visibility

✦ Engagement

✦ Audience

**Book IX
Chapter 5**

**Measuring
Other Social
Media Networks**

You can reach the Insights Dashboard by following these steps:

1. **Log into your page at www.google.com/business.**

2. **Click the Manage This Page button on the screen that appears.**

3. **Scroll down to the Insights section and click the View Insights Button.**

4. **On the screen that appears, select the tab you want: Visibility, Engagement, or Audience**

   The Insights section displays data trends over time. Set a date range for your data by selecting an option from the drop-down list in the upper-right corner of the graph. You can choose from Last 7 Days, Last 30 Days, Last 90 Days, or All-time.

Visibility

The Visibility tab (which is selected by default) displays cumulative views of a Google+ page (see Figure 5-3). To break this graph down into photo views (from any Google property including Search), post views, or profile views, click the down-pointing arrow to the right of Total Views.

Click here to break down data into photo, post, and profile views.

Select a time period.

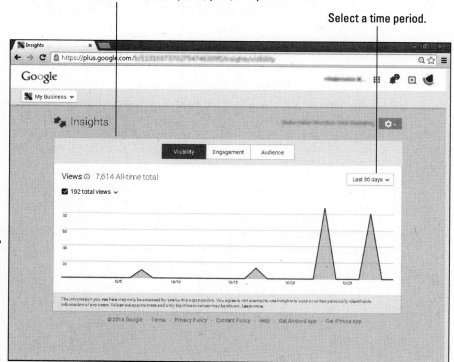

Figure 5-3:
The Visibility section for Google+ Insights, set for Last 30 Days.

Engagement

If you click the Engagement tab shown in Figure 5-3, you can see the total number of actions generated by your content, filtered by the date range you specify. You can filter this data to see cumulative data for

✦ **+1 clicks:** Clicks on your Google+ page posts

✦ **Shares:** Times posts have been shared

✦ **Comments:** Times someone commented on your Google+ posts

The Engagement tab also allows you to drill down to view engagement details on each of your specific posts, or to see the average number of actions by type of content. Click on the Recent Posts in the list that appears below the graph. That way, you can determine which posts are the most successful for your audience.

Audience

The third tab on the Insights Dashboard provides detail about the people who are reaching and responding to your Google+ page. You can find:

✦ **Followers:** Number of new followers on your local page

✦ **Followers by Country:** Breakdown of the locations of your international followers

✦ **Gender and Age:** Demographic analysis of your followers

Rippling through Google

You can find a fascinating diagram showing the path your Google+ presence has traveled when it's shared with others. These diagrams, which are called Google+ Ripples, not only show you how your posts, page, and profile have traveled from one person to another, but also help you discover new folks that you might want to follow.

Ripples help you visualize the ever-widening range of your content as people publicly refer it to others. You can also see who's doing the referring. After you post a publicly shared update on Google+, a diagram like the one in Figure 5-4 will be visible to everyone. The top portion of the figure shows the graph; the bottom displays matching statistics.

To view the Ripples path of any publicly shared post in your stream, click the down-pointing arrow at the top of the post and select View Ripples from the drop-down list that appears. Privately shared posts aren't included or visible in Ripples.

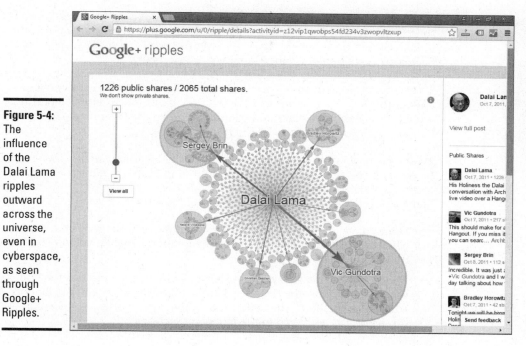

Figure 5-4:
The influence of the Dalai Lama ripples outward across the universe, even in cyberspace, as seen through Google+ Ripples.

External statistics sites for Google+

At least one site provides alternative or supplemental metrics for Google+. For an independent view, sample the 14-day free trial at Simply Measured. It offers a Google+ Page Report that includes performance, audience, content and engagement measures at `http://simplymeasured.com/freebies/ google-plus-analytics.`

Measuring LinkedIn Success

LinkedIn is a helpful place to meet professionals and extend your network. However, if you aren't getting referrals or if people aren't viewing your profile or asking you to connect to their networks, you're either doing something wrong or LinkedIn is the wrong social network for you.

One of your LinkedIn marketing goals is probably to drive more traffic to your website. As always, you can see how many people are coming to your site from LinkedIn by using Google's Social Analytics (see Chapter 1 of this minibook).

A March 2014 study by Oktopost reported that LinkedIn generated more than 80 percent of business-to-business (B2B) leads generated by social media. Other social networks were sorry trailers: Twitter (12.73 percent), Facebook (6.73 percent), and Google+ (0.21 percent).

To see how the results for your B2B business translate into conversions, look at the Social Value report in Google Analytics (see Chapter 6 of this minibook), which you can find by scrolling down the Overview page. (Choose Acquisition ➪ Social ➪ Overview.)

To see LinkedIn performance metrics, log in as an administrator. When you hover over the profile icon at the far right of the top navigation, a drop-down menu appears for Account & Settings. Click the row for your Company Page/Manage. On the next screen that appears, follow these steps:

+ **Home:** This tab shows the number of followers in the top right, along with directions for sharing an update and performance details on recent updates.

+ **Analytics:** On this tab, you can see key performance metrics for Updates, Reach, and Followers, described in the following sections. You can obtain additional detailed information within these categories, as shown in the three graphs described in the following sections.

Updates

The Updates section, shown in Figure 5-5, contains a table with your most recent updates. Each update displays:

+ **Preview:** The first few words of each post.

+ **Date:** The date each update was posted.

+ **Audience:** Whether the post was sent to all followers or a targeted subset of followers.

+ **Sponsored:** Whether an update was promoted.

+ **Impressions:** The number of times each update was shown to LinkedIn members.

+ **Clicks:** The total number of clicks on content, company name, or logo within the post (doesn't include engagement numbers, as described later in this list).

+ **Interactions:** The number of times people liked, commented on, or shared an update.

+ **Followers Acquired:** The number of followers gained from a specific sponsored update?

Updates section

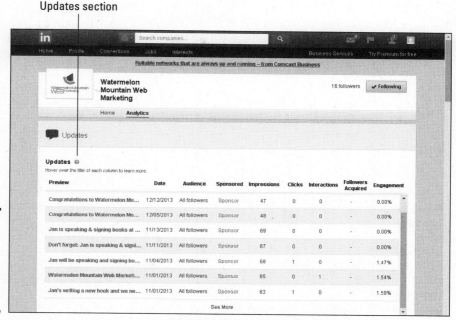

Figure 5-5:
LinkedIn
offers
analytical
detail for
Updates.

✦ **Engagement:** A measure uniquely defined by LinkedIn, this percentage is calculated by adding the number of interactions to the number of clicks and the number of followers acquired, and then dividing the result by the number of impressions.

Reach & Engagement

Reach & Engagement graphs, which appear below the Updates section of the Insights Dashboard, display trends for Impressions and Engagement over time. In the top right of this section, select from nine different time intervals, ranging from Today to Last 6 Months, as shown in Figure 5-6.

On the Reach graph on the left, you can toggle between Impressions (total number of times any update was viewed) for that time period, or Unique (number of unique LinkedIn viewers) for your updates. Numbers for both organic (unpaid) and sponsored (paid) updates are available.

On the Engagement graph on the right, you can rotate the display for the selected time frame to show Clicks, Likes, Comments, Shares, Followers Acquired, or Engagement Percent.

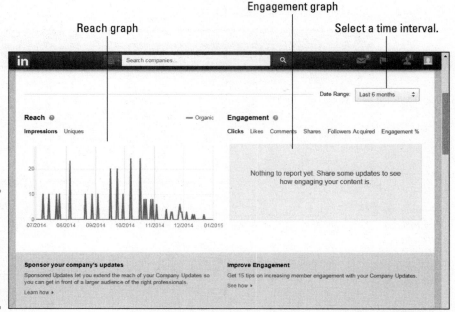

Reach graph

Engagement graph

Select a time interval.

Figure 5-6: LinkedIn offers analytical detail for Reach & Engagement.

Reproduced with permission of Watermelon Mountain Web Marketing, watermelonweb.com

Followers

The Followers section, shown in Figure 5-7, is divided into four areas. It offers data on follower demographics, acquisition trends over time, and competitive comparison:

✦ **Total:** The number of LinkedIn members following your Company Page.

The number displayed here is updated only once a day, so it may differ from the number on the Home tab, which updates in real-time.

✦ **Follower Demographics:** A breakdown of your followers by Seniority, Industry, Company Size, Job Function, and Employee/Non-Employee status. Select which detail appears by using the drop-down list in the upper-right corner of the graph.

✦ **Follower Trends:** Changes in your number of followers over time. Select the desired date range for this trend from the Date Range drop-down list.

✦ **How You Compare:** This list, not shown in Figure 5-7, compares your number of followers to the number of followers for similar businesses' Company Pages.

Select a time interval.

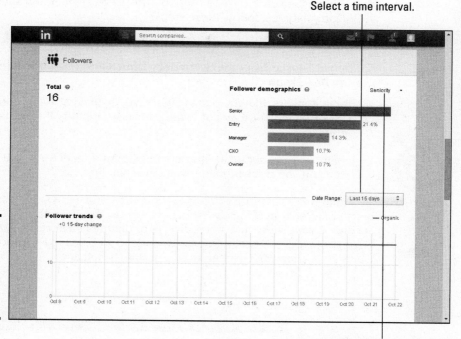

Choose follower demographics.

Reproduced with permission of Watermelon Mountain Web Marketing, watermelonweb.com

Figure 5-7:
LinkedIn
offers
analytical
detail for
Followers.

More qualified B2B leads arise from discussion groups than from company pages or updates.

If you aren't attracting a lot of Company Page views, take a look at the first two sentences of your profile. Because people initially see only those lines, see whether you can make them more compelling. You may find that the page description metatag you wrote for your website is just the ticket. (See Book II, Chapter 2 for more on metatags.)

Monitoring Social Mobile Impact

Mobile analytics is a bit different than web-based analytics. Because almost every social media service has a mobile application, as we discuss in Book VIII, Chapter 5, it's helpful to compare the effectiveness of social media in mobile versus web-based environments.

You can most easily compare these platforms by segmenting social visitors. In Google Analytics, follow these steps:

1. **Choose Acquisition ⇨ Social ⇨ Network Referrals.**

2. **Select Source from the Secondary Dimension drop-down list below the line graph.**

   A list appears, like the one in Figure 5-8, displaying social source referral URLs that may or may not include an `m.` to identify it as a mobile address.

You might want to set up a separate conversion funnel for social mobile users so you can track mobile results independently.

New subdomain identifiers `l.facebook.com` and `lm.facebook.com` began to appear in Google's list of social network referrals in Spring 2014. Facebook uses these internal redirects to distinguish access via http versus https protocol: `l.facebook` corresponds to web-based Facebook access, while `lm.facebook` corresponds to mobile-based access.

Social source referral URLs

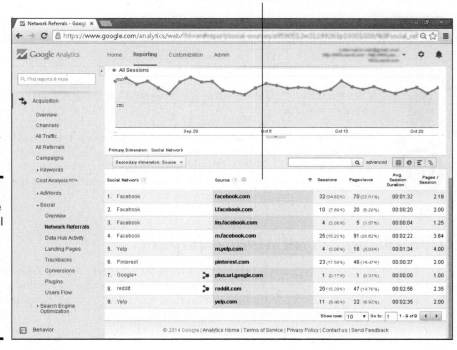

Figure 5-8: You can see which social mobile referrals came from mobile (m.) sites in Google Analytics.

Like with all analytics, which elements you decide to measure and compare depend on your goals and objectives. Are you measuring the success of your own mobile site, the use of your social media pages on mobile devices, the number of visitors from social mobile pages to your primary website, or the level of foot traffic to a brick-and-mortar store? You can see some of these statistics in Figure 5-9, in a report provided by Apsalar, a vendor of mobile analytics services.

Standard site parameters, such as amount of social mobile traffic, click-through rate (CTR), number of impressions, number of page views, visit duration, and number of new versus repeat visitors still apply, of course.

Watch for variations between mobile visitors and web visitors to your social media sites on conversion rates, newsletter subscriptions, and brand recall.

Naturally, you should watch for metrics specific to mobile use, such as

✦ Mobile phone versus tablet

✦ Use by operating system (iOS versus Android, primarily)

Sort by campaign sources

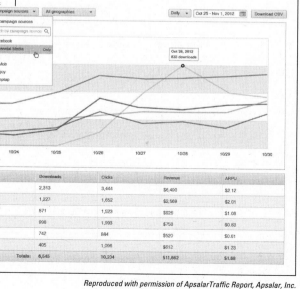

Figure 5-9: Apsalar provides helpful mobile-only statistics to assess performance of your mobile social pages and mobile ad campaigns.

You can see these details in Google Analytics by choosing Audience ⇨ Mobile ⇨ Devices. (This approach doesn't necessarily distinguish mobile social networks from other mobile users.)

✦ Mobile payment methods, codes, and coupons

✦ Click-throughs from a social mobile site to your regular, tablet, or mobile site

✦ Click-to-call rate versus actual clicks to your primary, mobile, or tablet-specific site

✦ Behavioral differences between users of your social media pages on the web versus on a mobile platform

Table 5-1 provides some third-party resources for mobile analytics.

Table 5-1   **Mobile Analytics Resources**

Name	*URL*	*What You Can Find*	*Cost*
Apsalar	Free version at `https://apsalar.com/app/login?action=register` Paid version at `https://apsalar.com/pricing-2`	Mobile app analytics including real-time daily cohorts and user-centric conversion funnels, cross-app analytics, and revenue and engagement data	Free for in-app versions; business levels start at $999/month
Flurry from Yahoo!	`www.flurry.com`	Mobile app analytics for usage, category benchmarks, and audience segmentation	Free
Mixpanel	`https://mixpanel.com`	Mobile app analytics	Free for small data sets; see `https://mixpanel.com/pricing`
Netbiscuits	`www.netbiscuits.com`	Mobile analytics	Free

Chapter 6: Comparing Metrics from Different Marketing Techniques

In This Chapter

✔ Comparing metrics among social media

✔ Integrating social media metrics with web metrics

✔ Analyzing social media with advertising metrics

✔ Juxtaposing social media with other online marketing

✔ Contrasting online with offline metrics

By now, you may be asking yourself whether web *metrics* (the science of measurement) are worth the trouble. They certainly matter if you have a business with a finite amount of time, money, or staff — which covers just about every business.

Metrics aren't about determining whether your company is the best in any particular marketing or advertising channel. They're about deciding which channels offer your company the best value for achieving your business objectives. Not to denigrate your instinct, but metrics are simply the most objective way to optimize your marketing effort.

Marketing isn't rocket science. If your metrics show that a particular tactic is working, keep doing it. If they show it isn't working, try something else.

Establishing Key Performance Indicators

The most important items to measure — the ones that reflect your business goals and objectives — are *key performance indicators* (KPIs). They may vary by type of business, but after they're established, they should remain consistent over time.

An e-retailer, for instance, may be more interested in sales by product category or at different price points, though a business-to-business (B2B) service company might want to look at which sources produce the most qualified prospects. The trick is to select five to ten relevant metrics for your business.

If something isn't measured, it can't be evaluated. If it can't be evaluated, it isn't considered important.

While you read this chapter, you can establish your own KPIs. Then you can combine them with other information about how your various marketing efforts contribute to sales and leads, to your bottom line, and to your return on investment (ROI). Armed with this information, you'll be in a position to make strategic business decisions about your marketing mix, no matter what size your company.

Enter at least one KPI for each business goal on your Social Media Marketing Plan (see Book I, Chapter 2). Some business goals share the same KPI. Schedule a review of the comparative metrics on your Social Media Activity Calendar (discussed in Book I, Chapter 4) at least once per month — or more often if you're starting a new endeavor; you're running a brief, time-constrained effort; or you handle a large volume of traffic.

Overcoming measurement challenges

Measuring success among forms of social media, let alone between social media and any other forms of marketing, is a challenge. You're likely to find yourself comparing apples to not only oranges but also mangoes, pineapples, kiwis, pears, and bananas. In the end, you have to settle for a fruit salad or smoothie.

Install the same statistical software, whether it's Google Analytics or another package, on all your sites. Your sites may not have identical goals (for instance, users may not be able to purchase from your LinkedIn profile or request a quote from your wiki), but using the same software will ensure that metrics are consistently defined. In fact, the availability of compatible analytics packages may influence your selection of a host, development platform, or even web developer.

Using A/B testing

You may want to apply *A/B testing* (comparing a control sample against other samples in which only one element has changed) to your forays into social media. Just as you might use A/B testing to evaluate landing pages or emails, you can also compare results between two versions of a blog post or compare performance of two different headlines for an update on a social media service, while keeping all other content identical.

If you're comparing performance (click-throughs to your site) of content placed in different locations — for example, on several different social bookmarking sites or social news services — use identical content for greater accuracy.

Don't rely on absolute measurements from any online source. Take marketing metrics with a shaker full of salt; look more at the trends than at the exact numbers. Be forewarned, though, that the temptation to treat numbers as sacrosanct is hard to resist.

To no one's surprise, an entire business has grown up around web metrics. If you have a statistical bent, join or follow the discussions on the resource sites listed in Table 6-1.

**Book IX
Chapter 6**

Comparing Metrics
from Different
Marketing
Techniques

Table 6-1	Online Metrics Resources	
Site Name	*URL*	*What It Offers*
eMetrics	`www.emetrics.org`	Events and conferences on marketing optimization
HubSpot	`http://blog.hubspot.com/marketing/how-to-run-an-ab-test-ht`	A/B testing how-to FAQs article
Huge	`www.hugeinc.com/ideas/report/social-roi`	Guide to tracking social media ROI
Marketing Experiments	`www.marketingexperiments.com/improving-website-conversion/ab-split-testing.html`	Information on A/B split testing
Digital Analytics Association	`www.digitalanalyticsassociation.org`	Professional association for analytics practitioners
Web Analytics Demystified Blog	`http://blog.webanalyticsdemystified.com`	Digital measurement techniques
Web Analytics World Blog	`www.webanalyticsworld.net`	Current news on the web analytics and digital marketing front
WebProNews	`www.webpronews.com`	Breaking news blog for web professionals, including analytics topics
Webtrends	`http://webtrends.com/resources/overview`	Resources for analytics and other marketing topics

Comparing Metrics across Social Media

We talk throughout this book about various genres of social media services. Each genre has its own arcane measurements, from hashtags to comments, from posts to ratings, from membership numbers to sentiment.

Use medium-specific metrics to gauge the efficacy of different campaigns within that medium or to compare results from one site within a genre to another.

However, to assess the overall effectiveness of social media efforts and your total marketing mix, common metrics cross boundaries. Surprise! These common metrics look a lot like the statistics discussed in Chapter 1 of this minibook. By using the right tools, or by downloading analytics to a spreadsheet and creating your own graphs, you can compare data for various social media.

Online traffic patterns may vary for all sorts of reasons and for different businesses. Watch for cyclical patterns across a week or compare the same time frames a year apart. Merchants often do this for same-store sales to compare how a store is performing compared to past years.

Carefully aggregate measurements over exactly the same time frame and dates. You obviously don't compare weekly data from a blog to monthly data for a website. But neither should you compare Tuesday traffic on one source to Saturday traffic on another, or compare November and December clicks for an e-commerce site that sells gift items (which is probably quite high) to January and February clicks (which are probably low). Compare, instead, to the same time frames from the preceding year.

In most cases, these metrics become some of the KPIs on your list:

+ **Traffic (visits):** The overall measure of the number of visits (not visitors) made to your site or to a particular social media presence over a set period. Facebook (see Figure 6-1) offers page administrators traffic data in its free analytics at www.facebook.com/insights (you must be logged in). Google Social Analytics enables you to compare traffic from different social media sources, as we discuss in Chapter 1 of this minibook.

+ **Unique users:** The number of different users (or, more specifically, IP addresses) who visited. Depending on your business model, you may want to know whether you have ten visits apiece from 100 ardent fans (multiple repeat users) or 1,000 users, each of whom drops in once. This type of detail is available for some, but not all, social media services.

+ **Keywords:** The list of search terms or tags used to find a particular web posting. Phrases are often more useful than individual words.

+ **Referrers:** A list of traffic sources that tells you how many visitors arrive at your web entities from such sources as search engines, other websites, paid searches, and many, but not all, other social media services. Some even identify referrers from web-enabled cellphones.

You can find a section like this in most analytics programs. Those traffic sources may be aggregated and displayed graphically for easy review, as shown in Shoutlet's Social Analytics feature (see Figure 6-2). This feature compares the performance of social posts across networks for a holistic view of campaign metrics.

Book IX
Chapter 6

Comparing Metrics
from Different
Marketing
Techniques

Figure 6-1:
Facebook's
Insights
analytics
tool displays
Facebook
traffic over a
customized
report time
frame.

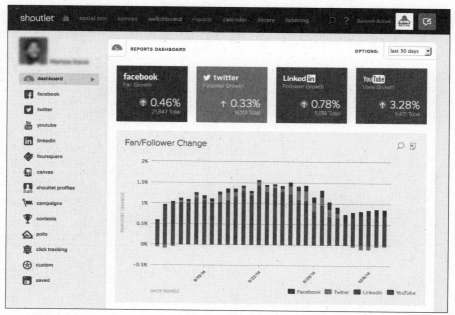

Figure 6-2:
The Shoutlet
analytics
report
provides the
total number
of referrals
by source
in the top
boxes, and
a graph
depicting
the relative
growth of
traffic by
source at
the bottom.

Keeping track of users' paths among many components of a complicated web presence isn't easy, but it's worth it. You may find that your marketing strategy takes B2B prospects from LinkedIn to your blog and then to a microsite. Or you may watch business-to-consumer (B2C) clients follow your offers from a social news service to a store widget on Facebook before they conclude with a purchase on your site. We talk more about tracking your links in the following section.

✦ **Click-through rate (CTR):** The number of click-throughs to your site from a particular source divided by the number of visitors (traffic) that arrived at that source. If 40 people view your Facebook stream in one day, for instance, and 4 of them click-through to your primary site, the CTR is 10 percent (4 ÷ 40). You may need to derive this data by combining traffic measurements from particular social media services with information from the Referrers or Entry Pages sections of your analytics program. In some cases, the CTR becomes the conversion measure for a particular social media service.

Table 6-2 suggests some useful KPIs that can track by genre and social media platform.

Table 6-2	Social Media by Genre and KPI	
Social Genre	*Site Examples*	*Useful KPIs to Check*
Bookmarking	Delicious, StumbleUpon	traffic, keywords, CTR
Community	Forums, Ning, Google Groups, Yahoo! Groups	traffic, users, time, keywords, CTR
Information	Blogs, webinars, wikis	traffic, users, time, keywords, referrers, CTR
Media sharing	Podcasts, YouTube, Pinterest, Instagram	traffic, users, time, keywords, CTR, number of views, Likes, Followers
Network	Facebook, LinkedIn, Google+, Twitter	traffic, users, time, keywords, CTR
News	Digg, reddit	traffic, keywords, CTR
Review	Angie's List, Epinions, TripAdvisor, Yelp, Urbanspoon	traffic, CTR, user ratings, leads
Shopping	Kaboodle, ThisNext	traffic, keywords, CTR

**Book IX
Chapter 6**

Comparing Metrics
from Different
Marketing
Techniques

Tagging links

Tagging your links with identifying code is especially helpful for tracking clicks that arrive from e-newsletters, email, widgets, banner ads, and links from a mobile phone because they otherwise aren't distinguishable in the referrer list.

Tagging links offers one other advantage: the ability to track the impact of *dark social media traffic.* Dark traffic arrives at your site via an intermediate stop on some site other than the social media page on which you posted your original link. (For instance, someone shares the link you placed on Facebook with one of their friends via email or text message.) Unless you tag your links, Google can't identify traffic from these sources, so it gets reported as direct traffic.

An unidentified referrer is usually displayed on a row with only a / (slash) in its name. This unspecified / category includes people who type your URL on the address bar of their browsers because they remembered it, were told about it, or have bookmarked your site.

Tagging links manually

If you have only a few such unspecified sources, simply tag the inbound link with additional, identifying information. Add `?src=` and the landing page URL. Follow that, in any order, with the source (where the link appeared, such as MerchantCircle), the medium (pay-per-click, banner, email, and so forth), and campaign name (date, slogan, promo code, product name, and so on). Separate each variable with an ampersand (`&`). The tagged link will look something like `www.`*`yoursite`*`.com/landingpage?src=yahoo&banner& july14`.

Google AdWords does this tracking for you automatically. Be sure that you have linked your Analytics and AdWords accounts together and enable auto-tagging. You can still use either the manual method described in this section or the Google tag builder described in the following section for all non–AdWords campaigns.

Using Google's URL builder to tag links

Google's automated tool for creating tagged links can be used for any advertising campaign or medium, not just Google AdWords. Follow these steps:

1. **Go to `https://support.google.com/analytics/ answer/1033867`.**

2. **Enter your website's address in the Website URL text box.**

3. **In the Campaign Source text box, enter the referrer, such as Facebook, newsletter, Google Ads, and so on.**

4. **Enter the type of ad in the Campaign Medium text box.**

   For example, the ad type may be promoted post, banner, retargeting, or print.

5. **(Optional) Enter keywords or target audience demographics in the Campaign Term text box.**

6. **(Optional) Include text from the body or headline of each ad in the Campaign Content text box to differentiate ads.**

   This step is often helpful for A/B testing when you're trying to decide which headline or offer works better in an ad.

7. **In the Campaign Name text box, enter an easily identifiable product name, slogan, promo code, holiday, or theme.**

8. **Click the Submit button.**

   Your custom URL, which appears below the button, looks something like `http://www.watermelonweb.com/?utm_campaign=holidayparties2014&utm_medium=banner&utm_source=chambernewsletter`.

As far as the user is concerned, the link automatically redirects to the correct landing page. However, you can count each distinctive URL in a list of referrers or, in the case of Google Analytics, by choosing Acquisition ⇨ Campaigns, as shown in Figure 6-3.

You can use tagged links to identify traffic coming from offline sources. Create an obvious, easy-to-remember URL for print, radio, or TV ads that looks something like `http://dell.com/tv`. Then ask your programmer to create a redirect from the obvious URL to your tagged link. Because the tagged link will show up as the referrer in Google Analytics, you can determine how successfully your offline advertising drives traffic to your site. The redirect link will look something like this one from Dell: `http://accessories.us.dell.com/sna/category.aspx?c=us&category_id=5914&cs=19&l=en&s=dhs`. Redirects are a great way to distinguish how often your video ads are seen on YouTube versus television, for example.

The process of tagging links may be time-consuming, but being able to monitor a particular campaign more accurately is worth your trouble.

Generate a separate, unique, shortened link for tweets, LinkedIn updates, and mobile sites, if needed. *Always* test to ensure that the modified link works correctly.

**Book IX
Chapter 6**

Comparing Metrics
from Different
Marketing
Techniques

Click Campaigns under Acquisition

Campaign names

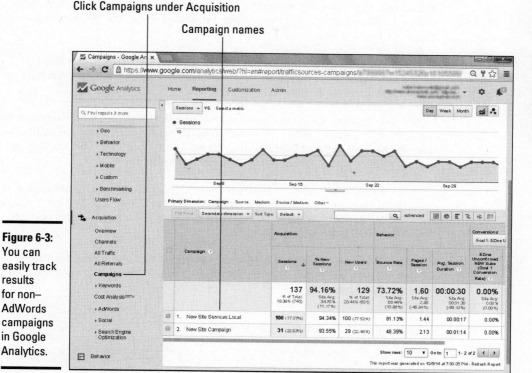

Figure 6-3:
You can
easily track
results
for non–
AdWords
campaigns
in Google
Analytics.

Reproduced with permission of Brad Cavanaugh, Air One, Inc.

Analyzing the clickstream

Clickstream analysis is a fancy name for tracking users' successive mouse clicks (the *clickstream*) to see how they surf the web. Clickstream analytics are usually monitored on an aggregate basis.

Server-based clickstream analysis provides valuable insight into visitor behavior. For instance, by learning which paths users most frequently take on a site and which routes lead to sales, you can make changes in content and calls to action, as well as identify ways to simplify navigation and paths to check out.

On a broader level, clickstream analysis gives you a good idea where your visitors were before they arrived at your website or social media service, and where they went afterward.

Aggregated data about user behavior or industry usage is useful while you design your social media marketing strategy. This analysis may also help explain why a campaign is or isn't working.

In the end, however, the only data that truly matters is the data that shows what's happening with your business, your web presence, your customers, and your bottom line.

You can easily see your upstream analysis (where visitors came from). That's the same as your referrers. What's harder to see is where visitors go when they leave your site.

Figure 6-4 displays a clickstream analysis of where visitors were before arriving at Twitter in 2014. The URLs of the top five upstream sites are available free on the Competitive Intelligence tab for a site on Alexa. To view downstream clicks, you must upgrade to Alexa's paid version.

Or you can try the Interest Affinity or Site Affinity Index on Quantcast for quantified sites. It doesn't provide specific clickstream data, but it compares the interest in other sites or areas by those who use a specific property to that of average Internet users.

Clickstream data vary over time while users run hot and cold about a particular service, while the user population changes, or while a social media technique evolves.

Top five upstream sites

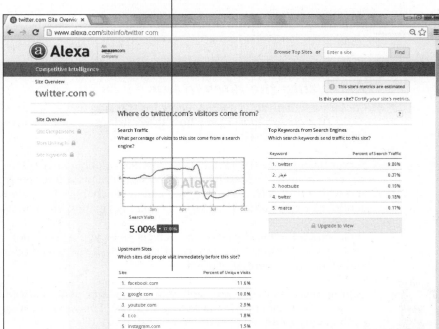

Figure 6-4: Alexa displays the top five upstream sources for visitors before they arrive at a specific site; in this case, Twitter.

**Book IX
Chapter 6**

Comparing Metrics
from Different
Marketing
Techniques

You can find a free open-source tool for clickstream analysis of users' paths through your website at `http://sourceforge.net/projects/statviz`.

You can also set up a clickstream analysis for sites in Google Analytics by choosing Audience⇨Users Flow. For more information, visit `https://support.google.com/analytics/answer/2519989`.

Tracking your own outbound links

Google Analytics lets you track outbound, downstream clicks from your own pages. Your programmer must tag all outbound links you want to track, which involves some JavaScript customization. Send your programmer to `https://support.google.com/analytics/answer/1136920`.

For additional help, have your programmer visit Google's Universal Analytics Upgrade Center at `https://developers.google.com/analytics/devguides/collection/upgrade`. If you haven't already upgraded to Google's Universal Analytics, you'll find that upgrading makes the entire tracking process easier.

If you need to tag many external links, try the automated tagging solution we discuss in the section "Using Google's URL builder to tag links," earlier in this chapter.

To see the number of clicks to each external link in Google Analytics, choose Behavior⇨Events⇨Overview, and look under whatever category name your programmer set up to track these external links.

Integrating Social Media with Web Metrics

In addition to creating your hub website, you may have developed sites either as subdomains within your primary domain name or with auxiliary domain names. These sites may take several forms:

✦ **Microsites:** These small, dedicated sites that have their own domain names are usually developed for a specific event, product or product line, service, or another promotion, or as specialized landing pages for an advertising campaign. Whether the microsite is permanent or temporary, you must make a strategic choice to create one, judging cost, branding needs, search engine optimization (SEO), and other marketing efforts against potential benefits.

✦ **Blogs:** All blogs and other information-sharing sites, such as webinars and wikis, can be fully tracked with analytical software. Some sites, such as Ning (`www.ning.com/ning3help/set-up-google-analytics`)

and Blogger (`www.bloggertipstricks.com/install-google-analytics.html`), offer Google Analytics integration, but not all hosted solutions do so. Although you can obtain statistics from certain hosted communities or third parties, you may not be able to customize them or integrate them with your other statistics.

✦ **Communities:** All Ning communities, as well as forums, chat rooms, and message boards, fall into this category. Although they may have their own internal statistics, also investigate whether you can customize those statistics to meet your needs before you select software or a hosted platform. For instance, Yahoo! Groups (`https://groups.yahoo.com/neo`) and Google Groups (`https://groups.google.com/forum/#!overview`) are inexpensive community alternatives, but they provide only limited statistics.

For statistical purposes, as well as SEO, own the domain names of micro-sites, blogs, and communities pages, rather than host them on another server (`http://myblog.wordpress.com`). Sites can almost always be tracked with your preferred analytics package if they're separately registered domains (`www.mymicrosite.com`), were created as sub-domains (`http://blog.yourdomain.com`), or live within a directory (`www.yourdomain.com/blog/blog-title`).

The use of KPIs at these additional sites makes it easier to integrate user activity on your social media channels with what happens after users arrive at your primary website. To complete the analysis, add a few more comparative indicators, each of which you can analyze independently:

✦ **Conversion rate:** You're already computing the percentage of visitors who complete tangible goals on your primary website, whether they purchase a product or complete a request form. Now compare the conversion rate (for the same available goal) by traffic source to the average conversion rate across all sources for that goal. Figure 6-5 displays the Social Value option in Google Analytics, which analyzes conversion rate to assess the relative value of links from various social media. (Go to Acquisition ➪ Social ➪ Overview and scroll down.)

✦ **Sales and lead generation:** These numbers may come from your store-front package or be based on measurements tracked offline. We discuss them in greater depth in Book I, Chapter 2.

✦ **Downloads:** Track the number of times users download video or audio files, slide-show PDF files, white papers, or application forms from your sites.

To track downloads, email links, and phone calls derived from clicks, you can use the same approach that you do for tracking outbound links, as discussed in the section "Tagging links," earlier in this chapter. Visit the event tracking guide for more information (`https://developers.google.com/analytics/devguides/collection/analyticsjs/events`).

Book IX
Chapter 6

Comparing Metrics
from Different
Marketing
Techniques

✦ **Pages per view, pages viewed:** Microsites, communities, and blogs usually offer enough content to make these parameters reasonable to measure. Tracking this information by social source, however, as shown in Figure 6-5, can be valuable. Page views are available for most blogs but not necessarily for all other services.

✦ **Time per visit:** The average length of time spent viewing material is a good, but not exact, proxy for the number of pages per view. Naturally, users spend less time reading a single tweet than they might spend on your blog or website, but fractions of a second are indications of trouble everywhere.

✦ **Bounce rate:** For another indication of interest in your content, determine the percentage of visitors who leave without visiting a second page (related to time per visit). Like with pages per view or time per visit, the bounce rate may be a bit misleading. If many people have bookmarked a page so that they can immediately find the information they want, your bounce rate may be higher than expected, although pages per view or time per visit may be low. You may want to sort bounces by upstream source.

Click this option see the relative value of links from social media.

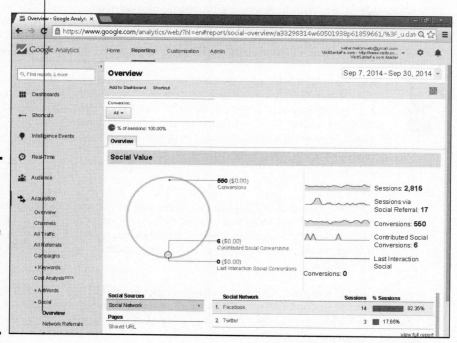

Figure 6-5:
Google Analytics displays Social Value in chart and linear forms as part of the Social Overview page.

Using Advertising Metrics to Compare Social Media with Other Types of Marketing

Because you generally don't pay social media services, social media marketing is incredibly appealing as a cost-effective substitute for paid ads. You can convert the advertising metrics in the following sections to compare the cost effectiveness of your various social media efforts or to analyze social media outlets versus other forms of promotion, online and off.

Obtaining metrics for paid advertising

With the exception of pay-per-click advertising, which exists only online, the metrics used for paid advertising are the same whether you advertise online or offline. Most publishers offer advertisers a *media kit* that includes demographics, ad requirements, and ad rates based on one or more pricing models.

Advertising costs vary over time based on demand and availability, as well as the overall economy. Ad prices are generally based on *what the market will bear* — that is, the most that an advertiser is willing to bid. New, real-time bidding schemes for online advertising may make prices even more volatile. Life is negotiable in many advertising marketplaces, except for those that operate as self-service networks. It never hurts to ask for what you want. For more information, see *Google AdWords For Dummies,* 3rd Edition, by Howie Jacobson, Joel McDonald, and Kristie McDonald (Wiley Publishing, Inc.).

Many social media sites don't charge for posting content because their true goal is to sell either premium services or advertising. Your content generates what they sell: an audience. The more user eyeballs a social media service can deliver to its advertisers, the greater its own advertising revenue. In essence, you manufacture their product in exchange for getting some of that traffic for yourself.

CPM

Cost per thousand (CPM) impressions, one of the most consistently used metrics in advertising, work across all forms of media. CPM is based on the number of times an ad is viewed, whether it's calculated for ads on TV, billboards, or in print magazines; received as dedicated emails; or viewed on web pages.

CPM is simple to calculate: Divide the cost by 1/1000 (.001) of the number of impressions (views). The more narrowly defined the audience, the higher the CPM. You can find a handy CPM calculator at www.clickz.com/static/cpm-calculator.

Book IX
Chapter 6

Comparing Metrics
from Different
Marketing
Techniques

For instance, the CPM for a 30-second broadcast Super Bowl ad in 2014 averaged almost $36, but the actual dollar cost — $4 million — was high because the audience was 111.5 million TV viewers. By contrast, CPM for a small, highly targeted audience of CEOs in high-tech companies may run $100 or more.

Because you may have difficulty tracking from impression to action in some channels, CPM models are often used to measure branding campaigns. Figure 6-6 compares the range of CPM rates for a variety of media. CPM rates vary widely within each category based on a variety of factors.

Figure 6-6:
The relative range of CPM rates for various forms of advertising in 2014.

Range of CPMs for Different Advertising Methods		
Media Type	Lower Range	Upper Range
Social Media	$1.00	$4.00
Display Advertising	$2.80	$4.86
Billboard	$3.00	$5.00
PPC Keywords	$4.00	$20.00
Magazine	$8.00	$20.00
Direct Mail	$26.00	$27.00

Sources: http://smallbusiness.chron.com/typical-cpm-74763.htmlb and www.ehow.com/info_12200588_average-banner-cpm.html

CPA and CPC

Compare CPM with a *cost-per-action* (CPA) advertising model and its subset, *cost-per-click* (CPC) ads. CPA advertising triggers payment only when a user takes a specific action, such as downloading a white paper; signing up for a newsletter; registering for a conference; or becoming a fan, friend, or follower. At the far end of the CPA spectrum, when CPA is based on a user purchase, it approaches a sales commission model.

In the classic definitions of CPA, CPC, and CPM, rates don't include the cost of producing an ad, the commission paid to an agency, or your own labor to research and review ad options. From a budget point of view, you need to include all these factors in your cost estimates.

A web-only metric, CPC (or sometimes *PPC,* for pay-per-click) falls within the CPA model because advertisers are charged only when a viewer clicks a link to a specified landing page. The CPC model is often used for ads in the rightmost columns of search engines and also for clicks obtained from banner, video, and online classified ads, and from shopping comparison sites and paid directory listings. For additional resources for paid online advertising, consult Table 6-3.

Table 6-3	Online Advertising Resources	
Name	*URL*	*What You Can Find*
ADOTAS	`http://research.adotas.com`	Online advertising research and news
Interactive Advertising Bureau	`www.iab.net/wiki/index.php/category:glossary`	Glossary of interactive advertising terms
	`www.iab.net/guidelines/508676/508767/display guidelines`	List of standard online ad sizes
DoubleClick by Google	`www.google.com/doubleclick`	Ad management and solutions
Small Business Association	`www.sba.gov/content/online-advertising`	Resources for online advertising
Internet Advertising Competition	`www.iacaward.org/iac`	Annual Internet ad competition produced by the Web Marketing Association
The Webby Awards	`www.webbyawards.com`	Interactive advertising competition
Word of Mouth Marketing Association	`http://womma.org`	Membership group, resources, events

Always ask which statistics a publisher provides to verify the results of your ads. Some confirm impressions, as well as clicks or other actions (check against your own analytics program); some provide only impressions; and some publishers can't — or won't — provide either one.

Even if you pay a flat fee, such as for an annual directory listing, you can compute CPC and CPM after the fact, as long as the publisher provides you with the number of impressions and you can identify click-throughs.

Reach

Reach is the estimated number of potential customers (qualified prospects) you can target in a specific advertising medium or campaign. You can apply the concept of reach, by extension, to specific social media channels, anticipated traffic on your website, or other populations, such as the addresses

**Book IX
Chapter 6**

Comparing Metrics
from Different
Marketing
Techniques

on your email list. Reach is sometimes expressed as a fraction of the total audience for an advertising campaign (for example, potential customers divided by total audience).

The number of potential customers may be the total number of viewers in a highly targeted campaign, or only a segment of them. In the case of the Super Bowl example in the earlier section "CPM," for instance, a beer ad may be targeted at males ages 25 to 64; only that demographic percentage of the audience should be calculated in reach.

For the best results, identify advertising venues where the number of potential customers (reach) represents a large share of potential viewers (impressions). Return to your early market research for viewer demographics from Quantcast or review media kits to estimate the reach of each publication or social media site you're considering.

Applying advertising metrics to social media

Because publishers receive no payments for most social media appearances, comparing free social media marketing to paid advertising requires a little adjustment. How can you compare the CPM or CPC for something that's free versus something you pay for? Though you can acquire information about page views *(impressions),* clicks, and other actions (conversion goals) from your analytics program, cost requires a little thought.

One possibility is to modify the cost of advertising to include labor and hard costs for production, management, and commission, and any fees for services, such as press release distribution. Then estimate the hard costs and the amount of work in labor dollars required to create and maintain various elements of your social media presence. If you outsource the creation of ads or social media content to contractors such as copywriters, videographers, photographers, or graphic designers, include those expenses.

Don't go crazy trying to calculate exact dollar amounts. You simply estimate the relative costs of each medium or campaign to compare the cost-effectiveness of one form of promotion to another. Social media marketing may be relatively inexpensive, but if you see only one action or impression after 20 hours of labor, you need to decide whether it's worth it.

Juxtaposing Social Media Metrics with Other Online Marketing

Regardless of any other online techniques you use, you can combine links with source tags, analytics program results, and advertising metrics to compare social media results to results from other online techniques.

Refine your list of KPIs for these elements:

✦ **Email newsletters:** Whether you use your own mailing list or rent one, you measure

- *Bounces:* Bad email addresses

- *Open rate:* The percentage of good addressees that open your news-letter, roughly equivalent to reach as a percentage of impressions

- *Click-through rate (CTR):* The percentage of people who click through to a web page after opening a newsletter

- *Landing pages:* Where newsletter recipients "go" when they click a link in a newsletter

Well-segmented, targeted lists result in better reach. If you rent lists, be sure to include the acquisition cost per thousand names, as well as the transmission cost, in your total cost for CPM (cost per thousand) comparison. Most newsletter services and list-rental houses provide all these metrics.

✦ **Coupons, promotion codes:** Online coupons can be tracked similarly to regular banner ads. However, for both promotion codes and coupons, track which offers produce the best results, which are almost always sales or registrations.

✦ **Press releases:** Sometimes press releases are hard to track online because many free press distribution services don't provide informa-tion on page views or click-throughs. By contrast, most paid distribution services tell you the click-through rate and the number of impressions (or number of times someone viewed your release) on their servers. Although these services can tell you where the release was distributed, they don't know what happened afterward. A press release is a good place to include an identifier in the links, as described earlier in the "Tagging links" section. The tag enables you to track entry pages. You may also see a spike in daily or hourly traffic to your site shortly after the distribution time.

✦ **Product placement in games and other programs:** Advertisers can now place the equivalent of banner ads or product images within online video games. If the ads are linkable, you can find the CTR and impressions to calculate CPM and CPC (cost per click). Offline games with product place-ment must be treated as offline marketing elements.

✦ **Online events:** Track live concerts, chats, speeches, and webinars with KPIs for registration — request an email address, at minimum — even if the event is free. Though not everyone who registers attends, this approach also provides a helpful set of leads and a built-in audience

Book IX
Chapter 6

Comparing Metrics
from Different
Marketing
Techniques

to notify of future events. Of course, you can also check referrers and entry pages.

✦ **Disaggregated components, such as third-party blogs, chat rooms, RSS feeds, regular email, or text messaging:** Tagged links that pass through from these forms of communication are probably your best bet.

You can incorporate a special tag for links forwarded by others, although you might not be able to tell how they completed the forwarding (for example, from a Share This feature versus email) unless you have implemented social media plug-ins. It all depends on what you're trying to measure.

TIP

Be sure to register for optional analytics when you install a Share function from sites such as AddThis or ShareThis, which integrate with Google Analytics. Then you can see where and how often users forward your link through these services.

Contrasting Word-of-Web with Word-of-Mouth

Word-of-mouth is, without a doubt, the most cost-effective form of advertising. Ultimately, that force powers all social media, with its peer-to-peer recommendations and referrals.

REMEMBER

Try to keep your expectations in check. According to Microsoft research in 2012, less than 1 percent of social media content goes viral. In this case, *viral* is defined as reaching a much larger audience via peer-to-peer sharing compared to the audience reached by the original post.

Recent research on the impact of social media as a form of word-of-mouth is both intriguing and contradictory:

✦ mention (`www.mention.com`) found that 76 percent of more than 1 billion brand mentions on the web and social media were basically "meh" — neither positive nor negative. The remaining mentions are more likely to stand out.

✦ According to eMarketer, about 68 percent of social media users 18 to 34 years old, and 53 percent ages 33 to 35 are at least somewhat likely to be influenced to make a purchase based on a friend's social media posting.

✦ Lithium Technologies found that 70 percent of consumers read online reviews when considering a brand.

Keep these points in mind while you consider the positive and negative impacts of participation in social media. Review sites can have a significant impact on your marketing, but the impact of individual recommendations may be over-rated except in special cases.

You can monitor mentions of your company online and the tone of those responses, as discussed in Book II.

Your analytical task here is to compare the efficacy of "word-of-web" by way of social media to its more traditional forms. Tracking visitors who arrive from offline is the trickiest part. These visitors type your URL in the address bar of their browsers either because they've heard of your company from someone else (word-of-mouth) or as a result of offline marketing.

Offline marketing may involve print, billboards, radio, television, loyalty-program key-chain tags, promotional items, packaging, events, or any other great ideas you dream up.

By borrowing the following techniques from direct marketing, you can find ways, albeit imperfect, to identify referrals from offline sources or other individuals:

✦ **Use a slightly different URL to identify the offline source.** Make the URL simple and easy to remember, such as `http://yourdomain.com/tv`; `http://yourdomain.com/wrapper`; `http://yourdomain.com/nyt`; or `http://yourdomain.com/radio4`. These short URLs can show viewers a special landing page — perhaps one that details an offer or a contest encouraged by an offline teaser — or redirect them to an existing page on your site. Long, tagged URLs that are terrific for online sourcing and hard-to-remember shortened URLs are not helpful offline.

✦ **Identify referrals from various offline sources.** Use different response email addresses, telephone numbers, extensions, or people's names.

✦ **Provide an incentive to the referring party.** "Tell a friend about us. Both of you will receive $10 off your next visit." This technique can be as simple as a business card for someone to bring in with the referring friend's name on the back. Of course, the card carries its own unique referral URL for tracking purposes.

✦ **Stick to the tried-and-true method.** Always ask, "May I ask how you heard about us?" Then tally the results.

You can then plug these numbers into a spreadsheet with your online referral statistics to compare offline methods with online social media.

HubSpot (`www.hubspot.com`) compared the subjective importance of various sources of B2B lead sources by marketing channel, including some offline activities, in its *2013 State of Inbound Marketing* survey. The results, shown in Figure 6-7, indicate that marketing professionals view online activities as more important sources of leads than traditional offline marketing venues, with social media, natural search (SEO), and email seen as the most important. Think about where you're spending your marketing dollars.

Figure 6-7:
In a
HubSpot
survey,
businesses
rated social
media, SEO,
and email
as more
valuable
sources of
leads than
traditional
marketing
activities.

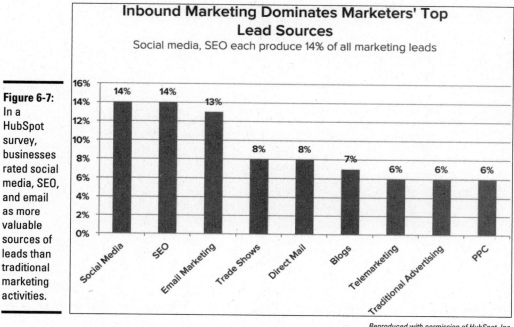

Inbound Marketing Dominates Marketers' Top Lead Sources

Social media, SEO each produce 14% of all marketing leads

Social Media 14% | SEO 14% | Email Marketing 13% | Trade Shows 8% | Direct Mail 8% | Blogs 7% | Telemarketing 6% | Traditional Advertising 6% | PPC 6%

Chapter 7: Making Decisions by the Numbers

In This Chapter

✔ Making decisions based on metrics

✔ Diagnosing and fixing problem campaigns

✔ Keeping your online marketing grounded

The 2014 *Social Media Marketing Industry Report* from Social Media Examiner showed that only 37 percent of professionals whose companies use social media said that they are able measure their return on investment (ROI). By using the tools for assessing qualitative and quantitative results, including ROI, you can certainly count yourself among those happy few who do!

However, there's no point in collecting metrics just to save them in a virtual curio cabinet. The challenge is to figure out how to use the numbers to adjust your online marketing campaigns, whether they need fine-tuning or a major overhaul. In this chapter, we show you how to analyze problems, see what your data reveal, and then use the results to modify your marketing approach.

Using Metrics to Make Decisions

In spite of the hype, social media is, at its core, a form of strategic marketing communications. As a business owner, you must balance the subjective aspects of branding, sentiment, goodwill, and quality of leads with the objective performance metrics of traffic and click-through rate (CTR) and the business metrics of customer acquisition costs, conversion rate, sales value, and ROI. The balance point is unique to each business at a specific time. Alas, no fixed rules exist.

As part of your balancing act, you'll undoubtedly also tap your instincts, incorporating casual feedback from customers, the ever-changing evolution of your market, your budget, and your assessment of your own and your staff's available time and skills.

Even after you feel confident about your marketing program, keep watching your metrics as a reality check. Data has a funny way of surprising you.

Don't become complacent. Continue to check your performance and business metrics at least monthly. How do they compare to what your instinct is telling you?

Knowing When to Hold and When to Fold

Watch for a few things in your metrics. As always, you evaluate comparative results, not absolute numbers. Keep an eye on these characteristics:

✦ Negative and positive trends that last for several months

✦ Abrupt or unexpected changes

✦ No change in key performance indicators (KPIs), in spite of social media marketing activities

✦ Correlations between a peak in traffic or sales with a specific social marketing activity

Layering activity timelines with metrics, as shown in Figure 7-1, is a simple, graphical way to spot this type of correlation. Establishing baseline metrics for your hub presence first truly helps in this process. It also helps if you add social media techniques one at a time — preferably with tracking codes.

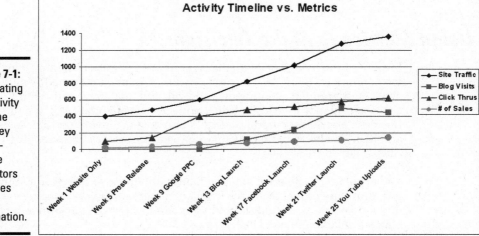

Figure 7-1: Correlating an activity timeline with key performance indicators provides useful information.

Don't make *irreversible* decisions based on one event or from an analytical time frame that's too short for the marketing channel you're trying to implement. There are no rules for a time frame that is too short or too long. Your overall campaign may be designed to take off like a rocket in less than a week, or it may be set up to take 6 to 12 months to bear fruit. Be patient. Monitor your social media campaigns and rely on your business instincts.

You may find a time delay between the initiation of an effort and its impact on metrics, for these reasons:

✦ Viewers may wait to see a history of posts before engaging, let alone clicking through to your main hub.

✦ By definition, establishing a relationship with viewers or prospects takes time, just as it does in real life.

✦ Our brains haven't changed in spite of the Internet: As every brand marketer knows, most people still need to see something seven times to remember it.

✦ Many types of social media display a greater cumulative effect over time as viral marketing takes hold.

✦ Your mastery of a new medium usually improves as you climb the learning curve.

With positive results, the answer is simple: Keep doing what you're doing, and even more so. After you identify the elements responsible for your success, repeat them, amplify them, multiply them, and repurpose them.

Neutral or negative results force you to evaluate whether you should drop the activity or invest the effort needed to identify the problem and try to fix it. Ultimately, only you can decide whether you want to continue sinking time and effort into a social marketing method that doesn't produce the results you want.

Make a chart for yourself like the one from Social Media Examiner shown in Figure 7-2. It shows how 2,800 marketers rank their accomplishments from using social media. How do your efforts stack up?

Figure 7-2:
Compare
the benefits
you receive
from social
media with
the benefits
identified by
marketers
in other
businesses.

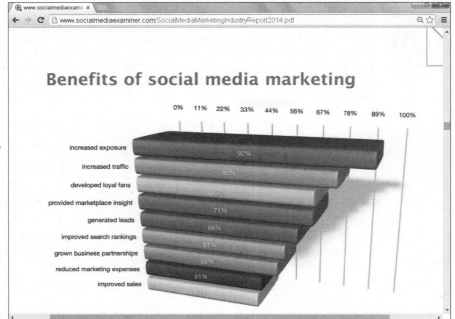

Trekking through social media

Inspired by a love of the outdoors, KEEN, Inc., manufactures hybrid outdoor and casual footwear with an innovative design that supports the lifestyles and outdoor adventures of active people around the world. Founded in 2003, KEEN is one of the fastest-growing brands in the outdoor industry and has quickly become a well-respected brand, with a loyal following. Through its Hybrid Care giving program, KEEN has partnered with nonprofit organizations around the world that are working towards building stronger communities and a healthier planet, and stands behind those partners that are actively working to inspire responsible outdoor participation and land and water conservation.

According to Eric King, KEEN's Social Strategist, the company's social media presence has evolved to "meet our fans wherever they are." KEEN started with Facebook in 2008 as part of a sustainability campaign targeting college students, and has added other channels incrementally since then. "Since social marketing is constantly evolving, it can be tricky to know exactly what to plan for, but we try to do everything possible to stay on top of the latest tools and trends and be nimble enough to take advantage of the right opportunities that come along," King says.

Reproduced with permission from KEEN FOOTWEAR

King's approach is driven by content. "We decide which content we need first, create that content, and then determine the most appropriate posting dates and times by looking at our analytics. We do schedule most of our content in advance, but also leave some slots open for opportunities that come up in real-time."

KEEN aims for a broad range of content, including product photography, brand storytelling, Ambassador and Hybrid Care partner updates, sneak peeks, and fan photos. The effort is managed by one dedicated person in-house, plus employee contributors and some outside content creators.

King tries to tailor content for each social media channel separately, considering everything from age demographics to topic affinities. He then researches which themes or content mediums will work best for each channel. "For example," he finds, "Instagram and Tumblr are ideal for posting lookbook-style inspirational images, while Facebook and Twitter are better suited for asking our community questions and then responding to their suggestions."

(continued)

(continued)

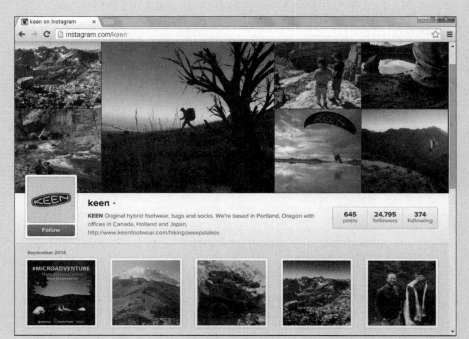

Reproduced with permission from KEEN FOOTWEAR

To keep track of all this social media traffic, KEEN uses a sophisticated analytics program called Crimson Hexagon for "social listening." KEEN manages the analysis in-house, going beyond just the numbers to understand the why. As King explains, "We study what's being said about KEEN online, how much of the conversation is positive or negative, how it compares to what's being said about our competitors, and then how we can use all this information to inform future strategy."

King's advice to other marketers is straightforward: "Know exactly what your goals are and how you plan on tracking them at the start of every year and every campaign. Be consistent with your tracking and set clear KPIs [key performance indicators] that can be tied back to definitive numbers. Finally, make sure that everyone who is involved is on the same page and working toward one common goal."

He follows his own advice. KEEN's goals, which are to increase brand awareness and engagement, have evolved over time as KEEN has "placed more priority in listening to what our fans have to say . . . so we can be more intentional with how we're communicating with them. . . . We want to make it clear that we're listening and that we care about what the community has to say."

KEEN's web presence:

✔ www.keenfootwear.com

✔ http://www.facebook.com/KEEN

✔ http://twitter.com/keen

✔ http://pinterest.com/keenfootwear

✔ http://instagram.com/keen

✔ www.youtube.com/user/keenoutdoor

✔ www.keenfootwear.com/blog

Diagnosing Problems with Social Media Campaigns

Put on your business hat when you detect a problem. Some techniques may be worth modifying and trying again, but others should be dropped. Ultimately, it's a business decision, not a technological one.

Be patient when assessing cost of customer acquisition and ROI, although a few trend lines in your metrics might give you pause:

✦ Traffic to a social media service never picks up, or falls and remains low after an initial burst.

✦ Traffic to the social media site holds steady, but the click-through rate (CTR) to your master hub or other sites is low.

✦ Follow-through on intermediate calls to action is low in performance metrics.

✦ Traffic and click-throughs increase, but the leads aren't well qualified.

✦ Traffic and engagement, which had been increasing for quite a while, fall and continue to fall; small dips and rises are natural.

✦ A conversion rate tracked back to a social media service is unintentionally lower than from other sources, and average sales value is lower. (Good strategic reasons for these results might exist, of course. You might deliberately target the younger student audience on Foursquare with less-expensive options than those offered to an older, more affluent audience on Facebook.)

✦ The cost of customer or lead acquisition is much higher than for other channels, making the ROI unattractive. For example, a high-maintenance blog might generate a few leads but be relatively expensive compared to prescheduled tweets that drive more traffic successfully.

Fixing Problems

Underlying problems with low traffic on social media usually can be slotted into a few categories:

✦ Problems locating your social media presence

✦ Mismatch between channel and audience

✦ Poor content

✦ No audience engagement

✦ Problems with the four P's of marketing: Product, price, placement or position (distribution), and promotion

After these problems are diagnosed, they can be handled in roughly the same way, regardless of the social media venue used.

Before you panic, make sure that you've set reasonable expectations for performance and business metrics. Research the range of responses for similar companies or view your competitors' social media sites to see how many responses, comments, and followers they have. Although you can't foretell their ROI, you can assess their traffic and inbound links. Your results from social media may be just fine!

Use the social monitoring tools described in Book II, Chapter 3 to discover how your competitors are doing on social media compared to your business. Many of these tools enable you to check any domain name.

Be careful with interpretation, however; if your competitors began working on their social media campaigns long before you did, they are likely to have very different results.

Remember that the social media audience is quite fickle. A constant demand exists for changes in content, approach, tools, and tone to keep up.

Your social presence can't be found

Driving traffic to your social media presence is as challenging as driving people to your site. If traffic is still low after about four weeks, ensure that all your social media sites are optimized for external search engines such as Google and internal (on-site) search tools used by different social media services. Turn to Book II, Chapter 2 for optimization techniques.

The source of the problem may be poorly selected search terms or tags, a headline or description that contains no keywords, or content that hasn't been optimized. Unless your hub presence, whether it's a blog or website, is well optimized itself, your social media presence may suffer, too.

Be sure that posts occur often enough for your social media page to appear in real-time search results.

Inappropriate match between channel and audience

The symptoms for a mismatch usually show up quickly: People take little or no interest in your social media postings, you suffer from low CTR, and your bounce rate is high whenever visitors do click through.

To start with, you may have chosen an inappropriate social media service or the wrong group within a network. For example, young tech males like reddit, but if you want a social site about weddings and interior decor, try Pinterest instead.

The solution: Return to your Social Media Marketing Plan (see Book I, Chapter 3). Review the demographics and behavioral characteristics for the social media service you're using. They may have changed over time; for example, Facebook is still enormously popular with 18- to 29-year-olds, in spite of recent growth in older users, but that may not last. The youngest of social media users are already migrating toward Snapchat! Find a social venue that's a better fit, revise your plan, and try again.

Use Quantcast or Alexa to check demographics on social media sites if you aren't sure.

Poor content

Content problems are a little harder to diagnose than visibility problems, especially if the problem appears with your first posts. In that case, the problem may also look like a channel mismatch, with content that simply doesn't appeal to your target market or is inappropriate for the channel.

However, if you experience a persistent dip in traffic, comments, or CTR from your blog, Facebook stream, Pinterest, podcast, YouTube, or any other social media account, you have other difficulties. Perhaps the content isn't timely, or isn't updated frequently enough.

Or perhaps content quality itself has degraded. Content creators are commonly enthusiastic at the beginning of a project but may lose interest after a period of time. Or they may have a backlog of media and ideas that can be repurposed and posted initially; after that's depleted, they may run out of ideas. As a result, later content may not be as valuable to your market, lack appropriate production values, or simply become boring.

Watch for burnout. After the backlog of media is used up, the insistent demands for new content can easily become a burden. Creators often lose interest, or they focus on quantity rather than on quality.

Compare the individual posts that produced an increase in traffic, responses, or CTR to ones that are failing. Tally posts by the names of their creators and what the posts were about. Start by asking previously successful creators to develop new material along the lines of older, successful content. If that doesn't work, watch the most popular tags to see what interests visitors and try to tie new content into those topics, if appropriate.

Finally, try assigning fresh staff members, recruiting guest writers and producers, or hiring professionals for a while. If this change produces better results, you have indicators for a long-term solution.

Lack of audience engagement

If you see traffic to the social media service holding steady but lack follow-throughs from calls to action, or you have an unusually low CTR to your hub site, you may not be engaging your audience. Watch especially for engagement parameters that never take off or that dip persistently.

Review user comments, retweets, and other interactions on each service. You can use the internal performance metrics for Twitter, Facebook, and your blog to assess numerical results of engagement. Then review the chain for interaction between social media visitors and your staff. Are visitor responses being acknowledged? Is there follow-up? One of the biggest challenges in social media is establishing a relationship with your visitors and maintaining a back-and-forth conversation. A lack of engagement may presage a lack of brand recognition, loss of customer loyalty, and reduced referrals from visitors to their friends or colleagues.

The four P's of marketing

Perhaps you're getting traffic and click-throughs to your hub site and generating plenty of leads but still not closing or converting to sales. It might be time to go back to the basics.

Review a web analytics report generated before you started your social media marketing efforts. Make sure your website is well optimized for search, your online store (if you have one) is working well, and your conversion rate is solid. Fix any problems with your website before you try to adjust your social media campaign.

Product, price, placement or position (distribution), and promotion — the four P's — are considered the basic elements of traditional marketing. These terms apply to social media and other forms of online marketing, as well.

Product

Your *product* is whatever good or service you sell, regardless of whether the transaction takes place online or off. Product also includes such elements as performance, warranties, support, variety, and size. Review your competition to see which features, benefits, or services they offer, and which products they're featuring in social media. If you have an online store, look at your entire product mix and merchandising, not just at individual products. Ask yourself these questions:

✦ Are you selling products that the people you're targeting with social media want to buy?

✦ Do you have enough products or services to compete successfully in this environment?

✦ Are you updating your offerings regularly and promoting new items often?

Price

Price comparison sites such as Shopping.com and discount stores online already put price pressure on small businesses. Now mobile social media shopping sites, with the rapid viral spread of news about special offers and price breaks, have put cost-conscious shoppers firmly in the driver's seat.

No longer can you check only competitors' websites and comparison-shopping sites for prices. Now you must check to see what they offer visitors to their Facebook, Twitter, or LinkedIn pages; their blog readers; those who receive their e-newsletter; and social shopping page customers to gain new customers and hold onto them as loyal, repeat buyers. Any single product or service may now have multiple prices, depending on who's buying.

Use social shopping and other sites to assess your prices against your online competition. Are yours significantly higher or lower, or are they price competitive?

Your small business can have difficulty competing in the market for standard manufactured goods such as baby clothes or DVDs unless you have excellent wholesale deals from manufacturers or distributors. But you can compete on price on customized goods or services or by offering unique benefits for buying from your company.

If you must charge higher prices than your social media competitors, review your value proposition so that people perceive an extra benefit. It might be a $5 promotional code for a discount on another purchase, a no-questions-asked return policy, exclusivity, or very accessible tech support.

Be careful not to trap yourself into matching prices against large companies with deep pockets. Make tactical financial decisions about loss leaders and discounts for users of particular social media. Consider a less-than-full-featured product or service package for social media users if needed (sometimes called the *freemium* business model).

Placement or position

Placement or position refers to how products and services are delivered to consumers (distribution channels). Where and how are your products and services available? Your website needs to serve as a 24/7 hub for customer research, support, and sales online, but social media offers brand-new opportunities to serve your clients. Best Buy, for example, has already become famous for its *twelpforce,* in which employees use Twitter to field customer support questions and make product recommendations.

With multiple social marketing outlets, you must be alert for the effects of *channel cannibalization* (the use of multiple distribution channels that pull sales from each other). Products or services sold directly from social media outlets may depress the sales numbers on your website.

Promotion

Your online and social media marketing plans fall into the *promotion* category, which includes all the different ways you communicate with customers and prospects, both online and offline. This also includes making people aware of your multiple points of visibility online, almost as though you're marketing another product. Careful cross-promotion among all your online venues is now as critical as integrating online and offline advertising. Are people aware of all your social media pages? Are you using the right calls to action on those pages to get people to buy?

Don't continue investing in a social media technique just because everyone else is doing it.

Adjusting to Reality

Many times, expectations determine whether a marketing technique is seen as a success, a waste of time, or something in between. It isn't possible for a particular social media service to produce extraordinary changes in traffic or conversions. In most cases, though, your victories will be hard-won, while you cobble together traffic from multiple social media sources to build enough of a critical mass to gain measurable sales.

Achieving that goal usually involves many people, each of whom may become a committed champion of the method she has been using. When you decide to pull the plug on one of your social media techniques — or just decide to leave it in a static state — try to still keep your employees engaged.

Unless social media participants have proved themselves to be nonperformers, try to shift them into another channel so that they can retain a direct relationship with customers.

Avoid the temptation to recentralize your social media marketing in one place, whether it's PR, marketing communications, management, or customer support. Instead, try to maintain the involvement of someone from each of those functional areas, as well as subject area experts from such diverse departments as manufacturing, sales, and research and development (R&D).

Marketing is only part of a company, but all of a company is marketing.

As wild a ride as social media may seem, it's more of a marathon than a sprint. Given that it may take months to see the return on your marketing efforts, you may need to nourish your social media sites for quite a while.

Feeding the hungry maw of the content monster week in and week out isn't easy. You need to not only keep your staff engaged and positive, but also keep your content fresh. Take advantage of brainstorming techniques that involve your entire team to generate some new ideas each month. Here are a few suggestions to get you started:

✦ Create unique, themed campaigns that last one to three months. Find an interesting hook to recruit guest posts or writers, perhaps letting a few people try your product or service and write about it.

✦ Distribute short-term deals using some of social media channels described in Book VIII, such as providing location-based coupons on cellphones or distributing offers to Meetup attendees.

✦ Write a Wikipedia entry about your product or business from a consumer's point of view.

✦ Make friends on Facebook by incorporating an interactive application, such as a poll or sweepstakes entry.

✦ Reach one or more of your discrete niche markets by using some of the smaller alternative social media services listed in Book VIII, Chapter 3, or in Book II, Chapter 3.

✦ If you aren't gaining traction with groups on LinkedIn or Facebook, post on someone else's old-fashioned forum, message board, or chat room on a relevant topic.

✦ Tell a story about your product or service in pictures or video and upload it to Instagram, Vine, Pinterest, YouTube, or another image service.

Every marketing problem has an infinite number of solutions. You have to find only one of them!

Index

• *H* •

About the Authors

Jan Zimmerman has found marketing to be the most creative challenge of owning a business for the more than 35 years she has spent as an entrepreneur. Since 1994, she has owned Sandia Consulting Group and Watermelon Mountain Web Marketing (www.watermelonweb.com) in Albuquerque, New Mexico. (*Sandia* is Spanish for *watermelon*.) Jan's web marketing clients at Watermelon Mountain are a living laboratory for experimenting with the best social media, search engine optimization, and other online marketing techniques for bottom-line success. Her consulting practice, which keeps Jan aware of the real-world issues facing business owners and marketers, provides the basis for her pragmatic marketing advice. Ranging from hospitality and tourism to retail stores, B2B suppliers, trade associations, colleges, and service companies, her clients have unique marketing needs but share similar business concerns and online challenges. Throughout her business career, Jan has been a prolific writer. She has written three editions of *Web Marketing For Dummies*, four editions of another book about marketing on the Internet, as well as the books *Doing Business with Government Using EDI* and *Mainstreaming Sustainable Architecture*. She has also co-authored two previous editions of *Social Media Marketing All-in-One For Dummies* and co-authored the third edition of *Facebook Marketing All-in-One For Dummies*. Her concern about the impact of technological development on women's needs led to her book *Once Upon the Future* and the anthology *The Technological Woman*.

The writer of numerous articles and a frequent speaker on Web marketing and social media, Jan has long been fascinated by the intersection of business, technology, and human communication. In her spare time, she crews for the hot air balloon named *Levity* to get her feet off the ground and her head in the clouds.

Jan can be reached at books@watermelonweb.com or 505-344-4230. Your comments, corrections, and suggestions are welcome.

Deborah Ng is a former freelance writer who used her gift of gab to grow a successful blog into the number one online community for freelance writers before selling in 2010. Deb is the former community manager for several online brands and can currently be found enjoying her role as Director of Community for New Media Expo. When she's not oversharing on the social networks, Deb blogs at Kommein.com and enjoys her time with her extremely handsome husband and brilliant son.

Dedication

Jan Zimmerman:

In memory of my beloved mother, Adeline R. Zimmerman

Never, ever give up.

Authors' Acknowledgments

Jan Zimmerman: No nonfiction writer works alone, and this book is no exception. The more books I write, the more I realize how much I depend on others. In particular, this edition couldn't have been written without my wonderful employees: web marketing assistant, Esmeralda Sanchez, whose dedication to the task made this book possible, and Shawna Araiza, a highly experienced, senior web marketing associate at Watermelon Mountain Web Marketing.

Together with research support from Patricia Jephson and Diane Duncan Martin, they conducted background research, compiled sites for the numerous tables in this book, created graphics, and rooted out arcane online facts. Among them, they checked thousands of links and reviewed hundreds of sites for screen shots. (Not many people are asked to search for a good marketing post on Facebook!) Finding exemplary companies for case studies — and clearing several hundred copyrights — required endless calls and e-mails, for which Shawna and Esmeralda deserve all the credit.

I owe my staff a great debt for handling the research on this book at a very complicated time of my life, and working doubly-hard to try to keep the book close to schedule — not to mention their patience and computer support. I am especially grateful to Shawna for taking over much of our client workload so I had to write.

As always, my family, friends, and cats earn extra hugs for their constant encouragement. I'm lucky to have friends who accept that I cannot be there for them as much as they are there for me. The garden, the house, the car, and the cats, alas, are not so forgiving. Special thanks to my clients, who teach me so much and give me the opportunity to practice what I preach.

I'd also like to thank Kim Darosett, senior project editor at Wiley, for her flexibility and patience, and copy editor Laura Miller and technical editor, Michelle Krasniak, for their knowledgeable assistance. Together, they made this book much better than it started out. My thanks to all the other staff at Wiley — from the art department to legal — who have provided support. If errors remain, they are indubitably mine.

My appreciation also to my agent, Margot Hutchison of Waterside Productions. Margot and her extraordinary family continue to teach us, at `http://teamsam.com`, lessons about what's truly important in life. If you profit from reading this book, please join me in donating to The Magic Water Project in memory of Sam Hutchison at `www.magicwater.org`. Thank you in advance, dear readers, for making a contribution "because of Sam."

Deborah Ng: For Dummies books aren't award-winning works of non-fiction. No one will be talking about this book during book club meetings or on talk shows. Nevertheless, there's still a whole lot of passion, labor, and love going into these books, and I'm so proud and honored to be a part of the For Dummies family.

I'm forever grateful to my mother, Arline Dederick, and my sisters Diana Hayes, Desiree Pacuk, and Dawn Vota for encouraging me to write at an early age, and making sure I stuck with it. But mostly for not rolling their eyes too much as I describe my latest projects — and there are lots of them.

I have a solid network of friends who keep me grounded and make sure there's a glass of wine available when I close my laptop. Thank you also to my "Welcomer" friends, Celina Pellicane, Helen Raczkowski, Maureen Schenfeld, and Jennifer Hoffman, a true survivor. Without all of you, I would go crazy. Thank you for keeping me sane and keeping me real. Thank you also to my White Meadow friends who are neighbors in the truest sense of the word.

Finally, but by no means least, thank you to my editors: Amy Fandrei for your continued patience and faith in me for the past five years, and Kim Darosett also for your kind patience and guidance. I'm so fortunate to be able to work with you both, even if you do make me take a lot of screenshots.

Publisher's Acknowledgments

Acquisitions Editor: Amy Fandrei

Senior Project Editor: Kim Darosett

Copy Editor: Laura Miller

Technical Editor: Michelle Krasniak

Editorial Assistant: Claire Brock

Sr. Editorial Assistant: Cherie Case

Production Editor: Vinitha Vikraman

Cover Image: ©iStock.com/hocus-focus

Apple & Mac

iPad For Dummies, 6th Edition
978-1-118-72306-7

iPhone For Dummies, 7th Edition
978-1-118-69083-3

Macs All-in-One For Dummies, 4th Edition
978-1-118-82210-4

OS X Mavericks For Dummies
978-1-118-69188-5

Blogging & Social Media

Facebook For Dummies, 5th Edition
978-1-118-63312-0

Social Media Engagement For Dummies
978-1-118-53019-1

WordPress For Dummies, 6th Edition
978-1-118-79161-5

Business

Stock Investing For Dummies, 4th Edition
978-1-118-37678-2

Investing For Dummies, 6th Edition
978-0-470-90545-6

Personal Finance For Dummies, 7th Edition
978-1-118-11785-9

QuickBooks 2014 For Dummies
978-1-118-72005-9

Small Business Marketing Kit For Dummies, 3rd Edition
978-1-118-31183-7

Careers

Job Interviews For Dummies, 4th Edition
978-1-118-11290-8

Job Searching with Social Media For Dummies, 2nd Edition
978-1-118-67856-5

Personal Branding For Dummies
978-1-118-11792-7

Resumes For Dummies, 6th Edition
978-0-470-87361-8

Starting an Etsy Business For Dummies, 2nd Edition
978-1-118-59024-9

Diet & Nutrition

Belly Fat Diet For Dummies
978-1-118-34585-6

Mediterranean Diet For Dummies
978-1-118-71525-3

Nutrition For Dummies, 5th Edition
978-0-470-93231-5

Digital Photography

Digital SLR Photography All-in-One For Dummies, 2nd Edition
978-1-118-59082-9

Digital SLR Video & Filmmaking For Dummies
978-1-118-36598-4

Photoshop Elements 12 For Dummies
978-1-118-72714-0

Gardening

Herb Gardening For Dummies, 2nd Edition
978-0-470-61778-6

Gardening with Free-Range Chickens For Dummies
978-1-118-54754-0

Health

Boosting Your Immunity For Dummies
978-1-118-40200-9

Diabetes For Dummies, 4th Edition
978-1-118-29447-5

Living Paleo For Dummies
978-1-118-29405-5

Big Data

Big Data For Dummies
978-1-118-50422-2

Data Visualization For Dummies
978-1-118-50289-1

Hadoop For Dummies
978-1-118-60755-8

Language & Foreign Language

500 Spanish Verbs For Dummies
978-1-118-02382-2

English Grammar For Dummies, 2nd Edition
978-0-470-54664-2

French All-in-One For Dummies
978-1-118-22815-9

German Essentials For Dummies
978-1-118-18422-6

Italian For Dummies, 2nd Edition
978-1-118-00465-4

Available in print and e-book formats.

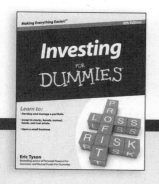

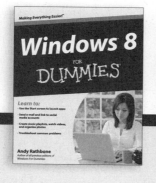

Available wherever books are sold. **For more information or to order direct visit www.dummies.com**

Math & Science

Algebra I For Dummies,
2nd Edition
978-0-470-55964-2

Anatomy and Physiology
For Dummies, 2nd Edition
978-0-470-92326-9

Astronomy For Dummies,
3rd Edition
978-1-118-37697-3

Biology For Dummies,
2nd Edition
978-0-470-59875-7

Chemistry For Dummies,
2nd Edition
978-1-118-00730-3

1001 Algebra II Practice
Problems For Dummies
978-1-118-44662-1

Microsoft Office

Excel 2013 For Dummies
978-1-118-51012-4

Office 2013 All-in-One
For Dummies
978-1-118-51636-2

PowerPoint 2013
For Dummies
978-1-118-50253-2

Word 2013 For Dummies
978-1-118-49123-2

Music

Blues Harmonica
For Dummies
978-1-118-25269-7

Guitar For Dummies,
3rd Edition
978-1-118-11554-1

iPod & iTunes
For Dummies, 10th Edition
978-1-118-50864-0

Programming

Beginning Programming
with C For Dummies
978-1-118-73763-7

Excel VBA Programming
For Dummies, 3rd Edition
978-1-118-49037-2

Java For Dummies,
6th Edition
978-1-118-40780-6

Religion & Inspiration

The Bible For Dummies
978-0-7645-5296-0

Buddhism For Dummies,
2nd Edition
978-1-118-02379-2

Catholicism For Dummies,
2nd Edition
978-1-118-07778-8

Self-Help & Relationships

Beating Sugar Addiction
For Dummies
978-1-118-54645-1

Meditation For Dummies,
3rd Edition
978-1-118-29144-3

Seniors

Laptops For Seniors
For Dummies, 3rd Edition
978-1-118-71105-7

Computers For Seniors
For Dummies, 3rd Edition
978-1-118-11553-4

iPad For Seniors
For Dummies, 6th Edition
978-1-118-72826-0

Social Security
For Dummies
978-1-118-20573-0

Smartphones & Tablets

Android Phones
For Dummies, 2nd Edition
978-1-118-72030-1

Nexus Tablets
For Dummies
978-1-118-77243-0

Samsung Galaxy S 4
For Dummies
978-1-118-64222-1

Samsung Galaxy Tabs
For Dummies
978-1-118-77294-2

Test Prep

ACT For Dummies,
5th Edition
978-1-118-01259-8

ASVAB For Dummies,
3rd Edition
978-0-470-63760-9

GRE For Dummies,
7th Edition
978-0-470-88921-3

Officer Candidate Tests
For Dummies
978-0-470-59876-4

Physician's Assistant Exam
For Dummies
978-1-118-11556-5

Series 7 Exam For Dummies
978-0-470-09932-2

Windows 8

Windows 8.1 All-in-One
For Dummies
978-1-118-82087-2

Windows 8.1 For Dummies
978-1-118-82121-3

Windows 8.1 For Dummies,
Book + DVD Bundle
978-1-118-82107-7

Available in print and e-book formats.

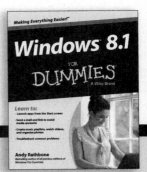

Available wherever books are sold. **For more information or to order direct visit www.dummies.com**

Take Dummies with you everywhere you go!

Whether you are excited about e-books, want more from the web, must have your mobile apps, or are swept up in social media, Dummies makes everything easier.

For Dummies is the global leader in the reference category and one of the most trusted and highly regarded brands in the world. No longer just focused on books, customers now have access to the For Dummies content they need in the format they want. Let us help you develop a solution that will fit your brand and help you connect with your customers.

Advertising & Sponsorships

Connect with an engaged audience on a powerful multimedia site, and position your message alongside expert how-to content.

Targeted ads • Video • Email marketing • Microsites • Sweepstakes sponsorship

Custom Publishing

Reach a global audience in any language by creating a solution that will differentiate you from competitors, amplify your message, and encourage customers to make a buying decision.

Apps • Books • eBooks • Video • Audio • Webinars

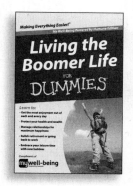   

Brand Licensing & Content

Leverage the strength of the world's most popular reference brand to reach new audiences and channels of distribution.

For more information, visit www.Dummies.com/biz

Dummies products make life easier!

- DIY
- Consumer Electronics
- Crafts
- Software
- Cookware
- Hobbies
- Videos
- Music
- Games
- and More!

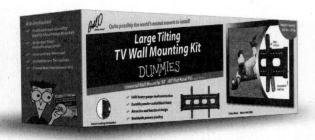

For more information, go to **Dummies.com** and search the store by category.

FOR
DUMMIES
A Wiley Bran

For Dummies is a registered trademark of John Wiley & Sons, Inc.